The Documentary History of
the Supreme Court of
the United States, 1789–1800

Volume One
Part 1
Appointments and Proceedings

The Documentary History of the Supreme Court of the United States, 1789–1800

Volume One

Part 1

Appointments and Proceedings

With a Foreword by Warren E. Burger,
Chief Justice of the United States

Maeva Marcus, *Editor*
James R. Perry, *Editor*
James M. Buchanan, *Associate Editor*
Christine R. Jordan, *Associate Editor*
Stephen L. Tull, *Assistant Editor*
Sandra F. VanBurkleo, *Assistant Editor*
Sarah E. Blank, *Assistant Editor*
Nancy L. Matthews, *Assistant Editor*
Marc Pachter, *Illustrations Editor*

COLUMBIA UNIVERSITY PRESS
NEW YORK   1985

The Press gratefully acknowledges the assistance of DeWitt Wallace and of The William Nelson Cromwell Foundation in the publishing of this volume.

Library of Congress Cataloging in Publication Data
Main entry under title:

The Documentary history of the Supreme Court of the United States, 1789-1800.

Includes index.
Contents: v. 1. pt. 1. Appointments and proceedings.
pt. 2. Commentaries on appointments and proceedings.
1. United States. Supreme Court--History--Sources.
I. Marcus, Maeva, 1941-   . II. Perry, James R.,
1950-   . III. United States. Supreme Court.
KF8742.A45D66 1985   347.73'2609   85-3794
ISBN 0-231-08867-1 (v. 1, pt. 1)   347.3073509
0-231-08868-x(v. 1, pt. 2)
0-231-04552-2 (v. 1)

Columbia University Press
New York   Guildford, Surrey

Printed in the United States of America

Clothbound editions of Columbia University Press Books are Smyth-sewn and printed on permanent and durable acid-free paper

To the Memory of Elizabeth Hughes Gossett, 1907–1981

Contents

Part 1

Appointments to the Bench

Part 2

Commentaries

Contents   xxxi

List of Illustrations

Foreword

Warren E. Burger

Chief Justice of the United States

As the bicentennial anniversaries of the Constitution and the Supreme Court draw near, it is dismaying to realize that no accurate and complete record exists of the work of the Supreme Court from 1790 to 1800, which constitutes an important part of its formative period. To fill this gap the Supreme Court Historical Society, with the support of the National Historical Publications and Records Commission and the Supreme Court itself, undertook what turned out to be a massive project to gather the materials necessary to reconstitute, as nearly as possible, the record of those years. The task has proven far more difficult than anticipated, since many of the official papers of the Supreme Court were destroyed or damaged by fires at different times during the nineteenth century. However, with the cooperation and assistance of historians, archivists, and librarians throughout the United States, the staff of the Documentary History project has amassed a unique collection of documents illuminating the history of the Court.

With the publication of Volume 1 of *The Documentary History of the Supreme Court of the United States, 1789-1800,* the Supreme Court Historical Society is pleased to present to the public, and especially to historians, lawyers, judges, teachers, and students, information about the development of the Court that hitherto has been inaccessible. Until the Documentary History project began its work, little attention had been given to the first decade of the Court's history, yet in that ten years the groundwork was laid for important aspects of constitutional adjudication. The publication of this material provides the raw documentation for scholars to study and interpret. We learn, for example, that Alexander James Dallas, the unofficial reporter for the Supreme Court, not only omitted cases from his reports but took certain liberties with those he did include. In the case of *Ware v. Hylton* (3 *Dallas* 199 [1796]), for example, the only case John Marshall argued in the Court (and which he lost), the arguments of counsel and the opinions of the Justices are not verbatim. The decision, not popular with the debtor class of that day, not surprisingly held that the treaty of 1783 with England controlled over contrary state law relating to payment. That is what John Marshall would have decided as a judge.

It is unfortunate that the federal courts, which so often look to the original understanding of our Constitution for guidance in their judgments, should have such a scarcity of material to consult concerning what the first generation of federal judges did and thought. *The Documentary History of the Supreme Court of the United States, 1789-1800,* concerns only the Supreme Court, but the wealth of material it contains points to how much remains to be investigated in the records of the other federal courts. It is my sincere hope that the publication of this unique series will stimulate interest in the history of the Third Branch of government and inspire additional studies of our early federal court system that would provide a great contribution to the forthcoming bicentennial celebration of 1987.

Dr. Maeva Marcus and her staff deserve our thanks for an important task well done.

Acknowledgments

A project of the scope of *The Documentary History of the Supreme Court of the United States, 1789-1800,* could not be undertaken without the support of many individuals and institutions. Preeminent among them is the Supreme Court of the United States. The leadership of Chief Justice Warren E. Burger and the encouragement of the entire Court have been essential to the success of the project. The chief justice's interest in history and his commitment to making the public more aware of the Court's origins caused him to be among the first to endorse the idea of publishing a documentary history of the Supreme Court's first decade. His generous assistance and that of the other members of the Court benefited the Documentary History project in countless ways, for which we are all very grateful.

Another organization providing vital support to this Documentary History project is the Supreme Court Historical Society. Elizabeth Hughes Gossett— to whom this volume is dedicated—was the Society's first president. The youngest child of Chief Justice Charles Evans Hughes, Mrs. Gossett had a special appreciation for the history of the Court. She immediately recognized the significance of the project and gave it her enthusiastic support until her death in 1981. Her successors as leaders of the Society, Robert T. Stevens, Linwood Holton, and Kenneth Rush, have continued to contribute in many ways to the publication of this series. The late Professor William F. Swindler, the Society's first director of publications, was instrumental in the creation of the project and provided us cheerful encouragement and an endless fund of knowledge. Gary Aichele, executive director of the Supreme Court Historical Society, served as the project's administrator and greatly facilitated its work.

Funding the Society's support of the project, the National Historical Publications and Records Commission has provided the financial assistance without which the *Documentary History* could not have been produced. Members of the staff of the Commission have been especially supportive: Frank G. Burke, executive director, Roger Bruns, director of publications, and George Vogt, director of the records program, advised us on matters financial and substantive; Sara D. Jackson and Mary Giunta guided us through the voluminous collections of documents at the National Archives with unfailing good spirits and advice. Fred Shelley, former deputy director of the Commission, also contributed his encouragement and expertise.

Various other private organizations and individuals also provided important financial assistance to the Documentary History project at times when it was greatly needed. Among these organizations are the Morris and Gwendolyn Cafritz Foundation, the William Nelson Cromwell Foundation, American Telephone and Telegraph, and the Cudahy Foundation. Law firms that have contributed to the project include Wilmer, Cutler & Pickering; Arendt, Fox, Kintner, Plotkin & Kahn; Hogan & Hartson; Arnold & Porter; Steptoe & Johnson; and Crowell & Moring. Among the many individuals who have supported the work of the Documentary History project are Elizabeth and William Gossett, J. Roderick Heller, Earl Kintner, Whitney North Seymour, and Robert T. Stevens.

The editors also wish to recognize the valuable contribution of our editorial advisory committee. We owe a special word of thanks to David Chesnutt, who shared with us his broad knowledge of documentary editing and the technical aspects of the process of publication, and to Merrill Jensen, whose untimely death deprived us of an advisor who not only had a remarkable depth of knowledge but who gave unstintingly of his time.

In addition to the chief justice and the associate justices, many people at the Court have provided help to the project. Mark W. Cannon, administrative assistant to the chief justice, has been a continuing source of strength. James A. Robbins, James R. Donovan, Alexander L. Stevas, Gail A. Galloway, and Francis J. Lorson aided us in a number of important ways. Because of the nature of the Documentary History project, the help of members of the Court's library staff has been invaluable. We thank all of them, especially Librarian Roger F. Jacobs and reference librarians Patricia M. Evans and Sara J. Sonet.

A number of people have helped us with specific research problems. John J. McCusker came to our aid in the calculation of monetary exchange rates. James Oldham gave us the benefit of his work in English legal history. Gerard H. Clarfield and Noble E. Cunningham, Jr., cleared up a problem with the identification of Timothy Pickering's handwriting. Andrew Oliver, an expert in early American portraiture, agreed when the project began to serve as illustrations editor; his death in 1981 deprived us of a generous and delightful colleague, and we acknowledge here his early contributions to the project. The staff of the National Portrait Gallery also provided invaluable assistance in locating illustrations for the project.

One of the pleasures of working on a documentary editing project for the early national period is the existence of other editing projects of the same era. We have benefited greatly from the help of the editorial staffs of many of these projects and would like to express our appreciation to them: The Documentary History of the Ratification of the Constitution, The Documentary History of the First Federal Congress, as well as the papers projects for John Jay, George Washington, John Adams, Alexander Hamilton, James Madison, Nathanael Greene, John Marshall, James Iredell, and Benjamin Henry Latrobe.

When searching for primary sources for a project as extensive as a documentary history of the Supreme Court, the aid of the repositories holding documents is indispensable. We put heavy burdens on certain institutions with large collections which were particularly relevant to our work. The staffs of the Library of Congress Manuscript Room, Rare Book Room, and Newspaper and Periodical Reading Room met every request cheerfully and with valuable professional advice. The same is true of the highly competent staffs of the National Archives and its records centers, where we spent a great deal of time sifting through record groups with their patient assistance.

Other repositories also provided extensive staff time and expertise. We are especially grateful to the American Philosophical Society, the Boston Public Library, Brown University's John Carter Brown Library and John Hay Library, Columbia University's Butler Library, the Connecticut Historical Society, the Connecticut State Library, the Dickinson College Library, Duke University's Perkins Library, the Essex Institute, Harvard University's Houghton Library, the Historical Society of Pennsylvania, the Huntington Library, the Maryland Hall of Records, the Maryland Historical Society, the Massachusetts Historical Society, the New England Historic Genealogical Society, the New Hampshire Historical Society, the New Hampshire State Library, the New Jersey Historical Society, the Newport Historical Society, the New-York Historical Society, the New York Public Library, the New York State Library, the North Carolina Department of Archives and History, William Paterson College's Askew Library, the Rhode Island Historical Society, Rutgers University's Alexander Library, the University of South Carolina's South Caroliniana Library, the Suffolk County (Massachusetts) Court House, Swarthmore College's Friends Historical Library, the University of Georgia Library, the University of North Carolina Library, the University of Virginia's Alderman Library, the Virginia Historical Society, Mystic Seaport's G. W. Blunt White Library, and Yale University's Sterling Memorial Library.

In addition to the repositories themselves, we would like to acknowledge the efforts of many individuals who work at those institutions: Elizabeth Abbe, Robert G. Anthony, Jr., Clark L. Beck, Jr., Ruth Blair, Lawrence Boyer, Ann K. Bratton, Robert Byrd, Thomas E. Camden, Paul I. Chestnut, C. Fred W. Coker, John D. Cushing, Eunice G. DiBella, Thomas J. Dunnings, Jr., Mark Gallicchio, Anne Goodrich, Lawrence Hackman, Charles J. Kelly, Eileen Kennedy, Gary J. Kohn, Bruce Laverty, Ellen D. Mark, Memory F. Mitchell, Ruth S. Nicholson, James K. Owens, Edward Papenfuse, Peter Parker, Gayle P. Peters, John Platt, John Powers, Charles Reeves, Richard H. Richardson, Marianne L. Roos, Mattie Russell, John Shelly, Nathaniel Shipton, Richard A. Shrader, Paul Sifton, Robert Sparks, Jeffrey Stafford, Linda Stanley, Patricia Stark, Douglas Stein, George Stephenson, Gregory A. Stiverson, Allen Stokes, Diane Telian, Patricia Vanorny, Glen Vencivengo, and Loretta Zwolak.

Over the years, the project has been assisted by student interns who served for a summer or a semester during the academic year. The contributions of the following individuals are greatly appreciated: Greg Andrews, Jeffrey M. Bandman, Stuart Bender, Inez M. Bulatao, Britt C. Byrne, Carol Cahn, Shermin H. Chow, Elizabeth A. Connolly, Stephen L. Cox, Christina M. De-

Concini, Sheree DeCovny, Abigail Friedman, Heidi A. Garland, Neil Gath, Cordelia Gould, Elizabeth A. Heck, Cathy Mantegna, Stephanie Marcus, Gary A. Massey, Ann L. O'Connor, Paul C. Pebley, Anne V. Power, Julie Reuben, Bruce A. Reznik, Betsy J. Salveson, Eric Schine, Peter Shabecoff, Kim A. Snyder, Jane Spanier, Nancy Spiegel, Claire E. Stager, Jill I. Stanton, Robert Teir, Shelley Wall, Daniel E. Waltz, Wendy Weinberg, Catherine M. Wiles. We also would like to thank those who coordinated the intern programs: David J. Brandenburg at American University, Joy Colangelo at the University of California at Santa Cruz, Linda Lear at George Washington University, and Millie Tan Steward and Fiona Hodgson at Brandeis University.

Finally we would like to acknowledge the support and assistance of the able people at International Computaprint Corporation. We would especially like to thank J. Robert Dinon, Eileen Colahan, and Eric Cassel, who provided patient and expert guidance to us as we worked our way through the often unsettling problems of setting eighteenth-century texts into type. Without the help of these people and all the individuals and institutions mentioned above, the creation of this volume and the project itself would not have been possible.

Introduction

Because of its unique position in the national government the Supreme Court[1] is a much-studied institution. Such attention is not misplaced, for the Court is surely the most novel creation of the Constitution. Yet there is a gap in our knowledge of the evolution of the Court: its crucial formative years, 1789-1800, have been the subject of few scholarly works.[2]

This first decade of the Supreme Court's history warrants more study. During these years, the Court considered questions central to the creation of a workable national government out of the constitutional blueprint. From the cases brought before it, the Court decided issues bearing upon the nature of the federal relationship, the meaning of separation of powers, the Court's function in enforcing the foreign policy of the United States government, the definition of war, the supremacy of national treaties over state laws, the nature of citizenship, and the relationship between the common law of England and the laws of the United States.

George Washington understood the significance of the Court. He wrote to the justices before they set out on their first circuits: "I have always been persuaded that the stability and success of the National Government, and consequently the happiness of the People of the United States, would depend in a considerable degree on the Interpretation and Execution of its Laws.— In my opinion, therefore, it is important that the Judiciary System should not only be independent in its operations, but as perfect as possible in its formation.—" Washington asked the justices to keep him informed of their activities "in such an unexplored field."[3] Unfortunately, they rarely complied.

Today, historians interested in the operation of the federal judicial system during its first decade are faced with a paucity of accurate, accessible, published primary materials with which to examine the period. As a first step to correct this situation, the Supreme Court Historical Society and the Supreme Court of the United States, with the encouragement of Chief Justice Warren E. Burger,

---

1. Throughout this series, "Court" and "Supreme Court" should always be taken to mean Supreme Court of the United States.

2. Julius Goebel, in his mammoth first volume of the Oliver Wendell Holmes Devise History of the Supreme Court of the United States, *Antecedents and Beginnings to 1801* (New York: Macmillan, 1971), devotes only three chapters to the Supreme Court.

3. George Washington to the Chief Justice and Associate Judges of the Supreme Court of the United States, April 3, 1790, James Wilson Papers, PHi.

launched a historical research project, *The Documentary History of the Supreme Court of the United States, 1789-1800.*

This multi-volume documentary history will provide scholars and lawyers with the first accurate record of all cases heard by the Supreme Court between 1790 and 1800. It will also present an ample selection of contemporary comment about the justices and their duties, the business of the Court, and the function of the Court in the constitutional framework. A compilation of official records, private papers, and other primary sources, this series will bring together and make readily available hitherto unpublished materials. They will document the Court's important role in creating administrative procedures for the American judicial system and establishing the legal precedents that enabled the new government to prosper.

In an effort to assemble as complete a collection as possible, the staff of the Documentary History project conducted a massive search. The official records of the Supreme Court are preserved in the National Archives, but they are incomplete for the first decade. Some early Supreme Court papers have been destroyed by fire, many in 1898 when a gas explosion occurred in the sub-basement of the Capitol. (The Court met and kept its records in the Capitol from 1801 to 1935.) In order to reconstruct the most comprehensive official file possible for each case the Court considered in its initial decade, we have searched for case papers in the archives of lower federal and state courts, as well as in private collections. We also have gathered contemporary newspaper reports of these cases, a valuable supplement to the official documentation.

Although collecting official papers has been our first priority, we also have looked for nonofficial material relevant to the history of the Court in its early years. To aid us in this search, we compiled several lists: names of people directly connected to the Court or its business, specific cases, ships involved in admiralty cases, and issues considered by the Court in particular cases. We had hoped to be able to pinpoint the location of documents we needed by using these lists in conjunction with the finding aids and card catalogs of manuscript repositories. Because our search concerned a subject rather than a person, however, the aids and catalogs at many institutions were inadequate. We therefore made the decision to check the major manuscript collections for the period 1787-1801. At the present time we have examined the pertinent holdings of more than one hundred repositories throughout the United States. These range in size from small, but significant, collections to the massive holdings of the Library of Congress, the National Archives and its regional branches, major historical societies, universities, and state archives. In an attempt to locate manuscripts in smaller repositories whose collections did not warrant a personal visit, the staff of the Documentary History project contacted by mail almost seven hundred state and local archives and libraries, historical societies, universities, and museums. We also sought out papers in private hands. Advertisements were sent to every leading historical journal—as well as collectors' magazines—for all fifty states and England. Our quest has not been limited to manuscripts. We have read published primary and secondary sources to obtain pertinent information. And we have begun a search for all relevant material in contemporary newspapers.

The nature of this newspaper search must be explained. To read all newspapers published during the years 1787-1801 would be impossible, so we have established priorities for the order in which we examine them. We have concentrated on newspapers published in New York and Philadelphia, the respective capitals of the United States and the cities in which the Supreme Court held its sessions until the government moved to Washington, D.C. Our next priority has been to read newspapers from cities in which the circuit courts of the United States sat; that includes one or two cities in each state of the union. Within this category we have tried to look at newspapers from different geographic sections of the country in order to gain a variety of perspectives on the Court. When available, and when time has allowed, we also have read newspapers from other major cities. Because of its magnitude, the newspaper search is still under way as volume 1 of *The Documentary History of the Supreme Court of the United States, 1789-1800,* goes to press. We suspect that it will continue until our last volume is completed.

At this date, our search has yielded almost eighteen thousand documents. Despite this impressive number, we make no claim to having discovered every item dealing with the Supreme Court during its first ten years. When the subject of a documentary history is an eighteenth-century institution, every eighteenth-century manuscript collection, and many nineteenth-century ones as well, would have to be read to ensure the location of every mention of that institution. Given the constraints of time and budget, this was manifestly impossible. Nevertheless, *The Documentary History of the Supreme Court of the United States, 1789-1800,* will constitute a collection of materials that no individual scholar could hope to duplicate.

We do not intend to publish all the documents we have collected. Our series of seven volumes will contain only those documents we believe to be most useful and of most interest to scholars, lawyers, and the reading public. (The criteria for selecting items will be explained in each volume.) Volume 1 presents documents that establish the structure of the Supreme Court and recount the official record of the Court's activity during its first decade. It will serve as an introduction and reference tool for the subsequent volumes. The second volume will consist of items bearing on the origins of the federal judiciary. These documents will provide a framework for understanding the development of Article III of the Constitution and legislation dealing with the judicial system during the first ten years of its existence. The special focus of the volume will be references to the structure and role of the Supreme Court. Volume 3 will treat the justices on circuit and include, among other things, a circuit court calendar for each of the three circuits from 1790 to 1800 and a collection of all grand jury charges that we have found, both in print and in draft form. The four volumes that follow will concentrate on the specific cases that came before the Supreme Court and, if space permits, miscellaneous documents dealing with a variety of topics such as the extrajudicial activities of the justices and plans for where the Court was to sit in New York, Philadelphia, and Washington.

As all the material we have amassed cannot be published in seven volumes, we hope to produce in microform a considerable portion of the remaining unpublished documents. But even if this is not possible, our collection will serve as a central archive open to scholars who individually cannot afford to undertake the search our staff conducted.

By gathering and then publishing many of these items, we will be preserving the documentary basis for future studies of the history of the early Court. Often manuscripts housed in repositories both public and private are not well preserved. Repeated handling, fading ink, crumbling paper, and even theft take their toll. The volumes of *The Documentary History of the Supreme Court of the United States, 1789-1800,* as well as any unpublished portion of our collection, will give scholars, for many future generations, an opportunity to investigate the first decade of the Court's history—an opportunity that most likely would have been lost had these documents been left to decay.

But what will scholars find when they look at our volumes? They will find a collection of materials that will allow them to analyze the origin and evolution of the Supreme Court. The series will contain important material that hitherto has not been readily available or frequently used by scholars. In the first volume, for example, readers will become aware of cases the Court heard that are not reported by Alexander James Dallas.[4] Scholars can compare the fine minutes of the Court's proceedings with the original draft minutes and derive a more detailed idea of how the Court operated. Among other things, they can see the confusion that existed over various points of procedure, the clerks' struggle to record events properly, and the omission from the fine minutes of certain items that appear in the original draft minutes. In addition, scholars can examine for the first time a formulary kept by the clerk of the Court that adds to our knowledge of the use of common law forms in the federal courts. Material presented in volume 1 allows scholars to study in depth the process of appointment to the bench of the Supreme Court during its first decade. In short, this and the subsequent volumes will add immeasurably to existing information about this period of the Court's history.

As the bicentennial of the Constitution approaches, every effort should be made to acquaint the American people with the establishment of their government. In the case of the judiciary, the task is more difficult because relatively little work has been done on the initial years of its existence. The history of the Supreme Court begins, in most people's memories, with Chief Justice John Marshall and *Marbury v. Madison.* But the Court that was headed by Marshall

---

4. A[lexander] J[ames] Dallas, *Reports of Cases Ruled and Adjudged in the Several Courts of the United States and of Pennsylvania,* vols. 2-4 (Philadelphia, 1798-1807).

built on the foundation laid by the Courts of Chief Justices John Jay, John Rutledge, and Oliver Ellsworth. The earliest justices were committed firmly to the principles of the new Constitution and understood that the way in which they performed their duties would have much to do with the success of the new government. When all the volumes of *The Documentary History of the Supreme Court of the United States, 1789-1800,* are published, the source material necessary for a full evaluation of the contribution of the pre-Marshall Courts will be available, and the first decade of the Court's history should receive, at last, its proper due.

Guide to Editorial Method

This guide to editorial method presents the rules by which we edit documents for publication. On occasion, however, textual idiosyncrasies require special treatment, including modification of our general guidelines. Any such deviation is explained in a headnote or in annotation to the particular document. Each volume in this series will be preceded by a guide to editorial method which will include decisions on problems not encountered before. Similarly, we will update other elements of the editorial apparatus, such as the descriptive symbols for documents and all lists of abbreviations.

Our first and most important editorial principle is that we reproduce the text of the original document as accurately as possible. We do not correct authorial omissions or errors, and we do not note them unless there is a possibility of a misreading. We retain original spelling, capitalization, and punctuation. We also retain the peculiarities of eighteenth-century writing styles: superior letters and any punctuation beneath them, dashes and ellipses, as well as other less familiar marks or constructions. The editorial decisions relating to many of these eighteenth-century practices are discussed below.

A second major principle has particular relevance to publishing handwritten documents; i.e., we concern ourselves more with the function than with the form of textual marks, particularly when variations reflect a writer's individual style. For example, the purpose of a contraction mark within an abbreviated word is to indicate the omission of letters irrespective of whether the bar is long or short, straight or curved, or whether it touches any letter. It would be prohibitively expensive to reproduce in a printed form the great variety employed in the shape and placement of contraction marks. We therefore have standardized the form and placement of the contraction mark to reflect its function within the word. Similarly, the shape of an ampersand is considered of less importance than its use in place of a word spelled out; we therefore standardize the different shapes to one form. On the other hand, where textual variation can be retained with less expense, we do so. Thus, ellipses can be formed by a straight line, a series of stops, or several asterisks, and we reproduce these several forms. Keeping in mind our effort to present literal transcriptions of texts with more emphasis on function than form, we leave out apparently functionless stray marks. We also omit pagination and running heads that appear in the original, since our volume has its own pagination and running heads. We also ignore redundancy in the text and reduce double periods, commas, ditto marks, ellipses, and underscoring to single marks. Generally, we alert the reader to those areas where editorial exigencies require the invocation of the rule of function over form.

Two final factors influence the manner in which we edit documents for publication. The first is a realization of typographical limitation. Thus, it may not be feasible to place text on a printed page exactly where a person wrote it in a manuscript. In this case, we keep in mind the reason for the original placement and then locate it where we can. When some ambiguity exists as to a writer's original intention or where we think that the reader may need further information as to original placement, we discuss it in a note. Another example of typographical necessity concerns recording the presence of postmarks. When a postmark consists of a circle around the edge of which appear the word "Philadelphia" and the date "Aug 17," we are constrained to reproduce it in a linear fashion as "Philadelphia   Aug 17." Punctuation and other text that cannot be reproduced is omitted from the published version and noted. Thus, a period that has been crossed out in the text would not appear as part of the document, but would be noted instead. In recording the presence of seals or their equivalents, we will distinguish between those that are imprinted on wax or a similar substance, those that are handwritten and stylized, and those that merely read "L S."

The final factor influencing our editing involves a concern for fitting as many documents as possible into the volume and making them as readable as we can. Thus, in order to save lines, we reduce some vertical spacing. Multiple-line closings to letters are reproduced as a single stream of text with extra space indicating original line divisions. The following closing

> I am,
>   Dear sir,
>   Your most humble
>   and obedient servant.

would appear in type as

I am,   Dear sir,   Your most humble   and obedient servant.

In addition, we have adjusted vertical spacing to enhance readability. Thus, in the minutes of the Supreme Court, we have inserted spacing between cases to separate them and make them easier to read.

In order to implement our two major principles—literal reproduction informed by a concern for function rather than form—we have tried to develop a sensitivity to conventions of handwriting in the early national period. Especially helpful has been a survey of contemporary copybooks and grammars as well as the scholarly literature of eighteenth-century handwriting. These reference works, as well as consultations with Laetitia Yeandle, curator of manuscripts at the Folger Shakespeare Library in Washington, D.C., have shaped our transcription of documents. In addition, an awareness of printing conventions in the late eighteenth century has been important in making decisions as to how to render these texts into print. Typesetters exerted a powerful influence on penmanship into the early nineteenth century, mainly through their attempts to standardize idiosyncratic handwriting and variable marks. Wherever compromises had to be made in transferring handwriting into type, preference has been given to the practice of contemporary typesetters.

Selecting Documents for Publication

Our central concern is to publish the greatest number of relevant documents that we can in the limited space available. The criteria for selecting documents to be published are explained in each volume of this series. For the first volume, they are discussed in the introductions to the three major sections: "Appointments to the Bench," "The Clerks and Their Record," and "Commentaries." In the situation where we have multiple versions of a document—e.g., recipient's copy, sender's copy, letterpress copy—we select one to publish according to guidelines explained in the section on "Descriptive Symbols for Documents." If there are differences between the version of a document chosen for publication and other versions in our possession, we note the significant variations, except in instances where noting the variations would exceed the space required to actually publish the document, in which case we present both versions. We have made a special effort to locate recipients' copies of documents, but have not made any effort to find all other extant versions.

Because eighteenth-century newspaper editors frequently reprinted articles that had appeared earlier in other newspapers, the selection of which version to publish in this series is especially involved. In general, when articles are the same—allowing always for some insignificant typographical variation—we publish the version which appeared closest in time to the event described. In the case of two items appearing at the same time, we choose the one published in the newspaper in closest proximity to the event described. In the source note, we present the names of the two most geographically distant newspapers that carried the same news item in order to suggest the distribution of the information conveyed; we also note publication of the item in the capital. A complete table of such coverage will appear in the last volume of this series. When another article varies somewhat from the one already published but does not present further information, we note the variant version and the geographic distribution of its appearance. If such an article were to contain only one minor bit of additional information, we would note the extra data at an appropriate point and give the geographic distribution of this variant article. On the other hand, when an article is significantly different and conveys additional information, it is published and the geographic spread of its reprintings is noted.

Excerpting, Calendaring, and Tabulating
Documents for Publication

In addition to selective publication, we have been able to save space by presenting excerpts of documents if only portions relate to our subject. When we publish a complete letter, we present the place and date line, the salutation, the body of the text, and the closing where these elements appear in the original; relevant material on the address cover appears in the source note to the document. When publishing an excerpt, however, we leave out the place and date line (which is part of the document title anyway), the salutation, and the closing; for the body of the text, we present only the material of significance to our topic, with ellipses to indicate editorial deletion.[1] It should be noted that, unlike other editorial interventions, these ellipses are not bracketed. In order to distinguish between editorial and authorial ellipses, we annotate the latter where they occur. When presenting an excerpt, we sometimes must provide editorial summaries of text that we have not published in order to retain the sense of the original; these editorial summaries, like all such editorial interventions, appear in italics within square brackets. We also delete any post-1800 additions to the documents, because we want to present the texts as they appeared at the end of the time spanned by this documentary history.

We can include more documents by using calendars and tables wherever possible. Thus, because newspapers often reprinted items published elsewhere, we will tabulate, when appropriate, newspaper coverage of the Supreme Court, the justices, and Court-related topics. These tables will appear in appendixes in the last volume of the series. For the most part, case papers, which are repetitive and formally structured, also will be calendared.

Titling Documents

All document titles are constructs supplied by the editors. In general, a title to a letter includes the sender and recipient followed by the date and place of

---

1. The following rules have governed our placement of ellipses at the beginning and end of excerpts. Where material has been elided at the beginning of the document, we begin with a flush-left ellipsis with the text following immediately. At the end of the elided passage, we use a mark of punctuation—if there is one—and then an ellipsis. If there is a second excerpt within the same document, a variety of rules govern different situations. First, if excerpt one stops at the end of one paragraph, and excerpt two begins in the middle of the next, the ellipsis would be indented immediately preceding the text of excerpt two. If the first excerpt ends in the middle of one paragraph and the second starts at the beginning of the next, the ellipsis will follow excerpt one and a paragraph indentation will precede excerpt two. If excerpt one ends in the middle of one paragraph and excerpt two begins in the middle of the next, an ellipsis will follow excerpt one and an ellipsis will also be indented before excerpt two. Finally, where the first excerpt stops at the end of one paragraph and the second starts at the beginning of another paragraph, with one or more complete paragraphs between, an ellipsis will be indented on its own line between the two.

composition. Whenever names, dates, or places are not specified in the original document but we can infer the missing data without a doubt, we include it within square brackets as part of the title. If our inference is subject to debate, we place the data with a question mark within square brackets. Pseudonymous authors are identified where possible. Documents with conjectural dates are located chronologically near the earliest date that can be determined for them.

For items republished from newspapers, we use the short-title newspaper names devised by Clarence S. Brigham in his two-volume *History and Bibliography of American Newspapers, 1690-1820* (Worcester, Massachusetts: American Antiquarian Society, 1947), and in his "Additions and Corrections to *History and Bibliography of American Newspapers, 1690-1820,*" included in the *Proceedings of the American Antiquarian Society* 71 (1961): 15-62. We try to date and place an article as closely as possible to the event described. If the item that we are publishing has its own identifiable date and place of origin and these are different from those of the newspaper itself, we use in our title the date and place for the article. If the item does not have a date and place different from the newspaper itself, we use the latter in our title. The date and place of the newspaper itself appear as part of the source note in both cases. The source note to an item republished from a newspaper also explicitly states from where the date and place in the title have been taken. Finally, if a newspaper article has a title providing additional information, that information is presented in the title.

Annotating Documents

In order to be able to publish as much as possible of the primary source material that we have collected, we annotate documents minimally. The first note for a document is an unnumbered source note. This note includes a descriptive symbol identifying the type of document it is (see "Descriptive Symbols for Documents") and the repository and collection where it is located (see "Repository Symbols"). Subcollections are given if collections are particularly large, making retrieval of a document difficult. When other versions of a document exist, their descriptive symbols, repository symbols, and collection locations follow immediately. Also included in the source note are the address, any endorsements that provide additional information, and other relevant data, such as the physical condition of the document if it affects legibility. For the rules on noting newspaper coverage and the reprinting of articles, see the section above on selecting documents for publication.

Subsequent annotation provides information which illuminates the text in relation to the Court as an institution. We do not identify individuals unless the content of the document indicates that they are of some importance to the history of the Court. Thus, litigants and lawyers are identified, jurors and deponents are not. People who appear in their official capacities, such as marshals or clerks, and who are identified as such in the document are not noted further. Places are identified minimally. The state where a place is located is not given for each mention of the locality; instead, the reader can look under the name of the locality in the index, where the state will be identified. Background information on issues is provided as succinctly as possible. Published primary and secondary material that gives further information is kept to a minimum in notes. Where annotation information for a particular document is supplied in a part of the document we are not publishing, or where information is common knowledge, we do not provide a citation. Legal terms not included in the glossary at the end of each part of this volume are defined at the point they occur; except where noted, our definitions are derived from *Black's Law Dictionary*, 4th ed. rev. (St. Paul, Minnesota: West Publishing, 1968).

Transcribing Ambiguous Text

Our effort to transcribe documents literally has given rise to a set of rules for transcription of ambiguous texts, where a writer's intention is not certain. Thus, we may not be able to distinguish whether an author meant to record a period or a comma, an upper or lowercase letter, a contraction bar or an ellipsis. In an effort to resolve such textual ambiguity, we refer first to the writer's prior practice and transcribe accordingly. If a writer consistently capitalized or spelled a word in a distinct, idiosyncratic manner, then we follow this previous practice. Having decided not to modernize in our transcription, we recognize that a sensitive interpretation of text based upon an author's style is a crucial editorial role. If a writer's previous practice does not provide clear guidance in transcribing textual ambiguity, we follow modern practice. In particular, if a word is clearly identifiable, but individual letters cannot be traced because of the author's hasty scrawl, modern spelling is adopted in the absence of evidence that the writer was in the habit of using a variant spelling. Where an ambiguous usage has no modern equivalent, we make an editorial choice, and that becomes our rule for the future. In this guide, we carefully note where we modernize and where we have made editorial choices in transcribing ambiguous text.

Transcribing from Printed Sources

As with correspondence, we reproduce text from printed sources as closely as possible to the way that it appears in the original. Three problems characteristic only of printed media have been treated specially. First, letters inverted in the original are corrected and then annotated. Thus, when a "u" is mistakenly typeset in the original instead of an "n," we print the "n" in our text and present the original version in a note. Second, when a word has been divided from the next word in the wrong place—e.g., "agreeabl yto"—or not divided at all, we publish a corrected version and annotate the original. Finally, letters that did not imprint in the original are supplied within brackets; if the correct letter is conjectural, it is followed by a question mark within the brackets.

Eighteenth-Century Punctuation

Two marks of punctuation used in the eighteenth century and reproduced in this series were the virgule (/) and the equals sign (=), two short parallel lines used as a hyphen. The virgule could be employed either alone or in conjunction with another mark of punctuation to stop or otherwise demarcate a sentence. The equals sign was used sometimes in place of a hyphen to draw together two separate words or parts of words: e.g., "New=York."

The dash also was used to punctuate in the eighteenth century. Appearing as a short, horizontal line, straight or curved, located on the baseline or slightly above, it was employed where a sentence broke off abruptly or was interrupted, where a significant or solemn pause was required, or at an unexpected turn of sentiment. In addition to appearing alone, the dash also could be used in conjunction with another mark of punctuation. In the latter case, a writer could create shading within punctuation; for example, the period-dash combination connoted elongation in a pause, dramatic stoppage, or a particularly august statement. We retain the dash wherever its use could be interpreted to have some value as punctuation.

Writers sometimes omitted punctuation. When this has been done in a series of items and no additional space left between them, we annotate those items that might cause the reader difficulty. Where missing punctuation might cause the reader to misinterpret the division between two thoughts, we supply extra space to divide the thoughts. When a thought ends without punctuation at the edge of the document page, and a new thought begins on the next line, we add whatever mark of punctuation the writer customarily used and put it in square brackets. Punctuation left out between two items in a series, because the first item falls at the end of a line and the second comes at the beginning of the next line, is supplied in square brackets.

Eighteenth-Century Abbreviation

Two modes of abbreviating words were available to eighteenth-century writers: abbreviation in the middle of a word (contraction) and abbreviation at the end of the word (suspension). A selective list of abbreviations that appear in this volume and that may be unfamiliar is in the appendix of "Signs and Abbreviations." Idiosyncratic abbreviations that may cause confusion are noted where they occur. Contraction involved the omission of letters in the middle of a word, as where "Honorable" was written as "Honble." Contractions of this type could appear without punctuation, or they could be punctuated in several different ways. The use of the apostrophe to indicate mid-word abbreviation was not unknown, but it was infrequent. On occasion, writers would indicate the location of missing letter(s) by using one or more ellipses. An ellipsis might appear as a straight line ("His Maj＿＿y" to mean "His Majesty"); or it might appear as a series of stops or asterisks ("His Maj . . . y" or "His Maj***y").

In addition to the use of apostrophes and ellipses, eighteenth-century writers often indicated that letters had been dropped by the use of contraction bars, which we retain. Explicit rules had dictated the form and placement of these marks in medieval Latin usage, but by the late eighteenth century personal preference determined practice. The form of the bar might be straight, curved, wavy, or sweeping and usually bore no relation to any set of rules indicating different functions. It might be placed in empty space, through the letters at the end of a word, through the ascenders of letters, or, beginning beneath endletters, it might move up and through an entire word or cluster of letters. Contemporary printers, aware that old distinctions were virtually meaningless, usually standardized all bars to curved or straight, depending upon their personal preferences or supply of type. In general, printers adopted uniformly straight contraction bars. When printed, these bars were usually placed over the letter immediately before the letter(s) omitted.

Given these contemporary conventions of writing and printing contraction marks, we have adopted the following rules. We read as a contraction bar any mark passing through or above any of the characters making up the part of the word on the baseline (thus explicitly excluding, for the moment, marks involving superior letters). We standardize all contraction marks to short straight bars and place them over the letter immediately preceding the part of the word left out. If an author has left letters out of two parts of a word and indicated the omission with a single contraction mark, we record that mark over the letter preceding the first part of the word omitted. In a contracted word where a "t" has been crossed so as to indicate the possible intention of its serving a second purpose as a contraction mark and where it is the writer's practice to use contraction bars, we read it as one.

Eighteenth-century writers also contracted words through the use of superior letters. Although superior letters could be used in the middle of a word ("M^{d}m"), this was rarely done. More commonly, contractions using superior letters involved either one superior letter or a cluster of them at the end of a word ("Feb^y" or "Esq^{rs}"). When in doubt as to whether a letter or cluster of letters might be superior or not, we bring it down to the baseline, unless a writer's prior practice was to use superior letters.

The placement of punctuation marks—usually periods, commas, or colons—beneath superior letters was quite common. Writers also used ellipses beneath superior letters to indicate contraction. We reproduce an ellipsis drawn beneath any part of a superior-letter construction as an ellipsis beneath all superior letters. It should be noted that it is often difficult to determine whether a mark beginning over the baseline letters and continuing under the superior letters was meant to be a contraction mark or an ellipsis. Because most writers used both contraction marks and ellipses, we cannot refer to previous usage to resolve this dilemma. We resort, therefore, to an arbitrary rule: if a mark involves more baseline than superior letters, we read it as a contraction bar; if it involves more superior letters, we read it as an ellipsis. In situations of perfect ambiguity, we favor the contraction bar, which was more commonly employed. In an abbreviated word where a "t" has been crossed so as to indicate the possible intention of its serving a second purpose as an ellipsis under superior letters and where it is the writer's practice to use ellipses, we read it as one.

In reproducing punctuation beneath superior letters, we have had to develop rules to cover a wide array of punctuation combinations. Where a single punctuation mark lies beneath a single letter, the mark is placed beneath that letter. Where there are fewer punctuation marks than superior letters, the marks are right-justified beneath the superior letters. In those instances where the number of punctuation marks exceeds the number of superior letters under which they lie, the number of punctuation marks will be reduced to equal the number of superior letters. A special case of this is where multiple marks of punctuation appear beneath a single superior letter; in this instance, two marks will be retained. Our concern in establishing this rule is to retain the fact of multiple punctuation marks rather than to try to reproduce the precise form in which the multiple punctuation appears: thus, where an eighteenth-century writer might have placed five stops under the three superior letters in "Honble," we reduce this to three. Where superior letters have both punctuation and ellipses beneath, the punctuation is reproduced according to the rules explained above and the ellipsis is placed beneath all superior letters.

The second major mode of abbreviation, through suspension, involved simply the omission of endletters. A mark of abbreviation, whether a stop, colon, dash, or semicolon, usually would follow. Also possible in punctuating a suspension was the use of the virgule, either alone or in conjunction with another mark of punctuation. A writer could also use a contraction mark in addition to, or in place of, a mark of punctuation. In transcribing an abbreviation connected to the following word by a penstroke, we do not insert a space after the abbreviation, thus maintaining a common eighteenth-century practice. Whole words connected by a penstroke are separated, however. Suspension and contraction were sometimes used together. Words could be shortened by every imaginable combination of omitted characters, ellipses, contraction bars, and superior letters with or without punctuation beneath.

Eighteenth-Century Signs

Unlike abbreviations, where words were shortened either through contraction or suspension, signs were used in the eighteenth century in place of the text not written out. The sign, therefore, did not indicate missing material; it represented the material in another form. A list of signs appears at the back of each part of this volume in a compilation of "Signs and Abbreviations." Two commonly recognized signs are the "℥" or "℥" (per sign) meaning "Per" or "per" and the "&" (ampersand) meaning "and." Both of these signs were written in many different forms. We reproduce these signs, as well as others, by designing a special character to represent each; we retain the function of the signs without trying to reproduce their multifarious forms. Two unusual signs (no longer used) were ^{9} and $^℮$. The first was used at the end of a word in place of the letters "us" or "os" or "ost"; the second symbol replaced "is" or "es" or, more generally, any word ending. It should be noted that, like eighteenth-century writers and printers, we have used a "y" to transcribe the thorn mark, an Old English and Icelandic runic character for "th."

Reference marks are a special class of signs. Eighteenth-century writers employed them to direct readers to passages of text in margins or on other pages in those situations where the insertions could not be interlined. The asterisk is the most common reference mark, and we reproduce it as "*." But marks called obelisks were also used. We retain in their original form those obelisks with distinctive shapes, such as daggers, double daggers, and parallel lines. But an obelisk also could appear as a cross or an "X" with an arbitrary arrangement of decorative dots and flourishes. Because of the expense of reproducing the idiosyncratic forms of this latter type of obelisk, we have indicated their use by the symbol "⊗." Any confusion that might result from standardizing this latter type of obelisk to the same form is explained in a note to the specific passage.

Whenever a reference mark has been used to indicate where a writer intended a passage be inserted, we reproduce the reference mark itself and then move the corresponding reference mark (if any) as well as the insertion to the designated location. We treat the inserted passage and its accompanying reference mark as if they were interlineations and therefore drop the type size to that used for interlineations.

Transcribing Unreadable Text

We have transcribed the texts for this documentary edition mainly from photocopies or microform. In those instances where we transcribe directly from original documents, we mention the fact in the source note to the document. When transcribing from photocopies, it frequently is difficult to discern whether a mark is one of punctuation, a spot of ink, or a flaw in the copy.

Situations also occur where text is unreadable because of heavy crossing out, destruction by fire or other accident, or poor handwriting. For text that is crossed out and therefore illegible, we indicate the extent of the obliteration by using the following phrasing in italics within square brackets:

[*letter(s) inked out*] for less than a word
[*word inked out*]
[*phrase inked out*] for more than a word up to a full line
[*passage inked out*] for more than a line

For text that is missing because of fire or other accident, we indicate the extent of the loss by using the following phrasing in italics within square brackets:

[*letter(s) missing*] for less than a word
[*word missing*]
[*phrase missing*] for more than a word up to a full line
[*passage missing*] for more than a line

If the text that is poorly written, inked out, or missing is obvious, we supply it in roman type within square brackets. For example, where the phrase "United S[*letters missing*] of America" might have occurred, we substitute "United S[tates] of America." If the insertion is more conjectural than in this example or if we are not able to surmise the proper spelling because the writer has not used the word before and has a reputation for idiosyncratic spelling, a question mark is placed after the last letter before the square bracket closure. We rely on any documentation available, such as contemporary copies, to supply illegible text. We indicate the reason for such conjectural readings either in a headnote or in annotation to the specific document. Inasmuch as we use square brackets to enclose editorial conjectures, comments, or insertions, we annotate those instances where a writer actually used square brackets in his own text, though the latter are few in number.

The problem of text written over other text or over a passage that has been erased poses some difficulty. Where a writer has placed a second word over one initially written (whether he did or did not attempt to erase the first effort), we publish as part of the text the word finally chosen and note the initial choice. Where words have been written over or around text that the author has completely erased and thereby made illegible, we do not note the erasure. This is a necessity because many erasures, especially on photocopies or microform, are invisible, and to note some but not others would be misleading.

Embellishment

We delete from our transcription all textual marks that are of strictly decorative or design function. Thus, end-of-line dashes used to justify texts to the right margin are deleted as unnecessary since our typeset lines do not break at the same point as the document lines. Dashes employed in the same fashion within braces are not reproduced either. Any dash, however, that might serve some purpose as punctuation is retained. Elaborately self-conscious changes in the style of handwriting—textual enlargement, ornate capital letters—are not reproduced as such; nor are idiosyncratic decorative or aesthetic marks whether meant to balance or serve some other purpose inherent in the layout of the original document page. To reproduce such idiosyncratic embellishment would be technologically difficult and prohibitively expensive. We make this decision fully aware that the meaning of a document inheres as much in its appearance as in the words it contains. But the meaning that derives from the physical appearance of a document can be discerned only by examining it in person. The experience of personal contact with a document cannot be duplicated in a typeset edition.

Guide to Editorial Apparatus

Descriptive Symbols for Documents

The following table includes the symbols used to describe the documents available for publication and citation. When more than one version of a document exists, preference for publication is given in descending order according to this table. Thus, we publish a recipient's copy of a document in preference to a draft. In the source note, all versions are listed, the first being the one we are publishing.

R   Recipient's copy of a letter or other document. We determine whether a letter or document is a recipient's copy by any indication of endorsements, the presence of an address cover, or the collection in which it was found. If the letter or document is identifiably a duplicate, triplicate, presscopy, or polygraph copy made and sent to offset possible loss of the original, then we mention that fact in the source note; but the letter or document is still considered a recipient's copy.

D   Document. When used to describe commissions and other official documents, this symbol indicates that we cannot identify whether the document is a recipient's copy or a retained copy. When applied to diaries, notes, and journal entries, this symbol means that we are describing an original. If the document is identifiably a duplicate, triplicate, presscopy, or polygraph copy, that fact is explained in the source note; but the document is still marked as "D."

L   Letter. We use this symbol when we cannot determine whether a letter is a recipient's copy or a retained copy. If the letter is identifiably a duplicate, triplicate, presscopy, or polygraph copy, then that fact is mentioned in the source note; but the document is still considered an "L."

C   Retained copy of a letter or other document. It is assumed that such copies are kept for personal or official files unless otherwise stated. This designation also is used (with appropriate editorial explanation) for copies of letters sent to individuals other than the addressee. If the letter or document is identifiably a duplicate, triplicate, or polygraph copy, that fact is mentioned in the source note; but the document is still marked with a "C."

Pc   Presscopy. Used only for a retained copy of a letter or document. A presscopy was made by impressing thin dampened paper onto the original document, thereby transferring some ink to the thin paper. The result is frequently blurred and difficult to read.

Lb   Letterbook copy. A letterbook copy of a letter or document is a retained version copied into a bound volume.

Df   Draft of a letter or document.

Pr   Printed version of a letter or document. Usually published substantially later than a contemporary version.

Tr   Transcript of a letter or document made substantially later than a contemporary version. If a transcript is typewritten, that fact is mentioned in the source note. When the origin of a transcript can be identified, an explanation is provided in the source note.

The symbols above are used in combination with the following descriptive symbols.

A   Autograph text (text in the handwriting of the author).

[A?]   Probably autograph text.

S   Signed by the author.

[S?]   Signature cropped, clipped, or obliterated.

Seals are represented by the following symbols.

SEAL   An official seal.

Seal   A handwritten drawing of a seal.

LS, etc.   The abbreviations "LS," "L.S.," "LS.," and "L.S" appear as in the original document.

Three special situations must be noted. First, if we transcribe from a photocopy made from another photocopy or facsimile, we mention that fact in the source note. If we are relying on a text which is itself an extract or abstract, we note that also. Finally, if we translate the text from another language, we explain that in the source note.

Repository Symbols

The following list includes all repository symbols used in this volume.

CSmH	Henry E. Huntington Library, San Marino, California
Ct	Connecticut State Library, Hartford, Connecticut
CtHC	Hartford Seminary Foundation, Hartford, Connecticut
CtHi	Connecticut Historical Society, Hartford, Connecticut
CtNlHi	New London County Historical Society, New London, Connecticut
CtY	Yale University, New Haven, Connecticut
DLC	United States Library of Congress, Washington, D.C.
DNA	United States National Archives and Records Service, Washington, D.C.

	RG 21	Records of District Courts of the United States
	RG 46	Records of the United States Senate
	RG 59	General Records of the Department of State
	RG 76	Records of Boundary and Claims Commissions and Arbitrations
	RG 94	Records of the Adjutant General's Office, 1780s-1917
	RG 217	Records of the United States General Accounting Office
	RG 233	Records of the United States House of Representatives
	RG 267	Records of the Supreme Court of the United States
	RG 360	Records of the Continental and Confederation Congresses and the Constitutional Convention

DUSC	United States Supreme Court, Washington, D.C.
DeHi	Historical Society of Delaware, Wilmington, Delaware
DeU	University of Delaware, Newark, Delaware
G-Ar	Georgia State Department of Archives and History, Atlanta, Georgia
GEpFAR	United States Federal Archives and Records Center, East Point, Georgia

	RG 21	Records of District Courts of the United States

ICHi	Chicago Historical Society, Chicago, Illinois
LNT	Tulane University, New Orleans, Louisiana
MB	Boston Public Library, Boston, Massachusetts
MBNEH	New England Historic Genealogical Society, Boston, Massachusetts
MBSufC	Suffolk County Court House, Boston, Massachusetts

MH-H	Harvard University, Houghton Library, Cambridge, Massachusetts
MHi	Massachusetts Historical Society, Boston, Massachusetts
MNF	Forbes Library, Northampton, Massachusetts
MScitHi	Scituate Historical Society, Scituate, Massachusetts
MWA	American Antiquarian Society, Worcester, Massachusetts
MWalFAR	United States Federal Archives and Records Center, Waltham, Massachusetts
	RG 21 Records of District Courts of the United States
MdAA	Hall of Records Commission, Annapolis, Maryland
MdFre	C. Burr Artz Public Library, Frederick, Maryland
MdHi	Maryland Historical Society, Baltimore, Maryland
MeHi	Maine Historical Society, Portland, Maine
MiU-C	University of Michigan, William L. Clements Library, Ann Arbor, Michigan
N	New York State Library, Albany, New York
NHi	New-York Historical Society, New York, New York
NN	New York Public Library, New York, New York
NNC	Columbia University, New York, New York
NNPM	Pierpont Morgan Library, New York, New York
Nc-Ar	North Carolina State Department of Archives and History, Raleigh, North Carolina
NcD	Duke University, Durham, North Carolina
NcU	University of North Carolina, Chapel Hill, North Carolina
Nh	New Hampshire State Library, Concord, New Hampshire
NhHi	New Hampshire Historical Society, Concord, New Hampshire
Nj	New Jersey State Library, Trenton, New Jersey
NjBaFAR	United States Federal Archives and Records Center, Bayonne, New Jersey
	RG 21 Records of District Courts of the United States
NjMoNP	Morristown National Historical Park, Morristown, New Jersey
NjP	Princeton University, Princeton, New Jersey
NjR	Rutgers—The State University, New Brunswick, New Jersey
OCHP	Cincinnati Historical Society, Cincinnati, Ohio
PCarlH	Cumberland County Historical Society and Hamilton Library Association, Carlisle, Pennsylvania
PHarH	Pennsylvania Historical and Museum Commission, Harrisburg, Pennsylvania
PHi	Historical Society of Pennsylvania, Philadelphia, Pennsylvania
PP	Free Library of Philadelphia, Philadelphia, Pennsylvania
PPFAR	United States Federal Archives and Records Center, Philadelphia, Pennsylvania
	RG 21 Records of District Courts of the United States

PPIn	Independence National Historical Park, Philadelphia, Pennsylvania
PPL	Library Company of Philadelphia, Philadelphia, Pennsylvania
PPRF	Rosenbach Foundation, Philadelphia, Pennsylvania
PSC-Hi	Friends Historical Library of Swarthmore College, Swarthmore, Pennsylvania
PU-L	University of Pennsylvania, Biddle Law Library, Philadelphia, Pennsylvania
PWacD	David Library of the American Revolution, Washington Crossing, Pennsylvania
RHi	Rhode Island Historical Society, Providence, Rhode Island
RPJCB	John Carter Brown Library, Providence, Rhode Island
ScC	Charleston Library Society, Charleston, South Carolina
ScCAH	South Carolina Department of Archives and History, Columbia, South Carolina
ScHi	South Carolina Historical Society, Charleston, South Carolina
ScU	University of South Carolina, Columbia, South Carolina
UkLPR	Public Record Office, London, United Kingdom
Vi	Virginia State Library, Richmond, Virginia
ViHi	Virginia Historical Society, Richmond, Virginia
ViMtV	Mount Vernon Ladies' Association of the Union, Mount Vernon, Virginia
ViU	University of Virginia, Charlottesville, Virginia
ViW	College of William and Mary, Williamsburg, Virginia

Short Titles and Abbreviations

Ames	Seth Ames, ed., *Works of Fisher Ames,* 2 vols. (Boston: Little, Brown, 1854).
Annals	*Annals of the Congress of the United States,* 42 vols. (Washington, D.C.: Gales and Seaton, 1834-1856).
ASP	*American State Papers: Documents, Legislative and Executive, of the Congress of the United States,* 38 vols. (Washington, D.C.: Gales and Seaton, 1832-1861). This series is divided into ten classes: *Foreign Relations, Indian Affairs, Finance, Commerce and Navigation, Military Affairs, Naval Affairs, Post-Office Department, Public Lands, Claims,* and *Miscellaneous.*
BDAC	U.S., Congress, House, *Biographical Directory of the American Congress, 1774-1961,* 85th Cong., 2d sess., H. Doc. 442, Serial 12108.

*Black's Law
Dictionary*   Henry Campbell Black, *Black's Law Dictionary,* 4th ed. (St. Paul, Minn.: West Publishing, 1951).

CCD   Circuit Court for the district of: e.g., CCD Massachusetts means Circuit Court for the district of Massachusetts.

DAB   *Dictionary of American Biography.*

Dallas, 1   Alexander James Dallas, *Reports of Cases Ruled and Adjudged in the Courts of Pennsylvania* (Philadelphia: T. Bradford, 1790).

Dallas, 2-4   Alexander James Dallas, *Reports of Cases Ruled and Adjudged in the Several Courts of the United States, and of Pennsylvania,* vol. 2 (Philadelphia: Aurora, 1798); vol. 3 (Philadelphia: J. Ormrod, 1799); vol. 4 (Philadelphia: Printed for P. Byrne, by Fry and Kammerer, 1807).

DC   District Court for the district of: e.g., DC Virginia means District Court for the district of Virginia.

DNB   *Dictionary of National Biography.*

FFC   Linda Grant De Pauw, ed., *Documentary History of the First Federal Congress of the United States of America,* 3 vols. to date (Baltimore: Johns Hopkins University Press, 1972-1977).

FFE   Merrill Jensen and Robert A. Becker, eds., *Documentary History of the First Federal Elections, 1788-1790,* 1 vol. to date (Madison: University of Wisconsin Press, 1976).

HRJ   *Journal of the House of Representatives of the United States,* vols. 1-9 (Washington, D.C.: Gales and Seaton, 1826).

JCC   *Journals of the Continental Congress, 1774-1789,* vols. 1-15, ed. Worthington C. Ford; vols. 16-27, ed. Gaillard Hunt; vols. 28-34, ed. John C. Fitzpatrick (Washington, D.C.: Government Printing Office, 1904-1937).

LPAH   *The Law Practice of Alexander Hamilton,* vols. 1-2, ed. Julius Goebel, Jr.; vols. 3-5, ed. Julius Goebel, Jr., and Joseph H. Smith (New York: Columbia University Press, 1964-1981).

MBBP   John Hill Martin, *Martin's Bench and Bar of Philadelphia* (Philadelphia: Rees Welsh, 1883).

MJI   Griffith John McRee, *Life and Correspondence of James Iredell,* 2 vols. (1857; reprint ed. in 1 vol., New York: Peter Smith, 1949).

OED   *Oxford English Dictionary.*

PAH   Harold C. Syrett, ed., *The Papers of Alexander Hamilton*, 26
                vols. (New York: Columbia University Press, 1961-1979).

PGM   Robert A. Rutland, ed., *The Papers of George Mason, 1725-
                1792*, 3 vols. (Chapel Hill: University of North Carolina
                Press, 1970).

PGW, Diary   *The Diaries of George Washington*, vols. 1-3, ed. Donald Jack-
                son; vols. 4-6, ed. Donald Jackson and Dorothy Twohig
                (Charlottesville: University Press of Virginia, 1976-1979).

PJA   Robert J. Taylor, ed., *Papers of John Adams*, 4 vols. to date
                (Cambridge: Belknap Press of Harvard University Press,
                1977-1979).

PJA, Diary   Lyman H. Butterfield, ed., *Diary and Autobiography of John Ad-
                ams*, 4 vols. (Cambridge: Belknap Press of Harvard Univer-
                sity Press, 1961).

PJA, Legal   L. Kinvin Wroth and Hiller B. Zobel, eds., *Legal Papers of
                John Adams*, 3 vols. (Cambridge: Belknap Press of Harvard
                University Press, 1965).

PJI   Don Higginbotham, ed., *The Papers of James Iredell*, 2 vols. to
                date (Raleigh: Department of Cultural Resources of the Di-
                vision of Archives and History, 1976).

PJJ   Richard B. Morris, ed., *John Jay*, 2 vols. to date: vol. 1, *The
                Making of a Revolutionary*, and vol. 2, *The Winning of the Peace*
                (New York: Harper & Row, 1975-1980).

PJM   *The Papers of John Marshall*, 3 vols. to date: vol. 1, ed. Her-
                bert A. Johnson; vol. 2, ed. Charles T. Cullen and Herbert
                A. Johnson; vol. 3, ed. William C. Stinchcombe and Charles
                T. Cullen (Chapel Hill: University of North Carolina Press,
                1974-1979).

PMad   *The Papers of James Madison*, 14 vols. to date: vols. 1-7, ed.
                William T. Hutchinson and William M. E. Rachal (Chicago:
                University of Chicago Press, 1962-1971); vol. 8, ed. Robert
                A. Rutland and William M. E. Rachal (Chicago: University
                of Chicago Press, 1975); vols. 9-10, ed. Robert A. Rutland
                (Chicago: University of Chicago Press, 1977); vols. 11-13, ed.
                Robert A. Rutland and Charles F. Hobson (Charlottesville:
                University Press of Virginia, 1977-1981); vol. 14, ed. Robert
                A. Rutland and Thomas A. Mason (Charlottesville: University
                Press of Virginia, 1983).

PTJ	Julian P. Boyd, ed., *The Papers of Thomas Jefferson*, 20 vols. to date (Princeton: Princeton University Press, 1950-1982).
RFC	Max Farrand, ed., *The Records of the Federal Convention of 1787*, 4 vols. (1937; reprint ed., New Haven: Yale University Press, 1966).
ROC	*The Documentary History of the Ratification of the Constitution*, 4 vols. to date: vols. 1-3, ed. Merrill Jensen; vol. 13, ed. John P. Kaminski and Gaspare J. Saladino (Madison: State Historical Society of Wisconsin, 1976-1981).
SEJ	*Journal of the Executive Proceedings of the Senate of the United States of America*, vols. 1-3 (Washington, D.C.: Duff Green, 1828).
SLJ	*Journal of the Senate of the United States of America*, vols. 1-5 (Washington, D.C.: Gales and Seaton, 1820-1821).
Stat.	*The Public Statutes at Large of the United States*, vols. 1-17 (Boston: Little, Brown, 1845-1873); vols. 18-94 (Washington, D.C.: Government Printing Office, 1875-1981).

Newspaper Coverage, 1787-1801

As extensive as our newspaper search has been (see the "Introduction" for our guidelines), we have not been able to locate complete runs for every newspaper we wanted to read. We have given priority to reading all hard copy and microcopy available at the Library of Congress. Next, we have sought to borrow microform copy on interlibrary loan from a number of libraries and historical societies. Despite our best efforts, we often have been unable to secure all copies of every newspaper.

The list that follows presents the newspapers that were read and the extent of the coverage for each. Our short titles correspond to those used by Clarence S. Brigham in his two-volume *History and Bibliography of American Newspapers, 1690-1820* (Worcester, Massachusetts: American Antiquarian Society, 1947) and in his "Additions and Corrections to *History and Bibliography of American Newspapers, 1690-1820*," included in the *Proceedings of the American Antiquarian Society* 71 (1961): 15-62. Brigham's bibliography and supplement provide full newspaper titles, changes in those titles, dates of publication, as well as printers and publishers. Following the name of the newspaper, we place in parentheses the years that the newspaper was published between 1787 and 1801—the years included in our search. Finally, we indicate how many issues of the newspaper we were able to find and read. We note the coverage by these terms:

"full" means all issues (sometimes with a few exceptions) were available
"very good" means three-quarters or more was available
"good" means one-half to three-quarters was available
"poor" means less than one-half was available
"scattered" means only a few issues were available.

CONNECTICUT

Hartford
American Mercury (1787-1801): 1787-1791 missing, 1792-1797 very good, 1798 missing, and 1799-1801 full.
Connecticut Courant (1787-1801): full.
Hartford Gazette (1794-1795): good.

New Haven
Connecticut Journal (1787-1801): full.

DELAWARE

Wilmington
Delaware and Eastern-Shore Advertiser (1794-1799): scattered.
Delaware Gazette (1787-1799): scattered.

GEORGIA

Augusta
Augusta Chronicle (1789-1801): 1789-1794 very good, 1795 good, 1796-1801 missing.
Augusta Herald (1799-1801): scattered.
Georgia State Gazette (1787-1789): full.
Southern Centinel (1793-1799): scattered.

Savannah
Columbian Museum (1796-1801): 1796-1797 good, 1798-1801 poor.
Gazette of the State of Georgia (1787-1788): full.
Georgia Gazette (1788-1801): very good.

MARYLAND

Annapolis
Maryland Gazette (1787-1801): 1787-1789 scattered, 1790 very good, 1791-1794 missing, 1795-1798 very good, 1799-1801 missing.

Baltimore
American (1799-1801): very good.
Baltimore Daily Intelligencer (1793-1794): full.
Baltimore Daily Repository (1791-1793): full.

Baltimore Evening Post (1792-1793): scattered.
Baltimore Telegraphe (1795-1801): scattered.
Edwards's Baltimore Daily Advertiser (1793-1794): scattered.
Federal Gazette (1796-1801): full.
Federal Intelligencer (1794-1795): full.
Maryland Gazette (1787-1792): 1787-1790 poor, 1791-1792 missing.
Maryland Journal (1787-1797): 1787-1792 full, 1793-1794 good, 1795-
     1797 missing.

Easton

Maryland Herald (1790-1801): scattered.
Republican Star (1799-1801): scattered.

MASSACHUSETTS

Boston

American Apollo (1792-1794): very good.
American Herald (1787-1788): very good.
Argus (1791-1793): 1791 poor, 1792-1793 full.
Boston Gazette (1787-1798): full.
Boston Gazette (1800-1801): full.
Boston Price-Current (1795-1798): scattered.
Columbian Centinel (1790-1801): full.
Courier (1795-1796): poor.
Federal Gazette (1798): poor.
Federal Orrery (1794-1796): good.
Herald of Freedom (1788-1791): 1788-1790 good, 1791 scattered.
Independent Chronicle (1787-1801): full.
Massachusetts Centinel (1787-1790): full.
Massachusetts Gazette (1787-1788): full.
Massachusetts Mercury (1793-1801): 1793-1796 poor, 1797-1801 full.
Russell's Gazette (1798-1800): full.
Times (1794): scattered.

NEW HAMPSHIRE

Exeter

Herald of Liberty (1793-1796): scattered.
Lamson's Weekly Visitor (1795): good.
New Hampshire Gazetteer (1789-1793): scattered.
Political Banquet (1799-1800): scattered.
Ranlet's Federal Miscellany (1798-1799): scattered.

Portsmouth

Federal Observer (1798-1800): scattered.
New-Hampshire Gazette (1787-1801): 1787-1789 missing, 1790-1792 very
     good, 1793-1794 missing, 1795-1801 very good.

New-Hampshire Spy (1787-1793): 1787-1788 very good, 1789-1793 missing.

Oracle of the Day (1793-1799): 1793-1796 missing, 1797-1798 full, 1799 missing.

Republican Ledger (1799-1801): scattered.

United States Oracle (1800-1801): full.

NEW JERSEY

Trenton

Federalist (1798-1801): full.

Federal Post (1788-1789): poor.

New-Jersey State Gazette (1792-1796): 1792-1794 missing, 1795-1796 very good.

New-Jersey State Gazette (1799-1800): good.

State Gazette (1796-1799): scattered.

NEW YORK

Albany

Albany Register (1788-1801): scattered.

New York

American Citizen (1800-1801): poor.

American Minerva (1793-1796): 1793-1794 poor, 1795-1796 missing.

Argus (1795-1800): very good.

Commercial Advertiser (1797-1801): full.

Daily Advertiser (1787-1801): 1787-1793 full, 1794-1795 poor, 1796-1797 missing, 1798-1801 very good.

Diary (1792-1798): 1792-1793 poor, 1794 full, 1795 scattered, 1796-1798 good.

Forlorn Hope (1800): full.

Gazette of the United States (1789-1790): full.

Greenleaf's New York Journal (1794-1800): scattered.

Impartial Gazetteer (1788): good.

Mercantile Advertiser (1798-1801): scattered.

Minerva (1796-1797): full.

New-York Daily Gazette (1788-1795): 1788-1789 full, 1790-1795 missing.

New-York Gazette (1795-1801): scattered.

New-York Journal (1787-1793): very good.

New-York Morning Post (1787-1792): scattered.

New York Packet (1787-1792): scattered.

New-York Weekly Museum (1788-1801): 1788-1791 scattered, 1792-1794 very good, 1795-1796 missing, 1797-1801 very good.

Time Piece (1797-1798): full.

NORTH CAROLINA

Edenton
State Gazette of North-Carolina (1788-1799): very good.

Fayetteville
North-Carolina Minerva (1796-1799): good.

New Bern
Newbern Gazette (1798-1801): scattered.
North-Carolina Gazette (1787-1798): scattered.
State Gazette of North-Carolina (1787-1788): scattered.

Raleigh
North-Carolina Minerva (1799-1801): good.
Raleigh Register (1799-1801): full.

Salisbury
North-Carolina Mercury (1798-1801): scattered.

Wilmington
Wilmington Centinel (1788): full.

PENNSYLVANIA

Norristown
Norristown Gazette (1799-1800): scattered.

Philadelphia
Aurora (1794-1801): full.
Claypoole's American Daily Advertiser (1796-1800): full.
Complete Counting House Companion (1787-1790): scattered.
Country Porcupine (1798-1799): scattered.
Daily Advertiser (1797): good.
Dunlap's American Daily Advertiser (1791-1795): full.
Evening Chronicle (1787): scattered.
Federal Gazette (1788-1793): full.
Freeman's Journal (1787-1792): full.
Gales's Independent Gazetteer (1796-1797): full.
Gazette of the United States (1790-1801): 1790-1793 full, 1794-1798 good,
        1799 missing, 1800-1801 very good.
General Advertiser (1790-1794): full.
Independent Gazetteer (1787-1796): full.
National Gazette (1791-1793): full.
New World (1796-1797): very good.
Pennsylvania Evening Herald (1787-1788): full.
Pennsylvania Gazette (1787-1801): 1787-1796 full, 1797-1801 missing.
Pennsylvania Journal (1787-1793): full.

Pennsylvania Mercury (1787-1792): full.
Pennsylvania Packet (1787-1790): full.
Philadelphia Gazette (1794-1801): full.
Philadelphia Minerva (1795-1798): full.
Porcupine's Gazette (1797-1799): full.
Poulson's American Daily Advertiser (1800-1801): full.
True American (1798-1801): scattered.
Universal Gazette (1797-1800): full.

York
  Pennsylvania Herald (1789-1800): 1789-1793 full, 1794-1795 missing,
     1796-1798 full, 1799-1800 missing.
  York Recorder (1800-1801): full.

RHODE ISLAND

Newport
  Companion (1798-1799): scattered.
  Guardian of Liberty (1800-1801): scattered.
  Newport Mercury (1787-1801): 1787-1791 very good, 1792-1801 full.

Providence
  Providence Gazette (1787-1801): very good.
  Providence Journal (1799-1801): full.
  State Gazette (1796): poor.
  United States Chronicle (1787-1801): 1787-1799 very good, 1800-1801
     missing.

SOUTH CAROLINA

Charleston
  City Gazette (1787-1801): 1787-1788 missing, 1789 full, 1790-1795 miss-
     ing, 1796 full, 1797 missing, 1798-1801 very good.
  Columbian Herald (1787-1796): 1787-1792 missing, 1793-1794 poor,
     1795 missing, 1796 poor.
  Federal Carolina Gazette (1800): scattered.
  South-Carolina State-Gazette (1794-1801): 1794-1796 poor, 1797 missing,
     1798-1799 poor, 1800-1801 missing.
  State Gazette of South-Carolina (1787-1793): 1787-1790 good, 1791-1792
     missing, 1793 very good.
  Times (1800-1801): full.

VERMONT

Bennington
  Vermont Gazette (1787-1796): 1787-1792 full, 1793 poor, 1794-1796
     missing.

Rutland
  Farmers' Library (1793-1794): full.
  Herald of Vermont (1792): full.
  Rutland Herald (1794-1801): 1794-1800 full, 1801 missing.

VIRGINIA

Norfolk
  Norfolk Weekly Journal (1797-1798): full.
  Virginia Chronicle (1792-1795): good.

Richmond
  Examiner (1798-1801): scattered.
  Friend of the People (1800): scattered.
  Observatory (1797-1798): scattered.
  Press (1800): scattered.
  Richmond and Manchester Advertiser (1795-1796): poor.
  Richmond Chronicle (1795-1796): scattered.
  Virginia Argus (1796-1801): 1796-1798 missing, 1799-1801 good.
  Virginia Federalist (1799-1800): scattered.
  Virginia Gazette, and General Advertiser (1790-1801): 1790-1796 very
      good, 1797-1798 scattered, 1799 very good, 1800-1801 scattered.
  Virginia Gazette and Independent Chronicle (1787-1789): scattered.
  Virginia Gazette, and Richmond and Manchester Advertiser (1793-1795): very
      good.
  Virginia Gazette & Richmond Chronicle (1793-1795): scattered.
  Virginia Gazette, and Weekly Advertiser (1787-1797): 1787-1789 full, 1790-
      1797 missing.
  Virginia Independent Chronicle (1787-1790): full.

The Documentary History of
the Supreme Court of
the United States, 1789–1800

Volume One
Part 1
Appointments and Proceedings

Appointments to the Bench

During the 1790s the bench of the Supreme Court consisted of one chief justice and five associate justices. From the first appointments made by George Washington through the appointment of John Marshall as chief justice in 1801, seventeen justices were appointed and commissioned. These seventeen appointments were distributed among fourteen men: eleven men received one appointment each and three men (John Rutledge, William Cushing, and John Jay) were appointed on two different occasions. Of the seventeen commissioned justices, only fourteen served on the Court: four as chief justice and ten as associate justice. John Rutledge served in both capacities during the decade, first as associate justice and later as chief justice. In addition, three men who received commissions did not serve in the positions conferred. Robert Hanson Harrison, commissioned as associate justice in 1789, did not serve on circuit and never sat with the Supreme Court because of poor health. Reasons of health also prevented Associate Justice William Cushing from accepting a commission promoting him to chief justice in 1796 (but he continued to serve as an associate justice). Finally, John Jay, who had been chief justice from 1789 to 1795, declined his 1800 reappointment.

This section includes complete documentation for the seventeen separate appointments made during this period. The seventeen are arranged in the order that they were approved by the Senate. Preceding each appointment is a brief biography of the appointee, focusing on his legal career leading up to his elevation to the bench. The documents that follow the biography trace chronologically the course of the appointment process. Appearing first are all papers that concern efforts to ascertain whether the eventual appointee would accept the honor or whether the president would be interested in considering that person's nomination. These papers are published only if they involve the president or those acting for him. Next come the official documents relating to the appointment: nomination by the president to the Senate, receipt of the nomination by the Senate, Senate action, notification to the president of Senate action, commission, cover letter, and record of oaths. Some of this official documentation is highly repetitive and, therefore, has been presented in abstract form with references to full printings. Abstracts, like other editorial interventions in the text, appear in italics and within brackets. Following the official documentation are printed—in chronological order—any letter of acceptance or declination, any letter of resignation or notice of death, and any other documentation that is subsequent to the appointment and that involves the appointee, the president, or those acting for the president.

Special mention should be made of the justices' oaths. Two oaths or affirmations were required before a justice could act in his official capacity. First, Article VI, section 3 of the Constitution states that the justices "shall be bound by Oath or Affirmation, to support this Constitution."[1] In addition, section 8 of "An Act to establish the Judicial Courts of the United States" stipulates a specific oath for the justices.[2] Before a justice could take his seat on any bench—either of a circuit court or of the Supreme Court—

he had to have taken both oaths. Hence, John Rutledge, who did not attend the first session of the Supreme Court in February, 1790, took his oaths before May 12, 1790, when he joined James Iredell on the bench of the Circuit Court for the district of South Carolina. In the minutes of the Supreme Court, justices were not listed as present by the clerk until after they had taken their oaths. William Cushing and John Blair, who first sat as associate justices when the Supreme Court opened on February 2, 1790, are listed as present on their first day in attendance; thus, they had to have taken their oaths prior to the Court's convening. Finally, it should be noted that those justices appointed under a temporary commission and later appointed under a permanent commission took their oaths two times, once for each commission.

1. *ROC*, 1:316.
2. *Stat.*, 1:76.

John Jay: Appointment as
Chief Justice in 1789

Born in New York City on December 12, 1745, John Jay was the son of Peter and Mary (Van Cortlandt) Jay, whose families were among the wealthiest and most influential in the province.[1] Jay's mother looked after his early education by teaching him English grammar and Latin. In 1753 Jay entered Reverend Peter Stouppe's grammar school in New Rochelle, several miles from Rye, where his family had moved shortly after Jay's birth.[2] He remained at Reverend Stouppe's for the next three years before returning home to complete his education under the guidance of George Murray.[3]

Jay entered King's College (later Columbia) in 1760 at the age of fourteen.[4] His course of instruction there closely paralleled those at Oxford and Cambridge and consisted mostly of the study of Greek and Latin with some instruction also in public law, philosophy, and natural science. Among his classmates were some of the sons of New York's elite: Robert R. Livingston, Peter Van Schaack, Egbert Benson, and Richard Harison.[5]

By February, 1763, Jay had decided on a career in law.[6] After graduating from King's College with honors in May, 1764, Jay entered the law offices of New York City attorney Benjamin Kissam.[7] There he spent the next twenty-two months drafting and preparing an assortment of legal instruments and assisting Kissam's chief clerk, Lindley Murray. The tedium of incessant copywork was broken in October, 1765, by the lawyers' strike protesting the Stamp Act and the consequent closure of the courts. Jay put the unexpected respite to good use. He returned to the family homestead at Rye where he spent the better part of the winter and spring of 1766 reading the classics.[8] After this extra study, Jay received a Master of Arts degree from King's College in May, 1767. With the Stamp Act crisis over, Jay returned to Kissam's office where he became chief clerk at the end of 1766.[9]

Two years later, having completed his duties as clerk, Jay joined the bar and soon thereafter formed a partnership with his old schoolmate and fellow New Yorker Robert R. Livingston, Jr.[10] Although Jay and Livingston dissolved their partnership after three years, Jay's own practice continued to grow; it included appearances before New York's Supreme Court of Judicature, the Court of Chancery, the Mayor's Court of New York City, and the inferior courts of Westchester, Ulster, Orange, Queens, and Dutchess Counties. By 1774 he was one of the most successful attorneys in the province.[11]

While Jay's law practice occupied much of his day, he did find time for other pursuits. With other King's College graduates, Jay formed the Debating Society of New York City in 1768. This group considered such timely questions as "Whether in an absolute Monarchy it is better That the Crown should be elective than hereditary."[12] Later, Jay joined with other members of the bar of the Supreme Court of Judicature to form the "Moot," a society that met to debate questions of law.[13] In 1769 he was appointed a clerk on a commission charged with settling a boundary dispute between New York and New Jersey. Jay's life, however, was not occupied entirely by serious matters. As a manager of the socially important Dancing Assembly of New York City, Jay maintained a strategic position of eminence and command over the social season.[14]

John Jay by Gilbert Stuart (1755-1828). Oil on canvas, 1783. Courtesy Diplomatic Reception Rooms, United States Department of State.

Having prospered in his chosen profession, Jay's thoughts turned to marriage. On April 28, 1774, he wed Sarah Van Brugh Livingston (1756-1802), the seventeen-year-old second cousin of his law partner, Robert R. Livingston, Jr.[15] She was the daughter of William Livingston (1723-1790), a leading lawyer in colonial New York,[16] and Susannah (French) Livingston (baptized 1723, died 1789),[17] described as the daughter of a wealthy New Jersey landowner.[18] Sarah and John Jay's marriage produced six children, two of whom—Peter Augustus and William—followed their father into law.[19]

In the spring of 1774, events in Boston and New York altered the course of his life. When news of the closing of Boston's port reached New York in early May, 1774, the city's merchants reacted by forming the Committee of Fifty-One to maintain communication with other colonies. Jay was appointed to a subcommittee formed to draft a reply to a Boston town meeting resolution calling for a nonimportation agreement until the Boston Port Act was repealed. Less than a week later, the subcommittee produced a call for a congress of deputies from all colonies to meet and determine a proper response to the Crown's action.[20]

Elected to the First Continental Congress in 1774,[21] Jay followed the moderate New York delegation on almost every issue. He supported Joseph Galloway's plan of union and quickly became a spokesman for those seeking conciliation and accommodation with England.[22] Yet Jay's signing of the Continental Association agreements calling for economic sanctions against Great Britain, and his authorship of the "Address to the People of Great Britain," won him more support from New York's Sons of Liberty than from his conservative friends.[23]

Upon his return to New York, Jay threw himself into the business of politics. He was elected to the Committee of Sixty, a more radical successor to the now defunct Committee of Fifty-One. The Committee of Sixty was charged with enforcing the nonimportation agreements.[24] In the Second Continental Congress, Jay, still committed to reconciliation, joined with James Duane and John Dickinson to convince other delegates that one more petition to the king was in order, even though colonial agents had sent word that Parliament not only had ignored Jay's "Address to the People of Great Britain" but also was making arrangements to send troops to enforce parliamentary rule. A congressional committee was formed consisting of Jay, Dickinson, Benjamin Franklin, Thomas Johnson, and John Rutledge; and on June 19 it submitted to Congress the final draft of what became known as the "Olive Branch Petition."[25]

In April, 1776, Jay returned to New York to attend to his ailing parents and wife.[26] Elected to the Third New York Provincial Congress, he helped draft a resolution supporting the Declaration of Independence, chaired a committee to detect loyalist conspiracies (in which he uncovered a plot to assassinate General Washington), and played a major role in the committee that drafted New York's constitution. With the adoption of this constitution in April, 1777, the Fourth Provincial Congress promptly elected Jay chief justice of the newly formed state Supreme Court of Judicature.[27]

Jay's duties as chief justice required him to adjudicate criminal cases both in the Supreme Court of Judicature and in specially commissioned courts of oyer and terminer. This responsibility was something new and not altogether agreeable to Jay. By the spring of 1777, New York had become a battleground for two opposing armies, resulting in the disruption of civil authority. Jay quickly determined that the only way to restore order and protect the public welfare was through a firm rule of law. Consequently he led the court in meting out stiff fines and sharp punishments to criminal offenders brought before his court. Records show the extent of his adherence to his resolve: in one session of the Court of Oyer and Terminer and Goal Delivery in and for the County of Albany in May, 1778, Jay and his colleagues sentenced ten outlaws to the gallows (although the court recommended that three of them should be pardoned).[28]

Jay's unpleasant task of sitting in judgment over criminals soon ended. On November 4, 1778, the New York legislature appointed him to assist New York's delegation to the Continental Congress in negotiating a land dispute between Vermont and New

York. Unexpectedly, however, on December 10, only three days after his arrival in Philadelphia, Congress elected him president after Henry Laurens resigned in a dispute over the censure of Silas Deane, a former congressman who had been recalled from a mission to France.[29] Jay presided over a Congress beset by countless problems. Most pressing were attempts to stabilize the country's finances both at home and overseas (a nearly impossible task owing to the nation's wildly fluctuating currency). The difficulties of provisioning the army were exacerbated by the state of the new nation's finances. Matters with the army were further complicated by clashes among some of its commanders. Jay also was present during the dispute over the sloop *Active* and took part in the drafting of a congressional resolution holding "that no act of any one State can or ought to destroy the right of appeals to Congress." The resolution, once adopted, paved the way for the establishment of the first federal court, the Court of Appeals in Cases of Capture.[30]

Toward the end of March, 1779, Congress voted to remove its foreign commissioners and appoint in their stead individual ministers to several European states. Jay, still serving as president of Congress, was elected as minister plenipotentiary to Spain on September 27, 1779. After a difficult crossing in which his ship was almost destroyed by a storm and nearly captured by an English frigate, Jay and his party arrived in Cádiz on January 22, 1780.[31] For the next two and one-half years Jay attempted to negotiate an American-Spanish alliance as well as Spanish loans to the specie-starved United States.[32] On June 13, 1781, Congress appointed Jay one of the American commissioners to negotiate a peace treaty with Great Britain. Jay continued his efforts in Spain until May, 1782, when he left to join the peace negotiations in Paris at the request of Benjamin Franklin.[33]

After the signing of the Treaty of Peace (September 3, 1783) between the United States and Great Britain, Jay left his family in France and journeyed to England where he spent the next four months attending to family business, sightseeing, and taking the restorative waters at Bath.[34] Rejoining his family in January, he spent the next few months in France before leaving for the United States on May 16. Although expecting to retire from public office, Jay, during his Atlantic crossing, was elected by the Confederation Congress to be secretary for foreign affairs. With some hesitation Jay accepted the post and was sworn in on December 21, 1784. As secretary, Jay had to contend with two problems remaining from the revolution: the occupation of British outposts in the Northwest Territory and the question of British debts. The issues were intertwined. England insisted that it would not abandon the outposts until its citizens were guaranteed recovery of debts owed them by Americans.[35]

During Jay's tenure as secretary, the movement toward a strong national government reached fruition with the creation of the Constitution. Jay aided the efforts of Alexander Hamilton and other New Yorkers working for the ratification of the Constitution in that state by contributing to what became known as *The Federalist* papers. Jay wrote numbers 2-5 on the subject of foreign affairs and number 64 on the treaty making power.[36]

Jay's service as secretary for foreign affairs ended when George Washington nominated him as chief justice of the United States on September 24, 1789. The nomination was confirmed two days later. Awaiting the arrival of his successor as secretary of state, Thomas Jefferson, Chief Justice Jay held the post *ad interim* until March 22, 1790. In the late spring of 1792, while still sitting on the Court, Jay was nominated governor of New York by federalists in that state but was defeated by George Clinton in a controversial election that left Jay's supporters embittered. On April 19, 1794, the Senate confirmed Chief Justice Jay's appointment as envoy extraordinary to the Court of His Britannic Majesty. His mission was to negotiate a peaceful settlement of controversies with Great Britain, including British occupation of the northwest posts, the British debt question, and the issue of spoliations made by British ships on American vessels during the Anglo-French war. His efforts resulted in the Treaty of Amity, Commerce, and Navigation which was signed on November 19, 1794.[37]

During the chief justice's absence in England, New York federalists once again nominated him governor. Upon his arrival in New York on May 28, 1795, Jay learned of his nomination and that early vote counts indicated a victory. On June 5 the official results were announced: Jay was governor of New York.[38] He resigned his commission as chief justice on June 29, 1795, thus ending his career on the Supreme Court.[39]

As governor of his native state Jay worked for the revision of the New York criminal code and signed legislation for the gradual abolition of slavery.[40] On November 8, 1800, he declined renomination for governor, seeking instead a retirement from public life. This plan was briefly interrupted by President Adams's nomination of Jay as chief justice on December 18, 1800, in place of Oliver Ellsworth, who had just resigned. Although the Senate immediately confirmed the nomination, Jay was set in his determination to retire to his farm in Bedford, New York, and he returned his commission.[41] Upon the completion of his second term as governor in the spring of 1801, Jay retired from public life and spent his remaining twenty-eight years on his estate.[42]

1. Herbert Alan Johnson, *John Jay, 1745-1829* (Albany: University of the State of New York, 1970), p. 1; *PJJ*, 1:33; *DAB*. Peter Jay (1704-1782) was descended from Augustus Jay, a French Huguenot refugee who was able to assemble a respectable fortune through his mercantile business and his marriage—his bride Anna Maria Bayard was related to the Van Cortlandt, Van Rensselaer, and Schuyler families. Peter Jay followed in his father's footsteps by taking up the mercantile business and marrying wealth. His wife, Mary Anna Van Cortlandt (1705-1777), was a granddaughter of the first lord of the manor of Philipsburg. *PJJ*, 1:29-30.

2. Johnson, *John Jay*, p. 2; *PJJ*, 1:33.

3. Johnson, *John Jay*, p. 2. On his death in 1784, George Murray was a schoolmaster. *Collections of the New-York Historical Society* 36 (1903): 414.

4. John Jay entered King's College on August 29, 1760. Frank Monaghan, *John Jay* (New York: Bobbs-Merrill, 1935), p. 26.

5. Johnson, *John Jay*, p. 2.

6. On February 15, 1763, John Jay's father wrote to Jay's brother that John "is still determined to Study the Law" which seems to indicate that John and his father had previously discussed his career choice. *PJJ*, 1:44.

7. George Van Santvoord, *Sketches of the Lives, Times and Judicial Services of the Chief Justices of the Supreme Court of the United States*, 2d ed. (Albany: Weare C. Little, 1882), p. 6; *PJJ*, 1:62-67. At the time of Jay's clerkship, Benjamin Kissam (d. 1782) was an established lawyer practicing in New York City. William Richard Cutter, *Genealogical and Family History of Southern New York and the Hudson River Valley*, 3 vols. (New York: Lewis Historical Publishing Company, 1913), 2:499; Herbert Alan Johnson, "John Jay: Lawyer in a Time of Transition, 1764-1775," *University of Pennsylvania Law Review* 124 (1976): 1261.

8. Johnson, *John Jay*, pp. 3-4.

9. *PJJ*, 1:81-84; Johnson, *John Jay*, pp. 4-5.

10. *PJJ*, 1:86. Robert R. Livingston, Jr. (1746-1813), graduated from King's College in the class of 1765. He then studied law in the office of his cousin, William Livingston, and later with Judge William Smith, Jr. He was admitted to the bar in 1770. *DAB*.

11. *PJJ*, 1:86; Johnson, *John Jay*, p. 6.

12. *PJJ*, 1:87-91; Paul M. Hamlin, *Legal Education in Colonial New York* (New York: New York University, Law Quarterly Review, 1939), p. 204n. According to extant records, the debate cited above was held at the first meeting of the Debating Society on January 22, 1768, in New York City. In this particular debate, John Jay, in the affirmative, joined with his mentor, Benjamin Kissam, in opposing Peter Van Schaack, Stephen DeLancey, and John Vardill who took the negative. Jay and Kissam won the debate. Hamlin, *Legal Education*, p. 204n.

13. *PJJ*, 1:86. The Moot was organized in 1770 and disbanded in 1775. Among its founding members were Benjamin Kissam, William Livingston, Gouverneur Morris, James Duane, Robert R. Livingston, Jr., Egbert Benson, Peter Van Schaack, Stephen DeLancey, and William Smith. Ibid., pp. 86, 87n; Hamlin, *Legal Education*, p. 202.

14. *PJJ*, 1:118, 116.

15. Laura Jay Wells, *The Jay Family* (New York: J. B. Watkins, 1938), p. 21n; *PJJ*, 1:123-24; Edwin Brockholst Livingston, *The Livingstons of Livingston Manor* (New York: Knickerbocker Press, 1910), pp. 539-42, 553-55.

16. *DAB*, entry for William Livingston.

17. Livingston, *Livingstons of Livingston Manor*, pp. 539, 553.

18. *DAB*, entry for William Livingston.

19. Wells, *Jay Family*, pp. 34-35, 41. William Jay became a judge in Westchester County, New York, and Peter a successful lawyer.

20. *PJJ*, 1:129, 132n.

21. Ibid., p. 135. In addition to John Jay, the New York delegation numbered among its members John Alsop, Philip Livingston, and James Duane, all of whom were members of the Committee of Fifty-One. Ibid., pp. 132-35.

22. Ibid., p. 136; Jack N. Rakove, *The Beginnings of National Politics: An Interpretive History of the Continental Congress* (Baltimore: Johns Hopkins University Press, 1979), pp. 53-54.

23. Johnson, *John Jay*, pp. 10-11; Monaghan, *John Jay*, pp. 62-65; *PJJ*, 1:135-37.

24. Monaghan, *John Jay*, p. 64; *PJJ*, 1:141.

25. *PJJ*, 1:147-49.

26. Ibid., p. 263.

27. Ibid; Johnson, *John Jay*, pp. 13-15. John Jay was elected on May 3, 1777, and began service on September 9, at the first session of the court at Kingston, New York. *PJJ*, 1:394, 478.

28. *PJJ*, 1:478-79; Johnson, *John Jay*, p. 16; Monaghan, *John Jay*, p. 102.

29. *PJJ*, 1:510; Johnson, *John Jay*, pp. 16-18.

30. *PJJ*, 1:507-12. For further discussion of the development of the Court of Appeals in Cases of Capture, see Henry J. Bourguignon, *The First Federal Court: The Federal Appellate Prize Court of the American Revolution, 1775-1787* (Philadelphia: American Philosophical Society, 1977), pp. 101-34.

31. *PJJ*, 1:649, 651n, 666-68, 692; Johnson, *John Jay*, p. 20.

32. *PJJ*, 1:715-17.

33. Johnson, *John Jay*, p. 22. Five commissioners were appointed: Benjamin Franklin, John Jay, John Adams, Thomas Jefferson, and Henry Laurens. Adams did not join the negotiations until October 23, 1782, having been detained in the Netherlands on business. Jefferson never joined the negotiations. Henry Laurens was captured en route by British cruisers and was released shortly before the completion of the negotiations. Ibid., pp. 24-25.

34. *PJJ*, 2:579, 619-25.

35. Johnson, *John Jay*, pp. 29-30.

36. Irving Dilliard, "John Jay," in *The Justices of the United States Supreme Court 1789-1969: Their Lives and Major Opinions*, ed. Leon Friedman and Fred L. Israel, 4 vols. (New York: R. R. Bowker, 1969), 1:7-8; *DAB*.

37. *DAB;* see documents published below for John Jay's nomination and confirmation in 1789; *BDAC*, p. 13; Monaghan, *John Jay*, p. 336; *SEJ*, 1:151-52; Johnson, *John Jay*, p. 43.

38. Monaghan, *John Jay*, p. 405.

39. See documents published below for John Jay's resignation. He was inaugurated governor on July 1, 1795. Johnson, *John Jay*, pp. 45-46.

40. Dilliard, "John Jay," p. 18.

41. See documents published below, under "John Jay: Appointment as Chief Justice in 1800" for John Jay's nomination, confirmation, and declination, December, 1800-January, 1801; Johnson, *John Jay*, p. 47.

42. Henry Flanders, *The Lives and Times of The Chief Justices of the Supreme Court of the United States*, 2 vols. (New York: James Cockcroft, 1875), 1:423-24.

Nomination by George Washington ———————
September 24, 1789

. . . I nominate for the Supreme-Court of the United States[1]

> John Jay, of New York, Chief-Justice
> John Rutledge, of South Carolina,
> James Wilson, of Pennsylvania,
> William Cushing, of Massachusetts, ⎬ Associate Judges
> Robert H. Harrison, of Maryland,
> John Blair, of Virginia . . .

RS (DNA, RG 46, Anson McCook Collection); Lb (DLC, George Washington Papers); C (Contemporary copy in MHi, Miscellaneous Manuscript Collection).

1. In a letter to Alexander Hamilton written on September 25, 1789, George Washington enclosed "A List of persons holding Offices of a general Nature with the states to which they belong annexed." This list includes those states from which Supreme Court justices were chosen and serves to emphasize the geographic dispersion of seats on the Court. Alexander Hamilton Papers, DLC.

Nomination Received by Senate ———————
September 24, 1789

[*The Senate Executive Journal (RG 46, DNA) records receipt of this nomination on September 24, 1789.*]

Confirmation by Senate ———————
September 26, 1789

. . . The Senate proceeded to consider the Message from the President of the United States of the 24th instant, and the nomination of John Jay of New York to be Chief-Justice of the Supreme Court of the United States;—

And on the Question to advise and consent thereto,

It passed in the affirmative.

The Senate proceeded to consider the nomination of John Rutledge of South Carolina to be one of the associate Judges;

And on the question to advise and consent thereto,

It passed in the affirmative.

The Senate proceeded to consider the nomination of James Wilson of Pennsylvania to be one of the associate Judges;

And on the question to advise and consent thereto,

It passed in the affirmative.

The Senate proceeded to consider the nomination of William Cushing of Massachusetts, to be one of the associate Judges;

And on the question to advise and consent thereto,
It passed in the affirmative.
The Senate proceeded to consider the nomination of Robert H. Harrison
of Maryland, to be one of the associate Judges;
And on the question to advise and consent thereto,
It passed in the affirmative.
The Senate proceeded to consider the nomination of John Blair of Virginia,
to be one of the associate Judges;
And on the question to advise and consent thereto,
It passed in the affirmative.

. . .

Ordered, that the Secretary lay before the President of the United States,
the proceedings of the Senate upon his Message of 24ᵗʰ September 1789. . . .

D (DNA, RG 46, Executive Journal).

Notification to President of Senate Confirmation ——————
September 26, 1789

[*George Washington received a copy of the Senate's confirmation of the nomination of John Jay to be chief justice. This copy, attested to by Samuel A. Otis, secretary of the Senate, is not extant; but it was transcribed at the time into a letterbook (George Washington Papers, DLC).*]

Commission ——————————————————
September 26, 1789

George Washington President of the United States of America.
To all who shall see these Presents— Greeting.

Know Ye, That reposing special Trust and Confidence in the Wisdom, Uprightness, and Learning of John Jay of New York Esquire, I have nominated, and by and with the Advice and Consent of the Senate, do appoint him Chief Justice of the Supreme Court of the United States, and do authorize and empower him to execute and fulfil the Duties of that Office according to the Constitution and Laws of the said United States; and to have and to hold the said Office, with all the Powers, Privileges, and Emoluments to the same of Right appertaining, unto him the said John Jay during his good Behaviour.

(L. S.)
In Testimony whereof I have caused these letters to be made patent, and the Seal of the United States to be hereunto affixed. Given under my hand the twenty sixth day of September in the year of our Lord one thousand seven hundred and eighty nine.

Gᵒ Washington

Lb (DNA, RG 59, Miscellaneous Permanent and Temporary Commissions); C (DNA, RG 59, Miscellaneous Letters).

On October 5, 1789, George Washington noted in his diary that he had "Dispatched the Commissions to all the Judges of the Supreme and District Courts . . . and accompanied them with all the Acts respecting the Judiciary Department." *PGW, Diary,* 5:452.

Cover Letter to Commission
George Washington to John Jay
October 5, 1789 [New York, New York]

United States, October 5th 1789.

Sir,

It is with singular pleasure that I address you as Chief Justice of the supreme Court of the United States, for which office your Commission is here enclosed.

In nominating you for the important station which you now fill, I not only acted in conformity to my best judgement; but, I trust, I did a grateful thing to the good citizens of these united States: And I have a full confidence that the love which you bear our Country, and a desire to promote general happiness, will not suffer you to hesitate a moment to bring into action the talents, knowledge and integrity which are so necessary to be exercised at the head of that department which must be considered as the Key-stone of our political fabric.

I have the honor to be,   with high consideration and   sentiments of perfect esteem,   Sir,   Your most Obedient and   most Humble Servant,

G:Washington

The Honorable
John Jay.—

ALS (LNT, George and Katherine Davis Collection); Df (DNA, RG 59, Miscellaneous Letters); Lb (DLC, George Washington Papers).

John Jay to George Washington
October 6, 1789 New York, New York

New York   6 October 1789

Sir

When distinguished Discernment & Patriotism unite in selecting men for Stations of Trust and Dignity, they derive Honor not only from their Offices, but from the Hand which confers them.

with a mind and a Heart impressed[1] with these Reflections and their correspondent Sensations, I assure you that the Sentiments expressed in your Letter of Yesterday, and implied by the Commission it enclosed, will never cease to excite my best Endeavours to fulfill the Duties imposed by the latter, and as far as may be in my power, to realize the Expectations which your nominations, especially to important Places, must naturally create—

with the most perfect Respect Esteem & Attachment I have the Honor to be   Sir   your most obedient & most humble Servant

John Jay

the President of the United States—

ARS (DNA, RG 59, Miscellaneous Letters); ADfS (NNC, John Jay Papers).
  1. In draft, "strongly impressed."

Record of Oath
October 19, 1789 [New York, New York]

Pursuant to an Act of the United States in Congress assembled Entitled "An Act to regulate The Time and Manner of administering certain Oaths."

I   do solemnly swear that I will support the Constitution of the United States.

. . .

John Jay   Chief Justice of the Sup Court of the united states
                19ᵗʰ of October 1789—

DS (N, Secretary of State Office Miscellaneous).

Record of Oaths
October 19, 1789 New York, New York

Be it Remembered, That at the City of New York on the nineteenth Day of October in the year of our Lord one thousand seven hundred and eighty nine, personally appeared before me, Richard Morris Esquire Chief Justice of the Supreme Court of the State of New York, John Jay of the same City, Esquire, and did then and there in due form take an oath in the words following, to wit, "I John Jay do solemnly swear, that I will administer Justice without respect to persons, and do equal Right to the poor and to the rich, and that I will impartially discharge and perform all the Duties incumbent on me, as Chief Justice of the Supreme Court of the United States of America, according to the best of my abilities and understanding, agreeably to the Constitution and Laws of the United States, so help me God" and be it also Remembered, That at the same time and place before me, the said Richard Morris, he the said John Jay did in due form take another oath in the words following, to wit, "I John Jay do solemnly swear, that I will support the Constitution of the the United States, so help me God." —

Ri^dMorris

DS (DNA, RG 360). A signed copy also exists in the John Jay Papers, NNC.

John Jay to George Washington
June 29, 1795 New York, New York

private

New York   29 June 1795 —

my dear Sir

The enclosed contains my Resignation of the office of Chief Justice — [1] I cannot quit it, without again expressing to You my acknowledgments for the Honor you conferred upon me by that appointment; and for the repeated marks of Confidence & attention for which I am indebted to You.

It gives me pleasure to recollect and reflect on these circumstances — to indulge the most sincere wishes for your Health and Happiness — and to[2] assure you of the perfect Respect Esteem and Attachment with which I am

Dear Sir   your obliged & affectionate Friend   and Servant —

John Jay

The President of the United States —

ARS (DLC, George Washington Papers); ADf (NNC, John Jay Papers).
  1. See below, John Jay to George Washington, June 29, 1795.
  2. In draft, "and ~~for opportunities of~~ to."

John Jay to George Washington
June 29, 1795 New York, New York

New York   29 June 1795

Sir

Having been elected Governor of the State of New York, & the first Day of next month being assigned for my entering on the Execution of that office, it is proper that I should, and therefore I do hereby resign the office of Chief Justice of the united States —

The repeated marks of national confidence with which I have been honored, have made deep and lasting Impressions on my ~~Heart~~ mind and Heart — Permit me to assure You Sir! that no change of Situation will ever abate my attachment to the united States, or to You —

I have the Honor to be &^c &^c:

ALb (N, Governor's Letterbook). The recipient's copy of this must have been the enclosure mentioned by John Jay in his private letter to George Washington dated June 29, 1795 (q.v., above).

George Washington to John Jay ——————————————
July 2, 1795   Philadelphia, Pennsylvania

Philadelphia   2ᵈ July 1795

My dear Sir,

Your letter of the 29ᵗʰ ultᵒ resigning the Office of Chief Justice of the United States I received yesterday, &¹ with sincere regret. _

For the obliging sentiments you have expressed for me in your private letter which accompanied it, I as sincerely thank you. _

In whatever line you may² walk, my best wishes will always³ accompany you; they will particularly do so on the theatre you are about to enter upon; which I sincerely wish may be as smooth, easy and happy, as it is honorable⁴

With very great⁵ esteem & regard   I am _ My dear Sir   Your Obedᵗ & Affectᵉ

Gᵒ Washington

His Excellʸ
John Jay Esqʳ

ARS (NNC, John Jay Papers); ADfS (DLC, George Washington Papers); Lb (DLC, George Washington Papers).

1. The "&" interlined in draft.
2. The word "may" interlined in draft.
3. The word "always" interlined in draft.
4. In draft, "and particularly ⌃ [*word inked out*] the theatre you are going have entered upon; ⌃ may be as smooth, easy & happy, as it is honorable."
   - *interlinear:* They will / do so on / are about to
   - *interlinear:* sincerely / which I wish
5. In draft, "very great" interlined over "sincere."

John Rutledge: Appointment as Associate Justice in 1789

John Rutledge, born in Charleston, South Carolina, in September, 1739, was the son of Dr. John Rutledge[1] and Sarah (Hext) Rutledge one of South Carolina's wealthiest heiresses.[2] Rutledge's early education was supervised by his father, and, after the latter's death in 1750, was continued under the tutelage of the Reverend Mr. Andrews, an English clergyman. After several years of classical studies under Andrews, Rutledge entered a school run by David Rhind of Charleston, described as a "classical scholar."[3] Rutledge, after a short time at Rhind's school, began law study under his uncle Andrew Rutledge.[4] After his uncle's death in 1755, Rutledge continued his studies under the guidance of James Parsons of Charleston.[5] Having spent two years in apprenticeship at Parson's office, Rutledge sailed for London to attend the Middle Temple where, on February 9, 1760, he was called to the bar.[6]

Rutledge returned to his native South Carolina in December, 1760,[7] and, aided by his mother's wealth and by his family's social and political connections, quickly established himself among Charleston's elite.[8] Following his admission to the South Carolina bar in January, 1761,[9] Rutledge was elected in March to the Royal Assembly.[10] By 1763 his legal practice had become so profitable that he could refuse cases where the retainers were less than one hundred pounds.[11] At this time, Rutledge married Elizabeth Grimké, who was descended from an old Charleston family.[12] In 1764 he received his first Crown appointment when Governor Thomas Boone appointed him attorney general for the province.[13] The following year Rutledge joined the South Carolina delegation at the Stamp Act Congress and chaired the Committee on Resolutions that sent a memorial to the House of Lords requesting repeal of the act.[14]

In July, 1774, the conservative planters of South Carolina elected Rutledge chairman of the state's delegation to the First Continental Congress. In Congress, Rutledge supported Joseph Galloway of Pennsylvania in advocating an administrative separation from England rather than the complete break called for by radicals led by Patrick Henry. When the Second Continental Congress convened in Philadelphia in May, 1775, Rutledge again attended as a delegate from South Carolina and was appointed chairman of the Committee on Government. After the adjournment of Congress, he went back to South Carolina to participate in the Charleston convention (December, 1775) that had been called to draft a constitution for the newly formed Republic of South Carolina.[15]

Upon acceptance of the constitution, the Assembly, in March, 1776, elected Rutledge the first president of the South Carolina Republic. In March, 1778, a new constitution was proposed which called for changing the republic to a state, disestablishing the Anglican church, providing for popular election of the legislature, and withdrawing the executive's veto over that body. Rutledge, opposed to the popular election of the legislature, resigned in protest. His resignation, however, was short-lived; the invasion in early 1779 by British troops moved the legislature to elect Rutledge governor with virtually absolute power. In May, 1780, the British captured Charleston, and Rutledge

John Rutledge by John Trumbull (1756-1843). Oil on wood, 1791. Courtesy Yale University Art Gallery.

was forced to withdraw along with the remnants of the state government to the North Carolina border. The government remained in exile until the summer of 1781.[16]

As the war drew to a close, Rutledge worked hard to restore civil government to South Carolina. In 1782, unable to succeed himself as governor, Rutledge went to Congress as a representative from South Carolina. While serving there, he declined two positions in the new national government: judge on the Court of Appeals in Cases of Capture and minister to the Netherlands. In 1784 Rutledge accepted the position of chief judge of the recently created South Carolina Court of Chancery to which the legislature had elected him.[17]

When the Constitutional Convention met in Philadelphia in 1787, Rutledge attended as a delegate from South Carolina. With Oliver Ellsworth, he served on the select committee that shaped the compromise between the large and small states. He also sat on the Committee of Detail charged with writing the first draft of the Constitution. Completing his work, Rutledge returned to South Carolina to ensure the Constitution's safe passage through the state's ratifying convention.[18]

After the creation of the United States government, President Washington, faced with choosing six eminent jurists to fill the bench of the newly established Supreme Court, nominated—and the Senate confirmed—John Rutledge as senior associate justice. Although Rutledge accepted the commission, he was unable to attend any of the meetings of the Supreme Court but did serve on circuit. He did not remain long on the Court, however; in March, 1791, he resigned his commission to become chief justice of the South Carolina Court of Common Pleas. In June, 1795, assuming that John Jay would resign as chief justice of the Supreme Court in order to accept election as the governor of New York, Rutledge wrote to President Washington to offer his services. Washington gratefully accepted and sent Rutledge notice of his interim appointment; he informed him that he would be given his temporary commission when he arrived in Philadelphia to attend the Supreme Court term in August.[19]

On July 16, 1795, probably before Rutledge received word of his appointment, he attended a meeting at St. Michael's Church in Charleston. Joining other prominent South Carolinians on the speaker's platform, Rutledge, in a lengthy speech, vehemently attacked the provisions of the Jay Treaty, a treaty which he and his fellow Charlestonians considered favorable to British interests. News of Rutledge's speech prompted outraged pro-treaty partisans to demand that he not be given his temporary commission as chief justice; Washington, however, kept his word and instructed the secretary of state to issue it. But, since this was a recess appointment, a permanent one awaited the approval of the Senate, scheduled to meet in December. In the months following the Charleston speech, Rutledge came under the fire of pro-treaty newspaper editors and politicians, who were determined to prevent his confirmation as chief justice. Rumors of mental instability compounded his already precarious political situation and, on December 15, 1795, the Senate rejected his nomination by a vote of fourteen to ten.[20] Rutledge spent the remaining five years of his life as a private citizen. He died at Charleston, South Carolina, on July 18, 1800.[21]

1. *DAB*; Mabel L. Webber, comp., "Dr. John Rutledge and His Descendants," *South Carolina Historical and Genealogical Magazine* 31 (1929-30): 14. Dr. John Rutledge, a native of northern Ireland, had followed his brother, Andrew, to South Carolina about 1735. Little is known of his early life, but by 1748 he was prominent enough to be elected a member of the South Carolina General Assembly. Webber, "Dr. John Rutledge and His Descendants," pp. 8-10.

2. Leon Friedman, "John Rutledge," in *The Justices of the United States Supreme Court 1789-1969: Their Lives and Major Opinions*, ed. Leon Friedman and Fred L. Israel, 4 vols. (New York: R. R. Bowker, 1969), 1:33-34.

Sarah (Hext) Rutledge (1724-1792) was the daughter of Captain Hugh Hext and Sarah (Boone) Hext, who, upon the death of Captain Hext, married Andrew Rutledge, the older brother of Dr. John Rutledge. Sarah (Boone) Hext-Rutledge had inherited considerable property from her father, John Boone, and from her first husband, Hugh Hext. Upon Sarah (Boone) Hext-Rutledge's death in 1743, the property went to Sarah (Hext) Rutledge, the wife of Dr. John Rutledge. Webber, "Dr. John Rutledge and His Descendants," pp. 8-10.

3. Flanders, *Lives and Times of the Chief Justices,* 1:436; Friedman, "John Rutledge," p. 34; *DAB,* entry for John Rutledge.

4. Flanders, *Lives and Times of the Chief Justices,* 1:436; Friedman, "John Rutledge," p. 34.

5. Friedman, "John Rutledge," p. 34. James Parsons (1724-1779) emigrated to South Carolina sometime before 1750 from his native Ireland. Following a five year apprenticeship to an attorney of the Court of King's Bench, Parsons gained admission to that court's bar and later practiced for a number of years in the Irish Court of Chancery. Admitted to the South Carolina Court of Common Pleas as an attorney in 1750, he quickly rose to a position of eminence and wealth and was elected to the South Carolina Royal Assembly, 1752-1754 and 1760-1775. During the Stamp Act crisis, he opposed the Crown and soon thereafter became an active participant in the struggle for independence and served on various councils of safety and provincial congresses. He was elected to the first three General Assemblies and served for a year as vice president of the state. Hoyt Paul Canaday, Jr., "Gentlemen of the Bar: Lawyers in Colonial South Carolina" (Ph.D. diss., University of Tennessee, 1979), p. 182; Walter B. Edgar and N. Louise Bailey, eds., *Biographical Directory of the South Carolina House of Representatives,* vol. 2, *The Commons House of Assembly, 1692-1775* (Columbia: University of South Carolina Press, 1981), p. 508.

6. Friedman, "John Rutledge," p. 34. Rutledge was admitted to the Middle Temple on October 11, 1754, but seems not to have sailed for England until October, 1758. Edward Alfred Jones, *American Members of the Inns of Court* (London: Saint Catherine Press, 1924), p. 189; Richard Hayes Barry, *Mr. Rutledge of South Carolina* (New York: Duell, Sloan and Pearce, 1942), p. 14.

7. Barry, *Mr. Rutledge of South Carolina,* pp. 15-17.

8. Friedman, "John Rutledge," p. 34.

9. Webber, "Dr. John Rutledge and His Descendants," p. 15.

10. Barry, *Mr. Rutledge of South Carolina,* p. 47.

11. Friedman, "John Rutledge," p. 34. By 1770 Rutledge was employing law clerks in his office. He trained five apprentices, two of whom were William Hasell Gibbes and John Julius Pringle. Canaday, "Gentlemen of the Bar," pp. 188-89.

12. Nineteen-year-old Elizabeth Grimké, the daughter of Charleston lawyer Frederick Grimké and Martha (Emmes) Grimké, married John Rutledge on May 1, 1763. Their marriage produced ten children, eight of whom survived them. Elizabeth (Grimké) Rutledge died in June, 1792. Barry, *Mr. Rutledge of South Carolina,* p. 71; Webber, "Dr. John Rutledge and His Descendants," p. 15; Edgar and Bailey, *Biographical Directory of the South Carolina House of Representatives,* 2:580.

13. Friedman, "John Rutledge," pp. 34-35. Rutledge held the post of attorney general for only ten months.

14. Ibid.

15. Friedman, "John Rutledge," pp. 36-37; *DAB.*

16. Friedman, "John Rutledge," pp. 37-38; *DAB*; Robert W. Barnwell, Jr., "Rutledge, 'The Dictator,'" *Journal of Southern History* 7 (1941): 220.

17. Friedman, "John Rutledge," pp. 38-39; *DAB.*

18. Friedman, "John Rutledge," pp. 39-41. South Carolina's Constitutional Convention voted on May 23, 1788, by a vote of 149 to 73, to accept the Constitution. Jonathan Elliot, ed., *Debates in the Several State Conventions on the Adoption of the Federal Constitution,* 2d ed. in 5 vols. (Philadelphia: J. B. Lippincott, 1863), 4:338-40.

19. See documents published below for the nomination and confirmation of John Rutledge as an associate justice; Friedman, "John Rutledge," pp. 41-45; see below, under "John Rutledge: Appointment as Chief Justice in 1795," John Rutledge to George Washington, June 12, 1795, and George Washington to John Rutledge, July 1, 1795.

20. For John Rutledge's speech, see "Commentaries," under date of July 17, 1795; for the first report of Rutledge's receipt of the appointment as chief justice, see "Commentaries," under date of July 20, 1795; for the subsequent furor and rumors, see documents published in "Commentaries" between the dates of July 25 and December 14, 1795.

21. Clare Jervey, comp., *Epitaphs from St. Michael's, Charleston, South Carolina* (Columbia: State Co., 1906), p. 240.

Nomination by George Washington ⸻
September 24, 1789

[*For nomination of John Rutledge, see George Washington's nomination of John Jay dated September 24, 1789, and published above.*]

Nomination Received by Senate ⸻
September 24, 1789

[*The Senate Executive Journal (RG 46, DNA) records receipt of this nomination on September 24, 1789.*]

Confirmation by Senate ⸻
September 26, 1789

[*For confirmation of John Rutledge, see the Senate's confirmation of John Jay dated September 26, 1789, and published above.*]

Notification to President of Senate Confirmation ⸻
September 26, 1789

[*George Washington received a copy of the Senate's confirmation of the nomination of John Rutledge to be associate justice. This copy, attested to by Samuel A. Otis, secretary of the Senate, is not extant; but it was transcribed at the time into a letterbook (George Washington Papers, DLC).*]

Commission ⸻
September 26, 1789

George Washington President of the United States of America.
To all who shall see these Presents⸺ Greeting.

Know Ye, That reposing special Trust and Confidence in the Wisdom, Uprightness, and Learning of John Rutledge of South Carolina Esquire, I have nominated, and by and with the Advice and Consent of the Senate, do appoint him one of the Associate Justices of the Supreme Court of the United States, and do authorize and empower him to execute and fulfil the Duties of that Office according to the Constitution and Laws of the said United States; and to have and to hold the said Office, with all the Powers, Privileges, and Emoluments to the same of Right appertaining, unto him the said John Rutledge during his good Behaviour.

(L. S.) In Testimony whereof I have caused these letters to be made patent and the Seal of the United States to be hereunto affixed. Given under my hand the twenty sixth day of September in the year of our Lord one thousand seven hundred and eighty nine.

G⁰ Washington

Lb (DNA, RG 59, Miscellaneous Permanent and Temporary Commissions). For an example of a recipient's copy of a commission to be associate justice, see that published below for James Wilson and dated September 29, 1789. In Miscellaneous Letters, RG 59, DNA, there is a master copy for the commissions of the associate justices. The master copy is filled out as a commission for "John Rutledge, of South Carolina, Esquire." At the bottom appear the names, places of residence, and dates of commission for the other associate justices:

"William Cushing, of Massachusetts, Esquire dated 27ᵗʰ Septʳ 1789.
Robert H. Harrison, of Maryland, Esquire, dated 28ᵗʰ Septʳ 1789.
James Wilson, of Pennsylvania, Esquire, dated 29ᵗʰ Septʳ 1789.
John Blair, of Virginia, Esquire dated 30ᵗʰ Septʳ 1789."

On October 5, 1789, George Washington noted in his diary that he had "Dispatched the Commissions to all the Judges of the Supreme and District Courts . . . and accompanied them with all the Acts respecting the Judiciary Department." *PGW, Diary,* 5:452.

George Washington to John Rutledge ——————————
September 29, 1789 New York, New York

To the Honorable John Rutledge
        South Carolina. —

Dear Sir,

In requesting your candid attention to a subject, which I deem highly interesting to our Country, I am convinced that I address myself well. —

Regarding the due administration of Justice as the strongest cement of good government, I have considered the first organization of the Judicial Department as essential to the happiness of our Citizens, and to the stability of our political system. — Under this impression it has been an invariable object of anxious solicitude with me to select the fittest Characters to expound the laws and dispense justice. —

This sentiment, Sir, has over-ruled, in my mind, the opinions of some of your friends, when they suggested that you might[1] not accept an appointment to a seat on the supreme Bench of the United States — The hesitation, which those opinions produced, was but momentary, when I reflected on the confidence which your former services had established in the public mind, and when I exercised my own belief of your dispositions still further to sacrifice to the good of your Country. —

In any event I concluded that I should discharge the duty which I owe to the Public by nominating to this important office a Person whom I judged best qualified to execute its functions _ and you will allow me to repeat the wish that I may have the pleasure to hear of your acceptance of the appointment. _

My best respects are offered to Mʳˢ Rutledge and with sentiments of very great esteem and regard

I am, Dear Sir,   Your Most Obedient and   Affectionate Humble Servant _

(Signed) George Washington

New-York
Septʳ 29ᵗʰ 1789.

Lb (DLC, George Washington Papers); Df (DNA, RG 59, Miscellaneous Letters).
  1. In draft, "would" crossed out.

Cover Letter to Commission ────────────────────
George Washington to John Rutledge
September 30, 1789   [New York, New York]

To the Associate Judges of the Supreme Court,
and to the Attorney General of the United States. _

Sir,

I experience peculiar pleasure in giving you notice of your appointment to the Office of an Associate Judge in the Supreme Court of the United States. _ [1]

Considering the Judicial System [2] as the chief Pillar upon which our national Government must rest,[3] I have thought it my duty to nominate, for the high Offices in that department, such men as I conceived would give dignity and lustre to our National Character; _ [4] and I flatter myself that the love which you bear to our Country _ and a desire to promote general happiness will lead you to a ready acceptance of the enclosed Commission, which is accompanied with such Laws as have passed relative to your Office. _

I have the honor to be   With high consideration,   Sir,   Your Most Obedient Servᵗ

(Signed) George Washington

United States
Septʳ 30ᵗʰ 1789

Lb (DLC, George Washington Papers); Df (DNA, RG 59, Miscellaneous Letters). This letter was a form for the cover letter to the commission for each associate justice. For a recipient's copy of this cover letter, see that published below for William Cushing and dated September 30, 1789.
  1. In draft, "United States of America" with the last two words crossed out.
  2. In draft, two beginning phrases for this paragraph have been crossed out: "It is unnecessary for me to observe" and "I consider the Judicial Department."

3. In draft, sentence ended here and next one began "Under this impression" which was then crossed out.

4. George Washington expressed this view of the importance of nominations to the judiciary on other occasions as well. On October 10, 1789, Otho H. Williams wrote to Washington in support of Robert Smith for federal district judge for Maryland in the event that Thomas Johnson declined the appointment. On November 22, 1789, Washington responded to Williams that "in the Person of a Judge, the World will look for a character and reputation founded on service and experience" and Smith was too young and inexperienced. "In such important appointments as the Judiciary, much confidence is necessary, and this will not be given fully to an untried man." George Washington Papers, DLC.

John Rutledge to George Washington —————————————————
October 27, 1789   Charleston, South Carolina

Charleston S°Carolina   Oct.ʳ 27. 1789

Dᵣ Sir/

I have had the pleasure of receiving the Letter, of September 29ᵗʰ, with which you were so kind as to favour me, & request that you will be pleased to accept my warmest Acknowledgements, for the Opinion you express of my former Conduct, & present disposition.

I esteem it highly honourable, to be selected as one of the fittest Characters to fill the Supreme Judicial Department, & associated with Gentlemen of such Ability & Integrity as those whom you have chosen for that purpose.

The future plan of Life which I had formed was that of Ease & Retirement: But, on considering the Subject of your Letter, with the Attention which it merited & excited, I have determined to accept the Trust committed to me, &, by a faithful Execution of it, contribute my best Endeavour to promote the Stability of our political System, & Happiness of our Country.

Mⁿˢ Rutledge joins, with me, in best Respects to Mⁿˢ Washington.

I have the Honour to be, with the highest Sentiments of Esteem & Veneration   Dᵣ Sir   Yᵣ most obedᵗ & very   ħble Servᵗ

J: Rutledge

ARS (DLC, George Washington Papers). Endorsed "private."

Record of Oath ————————————————————————————
February 15, 1790

[*The minutes of the Circuit Court for the district of South Carolina mention that Associate Justices John Rutledge and James Iredell presented*] Certificates of their having duly taken the Oath to support the Constitution of the United States:

to Wit the said John Rutledge on the Fifteenth day of February last and the said James Iredell on this day —

D (GEpFAR, RG 21, CCD South Carolina Minutes, May 12, 1790). Although this document does not note that John Rutledge took the oath of office prescribed by the Judiciary Act, presumably he did so.

John Rutledge to George Washington ————————————
March 5, 1791 Charleston, South Carolina

Charleston   March 5. 1791

Sir/

This State having thought proper to create the Office of Chief Justice, & offer it to me, & the peculiar Circumstances of the Appointment being such that I conceive I could not with any Propriety refuse it, I beg Leave to inclose, & resign my Commission, of an Associate Judge, of the United States.

Permit me to return my Thanks for the Honor confer'd on me by that Commission, & to offer my sin[c?]rest Wishes, for a long Continuance of your Health & Happiness —

I have the Honour to be, with the greatest Respect; Sir   y.r most obed.t & very ħble Serv.t

J: Rutledge

The President of the United States/

ARS (DNA, RG 59, Miscellaneous Letters). Marked "Copy— original— (inclosing Commission) & Post." The letter published here may be the original or a duplicate copy. The commission has not been found. On July 29, 1791, Tobias Lear, secretary to President George Washington, forwarded the commission to Secretary of State Thomas Jefferson. Miscellaneous Letters, RG 59, DNA.

William Cushing: Appointment as
Associate Justice in 1789

William Cushing, the son of John and Mary (Cotton) Cushing,[1] was born at Scituate, Massachusetts, on March 1, 1732.[2] Both of his parents came from families long prominent in the province. On his mother's side, William Cushing was descended from the theologian Reverend John Cotton; on his father's side, from two jurists who had served on the commonwealth's highest court.[3] Cushing received his early education from Richard Fitzgerald, who operated a Latin school in Scituate, and from his grandfather, Josiah Cotton. Cushing was admitted to Harvard College in 1747 and, after a typical classical education, graduated in 1751. After serving for a year as preceptor of the grammar school at Roxbury, Massachusetts, and receiving an honorary Master of Arts from Yale, he again returned to Harvard, this time to study theology on a fellowship granted to him by the college. But something must have caused him to change his mind, for he quit the college on December 20, 1754, and began to read law in the office of Jeremiah Gridley, a prominent Boston lawyer.[4] For the next three years, Cushing assisted the elder attorney on his circuit around the commonwealth, read law, and tended to the chores of a busy law office.[5] It was during his apprenticeship with Gridley that Harvard awarded Cushing the degree of Master of Arts. In February, 1758, Gridley rewarded his young protégé's industry by personally moving for his admission as an attorney to the bar of the Superior Court of Judicature; four years later the same court admitted him as a barrister.[6]

Although Cushing returned to Scituate to open his law practice, the comfortable surroundings of home were not enough to overcome the lure of the frontier. The creation of Lincoln County in the district of Maine opened county officer appointments, and Cushing, along with his younger brother, Charles, seized upon the more promising opportunities on the northern frontier. The Cushing brothers were not disappointed. Charles became the county's high sheriff while William secured an appointment as a county judge of probate and as a justice of the peace, which enabled him to sit on the county Court of General Sessions of the Peace.[7] And so, in 1760 both brothers struck out for the northern village of Pownalborough (now Dresden) on the Kennebec River to begin their new employments.[8]

At Pownalborough, William Cushing engaged in a number of pursuits that provided him with an adequate, but not sumptuous, income. In addition to his duties as a probate judge, which were not overly burdensome (he handled only forty-five cases in five years), he dabbled for a time in land speculation and the timber business. He derived steadier income from the legal practice that he established at Pownalborough. Virtually the only educated lawyer in that part of the country, Cushing often was appointed acting attorney general in the absence of the king's attorney; this position brought him a number of additional cases a year. He served also as attorney for a private clientele that included an assortment of small farmers, laborers, and merchants who brought to court a variety of suits involving land title disputes, petty debts, and personal damages.[9] In addition to these pursuits Cushing tended to the legal affairs of a number of land

William Cushing attributed to James Sharples (ca. 1751-1811). Pastel on paper, ca. 1796-1797. Courtesy Independence National Historical Park.

companies. Included among these was a powerful consortium of wealthy landowners, trading under the name of the Kennebec Proprietors, who sought to exploit the region's rich timber resources by grabbing land title either through purchases or court action. As an attorney for land interests, he frequently associated with John Adams, who also was employed to advance similar claims in court. In a two year period, Cushing joined Adams in arguing at least thirteen cases and opposed him in one.[10] Despite his employment as an attorney for various land companies, Cushing's retainers did not amount to much, and he was able to do well only by combining his income from employments as public servant, private attorney, company lawyer, and sometime land speculator.[11]

William Cushing's adventures in the north woods ended with his father's resignation as judge of the Massachusetts Superior Court of Judicature in 1771. Leaving behind his duties and law practice in Lincoln County, he went to Boston and claimed his father's seat on the bench. In 1774, he married Hannah Phillips.[12] The following year, with the reorganization of the courts by the newly formed revolutionary council of state, he became a member of the new Superior Court of Judicature.[13] Two years later he became chief justice of that Court upon the resignation of John Adams from that office.[14] The condition of Massachusetts's statute law at that time was chaotic, and Cushing often turned to scripture to embellish the written law. In a charge to the grand jury impanelled to try the Shays insurrectionists of 1786, he reminded them that they had a sacred duty to decide against those "internal enemies" who failed to follow the biblical precept, "Pay What Thou Owest."[15] The jury subsequently returned guilty verdicts, and Cushing sentenced many of the rebels to the gallows.[16]

Cushing's twelve year tenure on Massachusetts's highest court—first on the Superior Court of Judicature and then on its successor, the Supreme Judicial Court[17]—was punctuated by extrajudicial service in the state's constitutional convention (1779), his election as vice president of the state's convention to ratify the federal Constitution (1788), and his service as a Massachusetts presidential elector in the first federal election held under the new Constitution. Having been convinced of the need for a strong national government as a result of his experience during Shays's Rebellion, Cushing worked diligently for adoption of the Constitution in the Massachusetts ratifying convention.[18]

President Washington nominated Cushing to the Supreme Court of the United States on September 24, 1789, thus launching the Massachusetts judge on a twenty-one year career on the federal bench. As senior associate justice on the Court during John Jay's mission to England in 1794 and 1795, Cushing was called upon to act as chief justice *ad interim*. Upon Jay's resignation and John Rutledge's rejection by the Senate, Washington nominated Cushing chief justice on January 26, 1796. Cushing's frail health, however, forced him to return the commission to Washington a week later.[19] Despite his poor health, Cushing remained on the bench for another fourteen years until his death on September 13, 1810, at his home in Scituate, Massachusetts. Seventy-eight years old at the time of his death, William Cushing was the last of Washington's appointees to leave the bench.[20]

1. Mary (Cotton) Cushing (d. 1767) was the daughter of Josiah Cotton, a lawyer of Plymouth, Massachusetts. James S. Cushing, *The Genealogy of the Cushing Family* (Montreal: Perrault Printing, 1905), p. 48.

2. *DAB.*

3. *DAB,* entry for William Cushing. William Cushing's grandfather, John Cushing (1662-1737), was a deputy to the General Court (1692), chief justice of the Inferior Court of Plymouth (1702-1710), a provincial councillor (1710-1728), and judge of the Superior Court of Judicature of Massachusetts (1728-1737). William Cushing's father, John (1695-1778), was town clerk of Scituate (1719-1744), judge of probate for Plymouth County (1739), justice of the Court of Common Pleas in Plymouth County (1738-1751), judge of the Superior Court of Judicature (1747-1771), and a provincial councillor (1746-1763). He was one of the judges presiding at the trial of the British soldiers involved in the Boston Massacre. Lemuel Cushing, *The Genealogy of the Cushing Family* (Montreal: Lovell Printing and Publishing, 1877), pp. 20-21, 31; James S. Cushing, *Genealogy of the Cushing*

Family, p. 48; "Brief Memoirs and Notices of Prince's Subscribers," *New-England Historical and Genealogical Register* 8 (1854): 41.

4. John D. Cushing, "A Revolutionary Conservative: The Public Life of William Cushing, 1732-1810" (Ph.D. diss., Clark University, 1959), pp. 1-4; Clifford K. Shipton, ed., *Sibley's Harvard Graduates,* vol. 13, *1751-1755* (Boston: Massachusetts Historical Society, 1965), pp. 26-27. Jeremiah Gridley (1701/2-1767). Gridley resided in Boston until May, 1755, when he moved to Brookline. Gridley had graduated from Harvard in 1725 and by 1755 was one of the most prominent lawyers in the province. In addition to his legal practice, Gridley was a public spirited man who dabbled in local politics, briefly edited a Boston literary magazine, and helped found the Fellowship Club which was later incorporated as the Marine Society (1754). He was a member of the order of Freemasons. *DAB.*

5. Shipton, *Sibley's Harvard Graduates,* 13:26-27; John D. Cushing, "Revolutionary Conservative," p. 4. For an account of a lawyer riding circuit in Massachusetts in 1771, see *PJA, Diary,* 2:35-44.

6. Shipton, *Sibley's Harvard Graduates,* 13:26-27; John D. Cushing, "Revolutionary Conservative," p. 4; Superior Court of Judicature [Record], 1757-1759, pp. 296-97 and [Record], 1760-1762, p. 400, MBSufC. At the August 1761 term of the Superior Court of Judicature, all attorneys who belonged to the court's bar formally became barristers. The move, supposedly that of Chief Justice Thomas Hutchinson, was an attempt to add dignity to the court. Subsequent admission as barrister required three years of practice in the inferior court. In 1766 this term of probation was lengthened to seven years: three years of law study, two years of service as an attorney in the inferior court, and two years of service in the Superior Court of Judicature. *PJA, Legal,* 1:lviii, lxxix; Arthur M. Alger, "Barristers at Law in Massachusetts," *New-England Historical and Genealogical Register* 31 (1877): 206-7.

7. John D. Cushing, "Revolutionary Conservative," pp. 4, 7-11. Lincoln County embraced millions of acres that lay between the Amorescoggin River northward to Nova Scotia—practically the entire state of present-day Maine.

Charles Cushing (1734-1810), who was in the class of 1755 at Harvard with John Adams, served as sheriff of Lincoln County for twenty years. Afterwards, he was appointed one of the clerks of the Supreme Judicial Court, and later, judge of the Court of Common Pleas at Boston. Frederic Allen, "The Early Lawyers of Lincoln and Kennebec Counties," *Collections of the Maine Historical Society* 6 (1859): 47n; *PJA,* 1:14n.

8. *DAB*; Herbert Johnson, "William Cushing," in *The Justices of the United States Supreme Court 1789-1969: Their Lives and Major Opinions,* ed. Leon Friedman and Fred L. Israel, 4 vols. (New York: R. R. Bowker, 1969), 1:60-61.

9. John D. Cushing, "Revolutionary Conservative," pp. 8, 13, 19-22, 54-56.

10. Joseph Williamson, "The Professional Tours of John Adams in Maine," *Collections and Proceedings of the Maine Historical Society,* 2d ser. 1 (1890): 303-8.

11. John D. Cushing, "Revolutionary Conservative," pp. 10-11. 25-26, 36, 54-56.

12. Ibid., pp. 59-63, 100-101. Hannah (Phillips) Cushing (1754-1834) was from Middletown, Connecticut. William and Hannah Cushing had no children. James S. Cushing, *Genealogy of the Cushing Family,* p. 91; *DAB.*

13. Appointments to the new Superior Court of Judicature included John Adams as chief justice and William Read, Robert Treat Paine, and Nathaniel Peaslee Sargent as associate justices. Adams never served on this court, preferring instead to remain in Congress. Robert Treat Paine refused his commission claiming that Adams's appointment was motivated by politics rather than judicial expertise. Read and Sargent also declined but the latter reconsidered and accepted the post a short while later. Jedidiah Foster and James Sullivan were appointed to the vacant seats. John D. Cushing, "Revolutionary Conservative," pp. 100-103.

14. Adams resigned his judicial post on February 10, 1777, never having sat on the bench. Ibid., p. 116-17.

15. Ibid., pp. 261, 289, 300.

16. Ibid., pp. 261-303.

17. The Supreme Judicial Court was the successor to the old Superior Court of Judicature that was reorganized following the adoption of the state constitution in 1780. Ibid., p. 204.

18. *DAB*; Johnson, "William Cushing," pp. 61-65.

19. For the nomination and appointment of William Cushing as an associate justice in 1789, see below; for documents relating to his appointment as chief justice in 1796, see below, under "William Cushing: Appointment as Chief Justice in 1796."

20. *DAB*; Johnson, "William Cushing," pp. 65, 69-70.

Nomination by George Washington ——————————————
September 24, 1789

[For nomination of William Cushing, see George Washington's nomination of John Jay dated September 24, 1789, and published above.]

Nomination Received by Senate ——————————————
September 24, 1789

[The Senate Executive Journal (RG 46, DNA) records receipt of this nomination on September 24, 1789.]

Confirmation by Senate ————————————————————
September 26, 1789

[For confirmation of William Cushing, see the Senate's confirmation of John Jay dated September 26, 1789, and published above.]

Notification to President of Senate Confirmation ——————
September 26, 1789

[George Washington received a copy of the Senate's confirmation of the nomination of William Cushing to be associate justice. This copy, attested to by Samuel A. Otis, secretary of the Senate, is not extant; but it was transcribed at the time into a letterbook (George Washington Papers, DLC).]

Commission ————————————————————————————
September 27, 1789

[The official copy of William Cushing's commission is similar to John Rutledge's, published above under date of September 26, 1789.]

Lb (DNA, RG 59, Miscellaneous Permanent and Temporary Commissions). William Cushing's name, place of residence, and date of commission are given in the master copy for the commissions of the associate justices in Miscellaneous Letters, RG 59, DNA; see source note for commission of John Rutledge dated September 26, 1789. For an example of a recipient's copy of a commission to be an associate justice, see James Wilson's, published below under date of September 29, 1789.

On October 5, 1789, George Washington noted in his diary that he had "Dispatched the Commissions to all the Judges of the Supreme and District Courts . . . and accompanied them with all the Acts respecting the Judiciary Department." *PGW, Diary*, 5:452.

Cover Letter to Commission ─────────────────────────
George Washington to William Cushing
September 30, 1789 [New York, New York]

United States, September 30ᵗʰ 1789.

Sir,

I experience peculiar pleasure in giving you notice of your appointment to the office of an associate Judge in the Supreme-Court of the United States.

Considering the Judicial System as the chief-Pillar upon which our national Government must rest, I have thought it my duty to nominate, for the high Offices in that Department, such men as I conceived would give dignity and lustre to our national character ─ and I flatter myself that the love which you bear to our country, and a desire to promote general happiness, will lead you to a ready acceptance of the enclosed commission, which is accompanied with such laws as have passed relative to your office.

I have the honor to be, with high consideration, and sentiments of esteem, Sir, Your most obedient Servant

G°Washington

The honorable
William Cushing Esquire.

RS (MHi, Robert Treat Paine Papers). For the form used as a model for this cover letter, see that published above for John Rutledge and dated September 30, 1789.

William Cushing to George Washington ─────────────
November 18, 1789 Boston, Massachusetts

Boston   November the 18ᵗʰ¹ 1789.

Sir,

On Saturday the 24ᵗʰ of October, at Taunton, while on the² circuit, I had the honor of receiving your letter of the 30ᵗʰ of September last with a commission for the office of an associate Justice of the Supreme court of the united States. Decency & duty would have prompted an earlier answer, but that two of our state courts, at Cambridge & Salem remaining to conclude the business of the year, Judge Sewall, who has been appointed to the office of district Judge, thought with me, that two immediate resignations would³ have endangered the falling through or a distant adjournment of those courts, to the public inconvenience & the injury of individuals; which, I doubt not, therefore, you will⁴ approve as an apology for the delay. You condescend, Sir, to consider the Judicial System as the chief pillar of our national government, and kindly to say, that you have nominated to that department such men as you concieved would give dignity and lustre to our national government.⁵ I should be glad if my poor abilities could in any measure give ground for such a hope respecting myself; but I beg leave to say, that my wish has been from the beginning, to have such a national government take place, as should effectually secure the union,[6] the authority, the peace & prosperity of these states. And since you have been pleased to express a desire of my ready acceptance of the office, I do now, with the greater confidence, but hoping for your candor, of which I shall stand in need, declare my acceptance of it.__ I must take the liberty to express my regret at being deprived of the honor[7] of paying my respects to you at Boston, and joining publicly in the universal joy occasioned by your honoring these northern States with a visit,__ owing to a bad cold joined to the foulness of the weather the monday & Tuesday after your arrival here.__ Without troubling you, Sir, with my sense of the great things you thought it your duty to do and Suffer for us during the war, I shall only add my hearty wish, that you may long preside over, and thereby continue to render happy, the people of America.

I have the honor to be, with the deepest respect, Sir, Your most obedient   obliged humble Servant

W^mCushing

George Washington Esq[r?]
President of the united States.

ARS (DNA, RG 59, General Records of the Department of State); ADfS (MHi, Norcross Collection).

1. In draft, "17th."
2. In draft, "our."
3. In draft, "might."
4. In draft, "will" has been interlined.
5. In draft, William Cushing wrote "government," then crossed it out and interlined "Character." He reverts to his initial wording in the final copy.
6. In draft, "to have such a national government as shall effectually Secure the union . . . "
7. In draft, "I must take the liberty to express my regret, that I could not have the honor . . . "

Record of Oaths ——————————————————————————
[on or before February 2, 1790]

[*There is no extant record of William Cushing taking his oaths. He had to have done so on or before February 2, 1790, when the Court first opened with Cushing listed as present. No mention is made in the Court's minutes of his taking the oaths in the Court that day.*]

Robert H. Harrison: Appointment as Associate Justice in 1789

Robert Hanson Harrison, the least well known of George Washington's appointees to the Supreme Court, was born in 1745 in Charles County, Maryland. Richard Harrison (d. 1780), his father, a member of the local gentry, served as a justice of the peace for Charles County and as one of its representatives in the Maryland House of Delegates. His mother, Dorothy (Hanson) Harrison (1721-1752), belonged to the prominent Hanson family of Maryland. She died when Harrison was six years old.[1] Very little is known about Robert H. Harrison's upbringing or education.

The first evidence of Harrison's plans to practice law appears in the minutes of the Fairfax County Court in Virginia, where, on August 22, 1765, the court ordered that Harrison's good character be certified to the examiners for attorneys.[2] Why Harrison moved to Virginia and when are not known. Perhaps it was because, like many Charles County families, the Harrisons had relatives and business interests across the Potomac River in Virginia. Robert H. Harrison's uncle, Rice Hooe IV, had owned land in northern Virginia since the early eighteenth century. Although Hooe probably had died some time in the late 1740s, there were a number of his relatives living in northern Virginia in the 1760s. Rice Hooe IV's son, Robert Townsend Hooe, and two of his Harrison cousins later became Alexandria merchants.[3] Before Harrison moved to Virginia, he may have known George Johnston, Sr. (ca. 1700-1766), who was a distinguished lawyer and representative of Fairfax County in the House of Burgesses and who also was a native of Maryland. Harrison married Johnston's daughter.[4] The minutes of the Fairfax County Court are missing for 1766 and 1767, but those of 1768 record Robert Harrison's involvement as an attorney in a case on September 20. After this date, Harrison's name appears regularly in the court's records.[5]

With his more prominent Fairfax County neighbors, George Washington and George Mason, Harrison was caught up in Revolutionary War fervor. George Washington presided over, and Harrison acted as clerk at, the meeting in Alexandria in 1774 which drew up the Virginia Resolves. In addition to other committee assignments, Harrison was appointed to the Alexandria Committee of Correspondence. Harrison joined the Militia Company of Alexandria and was later commissioned a lieutenant in the Third Virginia Regiment. He was holding the latter position when George Washington asked him to become one of his aides-de-camp on November 6, 1775. As a member of Washington's wartime family, Harrison was a trusted and valued aide. He served as Washington's military secretary through March, 1781, and handled negotiations over prisoner exchanges.[6]

After his service during the revolution, Harrison returned to Maryland to accept an appointment as chief judge of the General Court of that state. Harrison's return also may have been prompted by familial concerns. His father had died in 1780 and Harrison, finding his father's estate in need of constant attention, wished to spend more

Robert Hanson Harrison detail in *The Capture of the Hessians at Trenton* by John Trumbull (1756-1843). Oil on canvas, ca. 1786-1828. Harrison is in the foreground, Tench Tilghman (1744-1786), an aide-de-camp to General Washington, is in the background. Courtesy Yale University Art Gallery.

time on the estate and with his family. It may have been around this time that Harrison married again; his first wife had died by 1775, leaving him with two small daughters. His second wife was Grace Dent, of Charles County, Maryland. This marriage further cemented his ties to local and statewide gentry.[7]

Upon his return to Charles County, Harrison's career rarely took him beyond Maryland's bounds. He served as chief judge of the General Court between 1781 and 1790. Considered a highly skilled judge, he and his colleagues decided cases that included questions of treason and the confiscation of property.[8] In 1785 he declined an appointment from Congress to sit on a commission (which included fellow Marylander and future associate justice Thomas Johnson) to adjudicate the territorial dispute between Massachusetts and New York over lands west of the Genesee River. In 1787 Harrison declined to serve in the Maryland delegation to the Constitutional Convention in Philadelphia, and in October, 1789, refused an appointment as chancellor of Maryland.[9]

Although it took Harrison only two days to decline the appointment as chancellor, he took a longer time to refuse the position offered by his old Alexandria neighbor, commander-in-chief, and now president, George Washington. President Washington nominated Harrison to the Supreme Court on September 24, 1789, and the Senate confirmed the nomination two days later. Washington then wrote a personal letter urging Harrison to accept the post. Harrison considered the offer carefully and, a month later, wrote back to the president declining the appointment. He cited poor health and pressing domestic concerns. Washington wrote to him again, urging him to reconsider. On November 27, 1789, Alexander Hamilton, another former member of the Washington family of aides-de-camp, and now secretary of the treasury, added his encouragement: "We want men like you. They are rare in all times." Harrison apparently responded to their beckoning. He set out for New York on January 14, 1790, but never reached his destination. On January 21, he wrote to Washington that, because of poor health, he could not accept his appointment to the Court.[10] Less than three months later, on April 2, 1790, Harrison died at his family home, twenty miles from Port Tobacco, Charles County, Maryland.[11]

1. George T. Ness, Jr., "A Lost Man of Maryland," *Maryland Historical Magazine* 35 (1940): 316; Edward C. Papenfuse, et al., *Biographical Dictionary of the Maryland Legislature, 1635-1789* (Baltimore: Johns Hopkins University Press, 1979), under Richard Harrison.

2. We are grateful to Constance Ring of the Fairfax County Circuit Court Archives for supplying this information.

3. Harry Wright Newman, *Charles County Gentry* (1940; reprint ed., Baltimore: Genealogical Publishing, 1971), pp. 21-31, *passim*; Papenfuse, et al., *Biographical Dictionary of the Maryland Legislature, 1635-1789*, under Robert Townsend Hooe and Joseph Hanson Harrison; *PGW, Diary*, 3:205; George Mason Graham Stafford, comp., *General George Mason Graham of Tyrone Plantation and His People* (New Orleans: Pelican Publishing, 1947), pp. 235-45.

4. *History and Register of Ancestors and Members of the Society of the Colonial Dames of America in the State of Virginia, 1892-1930* (Richmond, 1930), p. 482; *PGW, Diary*, 1:218n; Ness, "Lost Man of Maryland," p. 318. The name and birth and death dates of his wife are unknown.

5. This information provided courtesy of Constance Ring, Archives of the Fairfax County Circuit Court.

6. Ness, "Lost Man of Maryland," pp. 316-23.

7. Ibid., pp. 319, 323-24; Papenfuse, et al., *Biographical Dictionary of the Maryland Legislature, 1635-1789*, under Richard Harrison; Newman, *Charles County Gentry*, pp. 21-22.

8. Ness, "Lost Man of Maryland," pp. 325-26. Paul S. Clarkson and R. Samuel Jett write that Harrison was "the ablest of four able men ultimately appointed from this court to the United States Supreme Court"; the other General Court judges appointed to the Supreme Court were Thomas Johnson, Samuel Chase, and Gabriel Duvall. Paul S. Clarkson and R. Samuel Jett, *Luther Martin of Maryland* (Baltimore: Johns Hopkins University Press, 1970), p. 59.

9. *JCC*, 28:125, 181, 440-41; Ness, "Lost Man of Maryland," pp. 327, 330.

10. For the documents relating to the appointment of Robert Hanson Harrison to be an associate justice, see below.

11. Ness, "Lost Man of Maryland," p. 331.

Nomination by George Washington
September 24, 1789

[*For nomination of Robert H. Harrison, see George Washington's nomination of John Jay dated September 24, 1789, and published above.*]

Nomination Received by Senate
September 24, 1789

[*The Senate Executive Journal (RG 46, DNA) records receipt of this nomination on September 24, 1789.*]

Confirmation by Senate
September 26, 1789

[*For confirmation of Robert H. Harrison, see the Senate's confirmation of John Jay dated September 26, 1789, and published above.*]

Notification to President of Senate Confirmation
September 26, 1789

[*George Washington received a copy of the Senate's confirmation of the nomination of Robert H. Harrison to be associate justice. This copy, attested to by Samuel A. Otis, secretary of the Senate, is not extant; but it was transcribed at the time into a letterbook (George Washington Papers, DLC).*]

Commission
September 28, 1789

[*The official copy of Robert H. Harrison's commission is similar to John Rutledge's, published above under date of September 26, 1789.*]

Lb (DNA, RG 59, Miscellaneous Permanent and Temporary Commissions). Robert H. Harrison's name, place of residence, and date of commission are given in the master copy for the commissions of the associate justices in Miscellaneous Letters, DNA, RG 59; see source note for commission of John Rutledge on September 26, 1789. For an example of a recipient's copy of a commission to be an associate justice, see James Wilson's, published below under date of September 29, 1789.

On October 5, 1789, George Washington noted in his diary that he had "Dispatched the Commissions to all the Judges of the Supreme and District Courts . . . and accompanied them with all the Acts respecting the Judiciary Department." *PGW, Diary,* 5:452.

George Washington to Robert H. Harrison ⸻
September 28, 1789 New York, New York

New York Sept.ʳ 28ᵗʰ 1789.

Dear Sir,

It would be unnecessary to remark to you, that the administration[1] of Justice is the strongest cement of good Government, did it not follow as a consequence that the first organization of the federal Judiciary is essential to the happiness of our Country, and to the stability of our political system. ⸺

Under this impression it has been the invariable object of my anxious solicitude to select the fittest characters to expound the Laws and dispense Justice. ⸺ To tell you that this sentiment has ruled me in your nomination to a seat on the Supreme Bench of the United States, would be but to repeat opinions with which you are already well acquainted⸺ opinions which meet a just co-incidence in the public mind.

Your friends, and your fellow-citizens, anxious for the respect of the Court to which you are appointed, will be happy to learn your acceptance ⸺ and no one among them will be more so[2] than myself.

As soon as the Acts which are necessary accompaniments of these appointments can be got ready, you will receive Official notice of the latter. ⸺ This letter is only to be considered as an early communication of my sentiments on this occasion and as a testimony of the sincere esteem and regard with which I am

Dear Sir   Your Most Obed.ᵗ and   Affectionate HᵇˡᵉServᵗ

G.ºWashington

The Honᵇˡᵉ
Rob.ᵗ H. Harrison

ARS (DNA, RG 233, Library of Congress Special Collection); Lb (DLC, George Washington Papers); DfS (DNA, RG 59, Miscellaneous Letters) with sections in hand of Washington. Addressed "Charles Ctʸ or   elsewhere   Maryland."
 1. In draft, "administration" is "due administration."
 2. In draft, following "so" is "on every account."

Cover Letter to Commission ⸻
George Washington to Robert H. Harrison
September 30, 1789 [New York, New York]

[*For the form used as a model for this cover letter, see that published above for John Rutledge under date of September 30, 1789.*]

Lb (DLC, George Washington Papers); Df (DNA, RG 59, Miscellaneous Letters). For an example of a recipient's copy of this letter, see that published above for William Cushing and dated September 30, 1789.

Robert H. Harrison to George Washington —————————
October 27, 1789 Annapolis, Maryland

Annapolis   October 27ᵗʰ 1789.

My Dear Sir,

I received on the 9ᵗʰ Instᵗ your very obliging & interesting Favor of the 28ᵗʰ Ultᵒ — and request you to be assured, that the perusal of it, for the matter and the manner of the communication, filled me with every emotion, which friendship & gratitude could inspire.

In the first place permit me, My Dear Sir, to apologize for the time, which has elapsed without this acknowledgement. On no occasion of my life have I been under an embarrasment so painful. It is at length with a difficulty almost inconceivable, after revolving every circumstance, & after many days & nights of anxious sollicitude, that I have come to a final determination that I cannot but decline the appointment. On the one hand, a sincere & lively gratitude for the honour conferred by the public, and the transcendent proof of your regard & confidence; an animated love to our Country; an attachment to the Government not yet compleatly organized; a conviction that it is incumbent on every virtuous Citizen to exert his endeavours in rendering it firm, respectable & happy: All these considerations pressed powerfully on my mind, and at times almost irresistibly urged my acceptance. On the other hand, considerations which at first sight may not appear so striking, laudable & weighty, disuaded & restrained me.

In the most favourable view of the Subject it appeared, that the duties required from a Judge of the Supreme Court would be extremely difficult & burthensome, even to a Man of the most active comprehensive mind; and vigorous frame. I conceived this would be the case, if he should reside at the Seat of Government; and, in any other view of my residence I apprehended, that as a Judge sollicitous to discharge my trust, I must hazard, in an eminent degree, the loss of my health, and sacrifice a very large portion of my private and domestic happiness. Should I however, enter on the duties, required by my appointment, I should be constrained to take the more unfavourable residence, from the circumstances of my family. It's number has been lately much encreased, by the unhappy event of a Brother's death.[1] In his last moments he seemed to derive great comfort from the reflexion, that his Infant children would be left to my care; and I consider myself under an indispensible obligation to superintend their affairs, & watch over them, as their Friend & Guardian. This obligation, since his death, has been greatly augmented. He did not confide the guardianship to me alone; but it has pleased Heaven, that my Associate & dear friend, who before had been rendered decrepit by a paralitic affection, has since the receipt of your Letter, sustained another Stroke.[2] There is little reason to expect, he will ever again be capable of attending to this trust, or to any other worldly affairs; and there is no other person to whose care and protection I could confide the Children and the management of their interests.

When I tell you, My dear Sir, in addition to these most interesting considerations, that I feel a distrust of my competency to the arduous & exalted Station, and a full pursuasion that my declining it will not be attended with any public detriment— I flatter myself, you will think [m?] think me at least justified to my own conscience.— It is my ardent wish to be justified in your opinion. Be assured that no circumstance of my life ever caused me so much anxiety & doubt. The alternative before me was either to act against the dictates of my own Judgement, to forego the considerations of my domestic happiness, and in a great measure to desert the interests of those, with whom I am connected by the dearest ties; or, in appearance, to slight the calls of my Country— it's proffered honours, and (what infinitely concerns me) the duty I owe to your inestimable disinterested friendship.— I entreat you to pardon the detail of private matters— and that you will continue to believe, that

I am My Dear Sir, with every sentiment of Attachment & respect Your Constant friend & Affect^te & Obliged H Servant

Rob:H: Harrison

The President
of
the United States &c

ARS (DNA, RG 360).
1. Robert Hanson Harrison's younger brother, William, died on July 21, 1789. He had served in the Maryland Senate and the Confederation Congress. Papenfuse, et al., *Biographical Dictionary of the Maryland Legislature, 1635-1789,* under William Harrison.
2. Robert H. Harrison probably is referring to Warren Dent (1744-1794), who, with Robert H. Harrison, also had been named co-executor of William Harrison's will. Dent, who was a brother-in-law of both William and Robert H. Harrison, was a Charles County merchant and magistrate. Newman, *Charles County Gentry,* pp. 21-22; Charles County (Wills), Vol. AI #10, pp. 226-31, MdAA; James McHenry to George Washington, November 14, 1789, published below; Papenfuse, et al., *Biographical Dictionary of the Maryland Legislature, 1635-1789,* under Warren Dent.

Robert H. Harrison to George Washington ——————
October 27, 1789 Annapolis, Maryland

Annapolis October the 27th 1789
Sir,
I received on the 12th Inst^t the Letter, which you did me the Honor to write on the 30th of last month, notifying my appointment, and enclosing my Commission, of an Associate Judge, in the Supreme Court of the United States— with such laws as had passed relative to the Office, and expressing a wish that the Commission should have my ready acceptance.
Permit me to assure You, Sir, that the distinguished honor, which has been done me, in the appointment— and the very flattering and obliging terms, in

which your communication, upon the Subject was made, excited in me, the most lively sensations of gratitude, and demand a return of my warmest acknowledgements.

But at the same time, Sir, that I make these acknowledgements _ and whilst I bear a love to our Country, and a desire to promote general happiness; and whilst I experience the highest respect and veneration for your opinion and wishes, & for the opinion and wishes of all, who concurred in my appointment, I must beg leave to add, that I feel myself most painfully obliged to decline it.

Permit me, Sir, to assign the reasons which on this occasion have influenced my conduct. It appears to me, in the most favourable view of the matter, that the duties required by the Act for establishing the Judicial department, will be, from the limited number of the Judges, considering the great extent of the States & and the frequency of the Courts, extremely difficult and burthensome to perform.

In my apprehension, this must be the case, even, if all appointed to the Bench of the Supreme Court, should reside at the Seat of the General Government. _ And, in any other view of residence, it seems to me, that the performance of the duties would be nearly impracticable for myself; or at least, that I could not accomplish them, without hazarding, in an eminent degree, the loss of health, and surrendering almost every consideration of private & domestic happiness. Should I accept the appointment, I should be constrained to take the more unfavourable residence. The number of my family has been encreased by the unfortunate event of a Brother's death, and I consider myself under an indispensable necessity of attending to the affairs of his Children, as their friend and Guardian _ both for their interest and for my own indemnity. These considerations, Sir, and one more, of still greater weight, _ a distrust of my competency to the arduous & exalted Station _ and the persuasion that my not accepting, will not be a matter of public detriment, induce me to determine that I cannot but decline the appointment.

Having taken the liberty to state, in a summary way, the true motives of my conduct, suffer me to subjoin, Sir, that my attachment to the General Government, is the same, it has ever been, and that it's Constitutional rights and laws, both from inclination & duty, will ever have my support.

I have the Honor to be, with Sentiments of the highest respect and veneration, Sir, Your Most Obed'Servant _

                                                                    Rob: H: Harrison

The President
      of
   the United States
   of America

ARS (DNA, RG 59, Letters of Resignation and Declination from Federal Office).

James McHenry to George Washington ——————
November 14, 1789   Annapolis, Maryland

Annapolis   14 Novr 1789

Dear Sir.

Since my arrival here I have had several conversations with judge Harrison on the subject of his late appointment, and from what he says I cannot but think he was greatly influenced in returning the commission from an apprehension you might be embarrassed should he have kept it longer for consideration. No one except myself is yet acquainted with what he has done; and he assured me this morning, before leaving town, that he thought he had been premature, and wished to be again in possession of the commission, although he was by no means certain that he would finally be enabled to come to a different determination.

Well knowing the value of this man, his goodness of heart and unalterable attachment to you, I thought it my duty to communicate these circumstances in hopes that it may not yet be too late to place him in a situation for further deliberation. My own opinion is that he will serve in case his brother in law dies, an event which I look upon to be at no great distance from a letter I have seen of Dr Brown's on the subject.

I hope most sincerely that your health has been improved by your journey. If the secret and public wishes of good men can conduce to this end it will be a long time before you will have any need of the faculty. But you have created a new fountain of blessings. In your nominations and appointments you have had respect to want and wretchedness, where united with worth and capacity, and have thereby drawn upon you more ~~blessings~~ prayers and gratitude than has ever fallen to the lot of any dead or living Sovereign prince or first magistrate whatever.

With the most sincere attachment I have the honor to be Dr Sir   your ob^t s^t

James McHenry

ARS (DLC, George Washington Papers).

James McHenry (1753-1816), a member of the Maryland legislature, knew both George Washington and Robert H. Harrison from the Revolutionary War. McHenry had been appointed to Washington's headquarters staff as a secretary on May 15, 1778, where Harrison was employed as Washington's senior secretary. McHenry, who became a leading federalist in Maryland, served in the House of Delegates through 1791, when he was elected to the Maryland Senate. In January, 1796, he joined Washington's cabinet as secretary of war and continued in the same post under John Adams until May, 1800. *DAB*.

George Washington to Robert H. Harrison ──────────
November 25, 1789   New York, New York

New York. Nov.ʳ 25ᵗʰ 1789.

My dear Sir,

Since my return from my Tour through the Eastern States, I have received your two letters, dated the 27ᵗʰ of last month; together with the Commission which had been sent to you as a Judge of the Supreme Court of the United States.

I find that one of the reasons, which induced you to decline the appointment, rests on an idea that the Judicial Act will remain unaltered._ But in respect to that circumstance, I may suggest to you, that such a change in the system is contemplated, and deemed expedient by many in, as well as out of Congress, as would permit you to pay as much attention to your private affairs as your present station does.

As the first Court will not sit until the first Monday in Feb.ʳʸ, I have thought proper to return your Commission, not for the sake of urging you to accept it contrary to your interest or convenience, but with a view of giving you a farther opportunity of informing yourself of the nature & probability of the change alluded to._ This you would be able to do with the less risque of mistake, if you should find it convenient to pass sometime here, when a considerable number of members of both houses of Congress shall have assembled; and this might be done before it would become indispensable to fill the place offered to you._ If, on the other hand, your determination is absolutely fixed, you can, without much trouble, send back the Commission, under cover,_

Knowing as you do the candid part which I wish to act on all occasions; you will I am persuaded, do me the justice to attribute my conduct in this particular instance to the proper motives, when I assure you that I would not have written this letter if I had imagined it would produce any new embarrassment._[1] On the contrary you may rest assured, that I shall be perfectly satisfied with whatever determination may be consonant to your best judgment & most agreeable to yourself

I am, my dear Sir, With sentim.ᵗˢ of real esteem & reg.ᵈ Your Most Obed.ᵗ & Affec.ᵉ Se[r?]

G.°Washington

PS.

As it may be satisfactory to you know[2] the determination of the other Associate Judges of the Supreme Court, I have the pleasure to inform you that all of them have accepted their Appointments.

ARS (DNA, RG 233, Library of Congress Special Collection); Lb (DLC, George Washington Papers); Df (DNA, RG 59, Miscellaneous Letters) with sections in hand of George Washington. The rationale presented by Washington in this letter follows that outlined in a document in John

Jay's handwriting and entitled "Remarks respecting Mr Harrisons objections." Miscellaneous Letters, RG 59, DNA.
  1. In draft, the phrase "on your part" follows the word "embarrassment."
  2. In letterbook copy, this sentence begins: "As you may wish to know."

Alexander Hamilton to Robert H. Harrison ——————————
November 27, 1789 New York, New York

My Dear Friend.

After having laboured with you in the common cause of America during the late war and having learnt your value, judge of the pleasure, I felt in the prospect of a reunion of efforts in the same cause_ for I consider the business of America's happiness as yet to be done_

In proportion to that sentiment has been my disappointment at learning that you had declined a seat on the Bench of the U. States_ Cannot your determination, My Dr Friend, be reconsidered_?

One of your objections I think will be removed_ I mean that which relates to the nature of the establishment_ Many concur in opinion that its present form is inconvenient, if not impracticable. Should an alteration take place your other objection will also be removed. For you can then be nearly as much at home as you are now.

If it is possible, My Dr Harrison, give yourself to us_ We want men like you. They are rare in all times.

            Your affect. friend
    Adieu Y^r Affect. Friend & obedt Svt

                                                A Hamilton

N. York Nov. 27. 1789.
    R. H. Harrison.

Tr (NNC, John C. Hamilton Transcripts).
    Secretary of the Treasury Alexander Hamilton (1757-1804) first met Robert H. Harrison during the Revolutionary War. Harrison was George Washington's secretary, when Hamilton joined Washington's staff as an aide-de-camp in March, 1777. *DAB*, entry for Alexander Hamilton; *PAH*, 1:195-96.

George Washington to James McHenry ——————————
November 30, 1789 New York, New York

... I have received your letter of the 14th inst^t_ and in consequence of the suggestions contained therein, added to other considerations which occurred to me, I have thought it best to return Judge Harrison his Commission, and I sincerely hope that upon a further consideration of the Subject he may be induced to revoke his former determination & accept the Appointm^t ...

ARS (CSmH, George Washington Papers); Lb (DLC, George Washington Papers); Df (DNA, RG 59, Miscellaneous Letters) with interlineations in handwriting of George Washington. ARS marked "Confidential."

James McHenry to George Washington ⸻⸻⸻⸻⸻
December 10, 1789   Annapolis, Maryland

... I received your letter of the 30 ultimo last night ...

I hope and trust Judge Harrison will be able to gratify his own inclinations. I have not heard from him since he left Annapolis. ...

ARS (DLC, George Washington Papers).

Robert H. Harrison to George Washington ⸻⸻⸻⸻⸻
January 21, 1790   Bladensburg, Maryland

Bladensburg   Jañy 21ˢᵗ 1790.

My dear Sir,

I left Home on the 14ᵗʰ Inst⸵ with a view of making a Journey to New York, and after being several days detained at Alexandria by indisposition came thus far on the way. I now unhappily find myself in such a situation, as not to be able to proceed further. From this unfortunate event and the apprehension that my indisposition may continue, I pray you to consider that I cannot accept the Appointment of an Associate Judge, with which I have been honoured. What I do, My dear Sir, is the result of the most painful and distressing necessity.

I intreat that you will receive the warmest returns of my gratitude for the distinguished proofs I have had of your flattering and invaluable esteem & confidence ⸺ and that you will believe that I am and shall always remain with the most affectionate attachment

My Dear Sir,   YʳMost Obedᵗ & Obligᵈ frᵈ & Sert

Rob:H: Harrison

ARS (DNA, RG 233, Library of Congress Special Collection).

Tobias Lear to Thomas Jefferson ⸻⸻⸻⸻⸻
July 29, 1791   [Philadelphia, Pennsylvania]

... I have the honor to transmit to you the enclosed Commissions, with the letters accompanying them, which have been returned to the President of the United States: ⸺

    . . .

Robert H. Harrison ⸺ One of the Associate Judges ⸺
declined Decʳ 26ᵗ 1789 ⸺ [1] ...

ARS (DNA, RG 59, Miscellaneous Letters); Lb (DLC, George Washington Papers).

Tobias Lear (1762-1816) became George Washington's private secretary in 1785 and remained in his service for seven years. In 1794 Lear moved to Alexandria and in 1795 was elected president of the Potomac Company. In 1798 Lear rejoined Washington as his military secretary when war with France seemed imminent. He remained with Washington until the latter's death in 1799 and later had a distinguished career in the foreign service. *DAB.*

1. We have not found any letter from Robert H. Harrison dated December 26, 1789, and enclosing his commission. The meaning of this entry is not clear, in view of Harrison's letter to George Washington on January 21, 1790 (q.v.), stating that he would not be able to serve on the Court.

James Wilson: Appointment as Associate Justice in 1789

Born in 1742 and raised on a farm in the shire of Fife, Scotland, James Wilson nonetheless was well prepared for the intellectual challenges that lay ahead of him. Wilson, whose parents wanted him to become a minister, received instruction in Latin, Greek, mathematics, penmanship, and rhetoric at the local parish school. After graduating at the age of fourteen, he obtained a scholarship to attend the University of St. Andrews. At the university's College of Saint Salvator, he studied Latin, Greek, mathematics, logic, moral philosophy, ethics, and natural and political philosophy and probably became familiar with the literature of the Scottish and English enlightenment. After he finished four years of study at Saint Salvator's, Wilson, still determined to become a minister, enrolled in Saint Mary's College, the school of divinity at the University of St. Andrews.[1]

Wilson's university career ended abruptly, however, with the death of his father. As the oldest son among seven children, Wilson had to help support his family. He became a tutor and seems to have remained one until his brothers could take over some of the burden of providing for the family. Wilson moved to Edinburgh in the spring of 1765, where he began a course in bookkeeping and accounting. But it was not long before Wilson concluded that, for a person of his education and low social rank, greater opportunities existed in America. Friends and relatives of the Wilson family already had crossed the ocean, and Wilson planned to make his way to Pennsylvania, where some had settled, as soon as he could. In the fall of 1765, Wilson's ship arrived in New York, and soon thereafter he continued on to Philadelphia.[2]

Wilson received an appointment as tutor at the College of Philadelphia, but he apparently decided that the study of law would lead to greater advancement in Pennsylvania. With financial help from his cousin, Robert Annan, Wilson in 1766 began to read law in the office of John Dickinson.[3] Less than a year later, Wilson moved to Reading, seat of Berks County, and began to practice law there. In November, 1767, he expanded his practice by gaining admission to the bar of neighboring Lancaster County. Two years later, the Supreme Court of Pennsylvania admitted Wilson to its bar. Meanwhile his practice in Reading continued to grow, but Wilson thought that even better prospects existed at Carlisle, in Cumberland County, so he moved there in the fall of 1770. At Carlisle his law practice thrived, he bought a home, and on November 5, 1771, he married Rachel Bird, whom he had been courting for several years.[4]

Soon after his marriage, Wilson became immersed in patriot politics. His appointment in July, 1774, as head of the Carlisle committee of correspondence and election to the first provincial conference at Philadelphia launched his participation in the events leading up to the revolution. In 1774, Wilson revised and published a manuscript he had written in 1768, *Considerations on the Nature and Extent of the Legislative Authority of the British Parliament,* in which he concluded that in no instance did Parliament have

James Wilson by Jean Pierre Henri Elouis (1755-1840). Watercolor on ivory, ca. 1792. Courtesy National Museum of American Art, Smithsonian Institution, Museum Purchase.

legislative authority over the Colonies—a radical position even in 1774. Wilson's reputation grew, both in America and England, as a result of this publication. After the meeting of the provincial conference, Wilson returned to Carlisle, where he was chosen as a delegate to the next Pennsylvania provincial convention. Following the adjournment of this second meeting in January, 1775, he helped organize the Cumberland militia. His efforts were rewarded by a commission as colonel of the Fourth Battalion of Cumberland County Associators. On May 6, 1775, Wilson was elected to the Second Continental Congress. There, on July 2, 1776, Wilson and two other Pennsylvania delegates—out of seven—cast their votes for independence.[5] Wilson's experience in the Continental Congress included service on a number of committees where he revealed his preference for a stronger national government. He favored cession of the states' western claims, the adoption of revenue and taxation powers for Congress, and the institution of a national appellate prize court.[6]

Wilson's service terminated in September, 1777, when the Pennsylvania Assembly did not reappoint him as a delegate. Wilson had bitterly opposed passage of the very democratic state constitution of 1776, and the new majority in the Assembly had not forgotten it. In February, 1777, the Assembly had removed Wilson from the congressional delegation but then could find no one to replace him, so Wilson had been reinstated. In September, however, Wilson's departure was final.[7]

In the summer of 1778, Wilson sold his property in Carlisle and moved to Philadelphia, where, he thought, his major interests would prosper. He threw himself into the practice of law, money-making schemes of various kinds, and politics. Wilson defended a number of tories accused of treason and developed a theory of what constituted treason in the eyes of the law and what proof was necessary to convict someone of that offense. His concept that two witnesses to the same overt act were required to prove guilt—a concept that eventually made its way into the American Constitution—provided greater safeguards to American citizens than Englishmen enjoyed. Wilson also represented many clients in admiralty cases; as a result, he became more and more convinced of the need for a federal court with power over the state courts. In 1780 Wilson, with Robert Morris and Thomas Willing, was instrumental in the creation of the Bank of Pennsylvania. Although the first Bank of Pennsylvania failed in September, 1781, Wilson and Morris already had begun efforts to organize a national bank. Their endeavors were successful, and the Bank of North America was chartered by the Confederation Congress in December, 1781. The state of Pennsylvania also granted the Bank a charter, but opposition to the national bank prompted the Pennsylvania Assembly to revoke the charter in 1785. When the Bank came under attack in 1785, the directors asked Wilson to defend the institution. He wrote *Considerations on the Power to Incorporate the Bank of North America,* in which he developed arguments in favor of the implied powers of the Confederation Congress to create a bank and the obligation of contracts. In 1787 Pennsylvania reinstituted the Bank's charter.

At the same time that Wilson was engaged in law practice and politics, he became more and more involved in land speculation and other business ventures. He soon owed a large amount of money to the Bank of North America, as well as to many individuals. While Wilson expected to make a profit from these activities, he also believed that he was working for his country's interest by promoting settlement schemes. In 1782, John Dickinson, the President of Pennsylvania's Supreme Executive Council, appointed Wilson to represent the state when the Confederation Congress considered conflicting claims between Pennsylvania and Connecticut over lands in the Wyoming Valley of Pennsylvania. The congressional commissioners supported Pennsylvania's claim.[8]

With a change in the political makeup of the Pennsylvania Assembly, Wilson was elected to the Confederation Congress in January, 1783. Although Wilson continued to be a delegate, with a few interruptions, until the Congress expired, he lost patience with its inept maneuverings and inability to take significant action to strengthen the bonds among the states. He paid close attention, however, to Congressional activity regarding western lands and looked out for his own interests as well as Pennsylvania's. During this period, Wilson could tend to the many nongovernmental activities that attracted him. He was president of the St. Andrews Society, a social and philanthropic organization composed of Scotsmen, from 1786 to 1796. He was an insatiable reader of political theory, history, and philosophy, and Philadelphia society soon recognized his preeminence in these fields. In 1786 the American Philosophical Society, the most prestigious learned society of the day, elected Wilson a member.[9]

In light of Wilson's political activities and learned reputation, it is not surprising that the Pennsylvania legislature chose him as a delegate to the federal convention in 1787. By this time Wilson's views on government had become clearly defined in his own mind. He advocated a strong national government, democratically elected by the people of the United States. In the convention he supported popular election of both branches of the legislature, as well as the executive. He openly opposed property qualifications for voting and restrictions on the admission of new states to the union. For the purposes of the new union, Wilson believed that the national government should be supreme, that the states should be virtually nonexistent. During his service in the Continental Congress and the Confederation Congress, Wilson had become acutely aware of the need for a national judiciary. In the constitutional convention, he not only favored a supreme court with judges appointed by the president but also moved the adoption of a measure giving Congress the power to establish inferior federal courts. Wilson also was a staunch supporter of judicial review. As a member of the Committee of Detail, he helped prepare a draft of the Constitution.[10]

Although the federal convention did not adopt all of Wilson's views, he was tireless in his efforts to obtain ratification of the Constitution. Elected a delegate to the Pennsylvania ratifying convention, he became the major spokesman for adoption. As the federalist delegates formed a solid majority, the result was not greatly in doubt. On December 12, 1787, the Pennsylvania Convention ratified the Constitution, 46 to 23.[11]

To cap his governmental activities during these years, Wilson fought for approval of a new constitution for the state of Pennsylvania. Modeled on the Constitution of the United States and written principally by Wilson, the new constitution represented the conservative reaction to the very democratic Pennsylvania constitution of 1776. Wilson's opposition to the 1776 document had earned him many enemies. His espousal of many democratic principles of government, both in the federal Constitution and in the new Pennsylvania state constitution, did little to change his image as an exponent of the conservative interests in Pennsylvania.[12]

As the new national government was being formed, Wilson made known his aspirations to be chief justice of the Supreme Court.[13] His disappointment on being nominated an associate justice can only be surmised. Nonetheless, he threw himself into the work of the Court and its concomitant circuit riding with characteristic industry.

Although attending the circuit courts was a time consuming duty, Wilson found time to engage in other activities. In the winter of 1790, the College of Philadelphia appointed him its first professor of law. The lectures, delivered that winter and the winter following, treated many significant issues in political philosophy and jurisprudence, and Wilson expected that they would establish him as America's foremost legal mind. But the lectures were not even published in his lifetime. Wilson entertained even greater expectations when he requested President Washington and the Pennsylvania legislature to commission him to produce a full digest of the laws of the United States and of Pennsylvania. The Pennsylvania legislature accepted his offer and Wilson began the digest, but never finished it. Wilson even found time to marry again, six years after the death of his wife Rachel. In the spring of 1793, he met and courted Hannah Gray who was less than twenty years old. On September 19, they were married, and she accompanied him on the remainder of the eastern circuit.[14]

As the years passed, however, Wilson began to spend more and more time trying to keep his financial empire afloat. He missed various sessions of the circuit court when he felt compelled to return to Philadelphia to look after his economic interests. Misgivings about Wilson's financial dealings surely must have influenced Washington's appointment of a chief justice when a vacancy occurred in 1795 and then again in 1796, for he passed over Wilson each time. Disappointment and constant worrying about how to pay his debts took a severe toll on Wilson's health, and he was less and less able to fulfill his judicial duties.[15] To escape his creditors, in the spring of 1797, Wilson left Philadelphia, hid in Bethlehem for a short time, continued on to Burlington, New Jersey, and there was arrested and jailed. Wilson managed to satisfy the judgment against him and immediately fled south. But disaster awaited him in North Carolina, too. Pierce Butler[16] had initiated legal proceedings against Wilson, who owed him $197,000, and Wilson was again put in jail.

Wilson's son, Bird, succeeded in arranging his release, but conditions hardly improved for Wilson. For the remainder of the spring and summer of 1798, Wilson, too weak and lethargic to act, lived in a hot, depressing room at the Horniblow Tavern, with only his wife for a companion. Insulated from criticism and talk of impeachment, Wilson spoke of extricating himself from his troubles, but nothing could be done. In July Wilson contracted malaria, and, in August, he had a stroke. Barely recognizable as the man whose intellectual achievements had contributed so much to the future of his country, broken in mind and body, Wilson died on August 21, 1798.[17]

1. Charles Page Smith, *James Wilson: Founding Father, 1742-1798* (Chapel Hill: University of North Carolina Press, 1956), pp. 3-16.

2. Ibid., pp. 17-21.

3. Ibid., pp. 21-24. John Dickinson (1732-1808) had been tutored privately before studying law with John Moland, a leading member of Philadelphia's bar. He later studied law in the Middle Temple, before returning to Philadelphia in 1757 to practice. *DAB.*

4. Smith, *James Wilson*, pp. 29-42. By the time of Rachel (Bird) Wilson's death in 1786, she had borne six children. Ibid., p. 212.

5. Ibid., pp. 51-61; *DAB.*

6. Smith, *James Wilson*, pp. 98-99; Bourguignon, *First Federal Court*, p. 93; *DAB.*

7. *DAB.*

8. Smith, *James Wilson*, pp. 116-28, 140-77.

9. Ibid., pp. 187-214.

10. Ibid., pp. 225, 251. Robert G. McCloskey, "James Wilson," in *The Justices of the United States Supreme Court 1789-1969: Their Lives and Major Opinions*, ed. Leon Friedman and Fred L. Israel, 4 vols. (New York: R. R. Bowker, 1969), 1:87-89; *DAB.*

11. McCloskey, "James Wilson," pp. 89-90; *ROC*, 2:22; *DAB.*

12. Smith, *James Wilson*, pp. 297-304; *DAB.*

13. See "Commentaries," James Wilson to George Washington, April 21, 1789.

14. *DAB*; Smith, *James Wilson*, pp. 308-14, 342-67. In 1802, following the death of James Wilson, Hannah (Gray) Wilson married Dr. Thomas Bartlett. She died in London, England, on March 14, 1808. Marcus D. Raymond, *Gray Genealogy*, (Tarrytown, New York: 1887), p. 192; American Antiquarian Society, "Index of Deaths in *Massachusetts Centinel* and *Columbian Centinel*, 1784-1840," typescript, 12 vols. (Worcester, Mass.: 1952).

15. McCloskey, "James Wilson," pp. 94-95; Smith, *James Wilson*, pp. 354, 361, 372-83.

16. Smith, *James Wilson*, pp. 383-85. Pierce Butler (1744-1822), formerly a senator from South Carolina. *DAB*.

17. Smith, *James Wilson*,, pp. 386-88; *DAB*. Destitute at the time of his death, Wilson was buried in the cemetery at Hayes Plantation (the home of Samuel Johnston, Associate Justice James Iredell's brother-in-law), because his family could not afford to return his body to his home in Pennsylvania. In 1906, Wilson's remains were disinterred and ceremoniously returned to Pennsylvania, where he was buried in Christ Church, Philadelphia. *Washington Daily News* (Washington, North Carolina), August 18, 1976.

Nomination by George Washington
September 24, 1789

[*For nomination of James Wilson, see George Washington's nomination of John Jay dated September 24, 1789, and published above.*]

Nomination Received by Senate
September 24, 1789

[*The Senate Executive Journal (RG 46, DNA) records receipt of this nomination on September 24, 1789.*]

Confirmation by Senate
September 26, 1789

[*For confirmation of James Wilson, see the Senate's confirmation of John Jay dated September 26, 1789, and published above.*]

Notification to President of Senate Confirmation
September 26, 1789

[*George Washington received a copy of the Senate's confirmation of the nomination of James Wilson to be associate justice. This copy, attested to by Samuel A. Otis, secretary of the Senate, is not extant; but it was transcribed at the time into a letterbook (George Washington Papers, DLC).*]

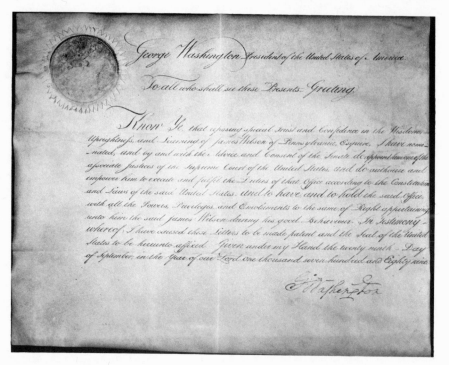

Commission of James Wilson, September 29, 1789. Courtesy Biddle Law Library, Rare Book Room, University of Pennsylvania.

Commission ──────────────
September 29, 1789

SEAL   George Washington President of the United States of America. To all who shall see these Presents — Greeting.

Know Ye, that reposing special Trust and Confidence in the Wisdom, Uprightness, and Learning of James Wilson of Pennsylvania, Esquire, I have nominated, and by and with the Advice and Consent of the Senate do appoint him one of the associate Justices of the Supreme Court of the United States, and do authorize and empower him to execute and fulfil the Duties of that Office according to the Constitution and Laws of the said United States — and to have and to hold the said Office, with all the Powers, Privileges, and Emoluments to the same of Right appertaining, unto him the said James Wilson during his good Behaviour. In Testimony whereof, I have caused these Letters to be made patent and the Seal of the United States to be hereunto affixed. Given under my Hand the twenty ninth Day of September, in the year of our Lord one thousand seven hundred and Eighty nine.

G?Washington

RS (PU-L, Rare Book Letters). The letterbook copy of James Wilson's commission (Miscellaneous Permanent and Temporary Commissions, RG 59, DNA) is similar to John Rutledge's, published above under date of September 26, 1789. Wilson's name, place of residence, and date of commission are given in the master copy for the commissions of the associate justices in Miscellaneous Letters, RG 59, DNA; see source note for commission of John Rutledge under date of September 26, 1789.

On October 5, 1789, George Washington noted in his diary that he had "Dispatched the Commissions to all the Judges of the Supreme and District Courts . . . and accompanied them with all the Acts respecting the Judiciary Department." *PGW, Diary,* 5:452.

Cover Letter to Commission
George Washington to James Wilson
September 30, 1789   [New York, New York]

[*The recipient's copy of the cover letter to James Wilson is similar to that received by William Cushing, published above under date of September 30, 1789.*]

ARS (PU-L, Rare Book Letters). For the form used as a model for this cover letter, see that published above for John Rutledge and dated September 30, 1789.

Record of Oath
October 5, 1789   Philadelphia, Pennsylvania

City of Philadelphia ss.

I do hereby certify that on the Fifth Day of October in the Year of our Lord One Thousand Seven Hundred and Eighty Nine, James Wilson Esquire, appointed an associate Justice of the supreme Court of the United States, personally appeared before me Samuel Powel Esquire Mayor of the said City, and voluntarily took the Oath of Office prescribed by an Act of Congress of the United States entitled "An Act to establish ₍the₎ Judicial Courts of the United States _"

SEAL

In Testimony whereof I have hereunto set my Hand and affixed my Seal the Day and Year first above written

Samuel Powel   Mayor

DS (PU-L, Rare Book Letters). Although this document does not note that James Wilson took the oath to support the Constitution, presumably he did so.

James Wilson to George Washington ——————————
October 18, 1789

Sir

Your Commission, appointing me one of the associate Justices of the Supreme Court of the United States, and your very obliging Letter, with which it was accompanied, I have had the Honour of receiving.

Be assured, Sir, that I entertain a just Sense of the delicate and pleasing Manner, in which you describe the Motives and the Objects of your Choice. Permit me to add _ I hope I do it with Justice and without Vanity _ that you are correct in your Conjecture concerning the Principles, which lead me to an Acceptance of the Commission.

I have taken the Qualification prescribed by the Law; and hold myself in Readiness to perform the Duties of my Office.

I have the Honour to be with Sentiments of the highest Respect and Esteem,

[corner of letter missing]

His Excellency
The President of the United States

AR[S] (DNA, RG 59, Miscellaneous Letters). The signature has been cut from this letter, but the handwriting is that of James Wilson. As was Wilson's frequent practice, the date was written below his signature and therefore was cut off with the signature. The date can be ascertained by a draft of this acceptance in Wilson's hand and dated October 18, 1789. Rare Book Letters, PU-L.

James Iredell to Timothy Pickering ——————————
August 25, 1798   Edenton, North Carolina

Edenton, N. C.   Aug. 25. 1798

Dear Sir,

It is with the truest concern I inform you of the unfortunate death of my Friend Judge Wilson, one of the Judges of the S. C. of the U. S., which ~~unfortunately~~ happened here on the night of the 21 _ Inst _ I take the liberty ~~here~~ to mention that it is of great consequence this vacancy should be supplied as early as it can be found convenient, as the ensuing Southern Circuit was assigned to Judge Wilson, in which business of the utmost consequence is depending: Tho' I should be disposed cheerfully to make great personal sacrifices for the public Interest, yet having been from home ~~the~~ almost the whole of the present year, & as I must leave it early possibly on an absence of many months the beginning of the next, it does not appear practicable to me notwithstanding my utmost wishes ~~to engage~~ to attend in S° C. upon the next[1] Circuit, and there would be a manifest impropriety, if it can be avoided, in my attending in this State, as there are some suits of great weight and con-

Defendant
sequence in which I am a ~~Party~~ as an Ēxor, which have been long depending,
and I think [*word inked out*] unreasonably delayed hitherto, and it might be
extended with the utmost prejudice to the Plaintiffs if any further delay should
take place. As I shall feel much anxiety on this subject, you will particularly
oblige me if you will take the trouble to inform me when the President has
                                                  in regard to
supplied this vacancy, and also ~~of~~ ^ the probability that the Gentleman ap-
                           fill in
pointed to ~~succeed~~ ^ ~~Judge Wilson~~ will be able to attend the S. Circuit this
fall __

I have the honor to be, &c __

The hon. T. Pickering Esq.

ADf (NcD, James Iredell Sr. and Jr. Papers). Marked "Substance of a Letter to M⟨r⟩ Pickering,
Secretary of State."
   1. James Iredell seems to have begun to write another word and then wrote "next" over it.
The earlier word is illegible.

Timothy Pickering to John Adams ————————————
September 6, 1798   Trenton, New Jersey

Department of State
Trenton   Sept⟨r⟩ 6. 1798.

Sir,
   Last evening I received from Judge Iredell the inclosed letter mentioning
the death of James Wilson Esq⟨r⟩ one of the Judges of the Supreme Court of
the United States; an event of which I embrace the earliest mail to give you
information.
   I hope M⟨rs⟩ Adams is recovering.
   I am with great respect   sir, your obed⟨t⟩ servant,

Timothy Pickering

The President of the
   United States.

ARS (MHi, Adams Manuscript Trust); APcS (MHi, Timothy Pickering Papers); Lb (DNA, RG
59, Domestic Letters).

John Blair: Appointment as
Associate Justice in 1789

John Blair, Jr., born in Williamsburg in 1732, was the son of John Blair, Sr., one of Virginia's leading colonial statesmen. John Blair, Jr., graduated with honors from the College of William and Mary in 1754 and then proceeded to London to study law at the Middle Temple (1755-1756) where he was called to the bar in 1757. During his stay in London, Blair became a protégé of Robert Dinwiddie, Virginia's lieutenant governor and a friend of his father. He also found time for courting; on December 26, 1756, Blair married Jean Blair of Edinburgh, Scotland.[1]

Upon his return to Williamsburg, Blair immediately began practice in the colony's General Court and became actively involved in the political affairs of his native state. In 1765, while representing the College of William and Mary in the House of Burgesses, Blair joined other conservative Virginians in opposing Patrick Henry's Stamp Act resolutions, which they considered too radical. Four years later, however, following the dissolution of the House of Burgesses, Blair helped to draft Virginia's nonimportation agreement. In 1771 he resigned from the House of Burgesses in order to become clerk of the governor's Council, a position once held by his father.[2] At the fifth Virginia convention, held at Williamsburg in May, 1776, Blair again represented the College of William and Mary and served on a committee charged with drafting a declaration of rights and a plan of government. After the adoption of the commonwealth's constitution, he again followed in his father's footsteps and became a member of the new governor's Council in June, 1776.[3]

Blair began his long judicial career when the state legislature—following the establishment of Virginia's judicial department in October, 1777—elected him one of five judges of the newly organized General Court. By 1779 he had become chief justice of that court, and, in November, 1780, he became chancellor of the three-member High Court of Chancery. As a judge on the General Court and, later, the High Court of Chancery, he also sat *ex officio* on the state's Court of Appeals.[4]

Elected a member of the Virginia delegation to the Constitutional Convention,[5] Blair opposed popular election of a single federal executive and favored instead a legislative election of a ruling executive council. Failing to persuade other members of the delegation to adopt his proposal, Blair realized that further debate would only produce a delay harmful to the new constitution and instead voted with George Washington and James Madison for its adoption. Blair later supported the Constitution at the Virginia ratifying convention, where he represented York County.[6]

Returning to Virginia after the Constitutional Convention, Blair again took up his judicial duties. In November, 1787, the case of *Commonwealth v. Posey* came before the Court of Appeals.[7] The case, which came on appeal from the General Court, involved a convicted arsonist who claimed that his indictment was deficient and that he was entitled to benefit of clergy. After hearing argument from the attorneys of both parties, the Court denied Posey's contention that he had benefit of clergy. Instead, the court

John Blair attributed to William Joseph Williams (1759-1823). Pastel on paper, ca. 1785-1795. Courtesy Mrs. Margaret Spencer St. John. On loan to The Colonial Williamsburg Foundation.

rested its decision on that in *Powlter's* case, an English precedent established nearly two centuries earlier and on the construction of various English statutes. By so doing, the majority of the justices—including Blair—reinforced the principle that long-settled English statutory constructions formed precedents to be followed as part of the law of Virginia.[8]

In January, 1788, a controversy erupted between Virginia's judiciary and its legislature. The legislature had passed a statute establishing state district courts and providing that they be staffed with judges from the Court of Appeals. Provoked by the additional burden placed upon them by this statute, Blair and his associates responded by drafting a remonstrance that prompted the legislature to suspend the offending statute in June, 1788.[9]

Following the reorganization of the Virginia judicial system, the legislature in 1788 chose Blair as one of five judges to sit on the new Virginia Supreme Court of Appeals.[10] This court first met in June, 1789. Three months later, however, Blair's service was interrupted by his nomination to the Supreme Court of the United States on September 24, 1789. Blair remained on the Supreme Court until October 25, 1795, when he resigned because of ill health. He spent the remainder of his days at his home in Williamsburg and died there on August 31, 1800.[11]

1. J. Elliott Drinard, "John Blair, Jr.," *Proceedings of the Thirty-Eighth Annual Meeting of the Virginia State Bar Association* (Richmond, 1927), p. 436; Fred L. Israel, "John Blair, Jr.," in *The Justices of the United States Supreme Court 1789-1969: Their Lives and Major Opinions*, ed. Leon Friedman and Fred L. Israel, 4 vols. (New York: R. R. Bowker, 1969), 1:109; *DAB*; Anton-Hermann Chroust, *The Rise of the Legal Profession in America*, 2 vols. (Norman: University of Oklahoma Press, 1965), 1:287. John Blair, Jr., was one of ten children of John Blair, Sr. (1687-1771), and Mary (Monro) Blair (1708-ca. 1768). Mary (Monro) Blair was the daughter of the Reverend John Monro of St. Johns Parish, King William County, Virginia. John Blair, Sr., was educated at the College of William and Mary and held many public positions. Appointed interim deputy auditor-general (ca. 1713), he later became auditor-general of the colony (1732), a position he held until his death. In 1727 he was appointed naval officer for the upper district of the James River. A member of the Virginia House of Burgesses (1734-1741) until his appointment as clerk of the Council (1741), Blair later became a member of the Council in 1743. For a brief period in 1758 and again in 1768, he was acting governor of Virginia. *DAB*, for John Blair, Sr.; Wilson Miles Cary, "Wilson Cary of Ceelys, and His Family," *Virginia Magazine of History and Biography* 9 (July, 1901), p. 110; Drinard, "John Blair, Jr.," pp. 436-37.

Jean Blair (1736-1792) was the daughter of Archibald Blair of Edinburgh, Scotland, who was described as a "writer." John Leslie Hall, "Ancient Epitaphs and Inscriptions, in York and James City Counties, Virginia" (Paper read before the Virginia Historical Society, December 21, 1891), p. 78; Francis J. Grant, ed., *Register of Marriages of the City of Edinburgh, 1751-1800* (Edinburgh: Printed for the Scottish Record Society by J. Skinner, 1922), p. 65.

2. Drinard, "John Blair, Jr.," pp. 437-38; *DAB*, for John Blair, Sr.

3. Drinard, "John Blair, Jr.," p. 439; Israel, "John Blair, Jr.," pp. 109-10; *DAB*.

4. Drinard, "John Blair, Jr.," p. 439; *DAB*, for John Blair, Sr. and Jr.

5. Drinard, "John Blair, Jr.," pp. 440-41. In addition to John Blair, the Virginia delegation included George Washington, Patrick Henry, Edmund Randolph, James Madison, George Mason, and George Wythe. Ibid., p. 441.

6. Drinard, "John Blair, Jr.," p. 441; Israel, "John Blair, Jr.," pp. 110-11; *DAB*.

7. 4 Call 109 (1787).

8. Ibid., pp. 109-11, 120-21; Drinard, "John Blair, Jr.," pp. 441-42; Israel, "John Blair, Jr.," p. 111.

9. Drinard, "John Blair, Jr.," p. 442.

10. Israel, "John Blair, Jr.," p. 111.

11. See below for documents relating to John Blair's nomination, appointment, and resignation as associate justice. For his retirement and death, see Israel, "John Blair, Jr.," p. 115, and *DAB*.

Nomination by George Washington ——————————————————
September 24, 1789

[For nomination of John Blair, see George Washington's nomination of John Jay dated September 24, 1789, and published above.]

Nomination Received by Senate ——————————————
September 24, 1789

[*The Senate Executive Journal (RG 46, DNA) records receipt of this nomination on September 24, 1789.*]

Confirmation by Senate ——————————————
September 26, 1789

[*For confirmation of John Blair, see the Senate's confirmation of John Jay dated September 26, 1789, and published above.*]

Notification to President of Senate Confirmation ——————
September 26, 1789

[*George Washington received a copy of the Senate's confirmation of the nomination of John Blair to be associate justice. This copy, attested to by Samuel A. Otis, secretary of the Senate, is not extant; but it was transcribed at the time into a letterbook (George Washington Papers, DLC).*]

Commission ——————————————————
September 30, 1789

[*The official copy of John Blair's commission is similar to John Rutledge's, published above under date of September 26, 1789.*]

Lb (DNA, RG 59, Miscellaneous Permanent and Temporary Commissions). John Blair's name, place of residence, and date of commission are given in the master copy for the commissions of the associate justices in Miscellaneous Letters, RG 59, DNA; see source note for commission of John Rutledge dated September 26, 1789. For an example of a recipient's copy of a commission to be associate justice, see James Wilson's, published above under date of September 29, 1789.

On October 5, 1789, George Washington noted in his diary that he had "Dispatched the Commissions to all the Judges of the Supreme and District Courts . . . and accompanied them with all the Acts respecting the Judiciary Department." *PGW, Diary,* 5:452.

Cover Letter to Commission ——————————————
George Washington to John Blair
September 30, 1789   [New York, New York]

[For the form used as a model for this cover letter, see that published above for John Rutledge under date of September 30, 1789.]

Lb (DLC, George Washington Papers); Df (DNA, RG 59, Miscellaneous Letters). For an example of a recipient's copy of this letter, see that published above for William Cushing and dated September 30, 1789.

John Blair to George Washington ——————————————
October 13, 1789   Williamsburg, Virginia

Williamsburg   Oct.ʳ 13ᵗʰ 1789.

Sir,

The honourable commission which you have been pleased to offer me in the service of the United States came to hand the tenth inst.ᵗ accompanied by your very polite letter, & the laws which have passed relative to the office.

When I considered the great importance, as well as the arduous nature of the duties, I could not but entertain some fears, that I might find them well adapted neither to my domestic habits, my bodily constitution, nor my mental capacity; in every other respect, the office promises me a very desirable situation, for which I know not how sufficiently to declare my gratitude.

I have determined to make an experiment, whether I may be able to perform the requisite services, with some degree of satisfaction, in respect both to the Public and my self; and I request permission to assure you, Sir, that if any extrinsic circumstance were necessary to induce my acceptance of the appointment, I could find none so powerful as the wish of the man, who possesses the love & veneration of every American, the respect & admiration of all the world.[1]

I have the honour to be,   with more deference & esteem than I know how to express,   Worthy Sir,   Your most obedient & affectionate   servant,

John Blair

ARS (DNA, RG 59, Miscellaneous Letters).

1. John Dawson, writing from Richmond, mentioned Blair's acceptance in a letter to Tench Coxe on October 26, 1789. Tench Coxe Papers, PHi.

Record of Oaths ——————————————
[on or before February 2, 1790]

[There is no extant record of John Blair taking his oaths. He had to have done so on

or before February 2, 1790, when the Court first opened with Blair listed as present.
No mention is made in the Court's minutes of his taking the oaths in Court that day.]

John Blair to George Washington ─────────────────
October 25, 1795   Williamsburg, Virginia

Williamsburg, October 25ᵗʰ 1795 ─

Sir,

A strange disorder of my head, which has lately compel'd me to neglect my
official duties, & in one instance, where that was not strictly the case, has been
the cause of their being attended to in a way by no means satisfactory to myself, has for some time past made me contemplate the resignation of my office,
as an event highly probable.

I knew the advantage of my situation; I had a just sense of the high obligation confer'd upon me thro your goodness, & perhaps I should say, too
partial opinion of my merit; & I confess, it was with reluctance that I thought
of quiting such a station, flattering my self that by some happy turn I might
be restored to a capacity of performing it's duties. These, however, at all
events, were not to be neglected; and in respect to them, I thought my self
limited to some short time of probation. The appointed term has now run out,
without producing the effect of which I had at first but a faint hope, or any
strengthening of that hope. The result is, that I return you now the commission
by which I have been so highly honoured: Perhaps, I ought to have returned
it sooner; & if any apology be due from me for not having done so, I can
only say, as above, that I was unwilling to quit my hold, & that I hope I have
not procrastinated my resignation, so as not to allow you sufficient time to
make up your mind, as to a person proper to supply the vacancy, & to give
such early notice of the appointment, as to have my successor ready to take
his seat in February at the next Supreme Court.

With every sentiment of gratitude, all imaginable deference, & the most
cordial wishes, for the success, & (if possible) for the ease of your public
administration, I am, Sir, Your truly affectionate, & most obedient servant,

John Blair

ARS (DNA, RG 59, Miscellaneous Letters). Addressed "Philadelphia." Postmarked by hand
"Wᵐsburg 26. Octʳ 1795."

James Iredell: Appointment as Associate Justice in 1790

Seventeen-year-old James Iredell arrived in America from Bristol, England, in November, 1768, to take up his duties as a newly appointed customs official. This certainly was not an auspicious time to be joining the British customs service in America; the colonists were opposed to the recently enacted British revenue laws and frequently expressed their opposition by attacking His Majesty's customs officials. James Iredell came to North Carolina as an impoverished merchant's son under difficult circumstances, but he made the most of the opportunities he found in his new home at Edenton, North Carolina.

Iredell had been born on October 5, 1751, in Lewes, Sussex County, England. His family lived in Bristol, where James Iredell's father, Francis Iredell, was a none-too-successful merchant. Both Francis Iredell and his wife, Margaret (McCulloh) Iredell, were related to well-connected men in government circles, and it was to these relatives that the Iredells turned after 1766, when Francis Iredell suffered a paralytic stroke that forced him to retire from business. In February, 1768, Sir George Macartney, a distant relative, secured for James Iredell a post as comptroller of customs for Port Roanoke at Edenton, North Carolina. Iredell's office required him to collect the customs duties for his cousin, Henry E. McCulloh, who was the collector of customs for the port and who, at that time, was in England. Iredell's salary went to the maintenance of his parents and siblings, and he supported himself from the fees.[1]

Little is known about Iredell's early upbringing or education. Surviving letters indicate that, at the time of his appointment, he was a well-educated, mature, and outgoing youth, deeply religious and very concerned about his family's welfare. Because Bristol was England's second largest port and had an extensive trade with the colonies, Iredell probably understood the general state of British and American trade relations. His awareness of the situation in America—particularly North Carolina—may have been heightened by the fact that his cousin, Henry E. McCulloh, was one of the largest landholders in that province. Iredell's friendly disposition and his prior knowledge of local affairs may have contributed to his good relations with his American neighbors, an enviable rapport not common among customs officials.[2]

While at Edenton, Iredell read law with Samuel Johnston, the town's leading citizen, a lawyer who had attended school in New Haven, Connecticut, and who was, at the time Iredell met him, clerk of the Edenton District Superior Court. Iredell was admitted to practice before the Inferior Courts of North Carolina in 1770 and before the Superior Courts in 1771. After Iredell completed his legal training with Samuel Johnston, he married Johnston's sister Hannah in 1773. The Iredells established their home in Edenton and raised two daughters and a son there.[3]

Iredell's career in government began to flourish in 1774, and, at the same time, he started to involve himself in American politics. On May 5, his cousin, Henry E. McCulloh, finally transferred the collectorship of customs to him, and in August of that year, Iredell was appointed deputy king's attorney for Hertford and Perquimans Coun-

James Iredell by an unknown artist. Watercolor? on ivory, ca. 1790-1799. Courtesy
James Iredell Association, Edenton, North Carolina.

ties. Later, in October, he was also appointed deputy king's attorney for Tyrrell
County.[4] Despite his official positions, Iredell espoused the colonists' view of Britain's
relationship to its empire. In a 1774 essay, entitled "To the Inhabitants of Great
Britain," Iredell wrote that Parliament had no jurisdiction over the colonies, because
the colonies originally had belonged to the Crown. Like Thomas Jefferson, Iredell en-
visioned a commonwealth system, wherein the British empire would be united by one
monarch, but each of its parts would have a distinct and independent legislature.[5]

If Iredell was a revolutionary, however, he was a reluctant one. He had, after all, come to the colonies as an officer of the Crown and his parents, siblings, and powerful relatives were still in England. Furthermore, Iredell knew that he would lose an inheritance from a rich uncle in Jamaica if he sided with the colonies. Throughout 1775, Iredell hoped for reconciliation. In 1776 he was serving as the king's attorney for his home county of Chowan and still clearing ships as a customs officer, but by July, he had made his decision, closed his customs office, and cast his lot with America.[6]

Iredell lost little time in becoming useful to the patriot cause. He paid a substitute to bear arms,[7] and instead applied his talents to the creation of a new legal and judicial system for the state of North Carolina. In 1776 North Carolina's Provincial Congress appointed Iredell to a committee to examine all of North Carolina's laws and to suggest revisions. Many of his recommendations were later adopted. In 1777 he once again served as the attorney for Chowan County, this time as state's attorney. Iredell's skills as a jurist were again called upon by the legislature when he was elected one of three Superior Court judges on December 20, 1777.[8] Iredell accepted the post reluctantly, because he disliked riding circuit throughout the state and wanted to remain in private practice. He resigned six months later, on June 13, 1778; he had waited until after he received news of the Franco-American alliance, which allowed him to quit his post without the imputation that he had resigned when the patriot cause was failing.[9] His retirement from state service lasted only one year, for in July, 1779, North Carolina's governor appointed Iredell interim attorney general for the state until October. In that month the legislature met, and he was elected to the post.[10] Surviving evidence indicates that during Iredell's tenure as attorney general, he paid scrupulous attention to due process and also opposed wholesale confiscation of estates of persons he considered legitimate British subjects, rather than enemy aliens or traitors.[11] Iredell served as attorney general until the end of 1781, when he resigned after news of Cornwallis's surrender at Yorktown.[12]

On his return to private practice, Iredell could express his views more freely than he had as attorney general, and his insistence on the constitutional rights of citizens became more pronounced. Iredell's most famous case during this period was *Bayard v. Singleton.* This case, first argued in the North Carolina Superior Court in May, 1786, and decided in November, 1787, gave Iredell an opportunity to voice again his earlier opposition to wholesale confiscation of loyalist property as well as his regard for constitutional rights. In arguing this case, James Iredell spoke in favor of the court's power to overturn unconstitutional statutes enacted by the legislature; the court agreed with Iredell.[13]

To Iredell, constitutions were fundamental law. His philosophy of an independent judiciary, capable of exercising the power of judicial review and protecting the fundamental law, had been expressed as early as 1783 in his *Instructions to Chowan County Representatives,* where he called for fixed salaries for state judicial officers:

As nothing can be of more consequence than to have the judiciary department of Government well filled, and rendered absolutely independent, we think liberal Salaries should be provided for the Judges and Attorney General, and made equally permanent with their commissions, otherwise they cannot be truly independent, which is a point of the utmost moment in a Republic where the Law is superior to any or all the Individuals, and the Constitution superior even to the Legislature, and of which the Judges are the guardians and protectors.[14]

Iredell's views on the fundamentality of constitutional law also led him to despair of North Carolina's refusal to adhere to provisions of the Treaty of Paris (1783) and the

Articles of Confederation. A strong nationalist, Iredell believed that North Carolina was bound by these instruments and should not pass laws contradicting their provisions.[15]

Iredell returned to state service in November, 1787, when the legislature appointed him commissioner to revise and compile the laws of North Carolina.[16] His work was published in 1791.[17] In November, 1788, he was elected to the governor's Council of State.[18] In 1788 James Iredell also served as a delegate to North Carolina's first ratifying convention, held at Hillsborough. Iredell fought for adoption of the Constitution. He led the delegates who favored the Constitution, wrote the "Marcus" essays, and spoke eloquently in convention debates; but he could not overcome the anti-federalist sentiment which predominated there. Iredell then transferred his attention to the press, where he arranged for the publication of the debates of the first convention and may have written further articles in favor of the Constitution, which was finally ratified by North Carolina at its second convention in Fayetteville in 1789.[19]

James Iredell's efforts on behalf of the Constitution gained him national prominence and brought him to President Washington's attention. Following the resignation of Robert H. Harrison as associate justice of the Supreme Court, Washington nominated Iredell to replace him on February 8, 1790; the Senate confirmed the nomination on February 10. At thirty-eight, Iredell was the youngest of Washington's appointees. Iredell was to serve on the Court for less than ten years before dying at his home in Edenton, North Carolina, on October 20, 1799.[20]

1. *PJI*, 1:xxxvii, xlviii-xlix, lv-lvi, 12-13; *DAB.*

2. *PJI*, 1:xxxviii, xlvii-xlix, lvi.

3. Samuel Johnston (1733-1816), North Carolina's political leader during the Revolutionary War, began his career as a public servant in 1759 when he was elected to the Assembly. He later sat in the Continental and Confederation Congresses, presided over both North Carolina conventions to consider the Constitution and served as governor from 1787 to 1789. Johnston represented North Carolina in the Senate during the First and Second Congresses. His last public service was as a Superior Court judge from 1800 to 1803. *DAB; PJI*, 1:xlix, li, liv.

4. *PJI*, 1:235-36, 248, 268.

5. Ibid., pp. lxii-lxiii, 251-68.

6. Ibid., pp. 345-46, xxxi, lviii.

7. Ibid., p. 462.

8. Ibid., pp. lxxviii, 463; Walter Clark, ed., *The State Records of North Carolina,* 16 vols. numbered 11-26 (Winston, Goldsboro, Charlotte: State of North Carolina, 1895-1906), vol. 12, *1777-1778* (Winston, 1895), pp. 234, 415.

9. *PJI*, 1:lxxviii-lxxix; 2:32-34, 425.

10. *PJI*, 2:98; Clark, *State Records of North Carolina,* vol. 13, *1778-1779* (Winston, 1896), pp. 855, 948.

11. *PJI*, 1:lxxxi, lxxxv.

12. *PJI*, 2: 321, 425.

13. 1 Martin (North Carolina) 42-48; James Iredell to Richard Dobbs Spaight, August 26, 1787, printed in *MJI,* 2:172-76.

14. *PJI*, 2:449.

15. *PJI*, 1:lxxxvi-xc.

16. James Iredell, *Laws of the State of North-Carolina* (Edenton, N.C.: Hodge & Wills, 1791), p. 609.

17. James Iredell, *Laws of the State of North Carolina,* (Edenton, N.C.: Hodge and Wills, 1791).

18. Clark, *State Records of North Carolina,* vol. 20, *1785-1788* (Goldsboro, 1902), p. 500.

19. Louise Irby Trenholme, *The Ratification of the Federal Constitution in North Carolina* (New York: Columbia University Press, 1932), pp. 121-22, 196-97, 199n, 238-39.

20. See documents published below for nomination and confirmation of James Iredell; Fred L. Israel, "James Iredell," in *The Justices of the United States Supreme Court 1789-1969: Their Lives and Major Opinions,* ed. Leon Friedman and Fred L. Israel, 4 vols. (New York: R. R. Bowker, 1969), 1:128, 132.

George Washington Diary Entry ————————————
February 6, 1790 [New York, New York]

... The resignation of M.ʳ Harrison as an Associate Judge making a nomination of some other character to supply his place necessary I determined after contemplating every character which presented itself to my view to name M.ʳ Iredall of N.º Carolina; because, in addition to the reputation he sustains for abilities, legal knowledge and respectability of character he is of a State of some importance in the Union that has given No character to a federal Office. — In ascertaining the character of this Gentleman I had recourse to every means of information in my power and found them all concurring in his favor. — [1]

AD (DLC, George Washington Papers).
    1. James Iredell's name had been mentioned in a complimentary fashion by George Washington at a dinner the president gave on February 4, 1790. See "Commentaries," Samuel Johnston to James Iredell, February 4, 1790.

Samuel Johnston to James Iredell ————————————
February 7, 1790 New York, New York

... It is now near nine O'Clock at night when the Mail will be closed, so that I have only time to tell you that I have just this minute received a ~~Letter~~ Message from the President by Major Jackson[1] to inquire of me whether you will accept the Office of Associate Judge in the Supreme Fœderal Court and to inform of his intention to appoint you to that Office in the place of M.ʳ Harrison who has resigned, on which I sincerely congratulate you and hope to have the pleasure of forwarding your Commission by the next Post— ...

ARS (Nc-Ar, Charles E. Johnson Collection). Addressed "Edenton." Postmarked "N-York Feb 7."
    1. Major William Jackson (1759-1828) was one of President Washington's secretaries. *PGW, Diary,* 5:156n; Charles William Littell, "Major William Jackson," *Pennsylvania Magazine of History and Biography* 2 (1878): 364.

Nomination by George Washington ————————————
February 8, 1790

United States, February 9.ᵗʰ 1790.
Gentlemen of the Senate,
    Among the persons appointed during your late Session, to offices under the national Government, there were some who declined serving. Their names and offices are specified in the first column of the annexed list. I supplied these vacancies, agreeably to the Constitution, by temporary appointments; which

you will find mentioned in the second column of the list. These appointments will expire with your present session, and indeed ought not to endure longer than until others can be regularly made— for that purpose I now nominate to you the persons named in the third column of the list, as being in my opinion qualified to fill the Offices opposite to their names in the first.

G?Washington

A List of vacancies and appointments which have taken place in the national Offices, during the late recess of the Senate, and of persons nominated for them by the President of the United States on the 8th day of February[1] 1790.

First Column.	Second Column.	Third Column.
Resignations.	Temporary Appointm[rs]	Nominations.
Robert H. Harrison— one of the Associate Judges of the Supreme Court	. . . .	James Iredell of North Carolina. . . .

RS (DNA, RG 46); Lb (DLC, George Washington Papers).
    1."9th of February" in draft. George Washington noted in his diary on February 8 that he had "Nominated . . . Mr Iredall as an Associate Judge." George Washington Papers, DLC.

Nomination Received by Senate
February 9, 1790

[*The Senate Executive Journal (RG 46, DNA) records receipt of this nomination on February 9, 1790.*]

Confirmation by Senate
February 10, 1790

. . . The Senate proceeded to consider the Nominations made by the President of the United States in his Messages of the 9th instant— And,
    . . .
On the question to advise and consent to the appointment of James Iredell, to be one of the Associate Judges of the Supreme Court—
    It passed in the Affirmative
    . . .
And, a certified Copy as usual, of the advice and consent of the Senate, was laid before the President of the United States. . . .

D (DNA, RG 46, Executive Journal).

Notification to President of Senate Confirmation ——————
February 10, 1790

[*Certification paraphrasing the Senate's confirmation of James Iredell to be an associate justice was sent to George Washington on February 10, 1790. This certification, attested to by Samuel A. Otis, secretary of the Senate, is not extant; but it was transcribed at the time into a letterbook (George Washington Papers, DLC).*]

Commission ————————————————————————
February 10, 1790

[*The recipient's copy of James Iredell's commission is similar to that published above for James Wilson under date of September 29, 1789.*]

RS (NcD, James Iredell Sr. and Jr. Papers). The official copy of James Iredell's commission (Miscellaneous Permanent and Temporary Commissions, RG 59, DNA) resembles that published above for John Rutledge under date of September 26, 1789.

Cover Letter to Commission ——————————————
George Washington to James Iredell
February 13, 1790 [New York, New York]

To the Honorable James Iredell
        North Carolina. _

Sir,

One of the Seats on the Bench of the Supreme Court of the United States having become vacant by the resignation of the Gentleman appointed to fill the same; I have thought fit, by and with the advice and consent of the Senate, to appoint you to that Office_ and have now the pleasure to enclose you a Commission to be one of the Associate Judges of the Supreme Court of the United States.[1]

You have, Sir, undoubtedly considered the high importance of a Judicial System in every civil Government,[2] It may therefore be unnecessary for me to say any thing that would impress you with this idea in respect to ours. _ I must, however, observe, that, viewing, as I do, the Judicial System of the United States as one of the main Pillars on which our National Government must rest; it has been my great object to introduce into the high Offices of that department such Characters, as, from my own knowledge or the best information, I conceived would give dignity and stability to the to the Government_ at the same time that they added lustre to our national Character.

I have the honor to be,   With due consideration,   Your Most Obedient Servant

(signed) George Washington

United States
February 13th 1790.

Lb (DLC, George Washington Papers); Df (DNA, RG 59, Miscellaneous Letters).
   1. On February 18, 1790, Samuel Johnston wrote to James Iredell that "I expect you will receive your Commission by this Post." Preston Davie Collection, NcU.
                                                                  a   in every civil
   2. In draft, this passage appears as "the high importance of the Judicial System to our national Government."

James Iredell to George Washington —————————————
March 3, 1790   Edenton, North Carolina

Edenton North Carolina   March 3ᵈ 1790

Sir,

I had this day the distinguished honour to receive the letter you were pleased to write me on the 13th Inst., accompanying a Commission by which I am appointed to the high and important office of one of the Associate Justices of the Supreme Court of the United States. In accepting this dignified Trust, I do it with all the diffidence becoming the humble abilities I possess, and[1] at the same time with the most earnest resolution to endeavour by an[2] unremitting application, and a faithful discharge of all its duties in the best manner in my power to evince the awful sense I entertain of its importance, and prove myself not entirely unworthy of a confidence which is so very flattering and pleasing to me. I hope you will accept, Sir, of my warmest thanks for the great honour you have conferred upon me, and will believe that I shall earnestly[3] feel the weight and dignity of the duties now[4] incumbent upon me as requiring every effort of my mind to execute them as I ought and hope to be able to do.

I have the honour to be,   with the greatest Respect   Sir,   Your most obedient and   most faithful Servant

Ja. Iredell

ARS (DNA, RG 59, Miscellaneous Letters); ADfS (Nc-Ar, Charles E. Johnson Collection).
   1. In draft, "but."
   2. In draft, James Iredell omitted the word "an."
   3. In draft, "constantly."
   4. In draft, Iredell omitted the word "now."

Record of Oaths ——————————————————————

May 12, 1790 Columbia, South Carolina

I do hereby certify that the Honorable James Iredell this day took the oath to support the Constitution of the United States And also the oath of office as one of the Associate Justices of the Supreme Court of the United States— as required by Law. before me at Columbia in S°Carolina this 12 May 1790.

J: Rutledge

ADS (NcD, James Iredell Sr. and Jr. Papers). This certification is written on the verso of James Iredell's commission.

Notification of Death ——————————————————

October 20, 1799 Edenton, North Carolina

[*No formal notification exists of the death of James Iredell. For the first mention of the date and place of Iredell's death, see "Commentaries," the* Newport Mercury, *under date of October 28, 1799.*]

Thomas Johnson: Appointment as Associate Justice in 1791

Thomas Johnson was born on his parents' farm in Calvert County, Maryland, on November 4, 1732. His father, also named Thomas, was a man of prominence in Cecil County, Maryland; he had been appointed a trustee of its schools in 1723 and had been elected as a delegate to the Lower House of Assembly (1725-1727, 1728-1731). In 1725 Thomas Johnson, Sr., had married Dorcas Sedgwick of Calvert County. They had twelve children, eleven of whom survived; Thomas was their fifth-born.[1]

Thomas Johnson, Jr., was educated at the family home in Calvert County and then sent to Annapolis to make his own way. Through Thomas Jennings, an Annapolis lawyer and register of the land office, Johnson secured work as a scrivener in the office of the clerk of the Maryland Provincial Court. He also read law with Stephen Bordley, one of the province's leading lawyers.[2] Johnson stayed in Annapolis and was admitted to the Annapolis Mayor's Court in 1756 and by 1759 to the Charles County Court. In September of the latter year, Johnson was admitted to the bar of the Provincial Court. In 1760 he gained admission to the bars of Frederick and Baltimore Counties.[3] Two years later, Johnson first won election to represent Anne Arundel County (where Annapolis is situated) in the Lower House of Assembly; he continued to be elected through 1774. In addition to starting a career and being elected to political office, he began a family. In 1766 he married Ann Jennings, the daughter of Thomas Jennings, his first employer. During their twenty-eight-year marriage, they had eight children.[4]

In his years as a delegate to the legislature, Johnson's reputation as a lawyer and articulate spokesman for American rights grew. Maryland's controversy with England centered on the issue of who had the power to establish the fees paid to proprietary officials. Johnson and other members of the Lower House of Assembly (including Samuel Chase) contended that the legislature held the power to set the fees but the governor and his council disregarded their objections. By 1774 this controversy was overshadowed by events in other colonies, and Johnson was elected to the Annapolis Committee of Correspondence and to the Continental Congress.[5]

In the Continental Congress, Johnson won the friendship and respect of John Adams, who confided the following to his diary on October 10, 1774: "Johnson of Maryland has a clear and a cool Head, an extensive Knowledge of Trade, as well as Law. He is a deliberating Man, but not a shining orator—His Passions and Imagination dont appear enough for an orator. His Reason and Penetration appear, but not his Rhetoric."[6] Johnson served on numerous committees in the first two Continental Congresses and nominated George Washington to be commander-in-chief. Adams later recalled that of all the Maryland delegates to the Continental Congress, Johnson was the most frequent speaker, and at first a moderate who supported John Dickinson, "but eer long he and all his State came cordially into our System."[7] Johnson left the Second Continental Congress shortly before the adoption of the Declaration of Independence in order to raise money and munitions from Frederick County for Washington and his army. He also was appointed commander of the state militia.[8]

Thomas Johnson by John Hesselius (1728-1778). Oil on canvas, ca. 1765. Courtesy Maryland Historical Society, Baltimore. Purchased from Mrs. Bessy J. C. Frey from bequest of Miss Josephine Cushing Morris.

During the following years, Johnson served his native state in several capacities. Soon after his appointment as commander of the militia, he and his forces marched to New Jersey to bring relief to Washington's forces. Upon arriving in New Jersey in February, 1777, Johnson found out that he had been elected the first governor of the state of Maryland and hurried back to take up his duties in that office.[9] Johnson was reelected twice, and when he could no longer succeed himself as governor, he was elected to the Maryland House of Delegates in 1780 from Frederick County, where his family owned iron furnaces. Johnson retired from the House of Delegates in 1782.[10]

Johnson did not hold any elected office between 1782 and 1786, but still put his legal skills to good use. In Maryland, he served on a committee to prepare legislation conferring jurisdiction upon the state court of admiralty. For the Confederation Congress, he served as a judge in the territorial dispute between Massachusetts and New York over lands west of the Genesee River.[11] Johnson was also engaged in one of his life-long interests: promoting navigation up the Potomac River. Since the 1770s he had been corresponding with George Washington with regard to this possibility and in 1785 joined with him and several other men to found the Potomac Company. Johnson served on the board of directors and succeeded Washington as president of the company.[12]

After his brief respite from state office, Johnson, in 1786, returned to state service. He represented Frederick County in the House of Delegates from 1786 through 1788 and also represented that county in the state ratifying convention, where he worked for adoption of the Constitution.[13] On April 20, 1790, Maryland's governor, John Eager Howard, appointed Johnson chief judge of the Maryland General Court. Johnson's stay on the state bench was brief, but during his tenure the Maryland General Court heard cases that involved conflicts between state law and the newly established federal government. One of the cases adjudicated, *Dulany v. Wells*, upheld the supremacy of the Treaty of Paris (1783) over state laws regarding the collection of debts owed to British creditors during the revolution. Johnson resigned his post on the state bench in October, 1791,[14] following his appointment to the Supreme Court.

President Washington had tried in 1789 to induce Thomas Johnson to accept a federal appointment. The President had considered him as a potential candidate for a high administration post but did not think that Johnson would be willing to leave Maryland. Washington finally decided to nominate Johnson as federal judge for the district of Maryland; the Senate confirmed the appointment on September 26, 1789. Johnson, however, declined the honor.[15]

Following the resignation of John Rutledge from the Supreme Court in March, 1791, Washington again turned his thoughts to Thomas Johnson as a replacement. On July 14, the president wrote to Johnson to inquire whether he would accept an appointment as associate justice. Johnson professed reservations about assuming the post because of its onerous circuit-riding duties and because of his poor health. But his reservations were overcome, and Washington appointed him to the Court on August 5, 1791, the first recess appointment made to the Court. Johnson held his temporary commission until November 7, 1791, when the Senate confirmed the appointment. Within a year, however, Johnson did indeed begin to find the duties too strenuous, and consequently resigned on January 16, 1793.[16]

After his resignation from the Supreme Court, Johnson still held one other federal post, that of a commissioner for the new capital on the Potomac. President Washington, knowing of Johnson's long-standing interest in the region, had appointed him a commissioner in January, 1791, and Johnson filled the position ably until his resignation in 1794.[17]

Johnson retired to his estate, Rose Hill, in Frederick, Maryland. He declined an appointment in 1795 as secretary of state, and again in 1801 as chief judge of the circuit court of the District of Columbia. He died at his home in Frederick on October 26, 1819.[18]

1. Edward S. Delaplaine, *The Life of Thomas Johnson* (New York: Frederick H. Hitchcock, Grafton Press, 1927), pp. 10-15; Edward C. Papenfuse et al., *Directory of Maryland Legislators, 1635-1789* (n.p., 1974) where Thomas Johnson, Sr.'s, service is noted. He was elected again to the Lower House of Assembly from 1735 to 1737 and from 1739 to 1741.

2. Delaplaine, *Life of Thomas Johnson,* pp. 13-18; Herbert Alan Johnson, "Thomas Johnson," in *The Justices of the United States Supreme Court 1789-1969: Their Lives and Major Opinions,* ed. Leon Friedman and Fred L. Israel, 4 vols. (New York: R. R. Bowker, 1969), 1:153.

3. This information provided courtesy of the Legislative History Project, MdAA.

4. Papenfuse et al., *Directory of Maryland Legislators, 1635-1789,* under Thomas Johnson, Jr.; Johnson, "Thomas Johnson," p. 153.

5. Delaplaine, *Life of Thomas Johnson,* pp. 46-58, 86-87, 94.

6. *PJA, Diary,* 2:150.

7. Johnson, "Thomas Johnson," p. 149; Delaplaine, *Life of Thomas Johnson,* p. 150; *PJA, Diary,* 3:330.

8. Delaplaine, *Life of Thomas Johnson,* pp. 173-75; Johnson, "Thomas Johnson," pp. 149-50.

9. Delaplaine, *Life of Thomas Johnson,* pp. 222-35.

10. Ibid., pp. 343, 351-52, 375; Papenfuse et al., *Directory of Maryland Legislators, 1635-1789.*

11. Johnson, "Thomas Johnson," p. 152.

12. Delaplaine, *Life of Thomas Johnson,* pp. 68-84, 384-96; Johnson, "Thomas Johnson," p. 151.

13. Papenfuse et al., *Directory of Maryland Legislators, 1635-1789;* Delaplaine, *Life of Thomas Johnson,* pp. 439-40.

14. Delaplaine, *Life of Thomas Johnson,* pp. 466, 476; Johnson, "Thomas Johnson," pp. 154-55; *DAB.*

15. Delaplaine, *Life of Thomas Johnson,* pp. 462-63; *SEJ,* 1:29, 31.

16. Delaplaine, *Life of Thomas Johnson,* pp. 474-82; for the letters between George Washington and Thomas Johnson, as well as the documents relating to the appointment, see below.

17. Delaplaine, *Life of Thomas Johnson,* pp. 470, 490.

18. Ibid., pp. 492-509.

George Washington to Thomas Johnson ⸻
July 14, 1791   Philadelphia, Pennsylvania

Philadelphia   July 14th 1791

Dear Sir

Without preface, or apology for propounding the following question to you _ [1] at this time _ permit me to ask you with frankness, and in the fullness of friendship, whether you will accept of an appointment in the Supreme Judiciary of the United States?

Mʳ Rutledge's resignation has occasioned a vacancy therein which I should be glad[2] to see filled by you. _ Your answer to this question by the Post (which is the most certain mode of conveying letters) as soon as you can make it convenient, will very much oblige

Dear Sir   Your most Obedient &   Affectionate HᵇˡᵉServᵗ

GᵒWashington

The Honᵇˡᵉ
Thoˢ Johnson Esqʳ

ARS (PHi, Dreer Collection); Lb (DLC, George Washington Papers). Duplicate copies of this letter were sent to Thomas Johnson; see below, Thomas Johnson to George Washington, July 27, 1791.

1. Letterbook copy omits "for propounding the following question to you."
2. In letterbook copy, "very glad."

Thomas Johnson to George Washington ————————————
July 27, 1791 ["Spurriers," Anne Arundel County,] Maryland

27 July 1791.

Sir.

I write this in my way from Annap.ˢ to Frederick to acknowledge the Receit of your kind Letter of the fourteenth Instant and the Duplicate of it; they reached me so early as the twenty second and twenty third the last on my Way to Annapolis.

Your earnestness that I should accept so strongly marks the Rank I hold in your Regard that I cannot but be in good Humor with myself and a Conversation with Mʳ Carroll,[1] which I hoped to have had at Annapl. would probably have informed me in some particulars that might lead my determination amongst others and not the least whether the southern Circuit would fall to

me; if it would at my Time of Life and otherwise circumstanced as I am ‸ be
(it would)

an insurmountable Objection. Mʳ Carroll is at his Manor where I purpose to call on him Tomorrow soon after I intend to trouble you with another Letter.

I am sir with the highest Respect Your most obedient and obliged Servant.

Th Johnson

ARS (DNA, RG 59, Miscellaneous Letters). Three days after Thomas Johnson wrote this letter to George Washington, he sent another one to the president (q.v., below) mentioning that "I wrote to you the other day from Spurriers." Spurriers was a tavern in Anne Arundel County, Maryland. Near present-day Savage, Maryland, it was in the part of Anne Arundel County that became Howard County in 1851. Charles Francis Stein, Jr., *Origin and History of Howard County, Maryland* (Baltimore: Published by the author in cooperation with the Howard County Historical Society, 1972), pp. 1, 59, 315-16.

1. Probably Daniel Carroll (1730-1796) of Forest Glen, Montgomery County, Maryland. Carroll, a merchant and planter, served with Johnson as a commissioner for the District of Columbia. Carroll had been a representative in the First Congress. Papenfuse et al., *Biographical Dictionary of the Maryland Legislature, 1635-1789;* Daniel Carroll to James Madison, April 9, 1792, James Madison Papers, DLC.

Thomas Johnson to George Washington ————————————
July 30, 1791   Frederick, Maryland
August 1, 1791   Georgetown, District of Columbia

Frederick 30 July 1791.

Sir.

I wrote to you the other Day from Spurriers on my way from Annapolis[1] undecided as to anything the Office of Judge and expecting MʳCarroll could assist with Light to determine me but he could not. I now write to Mʳ Jay, who is probably not in Philᵃ, and also to Mʳ Wilson[2] to inform you whether by the subsisting or designed Arrangement, which I suppose the Judges agree on amongst themselves, the next Southern Circuit would fall to me; if it would, I neither expect or desire any Alteration to accomodate me but my weak Frame and the Interest my Family have in me forbid my engaging in it: Let this single Circumstance, if you please, determine the one way or the other for my Answer.

I had almost resolved to see you at philadelphia but Potomack Affairs and M^r D Carroll's Letter call me to George Town on Monday, from whence it is likely this Letter will go. I feel real Unesiness that my Embarrassment should occasion delay in your filling up this Office as the Time is now so short: impute it to the true occasion and believe me that whether I receive the Commission or not the Manner in which you have been pleased to offer it is the greater part of it's Value and will with the many other Instances of your Confidence and Friendship be remembered with pleasure by

    sir   Your most obedient and   much obliged Servant

Th Johnson

George Town   1 August
It never occurred to me 'till Yesterday that the supreme Court was to sit on to-day, I imagine you found yourself oblige'd to fill up the Office I do not regret my Inattention for any Thing so much as keeping you in Suspence for which indeed I am sorry.

The president

ARS (DNA, RG 59, Miscellaneous Letters).
   1. Thomas Johnson to George Washington, July 27, 1791 (q.v., above).
   2. These letters to John Jay and James Wilson have not been found.

Temporary Commission ————————————————
August 5, 1791

George Washington President of the United States of
America
To all who shall see these Presents _ Greeting

Whereas the Office of one of the Associate Justices of the Supreme Court of the United States is at present vacant, Know Ye, that reposing special Trust and Confidence in the Wisdom, Uprightness, and Learning of Thomas Johnson of Maryland, I do appoint him one of the Associate Justices of the said Supreme Court of the United States, and do authorize and empower him to execute and fulfil the duties of that Office according to the Constitution and Laws of the said United States; and to have and to hold the said Office, with all the Powers, Privileges, and Emoluments to the same of Right appertaining, unto him the said Thomas Johnson during his good Behaviour, and until the end of the next Session of the Senate of the United States, and no longer.

In Testimony whereof I have caused these letters to be made Patent, and the Seal of the United States to be hereunto affixed.

SEAL   Given under my hand the fifth day of August in the year of our Lord one thousand seven hundred and ninety one, and of the Independence of the United States of America the Sixteenth.

G.°Washington

By the President

Th:Jefferson

RS (MdFre, Thomas Johnson Letters); Lb (DNA, RG 59, Temporary Presidential Commissions). A blank form for this temporary commission has at the bottom "Thomas Johnson, of Maryland, &c: dated 5ᵗʰ Augᵗ 1791" (Miscellaneous Letters, RG 59, DNA). An entry in a record book in RG 360, DNA, notes that Johnson's commission was made out on August 5.

Cover Letter to Temporary Commission ———————
Thomas Jefferson to Thomas Johnson
August 5, 1791   Philadelphia, Pennsylvania

Philadelphia   August 5ᵗʰ 1791.

Sir

The President of the United States desiring to avail the public of your Services as one of the associate Justices of the Supreme Court of the United States, I have now the honor of enclosing you the Commission, and of expressing to you the sentiments of perfect esteem with which I am

Sir   your most Obedient and   most humble Servant.

Th:Jefferson

Thomas Johnson esquire

RS (In possession of Thomas Booker Johnson of Dallas, Texas); Lb (DNA, RG 59, Domestic Letters).

Tobias Lear to Thomas Jefferson ———————————
August 7, 1791   [Philadelphia, Pennsylvania]

. . . By the President's command, T. Lear has the honor to enclose & transmit to the Secretary of State, a letter for the Honᵇˡᵉ Thomas Johnson[1] which the President requests may be sent with his commission, and suggests directing them to the care of the Post master at Baltimore as the most likely mean of their reaching their destination with safety & dispatch. . . .

ARS (DLC, Thomas Jefferson Papers). Endorsed "recᵈ Aug. 7. 91."
   1. See below, George Washington to Thomas Johnson, August 7, 1791.

George Washington to Thomas Johnson ————————
August 7, 1791   Philadelphia, Pennsylvania

The honorable Thomas Johnson Esquire

———————————

Philadelphia   August. 7. 1791.

Dear Sir,

I have been duly favored with your letters of the 27 & 30 of July; the last of which came to hand while the Judges of the Supreme Court were with me on an invitation to dinner.

I took this opportunity of laying your letter before the Chief Justice, (as you mentioned your having written to him and to M̠ͬ Wilson on the subject) in order that it might be communicated to the other Judges— after a few minutes consultation together, the Chief Justice informed me that the arrangement had been, or would be so agreed upon that you might be wholly exempted from performing this tour of duty at that time—[1] and I take the present occasion to observe that an opinion prevails pretty generally among the Judges, as well as others who have turned their minds to the subject, against the expediency of continuing the Circuits of the Associate Judges, and that it is expected some alterations in the Judicial system will be brought forward at the next session of Congress, among which this may be one.

Upon considering the arrangement of the Judges with respect to the ensuing circuit and the probability of future relief from these disagreeable tours, I thought it best to direct your commission to be made out and transmitted to you, which has accordingly been done, and I have no doubt but that the public will be benefitted, and the wishes of your friends gratified by your acceptance.

With sentiments of very great regard &̠̠ͨᵃ

G. Washington

Lb (DLC, George Washington Papers).
    1. Rather than riding the Southern Circuit, Thomas Johnson attended the Circuit Court for the district of Virginia in Richmond in the fall.

Thomas Johnson to George Washington ————————
August 13, 1791   Frederick, Maryland

. . . This Morning I received your Letters of the 7ᵗʰ & 8ᵗʰ Instant[1] and one from Mᵣ Jefferson covering my Commission— . . .

I feel myself obliged by the Circumstances attending your Appointment of me to Office— it is difficult to restrain warm Expressions— suffice it that your Choice [&?] Earnestness in my Favor shall not be disgraced by the Heart   I cannot so well answer for my Hand. . . .

ARS (DNA, RG 59, Miscellaneous Letters). Postmarked "ANNAPOLIS, August 15."
    1. The letter of August 8, 1791, did not relate to the Supreme Court.

Record of Oaths ————————————————————————
September 19, 1791   Frederick County, Maryland

State of Maryland and Frederick County ss.

Be it known that on the Si nineteenth day of September Seventeen Hundred and Ninety One M.r Thomas Johnson, within named appeard before me Richard Potts Chief Justice of the County Court of the fifth district in the State aforesaid, and qualified under the within Commission, by taking the Oath prescribed by the Act of Congress entitled an Act to regulate the time and Manner of administering certain Oaths; and also the Oath prescribed by the Act entitled An Act to establish the judicial Courts of the United States. _ Witness my hand and Seal the day and year above _

    Seal   Richard Potts

ADS (MdFre, Thomas Johnson Letters). Recorded on the verso of the temporary commission.

Nomination by George Washington ——————————————
October 31, 1791

. . . Certain Offices having become vacant, since your last Session, by the death, resignation or appointment to other Offices, of those who held them, I have, in pursuance of the power vested in me by the Constitution, appointed the following persons to fill these vacancies _ viz.t _

Thomas Johnson, of Maryland, one of the Associate Justices of the Supreme
    Court, vice John Rutledge, resigned. _ c[1] . . .

RS (DNA, RG 46); Lb (DLC, George Washington Papers).
  1. The "c" is written in a different hand and indicates Senate confirmation.

Nomination Received by Senate ——————————————
November 1, 1791

[*The Senate Executive Journal (RG 46, DNA) records receipt of this nomination on November 1, 1791.*]

Confirmation by Senate ——————————————————
November 7, 1791

. . . The Senate proceeded to consider the nominations of the President of the United States contained in his message of 31.st October 1791. and _

Resolved, That they advise and consent to the appointment of the persons therein named to the offices to which they are respectively nominated; [*The Senate postponed decision on the nomination of four individuals, but Thomas Johnson was not among them.*]

Ordered, that the Secretary communicate this resolution to the President of the United States.

D (DNA, RG 46, Executive Journal).

Notification to President of Senate Confirmation ——————— November 7, 1791

[*Certification paraphrasing the Senate's confirmation of Thomas Johnson to be an associate justice was sent to George Washington on November 7, 1791. This certification, attested to by Samuel A. Otis, secretary of the Senate, is not extant; but it was transcribed at the time into a letterbook (George Washington Papers, DLC).*]

Commission ——————————————————————————— November 7, 1791

GEORGE WASHINGTON, President of the United States
of America.

To all who shall see these Presents, GREETING.

Know Ye,[1] that reposing special trust and confidence in the wisdom, uprightness and learning of Thomas Johnson of Maryland[, I] have nominated and by and with the advice and consent of the Senate[,] do appoint him one of the Associate Justices of the Supreme Court of the United States, and do authorize and empower him to execute and fulfil the duties of that Office according to the Constitution and Laws of the said United States, and to have and to hold the said Office, with all the powers, privileges, and emoluments to the same of right appertaining, unto him the said Thomas Johnson during his good behavier

> In Testimony whereof I have caused these Letters to be made patent and the Seal of the United States to be hereunto affixed.
>
> SEAL   Given under my hand the seventh day of November in the year of our Lord one thousand seven[2] and ninety one, and of the independence of the United States of America the sixteenth. —

G:Washington

By the President

Th: Jefferson

RS (Photostat in MdAA, Gift Collection); Lb (DNA, RG 59, Miscellaneous Permanent and Temporary Commissions); D (GEpFAR, RG 21, CCD Georgia, Minutes, November 10, 1792) in which Johnson's name is spelled "Johnston." The RS appears to have been retraced (possibly because of fading); bracketed commas have been supplied where faint marks can be seen and where the punctuation is corroborated by the letterbook copy in the National Archives. For the form of an official copy of a commission, see that published above for John Rutledge under date of September 26, 1789. In the record book kept by the Secretary of Congress (RG 360, DNA) an entry indicates that Johnson's commisson was made out on November 10 and dated November 7, 1791.

   1. This commission consists of a printed form until this point. The rest of the commission is handwritten. This is the first instance of a printed form being used for a justice's commission.

   2. The clerk meant to write "seven hundred" as it appears in the letterbook copy in the National Archives.

Cover Letter to Commission
Thomas Jefferson to Thomas Johnson
November 10, 1791   Philadelphia, Pennsylvania

Philadelphia   November 10th 1791

Sir

   The President of the United States desiring to avail the Public of your services as one of the associate Justices of the Supreme Court of the United States, I have now the honor of enclosing you the Commission and of expressing to you the sentiments of perfect esteem with which I am,

   Sir,   Your most obedient and   most humble Servant.

Th:Jefferson

Thomas Johnson esquire

LS (Photostat in DLC, Thomas Jefferson Papers). For an official copy of this cover letter, see that published below for William Paterson under date March 4, 1793.

Record of Oaths
August 6, 1792   Philadelphia, Pennsylvania

Be it Remembered that on the 6th day of August 1792 at Philadelphia, I did administer to the within named Thomas Johnson the oath of office, and the one to support the Constitution which are prescribed by Law _

John Jay
Ch. Justice

ADS (Photostat in MdAA, Gift Collection); D (GEpFAR, RG 21, CCD Georgia, Minutes, November 10, 1792). This certification was written by Jay on Johnson's commission.

Thomas Johnson to George Washington ——————————
January 16, 1793 Frederick, Maryland

Frederick   16 Jañy[1] 1793.

sir.

This incloses a Resignation of my Commission of Judge: it would have better suited with my Inclination and my Ideas of propriety to have held it till after the next supreme Court but I am not very well and a Journey now to Philadelphia would be at least disagreeable.

On my first reading the Judiciary Act it appeared to me rather an Essay and I had no Doubt but that there would have been an Alteration as soon as the Attention of Congress could be again drawn to the Subject. The Experience we have had of the little that has been or could be done under the present System though excessively fatiguing to the Judges would I thought have insured their Discharge from Circuit Duty_[2] I am not conscious of being greedy of the Profits of Office and would voluntarily have given up part of the Salary as I believe all my Brethren would have done But I am informed the Judges of the supreme Court are still to go the Circuits with an Increase of power to one eventually.

I have not Self consequence enough to blame others for not thinking as I do as to wish Arrangements for my Accomodation[_] I have measured Things however and find the Office and the Man do not fit_ I cannot resolve to spend six Months in the Year of the few I may have left from my Family, on Roads at Taverns chiefly and often in Situations where the most moderate Desires are disappointed: My Time of Life Temper and other Circumstances forbid it.

I am tul truly sensible to the good Opinion and Confidence you have so often shewn towards me_ and with best Wishes and Sentiments of perfect Esteem

I remain Sir most respectfully   Your obed[t] Servant.

ThJohnson

The president_

I Thomas Johnson do hereby resign surrender and give up my Office of Associate Justice of the Supreme Court of the United States Witness my Hand this 16th Day of January 1793.

Th Johnson

ARS (DNA, RG 59, Miscellaneous Letters). In George Washington's executive journal under date of January 26, 1793, is a notation that this resignation had been received "a few days ago." George Washington Papers, DLC.

  1. The "J" is written over "Feb."
  2. A separate volume in this series will be devoted to the justices' circuit riding.

George Washington to Thomas Johnson ————————
February 1, 1793   Philadelphia, Pennsylvania

Thomas Johnson Esquire   Maryland.

Philadelphia   1st Feb.̥ 1793.

Sir,

While I acknowledge the receipt of your Letter of the 16 of february,[1] I cannot but express the regret with which I received the resignation of your Office of Associate Justice of the Supreme Court, & sincerely lament the causes which produced it—

It is unnecessary for me to say how much I should have been pleased had your health & other circumstances permitted you to continue in Office; for besides the difficulty of finding characters to fill the dignified & important station[2] of Judge, in whom are combined the necessary professional, local & other requisites, the resignation of persons holding that high Office conveys to the public mind a want of stability in that Department, where it is perhaps more essential[3] than in any other.— With sentiments of the highest esteem & regard, & sincere wishes for your health & happiness,

I am, Sir &.̥

G: Washington

Lb (DLC, George Washington Papers); Df (DNA, RG 59, Miscellaneous Letters).

1. The letter from Thomas Johnson to George Washington bore the date January 16, 1793. The draft of this letter from Washington had "January" here.

2. In draft, interlined above "office."

3. In draft, interlined above "necessary."

William Paterson: Appointment as
Associate Justice in 1793

William Paterson was born in County Antrim, Ireland, on December 24, 1745.[1] His parents, Richard and Mary Paterson, were of Scottish birth but moved to Ireland sometime before their son's birth. The Patersons did not stay long in their new country, however, and in 1747 they once again moved—this time to America. Richard Paterson, a tin plate worker, hoped to establish a tin plate manufactory as his two brothers had already done in Berlin, Connecticut. After landing at New Castle on the Delaware River, the Patersons moved from place to place until finally settling at Princeton, New Jersey. Richard Paterson, unsuccessful in his manufactory venture, established a general store there.[2]

In 1756 the College of New Jersey (later Princeton) relocated its campus from Newark to Princeton. Inspired by the robed scholars patronizing his father's store, Paterson aspired to attend the college located across the green, barely one hundred yards from his home. After studying Greek and Latin at a local preparatory school, Paterson enrolled at the college in 1759 at the age of thirteen. His course of study at Nassau Hall reflected the college's goal to provide training not only for the clergy but also for social and political leaders; in addition to the classics and theology, it included courses in history and moral philosophy.[3]

After graduation in 1763, he began to read law in the office of Princeton attorney Richard Stockton and also tended his father's store part-time.[4] During this period, Paterson helped form the Well Meaning Club, which included among its founding members Oliver Ellsworth, Luther Martin, Tapping Reeve, Jonathan Dickinson Sergeant, and Jonathan Edwards, Jr. This fraternity's purpose was to give its members a forum in which to sharpen their rhetorical skills. Paterson contributed a number of orations to the society. His frivolous "The Belle of Princeton" that celebrated the charms of Betsy Stockton gave way to a more familiar theme in the "Oration on the Degeneracy of the Times," which darkly warned of England's downfall for "want of principle."[5] Receiving an M.A. from the College of New Jersey in the fall of 1766, Paterson delivered a commencement address entitled "Patriotism."[6]

Paterson's legal tutelage in Stockton's office continued for another two years. At first Paterson found the study of law to be "disagreeable and dry" and likened it to "being entangled in the cobwebs of antiquity," but he soon realized that a proper study and understanding of the law required an "intense application and assiduity."[7] In November, 1768, Paterson passed an examination for admission to the New Jersey bar, but because of the governor's absence, he was not licensed to practice until December.[8]

With his license in hand, Paterson began to establish his law practice. In July, 1769, he settled in the small farming village of New Bromley, barely a day's ride from Princeton, and may have supplemented the income from his law practice by establishing a small general store.[9] His appointment as a provincial surrogate a month later opened a potentially lucrative position for him as the governor's representative in actions on

William Paterson attributed to James Sharples (ca. 1751-1811). Pastel on paper, ca. 1800-1804. Courtesy Office of the Curator, Supreme Court of the United States.

wills. The office, however, only generated a moderate amount of business, and so, in 1772, he left New Bromley for Raritan, on the South Branch, in Somerset County. There he joined his younger brother, Thomas, in establishing a general merchandising business trading under the name of Thomas Paterson and Company.[10]

During this time, Paterson accepted any legal business that was brought to him, usually consisting of the drafting of wills and the settling of estates.[11] The business that came his way was meager; between 1769 and 1774 he averaged only five cases per year. In 1775 this jumped to fifteen cases, but only because nine of them were cases in which he represented his father.[12] Although all young attorneys experience difficulties in setting up a law practice, Paterson's early legal career was hampered not only by his inexperience but also by his personality. Described by one biographer as a "self-effacing but ambitious young man," Paterson "chose to sit back where the action wasn't and wait for clients and status to seek him out." He once commented that the only goal he sought in life was "to live at ease, & pass thro' life without much noise and bustle."[13] Such an attitude might well have proven fatal to his legal career had it not been for a train of events far to the north; events at Lexington and Concord soon catapulted him into a life of commitment to the patriot cause.

Some time before spring, 1775, Paterson wrote an "Address on the Rise and Decline of Nations." He may have delivered this address to his brethren at the Cliosophic Society, the successor to the Well Meaning Club. In the fashion of many popular orators and pamphleteers of the day, Paterson portrayed England as a once-great nation now ruled by tyrannical and conspiratorial factions. He also pointed out that the passage of a multiplicity of laws engendered a "spirit of contention" and rendered "life vexatious and troublesome." England's involvement in a "rapid succession of expensive wars" had created not only a "national debt . . . swelled to an enormous sum" but also a standing army that had become a tool "of oppression . . . in the hands of an enterprising spirit to work out the ruin of a state." Paterson concluded: "All history declares, that the dissolute, the voluptuous, and effeminate have ever been subdued by the hardy, the temperate and the brave."[14]

Although Paterson seems to have been ideologically prepared to join the patriots in opposition to England, he also was aware of the consequences of such a move and proceeded with caution. He hesitated for two reasons. First, there was a practical consideration: as a young lawyer attempting to establish a new practice, he was concerned that his reputation would suffer if he sided with those calling for armed resistance. Secondly, Paterson was by nature cautious and, like other moderates, he preferred to wait for events to take a more defined course before committing himself to the political fray. But the skirmishes at Lexington and Concord resolved his indecision and he joined the revolution.[15]

In May, 1775, the freeholders of Somerset County appointed Paterson a deputy to the Provincial Congress.[16] He was soon selected secretary of the Congress, a post to which he was reappointed for the Second and Third Congresses. His activities in the provincial congresses led to other political appointments. In 1776 he served concurrently as the state's attorney general and as a member of the legislative council. The following year, while serving as an officer in the Somerset County battalion of minutemen, he was appointed to the state's Council of Safety. It was at this time that he married, on February 9, 1779, Cornelia Bell, daughter of John Bell, a wealthy Somerset County landowner.[17] Although Paterson was elected to the Continental Congress in 1780, the responsibilities of family life, coupled with the press of personal business and the rigors of circuit riding as attorney general, forced him to decline the post.[18]

The revolution not only brought Paterson into political prominence, it substantially increased his law practice. Between 1775 and 1782 his business jumped from 15 to 124 cases per year.[19] Some of this law business came from departing loyalist attorneys and some from his position as attorney general on circuit. He inherited the clients of two prominent loyalist attorneys, Bernardus LaGrange, who had been burned in effigy by New Jersey patriots, and Cortlandt Skinner, who had hastily departed New Jersey a few steps ahead of the militia. Paterson capitalized on LaGrange's misfortune by purchasing the attorney's confiscated Raritan River estate and establishing both his law office and his home there.[20] By 1782 he numbered among his clients such prominent members of New Jersey's elite as Governor William Livingston and Chief Justice Robert Morris.[21]

In 1783 Paterson resigned his position as attorney general to devote more time to his law practice. Unfortunately for Paterson, it was a year marked by death and sorrow. His youngest daughter, Frances, died in June and five months later, his wife, Cornelia, succumbed to childbirth complications.[22] A little over a year later, Paterson married Euphemia White, daughter of one of his clients and a close friend of his departed wife.[23] Paterson's law business, already lucrative by the close of the war, continued to prosper in the 1780s. His practice took him to twelve of the thirteen counties of New Jersey, four of which provided him with 947 cases over a period of eight years.[24] By 1787 his income had grown to almost £1000.[25]

In 1787 the New Jersey legislature chose Paterson to represent the state at the forthcoming federal convention at Philadelphia. Except for his brief service as a commissioner appointed by the Confederation Congress to resolve a dispute between New York and Massachusetts in 1785, this was Paterson's first foray into national politics.[26] Paterson's greatest contribution to the development of the constitution at Philadelphia came on June 15, when he submitted what would later be known as the New Jersey Plan, which had been drafted by several men representing the interests of the small states. These states feared that their interests would not be served by a national legislature where representation was based on population; among other proposals, the New Jersey Plan called for retention of the Confederation Congress's equal representation by state. Although the New Jersey Plan was defeated by a coalition of large states, its concerns about the national legislature were reflected in the final draft of the Constitution. On July 2 Paterson was appointed to a grand committee charged with drafting a compromise agreeable to the large and small states as well as to sectional interests. After debate in committee and on the floor the "Great Compromise"—establishing equal representation by state in the Senate and by population in the House of Representatives—was finally, and narrowly, agreed to on July 16, 1787.[27]

Interestingly, in view of William Paterson's subsequent appointment to the Supreme Court, the New Jersey Plan called for the creation of a supreme federal tribunal, the judges of which would be appointed by the executive, and given the authority

to hear & determine in the first instance on all impeachments of federal officers, & by way of appeal in the dernier resort in all cases touching the rights of Ambassadors, in all cases of captures from an enemy, in all cases of piracies & felonies on the high seas, in all cases in which foreigners may be interested, in the construction of any treaty or treaties, or which may arise on any of the Acts for regulation of trade, or the collection of the federal Revenue . . .[28]

One week after the vote on the "Great Compromise," William Paterson left the convention, but he did not abandon his concern for the future of the national government. In March, 1789, he took office as a newly elected senator from New Jersey. Less than a month after his arrival at the capital, Paterson was at work on a committee charged with bringing in a bill "for organizing the judiciary of the United States."[29] With the exception of Oliver Ellsworth, Paterson was the most influential member of the committee and when the draft version of the bill was drawn up, the first nine sections were in his hand.[30] In the Senate debate on the bill, Paterson established himself as a staunch federalist by demanding that the federal district courts be made independent of state tribunals.[31]

Senator Paterson returned to New York for the second session of Congress in January, 1790, but, following the death of Governor William Livingston, the New Jersey legislature appointed Paterson governor on November 23, 1790.[32] During his term of office, Paterson codified New Jersey's statutes and updated the state's rules of practice and procedure in the courts of common law and chancery.[33] With Alexander Hamilton and others, Paterson formed the Society for Establishing Useful Manufactures to promote a planned industrial city at New Jersey's Passaic falls. The scheme, however, never developed beyond the initial stages of planning.[34]

Governor Paterson's work in New Jersey ended when President Washington nominated him to the Supreme Court in 1793 to replace Thomas Johnson who had resigned. Paterson remained on the bench until his death, at age sixty, in Albany, New York, on September 9, 1806.[35]

1. County Antrim is now in Northern Ireland. John E. O'Connor, *William Paterson: Lawyer and Statesman, 1745-1806* (New Brunswick: Rutgers University Press, 1979), p. 287n.

2. Ibid., p. 7; Gertrude Sceery Wood, *William Paterson of New Jersey, 1745-1806* (Fair Lawn, N.J.: Fair Lawn Press, 1933), pp. 1-3. Little is known about Paterson's mother, Mary; she died at age forty-nine on January 15, 1772, and is buried in the Presbyterian Church of Princeton's cemetery. Wood, *William Paterson*, p. 1.

3. O'Connor, *William Paterson*, pp. 8-15.

4. Wood, *William Paterson*, p. 11. At the time that Paterson read law in his office, Richard Stockton (1730-1781) was a prominent member of the New Jersey bar and was licensed as an attorney (1754), as a counselor (1758), and as a sergeant (1764). He was a trustee of the College of New Jersey during Paterson's clerkship in his office. In addition to Paterson, Stockton trained other young lawyers including Elias Boudinot and Joseph Reed. *DAB*.

5. O'Connor, *William Paterson*, pp. 27-29. Paterson went on to form the Cliosophic Society which was a successor to the Well Meaning Club. He maintained membership in this organization throughout the remainder of his life and returned often to speak before it. Ibid., p. 30.

6. Wood, *William Paterson*, p. 11.

7. Ibid., p. 12.

8. Ibid., pp. 15-16.

9. Ibid., pp. 16-17. At least one historian rejects the contention that Paterson derived extra income from operating a store. Richard Haskett notes that if Paterson did receive any extra money while at New Bromley, it came from his father. "Village Clerk and Country Lawyer: William Paterson's Legal Experience, 1763-1772," *Proceedings of the New Jersey Historical Society* 66 (1948): 164-65.

10. O'Connor, *William Paterson*, pp. 33-34, 292n; Wood, *William Paterson*, p. 21.

11. Wood, *William Paterson*, p. 21.

12. Richard Haskett, "William Paterson, Attorney General of New Jersey: Public Office and Private Profit in the American Revolution," *William and Mary Quarterly*, 3d ser., 7 (1950): 33; O'Connor, *William Paterson*, pp. 292-93n.

13. O'Connor, *William Paterson*, p. 43; Haskett, "Village Clerk and Country Lawyer," p. 163.

14. O'Connor, *William Paterson*, pp. 51-64.

15. Ibid., pp. 68-71.

16. Ibid., p. 71.

17. Ibid., pp. 75, 79-81, 88-89, 116-17; Haskett, "William Paterson, Attorney General," p. 35. They eventually had three children: two daughters, and a son.

18. *DAB*.

19. Haskett, "William Paterson, Attorney General," p. 33.

20. O'Connor, *William Paterson*, p. 109; Haskett, "William Paterson, Attorney General," p. 38; Wood, *William Paterson*, p. 25.

21. O'Connor, *William Paterson*, p. 108.

22. Ibid., pp. 116-17.

23. Ibid., pp. 108, 117. Euphemia (White) Paterson (1746-1832) was the daughter of Anthony White, a New Jersey landholder and the granddaughter of Lewis Morris (1671-1746), chief justice of New York (1715-

1733) and governor of New Jersey (1738 - 1746). Wood, *William Paterson*, p. 199; O'Connor, *William Paterson*, pp. 108, 117; Elizabeth Morris Lefferts, comp., *Descendants of Lewis Morris of Morrisania* (New York: Tobias A. Wright, 1907), Chart L; *DAB*, entry for Lewis Morris.

24. Of these 947 cases, 544 were debt cases, and of these, Paterson represented the creditor in 455 suits. O'Connor, *William Paterson*, pp. 118-21.

25. Ibid., p. 118. During this period, Paterson took into his law office several students, including Aaron Burr, Andrew Kirkpatrick (later chief justice of the New Jersey Supreme Court), and Robert Troup. Ibid., pp. 28, 108; *DAB*, entry for Andrew Kirkpatrick.

26. Ibid., pp. 119, 133-34.

27. Alfred H. Kelly, Winfred A. Harbison, and Herman Belz, *The American Constitution: Its Origins and Development*, 6th ed. (New York: W. W. Norton, 1983), pp. 95-100; Clinton G. Rossiter, *1787: The Grand Convention* (New York: Macmillan, 1966), pp. 186-89. Although Paterson has often been called the father of the New Jersey Plan, a number of men had a hand in its formulation. As one historian of the convention has remarked, the plan "showed the strains of its multiple paternity." Rossiter, *Grand Convention*, p. 175.

28. *RFC*, 1:244.

29. Rossiter, *Grand Convention*, p. 165; O'Connor, *William Paterson*, p. 169. Also serving with Paterson on this committee were Oliver Ellsworth, William Maclay, Caleb Strong, Richard Henry Lee, Richard Bassett, William Few, and Paine Wingate. O'Connor, *William Paterson*, p. 169.

30. O'Connor, *William Paterson*, p. 170.

31. Ibid., pp. 171-72.

32. Ibid., p. 183; Wood, *William Paterson*, p. 117.

33. Michael Kraus, "William Paterson," in *The Justices of the United States Supreme Court 1789-1969: Their Lives and Major Opinions*, ed. Leon Friedman and Fred L. Israel, 4 vols. (New York: R. R. Bowker, 1969), 1:167. Paterson's rules of practice and procedure later became known as "Paterson's Practice Laws." His revision of New Jersey's statutes was published as the *Laws of the State of New Jersey* (Newark: M. Day, 1800).

34. Kraus, "William Paterson," pp. 167-68.

35. Ibid., pp. 168, 173.

George Washington Journal Entry ——————————
February 19, 1793 [Philadelphia, Pennsylvania]

... In contemplating a Character to fill the vacancy, occasioned by Mr Johnson's resignation, on the bench of the Supreme Court of the U. S.— and seeking opinions thereon, The Att.^y Genl thought that Govr Patterson of New Jersey, who had been contemplated by the President, was a suitable Character to fill that office, notwithstanding his local situation. The Attorney was desired to converse with the Secretary of State on the subject, which he did; and informed, that the Secretary was decidedly of opinion that, considering the talents, respectability & integrity annexed to Govr Patterson's Character, he was a very proper person to be brought forward, notwithstanding his local situation.

D (DLC, George Washington Papers). According to the style of George Washington's journal, "Att.^y Genl" appears to the left of this passage in the margin, indicating the conversation was with Edmund Randolph. It should be noted here that Washington's journal was kept by his secretaries.

George Washington to William Paterson ——————————
February 20, 1793   Philadelphia, Pennsylvania

Philadelphia   February 20th. 1793

Sir,

The resignation of Mr Johnson, one of the Associate Judges, having occasioned a vacancy on the bench of the Supreme Court of the United States, it is incumbent upon me to bring forward a[1] suitable Character to fill that place. _ In performing[2] this part of my duty, I think it necessary to select a person who is not only professionally qualified to discharge that important trust, but one who is known to the public and whose conduct meets their approbation. _

Under this impression, Sir, I have turned my thoughts upon you; and if you will permit me to nominate you for this Office, I shall have the satisfaction to beleive that our Country will be pleased with, and benefitted by the acquisition.

As[3] an appointment to this office must be made[4] before the close of the present Session of the Senate, which is near at hand; and would be convenient if it could be done before the rising of the Supreme Court, which is now sitting in this City, in order that the Judges may make their arrangements for the ensuing Circuits,[5] it is necessary that I should know your determination as early as possible. _

With due Consideration[6] I have the honor to be Sir, Your most Obed.t Serv.t

G:Washington

Governor Patterson

LS (NjP, George Washington Papers); Lb (DLC, George Washington Papers); Df (DNA, RG 59, Miscellaneous Letters).

1. In draft, "[Character?]" follows.
2. In draft, this word has been interlined above an inked out word.
3. In draft, this has been interlined above "The necessity of making."
4. In draft, "must be made" has been interlined.
5. In draft, "and would be convenient if it could be done before the rising of the Supreme Court which is now sitting in order that the Judges may make their arrangemts of the Circuits" is interlined.
6. "With due Consideration" not in the closing of letterbook copy.

George Washington Journal Entry ——————————
February 20, 1793   [Philadelphia, Pennsylvania]

. . . In consequence of what passed yesterday respecting the nomination of Gov.r Patterson, he was this day written to upon this subject. . . .

D (DLC, George Washington Papers).

William Paterson to George Washington ─────────────
February 25, 1793   New Brunswick, New Jersey

New Brunswick,
25ᵗʰ Febʸ 1793.

Sir,

On my return from an excursion into the country, I found your letter of the 20ᵗʰ of this month. I consent to be nominated for the office of an associate judge.

With high respect,   I have the honor to be,   sir,   Your obedᵗ hb. servᵗ

Wᵐ Paterson

ARS (DNA, RG 59, Miscellaneous Letters).

George Washington Journal Entry ─────────────
February 26, 1793   [Philadelphia, Pennsylvania]

... Letter from Govʳ Patterson consenting to be nominated as a Associate
    Judge.─ ...

D (DLC, George Washington Papers).

Nomination by George Washington ─────────────
February 27, 1793

United States, February 27ᵗʰ 1793.

Gentlemen of the Senate,

I nominate William Paterson,[1] at present Governor of the State of New Jersey, to be one of the Associate Judges[2] of the Supreme Court of the United States;─ vice, Thomas Johnson, resigned.─

G°Washington

RS (DNA, RG 46); Lb (DLC, George Washington Papers). In George Washington's executive journal under date of February 27, 1793, is a notation that this nomination had been made. George Washington Papers, DLC.

1. In letterbook copy, William Paterson's name is spelled "Patterson."
2. Appears as "Justices" in letterbook copy.

Nomination Received by Senate ─────────────
February 27, 1793

[*The Senate Executive Journal (RG 46, DNA) records receipt of this nomination on February 27, 1793.*]

Nomination Nullified
February 28, 1793

United States, February 28th 1793.

Gentlemen of the Senate,

I was led, by a consideration of the qualifications of William Paterson,[1] of New Jersey, to nominate him an Assⁿciate Justice of the Supreme Court of the United States._ It has since occurred that he was a member of the Senate when the law creating that Office was passed, and that the time for which he was elected is not yet expired._ I think it my duty therefore to declare, that I deem the nomination to have been null by the Constitution[2]

G:Washington

RS (DNA, RG 46); Lb (DLC, George Washington Papers). In George Washington's executive journal under date of February 28, 1793, is a notation of the withdrawal of William Paterson's nomination because his term as Senator would not expire "until the 3ᵈ of March." George Washington Papers, DLC.

1. "Patterson" in letterbook copy.
2. Article I, section 6 of the Constitution states: "No Senator or Representative shall, during the Time for which he was elected, be appointed to any civil Office under the Authority of the United States which shall have been created, or the Emoluments whereof shall have been encreased during such time; and no Person holding any Office under the United States, shall be a Member of either House during his Continuance in Office." ROC, 1:309.

Nullification of Nomination Received by Senate
February 28, 1793

[*The Senate Executive Journal (RG 46, DNA) records receipt of the above letter from George Washington on February 28, 1793.*]

Nomination by George Washington
March 4, 1793

. . . I nominate

William Paterson, at present Governor of the State of New Jersey, to be one of the Associate Justices of the Supreme Court of the United States; vice, Thomas Johnson, resigned._ . . .

RS (DNA, RG 46); Lb (DLC, George Washington Papers). In George Washington's executive journal under date of March 4, 1793, is a notation of the nomination of William Paterson. George Washington Papers, DLC.

Nomination Received by Senate ——————————————————
March 4, 1793

[*The Senate Executive Journal (RG 46, DNA) records receipt of this nomination on March 4, 1793.*]

Confirmation by Senate ————————————————————
March 4, 1793

. . . On motion

It was agreed by unanimous consent so far to dispense with the rule as that the nominations be taken into consideration at this time.[1]

Resolved, That the Senate advise and consent to the appointments agreeable to the nominations respectively.

Ordered, That the Secretary lay this resolution before the President of the United States. . . .

D (DNA, RG 46, Executive Journal).

1. According to the Senate Executive Journal, the Senate on August 21, 1789, "Resolved, That when nominations shall be made in writing by the President of the United States to the Senate, a future day shall be assigned, unless the Senate unanimously direct otherwise for taking them into consideration." RG 46, DNA.

Notification to President of Senate Confirmation ——————
March 4, 1793

[*Certification paraphrasing the Senate's confirmation of William Paterson to be an associate justice was sent to George Washington on March 4, 1793. This certification, attested to by Samuel A. Otis, secretary of the Senate, is not extant; but it was transcribed at the time into a letterbook (George Washington Papers, DLC).*]

Commission ————————————————————————
March 4, 1793

George Washington President of the United States of America.
To all who shall see these Presents _ Greeting.

Know Ye, That reposing special Trust and Confidence in the Wisdom, Uprightness, and Learning of William Paterson of New Jersey, I have nominated, and by and with the Advice and Consent of the Senate, do appoint him one of the Associate Justices of the Supreme Court of the United States, and do authorize and empower him to execute and fulfil the Duties of that Office according to the Constitution and Laws of the said United States, and to have and to hold the said Office with all the Powers, Privileges, and Emoluments to the same of Right appertaining, unto him the said William Paterson during his good behaviour.

(L. S.)   In Testimony whereof I have caused these letters to be made patent and the Seal of the United States to be hereunto affixed. Given under my hand the fourth day of March in the year of our Lord one thousand seven hundred and ninety three, and of the Independence of the United States of America the Seventeenth.

G° Washington.

By the President

Th: Jefferson.

Lb (DNA, RG 59, Miscellaneous Permanent and Temporary Commissions); D (GEpFAR, RG 21, CCD Georgia, Minutes, April 25, 1793); D (NjBaFAR, RG 21, CCD New Jersey, Minutes, October 2, 1793). The Georgia circuit court minutes misspell William Paterson's name as "Patterson." For a recipient's version of this commission, see that published above for Thomas Johnson under date of November 7, 1791.

    According to an entry in the records of the Secretary of Congress (RG 360, DNA), Paterson's commission passed the seal of the United States on March 5, 1793. In George Washington's executive journal under date of March 6, 1793, is a notation that Washington had signed Paterson's commission. George Washington Papers, DLC.

Cover Letter to Commission ————————————————
Thomas Jefferson to William Paterson
March 4, 1793   Philadelphia, Pennsylvania

William Paterson Esquire—

Philadelphia   March 4ᵗʰ 1793

Sir

    The President of the United States desiring to avail the public of your services, as one of the associate Justices of the Supreme Court of the United States, I have now the honor of enclosing you the Commission, and of expressing to you the sentiments of perfect respect, with which I am, Sir, &c

Th: Jefferson

Lb (DNA, RG 59, Domestic Letters). For a recipient's version of this cover letter, see that published above for Thomas Johnson under date of November 10, 1791.

Record of Oaths
March 11, 1793 New Brunswick, New Jersey

... United States New Brunswick, New Jersey March 11th A. D. 1793 then the within named William Patterson[1] Esq[r] took the oath of Office of an Associate Justice of the Supreme Court of the United States agreeabl[e] to law and the Constitution and also the oath to support the Constitution of the United States as required by the same, before me.

> William Cushing one of Assoc[iate]
> Justices of the Supreme Court of
> the United States.

D (GEpFAR, RG 21, CCD Georgia, Minutes, April 25, 1793); D (NjBaFAR, RG 21, CCD New Jersey, Minutes, October 2, 1793). The page on which this is written is torn along the margin; therefore, bracketed readings have been supplied. This oath, which follows a transcription of Paterson's commission, probably was written directly on the commission.
1. Spelled as "Paterson" in New Jersey circuit court minutes.

William Paterson to Thomas Jefferson
March 12, 1793 New Brunswick, New Jersey

New Brunswick,
12[th?] March, 1793.

Sir.

Your letter of the 4[th?] of this month, and the commission therewith transmitted, I received a few days ago — I have been initiated into office, by taking the necessary oaths before judge Cushing.[1]

I am, sir, with great respect, Y[r] obed[t] hb. serv[t]

W[m] Paterson

ARS (DNA, RG 59, Miscellaneous Letters). Addressed "Philad[a]." Endorsed "rec[d] 14 March 1793."
1. William Cushing had written to William Paterson on March 5, 1793, from Philadelphia (Robert Treat Paine Papers, MHi). In this letter, Cushing had congratulated Paterson on his appointment, discussed circuit court arrangements, and mentioned that he would stop to see Paterson shortly. Apparently it was during this visit that Cushing delivered the oaths to Paterson; see above, Record of Oaths, March 11, 1793.

John Rutledge: Appointment as Chief Justice in 1795

[For biographical headnote, see "John Rutledge: Appointment as Associate Justice in 1789."]

John Rutledge to George Washington ─────────────
June 12, 1795   Charleston, South Carolina

Charleston   June 12. 1795.

Dear Sir/

Finding that Mr Jay is elected Governor of New-York, & presuming that he will accept the Office, I take the Liberty of intimating to you, <u>privately</u>, that, if he shall, I have no Objection to take the place which he holds, if you think me as fit as any other person, & have not made Choice of one to succeed him: in either of which Cases, I could not expect, nor would I wish for, it.

Several of my Friends were displeased at my accepting the Office of an Associate Judge, (altho' the senior,) of the Supreme Court, of the United States, conceiving, (as I thought, very justly,) that my Pretensions to the Office of Chief-Justice were, at least, equal to Mr Jay's, in point of Law-Knowledge, with the Additional Weight, of much longer Experience, & much greater Practice ─ I was not, however, so partial, to myself, as, not to think, that you had very sufficient Reasons, for preferring him to any other, tho', I, certainly, would not have taken the Commission, but, for your, very friendly & polite, Letter, which accompanied it ─ When I resigned it, I fully explained, to you, the Causes which induced me to accept the Office which I now hold ─ this I discharge, with Ease to myself, & Satisfaction to my Fellow-Citizens: But, when the Office of Chief-Justice, of the United States, becomes vacant, I feel that the Duty which I owe to my Children should impel me, to accept it, if offer'd: tho' more arduous & troublesome than my present Station, because, more respectable & honorable.

I have held many Posts, of high Rank, & great Importance, & have been under the Necessity of refusing others: but, they were offer'd, spontaneously, & handsomely ─ I have Reason to believe, that I discharged all that I held, with Fidelity & Honour ─ I never sollicited a Place, nor do I mean this Letter as an Application ─ it is intended, merely, to apprize you, of what I would do, if elected; & this I do, on an Idea, that you may, probably, have concluded, from the Resignation of my Continental-Commission, that it was my Determination, to remain, always, at Home.

I ask pardon for taking up so much of your Time, (which is always precious) & will intrude no longer, than to request, if an Appointment has taken place, or, the Nomination of any person [*word inked out*] settled, in your [*word inked out*] Mind, that the Contents of this Letter may be, for Ever, unknown, (as they are at present,) to any but yourself; and, to assure you, that, if, after reading this Letter, you shall nominate another, in preference of me, that Circumstance, can, never, lessen the respectful, & great, Esteem, & Veneration, which I have always professed, &, always shall have, for your Person & Character.

That God may long continue to preserve, in perfect Health, of Mind & Body, a Life, so inestimable, as yours, not only to this Country, but, I may truly add, to the Liberties of Mankind, in General, is the sincere & fervent Wish, & Hope, of

D.ʳ Sir   y.ʳ sincerely affectionate,   obliged, & obed.ᵗ Serv.ᵗ

J: Rutledge

George Washington
President of the United States of America.

ARS (DLC, George Washington Papers). Endorsed mistakenly "18ᵗʰ June 1795."

Edmund Randolph to John Rutledge ———————
July 1, 1795 Philadelphia, Pennsylvania

Department of State, July 1.ˢᵗ 1795.

Sir

It is with great pleasure, that I announce to you the wish of the President
to nominate ^you to the Chief-Justiceship of the United States, vacant by the resignation of Governor Jay. I hope, that it will be agreeable to you. In that event your presence will be very desireable at the ensuing meeting of the Supreme Court, on the third day of the next month. I therefore beg the favor of you to inform me by the earliest opportunity of your determination, and in case of acceptance, to proceed, as soon as it may be convenient to this City. The Commission, if you shall permit it to be issued in your name, will bear date on this day.

I have the honor to be, Sir, with great   respect & esteem, Yr. mo. ob. serv.

Edm: Randolph.

Lb (DNA, RG 59, Domestic Letters).

Temporary Commission
July 1, 1795

George Washington President of the United States of America.
To all who shall see these Presents_ Greeting.

Whereas the office of Chief Justice of the Supreme Court of the United States is at present vacant_ Know Ye, That reposing special Trust and Confidence in the Wisdom, Uprightness, and Learning of John Rutledge of South Carolina, I do appoint him Chief Justice of the Supreme Court of the United States, and do authorize and empower him to execute and fulfil the duties of that office according to the Constitution and Laws of the said United States, and to have and to hold the said office with all the Powers, Privileges, and Emoluments to the same of Right appertaining unto him the said John Rutledge during his good Behaviour, and until the end of the next Session of the Senate of the United States and no longer.

(L. S.)

In Testimony whereof I have caused these letters to be made patent and the Seal of the United States to be hereunto affixed. Given under my hand the first day of July in the year of our Lord one thousand seven hundred and ninety five, and of the Independence of the United States of America the nineteenth.

G? Washington.

By the President

Edm: Randolph.

Lb (DNA, RG 59, Temporary Presidential Commissions). As George Washington explained to John Rutledge in a letter of July 1, 1795 (q.v., below), Rutledge's temporary commission would be dated July 1 but kept in Philadelphia pending Rutledge's arrival. According to the official record, the temporary commission passed the seal of the United States on August 12, two days after Rutledge's arrival in Philadelphia (RG 360, DNA). Edmund Randolph sent it to Rutledge the same day; see Edmund Randolph to John Rutledge, August 12, 1795, published below.

George Washington to John Rutledge
July 1, 1795   Philadelphia, Pennsylvania

John Rutledge Esq?

Philad? 1st July 1795.

D?Sir,

Your private letter of the 18th ult?[1] and M? Jay's resignation of the office of Chief Justice of the US.[2] both came to my hands yesterday.

The former gave me much pleasure, and without hesitating a moment, after knowing you would accept the latter, I directed the Secretary of State to make you an official offer of this honorable appointment: _ to express to you my wish that it may be convenient & agreeable to you to accept it: _ to intimate, in that case, my desire[3] & the advantages that would attend your being in this city the first monday in August (at which time the next session of the supreme Court will commence): _ and to inform you, that your Commission as Chief Justice will take date on this day July the first,[4] (when M.r Jay's will cease) _ but that it would be detained here, to be presented to you on your arrival.

I shall only add, that the Secretary will write to you by post, & by a water conveyance also, if there be any vessel in this harbour which will sail for Charleston in a few days _ and that, with much sensibility for your good wishes, & an assurance of the sincerest esteem and regard,

I am, my dear Sir &.c

G.ºWashington

Lb (DLC, George Washington Papers); ADfS (DLC, George Washington Papers).
    1. John Rutledge's letter was dated June 12, 1795. It had been endorsed on receipt as dated June 18, 1795. See source note for John Rutledge to George Washington, June 12, 1795, published above.
    2. See two letters from John Jay to George Washington, published above and dated June 29, 1795.
    3. In draft, "desire" has been interlined over "~~wish~~."
    4. In draft, George Washington interlined "July the first."

Cover Letter to Temporary Commission ———
Edmund Randolph to John Rutledge
August 12, 1795   [Philadelphia, Pennsylvania]

The Secretary of State has the honor of inclosing to the hon.ble M.r Rutledge the Commission of Chief Justice of the United States.[1]
August 12. 1795.

Lb (DNA, RG 59, Domestic Letters).
    1. The temporary commission of John Rutledge passed the seal of the United States on August 12, 1795; see note to temporary commission of John Rutledge under date of July 1, 1795.

Record of Oaths ———
August 12, 1795   [Philadelphia, Pennsylvania]

[*The minutes of the Supreme Court (q.v.) record John Rutledge's oaths as being taken on August 12, 1795.*]

Nomination by George Washington ——————————
December 10, 1795

. . . I nominate the following persons to fill the Offices annexed to their respective names;— which became vacant during the recess of the Senate.

John Rutledge, of South Carolina, to be Chief Justice of the Supreme Court
    of the United States, vice John Jay, resigned.   not c[1] . . .

RS (DNA, RG 46); Lb (DLC, George Washington Papers). The letterbook copy begins: "this
day the following Nominations were submitted to the Consideration of the Senate."
   1. Not confirmed. Written in a hand different from that in the rest of the document.

Nomination Received by Senate ——————————
December 10, 1795

[*The Senate Executive Journal (RG 46, DNA) records receipt of this nomination on
December 10, 1795.*]

Rejection by Senate ——————————
December 15, 1795

[*December 11:*] The Senate took into consideration the message of the President
of the United States of the 10th instant, and the nominations therein mentioned
of John Rutledge and others.

    Ordered, that the further consideration thereof be postponed to Tuesday
next.

[*December 15:*] Agreeable to the order of the day, the Senate took into consideration the message of the President of the United States of the 10th instant,
and the nominations therein contained, of

    John Rutledge Esqr. and others, to offices therein mentioned, and

    Resolved, that they advise and consent to the appointments respectively,
agreeable to the nominations; except to that of John Rutledge, postponed.

    Ordered, that the Secretary lay this resolution before the President of the
United States.

    On motion,

    The Senate resumed the consideration of the message of the President of
the United States of the 10th instant, containing the nomination of John Rutledge, to be Chief Justice of the United States, and

    On motion to advise and consent to the appointment agreeable to the nomination

It passed in the negative $\begin{cases} \text{Yeas 10.} \\ \text{Nays 14.} \end{cases}$

The yeas and nays being required by one fifth of the Senators present. Those who voted in the affirmative, are,

M!. Bloodworth,	M!. Martin,
" Brown,	" Mason,
" Burr,	" Read,
" Butler,	" Robinson and
" Langdon,	" Tazewell.[1]

Those who voted in the negative, are,

M!. Bingham,	M!. Livermore,
" Cabot,	" Marshall,
" Ellsworth,	" Paine,
" Foster,	" Ross,
" Frelinghuysen,	" Rutherfurd,
" King,	" Strong and
" Latimer	" Trumbull.[2]

Ordered, that the Secretary lay this resolution before the President of the United States.[3] . . .

D (DNA, RG 46, Executive Journal).

1. Timothy Bloodworth (North Carolina), Alexander Martin (North Carolina), John Brown (Kentucky), Stevens T. Mason (Virginia), Aaron Burr (New York), Jacob Read (South Carolina), Pierce Butler (South Carolina), Moses Robinson (Vermont), John Langdon (New Hampshire), and Henry Tazewell (Virginia).

2. William Bingham (Pennsylvania), Samuel Livermore (New Hampshire), George Cabot (Massachusetts), Humphrey Marshall (Kentucky), Oliver Ellsworth (Connecticut), Elijah Paine (Vermont), Theodore Foster (Rhode Island), James Ross (Pennsylvania), Frederick Frelinghuysen (New Jersey), John Rutherfurd (New Jersey), Rufus King (New York), Caleb Strong (Massachusetts), Henry Latimer (Delaware), and Jonathan Trumbull (Connecticut).

The following senators did not vote: William Bradford (Rhode Island), James Gunn (Georgia), John Henry (Maryland), Richard Potts (Maryland), John Vining (Delaware), and George Walton (Georgia). Senators Bradford and Vining arrived the next day and would have cast their votes against Rutledge; see "Commentaries," Jacob Read to Ralph Izard, December 19, 1795.

John Adams reported that, according to George Walton, if the two Georgia senators had arrived in time for the vote, they would have voted against Rutledge; see "Commentaries," John Adams to Abigail Adams, December 21, 1795.

3. On December 21, 1795, *Dunlap's American Daily Advertiser* (Philadelphia) printed a report of the Senate's rejection of John Rutledge's nomination. In this article, the ten senators who had voted in favor of Rutledge were listed, but the vote itself was reported incorrectly as 14 to 8. The *Georgia Gazette* (Savannah) printed the same report with the same numerical error on January 7, 1796, as did the *Rutland Herald* (Rutland, Vermont) on January 11, 1796. The latter newspaper also misspelled Senator Butler's name as "Burier." The *City Gazette* (Charleston) on January 4, 1796, printed this report but gave the vote as 12 to 10. Another brief article about the Senate's action appeared in the *Boston Gazette* on December 28, 1796, which reported the vote as 14 to 9.

Notification to President of Senate Rejection ————————
December 15, 1795

[*Certification paraphrasing the Senate's rejection of John Rutledge to be chief justice was sent to George Washington on December 15, 1795. This certification, attested to by Samuel A. Otis, secretary of the Senate, is not extant; but it was transcribed at the time into a letterbook (George Washington Papers, DLC).*]

John Rutledge to George Washington ——————————————
December 28, 1795   Charleston, South Carolina

Chaᵗton   Decᵣ 28. 1795

Dear sir/

It is with great Reluctance that I feel myself under the Necessity of resigning the Commission, with which you honoured me last Summer, but, after having made a fair Experiment of the Strength of my Constitution, I find it totally unequal to the discharge of the duties of the Office, & therefore consider it as incumbent on me, to quit, the Station—[1] permit me, however, to inform you, that on my return to this State, I found a Variety of Causes, ready for Trial, before the Circuit Court, on all of which I gave Decrees in the Course of a Fortnight— That after having rested from the Fatigues of the Court for a day or two, I set out, tho' in ill Health, to attend my duty at Augusta, but, the death of the Clerk of the Court, at Savannah, the Want of the Records, & the Absence of Mᵣ Justice Pendleton, in whom the right of appointing another Clerk was vested, prevented my proceeding to Business, at Augusta: I then set out for Raleigh, in NᵒCarolina, but was so indisposed on the Road, as to be incapable of reaching it & was ultimately obliged to return to this Place, convinced by Experience, that it requires a Constitution less broken than mine, to discharge with Punctuality & Satisfaction, the Duties of so important an Office— I cannot however take Leave of the Station, without thanking you very sincerely, for the various Marks of Friendship & Confidence, which you have been pleased to shew me, & most ardently wish you every Happiness, that this Life can afford. I have the Honor to be with the greatest Respect dᵣ sir

yᵣ obliged & most obedᵗ   hble servᵗ

J. Rutledge

The President of the United States

ARS (DNA, RG 59, Miscellaneous Letters).

1. It is not known if John Rutledge knew that his nomination had been rejected when he wrote this letter. He was paid for his service as chief justice of the Supreme Court through December 28, 1795, the date of this letter of resignation. Miscellaneous Treasury Account #7905, RG 217, DNA.

William Cushing: Appointment as Chief Justice in 1796

[For biographical headnote, see "William Cushing: Appointment as Associate Justice in 1789."]

Nomination by George Washington
January 26, 1796

... The following Nominations were this day submitted to the Senate.

> United States
> Jan.ʸ 26. 1796.

Gentlemen of the Senate,

I nominate William Cushing, of Massachusetts, to be Chief Justice of the Supreme Court of the United States.

Samuel Chase, of Maryland, to be one of the associate Justices of the Supreme Court of the United States; vice John Blair resigned ...

Lb (DLC, George Washington Papers).

Nomination Received by Senate
January 26, 1796

[*The Senate Executive Journal (RG 46, DNA) records receipt of this nomination on January 26, 1796.*]

Confirmation by Senate
January 27, 1796

... The Senate proceeded to the consideration of the message of the President of the United States of the 26ᵗʰ instant, nominating William Cushing, and others, to office respectively.

Resolved, that they do advise and consent to the appointment agreeable to the nominations respectively.

Ordered, that the Secretary lay this resolution before the President of the United States.

D (DNA, RG 46, Executive Journal).

Notification to President of Senate Confirmation ——————
January 27, 1796

[*Certification paraphrasing the Senate's confirmation of William Cushing to be chief justice was sent to George Washington on January 27, 1796. This certification, attested to by Samuel A. Otis, secretary of the Senate, is not extant; but it was transcribed at the time into a letterbook (George Washington Papers, DLC).*]

Commission ———————————————————————
January 27, 1796

George Washington President of the United States of America.
To all who shall see these Presents— Greeting.

Know Ye, That reposing special Trust and Confidence in the Wisdom, Uprightness, and Learning of <u>William Cushing</u> of Massachusetts, I have nominated and by and with the Advice and Consent of the Senate do appoint him <u>Chief Justice of the Supreme Court</u> of the United States, and do authorize and empower him to execute and fulfil the Duties of that office according to the Constitution and Laws of the said United States, and to have and to hold the said office with all the powers, privileges, and Emoluments to the same of Right appertaining, unto him the said William Cushing during his good Behaviour.

(L. S.)

In Testimony whereof I have caused these Letters to be made Patent and the Seal of the United States to be hereunto affixed. Given under my hand the Twenty seventh day of January in the year of our Lord one thousand seven hundred and ninety six, and of the Independence of the United States of America the Twentieth.

G⁰ Washington.

By the President

Timothy Pickering.
Secretary of State

Lb (DNA, RG 59, Miscellaneous Permanent and Temporary Commissions).

Cover Letter to Commission ————————————————
Timothy Pickering to William Cushing
January 27, 1796 [Philadelphia, Pennsylvania]

William Cushing, Esq.

Department of State. January 27. 1796.

Sir

The President of the United States desiring to avail the public of your services as Chief Justice of the Supreme Court of the united States, I have now the honor of inclosing the Commission; and of expressing to you the sentiments of perfect respect with which I am Sir.

your most obed. serv.

Timothy Pickering.

Lb (DNA, RG 59, Domestic Letters).

William Cushing to George Washington ————————————
February 2, 1796 Philadelphia, Pennsylvania

Philadelphia Feby 2. 1796

[Dea]r Sir,

After the most respectful & grateful acknowledgment of my obligations to you for the appointment you have been pleased to make of me to the office of chief Justice of the United States, and to the hon. the Senate for their advice & consent to the Same; And after Considering the additional Care & duties attending[1] on that important Office, [&?] which, I apprehend my infirm &
the weight of,
declining state of health unequal to ˄ I must beg leave to retain the place I
on bench
have hitherto held, ˄ during the little time I may be able, in some measure, to perform the duties of it— And pray that the return of the Commission for
inclosed
the office of chief-Justice ˄ may be accepted— and that another person be appointed thereto[_ ?][2]

I have the honor to be, with the greatest respect, Sir, your most Obedient Servant

W. C—

ADfS (Photostat in MScitHi). This draft is damaged; therefore, readings have been supplied in brackets.

1. The "i" is written over an "a," and the "g" is written over a "t."

2. According to an unverified account, on the same day that the Senate confirmed William Cushing's nomination as chief justice, "there was a large dinner-party at the President's. Cushing was one of the guests. On entering the dining-room, Washington, from the head of the table,

directing his look to him, said in an emphatic tone, 'the Chief Justice of the United States will please take his seat on my right.' The Judge had heard nothing of the nomination, and was much affected at the announcement. His commission was made out, which he received the next day, and held for about a week, when, upon the ground of ill-health, he determined to resign it. Washington, for whom he entertained a profound veneration, endeavored to dissuade him from his purpose; but without avail." Flanders, *Lives and Times of the Chief Justices,* 2:46.

Samuel Chase: Appointment as Associate Justice in 1796

Samuel Chase, born in Somerset County, Maryland, on April 17, 1741, was the child of the Reverend Thomas Chase, an Episcopal clergyman who had immigrated from England, and Martha (Walker) Chase, the daughter of a Maryland farmer. Samuel Chase was instructed in the classics by his father and by the age of eighteen was ready to begin reading law in the offices of Annapolis attorneys John Hammond and John Hall.[1] In 1761, after two years of legal study, Chase gained admission to the bar of the Mayor's Court of Annapolis. His practice initially consisted of cases in the Mayor's Court, but it soon expanded to include the Court of Chancery as well as courts in the counties surrounding Annapolis.[2] A year after being admitted to practice as a lawyer, he married Ann (Nancy) Baldwin who lived nearby.[3]

Elected to the Maryland General Assembly in 1764, Chase soon earned a reputation as an opponent of the governor. His participation in the activities of the Sons of Liberty[4] brought him condemnation from the mayor and Board of Aldermen of Annapolis who singled him out as a "busy restless Incendiary—a Ringleader of Mobs—a foul mouth'd and inflaming son of Discord and Faction—a common Disturber of the public Tranquility, and a Promoter of the lawless excesses of the multitude." Unrepentant, Chase responded that his accusers were "despicable Pimps, and Tools of Power, emerged from Obscurity and Basking in proprietary Sunshine."[5] Such vitriolic exchanges would characterize Chase's public career. Some part of his troubles resulted from his impulsive and sometimes abrasive personality, which served to strain friendships and outrage his enemies.[6]

Chase's activities in the early years of the revolution lend some credence to the mayor's characterization of the young Marylander as a restless and busy incendiary. His reputation as a tireless agitator got him elected in 1774 to the Maryland Committee of Correspondence, and in June of that year he represented Anne Arundel County (including Annapolis) in Maryland's provincial convention.[7] A few months later, as a delegate to the First Continental Congress, Chase journeyed with four other Marylanders to Philadelphia. There Chase served on a committee charged with drafting a report on laws affecting trade and commerce. Although he was known in Maryland for his outspoken opposition to the Crown's rule, Chase considered himself a moderate, and he refused to join congressional radicals in calling for a total break with England. Instead, he hoped to work out a solution that would keep the empire intact. Chase chose only to support a move for a trade embargo with England. He returned to Maryland after the adjournment of the First Continental Congress and soon after participated in another provincial convention as a representative from Anne Arundel County.[8]

As a delegate to the Second Continental Congress, Chase kept very busy with committee work. In the spring of 1776, he was selected to join Benjamin Franklin and Charles Carroll of Carrollton on a mission to Canada seeking union between Canada and the southern colonies. The venture failed, and Chase returned to Philadelphia to discover that Maryland had instructed its congressional delegation to vote against independence. Winding up his remaining congressional business, Chase went back to An-

Samuel Chase by John Wesley Jarvis (1780-1840). Oil on panel, 1811. Courtesy National Portrait Gallery, Smithsonian Institution.

napolis and successfully worked with others in convincing the state legislature to change its instructions with regard to independence. Although he missed the vote for independence on July 2, Chase did return to Philadelphia in time to sign the final copy of the Declaration of Independence on August 2.[9]

For the next few years Chase engaged in a frenetic round of committee duties. As a member of Maryland's delegation to the Second Continental Congress, Chase served on twenty-one committees in 1777 and increased this to thirty the following year.[10]

Then, toward the end of 1778, Chase's public life ran headlong into scandal. Using information available to him as a member of Congress, Chase cornered the lucrative flour market in Maryland. His speculative activities were soon revealed, causing a torrent of public criticism. Alexander Hamilton published a series of blistering attacks in the *New-York Journal* denouncing Chase as a war profiteer. As a result of these criticisms, Chase was not returned to Congress in November, 1778; for the first time since 1764, he was without a public office.[11]

Although Chase's rather stormy exit from Congress removed him from national politics, it did not remove him from public criticism. He returned to Annapolis to fight the continuing charges of misconduct in the flour speculation incident. Chase finally was vindicated when the Maryland House of Delegates voted in January, 1782, to exonerate him of all charges placed against him in the flour scandal.[12]

In August, 1783, Maryland Governor William Paca sent Chase on a mission to England to arrange for the return of Maryland's pre-Revolutionary shares in the Bank of England. Chase realized this was an opportunity to rebuild both his and the state's finances, for if successful, he could receive well over £2,000 sterling in commissions. The negotiations, however, did not succeed—the issue was not settled until 1804—and Chase returned to Maryland sometime after August, 1784. While Chase did not receive any commissions, since the bank stock was not returned, his stay in England was not without personal reward. His first wife, Nancy (Baldwin) Chase, had died sometime between late 1776 and the winter of 1779 leaving Chase to tend a sizable family. On March 3, 1784, he married Hannah Kitty Giles, the daughter of Samuel Giles, a physician in Kentbury, Berks, England.[13]

Throughout the period in which he was involved in revolutionary politics, Chase's law practice continued to expand. By the late 1770s Chase had enough business that he could begin to take in young law students as clerks. Among the students Chase trained over the course of two decades were William Pinkney, Hugh Henry Brackenridge, and Kensey Johns, who later became chief justice of Delaware. Unlike many attorneys who employed law clerks, Chase took care to provide them with a well-rounded education. In addition to their legal training, Chase's students read history, politics, geography, rhetoric, logic, and philosophy.[14]

After his return from the bank stock negotiations in England, Chase became involved in a number of business ventures that proved disastrous. He overextended his credit by purchasing confiscated loyalist properties and compounded his financial woes by entering into a number of unsuccessful war supply speculation schemes. He hoped that by moving to Baltimore in 1786 he could generate enough legal business to meet his creditors' demands, but by 1787 his financial situation was so desperate that he was forced to petition the Maryland General Assembly to declare himself bankrupt.[15]

Chase began his judicial career in 1788 when Governor William Smallwood appointed him to the newly formed Court of Oyer and Terminer and Gaol Delivery of Baltimore County. In 1790, however, he resigned from the court, claiming that the meager emoluments of the office produced insufficient income. But in a resignation letter to Governor John Eager Howard, Chase revealed other reasons for his dissatisfaction. Both the press and some unnamed citizens of Baltimore, Chase complained, were intent on smearing his judicial reputation to the point that he could not properly conduct his office. His complaint, which probably did have some measure of truth in it, was symptomatic of a larger problem that plagued his public career. Chase had an almost uncanny ability to engender controversy while in public office.[16]

Chase did not support the Constitution when it was sent out from Philadelphia for ratification. At meetings and in newspapers—writing under the pen name "Caution"— Chase denounced the Constitution as a tool serving the interests of a few rich merchants rather than farmers and mechanics. Maryland federalists reacted harshly and at least one denounced Chase as an "Arch Fiend of Hell" for "playing the Devil in Town wth his D—d anti nightly meetings" against the Constitution.[17]

With the ratification of the Constitution by Maryland, Chase's harangues against it ceased. After 1788, in fact, he gradually became an avid supporter of federalist ideology. A number of events contributed to this political conversion. Chase, for instance, worked closely with Maryland federalist James McHenry in an effort to locate the seat of the national government in Baltimore. Although the effort failed, the ties that developed between Chase and McHenry served to soften Chase's anti-federalism.[18] Furthermore, between 1791 and 1794 events in Baltimore convinced Chase that his future lay not with the republican but with the federalist cause. In 1791 Chase received two concurrent judicial appointments: in August Governor Howard appointed Chase chief judge of the General Court, and in December he was appointed chief justice of the newly reorganized Baltimore County criminal court, the Court of Oyer and Terminer and Gaol Delivery. These two positions generated political controversy for Chase.[19]

Following the arrest of some pro-French sympathizers at a disturbance at Fell's Point (Baltimore), Chase convened a Court of Oyer and Terminer to investigate the incident. The refusal of those arrested to post bond prompted Chase to order the prisoners to jail, but threats against him by vociferous sympathizers and lack of support from the sheriff and the town's leading citizens caused Chase to adjourn court. At the August term of the court, Chase faced a grand jury summoned to hear the Fell's Point case, but, as he feared, the jury, instead of indicting the arrested individuals, returned a presentment against him for accepting his two court positions, and a presentment against the governor for appointing him to the offices. Chase challenged his opponents to present their complaints to the legislature, which they did. There Chase argued that his appointments were constitutional and reminded the legislators that a judge could be removed from office only because of "misbehaviour on conviction in a court of law." Although he won his case in the legislature—it declined to remove him from his judicial posts—it was a temporary victory, for the legislature subsequently abolished the Court of Oyer and Terminer and with it Chase's position.[20]

By the spring of 1795, with his future as a state judge in question and his political philosophy transformed, Chase's conversion to a supporter of the federalist administration was complete. He perceived the Fell's Point riot and the subsequent attack on him and his court to be symptomatic of a breakdown of law and order not only in Maryland but, as the Whiskey Rebellion in Pennsylvania proved, elsewhere as well. The events in Maryland also convinced Chase that his future lay with the federal government rather than with the state. He had now become an ardent proponent of a strong national government and was willing, indeed eager, to become a part of the federalist administration.[21]

This political turnaround enabled Chase's friend James McHenry to approach President Washington on Chase's behalf. McHenry informed the president that Chase had mended his anti-federalist ways and that he was available for employment by the administration in a judicial post. In late 1795 Washington considered Chase for the attorney generalship before rejecting him because of rumors concerning "impurity in his conduct." McHenry's efforts eventually proved successful, however. On January 26, 1796,

Washington overcame his reservations and nominated Chase to the Supreme Court in the place of retiring Associate Justice John Blair. The following day the Senate confirmed Chase's appointment.[22]

Chase's troubles with anti-federalist legislators, however, did not end with his appointment to the Supreme Court. His charges to grand juries, spoken with all the fervent conviction of a recent political convert, irritated republican editors and politicians alike. By 1803 Chase's outspoken manner and indelicate, if not injudicious, treatment of politically sensitive cases led republican partisans to call for his impeachment in the United States House of Representatives. A committee was formed in early January to review Chase's judicial conduct, and it soon reported back recommending impeachment. On March 12, the House voted 73 to 32 to draw up eight articles of impeachment.[23] Six articles involved Chase's handling of the treason trial of John Fries[24] and the sedition trial of James T. Callendar.[25] One article charged that Chase "did descend from the dignity of a judge and stoop to the level of an informer" in the case of James Wilson (a Wilmington, Delaware, printer), while the last article concerned Chase's improper charge to a grand jury in Baltimore.[26]

The trial, held in the Senate from January 3 to March 1, 1805, resulted in Chase's acquittal on all eight counts. During his remaining six years on the bench, Chase was plagued by frequent attacks of gout and often was unable to participate in the Court's deliberations. Chase died in Baltimore on June 19, 1811, in his seventy-first year.[27]

1. *DAB*. John Hammond (1735-1784) and John Hall (1729-1797). Hammond was admitted to the Middle Temple in February, 1753; entered Oriel College, Oxford University in January, 1758; and gained admission to the English bar in 1760. The same year, Maryland's Provincial Court and Anne Arundel and Frederick County courts admitted him to practice. In 1761 he was admitted to the bar of the Court of Chancery. Hall studied law in Maryland and attained admission to the bar of the Maryland Provincial Court in 1753 and to the bar of the Chancery Court by 1761. The county courts of Anne Arundel and Frederick Counties also admitted him to practice. Papenfuse et al., *Biographical Dictionary of the Maryland Legislature, 1635-1789*, entries for John Hammond and John Hall.

2. Irving Dilliard, "Samuel Chase," in *The Justices of the United States Supreme Court 1789-1969: Their Lives and Major Opinions*, ed. Leon Friedman and Fred L. Israel, 4 vols. (New York: R. R. Bowker, 1969), 1:185; *DAB*.

3. James Haw et al., *Stormy Patriot: The Life of Samuel Chase* (Baltimore: Maryland Historical Society, 1980), p. 12. Ann Baldwin's father was an unsuccessful planter and had recently died in a debtor's prison. Her mother was a keeper of an ordinary, or tavern, in Annapolis. Ibid.

4. *DAB*. On August 26, 1765, at the height of the Stamp Act crisis Chase participated in a demonstration against Annapolis resident Zechariah Hood who had secured the stamp tax distributorship for the province. That day an effigy of Hood was paraded about the town, pilloried, flogged, hanged, and finally burned. A few weeks later, the mob returned and tore down a storehouse Hood was repairing. The unfortunate collector fled to the safety of New York. Although Chase is suspected of being a ringleader in the first demonstration, there is no evidence to suggest that he participated in the later incident. Haw et al., *Stormy Patriot*, p. 18.

5. Robert R. Bair and Robin D. Coblentz, "The Trials of Mr. Justice Samuel Chase," *Maryland Law Review* 27 (1967): 368.

6. Haw et al., *Stormy Patriot*, pp. 162-63, 249-50, 253, 171.

7. Ibid., p. 43; Bair and Coblentz, "The Trials of Mr. Justice Samuel Chase," p. 368; *DAB*.

8. Haw et al., *Stormy Patriot*, pp. 43-47.

9. Ibid., pp. 52, 58-68.

10. *DAB*.

11. Haw et al., *Stormy Patriot*, pp. 105-9. Chase was returned to Congress in November, 1781, and again in 1783 and 1784, but never accepted the position. Ibid., p. 108.

12. Ibid., pp. 108-15.

13. Ibid., pp. 103, 120-29. At the time of Nancy (Baldwin) Chase's death, the Chase household consisted of eight children—four children of Samuel and Nancy Chase, and four children of Chase's father Thomas—and

two adults—Samuel Chase and his sister-in-law, Rebecca Baldwin. The marriage to Hannah Kitty Giles produced two daughters. Ibid., pp. 12, 28, 102-3, 126-27, 160.

14. Ibid., pp. 120-21.

15. Dilliard, "Samuel Chase," p. 188; Haw et al., *Stormy Patriot*, p. 143.

16. Haw et al., *Stormy Patriot*, pp. 162-63, 249-50, 253, 171.

17. Dilliard, "Samuel Chase," p. 188; James Buchanan to Tench Coxe, August 24, 1788, Tench Coxe Papers, PHi.

18. Haw et al., *Stormy Patriot*, pp. 164, 166-67.

19. Ibid., pp. 167-68.

20. Ibid., pp. 167-74.

21. Ibid., pp. 164, 172, 174.

22. Ibid., pp. 175-76. See below for documents relating to Samuel Chase's nomination and appointment as associate justice.

23. Dilliard, "Samuel Chase," pp. 193-96.

24. 9 F. Cas. 826 (C. C. D. Pa. 1799) (No. 5, 126).

25. 25 F. Cas. 239 (C. C. D. Va. 1800) (No. 14, 709).

26. *Trial of Samuel Chase, An Associate Justice of the Supreme Court of the United States, Impeached by the House of Representatives, for High Crimes and Misdemeanors, before the Senate of the United States*, taken in shorthand by Samuel H. Smith and Thomas Lloyd, 2 vols. (Washington, D.C.: Printed for Samuel H. Smith, 1805), 1:5-8; Evald Rink, comp., *Printing in Delaware, 1761-1800* (Wilmington: Eleutherian Mills Historical Library, 1969), p. 181.

27. Dilliard, "Samuel Chase," p. 197; *Trial of Samuel Chase*, 2:484; Haw et al., *Stormy Patriot*, p. 248; *DAB*.

George Washington to James McHenry ——————
January 20, 1796 Philadelphia, Pennsylvania

... Sound, I pray you, and let me know without delay, if Mr Saml Chase would accept a seat on the supreme Judicial Court of the U. States, made vacant by the resignation of M^{r}Blair.— If his decision is in the affirmative, he will at once perceive the necessity of being here by the first monday (if possible) in next month, at which time that Court is to sit in this city.— ...

ARS (DLC, James McHenry Papers); Lb (DLC, George Washington Papers); Tr (MdHi, James McHenry Papers). Marked "Private."

James McHenry to George Washington ——————
January 21, 1796 "Near Baltimore," Maryland

... I shall obtain Mr Chaces sentiments which shall accompany my letter ... by next post. ...

ARS (DLC, George Washington Papers).

James McHenry to George Washington ——————
January 24, 1796 "Near Baltimore," Maryland

... As to your orders respecting Mr Sam. Chace. Without detaining you with the preliminary matter that indicated to me his mind, it may be sufficient to inform you generally that he will accept, and particularly that he requested me

to tell you, that "he receives your intention to nominate him to a seat on the supreme judicial bench of the U. States with the utmost gratitude." He added. "The President shall never have reason to regret the nomination," and I believe it. He agrees to be in Philadelphia by the first monday by next month.
. . .

ARS (DLC, George Washington Papers).

William Vans Murray to George Washington ⸻
January 24, 1796   Philadelphia, Pennsylvania

112 Spruce Sᵗ   24. Janʸ 96

Sir,

You will excuse me I am certain for the liberty I take in mentioning Mᵣ Chase. Without touching in the remotest degree upon any thing belonging to the conversation I had the honour of lately; & without intimating that I had been spoken to, or that Mᵣ Chase had been even thought of by you Sir, I have taken some little pains to discover the opinions of several very respectable men from Maryland of Mᵣ Chase ⸺ as one whose name would possibly among others naturally present itself to the recollection of the Executive, when the Judicial vacancies were contemplated ⸺ His competence & merit are admitted by the gentlemen whom I have chatted with. ⸺ With Mᵣ Gale, late of Baltimore,[1] I had this morning a conversation about Mᵣ Chase. He says that the recent attack on the Jurisdiction of the General Court has produced in Mᵣ Chase's mind great discontent ⸺ & that he thinks Mᵣ Chase anxious to be out of the reach of the Judicial changes, to which the fluctuating spirit of a State Government seems to render the General Court perpetually liable.[2]

You Sir will not deem it presumtion in me to declare, that after much reflexion upon Mᵣ Chase's competence and fitness; I think him worthy of the honour of filling a seat on the Federal Bench; to which I do believe he would carry an energy which a Jurisdiction, in many cases concurrent, requires, particularly in its infancy. He is now Chief Justice of the State of Maryland ⸺ a high testimony to his general worth. A party spirit roused a ~~vote~~ ^{Resolution} of Impeachment against him in seventeen hundred and ninety Four ⸺ It was confined to a supposed violation of the Constitution in his having accepted the Chief Justiceship & the Presiding Judgeship of a local Jurisdiction in Baltimore, called their criminal Court. His conduct as a Judge, morally considered would have undergone a similar scrutiny had there been any foundation. The Resolution failed.[3]

I am with the greatest Respect   Sir   Yᵣ mo. ob Serᵗ

W. V. Murray

ARS (DLC, George Washington Papers).

William Vans Murray (1760-1803), a lawyer and Maryland congressman who had studied law in England, was frequently consulted by President Washington about federal appointments for Marylanders. Murray later held diplomatic posts in the Netherlands and France in the Adams administration. *DAB.*

1. Probably George Gale (1756-1815), a Maryland land and mill owner, who had served in the First Congress. Gale was appointed supervisor of distilled liquors for the district of Maryland in 1791 and in 1792 became the first president of the Baltimore branch of the Bank of the United States. In 1795 Gale moved from Baltimore County to Cecil County. Papenfuse et al., *Biographical Dictionary of the Maryland Legislature, 1635-1789.*

2. In 1794 a bill had been proposed in the Maryland House of Delegates concerning the jurisdiction of the General Court. The text of the bill as published on April 30, 1795, in the *Maryland Gazette* (Annapolis) would have increased the jurisdiction of the county courts at the expense of the General Court. The bill that had been passed in 1794 had to be confirmed, according to its last provision, by the newly elected General Assembly in 1795. The state Senate failed to do so; therefore the act did not take effect. *Votes and Proceedings of the House of Delegates of the State of Maryland [1794]* (Annapolis: Frederick Green, 1795), pp. 7, 112; *Votes and Proceedings of the House of Delegates of the State of Maryland [1795]* (Annapolis: Frederick Green, 1796), pp. 7, 17, 53, 59-60. *Votes and Proceedings of the Senate of the State of Maryland [1795]* (Annapolis: Frederick Green, 1796), pp. 18, 21, 22.

3. See biographical headnote for Samuel Chase, published above.

Nomination by George Washington
January 26, 1796

[*For nomination of Samuel Chase as associate justice, see George Washington's nomination of William Cushing as chief justice, published above under date of January 26, 1796.*]

Nomination Received by Senate
January 26, 1796

[*The Senate Executive Journal (RG 46, DNA) records receipt of this nomination on January 26, 1796.*]

Confirmation by Senate
January 27, 1796

[*For confirmation of Samuel Chase as associate justice, see the Senate's confirmation of William Cushing as chief justice, published above under date of January 27, 1796.*]

Notification to President of Senate Confirmation ————————
January 27, 1796

[*Certification paraphrasing the Senate's confirmation of Samuel Chase to be an associate justice was sent to George Washington on January 27, 1796. This certification, attested to by Samuel A. Otis, secretary of the Senate, is not extant; but it was transcribed at the time into a letterbook (George Washington Papers, DLC).*]

Commission ————————————————————————————————
January 27, 1796

George Washington President of the United States of America.
To all who shall see these Presents — Greeting.

Know Ye, That reposing special Trust and Confidence in the Wisdom, Uprightness, and Learning of Samuel Chase of Maryland, I have nominated and by and with the Advice and Consent of the Senate do appoint him one of the Associate Justices of the Supreme Court of the United States, and do authorize and empower him to execute and fulfil the duties of that office according to the Constitution and Laws of the said United States, and to have and to hold the said office with all the Powers, Privileges, and Emoluments to the same of Right appertaining unto him the said Samuel Chase during his good Behaviour.

(L. S.)
In Testimony whereof I have caused these letters to be made patent and the Seal of the United States to be hereunto affixed. Given under my hand the Twenty seventh day of January in the year of our Lord one thousand seven hundred and ninety six, and of the Independence of the United States of America the Twentieth.

G° Washington.

By the President

Timothy Pickering.
Secretary of State.

Lb (DNA, RG 59, Miscellaneous Permanent and Temporary Commissions).

George Washington to James McHenry ——————————
January 28, 1796   Philadelphia, Pennsylvania

... Your letters of the 21st & 24th instant have been duly received. _ The last, in time on tuesday, to give in the nominations of yourself & Mr Chase for the Offices contemplated. _ [1] The day following they were advised & consented to by the Senate, _ and the Commissions will be ready for the reception of you both on your arrival in this City. _ of this be so good as to inform Mr Chase; and, if he is still at Baltimore, to remind him, that monday next is the day appointed for the sitting of the Supreme Court; without him, there is no certainty of a sufficient number of Judges to constitute it[.] ...

ARS (DLC, James McHenry Papers); Lb (DLC, George Washington Papers); Tr (MdHi, James McHenry Papers). Addressed "Baltimore" and sent "Care of the Postmaster there President U. S." Postmarked "25 IA."
   1. James McHenry was appointed secretary of war.

James McHenry to George Washington ——————————
January 31, 1796   "Near Baltimore," Maryland

... I received your favour of the 28th last night and had its contents immediately communicated to Mr Chace. He is extremely pleased with his appointment and I have strong hopes that its good effects as it respects the public will extend beyond the judicial department, but on this point it is unnecessary to be particular till I have the happiness to see you. He would have set out today at noon but the stage he had engaged disappointed him so that he will only commence his journey to-morrow. I pray you to receive him kindly and cordially. ...

ARS (DLC, George Washington Papers).

Record of Oaths ——————————
February 4, 1796   [Philadelphia, Pennsylvania]

[*The minutes of the Supreme Court (q.v.) record Samuel Chase's oaths as being taken on February 4, 1796.*]

Oliver Ellsworth: Appointment as
Chief Justice in 1796

Oliver Ellsworth was born in Windsor, Connecticut, on April 29, 1745. His father, David Ellsworth (1709-1782), a Windsor selectman, owned a medium-sized farm not far from the town.[1] His mother, Jemima (Leavitt) Ellsworth (1722-1790), was born near Windsor in the village of Suffield.[2] David Ellsworth wanted his son to be trained for the ministry, so he placed his son in the care of Reverend Joseph Bellamy (1719-1790).[3] A well-known disciple of Jonathan Edwards, Bellamy taught promising young theologians at his home in Bethlehem, Connecticut.[4] In 1762, Ellsworth entered Yale, his mentor's alma mater. Ellsworth's career at Yale was not what might have been expected from a future minister. After a number of mischievous incidents brought him before the school's disciplinary board, he was dismissed from the college in 1764.[5]

Ellsworth next entered the College of New Jersey (later Princeton) where he seems to have abandoned his prankishness for the rigors of theological study.[6] Ellsworth, however, did have one disciplinary incident there that in some ways foreshadowed his career as a lawyer and jurist. The incident seems to have involved an infraction of the college's rule prohibiting the wearing of hats in the college yard, something for which he also was disciplined at Yale. Ellsworth successfully defended himself before the college's disciplinary board by pointing out that a hat "must consist of a crown and a brim, and proved that the head-piece he had worn in the yard was without a brim," and therefore he was not in violation of the college's regulation.[7] Ellsworth put his talent for argument to good use at the College of New Jersey by helping to form the Well Meaning Club, a debating society that included among its members Luther Martin, William Paterson, and Tapping Reeve.[8]

Upon graduation in 1766, Ellsworth returned home to continue his theological study under a new tutor, Reverend John Smalley of the New Britain Society. Ellsworth's study with Smalley did not go well, however, and the two parted ways after only a year. The story persists that Ellsworth's sermons read more like legal briefs than words from a pulpit.[9] Not surprisingly, Ellsworth turned to the law, commencing his studies with Matthew Griswold, a prominent Connecticut lawyer.[10] But Griswold's tutorial fees were too great, and Ellsworth was forced to leave Griswold's office for that of Jesse Root, a younger—and presumably less expensive—mentor. After further study, Ellsworth was admitted to the Connecticut bar in 1771.[11]

Ellsworth married Abigail Wolcott, the daughter of a prominent East Windsor family, in 1772.[12] Together they settled on a farm owned by his father near Windsor where Ellsworth divided his time between farm labor and legal business. He had entered the legal profession burdened with debts incurred during the course of his studies. He was able to satisfy most of his obligations through tutoring and selling off timber from the farm, but his professional earnings for the first three years of law practice totaled a mere three pounds Connecticut currency.[13]

Ellsworth's meager income was not due to any lack of initiative or ability. When courts sat at Hartford—ten miles distant—Ellsworth commuted by foot to attend the

Oliver Ellsworth attributed to James Sharples (ca. 1751-1811). Pastel on paper, ca. 1796-1797. Courtesy Independence National Historical Park.

sessions. Rather, as might be expected, clients preferred veteran attorneys. After a few years of struggle, however, Ellsworth's fortunes began to improve. His marriage to Abigail allied him with her family's power and wealth, and Ellsworth combined the attendant political and social connections with his own considerable talent and industry to improve his situation.[14]

In 1773 Ellsworth began to involve himself in the politics of Connecticut with his election as a deputy from Windsor to the General Assembly. The following year, he was returned to the same post and also appointed justice of the peace for Hartford County.[15] In early 1775 he moved his family—which now included a daughter—to Hartford to be closer to the legal and political opportunities the capital offered. In April of that year, he attended an emergency session of the General Assembly called to respond to the skirmishes at Lexington and Concord and was appointed to the Committee of the Pay Table, charged with supervising the state's military expenditures. The committee appointment was fortuitous. The importance not only of the committee but also of its members grew as the state's military expenditures grew.[16] Ellsworth's diligence and enthusiasm in carrying out the work of the Committee of the Pay Table was rewarded by an appointment as state's attorney for Hartford County in 1777.

Later that year the General Assembly appointed him to the Continental Congress, a position he would hold until the autumn of 1783.[17] Ellsworth did not journey to Philadelphia to attend the Congress until October, 1778, instead remaining at Hartford where he tended to his local duties, his legal business, and the needs of his family. His absence from Philadelphia, however, did not prevent his colleagues in Congress from appointing him to a special committee convening at Providence, Rhode Island, to investigate the failure of a military expedition in that state.[18]

By October, 1778, Ellsworth was a member of Congress, a state's attorney for Hartford County, a member of the Committee of the Pay Table, and a justice of the peace. In the following two years he added more positions to his political résumé. In April, 1779, he won a seat as Hartford's deputy to the General Assembly; in May, 1779, he was appointed to the powerful and influential state Council of Safety; and in April, 1780, he was elected to the Governor's Council, then the most powerful political body in the state.[19]

Ellsworth was in attendance at the Continental Congress for a total of nineteen months in the period between fall, 1778, and summer, 1783.[20] While in Congress, Ellsworth was a member of committees dealing with treasury affairs, weights and measures, and international treaties. His experience on Connecticut's Committee of the Pay Table enabled him to extract badly needed money for military supplies from recalcitrant states. As a member of Congress's Committee of Appeals, Ellsworth recognized the need for a national appeals court after the Pennsylvania courts refused to follow the committee's decree in the case of the *Active*. Subsequently, he helped draft a report that led to the establishment, in January, 1780, of the Court of Appeals in Cases of Capture.[21]

Retiring from Congress in 1783, Ellsworth returned to his law practice and was active in local affairs. Still a member of the Governor's Council, Ellsworth became an ex officio member of the newly formed Connecticut Supreme Court of Errors in 1784. The next year, he resigned as a councillor (and, thereby, as a member of the Supreme Court of Errors) and took a seat on the bench of the Superior Court.[22]

In 1787, still a judge on the Superior Court, Ellsworth was appointed a delegate to the Constitutional Convention. As a delegate from Connecticut, Ellsworth naturally supported the efforts of the small states to retain their power in the national legislature by giving each state equal representation.[23] Unlike many in the convention, however, Ellsworth was willing to compromise. His proposal for a bicameral legislature consisting of one house whose membership would be chosen on the basis of population and a second house in which all states would be equally represented was eventually endorsed by the convention and formed a basis for the "Great Compromise" of July 16, 1787.[24] In addition, Ellsworth enthusiastically supported James Wilson's motion to have the judiciary share with the executive branch in the power to revise proposed national legislation.[25] As the convention's work took shape, Ellsworth joined James Wilson, John Rutledge, Nathaniel Gorham, and Edmund Randolph on the important Committee of Detail charged with drafting the final version of the proposed constitution.[26] Before the signing of the Constitution, however, Ellsworth's judicial duties in Connecticut forced him to leave the convention in late August.[27]

Ellsworth took an active part in the ratification of the Constitution in Connecticut. In early November, 1787, he published the first of his "Landholder" essays that argued for the adoption of the Constitution. He carried his campaign to the state's ratifying convention where he quickly and skillfully maneuvered the federalist forces to endorse the Constitution on January 9, 1788—the first New England state to do so.[28]

Following his active role as a delegate in Connecticut's ratifying convention, he was chosen to represent the state in the United States Senate in 1789.[29] His career there lasted nearly six years. In that time he established himself as an ardent federalist. As a member of the Senate's committee to organize a judicial system, he was the principal author of the Judiciary Act of 1789.[30]

In early 1796, as a result of the Senate's rejection of John Rutledge as chief justice, President Washington again faced the task of choosing someone to appoint as chief justice of the United States. He first turned to Associate Justice William Cushing, who was nominated and confirmed in January, 1796. Preferring to remain an associate justice, Cushing refused the appointment, and Washington nominated Oliver Ellsworth, who was distinguished by his public service, knowledge of the federal judiciary, and federalist principles. The Senate confirmed the appointment on March 4.[31] Ellsworth's tenure on the Court—like Chief Justice John Jay's earlier in the decade—was shortened by extrajudicial service. In 1799 President John Adams, hoping to avoid a war with France, asked Ellsworth to travel there to promote an understanding between the two countries. Arriving in Paris in March, 1800, he negotiated a commercial convention with that nation which was ratified by the Senate in February, 1801.[32] But the ministerial journey to the continent broke his health. In a letter to John Adams of October 16, 1800, Ellsworth resigned. On his return to the United States in 1801, Oliver Ellsworth retired to his estate, Elmwood, in Windsor, Connecticut, where he died on November 26, 1807.[33]

1. Ronald J. Lettieri, *Connecticut's Young Man of the Revolution: Oliver Ellsworth* (Deep River, Conn.: New Era Printing, 1978), pp. 10-11; William Garrott Brown, *The Life of Oliver Ellsworth* (New York: Macmillan, 1905), p. 11; Samuel H. Parsons, "Early Records of Windsor, Connecticut," *New-England Historical and Genealogical Register* 5 (1851): 458.

2. Jane Jennings Eldredge, *The Leavitts of America* (Woods Cross, Utah: Leavitt Family Association, 1924), pp. 53, 97; Brown, *Life of Oliver Ellsworth*, p. 11.

3. Lettieri, *Oliver Ellsworth*, p. 10; Brown, *Life of Oliver Ellsworth*, pp. 12-13; *DAB*, entries for Oliver Ellsworth and Joseph Bellamy.

4. *DAB*, entry for Joseph Bellamy.

5. Ibid. Ellsworth's offenses numbered at least three: he was disciplined for violating curfew, creating a ruckus in the college yard, and participating in a drinking party with friends. Lettieri, *Oliver Ellsworth*, pp. 10-11.

6. Lettieri, *Oliver Ellsworth*, p. 11.

7. Brown, *Life of Oliver Ellsworth*, p. 19.

8. Lettieri, *Oliver Ellsworth*, p. 11; O'Connor, *William Paterson*, p. 28; Brown, *Life of Oliver Ellsworth*, pp. 19-20.

9. Lettieri, *Oliver Ellsworth*, pp. 11-12; J. Hammond Trumbull, *The Memorial History of Hartford County, Connecticut, 1633-1884*, 2 vols. (Boston: Edward L. Osgood, 1886), 1:279-80; *DAB*.

10. Lettieri, *Oliver Ellsworth*, p. 13. Matthew Griswold (1714-1799): admitted to the bar, 1743; representative of Lyme, Connecticut, in the General Assembly, 1748, 1751, 1754-59, 1789-90; king's attorney (New London County), 1755-65; member of the Council, 1759-69; judge and then chief judge of the state's Superior Court, 1765-1769, 1769-1784; deputy governor of Connecticut, 1769-1784; head of Connecticut's Council of Safety during the revolution; honorary LL.D. from Yale, 1779; governor of Connecticut, 1784-1786; president of the state's ratifying convention, 1788. *DAB; ROC*, 3:340, 610.

11. Lettieri, *Oliver Ellsworth*, pp. 12-14.

12. Michael Kraus, "Oliver Ellsworth," in *The Justices of the United States Supreme Court 1789-1969: Their Lives and Major Opinions*, ed. Leon Friedman and Fred L. Israel, 4 vols. (New York: R. R. Bowker, 1969), 1:224. Abigail Wolcott was the niece of Roger Wolcott, governor of Connecticut (1751-1754). Lettieri, *Oliver Ellsworth*, p. 14.

13. Kraus, "Oliver Ellsworth," p. 224.

14. Ibid.; Lettieri, *Oliver Ellsworth*, pp. 14-16.

15. Lettieri, *Oliver Ellsworth*, p. 16. Ellsworth was justice of the peace with sixty-nine other Hartford County appointees. Each Connecticut town of that period averaged about seven justices.

16. Ibid., pp. 16-21. Such was the increase of business that by May, 1777, the committee grew by two more permanent members and two full-time clerks.

17. Brown, *Life of Oliver Ellsworth*, pp. 51-52.

18. Lettieri, *Oliver Ellsworth*, pp. 30-33.

19. Ibid., pp. 34-36.

20. Ibid., p. 39.

21. Kraus, "Oliver Ellsworth," pp. 225-26; Lettieri, *Oliver Ellsworth*, pp. 52-53.

22. Kraus, "Oliver Ellsworth," p. 226; *DAB*.

23. *DAB*. For a discussion of the small states' concerns, see the headnote to "William Paterson: Appointment as Associate Justice in 1793."

24. Rossiter, *Grand Convention*, pp. 186-87, 191, 189; Lettieri, *Oliver Ellsworth*, pp. 68-69.

25. *RFC*, 2:73-74.

26. Rossiter, *Grand Convention*, pp. 200-201. Pennsylvania's James Wilson and South Carolina's John Rutledge would eventually receive appointments to the Supreme Court. Virginia's Edmund Randolph would become the first attorney general of the United States. Nathaniel Gorham (1738-1796) of Massachusetts had been involved since early in the revolution in public service both at the state and national level; most recently he had been elected as president of the Confederation Congress on June 6, 1786. *DAB*, for Nathaniel Gorham.

27. Rossiter, *Grand Convention*, p. 164. Ellsworth first attended the convention on May 28. August 23 was the last day that he was recorded as present; on August 27 he was in New Haven. *RFC*, 3:587.

28. Lettieri, *Oliver Ellsworth*, pp. 77, 83, 85; *ROC*, 3:560.

29. Kraus, "Oliver Ellsworth," pp. 227-29.

30. Lettieri, *Oliver Ellsworth*, p. 87; Charles Warren, "New Light on the History of the Federal Judiciary Act of 1789," *Harvard Law Review* 37 (November 1923): 60.

31. For the rejection of John Rutledge as chief justice, see above, "John Rutledge: Appointment as Chief Justice in 1795"; for the nomination and confirmation of William Cushing as chief justice, and his declination of the appointment, see above "William Cushing: Appointment as Chief Justice in 1796"; and for the nomination and appointment of Oliver Ellsworth, see the documents published below.

32. Kraus, "Oliver Ellsworth," pp. 230, 233-34; *DAB*.

33. See the resignation of Oliver Ellsworth published below; Brown, *Life of Oliver Ellsworth*, p. 326; Kraus, "Oliver Ellsworth," p. 234.

Nomination by George Washington ——————————
March 3, 1796

United States
March the 3^{d} 1796.

Gentlemen of the Senate.

I nominate Oliver Elsworth, of Connecticut, to be Chief Justice of the Supreme Court of the United States; vice William Cushing, resigned. —   c^{1}

G^{o}Washington

ARS (DNA, RG 46, Anson McCook Collection); Lb (DLC, George Washington Papers). The letterbook copy begins: "The following nomination was this Day laid before the Senate."
    1. Indicates Senate confirmation. Written in a hand different from that in the rest of the document.

Nomination Received by Senate ——————————
March 3, 1796

[*The Senate Executive Journal (RG 46, DNA) records receipt of this nomination on March 3, 1796.*]

Confirmation by Senate ——————————
March 4, 1796

. . . The Senate proceeded to consider the message of the President of the United States of the 3^{d} instant, and the nomination therein contained of

Oliver Ellsworth, to be Chief Justice of the Supreme Court of the United States, vice William Cushing, resigned.

And on the question to advise and consent to the appointment agreeable to the nomination.

It passed in the affirmative { Yeas 21.
                                Nay 1.

The yeas and nays being required by one fifth of the Senators present, Those who voted in the affirmative, are,

Mr Bingham,	Mr Martin,
" Bloodworth,	" Paine,
" Bradford,	" Potts,
" Cabot,	" Robinson,
" Foster,	" Ross,
" Gunn,	" Rutherfurd,

    " Henry,   " Strong,
    " King,   " Trumbull,
    " Langdon,   " Vining,
    " Latimer,   and
    " Livermore, " Walton.[1]

M.[r] Mason,[2] voted in the negative.

So it was,

Resolved, that the Senate do advise and consent to the appointment agreeable to the nomination.

Ordered, that the Secretary lay this resolution before the President of the United States.

D (DNA, RG 46, Executive Journal).

1. William Bingham (Pennsylvania), Alexander Martin (North Carolina), Timothy Bloodworth (North Carolina), Elijah Paine (Vermont), William Bradford (Rhode Island), Richard Potts (Maryland), George Cabot (Massachusetts), Moses Robinson (Vermont), Theodore Foster (Rhode Island), James Ross (Pennsylvania), James Gunn (Georgia), John Rutherfurd (New Jersey), John Henry (Maryland), Caleb Strong (Massachusetts), Rufus King (New York), Jonathan Trumbull (Connecticut), John Langdon (New Hampshire), John Vining (Delaware), Henry Latimer (Delaware), Samuel Livermore (New Hampshire), and George Walton (Georgia).

2. Stevens T. Mason (Virginia).

Notification to President of Senate Confirmation ——————
March 4, 1796

[*Certification paraphrasing the Senate's confirmation of Oliver Ellsworth to be chief justice was sent to George Washington on March 4, 1796. This certification, attested to by Samuel A. Otis, secretary of the Senate, is not extant; but it was transcribed at the time into a letterbook (George Washington Papers, DLC).*]

Commission ——————
March 4, 1796

[*The official letterbook copy of Oliver Ellsworth's commission as chief justice is similar to William Cushing's, published above under date of January 27, 1796.*]

Lb (DNA, RG 59, Miscellaneous Permanent and Temporary Commissions); D (GEpFAR, RG 21, CCD South Carolina, Minutes, May 12, 1796) where Oliver Ellsworth's name is spelled with one "l."

Cover Letter to Commission ————————————
Timothy Pickering to Oliver Ellsworth
March 4, 1796   [Philadelphia, Pennsylvania]

[*The letterbook copy of the cover letter to Oliver Ellsworth's commission as chief justice (Domestic Letters, RG 59, DNA) is similar to William Cushing's, published above under date of January 27, 1796.*]

Record of Oaths ————————————————————
March 8, 1796   [Philadelphia, Pennsylvania]

[*The minutes of the Supreme Court (q.v.) record Oliver Ellsworth's oaths as being taken on March 8, 1796.*]

Record of Oath ————————————————————
March 8, 1796   [Philadelphia, Pennsylvania]

United States of America—
   Before me William Cushing Esquire one of Associate Judges of the Supreme Court of the United States of America, on the Eighth day of March in the Year of our Lord One thousand Seven hundred and Ninety Six and of the Independence of the United States the Twentieth, personally appeared Oliver Ellsworth within named, and as Chief Justice of the United States took the Oath of Office to Support the Constitution of the United States as by Law prescribed. Witness my hand at Philadelphia, the day and Year above mentioned—

Wm Cushing

————————

United States of America—
   I Certify that in the Supreme Court of the United States at Philadelphia on Tuesday the Eighth day of March Anno Domini One thousand Seven hundred and Ninety Six and of the Independence and Sovereignty of the United States of America the Twentieth, the Letters patent within contained appointing the honorable Oliver Elsworth Chief Justice of the said Supreme Court, as is therein mentioned, were openly read and published in Court—
              Witness my hand and the Seal of the said Court at Philadelphia the day and Year last mentioned.—

J: Wagner, dep^y Clerk. Sup. Court

D (GEpFAR, RG 21, CCD South Carolina, Minutes, May 12, 1796). Originally this probably was written on the verso of Oliver Ellsworth's commission. It was recorded with his commission in the minutes of the circuit court for South Carolina.

Oliver Ellsworth to John Adams ————————————————
October 16, 1800   Le Havre, France

The President of the   }
United States of America   }

Havre   Octr 16[th?] 1800

Sir

Constantly afflicted with the gravel, and the gout in my kidnies, the unfortunate fruit of sufferings at sea, and by a winters journey through Spain, I am not in a condition to undertake a voyage to America at this late season of the year; nor if I were there, would I be able to discharge my official duties. I must therefore pray you, Sir, to accept this my resignation of the office of Chief Justice of the United States.

After a few weeks spent in England, I shall retire, for winter quarters, to the South of France, and wait impatiently for the opening of the Spring.

I have the honour to be, Sir,   with very great respect,   Your most obedient

Oliver Ellsworth

ARS (MHi, Adams Manuscript Trust). Endorsed "rec^d Dec. 15. 1800 from The Chief Justices son."

Bushrod Washington: Appointment as Associate Justice in 1798

Born in Westmoreland County, Virginia, on June 5, 1762, Bushrod Washington was the son of John Augustine Washington, a brother of George Washington, and Hannah (Bushrod) Washington, a member of a distinguished Virginia family.[1] After an early education in the classics directed by a tutor in the home of Richard Henry Lee, Bushrod Washington entered the College of William and Mary in 1775 at age thirteen.[2] Upon his graduation in 1778, Washington left Williamsburg but returned there in the spring of 1780 to attend the law lectures of George Wythe, who had been appointed William and Mary's first professor of law. Washington remained at Williamsburg through the fall of 1780 attending Wythe's lectures and participating in debating sessions with other law students, including another young Virginian, John Marshall.[3]

When Lord Cornwallis invaded Virginia in early 1781, Washington enlisted in Colonel John Mercer's troop of cavalry, fought in the battle of Green Spring in Virginia, and was present at the British surrender at Yorktown. Washington then journeyed to Philadelphia, where, for the next two years, he read law in the office of James Wilson.[4] He returned to Westmoreland County in April, 1784, was admitted to the Virginia bar, and opened a law practice. His first years as a lawyer were spent attending to business (some of it his uncle George's) in and around Westmoreland County. During this time he married, in October, 1785, Julia Ann Blackburn, the daughter of Thomas Blackburn, who had been an aide-de-camp to George Washington during the revolution.[5]

A year later Bushrod Washington's interests turned to politics. He joined the Patriotic Society, an organization of tidewater Virginians who gathered to discuss political issues of the day. George Washington probably encouraged his nephew to become actively involved in politics and to run for election to the Virginia House of Delegates. Bushrod Washington became a candidate and won election in 1787. In 1788 as a member of the Virginia constitutional ratifying convention meeting in Richmond, he supported adoption of the Constitution.[6]

Growing weary of political life, Washington once again devoted his full energies to law practice. He left Richmond to return to Westmoreland County but remained only a short time. In November, 1788, he moved to Alexandria where he hoped his law business would grow.[7] Alexandria, however, proved to be disappointing to the young lawyer; his next move took him to the state capital at Richmond.[8] At that time, Richmond was at the height of its golden age of law. Patrick Henry, Arthur Lee, Alexander Campbell, John Marshall, and Edmund Randolph regularly argued before the courts there. It was in this setting that Washington's law practice began to prosper, and between 1792 and 1796 he appeared as counsel in nearly one-fourth of the cases heard before the Virginia Court of Appeals, many of them opposite his old schoolmate, John Marshall.[9] The increased business allowed Washington to employ clerks in his office for the first time.[10] A scholar by nature, he kept copious notes of the cases brought before the Court of Appeals at Richmond and later published them as *Reports of Cases Argued in the Court of Appeals of Virginia*.[11]

Bushrod Washington by Chester Harding (1792-1866). Oil on canvas, 1828. Courtesy Nat W. Washington, Ephrata, Washington.

Events in late 1798 shaped the course of the remainder of Bushrod Washington's life. First, in September, 1798, again at the urging of his uncle, he ran for Congress in Virginia along with John Marshall. Bushrod Washington did so reluctantly, preferring to devote his life to law rather than politics. He was saved from this unwanted political duty by the death of Associate Justice James Wilson months before Virginia's congressional election. President Adams instructed Secretary of State Timothy Pickering to approach John Marshall or Bushrod Washington with an offer of appointment to the

Supreme Court. Marshall refused Pickering's overtures, and so, on October 6, Pickering wrote to Washington in Richmond to inform him of his recess appointment to the Court.[12] Washington, just back from campaigning, eagerly accepted the appointment and made plans to join the southern circuit which would begin in late October. He soon realized, however, that he could not make the scheduled meeting of the circuit court at Charleston by October 25, so he rode directly to the court's second sitting at Augusta, Georgia, where he presided for the first time in his career in a judicial capacity.[13]

On December 20, 1798, the Senate confirmed John Adams's recess appointment of Washington as an associate justice.[14] His tenure on the court lasted thirty-two years. The sixty-seven year old justice died on November 26, 1829, while in Philadelphia on circuit court business.[15]

1. *DAB.*

2. *DAB;* David Leslie Annis, "Mr. Bushrod Washington, Supreme Court Justice on the Marshall Court" (Ph.D. diss., University of Notre Dame, 1974), p. 25.

3. Annis, "Bushrod Washington," pp. 26-29.

4. Albert P. Blaustein and Roy M. Mersky, "Bushrod Washington," in *The Justices of the United States Supreme Court 1789-1969: Their Lives and Major Opinions,* ed. Leon Friedman and Fred L. Israel, 4 vols. (New York: R. R. Bowker, 1969), 1:244; Annis, "Bushrod Washington," p. 30.

5. Annis, "Bushrod Washington," pp. 43-47.

6. Ibid., pp. 48-56; *DAB.*

7. Annis, "Bushrod Washington," p. 56.

8. Ibid., pp. 58, 60. The exact date of Bushrod Washington's move is conjectural. He was in Alexandria in December, 1789, and seems to have moved to Richmond sometime before 1792 when his reports on the Court of Appeals at Richmond begin. Ibid., pp. 59n, 60; Lawrence B. Custer, "Bushrod Washington and John Marshall: A Preliminary Inquiry," *American Journal of Legal History* 4 (January 1960): 39n.

9. Annis, "Bushrod Washington," pp. 61-62. Bushrod Washington argued in the Court of Appeals opposite John Marshall in at least fourteen cases and joined him in three others.

10. *DAB.*

11. Printed in Richmond in two volumes (1798-1799) by Thomas Nicolson. Annis, "Bushrod Washington," pp. 61-63; *DAB.*

12. Annis, "Bushrod Washington," pp. 66-67; see below for letters relating to the offer to John Marshall and the subsequent offer to Bushrod Washington.

13. Bushrod Washington to James Iredell, December 5, 1798, Charles E. Johnson Collection, Nc-Ar; Annis, "Bushrod Washington," pp. 70-71, 74.

14. See below for the Senate confirmation of Bushrod Washington.

15. Blaustein and Mersky, "Bushrod Washington," p. 256; Annis, "Bushrod Washington," p. 269.

John Adams to Timothy Pickering ————————————
September 13, 1798   Quincy, Massachusetts

Quincy   Sept. 13. 1798

Sir

I have received your Letter of the 6th with Judge Iredells Letter inclosed, informing of the Death of Judge Wilson.[1] The Reasons urged by Judge Iredell for an early Appointment of a Successor, are important. I am ready to appoint either General Marshall[2] or Bushrod Washington. The former I Suppose ought

to have the Preference. If you think so Send him a Commission_ If you think any other Person more proper, please to mention him to
sir your most obedient & humble servant

John Adams

Timothy Pickering Esqr
Secretary of state.

ALS (DLC, Adams Family Collection); ALbS (MHi, Adams Manuscript Trust).
1. See the following letters under "James Wilson: Appointment as Associate Justice in 1789": James Iredell to Timothy Pickering, August 25, 1798, and Timothy Pickering to John Adams, September 6, 1798.
2. For biographical sketch of John Marshall, see headnote to "John Marshall: Appointment as Chief Justice in 1801."

Charles Lee to Timothy Pickering
September 13, 1798 Alexandria, District of Columbia

Alexandria 13 September 1798

Dᴿ Sir

I am informed that the newspapers have announced the death of Judge Wilson. Should the President turn his attention to Virginia for a Successor to that office I know of no person better qualified than Mᴿ Bushrod Washington. I am not desired or expected by this gentleman to mention his name, but I have done it of my own accord believing that the appointment would be acceptable to him and useful to our country.

I am very respectfully your most obedient servant

Charles Lee

Col Pickering
Secretary of State

ARS (MHi, Adams Manuscript Trust). Marked "[Encl. 19 Sept 1798]"; this letter was enclosed in a letter from Timothy Pickering to John Adams on September 19.

John Adams to Timothy Pickering
September 14, 1798 Quincy, Massachusetts

. . . General Marshall or Bushrod Washington will succeed Judge Wilson, if you have not some other Gentleman to propose, who in your Opinion can better promote the public honor and Interest. Marshall is first in Age, Rank and public services, probably not Second in Talents. Although I have an Ancient esteem for Judge Rush and the Dʳ,[1] it is not sufficient to make any alteration in my Judgment in this Case. As Virginia has no Judge at present, she is as much intitled as Pennsylvania to Attention. . . .

ARS (DNA, RG 59, Miscellaneous Letters); ALbS (MHi, Adams Manuscript Trust).
    1. Jacob Rush, a Pennsylvania judge, and Dr. Benjamin Rush. See "Commentaries," Timothy Pickering to John Adams, September 7, 1798.

Timothy Pickering to John Adams ————————
September 20, 1798 Trenton, New Jersey

Department of State
Trenton   Sept. 20. 1798.

Sir,
    I am this moment honoured with your letters of the 13th and 14th, and have directed a Commission to be made out for a judge of the Supreme Court, in the place of Judge Wilson deceased, leaving a blank for the name, and which I shall transmit to you in the mail of this evening. I shall also this day write to General Marshall to inform him that you have designated him to fill the vacant seat, and urge his acceptance ^of it : probably no appointment would be more universally approved: but I am sorry to think there is little chance of his gratifying what must be the public wish as well as yours: in a word, there is little hope that an eminent lawyer, in the full tide of practice at the bar, and receiving eight or ten thousand dollars a year, will relinquish it for the meagre reward of thirty five hundred dollars, a large part of which must be expended in travelling expences. The case might be different, if Gen! Marshall was weary of the toils and vexations of business at the bar; or if he possessed a very independent fortune.
    I forwarded yesterday the Attorney General's letter, presenting the name of M[r] Bushrod Washington — a name that I have never heard mentioned but with respect, for his talents, virtues and genuine patriotism: But he is young, not more I believe than three or four and thirty. His indefatigable pursuit of knowledge and the business of his profession has deprived him of the sight of one eye — it will be happy if the loss of the other does not make him perfectly the emblem of Justice. It would seem that Virginia should fill the vacant seat; and if General Marshall should decline, M[r] Washington has decidedly a superior claim to any other gentleman there of the profession. — You will observe my motive in leaving a blank for the name of the Judge; — that as it is probable Gen! Marshall will decline, I may insert the name of Bushrod Washington, & send him the commission: otherwise a fortnight will be lost in making out a new commission, & sending it to Quincy for your signature.
    I am most respectfully, sir, your   obed[t] servant,

Timothy Pickering

The president of the U.States.

ARS (MHi, Adams Manuscript Trust); Lb (DNA, RG 59, Domestic Letters). In the Massachusetts Historical Society collection of Timothy Pickering papers, there is an extract of this letter in the hand of Pickering; the extract includes a section of paragraph two beginning with "Washington" and ending with "Justice."

Timothy Pickering to John Marshall ————————————————
September 20, 1798 Trenton, New Jersey

. . . I have just received a letter from the President directing me to make out a Commission for you to fill the Seat vacant on the Bench of the Supreme Court by the death of Judge Wilson. The Commission I shall send this day to Quincy for the President's Signature. I wish in the mean time to be informed whether it will be agreeable to you to accept the appointment. Your acceptance will gratify the President, all the public men whose opinions I am acquainted with, and your fellow citizens, at large throughout the United States. If there were any more persuasive motive, I would present it to your view. I request an early answer. . . .

Lb (DNA, RG 59, Domestic Letters).

Timothy Pickering to John Marshall ————————————————
September 20, 1798 Trenton, New Jersey

(private)

Trenton   Sept. 20. 98

Dᵣ Sir,

Your last conversation with me the evening before your departure from Philadelphia makes me apprehensive that you will decline the vacant seat in the supreme court: For this reason I request your opinion (information, if you can give it) whether Mᵣ Bushrod Washington will accept it? I have understood that he has thought of quitting the bar; and that this place on the Bench would probably be acceptable to him.

respectfully yours

T.Pickering

General Marshall.

ARS (Ct, Gray-Glines Collection); APcS (MHi, Timothy Pickering Papers). Addressed "Richmond."

John Adams to Timothy Pickering ————————————————
September 26, 1798   Quincy, Massachusetts

Quincy   September 26. 1798

Dear Sir

        read
I had the Honor of your Letter of the 19th, last night, and have ˄ the En-
closures.

D[r] Rushes Letter[1] gives me pleasure because the Number of disappointed
Candidates is diminished by, it, by one.

M[r] Sitgreaves's Letter[2] is frank, candid and agreeable: But although this
Gentleman has Merit and Talents held in high Esteem by his Country, as well
as by me, I cannot help thinking that a few years of service in Stations less
exalted than the Bench of the United States, may reasonably be expected from
him.

M[r] Lee's Letter[3] deserves great Attention: The Name, the Connections, the
Character, the Merit and Abilities of M[r] Washington, are greatly respected:
But I still think that General Marshall ought to be preferred. Of the three
Envoys,[4] the Conduct of Marshall alone has been entirely Satisfactory, and
ought to be marked by the most decided approbation of the Public, He has
raised the American People, in their own Esteem. And if the Influences of
Truth and Justice, Reason and Argument is not lost in Europe he has raised
the Consideration of the United States in that quarter of the world. He is older
at the Bar than M[r] Washington, and you and I know by Experience that Seniority at the Bar, is nearly as much regarded, as it is in the Army. If M[r] Marshall should decline I should next think of M[r] Washington.[5] It is true that some
regard to states ought to be always remembered. But Pennsylvania has always
had a Judge. Virginia has had none, since the Resignation of M[r] Blair. As far
as states can have reasonable pretentions therefore, those of Virginia are at
least equal to those of Pennsylvania.

Thus the subject appears to me: If you are of a different opinion, I pray you
to inform me, or if any more meritorious Candidate than M[r] Marshall occurs
to you I hope you will mention him, to

sir your most obedient and   humble servant

John Adams

Timothy Pickering, Esqr
Secretary of State.

ARS (DNA, RG 59, Miscellaneous Letters); ALbS (MHi, Adams Manuscript Trust).
    1. See "Commentaries," Benjamin Rush to John Adams, September 14, 1798.
    2. See "Commentaries," Samuel Sitgreaves to Timothy Pickering, September 16, 1798.
    3. See above, Charles Lee to Timothy Pickering, September 13, 1798.
    4. President John Adams's special envoys to France were Charles Cotesworth Pinckney, El-
bridge Gerry, and John Marshall.

5. John Adams's favorable comments about John Marshall and preference for his appointment to the Court were mentioned in two letters from Timothy Pickering to George Cabot, one on November 6, 1798, and the other on November 10, 1798. Timothy Pickering Papers, MHi.

John Marshall to Timothy Pickering
September 28, 1798   Richmond, Virginia

... By the mail of last night I had the pleasure of receiving your two letters of the 20ᵗʰ & 21ˢᵗ inst. I pray you to make my respectful & grateful acknow-legements to the President for the very favorable sentiments concerning me which are indicated by his willingness to call me to so honorable & important a station as that of a Judge of the United States. The considerations which are insurmountable oblige ^me^ to decline the office I can assure you that I shall ever estimate properly both the dispositions of the President & the polite & friendly manner in which you have communicated them. I am confident that Mʳ Washington woud with pleasure accept the appointment & I am equally confident that a more proper person coud not be nam'd for it. ...

ARS (MHi, Adams Manuscript Trust). Marked "[Encl. 5 Oct 1798]"; enclosed in a letter from Timothy Pickering to John Adams of October 5.

Timothy Pickering to Charles Lee
September 28, 1798   Trenton, New Jersey

... Your letter mentioning Mr Bushrod Washington to fill the vacant seat on the bench of the Supreme Court,[1] I forwarded to the President; but before it could reach him he was disposed in favor of Mr W. in case Gen'l Marshall should decline the appointment. ...

APcS (MHi, Timothy Pickering Papers); Lb (DNA, RG 59, Domestic Letters).
    1. See above, Charles Lee to Timothy Pickering, September 13, 1798.

John Adams to Timothy Pickering
September 29, 1798   Quincy, Massachusetts

... I have received your favour of September 20ᵗʰ and return you the Com-mission for a Judge of the Supream Court Signed, leaving the Name and Date blank. You will fill the Blank with the Name of Marshall if he will accept it: if not with that of Bushrod Washington. I cannot blame the former if he Should decline: of the latter I have always heard the most agreable Accounts.
...

ARS (DNA, RG 59, Miscellaneous Letters); ALbS (MHi, Adams Manuscript Trust). The letter-book copy is dated "Sept 28ᵗʰ."

Temporary Commission ————————————————————————
September 29, 1798

John Adams, President of the United States of
America,
To all who shall see these Presents, Greeting:

Whereas the Office of one of the Associate Justices of the Supreme Court
of the United States is at present vacant, Now Know Ye, That reposing especial Trust and Confidence in the Wisdom, Uprightness and Learning of
Bushrod Washington of Virginia I do appoint him one of the Associate Justices
of the said Supreme Court of the United States, and do authorize and empower
him to execute and fulfil the Duties of that Office according to the Constitution
and Laws of the said United States; and to have and to hold the said office
with all the Powers, Privileges and Emoluments to the same of Right appertaining, unto him the said Bushrod Washington during his good Behaviour,
and until the end of the next Session of the Senate of the United States, and
no longer.

In Testimony whereof, I have caused these Letters to be made
Patent and the Seal of the United States to be hereunto affixed.
SEAL   Given under my hand, at the City of Philadelphia, the twenty
ninth day of September, in the Year of our Lord one thousand
seven hundred and ninety-eight, and of the Independence of the
said States the Twenty-third.

John Adams

By the President,

Timothy Pickering, Secretary of State.

RS (PPIn); Lb (DNA, RG 59, Temporary Presidential Commissions); D (GEpFAR, RG 21, CCD
Georgia, Minutes, November 9, 1796).

Timothy Pickering to John Adams ————————————————
October 5, 1798   Trenton, New Jersey

                                                              Marshall,
... Last evening I received the inclosed letter from General ᷓ declining, as I
expected, the offer of a seat on the Bench of the Supreme Court. I transmit
his letter, as well that his own grateful sense of the offer might be seen, as for
the strong expressions of the opinion of so good a judge on the fitness of
conferring the office on Mr Washington, whose talents and character are so
perfectly well known to him. I have filled the blank in the Commission with
Mr Washington's name; and shall forward the commission by tomorrow's
mail— the first for Richmond. ...

ARS (MHi, Adams Manuscript Trust); Lb (DNA, RG 59, Domestic Letters); C (MHi, Timothy
Pickering Papers).

Cover Letter to Temporary Commission ———————
Timothy Pickering to Bushrod Washington
October 6, 1798   Trenton, New Jersey

Department of State
Trenton New Jersey, 6 Oct.ʳ 98.

Sir,

The President of the United States being desirous of availing the public of your services as one of the associate justices of the Supreme Court of the United States, I have now the honor of enclosing the commission and of expressing the sentiments of respect with which

I am Sir,   Your most obed. serv.ᵗ

Timothy Pickering

Bushrod Washington Esq.ʳ
Richmond
Virginia—

APcS (MHi, Timothy Pickering Papers); Lb (DNA, RG 59, Domestic Letters).

John Adams to Timothy Pickering ———————
October 14, 1798   Quincy, Massachusetts

... I received last night your favor of the 5ᵗʰ ... thank you for dispatching ... the commission to Mr. Bushrod Washington. ...

ALbS (MHi, Adams Manuscript Trust).

Bushrod Washington to Timothy Pickering ———————
October 16, 1798   Richmond, Virginia

Richmond   October 16ᵗʰ 1798

Sir

I had the pleasure last evening, of recieving your favor of the 6ᵗʰ instant covering a Commission for a seat on the bench of the Supreme Court of the United States, which the President has been pleased to confer upon me.

I am fully sensible of the honor done me by this appointment, and accept it with gratitude. My abilities, such as they are, can never be exerted with more satisfaction to myself, than in the service of my Country—

Permit me, Sir, to express the high respect and esteem which I entertain for your character, and to return you my thanks for the flattering manner in which you have communicated to me my appointment.

I have the honor to be, Sir,   y.ʳ mo. obed. Servant

Bushrod Washington

ARS (DNA, RG 59, General Records of the Department of State). Addressed "Trenton." Postmarked "RICHMOND, Oct. 17. 1798." Marked "rec^d 23."

Record of Oaths
November 9, 1798   [Augusta, Georgia]

... The Honble Bushrod Washington Esqr was this morning duly qualified as an associate Justice of the Supreme Court of the United States agreeable to law and the constitution, by the Honble Joseph Clay Jun^{r1} ...

D (GEpFAR, RG 21, CCD Georgia, Minutes, November 9, 1798).
   1. Joseph Clay (1764-1811) was the United States district judge for Georgia. *DAB.*

Nomination by John Adams
December 19, 1798

... I nominate ... Bushrod Washington of Virginia to be one of the associate justices of the supreme court of the United States. ...

RS (DNA, RG 46).

Nomination Received by Senate
December 19, 1798

[*The Senate Executive Journal (RG 46, DNA) records receipt of this nomination on December 19, 1798.*]

Confirmation by Senate
December 20, 1798

... The Senate proceeded to consider the message of the President of the United States of the 19th instant, and the nominations contained therein ...
  Whereupon,
  Resolved, that they do advise and consent to the appointments agreeably to the nominations respectively [*with some exceptions*].
  Ordered, that the Secretary lay this resolution before the President of the United States. ...

D (DNA, RG 46, Executive Journal).

Notification to President of Senate Confirmation ——————
December [20-27], 1798

[No record survives notifying President John Adams of the Senate's confirmation of Bushrod Washington. Notification must have occurred on or after December 20, 1798—the date of Senate confirmation—and on or before December 27, 1798—the date of the cover letter to the commission.]

Commission ————————————————————
December 20, 1798

John Adams, President of the United States of America,
   To all who shall see these Presents, Greeting:

   Know Ye, That reposing especial trust and confidence in the Wisdom, Uprightness and Learning of Bushrod Washington of Virginia, I have nominated, and by and with the Advice and Consent of the Senate do appoint him one of the Associate Justices of the Supreme Court of the United States, and do authorize and empower him to execute and fulfil the duties of that office according to the Constitution and Laws of the said United States, and to have and to hold the said office with all the Powers, Privilges, and Emoluments to the same of Right appertaining unto him the said Bushrod Washington during his good Behaviour.

(L. S)
   In Testimony whereof, I have caused these letters to be made Patent and the Seal of the United States to be hereunto affixed. Given under my hand the Twentieth day of December, in the year of our Lord, one thousand seven hundred and ninety eight and of the Independence of the United States of America, the Twenty third.

John Adams,

By the President.

Timothy Pickering,
Secretary of State.

Lb (DNA, RG 59, Miscellaneous Permanent and Temporary Commissions).

Cover Letter to Commission —————————————————————
Timothy Pickering to Bushrod Washington
December 27, 1798   [Philadelphia, Pennsylvania]

De[p]artment of State, 27[th] Dec[r] 1798.

[Sir,]

[I] have [the] honor to enclose a new commission for you as one of the Associate Justices of the Supreme Court of the United States[,] which has been issued in consequence of [th]e President['][s having nominated you to the Senate and [th]eir c[on]cur[r]ence[.]

I have the honor to be sir   With great respect   your most obed. Serv[t]

Timothy Pickering

Bushrod Washington Esq[r]
Richmond

APcS (MHi, Timothy Pickering Papers); Lb (DNA, RG 59, Domestic Letters). Sections of the press copy are illegible; most readings in brackets have been supplied from the letterbook copy.

Record of Oaths ————————————————————————————
[on or before February 4, 1799]

[*There is no extant record of Bushrod Washington taking his oaths following issuance of his permanent commission. He had to have done so on or before February 4, 1799, when the Court opened with Washington listed as present. No mention is made in the Court's minutes of his taking the oaths in Court that day.*]

Alfred Moore: Appointment as Associate Justice in 1799

Alfred Moore was born on May 21, 1755, in Brunswick County, North Carolina, into the politically prominent family of Judge Maurice Moore and Anne (Grange) Moore.[1] Judge Moore remarried after the death of his first wife, and nine-year-old Alfred was sent off to Boston to complete his studies. After finishing his schooling in Boston, Moore returned to North Carolina to study law under the direction of his father.[2]

Not long after his return to his native state, a number of important events occurred in Moore's life. His marriage to Susanna Elizabeth Eagles of Brunswick County, North Carolina, and his admission to the North Carolina bar in 1775, began his family and his career.[3] These pursuits, however, were interrupted by the outbreak of the revolution. On September 1, 1775, the North Carolina provincial congress elected him a captain in the First North Carolina Regiment, and Moore marched off to war along with his father, brother, and uncle. For the next two years, Moore participated in a number of engagements, among them the battle of Moore's Creek Bridge (North Carolina) and the defense of Charleston.[4]

The war inflicted great personal loss on Alfred Moore. His brother, Maurice, was killed in 1776; his father, a colonel in the First North Carolina Regiment, and his uncle, James Moore, former commander of the Regiment and then brigadier general of the North Carolina forces, died in the spring of 1777.[5] Although Moore resigned his regimental commission in March, 1777,[6] and went home to care for his family and plantation, he continued his military activities in the local militia. Ironically, it was Moore's return to manage the plantation that caused its ruin. Moore's activities as a commander of the militia unit that constantly harassed the enemy became known to the British, and they retaliated by plundering his plantation and destroying his house. Undaunted by these misfortunes, Moore continued his militia service and sat as a judge advocate of the North Carolina forces in the closing days of the revolution.[7]

With peace returning to North Carolina, Moore turned his attention to political rather than military affairs. In 1782 he served in the state legislature as senator from Brunswick County before being elected by the state General Assembly, on May 3 of that year, to succeed James Iredell as attorney general. Moore held this position for nearly nine years, during which time he exhibited great ability. He prosecuted mostly cases of fraud but occasionally took on a case having more significance.[8] One of these was *Bayard v. Singleton*[9] involving a North Carolina statute dealing with attempts to recover "Lands and Tenements, Goods and Chattels" from purchasers who had received title from the state commissioners of forfeited estates.[10] While declaring the statute unconstitutional, the court, on the basis of the civil law and the common law of England, found for the defendant who purchased the land under that act. Moore had represented the defendant, Singleton. His victory opened the way for the dismissal of twenty-seven other suits brought up on similar grounds.[11]

As attorney general, Moore was active in state and national politics. The North Car-

Alfred Moore by Edward Greene Malbone (1777-1807). Watercolor on ivory, ca. 1805. Courtesy Office of the Curator, Supreme Court of the United States.

olina legislature appointed Moore, a staunch federalist, to the Annapolis Convention of 1786, but illness prevented his attendance. In 1788 he was defeated in the election of delegates to the state's ratifying convention, which rejected the federal Constitution. Less than a year later, however, a new convention was called and Moore joined James Iredell and William R. Davie in a successful campaign for ratification.[12]

In 1791 Moore attempted to disengage himself from public service. He resigned as attorney general after a disagreement with the legislature over the creation of a solicitor general's office that Moore claimed was an unconstitutional infringement on his office's powers. In addition to his dissatisfaction with the legislature's move, Moore wanted to spend more time on his plantation and his law practice. But his retirement was short-lived. He reentered public service when elected to the state legislature in 1792. In 1795 Moore failed, by one vote, in his bid for the United States Senate, but three years later was appointed to serve as a federal commissioner to conclude a treaty with the Cherokee Indian nation.[13]

In 1798 Moore began a judicial career that proceeded quickly from the state to the national level. On December 7, the General Assembly elected him to the state's Superior Court.[14] His service on the Superior Court lasted less than a year, for on December 4, 1799, President John Adams nominated him associate justice of the Supreme Court of the United States to fill the vacancy caused by the death of James Iredell. The Senate confirmed the nomination on December 10.[15] On April 21, 1800, at the meeting of the circuit court at Savannah, Georgia, Moore took the oaths of office.[16] His Court career lasted until 1804 when he resigned because of ill health. Upon leaving the Court, Moore returned to North Carolina where he worked toward establishment of the University of North Carolina. He died on October 15, 1810.[17]

1. Leon Friedman, "Alfred Moore," in *The Justices of the United States Supreme Court 1789-1969: Their Lives and Major Opinions,* ed. Leon Friedman and Fred L. Israel, 4 vols. (New York: R. R. Bowker, 1969), 1:269; *DAB.* Maurice Moore (1735-1777) was a lawyer who served in the North Carolina House of Commons, 1757-1760, 1762, 1764-1771, and 1773-1774. He sat on the governor's council, 1760-1761. In 1765 he wrote *The Justice and Policy of Taxing the American Colonies in Great Britain, Considered* while sitting as an associate provincial judge. Removed from office by Governor Tryon for his activities in the Stamp Act crisis, Judge Moore was reinstated in 1768 and served in that position until 1773. He attended North Carolina's Third Provincial Congress and was elected to—but did not attend—the Fifth Provincial Congress. Alfred Moore's great uncle, James Moore (d. 1706), was governor of the Province of South Carolina (1700) and his uncle, James Moore (1737-1777), was a prominent leader in revolutionary North Carolina. Little is known of Alfred Moore's mother, Anne (Grange) Moore. *DAB,* under Maurice Moore and James Moore.

2. Friedman, "Alfred Moore," p. 269; Samuel A. Ashe, ed., *Biographical History of North Carolina from Colonial Times to the Present,* 8 vols. (Greensboro, N.C.: Charles L. Van Noppen, 1905-1917), 2:303.

3. *DAB.*

4. *DAB;* Marilu B. Smallwood, *Some Colonial and Revolutionary Families of North Carolina,* vol. 2 (Gainesville, Fla.: Storter Printing, 1969), pp. 311, 307; Friedman, "Alfred Moore," p. 269.

5. Smallwood, *Some Colonial and Revolutionary Families of North Carolina* 2:311; *DAB,* under Maurice Moore and James Moore.

6. *DAB.*

7. Friedman, "Alfred Moore," p. 270.

8. *DAB;* Friedman, "Alfred Moore," p. 270; Ashe, *Biographical History of North Carolina* 2:304-5.

9. 1 Martin (North Carolina) 42 (1787).

10. Iredell, *Laws of the State of North Carolina,* pp. 553-54.

11. 1 Martin (North Carolina) 46-48 (1787).

12. Friedman, "Alfred Moore," p. 271.

13. Ibid., pp. 271-72.

14. *DAB.*

15. See documents published below for nomination and confirmation of Alfred Moore.

16. See record of oaths published below. Moore did not sit with the Supreme Court at the February term, 1800, at Philadelphia. He did, however, ride the southern circuit which commenced at Savannah on April 21. Moore journeyed to Philadelphia for the August 1800 term. Although Moore appears in the Court's minutes on August 6, the third day of the term, his commission was not read until August 9, 1800, the first day a sufficient number of justices were present to form a quorum. See "Fine Minutes," August 6 and 9, 1800.

17. Friedman, "Alfred Moore," p. 279.

Nomination by John Adams ──────────────────────
December 4, 1799

Gentlemen of the Senate,

   I nominate Alfred Moore of North-Carolina to be an associate justice of the Supreme Court of the United States, in the room of the late justice Iredell, deceased.

                                                        John Adams

United States   }
December 4. 1799.   }

RS (DNA, RG 46).

Nomination Received by Senate ──────────────────
December 5, 1799

[*The Senate Executive Journal (RG 46, DNA) records receipt of this nomination on December 5, 1799.*]

Confirmation by Senate ─────────────────────────
December 10, 1799

[*December 6:*] The Senate proceeded to consider the message of the President of the United States of the 4th instant, and the nomination contained therein, of Alfred Moore, to office — and
   On motion,
   Ordered, that the further consideration thereof be postponed. . . .

[*December 9:*] The Senate resumed the consideration of the message of the President of the United States of the 4th instant, and the nomination contained therein, of Alfred Moore, to office.
   On motion,
   Ordered, that the further consideration thereof be postponed. . . .

[*December 10:*] The Senate resumed the consideration of the message of the President of the United States of the 4th instant, and the nomination, contained therein of Alfred Moore, to office.
   Whereupon,
   Resolved, that they do advise and consent to the appointment agreeably to the nomination.
   Ordered, that the Secretary lay this resolution before the President of the United States. . . .

D (DNA, RG 46, Executive Journal).

Notification to President of Senate Confirmation ——————
December 10, 1799

[*Certification paraphrasing the Senate's confirmation of Alfred Moore to be associate justice was sent to John Adams on December 10, 1799 (Senate Confirmations and Rejections of Presidential Nominations, RG 59, DNA). This certification was attested to by Samuel A. Otis, secretary of the Senate.*]

Commission ——————————————————
December 10, 1799

John Adams President of the United States of America. To all who shall see these presents Greeting.

Know Ye that reposing especial trust and confidence in the wisdom uprightness, and learning of Alfred Moore of North Carolina, I have nominated, and by and with the advice and consent of the Senate do appoint him one of the Associate Justices of the Supreme Court of the United States, and do authorize and empower him to execute and fulfil the duties of that office according to the constitution and Laws of the said United States and to have and to hold the said office with all Powers privileges and emoluments to the same of right appertaining unto him the said Alfred Moore during his good behaviour. In Testimony whereof[1] I have caused these letters to be made patent and the Seal of the United States to be hereunto affixed. Given under my hand the tenth day of December in the year of our Lord one thousand seven hundred and ninety nine and of the Independence of the United States of America the twenty fourth

signed   John Adams

By the President.

Timothy Pickering
Secretary of State

D (GEpFAR, RG 21, CCD Georgia, Minutes, April 22, 1800).

1. In making this copy of the commission, after the phrase, "In Testimony," the clerk of the circuit court originally wrote the word "of" and the phrase "I have." As the word and the phrase overlap, it is impossible to know which was written first. Finally, the clerk wrote the "where" in "whereof" over his earlier efforts.

Cover Letter to Commision ————————————————————
Timothy Pickering to Alfred Moore
December 13, 1799 Philadelphia, Pennsylvania

Department of states_
Philadelphia, 13. Dec.ʳ 1799

Sir

The President of the United States being desirous of availing the public of your services as an Associate Judge of the Supreme Court of the United States, I have now the honor to enclose the commission, and to be,

Very respectfully,   Your most obed. serv.ᵗ

Timothy Pickering

Honble. Alfred Moore Esq.ʳ

APcS (MHi, Timothy Pickering Papers). This letter and its enclosure were forwarded to Alfred Moore through the agency of Sherwood Haywood. See below, Timothy Pickering to Sherwood Haywood, December 13, 1799.

Timothy Pickering to Sherwood Haywood ————————————
December 13, 1799 Philadelphia, Pennsylvania

Department of state
Philadelphia, 13ᵗʰ Dec.ʳ 1799

Sir

The enclosed is a Commission appointing Alfred Moore Esq.ʳ one of the Judges of the Supreme Court of the United States. As it is uncertain whether it will find him at Hillsborough or Wilmington, I beg the favor of you to give it the proper direction and transmit it to him.

I am, sir, very respectfully   your most obed. serv.ᵗ

Timothy Pickering

Sherwood Haywood Esq.ʳ
Raleigh

APcS (MHi, Timothy Pickering Papers).

Sherwood Haywood (1762-1829), brother of state treasurer John Haywood, was the federal commissioner of loans for North Carolina. Sherwood Haywood, who had been clerk of the state Senate from 1786 to 1798, followed his brother in moving to Raleigh. Ashe, *Biographical History of North Carolina*, 6:305-6; *SEJ*, 1:298; John L. Cheney, Jr., ed., *North Carolina Government, 1585-1979, A Narrative and Statistical History* (Raleigh: North Carolina Department of the Secretary of State, 1981), pp. 217-37.

Record of Oaths ——————————————————————————
April 21, 1800   [Savannah, Georgia]

District of Georgia

The within named Alfred Moore took the oath prescribed by the Act to establish the Judicial Courts of the United States to be taken by their Judges, and the oath to support the constitution of the United States this twenty first day of April Eighteen hundred before me.

signed   Joseph Clay Junr

signed   Joseph Clay Jun.
Judge of the said District

D (GEpFAR, RG 21, CCD Georgia, Minutes, April 22, 1800).

John Jay: Appointment as
Chief Justice in 1800

[For biographical headnote, see "John Jay: Appointment as Chief Justice in 1789."]

Nomination by John Adams
December 18, 1800

Gentlemen of the Senate

I nominate John Jay Esqr Govenor of the State of New York to be Chief Justice of the United States in the place of Oliver Elsworth who has resigned that office

John Adams

United States }
Dec 18ᵗʰ 1800. }

ARS (DNA, RG 46).

Nomination Received by Senate
December 18, 1800

[*The Senate Executive Journal (RG 46, DNA) records receipt of this nomination on December 18, 1800.*]

Confirmation by Senate
December 19, 1800

. . . The Senate proceeded to consider the message of the President of the United States of the 18[ᵗʰ?] instant, and the nomination, contained therein, of John Jay, to office.

Whereupon,

Resolved, that they do advise and consent to the appointment agreeably to the nomination.

Ordered, that the Secretary lay this resolution before the President of the United States. . . .

D (DNA, RG 46, Executive Journal).

Notification to President of Senate Confirmation ————————
December 19, 1800

[*Certification paraphrasing the Senate's confirmation of John Jay to be chief justice was sent to John Adams on December 19, 1800 (Senate Confirmations and Rejections of Presidential Nominations, RG 59, DNA). This certification was attested to by Samuel A. Otis, secretary of the Senate.*]

Commission ————————————————————————————
December 19, 1800

John Adams, President of the United States of America,
    To all who shall see these presents — Greeting:

Know ye, That reposing special Trust and Confidence in the Wisdom, Uprightness and Learning of John Jay of New York, I have nominated, and by and with the advice and consent of the Senate do appoint him Chief Justice of the Supreme Court of the United States, and do authorize and empower him to execute and fulfil the Duties of that Office according to the Constitution and laws of the said United States; and to Have and to Hold the said Office with all the powers, privileges and Emoluments to the same of right appertaining unto him the said John Jay during his good behaviour.

> In Testimony whereof, I have caused these Letters to be made Patent, and the Seal of the United States to be hereunto affixed. Given under my Hand at the City of Washington the Nineteenth
(L S)   day of December, in the year of our Lord, one Thousand Eight Hundred; and of the Independence of the United States of America, The twenty fifth,

John Adams

By the President

J. Marshall   Secretary of State

Lb (DNA, RG 59, Miscellaneous Permanent and Temporary Commissions).

John Adams to John Jay ————————————————————
December 19, 1800 Washington, District of Columbia

Washington   Dec 19 1800

Dear Sir
    Mr. Elsworth afflicted with the gravel & the gout in his kidneys, & intending to pass the winter in the South of France, after a few weeks in England, has

resigned his office of Chief Justice, & I have nominated you to your old station. This is [*letters inked out*] independent of the inconstancy of the people, as
it is of the will of a President. In the future administration of our Country,
the firmest security we can have, against the effects of visionary schemes or
fluctuating theories, will be in a solid judiciary & nothing will cheer the hopes
of the best men so much, as your acceptance of this appointment. You have
now a great opportunity to render a most signal service to your Country. I
therefore pray you most earnestly to consider of it seriously & accept it. You
may very properly resign the short remainder of your Gubernatorial period,
& Mr. Van Ranselaer[1] may discharge[2] the duties. I had no permission from
you to take this step but it appeared to me that providence had thrown in my
way an opportunity not only of marking to the publick the spot where in my
opinion the greatest mass of worth remained collected in one individual but
of my furnishing my Country with the best security its inhabitants afforded
against the increasing dissolution of morals_ Your commission will soon follow this letter.

   With unabated friendship and the highest esteem & respect I am Dear Sir
yours &c.

His Excellency John Jay Esqr.

ALb (MHi, Adams Manuscript Trust).
   1. Stephen Van Rensselaer (1764-1839), patroon of landed estates in upstate New York, was
lieutenant governor of New York from 1795 to 1801. Previous to his election as lieutenant governor he had served in both houses of the state legislature. *DAB*.
   2. John Adams seems to have written "may discharge may discharge" and then erased the first
"may discharge."

John Jay to John Adams —————————————————————————
   January 2, 1801   Albany, New York

                                                          Albany   2 Jan[y] 1801 _
Dear Sir
   I have been honored with your Letter of the 19th ult: informing me that I
had been nominated to fill the office of Chief Justice of the united States; and
Yesterday I rec[d] the Commission_ this nomination so strongly manifests your
Esteem, that it affords me particular Satisfaction_
   Such was the Temper of the Times, that the Act to establish the judicial
courts of the U. S., was in some Respects more accommodated to certain Prej-
udices and Sensibilities, than to the great and obvious Principles of sound Pol-
icy_ Expectations were nevertheless entertained that it would be amended, as
the public mind became more composed and better informed: but these Expectations have not been realized; nor have we hitherto seen convincing In-
dications of a Disposition in Congress to realize them. on the contrary, the

Efforts repeatedly made to place the judicial Departm.^t on a proper Footing, have proved fruitless —

I left the Bench perfectly convinced that under a System so defective, it would not obtain the Energy weight and Dignity which are essential to its affording due support to the national Governm.^t; nor acquire the public Confidence and Respect, which, as the last Resort of the Justice of the nation, it should possess. Hence I am induced to doubt both the Propriety and Expediency of my returning to the Bench under the present System, especially as it would give some Countenance to the neglect and Indifference with which the opinions & Remonstrances of the Judges on this important Subject have been treated —

Altho' I wish and am prepared to be and remain in Retirement, yet I have carefully considered what is my Duty, and ought to be my Conduct on this unexpected and interesting occasion. I find that, independent of other Considerations, the State of my Health removes every Doubt — it being clearly and decidedly incompetent to the fatigues incident to the office —

accept my warmest Acknowledgments for the Honor you have done me, and permit me to assure you of the Respect Esteem & Regard with which I am

Dear Sir   Your faithful Friend & Servt

John Jay

John Adams — President of }
the United States —

ARS (MHi, Adams Manuscript Trust).

John Marshall: Appointment as Chief Justice in 1801

John Marshall, born on September 24, 1755, in a rented ironworker's cottage near Germantown, Virginia, was the eldest of fifteen children of Thomas and Mary Randolph (Keith) Marshall. His father, a childhood friend and neighbor of George Washington, had moved west from Westmoreland County, seeking more land and opportunity for himself and his family. Soon Thomas Marshall became one of the leading citizens of Fauquier County, where Germantown was located, representing it in the House of Burgesses and the Virginia Convention of 1775.[1]

Growing up in a frontier county, the Marshall children received little formal education. At age fourteen, John Marshall was sent back east to Reverend Archibald Campbell's academy in Westmoreland County, where he and James Monroe became friends. The next year Marshall remained at home, and his father engaged a Scottish deacon, James Thomson, to tutor the Marshall children in Latin and Greek. These two years—plus three months at the College of William and Mary in 1780—concluded John Marshall's formal education.[2] Although Marshall's father may have intended to train his eldest child for the law, Marshall stated that at age eighteen he possessed more enthusiasm for contemporary political debates and military training than for Blackstone's *Commentaries*.[3] In early September, 1775, twenty-year-old John Marshall, a lieutenant in the Virginia militia, followed his father, a major, off to war.[4]

Marshall's militia service represented only his first skirmish of the war. In 1776 he was mustered into the Continental Army as a lieutenant with the Third Virginia Regiment. During his three years of active service, Marshall endured the miseries of Valley Forge and saw action throughout New Jersey and Pennsylvania. As a result of these experiences, he developed a profound and lifelong respect for George Washington.[5] The Continental Army also provided the first forum for Marshall's legal skills when on November 20, 1777, he was appointed a deputy judge advocate, a position giving him experience in the prosecution of courts-martial.[6] His enlistment over at the end of 1779, Marshall returned to Virginia where he met young Mary Willis Ambler (1766-1831), known as Polly. After a long courtship he married Polly on January 3, 1783.[7]

By the time of his marriage, Marshall had decided on a career in law. For approximately three months, in the spring and summer of 1780, he had been in Williamsburg attending the law lectures of George Wythe. These lectures were the sum total of Marshall's formal legal education. At the end of July, he left Williamsburg and returned to Fauquier County where he was admitted to practice before the county court on August 28, 1780.[8] Marshall could not immediately begin a law practice, however. Military service once again intervened, and he served in the army from October, 1780, until he resigned his commission in February, 1781. Events in Virginia disrupted the functioning of the courts, and this, too, delayed his career plans. Finally, after Cornwallis's surrender at Yorktown in 1781, the courts reopened, and Marshall began his law practice.[9]

Marshall, although young and untried, had already won the respect of his Fauquier County neighbors, who propelled him into state politics. In 1782 they elected him to

John Marshall by an unknown artist. Oil on glass, ca. 1797. Courtesy Mrs. Benjamin
T. Woodruff.

the General Assembly as a member of the House of Delegates. Later that year, the
General Assembly elected Marshall to the governor's Council of State (Privy Council).
The appointment to the Privy Council and the presence of the Ambler family in Rich-
mond prompted him to move to the capital city, where the state's highest courts met.
He thereafter made his home in Richmond. Marshall resigned his seat on the Privy
Council in April, 1784, but by May was back in the General Assembly. Fauquier
County had reelected him to the House of Delegates, even though he was only a
nominal resident by then. During his first term in the General Assembly, Marshall had

been appointed to the committee to review the laws of Virginia and report whether those laws ready to expire should be renewed. He served on similar committees throughout his years in the House of Delegates, allowing him to become intimately acquainted with Virginia's laws. Several other future Supreme Court justices worked on similar committees in their home states, James Iredell in North Carolina, and William Paterson in New Jersey.[10]

At the same time that he pursued a legislative career, Marshall developed a growing legal practice. By 1785 he had become a leader of the Richmond bar and a major political figure in the city. The Court of Appeals, the General Court, the High Court of Chancery, and the Court of Admiralty drew both the elite of the Virginia bar and a huge number of litigants. Marshall was admitted to the bar of the Virginia Court of Appeals, the state's highest court on April 29, 1785. In 1786 when Edmund Randolph became governor, he placed an advertisement in the *Virginia Independent Chronicle* (Richmond) stating that John Marshall would succeed to his business. That same year Marshall lost his first election in an attempt to become Virginia's attorney general. Marshall had other duties to keep him busy, however. From 1785 to 1788, he served as an alderman for the city of Richmond. During these years, his fellow aldermen chose Marshall to be recorder for Richmond, a job requiring him to keep the city's records, sign various orders, and serve on the Hustings Court.[11] He also tended to his growing family. He and Polly, who was an invalid most of her adult life, had ten children, six of whom survived.[12] In 1787 Marshall returned to the House of Delegates, representing Henrico County (the county in which Richmond is situated).[13]

Henrico County again chose Marshall in 1788 to be one of its delegates to the Virginia convention, held in June, to consider the Constitution. In this convention, Marshall, an advocate of ratification, emerged as a strong leader. In his third speech to the convention, Marshall forcefully defended the concept of a federal judiciary, pointing out that only a federal judiciary could protect the people from infringements of the Constitution. Thereafter, Marshall became a spokesman for the federalists in Virginia. After the establishment of the federal government, President Washington appointed him United States attorney for the district of Virginia. Marshall declined the position because it would have created a conflict with his law practice.[14]

In the late 1780s and 1790s, Marshall's law practice prospered. He also served as acting attorney general for Virginia from October, 1794, to March, 1795. Known as a lawyer's lawyer, he handled many cases on appeal referred to him by other attorneys when the cases were being heard in Richmond. Marshall was able to restrict his practice to the Richmond area and only argued at the county courts of the nearby counties.[15] One spectacular exception involved Richard Randolph, an older brother of John Randolph, who was later speaker of the House of Representatives. Rumors that Richard Randolph had murdered an illegitimate child born to him and his sister-in-law had finally become so public that he demanded a hearing. Marshall was one of the attorneys hired by Randolph to defend him, or more likely to defend his sister-in-law, at the Cumberland County court. The charges were ultimately dismissed and Randolph never went to trial.[16]

Marshall's most famous cases in Virginia dealt with contracts, British debts, and land purchases. In *Bracken v. College of William and Mary* he defended the right of the board of visitors of the college to change the school's curriculum and to dismiss the master of the grammar school. In *Ware v. Hylton,* the only case that Marshall argued in the Supreme Court, he defended the validity of Virginia statutes that prevented British creditors from recovering prerevolutionary debts, despite the existence of the Treaty of Paris of 1783 and the Constitution of the United States. Another cause in which Marshall was involved for more than a decade concerned the Fairfax lands in Virginia's Northern Neck. In addition to providing him with legal work, Marshall had a personal interest in the outcome of the resulting cases as he had purchased some of the land. Marshall's adroit handling of the legal issues in the state and federal courts, and his work in the House of Delegates (to which he was returned in 1789, 1790, and 1795-1797) to promote legislation favorable to the Fairfax heirs and the purchasers of the Fairfax lands, allowed him to secure legal title to land from the estate.[17]

Marshall's acquisition of this land, by giving him some financial security, may have contributed to his willingness to accept a federal appointment. Previously he had declined all appointments that would take him out of Virginia or disrupt his law practice. On June 5, 1797, he was commissioned a special envoy to France to negotiate a treaty of commerce and amity, an appointment he accepted soon thereafter. Elbridge Gerry and Charles Cotesworth Pinckney joined Marshall on this mission. No negotiations occurred. Instead, agents of the French government (X,Y, and Z) suggested a United States loan to France as well as a substantial bribe as a prerequisite to any official meeting. The American envoys firmly rejected these demands and informed President Adams that the mission had failed. When the XYZ affair was revealed in the United States, Marshall and his fellow commissioners were acclaimed as heroes.[18]

Upon his return to the United States, Marshall resumed his law practice but only briefly. His old commander-in-chief and friend, George Washington, urged him to run for Congress in 1799, and Marshall agreed to be a candidate. It was a difficult and long campaign for Marshall but he won a narrow victory. On December 2, 1799, he entered the Sixth Congress.[19]

Marshall's tenure in Congress was also brief. On May 7, 1800, President Adams, impressed with Marshall's leadership skills, nominated him secretary of war, a post he did not want. Five days later, Adams nominated Marshall secretary of state, a position he accepted. The Senate confirmed his appointment on May 13, 1800.[20]

But his career as secretary of state was short-lived too. In January, 1801, President Adams faced a crisis in the judiciary. Chief Justice Oliver Ellsworth had resigned from the Supreme Court, and John Jay, the former chief justice, had declined a new appointment. With the era of federalist rule ending, it was imperative that Adams act quickly to fill the vacancy. In what Adams later called the proudest act of his life, he turned to his secretary of state on January 19, 1801, and told John Marshall that he believed he must nominate him to be the fourth chief justice of the United States. On January 27, 1801, he was unanimously confirmed. Marshall's thirty-four-year career as chief justice placed an indelible stamp on the Court's and the nation's history. He died in Philadelphia on July 6, 1835.[21]

1. Leonard Baker, *John Marshall: A Life in Law* (New York: Macmillan, 1974), pp. 6-7, 24-25; *DAB*, entry for Thomas Marshall. John Marshall's mother, Mary Randolph (Keith) Marshall, was the daughter of an Anglican minister and a relative of the Randolphs, one of Virginia's leading families. Baker, *John Marshall*, pp. 6-7.

2. Baker, *John Marshall*, p. 13; *DAB*, entry for John Marshall; *PJM*, 1:37-38.

3. John Marshall, *An Autobiographical Sketch*, ed. John Stokes Adams (Ann Arbor: University of Michigan Press, 1937), pp. 4-5; *DAB*, entry for John Marshall.

4. Baker, *John Marshall*, pp. 4-5, 26-27.

5. Ibid., pp. 27-35; 38-56.

6. *PJM*, 1:15n; Baker, *John Marshall*, p. 51.

7. Baker, *John Marshall*, pp. 58-59, 71-73; *DAB*.

8. *PJM*, 1:37-41. George Wythe (1726-1806), a distinguished lawyer and mentor of Thomas Jefferson, was appointed to the first law professorship in the United States at the College of William and Mary in 1779. *DAB*.

9. Baker, *John Marshall*, p. 69; Marshall, *Autobiographical Sketch*, pp. 6-7.

10. *PJM*, 1:xlv-xlvi; Marshall, *Autobiographical Sketch*, p. 7; Baker, *John Marshall*, pp. 71, 90-95. For information on Iredell and Paterson see above, "James Iredell: Appointment as Associate Justice in 1790" and "William Paterson: Appointment as Associate Justice in 1793."

11. Baker, *John Marshall*, pp. 78, 87, 96-98; John J. Reardon, *Edmund Randolph: A Biography* (New York: Macmillan, 1975), p. 404, note 5; *PJM*, 1:xlvi.

12. Baker, *John Marshall*, p. 98.

13. *PJM*, 1:xlvi.

14. Ibid., pp. 252, 275-86; Baker, *John Marshall*, pp. 167-70.

15. *PJM*, 2:xxi-xxii, xxxvi.

16. Ibid., pp. 161-68.

17. Ibid., pp. 67-72, 140-50, xxxv-xxxvi; *PJM*, 3:xxix, 4-7; Baker, *John Marshall*, pp. 154-64, 293-98.

18. *PJM*, 3:79-86; Baker, *John Marshall*, pp. 213-93.

19. Baker, *John Marshall*, pp. 298-315.

20. Ibid., pp. 316-27, 331-32; *SEJ*, 1:352-54.

21. Baker, *John Marshall*, pp. 352-55, 767. For John Marshall's account of his conversation with John Adams, see "Commentaries," John Marshall to Joseph Story, under date of 1827.

Nomination by John Adams

January 20, 1801

Gentlemen of the Senate.

I nominate John Marshall Secretary of State to be a Chief Justice of the United States in the Place of John Jay who has declined his appointment

John Adams

United States
Jan 20th 1801.

ARS (DNA, RG 46, Anson McCook Collection).

Nomination Received by Senate

January 20, 1801

[*The Senate Executive Journal (RG 46, DNA) records receipt of this nomination on January 20, 1801.*]

Confirmation by Senate

January 27, 1801

. . . The Senate proceeded to consider the message of the President of the United States of the 20th instant, and the nomination contained therein of John Marshall, to office. Whereupon,

Resolved, that they do advise and consent to the appointment agreeably to the nomination.

Ordered, that the Secretary lay this resolution before the President of the United States. . . .

D (DNA, RG 46, Executive Journal).

Notification to President of Senate Confirmation ——————
January [27-31], 1801

[*No record survives notifying John Adams of the Senate's confirmation of John Marshall. The notification must have occurred on or after January 27, 1801—the date of Senate confirmation—and on or before January 31, 1801—the date of the commission.*]

Commission ————————————————————————
January 31, 1801

John Adams, President of the United States of America,
  To all who shall see these Presents, — Greeting:

Know ye, That reposing special Trust and Confidence in the Wisdom, Uprightness and Learning of John Marshall, of Virginia, I have nominated, and by and with the advice and consent of the Senate do appoint him Chief Justice of the Supreme Court of the United States, and do authorize and empower him to execute and fulfil the Duties of that Office according to the Constitution and Laws of the said United States; and to Have and to Hold the said Office, with all the powers, privileges and Emoluments to the same of Right appertaining unto him the said John Marshall during his good behaviour.

(L S)

In Testimony whereof, I have caused these Letters to be made Patent, and the Seal of the United States to be hereunto affixed. Given under my Hand at the City of Washington the Thirty first day of January in the year of our Lord one thousand Eight hundred and one; and of the Independence of the United States the Twenty Fifth.

John Adams

Lb (DNA, RG 59, Miscellaneous Permanent and Temporary Commissions).

John Adams to Samuel Dexter ————————————————————
January 31, 1801   Washington, District of Columbia

Washington   Jan 31 1801.

Dear Sir

I hereby authorize & request you to execute the office of Secretary of State so far as to affix the seal of the U. S. to the inclosed commission to the present Secretary of State John Marshall of Virginia to be chief Justice of the U. S. & to certify, in your own name on the commission as executing the office of Secretary of State pro hac vice[1]

Samuel Dexter Esqr.   Sec of the Treasury

ALb (MHi, Adams Manuscript Trust).

Samuel Dexter (1761-1816) at this time was serving both as secretary of war and as secretary of the treasury. Dexter, a lawyer by training, had been elected to Congress in 1792 and completed one term. In 1799 he was elected a senator from Massachusetts and held his Senate seat until John Adams appointed him secretary of war on May 13, 1800. On December 31, 1800, Adams also made him secretary of the treasury, and Dexter headed both departments for two months. *DAB.*

1. "For this occasion."

John Marshall to John Adams ————————————————————
February 4, 1801   [Washington, District of Columbia]

Feby 4th 1801

Sir

I pray you to accept my grateful acknowledgements for the honor conferd on me in appointing me chief Justice of the United States.

This additional & flattering mark of your good opinion has made an impression on my mind which time will not efface.

I shall enter immediately on the duties of the office & hope never to give you occasion to regret having made this appointment

With the most respectful attachment   I am Sir your Obed^t Servt

JMarshall

ARS (MHi, Adams Manuscript Trust).

John Adams to John Marshall ————————————————————
February 4, 1801   Washington, District of Columbia

Washington   Feb. 4. 1801

Dear Sir

I have this moment received your Letter of this morning and am happy in your Acceptance of the office of Chief Justice.

The Circumstances however of the Times render it necessary that I should request and Authorize you as I do by this Letter, to continue to discharge all the Duties of Secretary of State, untill ulteriour Arrangements can be made_ [1]

With great Esteem, I have the   Honor to be, Sir your Sincere   Friend

John Adams

John Marshall Esqr

ARS (DNA, RG 59, Miscellaneous Letters); ALb (MHi, Adams Manuscript Trust).

1. John Marshall continued to serve as secretary of state, *ad interim,* for the remainder of John Adams's administration. On March 4, 1801, President Thomas Jefferson asked Marshall "to perform the duties of the Secretary of state until a successor to that office shall be appointed" (Miscellaneous Letters, RG 59, DNA). Attorney General Levi Lincoln assumed the duties of the secretary of state, *ad interim,* beginning on March 5, 1801, the same day that James Madison was appointed to that post. Madison entered upon the duties of the office May 2, 1801.

Record of Oaths
February 4, 1801   [Washington, District of Columbia]

[*At the opening of the Supreme Court on February 4, 1801:*] A Commission from the President of the United States to John Marshall, Esquire of Virginia, bearing date the 31st day of January AD. 1801. and of the Independence of the United States the twenty fifth, and constituting the said John Marshall Chief Justice of the Supreme Court of the United States, is now read in open Court, and the said John Marshall having taken the oaths prescribed by Law, took his seat upon the Bench_ . . .

D (DNA, RG 267, General Records, Minutes).

The Clerks and Their Record

Section 7 of the Judiciary Act of 1789 granted authority to the Supreme Court to appoint a clerk. The statute specified that the clerk, before acting in his official capacity, either take an oath or affirm in the following words: "I, A. B., being appointed clerk of [the Supreme Court], do solemnly swear, or affirm, that I will truly and faithfully enter and record all the orders, decrees, judgments and proceedings of the said court, and that I will faithfully and impartially discharge and perform all the duties of my said office, according to the best of my abilities and understanding." Appointees were also required to post bond with sureties.[1] In accordance with their understanding of the duties of the office, the clerks of the Supreme Court between 1790 and 1800 created and maintained the official record of the Court: rough and fine minutes, rough docket notes and an engrossed docket, a counsellor roll and an attorney roll as well as a bound volume of attorney signatures, a file of certificates and character references in support of bar admissions, a formulary, a compilation of rules, a clerical inventory of case papers, and a small miscellaneous collection of documents. They also issued and received the legal instruments associated with litigation.

But the creation of the Court's record was not predetermined. The record that survives reveals an institution in the process of defining itself. The promise of the clerks to perform "according to the best of [their] abilities and understanding" concealed the basic problem that no one had a good understanding of how the Supreme Court would function, and therefore what records would be appropriate. In suits at common law, section 2 of "An Act to regulate Processes in the Courts of the United States," enacted in September, 1789, directed the clerks of the district and circuit courts to model their forms, modes of process, and rates of fees on those of the supreme courts of the states they were in. In causes of equity and admiralty jurisdiction, forms and modes of process were to follow the civil law, with fees the same as last allowed in state courts having supreme jurisdiction in such cases.[2] Presumably, the clerks of the Supreme Court also could turn to the states for guidance in record-keeping. For example, at the beginning of the Court's minutes in February term, 1790, John Tucker, newly appointed clerk of the Supreme Court, seems to have modeled the opening paragraph and the list of justices on the form used by him as clerk of the Supreme Judicial Court of Massachusetts.[3]

State practice was a start. For additional guidance, the clerks turned to the best legal minds available. Thus, in the drafts of orders and motions published in this volume we find drafts in the handwriting of Chief Justice John Jay, Chief Justice Oliver Ellsworth, and Attorney General Edmund Randolph, as well as in the hand of the clerk. In the formulary, we see the influence of two members of the Supreme Court bar—Jacob Read and William Lewis—in establishing certain forms. In the rough minutes the clerk labeled a paragraph on February 14, 1792, as "℥ Judge Iredell" suggesting that Associate Justice James Iredell shaped the phrasing of the passage. We will never know the full extent of the involvement of the justices and other prominent jurists in the development of the Court's record. On other occasions the clerks probably asked for and received advice on acceptable wording of the Court's business without noting that they had done so. The examples cited cannot be considered as comprehensive; rather, they are suggestive of one way by which the Court's record was created.

Other evidence reflects the uncertainty and tentativeness of the clerks who recorded the Court's business. The records of the Court include myriad textual errors, corrections, and revisions. This is especially true in the drafts of orders and motions and in the rough minutes. As described in the "Guide to Editorial Method" we reproduce the text as literally as possible, and therefore a comparison of the drafts of orders and motions and the rough minutes with the fine minutes, all published in this volume, reveals the process by which phrasing was refined until it assumed a finished form. An evolving system also can be seen in the types of records that the clerks created and the extent to which these records were maintained. For example, we present in this volume both an attorney roll and a bound volume of attorneys' signatures. We try to explain the genesis of each, but the fact remains that the existence of two overlapping registers of attorneys is indicative of a plan in flux. We also publish and discuss a contemporary list of rules from this period, a list that is different from that normally attributed to the first decade. Later clerks did not maintain this early list, but instead compiled a different one from the minutes of the Court. The Court's record thus was not conceived a priori, but was, rather, the result of the collective experience of the clerks, the justices, and other prominent jurists brought to bear on the problem of how to document the business of a new institution in a new nation.

Most important, this evolutionary process is inseparable from the clerks who kept the record. They brought to the task different backgrounds and talents as well as limitations. Furthermore, the turnover in clerks during the first decade and the absence of the appointed clerk from 1794 to 1798 contributed to a lack of continuity in the Court's record-keeping. In order to shed maximum light upon the Court's record, we have sought biographical information about the clerks. We also have examined the handwriting and probable purpose of each document, which are explained in the headnote for each document published in this section. A careful review of the surviving Court record reveals a great deal about how the men who held the office of clerk performed their duties.

On February 3, 1790, the Court appointed the first clerk, John Tucker.[4] Born on August 11, 1753, in Newbury, Massachusetts (near Newburyport), he was the son of the Reverend John and Sarah (Barnard) Tucker.[5] His early education was at nearby Dummer School, where the curriculum stressed Latin and Greek to prepare students for college. From the Dummer School, Tucker proceeded to Harvard where he graduated in 1774.[6] Shortly thereafter, he commenced the study of law with John Lowell (1743–1802), who resided in Newburyport until 1777 when he moved to Boston.[7] Having completed his training, "John Tucker of Newburyport, Gentleman" was admitted to the bar of the Superior Court of Judicature during June 1780 term when the court was sitting at Ipswich in Essex County.[8]

Tucker received his first clerical appointment from the same court, renamed the Supreme Judicial Court following the reorganization of the Massachusetts judiciary in 1781. During August 1783 term, when the Supreme Judicial Court was meeting at Boston in Suffolk County, Tucker was appointed clerk "in the room of Andrew Henshaw late of Boston Esq[r] deceased." He served with another clerk, Charles Cushing, brother of future Supreme Court justice William Cushing, who was at this time chief justice of the Massachusetts Supreme Judicial Court.[9]

John Tucker by Charles Annor (? - ?) after a lost portrait by Gilbert Stuart (1755-
1828). Oil on canvas, 1891. Courtesy Office of the Curator, Supreme Court of the
United States.

Tucker's future was shaped importantly by this appointment. First, Tucker married
Sarah (Prince) Henshaw, the widow of his clerical predecessor, on March 12, 1785.[10]
Secondly, the appointment gave Charles and William Cushing the opportunity to become familiar with Tucker's capabilities and character. When the time approached to
appoint a clerk of the Supreme Court, William Cushing knew Tucker well enough to
write to John Jay that "M[r] Tu[cker] . . . was, about five years [ago?] [ap]pointed one of
the Clerks of the [Supreme] Judicial Court of this State & has con[ducted to?] the gen-

eral approbation; is a Gentleman [of good?] sense & agreeable temper [*phrase illegible*] a man of virtue & integrity."[11] Theodore Sedgwick, a congressman from Massachusetts, and others contacted Jay in support of Tucker, now identified as a resident of Boston. When Jay responded to Cushing's letter, he noted, "Your character of M[r] Tucker corresponds with the accounts given of it by other Gentlemen." Jay further wrote that he would consult with the other justices about whom to appoint to the office. He concluded that the Supreme Court would need a clerk as soon as it convened and that it would be best if the clerk resided in the capital.[12]

When the Supreme Court began its first term at New York in February, 1790, Tucker was in the city. Oliver Ellsworth wrote that "being on the spot & well patronized he obtained the appointment."[13] As Jay had suggested in his letter to Cushing, the Court ordered that Tucker "reside, and keep his Office at the Seat of the National Government."[14] Despite this order, Tucker did not reside in New York or, later, in Philadelphia. He did not even resign his position as clerk of the Massachusetts Supreme Judicial Court. Rather, he took advantage of the complementary schedules of his two jobs. The Supreme Judicial Court in Massachusetts did not meet in January and the first meeting in February was scheduled for the third Tuesday of the month. Tucker was able to attend the February term of the Supreme Court without serious disruption of his official duties in Massachusetts. A similarly convenient schedule allowed Tucker to attend the August term of the Supreme Court.[15]

During his tenure as clerk, Tucker established a record of the minutes of the Court, a file of drafts of orders and motions, parchment rolls of attorneys and counsellors, and a file of certificates and character references.[16] But he remained clerk only long enough to create this system of record-keeping; he resigned before the beginning of the August 1791 term of the Court.[17] The reason for his resignation was later attributed to the lack of adequate compensation as clerk. Other factors also may have influenced his decision. The Court's move to Philadelphia in 1791 would have made it difficult for him to maintain the obligations of his clerkship in Massachusetts. In addition, a familial crisis involving the failing health of his father may have required his presence closer to home.[18]

Samuel Bayard, the son of Margaret (Hodge) and John Bubenheim Bayard, succeeded Tucker as clerk of the Court. Samuel Bayard was born in Philadelphia on January 11, 1767. During the Revolutionary War, his family moved for a time to its ancestral estate at Bohemia Manor, Maryland, then returned to Philadelphia, and finally settled on a farm outside that city. It was there that young Bayard completed his early education under the instruction of a private tutor. In 1784, he graduated as class valedictorian from the College of New Jersey (later Princeton) with an A.B. Thereafter, he studied law with, and then became the partner of, William Bradford, Jr.[19] Bayard was admitted to the Philadelphia bar on November 8, 1787 (the same year in which he received an A.M. from the College of New Jersey), and practiced law in that city for several years.[20] But he was not immediately successful as a lawyer. On June 28, 1789, William Bradford, Jr., wrote to his father-in-law Elias Boudinot, a congressman from New Jersey, "I wish you would keep him in mind if any appointment proper for him should occur to you. I am apprehensive that his business at Montgomery is very trifling_ the County is but small & poor and he has not the happiest art of carrying his talents to market." He continued in a more positive vein, "I think he possesses abilities which if properly exerted would enable him to figure in life: but at present he needs something to lift him from his retirement." Bradford had mentioned to Bayard

Samuel Bayard by James Frothingham (1786-1864). Oil on canvas, ca. 1830-1835. Courtesy Museum of Fine Arts, Boston. Bequest of Maxim Karolik.

the possibility of accepting a post as clerk of the federal district court for Pennsylvania, "which would not interfere with his professional pursuits in the state courts, would call him into notice, & be a stepping stone to more important posts."[21]

With the resignation of Tucker as Supreme Court clerk, Bayard saw the possibility of his attaining an even more prestigious post than clerk of a lower federal court. He spoke with Senator Caleb Strong and Congressman Theodore Sedgwick, both of Massachusetts, about his prospects. He also wrote to the justices.[22] On August 1, 1791, the Court officially appointed Bayard as clerk.[23]

During the time that Bayard served, the Court's record grew substantially. Bayard began a new bound volume of fine minutes, kept drafts of orders and motions as well as rough minutes, and maintained a docket book. In addition to continuing the parchment roll of counsellor signatures, he started a bound volume with signatures of attorneys admitted to the Supreme Court bar. He also added certificates and character references to the file begun by John Tucker. Also surviving from the period of Bayard's clerkship are his formulary, an inventory of case papers, rough dockets for February and August terms, 1798, and his compilation of orders and rules.

Unlike John Tucker, Samuel Bayard was not required by any Court order to reside in the capital. Therefore, when President George Washington in 1794 selected Bayard to go to London to prosecute admiralty claims for the United States, there was nothing to stop him from accepting the assignment as well as retaining his office of clerk of the Supreme Court. He arranged for someone to act as clerk in his absence, informed the justices, and then left for England in November, 1794.[24] He did not return to the United States until spring 1798.[25] During Bayard's stay in England, two men performed the duties of clerk: Jacob Wagner and David Caldwell.

Jacob Wagner (1772-1825) was responsible for maintaining the Court's record through 1797, most of the time that Bayard was gone. Wagner's name first appears affixed to a Court document dated August 5, 1794, before Bayard's departure; his title is given as deputy clerk. After Bayard left for England, Wagner continued to endorse Court documents with this title until August term, 1796, when he began to sign as clerk of the Court.[26] Wagner's early life is obscure. He was admitted to the Philadelphia bar on June 5, 1793, and maintained various Philadelphia addresses between 1794 and 1800.[27] Before beginning as deputy clerk at the Court, Wagner had started to work as a clerk at the Department of State. He continued to work at that department concurrently with the service he performed for the Court. On February 8, 1798, he was appointed chief clerk of the Department of State. It may have been this latter appointment, made in the same month that the Court met, that prompted Wagner to direct his attention away from the Court and turn over the duties of that position to David Caldwell.[28]

Born in Philadelphia on February 21, 1770, David was the son of Samuel Caldwell. The elder Caldwell was clerk of the federal district and circuit courts for Pennsylvania from the time of their first convening through his death on November 26, 1798. Before Samuel Caldwell's death, his physical disability made it difficult to fulfill the office of clerk, and David Caldwell took over the duties.[29] Thus, he was not unprepared when the Court required his services as clerk in the February 1798 term.

When Samuel Bayard returned from England in May, 1798, he did not establish his residence in Philadelphia. Instead, he settled in New Rochelle, Westchester County, New York. This was the home of Lewis and Susan (Stockton) Pintard, the parents of Bayard's wife, Martha Pintard. Bayard traveled to and from Philadelphia to act as clerk of the Court.[30] Meanwhile, in addition to familial ties, Bayard forged other links which bound him to Westchester County. In 1799 he was elected commissioner of schools of the Town of New Rochelle. In February of that same year, he was appointed assistant justice of the Court of Common Pleas and a justice of the peace for Westchester County. At the same time, he was named a master in chancery.[31] It may have been his success in the state of New York that made him decide not to continue as clerk of the

David Caldwell by Charles Balthazar Julien Févret de Saint-Mémin (1770-1852). Engraving, 1798. Courtesy National Portrait Gallery, Smithsonian Institution.

Court after August 1800 term. Also, he may not have wished to travel the additional mileage that would have been required of him as a commuting clerk because of the Court's move to Washington before the opening of the next term in 1801. In any event, he served as clerk through August 1800 term, and the Court appointed his successor, Elias Boudinot Caldwell, on the last day of that term, August 15.[32]

Born in Elizabethtown, New Jersey, on April 3, 1776, Elias Boudinot Caldwell was the son of the Reverend James and Hannah (Ogden) Caldwell. His parents named him after one of his father's parishioners, Elias Boudinot (1740-1821), who was a revolutionary statesman, prominent lawyer, trustee of the College of New Jersey (later Princeton), and subsequently a congressman. Orphaned at the age of five, Elias B. Caldwell was adopted by Boudinot. He received an A.B. from the College of New Jersey in 1796 and then studied law with his adoptive father.[33] At the time that he was deciding on a career and a place of residence, Caldwell learned from Samuel Bayard of his intention of resigning as clerk of the Supreme Court and his willingness to support Caldwell as a replacement. Bayard knew Caldwell through Elias Boudinot, who was the uncle of Bayard's wife and the father-in-law of Bayard's former law partner, William Bradford, Jr. Caldwell also sought the support of the justices.[34] By mid-May, 1800,

Elias Boudinot Caldwell by Thomas Sully (1783-1872) after a lost miniature. Oil on canvas, 1849. Courtesy Historical Society of Pennsylvania.

Caldwell was living in Baltimore, had been admitted to the bar there in April term, and was very dissatisfied with his situation.[35] Fortunately, his effort to secure the Court's clerkship succeeded, and he remained in that position until his death in 1825.[36]

At the time that Elias B. Caldwell took over as clerk, the Court's record reflected the circumstances of its creation by several preceding clerks and assistants. The minutes, presenting a chronological narration of the Supreme Court's daily proceedings from February term, 1790, through August term, 1800, existed in several forms. The bound fine minutes had been started by Bayard; a set of original minutes included Tucker's version of the fine minutes, in addition to subsequent rough minutes; and miscellaneous drafts of orders and motions also survived. The bound docket book, which recorded the progress of litigation in each case, covered the period from February term, 1791. Rough dockets for 1798 had been kept. A counsellor roll and an attorney roll had been started by Tucker; the former had been continued, but the latter had been superseded by Bayard's bound attorney list. Certificates and character references relating to application for admission to the Supreme Court bar were on file, too. A formulary begun by Bayard included forms for the period when Wagner had acted as clerk. Bayard also had compiled an inventory of case papers and a list of orders and rules. A few documents concerning the justices on circuit and all documents relating to cases completed the collection of records inherited by Elias B. Caldwell; these will be considered in subsequent volumes in this series devoted to the justices on circuit and the cases that came before the Court. In this volume, we publish all other documents described briefly above, the complete extant record of the Supreme Court of the United States from 1790 through 1800.

A headnote precedes each document in this section. The headnote discusses the purpose of each document, its physical condition if it affects legibility, and the changes in handwriting exhibited in it. Changes in handwriting reveal the role played by each clerk in the genesis of the Court's official record. It is very difficult, however, to identify the clerk responsible for any particular part of the record, because professional clerks in the eighteenth century sometimes possessed a range of formal and informal styles of handwriting. Our conclusions as to patterns of handwriting, therefore, must be considered as tentative. It is particularly difficult to pinpoint the identity of persons making single-letter corrections or inserting brief interlineations in the text. When the individual responsible for writing part of the text cannot be identified, that fact is noted in one of two ways. If the unknown handwriting appears only once, we note at that point that the text is in an unknown hand. If, however, the unknown hand appears more than once, we assign a letter identification to distinguish the common hand; thus, the reader will see references to passages written by "Hand A," "Hand B," "Hand C," etc. These passages are designated as the product of different hands, rather than clerks, in order to leave open the possibility that one clerk may have been responsible for writing in more than one "hand."

Finally, the reader should note three points before beginning to read the documents that follow. First, because of the intricate structural relationship among the "Fine Minutes," "Original Minutes," and "Drafts Relating to Court Proceedings," the reader may find it useful to read together the headnotes to all three. Secondly, because we do not note complete erasures, the development of the minutes through various stages—reflected by words changed, words crossed out, interlineations, partial as well as complete erasures—cannot be traced fully. Thirdly, for case-related text, we do not note factual errors, point out textual inconsistencies, or supply additional information, because we will be doing this in subsequent volumes.

1. "An Act to establish the Judicial Courts of the United States," *Stat.*, 1:76.

2. *Stat.*, 1:93-94.

3. Supreme Judicial Court [Record], 1790, p. 1r, MBSufC. John Tucker's service as clerk is discussed in his biography included in this introduction.

4. John McKesson acted as clerk on February 2, 1790, the day before John Tucker's appointment, when the commissions of the justices and of the attorney general were read. McKesson (1734-1798) received degrees from the College of New Jersey (later Princeton) (A.B. 1756; A.M. 1760) and an honorary A.M. from King's College (later Columbia) in 1758.

He was appointed to be a proctor in the Court of Vice Admiralty in Bermuda in 1759 and was admitted to the bar of the New York Supreme Court of Judicature in 1761. In addition to practicing law, McKesson was appointed to many clerical posts during his career: secretary to the New York Provincial Convention in 1775 and later to the Council of Safety, register in chancery in 1776, clerk of the New York Assembly in 1777, notary public in 1780, register of the New York Court of Admiralty in 1784, and secretary to the New York ratifying convention in 1788. By the time of his appointment as acting clerk of the Supreme Court of the United States, McKesson was serving as clerk of the New York Supreme Court of Judicature, Nisi Prius, Oyer and Terminer and General Gaol Delivery. See "Commentaries," *Gazette of the United States* under date of February 3, 1790; William M. MacBean, *Biographical Register of Saint Andrew's Society of the State of New York*, 2 vols. (New York, 1922), 1:17; McKesson Papers, NHi; [Robert] Hodge, [Thomas] Allen, and [Samuel] Campbell, *The New-York Directory, and Register, for the Year 1789* (New York, 1789).

5. John Tucker Prince, "Sketches of Several Branches of the Family of Tucker" (Boston, 1882), pp. 33, 39, unpublished manuscript in MBNEH.

6. W[illiam] D. N[orthend], *Catalogue of the Officers and Students of Dummer Academy, Byfield, Massachusetts, Instituted A.D. 1763* (Salem, Mass.: Salem Gazette Office, 1844), p. 21; Nehemiah Cleaveland, *The First Century of Dummer Academy . . .* (Boston: Nichols & Noyes, 1865), p. 24.

7. See "Commentaries," William Cushing to John Jay, November 18, 1789; *DAB*, entry for John Lowell.

8. The attorney general of Massachusetts had moved for John Tucker's admission at the November term, 1779, when the court met at Salem in Essex County (Superior Court of Judicature [Record], 1778-1780, pp. 122v, 191v, MBSufC).

9. Supreme Judicial Court [Record], 1783, pp. 151r, 178v, MBSufC; Supreme Judicial Court [Record], 1781-1782, p. 11v, MBSufC. See also *DAB*, entry for William Cushing.

10. Prince, "Sketches of Several Branches of the Family of Tucker," pp. 38-39; Boston Record Commissioners, *Report of the Record Commissioners*, 39 vols. (Boston: Municipal Printing Office, 1876-1909), vol. 30, *Boston Marriages, 1752-1809* (1903), p. 106.

11. See "Commentaries," William Cushing to John Jay, November 18, 1789.

12. See "Commentaries," Theodore Sedgwick to John Jay, September 23, 1789, and John Jay to William Cushing, December 7, 1789. John Jay also may have heard from Senator Rufus King of New York, whom Theodore Sedgwick believed to be one of John Tucker's acquaintances. Like Tucker, King had attended Dummer School and left for college in 1774. Massachusetts Congressman Fisher Ames, a Harvard classmate and intimate friend of Tucker, also contacted Jay. Cleaveland, *First Century of Dummer Academy*, pp. 30-31; see "Commentaries," Fisher Ames to John Jay, November 10, 1789. The relation between Ames and Tucker is mentioned in George Thatcher to Oliver Wolcott, Jr., June 13, 1796, Oliver Wolcott Jr. Papers, CtHi.

13. See "Commentaries," Oliver Ellsworth to Ephraim Kirby, February 15, 1790.

14. See "Fine Minutes," February 3, 1790.

15. *Catalogue of Records and Files in the Office of the Clerk of the Supreme Judicial Court for the County of Suffolk*, rev. ed. (Boston: Addison C. Getchell, 1897), pp. 119-25. John Tucker's handwriting and signature appear during this period throughout the official record of the Supreme Judicial Court [Record], 1790 and 1791, and Suffolk Minutes, 1790 and 1791, MBSufC.

16. For a more detailed discussion of these records, see the headnotes to "Original Minutes," "Drafts Relating to Court Proceedings," and "Admission to the Bar."

17. See "Fine Minutes," August 1, 1791.

18. See "Commentaries," George Thatcher to Oliver Wolcott, Jr., June 13, 1796. In this letter George Thatcher also states that John Tucker would like a position other than that of clerk of the Supreme Judicial Court so that he could stay more at home. See also "Commentaries," John Tucker, Sr., to [Paine Wingate], March 27, 1790. John Tucker, Sr., died on March 22, 1792. Prince, "Sketches of Several Branches of the Family of Tucker," p. 37.

After resigning, Tucker returned to Massachusetts where he continued as a clerk of the Supreme Judicial Court until his death in Boston on February 27, 1825. Prince, "Sketches of Several Branches of the Family of Tucker," pp. 39-40.

19. See *DAB*, entries for Samuel Bayard and for his father, John Bubenheim Bayard; Princeton University, *General Catalogue of Princeton University, 1746-1906* (Princeton, 1908), p. 102. For information on William Bradford, Jr., see note to his Supreme Court bar admission in "Fine Minutes," February 7, 1791.

20. *MBBP*, p. 247; *DAB*; Princeton, *Catalogue*, p. 102. Samuel Bayard is listed as an attorney at the same Philadelphia address in both the U.S., Department of Commerce and Labor, Bureau of the Census, *Heads of Families at the First Census of the United States Taken in the Year 1790: Pennsylvania* (Washington, D.C.: Government Printing Office, 1908) and Clement Biddle, *The Philadelphia Directory* (Philadelphia: James & Johnson, 1791).

21. John W. Wallace Collection, PHi; *DAB*, entry for Elias Boudinot. Montgomery County, where Samuel Bayard was practicing law, bordered on Philadelphia County.

22. See "Commentaries," Samuel Bayard to Caleb Strong, May 23, 1791.

23. See "Fine Minutes" under that date.

24. See *DAB* entry for Samuel Bayard's appointment by President Washington. See "Commentaries," Samuel Bayard to Edmund Randolph, October 25, 1794, for Bayard's pre-departure arrangements. Samuel Bayard to the Secretary of State, November 9, 1794, and December 26, 1794 (Despatches from Special Agents, RG 59, DNA), establish the timing of Bayard's departure.

25. Samuel Bayard to the Secretary of State, May 16, 1798. Despatches from Special Agents, RG 59, DNA.

26. David Hackett Fischer, *The Revolution of American Conservatism: The Federalist Party in the Era of Jeffersonian Democracy* (New York: Harper & Row, 1965), p. 369. For Jacob Wagner's service as clerk through 1797, bond of William Bingham and Thomas Willing dated December 12, 1797, and endorsed by Wagner as "Filed 13th Dec[r] 1797" in *Bingham v. Cabot*, Appellate Jurisdiction Records, RG 267, DNA. For the transition in Wagner's title from deputy clerk to clerk, venire of August 5, 1794, in *Oswald v. New York*, summons of March 6, 1796, in *Cutting v. South Carolina*, summons of August 12, 1796, in *Hollingsworth v. Virginia*, Original Jurisdiction Records, RG 267, DNA; writ of error of August 15, 1797, in *Bingham v. Cabot*, Appellate Jurisdiction Records, RG 267, DNA. Wagner had already been listed as clerk of the Supreme Court in Philadelphia directories for 1795 and 1796.

27. *MBBP*, p. 320. Philadelphia city directories list addresses for Jacob Wagner between 1794 and 1800.

28. As a clerk at the Department of State, Jacob Wagner endorsed as "rec[d] June 4" a letter from Jacob Mark and Company to Edmund Randolph, June 2, 1794 (Miscellaneous Letters, RG 59, DNA). We are grateful to the Department of State for supplying the date of Wagner's appointment as chief clerk. Wagner retained his post as clerk at the Department of State until March 31, 1807. His activities as clerk there are discussed in Noble E. Cunningham, Jr., *The Process of Government under Jefferson* (Princeton: Princeton University Press, 1978), pp. 94-97, 178-79; and in *Records of the Columbia Historical Society*, vol. 3 (Washington, D.C., 1900), p. 359.

After Wagner left his post at the Department of State, he moved to Baltimore. His decision to move there may have been influenced by his marriage on August 18, 1798, to Rachel Raborg of that city. After 1808 Wagner was a virulently partisan federalist editor and publisher in Baltimore, presiding over such papers as the Baltimore *North American*, the Baltimore (and later Georgetown) *Federal Republican*, and the Georgetown *Daily Federal Republican*. Wagner died on January 17, 1825, in Baltimore. His obituary appeared in the *Maryland Gazette* (Annapolis), January 20, 1825. For his marriage, see Robert W. Barnes, comp., *Marriages and Deaths from Baltimore Newspapers, 1796-1816* (Baltimore: Genealogical Publishing, 1978), p. 333. For newspaper activities, see Fischer, *Revolution of American Conservatism*, p. 369; Clarence S. Brigham, *History and Bibliography of American Newspapers, 1690-1820*, 2 vols. (Worcester, Mass.: American Antiquarian Society, 1947), entries for the (Baltimore) *North American* and *Federal Republican* and the (Georgetown) *Federal Republican* and *Daily Federal Republican*.

29. After his father's death, David Caldwell became clerk of the lower federal courts in Pennsylvania. He was appointed formally to the district court on November 27, 1798, and to the circuit court on May 11, 1801, holding this joint appointment until October 6, 1831. He died on November 11, 1835, and was buried in the cemetery of Third Presbyterian Church, Philadelphia. For biographical information on Samuel and David Caldwell, see John H. Campbell, *History of the Friendly Sons of St. Patrick and of the Hibernian Society for the Relief of Emigrants from Ireland: March 17, 1771-March 17, 1892* (Philadelphia: Hibernian Society, 1892), pp. 102-3. For evidence that David Caldwell assumed the duties of clerk before his father's death, David Caldwell to Richard Peters, November 22, 1798, Plumstead Papers, PHi, and *MBBP*, p. 12. On clerical appointments to the lower federal courts of Pennsylvania, *MBBP*, pp. 9, 12.

30. For Samuel Bayard's marriage to Martha Pintard in August, 1790, and his residence in New Rochelle, see *DAB* and Morgan H. Seacord and William S. Hadaway, *Historical Landmarks of New Rochelle* (New Rochelle: Huguenot and Historical Association and New Rochelle Trust Co., 1938), pp. 52-55; see also "Commentaries," Thomas B. Adams to William Cranch, July 15, 1799. For Bayard's movements from 1798 through 1800, we consulted the correspondence of his sister in the Margaret Bayard Smith Papers, DLC.

31. We are indebted to Richard N. Lander, Commissioner of Jurors of Westchester County, for information on Samuel Bayard's election to be commissioner of schools in 1799 and 1801. Bayard's judicial appointments in 1799 are recorded in the Minutes of the Council of Appointments, 4:106, New York State Library. He was reappointed as assistant justice and justice of the peace in February, 1800, and was elevated to be a judge of the Court of Common Pleas for Westchester County in October, 1800. Ibid., 4:195, 271.

32. For Elias B. Caldwell's appointment, see "Fine Minutes," for August 15, 1800. It is worth noting that on October 10, 1800, Alexander J. Dallas wrote that "The Records of the Supreme Court are removed to Georgetown" (Alexander J. Dallas to ?, George M. Dallas Collection, PHi). Furthermore, it is known that Samuel Bayard was in Washington in October, 1800 (Margaret Bayard Smith to Jane Kirkpatrick, October 19, 1800, Margaret Bayard Smith Papers, DLC). At that time, Bayard may have made a final check of the record that he was passing on to Elias B. Caldwell and signed his name after the August term, 1800, fine minutes.

Bayard stayed in New Rochelle until 1803, when he moved to New York City and began to practice law again. During his residence in New York, Bayard cooperated in founding the New-York Historical Society and was involved in newspaper publication. *DAB;* Brigham, *American Newspapers,* entries for the New York *Daily Advertiser,* 1785-1806, the New York *Daily Advertiser,* 1807, and the New York *People's Friend.*

In 1806 Bayard bought an estate in Princeton, New Jersey. There he held a series of offices: member of the New Jersey Assembly, 1813-1815; mayor of Princeton, 1817-1818; alderman 1821-1827; presiding judge of the Court of Common Pleas of Somerset County. He served the College of New Jersey (later Princeton) as librarian, 1806-1807; trustee, 1807-1810, 1822-1840; and treasurer, 1810-1828. He also served in several positions at Princeton Seminary: director, 1812-1840; vice president of the board of trustees, 1824-1831; and president of the board of trustees, 1831-1840. He was also ruling elder of the First Presbyterian Church in Princeton from 1807 to 1840 and trustee of the same in 1838. He died at Princeton on May 12, 1840. *DAB;* Princeton, *Catalogue,* p. 102; Helen Hamilton Stockton, "'Clermont'—Historic Mansion," *D.A.R. Magazine* 65 (1931): 550; Bayard Family Bible record, PHi.

33. Hallie L. Wright, "Sketch of Elias Boudinot Caldwell," with notes by Allen C. Clark, *Records of the Columbia Historical Society* 24 (1922): 204-11; *DAB,* entry for Elias Boudinot; Samuel Davies Alexander, *Princeton College during the Eighteenth Century* (New York: Anson D. F. Randolph, 1872), p. 291.

34. See "Commentaries," Elias B. Caldwell to William Gaston, February 28, 1800. For the relation of Elias Boudinot to William Bradford and Samuel Bayard, see *DAB* entries for Elias Boudinot and Lewis Pintard.

35. See "Commentaries," Elias B. Caldwell to William Gaston, May 12, 1800.

36. Elias B. Caldwell was admitted to practice before the Circuit Court of the District of Columbia on March 27, 1801, and successfully practiced thereafter as a lawyer. His political and social activities were varied. He commanded troops in the War of 1812, involved himself in the government of Washington, and helped found the American Colonization Society. He was also active in the Columbian Institute and in the Bible Society of the District of Columbia. For a brief period he edited the Georgetown *Washington Federalist.* Allen C. Clark's notes to Wright, "Sketch of Elias Boudinot Caldwell," pp. 211-13; Brigham, *American Newspapers,* 1:96.

Fine Minutes

The minutes of the Supreme Court present a chronological narration of daily proceedings. Judicial actions relating to litigation, procedural innovation, and admission to the bar were recorded in versions preceding the final transcription of these events in the fine, or engrossed, minutes. In this section, we publish the engrossed minutes; in the two sections that follow we present, first, the original, or rough, minutes and, second, drafts of orders, motions, proclamations, and judgments that preceded the engrossed minutes.

Below is a table which traces changes in handwriting through the fine minutes. We note individually in the text those instances where another hand is identifiable that does not fit this table.

February 1790 term-February 1792 term	Hand A
August 1792 term	Hand B
February 1793 term-February 1796 term	Hand C
August 1796 term-August 1797 term	Hand D
February 1798 term	Hand C
August 1798 term	Hand E
February 1799 term-August 1800 term	Hand F

What this table reveals is that Samuel Bayard, the clerk who began the engrossed minutes published here, did not personally transcribe the minutes from their initial to their finished, fine form. There is evidence, however, that the Court's appointed clerk was responsible for checking the accuracy of the transcription. For example, throughout the time that Hand A wrote the fine minutes, he spelled James Wilson's name with a double "l." This spelling followed that of John Tucker in his original version of the minutes.[1] In the engrossed minutes, this misspelling was corrected in almost all instances by a complete erasure of one of the "l's." Similarly the spelling of "council" usually was changed to "counsel" where the latter was the desired word. Other corrections appear to be in the handwriting of Samuel Bayard. Likewise, during the period when Bayard was in England and Jacob Wagner acted as clerk, we find instances where Wagner corrected the fine minutes. It is interesting that, even after the minutes had been transcribed for the last time, phrasing would be altered to express a thought more accurately or clearly. Thus on August 8, 1792, in the fine minutes the name of the court involved in a motion of the attorney general was revised, and this revision was not recorded in its entirety in the rough minutes.

The minutes are the main source of information about the day-by-day actions of the Court. Annotation to the minutes directs the reader to additional information about Supreme Court proceedings appearing in "Commentaries," especially in newspaper items. When a justice is absent for several days, we explain his absence only on the first day in order to avoid repetition in annotation. Those attorneys and counsellors whose admission to the Supreme Court bar is mentioned in the fine minutes are annotated at the time of their admission. For the members of the bar mentioned in this volume, we have supplied very brief identifications focusing on their previous bar admissions and their residences and activities at the time of admission to the Supreme Court bar; at the end of our series of volumes, we plan to print a directory of all attorneys with fuller biographies. Since case papers will be published in subsequent volumes in this series, case-related annotation, as well as all newspaper accounts focused narrowly upon particular cases, rather than on more general proceedings, will appear in those volumes.

We present the fine minutes, followed by the original minutes and the drafts of orders and motions in the hope that readers will compare them to achieve a better understanding of the development of the Court and its record-keeping. Our concern to save space in order to publish more documents precludes the presentation of related material on facing pages, even though such a format plainly would facilitate comparison. Furthermore, our decision to present minimal annotation dictates that we discuss these interrelationships only in a general structural framework, rather than focusing more specifically on textual comparisons.

D (DNA, RG 267, General Records). The minutes published here are from the first volume of manuscript engrossed minutes which extends from February term, 1790, through August term, 1805. Transcribed from the original document, rather than a photocopy.

1. See headnote to "Original Minutes" for more on the relationship of John Tucker's version of the fine minutes to the fine minutes published here.

At the Supreme Judicial Court of the United States,[1] begun and held at New York, (being the Seat of the national Government) on the first Monday of February, and on the first day of said month Anno Domini 1790. _

Present. _

The Honb!e John Jay Esquire Chief Justice

The Honb!e { William Cushing, and } Associate Justices _
{ James Wilson, Esq[rs][2] }

This being the day assigned by Law, for commencing the (first)[3] Sessions of the Supreme Court of the United States, and a sufficient Number of the Jus-
to form a quorum
tices ^ not being convened,[4] the Court is adjourned, by the Justices now present, untill to Morrow, at one of the Clock in the afternoon. _[5]

Tuesday, February 2nd, 1790. _

Present _

The Honb!e John Jay Esq[r] Chief Justice.

The Honb!e { William Cushing }
{ James Wilson, and } Associate Justices _
{ John Blair, Esq[rs] }

Proclamation is made and the Court is opened _

1. Presumably John Tucker, clerk of the Supreme Court, and, since 1783, a clerk of the Supreme Judicial Court of Massachusetts, from force of habit labeled the minutes of February 1, 1790, "Supreme Judicial Court of the United States" instead of Supreme Court. Tucker repeated the error at the opening of the August 1790 term.

2. Although the Court should have had six justices, only five were commissioned at this time. Robert H. Harrison had resigned on January 21, 1790, and James Iredell, who replaced him, was not commissioned until February 10. Justices John Blair and John Rutledge did not attend this session of the Court. Blair was present the next day; but Rutledge remained absent for the entire term. We do not know the reason for his absence, but it is mentioned by William Cushing and James Iredell. See "Commentaries," William Cushing to Charles Cushing, February 10, 1790; and James Iredell to Thomas Johnson, March 15, 1792, Thomas Johnson Letters, MdFre.

3. Parentheses surrounding the word "first" are in pencil. We are unable to determine whether or not they are contemporary.

4. The caret and interlined words "to form a quorum" are in pencil and may not be contemporary.

5. For newspaper coverage of the proceedings of this day, see "Commentaries," *Gazette of the United States* under date of February 3, 1790; *Independent Gazetteer* under date of February 3, 1790; and *Pennsylvania Packet* under date of February 6, 1790.

The New York Merchants Exchange where the Supreme Court first met. By an unknown artist. From a lost drawing. Courtesy Office of the Curator, Supreme Court of the United States.

Letters patent to the Honb^le John Jay Esquire, bearing date the 26th. day of September 1789. appointing him Chief Justice, of the Supreme Court of the United States,[6] are openly read, and published in Court. _

Letters patent to the Honb^le William Cushing Esquire, bearing date the 27th. day of September 1789. appointing him associate Justice of the Supreme Court of the United States, are openly read and published in Court. _

Letters patent to the Honb^le James Willson: Esquire, bearing date the 29th. day of September 1789. appointing him Associate Justice of the Supreme Court of the United States, are openly read and published in Court. _

Letters patent to the Honb^le John Blair Esquire bearing date the 30th_ day of September 1789. appointing him Associate Justice of the Supreme Court of the United States, are openly read and published in Court.

Letters patent to Edmund Randolph[7] of Virginia Esqr bearing date the 26th. day of September 1789. appointing him Attorney General for the United States[8] are openly read and published in Court.

6. Neither the Constitution nor "An Act to establish the Judicial Courts of the United States," September 24, 1789 (*Stat.*, 1:73-93), specified the exact title of the chief justice. The Judiciary Act of 1789 stated that "the supreme court of the United States shall consist of a chief justice and five associate justices" (ibid., p. 73), and each chief justice from John Jay through Morrison R. Waite (appointed 1874) was commissioned as "Chief Justice of the Supreme Court of the United States." From 1801 through 1863, congressional acts altering the number of justices on the Court continued to refer to the "Chief Justice." In addition, throughout this period "Chief Justice of the United States" appeared in judiciary-related legislation. On July 23, 1866, Congress enacted "An Act to fix the Number of Judges of the Supreme Court of the United States, and to change certain Judicial Circuits," in which the title became "Chief Justice of the United States" (ibid., 14:209). This title was repeated, in 1869, in "An Act to amend the Judicial System of the United States" (ibid., 16:44). After President Grant's 1874 commission of Morrison R. Waite under the older, more cumbersome title, each subsequent chief justice has been commissioned as "Chief Justice of the United States." William A. Richardson, "Chief Justice of the United States, or Chief Justice of the Supreme Court of the United States?," *New-England Historical and Genealogical Register*, 49 (1895): 275-79; Josiah M. Daniel, III, " 'Chief Justice of the United States': History and Historiography of the Title," *Supreme Court Historical Society Yearbook*, 1983, pp. 109-12.

7. Edmund Randolph (1753-1813) was attorney general of the United States from 1790 to 1794. In 1771 he had left the College of William and Mary to study law with his father, John Randolph, who was Virginia's attorney general. By 1774, Edmund Randolph had been admitted to practice before the Virginia General Court, the colony's highest court. John J. Reardon, *Edmund Randolph: A Biography* (New York: Macmillan, 1975), pp. 5, 12-15, 192, 248, 365.

8. The attorney general was understood by some to be an officer of the Court. On September 22, 1789, before the adoption of the Judiciary Act of 1789, Senator William Grayson of Virginia sent President Washington a letter recommending James Innes, Virginia's attorney general, for "the Office of Att^o general of the supreme Court" (George Washington Papers, DLC). The Judiciary Act of 1789, section 35, established the position of "attorney-general for the United States . . . whose duty it shall be to prosecute and conduct all suits in the Supreme Court in which the United States shall be concerned" (*Stat.*, 1:93). The letters patent of Edmund Randolph were read into the Court's record, and this was sufficient to enable him to practice before the Court either in a public or private capacity.

Edmund Randolph, the first attorney general of the United States, by an unknown artist. Oil on canvas, date unknown. Courtesy Virginia Historical Society.

Ordered, that Richard Wenman, be, and he is appointed Cryer of this Court.[9]

Adjourned untill to morrow at one of the Clock in the Afternoon. _ [10]

Wednesday February 3ʳᵈ 1789 _ 1790[11]

Present.

The Honbˡᵉ John Jay, Esquire Chief Justice.

The Honbˡᵉ ⎰ William Cushing ⎱
            ⎱ James Wilson and ⎰ Associate Justices.
            ⎰ John Blair, Esqures ⎱

Proclamation is made and the Court is opened.

Ordered, that John Tucker Esqⁱ[12] of Boston, be the Clerk of this Court. _ That he reside, and keep his Office at the Seat of the National Government, and that he do not practice either as an Attorney or a Counsellor in this Court while he shall continue to be Clerk of the same.

The said John Tucker in open Court, takes the Oath of Office by Law prescribed to be taken by the Clerk of the Court, and an Oath to support the Constitution of the United States; and also gives Bond (approved of by this Court to the United States, for the faithful discharge of his Duty as Clerk aforesaid, as by Law required.[13]

9. This is the only mention in the minutes of someone being appointed "Cryer" of the Court. The man appointed by the Court is probably Richard Wenman (fl. 1758-ca. 1793), listed as an upholsterer in the New York city directory of 1789. It is also possible that the crier appointed was the son of this man, also named Richard. (The Wenman family can be partially reconstructed from city directory entries in combination with incomplete parish records at Trinity Church in New York City.) The earliest record of the elder Richard Wenman is of his marriage to Ann Bush on January 1, 1758. Between 1772 and 1776, he received payment for various services rendered to the New York Supreme Court of Judicature, including "his Services as Cryer & Bell Ringer of the Supreme Court." In addition to his experience as a crier, the elder Wenman shared church contacts that may have led to his selection as crier of the Court. Chief Justice John Jay was a churchwarden of Trinity Church at this time, and John McKesson, who acted as clerk on the first day the Court convened, was involved in financial transactions with that church. "Register of Marriages," 1:29, 43, New York Trinity Church; *Collections of the New-York Historical Society* 31 (1898): 230–31; *Minutes of the Common Council of the City of New York, 1675–1776*, 8 vols. (New York: Dodd, Mead, 1905), 7:369, 457; 8:38, 83, 126, 135; "Minutes of the Vestry," 1:521-24, New York Trinity Church; Account Book, 1761-1798, pp. 99, 112-13, 116, John McKesson Papers, NHi.

Although no record survives of a new crier being appointed when the Court moved to Philadelphia, there is evidence that someone was paid to perform the task. Miscellaneous Treasury Accounts Nos. 5164, 6494, and 6793, RG 217, DNA.

10. For newspaper coverage of the proceedings of this day see, "Commentaries," *Gazette of the United States* under date of February 3, 1790; *Independent Gazetteer* under date of February 3, 1790; and *Pennsylvania Packet* under date of February 6, 1790.

11. "1790" is written in pencil and may not be contemporary.

12. For biographical sketch of John Tucker, see introduction to "The Clerks and Their Record."

13. The oath of office for the clerk and the provisions for bond were prescribed by law in the Judiciary Act of 1789, section 7 (*Stat.*, 1:76).

Ordered, that the Seal of this Court shall be the Arms of the United States, engraved on a circular piece of Steel of the Size of a Dollar, with these words in the Margin "The Seal of the Supreme Court of the United States"— And that the Seals of the Circuit Courts, shall be the Arms of the United States engraven on circular pieces of Silver of the Size of half a dollar, with these words in the Margin— Viz! In the upper part "the Seal of the circuit Court, in the lower part the name of the district for which it is intended.

Ordered, that the Clerk of this Court cause the before mentioned Seals to be made accordingly, and when done that he convey those for the Circuit Courts to the district Clerks respectively.

Adjourned to Friday the fifth day of February 1790.[14]

Friday February 5th— 1790.

Present.

The Honb!e John Jay Esq! Chief Justice.

The Honb!e ⎧ William Cushing ⎫
          ⎨ James Wilson, and ⎬ Associate Justices.
          ⎩ John Blair, Esq!s ⎭

Proclamation is made and the Court is opened.

Elias Boudinot[15] of New Jersey, Esq! ⎫
Thomas Hartley.[16] of Pennsylvania and ⎬
Richard Harrison[17] of New York Esq!s ⎭
are severally sworn as by Law required, and are admitted Counsellors of this Court.

14. For newspaper coverage of the proceedings of February 3, see "Commentaries," *Gazette of the United States* under date of February 6, 1790, and *Pennsylvania Packet* under date of February 6, 1790.

15. Elias Boudinot (1740-1821) in 1760 was licensed a counsellor and attorney at Elizabethtown, New Jersey. The Supreme Court of Pennsylvania admitted him to practice in 1770. At the time of his admission to the Supreme Court bar, Boudinot represented New Jersey in the United States House of Representatives. His brother, Elisha Boudinot, was admitted to the Supreme Court bar on February 9, 1790. *DAB; BDAC; MBBP,* p. 250.

16. Thomas Hartley (1748-1800) was admitted to the bars of Northampton and York Counties in Pennsylvania in 1769 and to the bar of the Supreme Court of Pennsylvania in 1779. A resident of York, Pennsylvania, Hartley was in New York as a representative to Congress from that state and became the first Pennsylvania lawyer to be admitted to the bar of the Supreme Court of the United States. *DAB;* Anton-Hermann Chroust, *The Rise of the Legal Profession in America,* 2 vols., (Norman: University of Oklahoma Press, 1965), 1:228-29; "Supreme Court List of Attorneys, 1742-1902," Records of the Eastern District, RG 33, PHarH; William C. Carter and A. J. Glossbrenner, *History of York County, Pennsylvania, from its Erection to the Present Time, 1729-1834,* 2d ed., enl. by A. Monroe Aurand, Jr. (Harrisburg: Aurand Press, 1930), p. 167.

17. Richard Nichols Harison (ca. 1747-1829) was practicing law in New York by 1767. The Supreme Court of Judicature of the province of New York admitted him to its bar on January 20, 1769, and, after a wartime suspension of his license, readmitted him to practice on April 21, 1786. He was attorney for the United States in the district of New York at the time he was sworn

Ordered, that (untill further Orders) it shall be requisite to the admission of Attorneys or Counsellors to practice in this Court; that they shall have been such for three Years past in the Supreme Courts of the State to which they respectively belong, and that their private and professional Character shall appear to be fair.

Ordered, that Counsellors shall not practice as Attornies; nor Attornies as Counsellors in this Court.[18]

Ordered, that they respectively take the following Oath, Viz! I   do solemnly swear that I will demean myself (as an Attorney or Counsellor) of the Court uprightly, and according to Law; and that I will support the Constitution of the United States.[19]

Ordered, that (unless and untill it shall be otherwise provided by Law) all Process of this Court. shall be in the Name of "the President of the United States—

Adjourned untill monday the Eighth day of Feb.ʸ 1790.[20]

Monday February 8th 1790.

Present.

The Honb:ᴵᵉ John Jay Esqʳ Chief Justice.

The Honb:ᴵᵉ { William Cushing
James Wilson, and
John Blair, Esqʳˢ } Associate Justices.

Proclamation is made and the Court is opened.

Egbert Benson—[21] John Lawrence—[22] Theodore Sedgwick—[23] William

---

a counsellor of the Supreme Court. *Officers and Graduates of Columbia College, General Catalogue, 1754-1894* (New York, 1894), pp. 85-86; *LPAH*, 1:311n; Paul M. Hamlin, *Legal Education in Colonial New York* (New York: New York University, Law Quarterly Review, 1939), p. 136.

18. Following English procedure and the practice of several states, the Supreme Court adopted a distinction between counsellors and attorneys. Only counsellors could plead a case before the Court. Attorneys could file motions and do other paperwork but could not conduct a case before the Court. On August 12, 1801, the Supreme Court changed this rule and ordered "that Counsellors may be admitted as Attornies in this Court, on taking the usual Oath." "Minutes of the Supreme Court of the United States, 1790-1805," General Records, RG 267, DNA.

19. Under a subsequent rule of February 7, 1791, counsellors and attorneys had the choice of taking an oath or an affirmation. See minutes of that date.

20. For newspaper coverage of the proceedings of February 5, see "Commentaries," *Gazette of the United States* under date of February 6, 1790, and *Pennsylvania Packet* under date of February 6, 1790.

21. Egbert Benson (1746-1833) was admitted in 1769 to the bar of the New York Supreme Court of Judicature. He practiced in New York City until 1772 when he moved to Red Hook in Dutchess County, New York. He was a congressman from New York when admitted to the Supreme Court bar. *BDAC; DAB.*

Smith‿[24] Morgan Lewis[‿][25] James Jackson‿[26] Fisher Ames‿[27] George Thacher[‿][28] Richard Varrick‿[29] and Robert Morris[30] Esq^{rs} are severally sworn according to Law, and admitted <u>Counsellors</u> of this Court.

22. John Laurance (1750-1810) was admitted to the bar in New York in 1772 and in January, 1775, to the bar of the Supreme Court of Judicature of that province. He was a congressman from New York City at the time of his admission to the bar of the Supreme Court of the United States. At the same time, he represented New York City in the state Senate and served as an alderman in New York City. John Schuyler, *Institution of the Society of the Cincinnati* (New York: Douglas Taylor, 1886), p. 242; *LPAH,* 1:292n; *DAB;* [Robert] Hodge, [Thomas] Allen, and [Samuel] Campbell, *The New-York Directory and Register for 1789* (New York, 1789).

23. At the time of his admission to the Supreme Court bar, Theodore Sedgwick (1746-1813) of Stockbridge was attending Congress as a representative from Massachusetts. First admitted to the Berkshire County, Massachusetts, bar in 1766, he was called as a barrister to the Supreme Judicial Court of Massachusetts in February, 1784, indicating an admission to practice as an attorney in that court two years earlier. *DAB;* Hollis R. Bailey, *Attorneys and their Admission to the Bar in Massachusetts* (Boston: William J. Nagel, 1907), p. 27.

24. William Loughton Smith (1758-1812) was admitted to the Charleston bar in 1784 and, at the time of his Supreme Court admission, was a member of Congress from South Carolina. *DAB;* George C. Rogers, Jr., *Evolution of a Federalist* (Columbia: University of South Carolina Press, 1962), pp. 26, 119, 167.

25. Morgan Lewis (1754-1844) graduated from the College of New Jersey (later Princeton) in 1773 and studied law under John Jay until interrupted by the revolution. He resumed his studies and was admitted to the bar of the Supreme Court of Judicature of New York in 1782. Lewis represented New York City in the state assembly at the time of his admission to the Supreme Court bar. *LPAH,* 1:293n; Hodge, Allen, and Campbell, *The New-York Directory* (1789); Richard A. Harrison, *Princetonians: A Biographical Dictionary,* vol. 2, *1769-1775* (Princeton: Princeton University Press, 1980), p. 311.

26. James Jackson (1757-1806), born in England, emigrated to Savannah at age fifteen. He was soon reading law and by 1776 had been named as the clerk of the Court of Common Sessions. By 1783 his private law practice was thriving. When admitted to the Supreme Court bar Jackson represented Georgia in the House of Representatives. William Omer Foster, Sr., *James Jackson: Duelist and Militant Statesman* (Athens: University of Georgia Press, 1960), pp. 1, 2, 25, 43, 182; Allen D. Candler, comp., *The Revolutionary Records of the State of Georgia,* vol. 1 (1908; reprint ed., New York: AMS Press, 1972), pp. 119, 277.

27. Fisher Ames (1758-1808) of Dedham, Massachusetts, was a member of the House of Representatives at the time of his admission to the bar of the Supreme Court. His first bar admission had been to the Court of Common Pleas in Suffolk County, Massachusetts, in 1781, and the Supreme Judicial Court of that state had admitted him in February, 1784. *DAB;* "Record-Book of the Suffolk [County] Bar," *Proceedings of the Massachusetts Historical Society* 19 (1881-1882): 155, 158.

28. George Thatcher (1754-1824) was called to the bar and began practice in York, District of Maine (Massachusetts), in 1778. At the time of his admission to the Supreme Court bar, he was a congressman from the District of Maine (Massachusetts). *BDAC.*

29. Richard Varick (1753-1831) was admitted to the bar in New York City on October 22, 1774. He was serving as mayor of New York City at the time of his admission to the Supreme Court bar. Charles Elliott Fitch, *Memorial Encyclopedia of the State of New York,* 3 vols. (New York: American Historical Society, 1916), 1:229; Hodge, Allen, and Campbell, *The New-York Directory* (1789); *DAB.*

30. Robert Morris (ca. 1745-1815) was admitted to the New Jersey bar in 1770 and licensed as a counsellor three years later. He was admitted to the Supreme Court bar in February, 1790; later that same year, the Senate consented to President Washington's nomination of Morris as a judge of the federal district court of New Jersey. *DAB; SEJ,* 1:63-64.

William Houston Esq[31] is also sworn as the Law directs, and is admitted an
Attorney of this Court.

Adjourned to Tuesday the ninth day of Feb[y] 1790.[32]

Tuesday February 9th. 1790.

Present.

The Honb[le] John Jay Esq[r] Chief Justice.

The Honb[le] ⎰ William Cushing ⎱
         ⎨ James Wilson and ⎬ Associate Justices.
         ⎰ John Blair, Esq[rs] ⎱

Proclamation is made and the Court is opened.

Samuel Jones_[33] Abraham Ogden_[34] Elisha Boudinot_[35] William Pater-

---

31. William Houstoun (1757-1812), licensed by the General Assembly of Georgia in 1782 to practice law, was elected to represent Georgia in the Confederation Congress from 1783 to 1786. He remained in New York to marry and practice law and was admitted to the New York bar on January 30, 1790, shortly before his admission to the Supreme Court bar. Edith Duncan Johnston, *The Houstouns of Georgia*, (Athens: University of Georgia Press, 1950), pp. 60, 318, 335, 339, 341; [Robert] Hodge, [Thomas] Allen, and [Samuel] Campbell, *The New-York Directory and Register for 1790* (New York, 1790).

32. The *Pennsylvania Mercury* (Philadelphia) on February 13, 1790, printed a fragmentary account of the proceedings of February 8. On February 18, 1790, the *Independent Chronicle* (Boston) noted the admission of three Massachusetts lawyers—Theodore Sedgwick, Fisher Ames, and George Thatcher—to the Supreme Court bar. Most newspapers, however, did not report the proceedings of February 8, 9, and 10, since the Court only admitted attorneys and counsellors on those days. After the Court's adjournment, newspapers published lists of the attorneys and counsellors admitted. See annotation for the parchment counsellor and attorney rolls.

33. Samuel Jones (1734-1819) was admitted to the bar of the Supreme Court of Judicature of New York on October 30, 1760. Following a wartime suspension of his license to practice, the highest court of the state readmitted him on April 29, 1786. At the time he was sworn a counsellor of the Supreme Court, he was New York City recorder and a representative of Queens County in the state Assembly. *DAB; LPAH*, 2:10n; Hodge, Allen, and Campbell, *The New-York Directory* (1789).

34. Abraham Ogden (1743-1798) graduated from the College of Philadelphia (later University of Pennsylvania) in 1761 and received his A.M. in 1765. He read law in New Jersey and by 1768 had been appointed surrogate for Morris County. Ogden moved his law office from Morristown to Newark after the Revolutionary War and was a member of the New Jersey legislature at the time of his admission to the Supreme Court bar. University of Pennsylvania, *Biographical Catalogue of the Matriculates of the College, 1749-1893* (Philadelphia, 1894), p. 8; E[dmund Drake] Halsey, *History of Morris County, New Jersey* (New York: W. W. Munsell, 1882), p. 24; William Ogden Wheeler, comp., *The Ogden Family in America*, ed. Lawrence Van Alstyne and Charles Burr Ogden (Philadelphia: J. B. Lippincott, 1907), pp. 103-4.

35. Elisha Boudinot (1749-1819) was licensed as a New Jersey counsellor in 1773. At the time of his admission to the Supreme Court bar, Boudinot practiced law in Newark, New Jersey. His brother, Elias Boudinot, had been admitted to the Supreme Court bar on February 5, 1790. J. J. Boudinot, ed., *The Life and Public Services, Addresses, and Letters of Elias Boudinot*, 2 vols. (Boston: Houghton, Mifflin, 1896), 2:392; 1:32; John Whitehead, *The Judicial and Civil History of New Jersey* (Boston: Boston History, 1897), p. 407; *DAB*, entry for Elias Boudinot.

son— [36] Ezekiel Gilbert— [37] and Cornelius [J], Bogert[38] Esq^{rs} are severally sworn as the Law directs, and are admitted as <u>Counsellors</u> of this Court.

Edward Livingston,[39] and Jacob Morton[40] Esq^{rs} are severally sworn according to Law, and admitted <u>Attornies</u> of this Court.

Adjourned untill February the tenth day, 1790.[41]

Wednesday Feby 10th. 1790.

Present.

The Honb^{le} John Jay Esqr Chief Justice.

The Honb^{le} $\left\{ \begin{array}{l} \text{William Cushing} \\ \text{James Wilson and} \\ \text{John Blair Esq}^{rs} \end{array} \right\}$ Associate Justices.

Proclamation is made and the Court is opened.

---

36. William Paterson (1745-1806), later associate justice of the United States Supreme Court, passed bar examinations in New Jersey in November, 1768, but was not licensed to practice law until the following month. Paterson served as New Jersey's attorney general during the Revolutionary War and represented New Jersey in the Senate when admitted to the Supreme Court bar. *DAB;* for information on Paterson passing his examination and receiving his license, see "Appointments to the Bench," headnote to "William Paterson: Appointment as Associate Justice in 1793."

37. Ezekiel Gilbert (1756-1841) was admitted to the bar of the Supreme Court of Judicature of New York on April 27, 1782. At the time of his admission to the Supreme Court bar, Gilbert represented Columbia County in the New York Assembly. *BDAC; LPAH,* 3:333n; Hodge, Allen, and Campbell, *The New-York Directory* (1789).

38. Cornelius J. Bogert (1754-1832) was admitted to the bar of the Supreme Court of Judicature of New York in October, 1775. The same year of his admission to the Supreme Court bar, he was elected to represent New York City in the state Assembly. Herbert S. Ackerman, *Five Bogert Families* (Ridgewood, New Jersey, 1950), p. 225; Hodge, Allen, and Campbell, *The New-York Directory* (1790).

39. Edward Livingston (1764-1836) was admitted to the bar of the Supreme Court of Judicature of New York in October, 1784. At the time of his admission to the bar of the Supreme Court, he lived in New York City and served as a clerk in the New York Court of Chancery. *DAB;* Donald M. Roper, ed., "The Elite of the New York Bar as seen from the Bench: James Kent's Necrologies," *The New-York Historical Society Quarterly* 56 (1972): 223; Hodge, Allen, and Campbell, *The New-York Directory* (1789).

40. Jacob Morton (1761-1836) was first called to the bar of the Supreme Court of Judicature of New Jersey in September term, 1782. He lived in New York City at the time of his admission to the bar of the Supreme Court of the United States. Richard A. Harrison, *Princetonians: A Biographical Dictionary,* vol. 3, *1776-1783* (Princeton: Princeton University Press, 1981), p. 236; Thomas E. V. Smith, *The City of New York in the Year of Washington's Inauguration, 1789* (New York, 1889), p. 25.

41. See note 32 above.

Bartholomew De Hart_[42] John Keep_[43] Peter Masterton,[44] and William Willcocks[45] Esq[rs] are now severally sworn as the Law directs, and are admitted Attornies of this Court.

New York February 10th. 1790_ Previous Proclamation being made, this Court is adjourned to the time and place appointed by Law.[46]

(signed.) "John Tucker Clk"[47]

At the Supreme Judicial Court of the United States,[48] begun and held at New York (being the Seat of the National Government) on the first Monday of August, and on the second day of said Month Anno. Domini 1790.

---

42. Balthazar DeHaert (ca. 1752-1830) was admitted to the bar of Orange County, New York, in 1773 and to the bar of the New York Supreme Court of Judicature on May 1 of the same year. DeHaert was a practicing lawyer and notary public in New York City when admitted to the Supreme Court bar. Franklin Ellis, *History of Monmouth County, New Jersey* (Philadelphia: R. T. Peck, 1885), p. 584; New Jersey Department of State, *New Jersey Index of Wills,* 3 vols. (1913; reprint ed., Baltimore: Genealogical Publishing, 1969), 2:1037; Samuel W. Eager, *An Outline History of Orange County* (Newburgh, New York: S. T. Callahan, 1846-1847), p. 646; Hodge, Allen, and Campbell, *The New-York Directory* (1789); *LPAH,* 1:1n.

Supreme Court clerk John Tucker misread Balthazar DeHaert's name from the attorney roll. DeHaert signed his first name as "Balth[r]," which was the common form of abbreviating Balthazar. See the parchment attorney roll published in this volume.

43. John W. Keese (1755-1809) was admitted to the bar of the New York Supreme Court of Judicature in April, 1786. At the time of his admission to the bar of the Supreme Court, he was a justice of the peace and a notary public. Schuyler, *Society of the Cincinnati,* p. 237; Hodge, Allen, and Campbell, *The New-York Directory* (1790); Smith, *City of New York,* p. 61.

The Court's clerk seems to have misread Keese's name on the attorney roll, which Keese signed as "J W Keese." The clerk apparently read the "se" at the end of the name as the letter "p."

44. Peter Masterton (baptized 1746) was called to the bar of the New York Supreme Court of Judicature in 1787. When admitted to the Supreme Court bar he practiced law in New York. William M. MacBean, *Biographical Register of St. Andrew's Society of the State of New York,* 2 vols. (New York, 1922-1925), 1:292; Hodge, Allen, and Campbell, *The New-York Directory* (1789).

45. William Wilcocks (1750-1826) was admitted to practice as an attorney in the Supreme Court of Judicature of New York on April 13, 1774. When sworn at the bar of the Supreme Court he resided in New York City and was a justice of the peace. Harrison, *Princetonians,* 2:54, 58; Hodge, Allen, and Campbell, *The New-York Directory* (1789).

46. See note 32 above. See also in "Commentaries," the *Federal Gazette* and *New-York Journal* under date of February 11, 1790.

47. Quotation marks were placed around John Tucker's name because the fine minutes published here were transcribed after he left office and the signature is not Tucker's. See headnotes to the "Fine Minutes" and the "Original Minutes."

48. See note 1 above.

Present.

The Honb^{le} John Jay Esqr Chief Justice.

The Honb^{le} { William Cushing
James Wilson
John Blair and
James Iredell Esq^{rs49} } Associate Justices.

Proclamation is made and the Court is opened.

Letters patent to the Honb^{le} James Iredell Esqr bearing date the 10th. day of February 1790. appointing him one of the Associate Justices of this Court; are openly read and published in Court.

Ordered, that the Clerk of this Court procure a Seal for the Circuit Court of the State of Rhode Island and Providence Plantations, similar to the circuit Seals ordered the last Term,[50] and when done that he cause the same to be conveyed to the Clerk of the district of Said State. &c.[51]

Richard Bassett,[52] and John Vining[53] Esq^{rs} are severally sworn as the Law directs, and are admitted Counsellors of this Court.

Adjourned to Tuesday the 3rd. day of August 1790.

Tuesday August 3d. 1790.

Present.

The Honb^{le} John Jay Esqr Chief Justice.

The Honb^{le} { William Cushing
James Wilson
John Blair, and
James Iredell Esq^{rs} } Associate Justices.

Proclamation is made and the Court is opened.

Barnabas Bidwell Esqr[54] is sworn as the Law directs and is admitted a Counsellor of this Court.

49. In a letter to Thomas Johnson on March 15, 1792, James Iredell stated that Rutledge was in New York but "confined with the gout" and unable to attend the Court. Thomas Johnson Letters, MdFre.

50. See minutes for February 3, 1790.

51. Rhode Island ratified the Constitution on May 29, 1790, thus joining the union.

52. Richard Bassett (1745-1815) was admitted to the bar of the Supreme Court of Delaware in or about 1778. At the time of his admission to the Supreme Court bar, Bassett was a senator from Delaware. See "Certificates and Character References," Certificate and Character Reference of Richard Bassett, Admitted as a Counsellor August 2, 1790; DAB.

53. John Vining (1758-1802) was admitted to the bar of New Castle County, Delaware, in 1782 and, at the time of his Supreme Court bar admission, was a congressman from Delaware. BDAC; J Thomas Scharf, History of Delaware, 1609-1888, 2 vols. (1888; reprint ed., Port Washington, N.Y.: Kennikat Press, 1972), 1:563.

New York, August 3d. 1790. Previous Proclamation being made, this Court is adjourned, next to meet at the time and place prescribed by Law.

Sign'd "John Tucker Clk"[55]

At the Supreme Court of the United States begun and held at Philadelphia (being the Seat of the national Government) on the first Monday of February and on the Seventh day of said month Anno Domini. 1791 —

Present.

The Honb^{le} John Jay Esqr Chief Justice.

The Honb^{le} { William Cushing
James Wilson, and
James Iredell Esq^{rs56} } Associate Justices.

Proclamation is made and the Court is opened.

Ordered, that the Counsellors and Attornies admitted to practice in this Court shall take either an Oath, or in proper Cases, an Affirmation of the Tenor prescribed by the Rule of this Court on that Subject made in February Term 1790.[57] Viz^t I   do solemnly swear or affirm (as the Case may be) that I will demean myself as an Attorney or Counsellor of this Court uprightly and according to Law; and that I will support the Constitution of the. United States.

William Lewis Esq^{r58} is affirmed according to the Order of Court, and is admitted to practice as a Counsellor of said Court.

54. Admitted to the bar of the Supreme Court on the basis of his experience in Connecticut, Barnabas Bidwell (1763-1833) immediately thereafter practiced law in Stockbridge, Massachusetts. He was admitted to the bar in Berkshire County, Massachusetts, in 1790 and to the bar of the Supreme Judicial Court of that state in October, 1794. See "Certificates and Character References," Certificate and Character Reference of Barnabas Bidwell, Admitted as a Counsellor August 3, 1790; William T. Davis, *History of the Judiciary of Massachusetts* (1900; reprint ed., New York: Da Capo Press, 1974), p. 287; Supreme Judicial Court [Record], 1794, p. 245, MBSufC; *DAB.*

55. See note 47 above.

56. John Blair was too ill to attend this session of Court (see "Commentaries," John Blair to Samuel Meredith, February 9, 1791). John Rutledge, elected chief justice of South Carolina on February 15, 1791 (Journal of the South Carolina House of Representatives, January 3, 1791-February 19, 1791, pp. 247-48, ScCAH), sent President Washington his resignation from the Supreme Court on March 5, 1791 (see "Appointments to the Bench," John Rutledge: Appointment as an Associate Justice in 1789).

57. See rule of February 5, 1790.

58. William Lewis (1751-1819) was admitted to the Philadelphia bar in 1773, to the Supreme Court of the province of Pennsylvania bar in 1776, and to the Supreme Court of Pennsylvania bar in 1778. At the time of his admission to the bar of the Supreme Court of the United States, he was the United States attorney for the district of Pennsylvania and a resident of Philadelphia. Lewis affirmed rather than swore because he was a member of the Society of Friends. *DAB;* William Primrose, "Biography of William Lewis," *Pennsylvania Magazine of History and Biography* 20 (April 1896): 32; "Supreme Court List of Attorneys, 1742-1902," Records of the Eastern District, RG 33, PHarH; Clement Biddle, ed., *The Philadelphia Directory* (Philadelphia: James & Johnson, 1791).

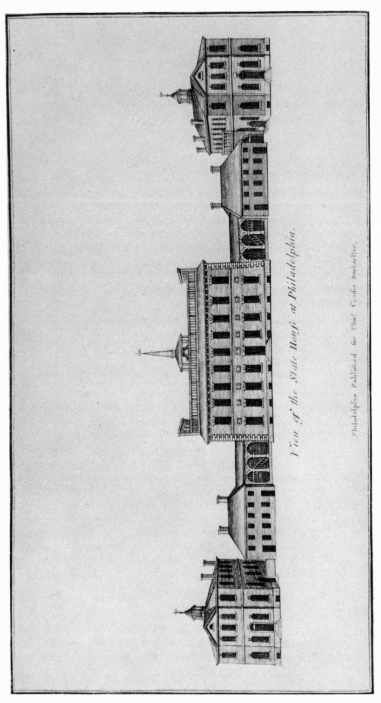

View of the State House at Philadelphia.

Philadelphia Published for Thos' Condie Bookseller.

View of the State House at Philadelphia. This engraving (1798) depicts the State House (center), where the Supreme Court met for its February 1791 term; it also includes a view of the City Hall (far left) where the Court was to meet for the rest of its sessions in Philadelphia. Attributed to Joseph Bowes (? - ?). Courtesy Library Company of Philadelphia.

William Bradford Junior,[59] and Alexander Willcocks[60] Esq^{rs} having been proposed by the Attorney General of the United States[61] for admission as Counsellors of this Court, they are sworn agreably to the Order thereof, and are admitted to practice accordingly.

Miers Fisher Esqr[62] having been proposed by the said Attorney General for Admission as a Counsellor of this Court he is affirmed agreably to the Order thereof and is admitted to practice accordingly.

Jonathan Dickinson Sergeant_[63] Jared Ingersoll_[64] Edward Tilghman,[65] and

---

59. William Bradford, Jr. (1755-1795), admitted to the York County, Pennsylvania, bar in 1779 and to the Supreme Court of Pennsylvania bar in 1780, was attorney general of Pennsylvania and a resident of Philadelphia at the time of his admission to the bar of the Supreme Court of the United States. *DAB;* John Gibson, ed., *History of York County Pennsylvania . . .* (Chicago: F. A. Battey, 1886), p. 436; "Supreme Court List of Attorneys, 1742-1902," Records of the Eastern District, RG 33, PHarH; Biddle, *The Philadelphia Directory* (1791); James Hardie, ed., *The Philadelphia Directory and Register,* 2d ed., (Philadelphia: Jacob Johnson, 1794).

60. In 1765 Alexander Wilcocks (1741-1801) was admitted to the bars of Northampton and York Counties in Pennsylvania and then to practice in the Supreme Court of the province of Pennsylvania. During the revolution, in 1778, the state Supreme Court readmitted him to the reorganized bar. At the time of his admission to the bar of the Supreme Court of the United States, Wilcocks was a resident of Philadelphia and its city recorder. University of Pennsylvania, *Biographical Catalogue* (1894), p. 8; Chroust, *Rise of the Legal Profession,* 1:228-29; Carter and Glossbrenner, *History of York County,* p. 58; "Supreme Court List of Attorneys, 1742-1902," Records of the Eastern District, RG 33, PHarH; Biddle, *The Philadelphia Directory* (1791).

61. During the two terms that the Court met in New York, in February and August, 1790, the justices admitted attorneys and counsellors without requiring that the admission be moved by anyone. This is the first instance of an admission being so moved. For a further discussion of the changes in procedure surrounding admission to the bar, see the introduction to "Admission to the Bar."

62. Miers Fisher (1748-1819), a resident of Philadelphia and a member of its Common Council at the time of his admission to the bar of the Supreme Court of the United States. In 1769 he was admitted to the bars of New Castle, Kent, and Sussex Counties in Delaware. He became a member of the bar of the Supreme Court of the province of Pennsylvania in 1770 and after the Revolution was readmitted in 1787. Fisher was a member of the Society of Friends. J. W. Jordan, ed., *Colonial Families of Philadelphia,* 2 vols. (New York: Lewis Publishing, 1911), 1:667-68; Biddle, *The Philadelphia Directory* (1791); "Supreme Court List of Attorneys, 1742-1902," Records of the Eastern District, RG 33, PHarH; Abraham Ritter, *Philadelphia and Her Merchants* (Philadelphia, 1860), p. 183.

63. Jonathan Dickinson Sergeant (1746-1793) was admitted to the New Jersey bar around 1765, to the Northampton County, Pennsylvania, bar in 1777, and to the bar of the Supreme Court of that state in 1778. At the time of his admission to the Supreme Court of the United States bar, he was a resident of Philadelphia. Edwin F. Halfield, "Jonathan Dickinson Sergeant," *Pennsylvania Magazine of History and Biography* 2 (1878): 438-41; John W. Jordan, ed., *Colonial and Revolutionary Families of Pennsylvania: Genealogical and Personal Memoirs,* 3 vols. (New York: Lewis Publishing, 1911), 2:657-58; Chroust, *Rise of the Legal Profession,* 1:228-29; "Supreme Court List of Attorneys, 1742-1902," Records of the Eastern District, RG 33, PHarH; Biddle, *The Philadelphia Directory* (1791).

64. Jared Ingersoll (1749-1822), admitted to the bar of the Supreme Court of the province of Pennsylvania in 1773 and, in 1779, readmitted to the Supreme Court of Pennsylvania, was a resident of Philadelphia and a member of its Common Council at the time of his admission to the

James Munroe[66] Esq.[rs.] having been proposed by the Attorney General of the United States for admission as Counsellors of this Court they are sworn agreably to the Order thereof and are admitted to practice accordingly.

Adjourned to Tuesday the 8th. day of February 1791.[67]

Tuesday February 8th. 1791.

Present.

The Honb[le] John Jay Esq[r] Chief Justice.

The Honb[le] { William Cushing
James Wilson, and
James Iredell Esq[rs.] } Associate Justices.

Proclamation is made and the Court is opened.

The Chief Justice laid before the Court a Letter he had received from the Judge of the district Court. of New York, which was read and is in the words following Viz[t] district of New York, January 20th. 1791 — Sir,
On complaint of the Collector, and proof on Oath, I committed Josiah Goreham Master of the Sloop Hiram to the Goal of this City on the 12th. of November last for a Breach of the Revenue Laws aggravated by Perjury — Charles Seely his. mate had, a few days before been committed for landing and storing a Quantity of Coffee before Report or Entry, and in the Night time; and both have ever since remained in Confinement for want of Sureties

---

bar of the Supreme Court of the United States. Franklin Bowditch Dexter, *Biographical Sketches of the Graduates of Yale College with Annals of the College History,* 6 vols. (New York: Henry Holt, 1885-1912), 3:184-85; "Supreme Court List of Attorneys, 1742-1902," Records of the Eastern District, RG 33, PHarH; Biddle, *The Philadelphia Directory* (1791); James Hardie, ed., *The Philadelphia Directory and Register* (Philadelphia: T. Dobson, 1793).

65. Edward Tilghman (1751-1815), admitted to the bar of the Supreme Court of the province of Pennsylvania in 1774 and readmitted, in 1785, to the Supreme Court of that state, resided in Philadelphia at the time of his admission to the Supreme Court of the United States bar. *DAB;* "Supreme Court List of Attorneys, 1742-1902," Records of the Eastern District, RG 33, PHarH; Biddle, *The Philadelphia Directory* (1791).

66. James Monroe (1758-1831), later to become the fifth president of the United States, was licensed to practice law by Virginia in June, 1782. At the time of his admission to the Supreme Court bar, Monroe was a senator from Virginia. *DAB;* Wilmer L. Hall, ed., *Journal of the Council of the State of Virginia,* vol. 3, *December 1, 1781-November 29, 1784* (Richmond: Virginia State Library, 1952), p. 108.

67. The *Gazette of the United States* (Philadelphia) of February 9, 1791, and the *Boston Gazette* of February 21, 1791, carried brief articles on the opening of the Court. The *Connecticut Courant* (Hartford), March 7, 1791, and the *New-Hampshire Gazette* (Portsmouth), March 12, 1791, noted the Court's opening and the absence of justices. See "Commentaries," *Gazette of the United States* under date of February 23, 1791, for an article listing the lawyers admitted to the Supreme Court bar on February 7 and 8.

for their appearance. An under Officer of the Customs was, about the time of. the removal of Congress, suspended by the Secretary of the Treasury for mal- conduct in pemitting Goods to be landed after Sunset— As there are Circum- stances which, in the Opinion of the principal Officers, rendered any criminal Intention questionable; it was determined that a Judicial Enqury should pre- cede his Removal or Restoration. In the mean time, deprived of the means of Subsistence, he is importunate for a Tryal— Each of these Cases,[68] and in gen- eral every Offence made subject to fine or corporal Punishment, one only excepted, are excluded from the Authority of the district Court by the Extent of the Punishment;[69] and it's criminal Cognizance thus circumscribed, is a Bur- then to the Community without any public Advantage— I think it therefore my duty to make this Representation, that if the Supreme Court should con- ceive it proper, a special Circuit Court may be appointed for this district, and the Prisoners as the suspended Officer, be punished or relieved as Justice shall require. I have the honor to be, with great Respect, sir, Your most obedient humble Servant

James Duane.

Honorable
The Chief Justice of the United States.

Thereupon Ordered, that a special Sessions of the Circuit Court be held at the City of New York in and for the district of New York on the twenty first day of February instant next;[70] and that authenticated Copies of this Order be trans- mitted by the Clerk of this Court to the Judge and the Clerk of the said district Court and to the Attorney of the United States for the said District.

It appearing from the Information of the Attorney General that divers persons charged with Offences against the Laws of the United States are now confined in the Goal of the City of Philadelphia,[71] and that as well for the Relief of the

---

68. The cases that required a special circuit court in New York were: *United States v. Seven Barrels of Coffee and One Barrel and One Keg of Muscovado Sugar* (Minutes, November 5, 6, and 22, 1790, and Admiralty Case Files, DC New York, RG 21, NjBaFAR); *United States v. Josiah Gorham, Jr., United States v. Asa Waugh, United States v. Charles Seely* (Minutes, November 5, 6, and 22, 1790, DC New York, RG 21, NjBaFAR; and Minutes, February 22-23, 1791, CCD New York, RG 21, NjBaFAR); *United States v. Samuel Dodge* (Minutes, February 22-23, 1791, CCD New York, RG 21, NjBaFAR).

69. The jurisdiction of the district courts was established in the Judiciary Act of 1789, section 9. *Stat.*, 1:76-77.

70. Section 5 of the Judiciary Act of 1789 empowered the Supreme Court to order special sessions of the circuit courts. *Stat.*, 1:75.

71. William Noble and Luther Stevenson were in jail in Philadelphia, charged with murder on the high seas. *United States v. William Noble and Luther Stevenson.* Minutes, February 21-22, 1791, and Criminal Case Files, CCD Pennsylvania, RG 21, PPFAR.

said Persons as of certain Seafaring men who are detained as Witnesses, it would be expedient that a special Sessions of the Circuit Court should be speedily held; Ordered that a special Sessions of the said Court for the trial of criminal Causes be held at the city of Philadelphia in and for the district of Pennsylvania on the twenty first day of February instant, next, and that authenticated Copies of this Order be transmitted by the Clerk of this Court to the Judge, and the clerk of the said district Court, and to the Attorney of the United States for the said district.

Edward Burd _ [72] Luther Martin _ [73] William Barton _ [74] Moses Levy _ [75] John F Mifflin _ [76] and Charles Heatly[77] Esqrs having been proposed by the Attorney

72. Edward Burd (1751-1833) was admitted to the Northampton County, Pennsylvania, bar in 1772. The Supreme Court of the province of Pennsylvania admitted him to practice in 1774 and readmitted him in 1778 following the establishment of the state Supreme Court bar. At the time of his admission to the bar of the Supreme Court of the United States, he was a resident of Philadelphia and prothonotary of the Supreme Court of Pennsylvania. Jordan, *Colonial Families of Philadelphia*, 1:106; Chroust, *Rise of the Legal Profession*, 1:229; "Supreme Court List of Attorneys, 1742-1902," Records of the Eastern District, RG 33, PHarH; J. Thomas Scharf and Thompson Westcott, *History of Philadelphia, 1609-1884*, vol. 2 (Philadelphia: L. H. Everts, 1884), p. 1559; Biddle, *The Philadelphia Directory* (1791).

73. Luther Martin (1748-1826) passed the Virginia bar in 1771 and began a full-time practice on the Eastern Shore of Virginia and Maryland in 1772. At the time of his admission to the bar of the Supreme Court, Martin was the attorney general of Maryland. Paul S. Clarkson and R. Samuel Jett, *Luther Martin of Maryland* (Baltimore: Johns Hopkins University Press, 1970), pp. 11, 303, 28, 33, 167.

74. William Barton (1755-1817) was admitted to the York County, Pennsylvania, bar in April, 1775, and to the Supreme Court of Pennsylvania bar in October, 1779. At the time of his admission to the bar of the Supreme Court of the United States, he resided in Philadelphia. E. A. J. Johnson, *The Foundations of American Economic Freedom: Government and Enterprise in the Age of Washington* (Minneapolis: University of Minnesota Press, 1973), p. 13; Gibson, *History of York County*, p. 436; *MBBP*, p. 247; U.S., Department of Commerce and Labor, Bureau of the Census, *Heads of Families at the First Census of the United States Taken in the Year 1790: Pennsylvania* (Washington, D.C.: Government Printing Office, 1908).

75. Moses Levy (1757-1826), admitted to the Philadelphia bar in 1778 and to the Pennsylvania Supreme Court bar in 1780, was a resident of Philadelphia at the time of his admission to the Supreme Court of the United States bar. *Catalogue of the Trustees Officers and Graduates of the . . . University of Pennsylvania, 1749-1880* (Philadelphia: Society of the Alumni, 1880), p. 31; *MBBP*, p. 287; "Supreme Court List of Attorneys, 1742-1902," Records of the Eastern District, RG 33, PHarH; Biddle, *The Philadelphia Directory* (1791).

76. John F. Mifflin (1759-1813) was admitted to the Philadelphia bar in 1779 and to the Supreme Court of Pennsylvania bar in 1781. At the time of his admission to the Supreme Court of the United States bar, he lived in Philadelphia. *University of Pennsylvania Catalogue, 1749-1880*, p. 31; *MBBP*, p. 294; "Supreme Court List of Attorneys, 1742-1902," Records of the Eastern District, RG 33, PHarH; Biddle, *The Philadelphia Directory* (1791).

77. Charles Heatly (d. 1814), a minister's son from Dublin, was admitted to the Irish bar in 1776, to the bar of the Philadelphia Court of Common Pleas in March, 1782, and to the Supreme Court of Pennsylvania bar in 1783. He was a Philadelphia attorney at the time of his admission to the Supreme Court bar. *MBBP*, p. 277; George Dames Burtchaell and Thomas Ulick Sadleir,

General of the United States, for admission as Counsellors of this Court, they are sworn agreably to the Order thereof and are admitted to practice accordingly.

William Rawle Esq![78] having been proposed by the said Attorney General for admission as a counsellor of this Court, he is affirmed agreably to the Order thereof, and is admitted to practice accordingly.

Jasper Moylan _ [79] Alexander J. Dallas _ [80] Thomas Leaming Junior,[81] and Peter S. du Ponceau[82] Esq![s] having been proposed by the said Attorney General for admission as Counsellors of this Court, they are sworn agreably to the order thereof and are admitted to practice accordingly.

eds., *Alumni Dublinenses: A Register of the Students, Graduates, Professors, and Provosts of Trinity College, in the University of Dublin* (London: Williams and Norgate, 1924), p. 386; "Supreme Court List of Attorneys, 1742-1902," Records of the Eastern District, RG 33, PHarH; Biddle, *The Philadelphia Directory* (1791).

78. William Rawle (1759-1836), a descendant of prominent Quaker families and an active member of the Society of Friends, was admitted to the Philadelphia bar in 1783 and to the Supreme Court of Pennsylvania bar in 1784. At the time of his admission to the bar of the Supreme Court of the United States, Rawle lived in Philadelphia. *DAB;* "Supreme Court List of Attorneys, 1742-1902," Records of the Eastern District, RG 33, PHarH; Biddle, *The Philadelphia Directory* (1791).

79. Jasper Alexander Moylan (ca. 1759-1812) was admitted to the Philadelphia bar in 1782 and to the Supreme Court of Pennsylvania bar in 1784. He was a Philadelphia resident at the time of his admission to the Supreme Court of the United States bar. Philadelphia *Aurora,* February 13, 1812; John H. Campbell, *History of the Friendly Sons of St. Patrick and of the Hibernian Society for the Relief of Emigrants from Ireland. March 17, 1771-March 17, 1892* (Philadelphia: Hibernian Society, 1892), p. 123; *MBBP,* p. 296; "Supreme Court List of Attorneys, 1742-1902," Records of the Eastern District, RG 33, PHarH; Biddle, *The Philadelphia Directory* (1791).

80. Alexander James Dallas (1759-1817), a resident of Philadelphia and secretary of the Commonwealth of Pennsylvania at the time of his admission to the Supreme Court of the United States bar, was admitted to the bar of Jamaica around 1780 and to the Supreme Court of Pennsylvania bar in 1785. *DAB;* Biddle, *The Philadelphia Directory* (1791); Hardie, *The Philadelphia Directory* (1793).

81. Thomas Leaming, Jr. (1748-1797), admitted to the New Jersey bar in 1772 and to the Supreme Court of Pennsylvania bar in 1787, lived in Philadelphia at the time of his admission to the Supreme Court of the United States bar. Jordan, *Colonial and Revolutionary Families of Pennsylvania,* 3:1222, 1224; "Supreme Court List of Attorneys, 1742-1902," Records of the Eastern District, RG 33, PHarH; Biddle, *The Philadelphia Directory* (1791).

82. Peter Stephen Du Ponceau (1760-1844) was a resident of Philadelphia, a notary public, and a "sworn interpreter" at the time of his admission to the Supreme Court of the United States bar. Du Ponceau had been admitted to the Philadelphia bar in 1785 and to the bar of the Supreme Court of Pennsylvania in 1786. *DAB;* Biddle, *The Philadelphia Directory* (1791); Hardie, *The Philadelphia Directory* (1793); "Supreme Court List of Attorneys, 1742-1902," Records of the Eastern District, RG 33, PHarH.

John Todd Junr Esq^{r83} having been proposed as aforesaid for admission as a Counsellor of this Court, he is affirmed according to their Order and is admitted to practice accordingly.

Joseph Anderson___[84] Joseph B. McKean[85] and Benjamin Chew Jun^{r86} Esq^{rs} having been proposed by the Attorney General aforesaid for admission as Counsellors of this Court, they are sworn agreable to the Order of Court and admitted to practice accordingly.

John Caldwell,[87] and Benjamin R, Morgan[88] Esq^{rs} having been proposed by the said Attorney General for admission as attornies of this Court, the said John is sworn, and the said Benjamin is affirmed according to the Order of Court and are admitted to practice accordingly.

83. John Todd, Jr. (1763-1793), a young Quaker lawyer, was admitted to the Philadelphia bar in 1785 and to the Supreme Court of Pennsylvania bar in 1787. Todd was a resident of Philadelphia at the time of his admission to the Supreme Court bar. Lyman H. Butterfield, ed., *Letters of Benjamin Rush,* 2 vols. (Princeton: Princeton University Press, 1951), 2:725n; *MBBP,* p. 318; "Supreme Court List of Attorneys, 1742-1902," Records of the Eastern District, RG 33, PHarH; Biddle, *The Philadelphia Directory* (1791).

84. Joseph Anderson (1757-1837) was admitted to the bar of New Castle County, Delaware, on November 24, 1785, and then to the Pennsylvania Supreme Court bar in April, 1787 (see "Certificates and Character References," Certificate of Sixteen Individuals, Admitted as Attorneys or Counsellors February 8, 1791). Anderson practiced law in Delaware through 1791. Less than three weeks after his admission to the Supreme Court bar, he was appointed a federal judge for that portion of the Ohio Territory now called Tennessee. *DAB;* Scharf, *History of Delaware,* 1:563.

85. Joseph Borden McKean (1764-1826) was admitted to the Chester County, Pennsylvania, bar in 1785 and to the Supreme Court of Pennsylvania bar in 1787. He lived in Philadelphia at the time of his admission to the bar of the Supreme Court of the United States. Frank M. Eastman, *Courts and Lawyers of Pennsylvania: A History, 1623-1923,* 3 vols. (New York: American Historical Society, 1922), 2:566; "Supreme Court List of Attorneys, 1742-1902," Records of the Eastern District, RG 33, PHarH; Biddle, *The Philadelphia Directory* (1791).

86. Benjamin Chew, Jr. (1758-1844), was admitted to the Philadelphia bar in 1786 and to the bar of the Supreme Court of Pennsylvania in 1787. At the time of his admission to the Supreme Court of the United States bar, he resided in Philadelphia. Jordan, *Colonial and Revolutionary Families of Pennsylvania,* 1:512; *MBBP,* p. 256; "Supreme Court List of Attorneys, 1742-1902," Records of the Eastern District, RG 33, PHarH; Biddle, *The Philadelphia Directory* (1791).

87. John Caldwell (ca. 1759-1820) was admitted to the Philadelphia bar in 1783 and to the Pennsylvania Supreme Court bar in 1785. Caldwell was a Philadelphia resident at the time of his admission to the Supreme Court bar. Baltimore *American,* April 26, 1820; *MBBP,* p. 254; "Supreme Court List of Attorneys, 1742-1902," Records of the Eastern District, RG 33, PHarH; Biddle, *The Philadelphia Directory* (1791).

88. Benjamin R. Morgan (ca. 1764-1840) was admitted to the Philadelphia bar in 1785 and to the Supreme Court of Pennsylvania bar in 1787. He lived in Philadelphia at the time of his admission to the Supreme Court of the United States bar and belonged to the Philadelphia Monthly Meeting of the Society of Friends. Eastman, *Courts and Lawyers of Pennsylvania,* 2:566-67; *MBBP,* p. 295; "Supreme Court List of Attorneys, 1742-1902," Records of the Eastern District, RG 33, PHarH; Biddle, *The Philadelphia Directory* (1791); William Wade Hinshaw, ed., *Encyclopedia of American Quaker Genealogy,* 6 vols. (1936-1950; reprint ed., Baltimore: Genealogical Publishing, 1969-1973), vol. 2, *Pennsylvania and New Jersey,* Thomas Worth Marshall, comp. (Baltimore: Genealogical Publishing, 1969), p. 601.

Nicholas and Jacob Vanstaphorst
  v̄s
State of Maryland.

The Marshall of the district of Maryland returns on the Summons in this Cause that he has in Obedience to the Writ caused to be summoned the State of Maryland by serving a copy of the said Process, on the Governor and Executive Council and Attorney General of said State in presence of <u>Joshua Barney</u> and <u>Robert Dorsey.</u>

Luther Martin Esq.ʳ Attorney General of the State of Maryland, having in Court directed John Caldwell Esq.ʳ to enter an appearance for the said State of Maryland; on motion of Edmund Randolph Esq.ʳ Attorney General for the United States, of Council for the plaintiffs, Ordered that the said appearance be entered, and on like motion it was Ordered by the Court, that the said State, plead in two months from the second day of this term or Judgment.

Philadelphia February 8th. 1791. This Court is adjourned, next to meet at the time and place appointed by Law.[89]

Sign'd "John Tucker Clk"[90]

At the Supreme Court of the United States, begun and held at Philadelphia (being the Seat of the National Government) on the first Monday in August and on the first day of the said Month, Anno Domini 1791.[91]

Present.

The Honb.ˡᵉ John Jay Esq.ʳ Chief Justice.

The Honb.ˡᵉ { William Cushing / James Wilson / John Blair and / James Iredell Esq.ʳˢ[92] } Associate Justices.

Proclamation is made and the Court is opened.

---

89. See "Commentaries," *Gazette of the United States* under date of February 23, 1791, for an article listing the lawyers admitted to the Supreme Court bar on February 7 and 8.

90. See note 47 above.

91. The minutes do not mention where the Court met. Newspapers reporting on the first day of the Court's proceedings, however, recorded that the Court had convened "at the new City-Hall." This report appeared in the *Federal Gazette* (Philadelphia) on August 2, 1791, and was reprinted in the *Boston Gazette* on August 15, 1791. A variant of this report appeared in the *Gazette of the United States* (Philadelphia) on August 3, 1791. The Court's meeting place was mentioned also in a brief article in the *General Advertiser* (Philadelphia), August 2, 1791. For further discussion of the Court's meeting places see note 112 below.

92. Only five justices held commissions at the beginning of this term. John Rutledge had resigned the previous March. See note 56 above.

Ordered, that Samuel Bayard[93] be the Clerk of this Court in the place of John Tucker Esquire of Boston resigned; he is accordingly directed to give bond as by Law directed, and is sworn to the faithful discharge of all the duties of his Office, and to support the Constitution of the United States.

On motion of the Attorney General John D. Coxe Esq[94] is admitted to practice as a Counsellor of this Court and is sworn according to Law, and order.

Nicholas & Jacob Vanstaphorst Pltffs
    vs   } In Case.
The State of Maryland Defd!

The Attorney General being of Council for the Plaintiffs moved the Court for a Commission to take the Depositions of certain Witnesses residing in Holland, with the consent of the Attorney and Counsel[95] on the part of the Defendant State.
The Court refused the Commission untill the Commissioners should be named.

The Court adjourned 'till to Morrow at ten oClock.

Tuesday August 2nd 1791.

Present.

The Honble John Jay Esquire Chief Justice.

The Honble { William Cushing
James Wilson
John Blair and
James Iredell Esqrs } Associate Justices—

Proclamation is made and the Court is opened.

On Petition David Leonard Barns Esquire[96] of Taunton in the State of Mas-

---

93. For a biographical sketch of Samuel Bayard, see the introduction to "The Clerks and Their Record."

94. John D. Coxe (1752-1824) was admitted to the Supreme Court of Pennsylvania bar in 1778. At the time of his admission to the bar of the Supreme Court of the United States, Coxe resided in Philadelphia. *University of Pennsylvania Catalogue, 1749-1880*, p. 30; *MBBP*, p. 260; "Supreme Court List of Attorneys, 1742-1902," Records of the Eastern District, RG 33, PHarH; Biddle, *The Philadelphia Directory* (1791); Hardie, *The Philadelphia Directory* (1793).

95. "Counsel" originally was spelled "Council," but "se" was written over the "ci."

96. David Leonard Barnes (1760-1812) was living in Taunton, Massachusetts, at the time of his admission to the Supreme Court bar. He had been admitted to the bar of the Court of Common Pleas in Suffolk County, Massachusetts, in July, 1783, and to the bar of the Supreme Judicial Court of that state in February, 1786. Judicial Conference of the United States, Bicentennial Committee, *Judges of the United States* (Washington, D.C.: Government Printing Office, 1978); "Record-Book of the Suffolk [County] Bar," p. 156; Supreme Judicial Court [Record], February-June, 1786, MBSufC.

sachusetts is admitted to practice as a Counsellor of this Court and is sworn accordingly.

On motion of William Bradford Junior Esquire Attorney General of Pennsylvania, Thomas Smith Esquire[97] of Carlisle in Pennsylvania is sworn and Jacob R. Howell[98] is solemnly affirmed and are admitted to practice as Counsellors in this Court, agreeably to Order.

William West Pltff in Error
v̄s
David L. Barns & others Def^dts

Mr Bradford offered to the Court a Writ, purporting to be a Writ of Error, Issued out of the Office of the Clerk of the Circuit Court for Rhode Island District directed to that Court and commanding the return of the Judgment and proceedings rendered by them in this Cause to this Court with such return &c.

On motion of Mr Bradford of Council for William West the said Writ and papers annexed to it were read.

Mr Bradford moved for a rule that the Defendant rejoin to the errors assigned in this Cause.

David L. Barns one of the Defendants and a Counsellor of this Court objected to the validity of the Writ in question and on that principle, to the rule moved for — The arguments on both sides being heard, the Court informed the parties that they would consider the question.

The Court adjourned till ten oClock to morrow.[99]

97. Thomas Smith (1745-1809) was admitted to the York County, Pennsylvania, bar in 1774 and to the bar of the Supreme Court of Pennsylvania in 1779. He was a resident of Carlisle, Pennsylvania, when he became a member of the bar of the Supreme Court of the United States. Burton Alva Konkle, *The Life and Times of Thomas Smith, 1745-1809: A Pennsylvania Member of the Continental Congress* (Philadelphia: Campion, 1904), pp. 4, 276-77, 49; "Supreme Court List of Attorneys, 1742-1902," Records of the Eastern District, RG 33, PHarH; Biddle, *The Philadelphia Directory* (1791).

98. Jacob Roberts Howell (ca. 1763-1793), a Philadelphia attorney of Quaker descent, was admitted to the bar of the Philadelphia Court of Common Pleas in March, 1785, and to the Pennsylvania Supreme Court bar in April, 1787. At the time of his admission to the Supreme Court bar, he was practicing law in Philadelphia. Hinshaw, *American Quaker Genealogy*, 2:378; *MBBP*, p. 279; "Supreme Court List of Attorneys, 1742-1902," Records of the Eastern District, RG 33, PHarH; Biddle, *The Philadelphia Directory* (1791); Hardie, *The Philadelphia Directory* (1793).

99. The *Columbian Centinel* (Boston) of August 13, 1791, noted the admission as a counsellor of David Leonard Barnes as well as other actions of August 1 and 2.

Wednesday August 3rd. 1791 _

Present.

The Honb^{le} John Jay Esquire Chief Justice.

The Honb^{le} { William Cushing } Associate Justices _
{ James Wilson }
{ John Blair and }
{ James Iredell Esq^{rs} }

On motion of the Attorney General Charles Swift Esqr[100] of the City of Philadelphia is admitted to practice as a Counsellor of this Court, and is sworn
agreably to their Order.

And now bond is given with two sureties, approved by the Court (Viz^t Charles
Pettit[101] and John Nicholson[102] Esquires) by Samuel Bayard their Clerk, for
the faithfull performance of the duties of his said Office &c. as by Law directed _ Ordered that this Bond be delivered by Mr Bayard to the Treasurer
of the United States, and that his receipt for the same be filed in the Clerks
Office of this Court.[103]

It appearing from the Information of the Attorney General, that a certain
Eleanor McDonald is confined in the Goal of this City of Philadelphia charged
with an Offence against the Laws of the United States,[104] and that for the relief
as well of the said Eleanor, as of such other Persons as may be charged with
Offences against the Laws of the United States it would ^be expedient that a
Special Sessions of a circuit Court in and for the district of Pennsylvania should
be speedily held.
Ordered, that a special Sessions of a circuit Court for the trial of criminal

100. Charles Swift (1757-1813), admitted to the Philadelphia bar in 1779 and to the Supreme
Court of Pennsylvania bar in 1781, lived in Philadelphia at the time of his admission to the bar
of the Supreme Court of the United States. Jordan, *Colonial Families of Philadelphia*, 1:118; "Supreme Court List of Attorneys, 1742-1902," Records of the Eastern District, RG 33, PHarH;
Biddle, *The Philadelphia Directory* (1791).
    101. Charles Petit (1736-1806); born in New Jersey; trained as a lawyer; served in a number
of government posts in New Jersey during the Revolutionary War; later moved to Philadelphia;
became an importing merchant; represented Pennsylvania in the Confederation Congress (1785-
1787). *BDAC*.
    102. John Nicholson (d. 1800) was comptroller general of Pennsylvania. *DAB*.
    103. See note 13 above.
    104. Eleanor McDonald was accused of stealing eleven gold doubloons from a vessel in the
Delaware River. William Lewis, judge of the District Court of Pennsylvania, wrote to William
Rawle, who was then attorney for the district of Pennsylvania, about the charges against Mc-
Donald. *United States v. Eleanor McDonald*, Criminal Case Files, CCD Pennsylvania, RG 21,
PPFAR; *SEJ*, 1:86, 88.

"Augt 2nd 1791

D^rSir
    One Eleanor McDonald has been charged before me on the Oath of Capt: Henry Williams of

causes be held at the City of Philadelphia in and for the district of Pennsylvania on the fifteenth day of August instant, and that authenticated copies of this Order be transmitted by the Clerk of this Court to the Judge and to the Clerk of the said district and to the Attorney of the United States for said District.[105]

William West Pltff
v̄s   } In Case.
David Barns & others Def^dts

The Court refused to grant the rule moved for, in this cause yesterday, being unanimously of opinion, that writs of orror to remove Causes to this Court from inferior ones, can regularly issue only from the Clerks office of this Court.

Supreme Court of the United States.

Jacob Van Staphorst &
Nicholas Van Staphorst   } Rule.
v̄s
The State of Maryland

It being suggested to the Court that several persons who are material Witnesses to both Parties in the above Cause reside in Amsterdam in Holland _ It is therefore Ordered on motion of Mr Randolph of Counsel[106] for the Plaintiffs and with the consent of Mr Ingersoll of counsel[107] for the Defendants, that a

---

the State of Massachusetts with stealing from him on Board his Vessel in the River Delaware, Eleven Doubloons & is now confined on the s^d charge On Considering the 9th Sect: of the Act to establish Courts & and the 16th Sect of the Act for the Punishment of Certain Crimes & it appears to me that the offence abovementioned cannot with Propriety be brought before the District Court and as the next Stated Circuit Court for the Pennsylvania District will not meet till the eleventh of October and then at York Town and as Capt: William's vessel will be ready to sail in a few Days the detaining him, his mate and Seamen to give Evidence will be attended with such evil to him, in addition to the Trouble of taking the Prisoner and several witnesses to so great a Distance, that I think you should speak to the Attorney General to move the Supreme Court to order a special ~~Court~~ Circuit Court to be held at Philadelphia for the Trial of the Prisoner.

I am Sir   Y^r [mo?] hb^le Servt
W:Lewis

W. Rawle Esqr"
(Records of the Office of the Clerk, RG 267, DNA).
McDonald was being held for theft on the high seas under the provisions of the Judiciary Act of 1789, section 9, which gave district courts jurisdiction of crimes committed on the high seas, and under section 16 of "An Act for the Punishment of certain Crimes against the United States," enacted in 1790, which prescribed the punishment for larceny on the high seas. *Stat.*, 1:76-77, 116.
105. See note 70 above.
106. "Counsel" originally spelled "Council," but "se" has been written over the "ci."
107. Idem.

Commission do issue to Rutger [J]an Schimmelpenninck, Pieter Stadnitski and Hendrick Vollenhoven as Commissioners on the part of the plaintiffs and to Nicolaas Bonds, Christian Van Eeghen, P. C. Nahuys and Wilhem Willink as Commissioners on the part of the Defendants, for the purpose of taking the Depositions of such witnesses as shall be brought before them, so that one of the said Commissioners named on the part of the Plaintiffs and one of the said commissioners named on the part of the Defendant do attend the execution thereof, and that the depositions so taken and certified under the hands and seals of the Commissioners so taking the same shall be read and received as evidence on the trial of the above Cause.

Sam¹Bayard Clk

At a Supreme Court of the United States begun and held at Philadelphia (being the seat of the national Government) on the first Monday of February, and on the Sixth day of said month _ Anno Domini 1792.

Present.

The Honb^le $\left\{ \begin{array}{l} \text{James Wilson} \\ \text{John Blair and} \\ \text{James Iredell Esq}^{rs108} \end{array} \right\}$ Associate Justices.

by law
This being the day assigned ^ for holding a Session of the Supreme Court of
                                                         to form a quorum
the United States,[109] and a sufficient number of the Justices ^ not being convened[110] the Court is adjourned by the Justices now present untill to morrow at twelve o'Clock.

Tuesday February 7th 1792.

Pursuant to adjournment.

The Honb^le $\left\{ \begin{array}{l} \text{James Wilson and} \\ \text{James Iredell Esq}^{rs111} \end{array} \right\}$ Associate Justices.

---

108. The Court did not achieve a quorum until William Cushing, delayed by illness, arrived on February 10. Poor health also caused Thomas Johnson, commissioned November 7, 1791, to miss this term of the Court. Chief Justice Jay was absent for the whole term as well, because of his wife's pregnancy and precarious state of health. See "Commentaries," John Jay to George Washington, January 27, 1792; William Cushing to George Washington, February 2, 1792; James Wilson to William Cushing, February 7, 1792; John Jay to Thomas Johnson, March 12, 1792.

109. The words "by law" and the caret have been written in pencil and may not be contemporary.

110. The phrase "to form a quorum" and the caret are written in pencil and may not be contemporary.

111. Associate Justice John Blair did not attend the Court sessions of February 7, 8, and 9. Perhaps he knew there would not be a quorum, for Blair again was present on February 10 when William Cushing arrived to make a quorum.

This day met but a sufficient number of Justices not being convened to constitute a Court, the Justices now present adjourn until to morrow at twelve o'Clock

Wednesday February 8th. 1792.

Pursuant. to adjournment.

The Honb^le { James Wilson and James Iredell Esq^rs } Associate Justices.

Met this day at the City Hall,[112] but there not being a sufficient number of Justices Convened the Court is adjourned by the Justices now present untill to morrow at twelve o'Clock.

Thursday February 9th 1792 —

Pursuant to adjournment.

The Honb^le { James Wilson and James Iredell Esq^rs } Associate Justices.

This day met at the City Hall, but there not being a sufficient number of Justices convened; the Court is adjourned by the Justices now present untill to morrow at twelve o'Clock.

Friday February 10th. 1792.

Pursuant to adjournment.

The Honb^le { William Cushing, James Wilson, John Blair and James Iredell Esq^rs } Associate Justices.

This day met at the City Hall, and there now appearing a sufficient number of Justices convened to constitute a quorum; proclamation is made and the Court is opened.

No business being before the Court, it is adjourned untill to morrow at eleven o'Clock.[113]

112. When the Supreme Court moved to Philadelphia in February, 1791, it met in the State House (Independence Hall) in the courtroom that ordinarily housed the Supreme Court of Pennsylvania. With the completion of Philadelphia's new City Hall in the summer of 1791, the Court moved to its new quarters, the Mayor's Court, on the first floor of City Hall, for the August 1791 term. The change was not noted in the minutes until February, 1792. Edward Burd to Jasper Yeates, February 8, 1791, in "Commentaries"; Robert P. Reeder, "The First Homes of the Supreme Court of the United States," *Proceedings of the American Philosophical Society* 76 (1936): 543-96.

113. The following newspapers printed reports of the Court's proceedings of February 10: *Federal Gazette* (Philadelphia), February 10, 1792; *Dunlap's American Daily Advertiser* (Philadelphia), February 11, 1792; *Gazette of the United States* (Philadelphia), February 11, 1792; the report in *Dunlap's* also appeared in the *Argus* (Boston), February 24, 1792.

Saturday February 11th. 1792.

Pursuant to adjournment.

The Honb^{le} {
William Cushing
James Wilson
John Blair and
James Iredell Esq^{rs}
} Associate Justices.

Met this day at the City Hall.

Proclamation is made and the Court is opened.

Eleazor Oswald who survived
Elizabeth Holt Administrators of
John Holt deceased
$\overline{vs}$
The State of New York
} Summons in Case.

And now the Return of the Marshall of the State of New York in this case is read in open Court by Mr Sergeant of Counsel[114] for the Plaintiff_ and a motion grounded thereon for a distringas to compel the appearance of said State

The Court informed Mr Sergeant, that they would consider his motion.

On motion of the Honorable Thomas Hartley Esquire, The Honorable William Few[115] and Abraham Baldwin[116] Esquires are admitted as Counsellors of this Court, and are sworn accordingly.

On motion of the Attorney General The Honorable John W. Kittera[117] is admitted a Counsellor of this Court, and is sworn accordingly.

By consent of Parties the Suit of
Jacob & Nicholas Van Staphorst Plaintiffs
$\overline{vs}$
The State of Maryland Defendant.
}

is continued over to the next term.

114. See note 106 above.

115. William Few, Jr. (1748-1828), was born near Baltimore. After moving to Georgia, he was admitted to the bar on August 1, 1783. Few was a senator from Georgia when admitted to the Supreme Court bar. *DAB;* Allan D. Candler, comp., *The Revolutionary Records of the State of Georgia,* 3 vols. (1905-1908; reprint ed., New York: AMS Press, 1972), 3:417.

116. Abraham Baldwin (1754-1807) was admitted to the Connecticut bar from Fairfield County in 1783. Shortly thereafter, he moved to Georgia and was admitted to the Georgia bar in 1784. At the time of his Supreme Court admission, he was serving as a congressman from Georgia. *DAB.*

117. John Wilkes Kittera (1752-1801), a congressman from Pennsylvania, had been admitted to the Philadelphia bar in 1782 and to the Supreme Court of Pennsylvania bar in 1785. He lived in Lancaster, Pennsylvania, at the time of his admission to the Supreme Court of the United States bar. *BDAC; List of the Members of the American Philosophical Society* (n.p., 1880) p. 18; *MBBP,* p. 284; "Supreme Court List of Attorneys, 1742-1902," Records of the Eastern District, RG 33, PHarH.

The Business before the Court for this day being finished it is adjourned by proclamation until monday at twelve o'Clock.

Monday February 13th 1792.

Pursuant to adjournment.

The Honb^{le} { William Cushing
James Wilson
John Blair and
James Iredell Esq^{rs} } Associate Justices.

This day met at the City Hall.

Proclamation is made and the Court is opened.

On motion of Mr Sergeant., H. H. Blackenridge Esquire[118] is admitted a Counsellor of this Court and is sworn accordingly.

The Court is adjourned by proclamation until to morrow at one o'Clock.

Tuesday February 14th. 1792.

Pursuant to adjournment.

The Honb: { William Cushing
James Wilson
John Blair and
James Iredell Esq^{rs} } Associate Justices.

This day met at the City Hall.

Proclamation is made and the Court is opened.

The Clerk in obedience to an order of the Court last term[119] having produced a receipt from the Treasurer of the United States of his bond which he has given for the faithful performance of the duties of his said Office,[120] and it being represented to the Court that agreeably to the practice of the Treasury, the said Bond ought to be lodged with the Register of the Treasury; the Court therefore direct that the said Bond be delivered to the said Register.

---

118. Hugh Henry Brackenridge (1748-1816) was admitted to the Philadelphia bar in 1780 and to the Supreme Court of Pennsylvania bar in 1783. A resident of Pittsburgh, Brackenridge was in Philadelphia on business at the time of his admission to the bar of the Supreme Court of the United States. *DAB;* Claude Milton Newlin, *The Life and Writings of Hugh Henry Brackenridge* (Princeton: Princeton University Press, 1932), pp. 57, 126-29; "Supreme Court List of Attorneys, 1742-1902," Records of the Eastern District, RG 33, PHarH.

The clerk misspelled Brackenridge as "Blackenridge."

119. See order of August 3, 1791.

120. This receipt could not be found in the Court's records. It was listed as still in existence in a bound inventory entitled "Index of Records & Papers in Supreme Court U. S. 20th Jan'y 1827" (General Records, RG 267, DNA).

Eleazer[121] Oswald who survived ⎫
Elizabeth Holt administrators of ⎪
John Holt deceased ⎬
   v̄s ⎪
The State of New York ⎭

On motion of the Counsel[122] for the Plaintiff leave is now given to withdraw the motion for a distringas v̄s the defendant State and for a discontinuance of the Suit to be entered thereon.

On motion of the Attorney General of the United States, George Read Esquire[123] Attorney for the United States in the district of Delaware is admitted a Counsellor of this Court, & is sworn accordingly.

Proclamation being previously made the Court is adjourned to the time and place appointed by Law.

Sam¹Bayard Clk

Monday August 6th. 1792.

At a Supreme Court of the United States, begun and held at Philadelphia (being the present seat of the National Government on the first Monday of August and on the sixth day of the said Month Anno Domini 1792 —

Present.

The Honble. John Jay Esqr Chief Justice.

⎛ William Cushing ⎞
⎪ James Wilson ⎪
The Honble ⎯⎨ John Blair ⎬ Associate Justices.
⎪ James Iredell & ⎪
⎝ Thomas Johnson Esq^rs ⎠

Proclamation is made and the Court is opened[124]

Letters patent bearing date the Seventh day of November Anno Domini 1791. directed to the Honble. Thomas Johnson of Maryland, constituting him an

---

121. The final "e" is written over an "o."

122. See note 106 above.

123. George Read, Jr. (1765-1836), was admitted to the bar at New Castle County, Delaware, in 1785. At the time of his admission to the Supreme Court bar, Read was the attorney for the United States for the district of Delaware. Henry C. Conrad, *History of the State of Delaware*, 3 vols. (Wilmington, 1908), 3:863; J. Thomas Scharf, *History of Delaware, 1609-1888*, 2 vols. (Philadelphia: L. J. Richards, 1888), 1:563; *SEJ*, 1:31.

124. The Court met at Philadelphia's "new City-Hall." See "Commentaries," *Gazette of the United States* under date of August 8, 1792.

Associate Justice of the Supreme Court of the United States, are now openly read and published in Court.[125]

On motion of the Attorney General of the United States, John Hallowell Esq[r][126] is admitted to practice as an Attorney of this Court and is solemnly affirmed accordingly —

Jacob. & Nicholas VanStaphorst
v̄s.   } In Case.
The State of Maryland

On motion of the Attorney General of counsel for the Plaintiffs, with consent
                                      ordered
of M[r] Ingersol of counsel for the Defendant, ˄ that this action be discontinued,[127] each party having agreed to pay their own costs.

Eleazer Oswald who survived &c.
Administrator of John Holt dec[d]
v̄s.   } In Case.
State of New York.

M[r] Ingersol of counsel for the Plaintiff moves in this cause for "a rule on the Marshall of the State of New York to return the writ issued against the said State" — The court informed M[r] Ingersol that they would consider his motion.

The Attorney General i̶n̶f̶ of the United States informs the Court that on Wednesday next he intends moving. for a Mandamus to be directed to the
                                              the
circuit Court for ˄ district of Pennsylvania,[128] commanding the said Court to proceed in a certain petition of William Hayburn applying to be put on the pension list of the United States, as an invalid Pensioner —

Proclamation is made and the Court is adjourned until to morrow at ten oClock.

---

125. Thomas Johnson replaced John Rutledge. See note 56 above.

126. John Hallowell (1768-1839), who studied law with fellow Quaker attorney Miers Fisher (see note 62 above), was admitted to the Philadelphia bar in 1788 and to the Supreme Court of Pennsylvania bar in 1789. He was a resident of Philadelphia at the time of his admission to the bar of the Supreme Court of the United States. Eastman, *Courts and Lawyers of Pennsylvania*, 2:557; Hinshaw, *American Quaker Genealogy*, 2:370, 540; "Supreme Court List of Attorneys, 1742-1902," Records of the Eastern District, RG 33, PHarH; Biddle, *The Philadelphia Directory* (1791); Hardie, *The Philadelphia Directory* (1793); Cornelius William Stafford, *The Philadelphia Directory for 1799* (Philadelphia: William W. Woodward, 1799).

127. The word "ordered" has been inserted in a different hand, possibly that of Samuel Bayard.

128. The word "the" has been interlined in a different hand, possibly that of Samuel Bayard.

Tuesday the 7th, of August 1792.

                          Pursuant to adjournment.

The Honble. John Jay Esqʳ Chief Justice.

The Honble. $\left\{\begin{array}{l} \text{William Cushing} \\ \text{James Wilson} \\ \text{John Blair} \\ \text{James Iredell \&} \\ \text{Thomas Johnson Esq}^{rs} \end{array}\right\}$ Associate Justices.

This day met at the City Hall.

Proclamation is made and the Court is opened.

Ebenezer Kingsley & others
   v̄.s. $\left.\begin{array}{l} \\ \\ \end{array}\right\}$ Error from Massachusetts.
Thomas Jenkins

By consent of parties agreed that this cause be continued to the next term.

The Attorney General moves the Court to be informed of the system of practice by which the attornies and counsellors of this Court shall regulate themselves and of the place in which rules in causes here depending shall be obtained.

The Court informed the Attorney General and the Gentlemen of the bar that if they have any remarks to offer on the subject of the mode of practice to be adopted here this Court are willing to hear them.

Eleazer Oswald who survived &c.
Administrator of John Holt decᵈ $\left.\begin{array}{l} \\ \\ \\ \end{array}\right\}$
   v̄s.
The State of New York

On motion of Mʳ Ingersol of counsel for the Plaintiff. ordered that the Marshall of the New York district return the writ to him directed in ^this cause before the adjournment of this Court, if a copy of this rule shall seasonably be serv'd upon him or his deputy _ or otherwise on the first day of the next term. And that in case of default, he do shew cause therefor, by affidavit taken before one of the Judges of the United States _

   Adjourned until to morrow at Ten o'Clock.

Wednesday the 8th. of August 1792 —

Pursuant to adjournment.

The Honorable John Jay Esquire Chief Justice.

Honble. {
William Cushing
James Wilson
John Blair
James Iredell &c
Thomas Johnson Esq^{rs}
} Associate Justices.

met at the City Hall.

Proclamation is made and the Court opened.

The Chief Justice in answer to the motion of the Attorney General, made yesterday., informs him and the Bar, that this Court consider the practice of the Courts of Kings Bench and of Chancery in England as affording outlines for the practice of this Court and that they will from time to time make such

alterations therein as circumstances may render necessar^{r}y.[129]

Edward Telfair for the
State of Georgia
vs.
Samuel Brailsford & oth^s
}

bill in Equity filed and motion by Mr Dallas of counsel for the Governor and State of Georgia — for an injunction to the Circuit Court for the District of Georgia to stay proceedings in a certain cause in which execution has issued — the argument of this motion is postponed until to morrow.

Agreeably to his motion of monday last the Attorney General proceeded to shew cause why a mandamus should issue to the Circuit Court for the ~~New York and~~[130] Pennsylvania-district for the purpose expressed in the said motion. The Court doubted of the authority of the Attorney General to make this motion ex officio. The argument on this point is adjourned.

Proclamation is made and the Court adjourned until to morrow at 10 o'Clock.

129. "An Act for regulating Processes in the Courts of the United States . . ." enacted by Congress on May 8, 1792 (*Stat.*, 1:276), confirmed the Supreme Court's rule-making power in common law and equity proceedings. By adopting the "practice of the Courts of Kings Bench and of Chancery" as guidelines for Supreme Court procedure, Chief Justice John Jay notified the members of the bar of the Court's recognition of its rule-making power.

130. The word "of" was altered to "for," the word "the" was added, and the words "New York and" were crossed out. All corrections were done in the same hand, possibly that of Samuel Bayard.

Thursday the 9th. of August 1792 —

Pursuant to adjournment.

The Honorable John Jay Esq: Chief Justice.

The Honble. { William Cushing
James Wilson
John Blair
James Iredell &
Thomas Johnson Esq^{rs} } Assoc^e Justic:

This morning met at the City Hall.

Proclamation is made and the Court opened.

Edward Telfair in behalf
of the State of Georgia
  v̄s.
Samuel Brailsford & a^{ls} } Bill of Equity.

The Court proceeded to hear the argument on the motion in this cause and having heard Counsel on the same, adjourn[131] until to morrow at ten oclock.

Friday the 10th. of August 1792 —

Pursuant to adjournment.

The Honble. John Jay Esq: Chief Justice.

Honble. { William Cushing
James Wilson
John Blair
James Iredell &
Thomas Johnson Esq^{rs} } Associate Justices.

This day met at the City Hall.

Proclamation is made and the Court opened.

The Court proceeded to hear the Attorney General in relation to the powers and extent of his office.[132]

The Court adjourn until to morrow at ten oclock.

131. An "ed" has been partly erased.
132. This argument was a continuation of the one begun on Wednesday, August 8, on a motion made by Edmund Randolph for a mandamus to be directed to the circuit court of Pennsylvania ordering it to proceed on the petition of William Hayburn to be put on the pension list of the United States.

Saturday the 11th. of August 1792.

Pursuant to adjournment.

The Honble. John Jay Esquire Chief Justice.

Honble. ⎰ William Cushing
        ⎱ James Wilson
          John Blair   ⎱ Asso: Justices.
          James Iredell &
          Thomas Johnson Esq^{rs}

This day met at the City Hall.

Proclamation is made and the Court opened.

Alexander Chrisholm Exec:
of Robert Farquhar dec^d ⎱ In case.
      v̄s.
The State of Georgia

Proclamation being previously made in the words following "Any person having authority to appear for the State of Georgia in the suit brought in this court by Alexander Chisholm citizen of South Carolina and Executor of Robert Farquhar of the same State, deceased, against the said State of Georgia, is required to come forth and appear accordingly," it was thereupon, moved by the Plaintiff. by Edmund Randolph Esquire his counsel that unless the said State of Georgia shall after reasonable previous notice of this motion cause an appearance to be entered in behalf of the said State, on the fourth day of next term, or shall then shew cause to the contrary, judgment shall be enter'd against the said State and a writ of enquiry of damages shall be awarded.
Ordered with consent of the Plaīnffs counsel, that the consideration of this motion be postponed until the first monday in February next.

The Court being divided[133] in their opinions on the subject of the Attorney Generals authority ex officio to move the Court for a mandamus to the circuit Court for the Pennsylvania district, to correct the error complained of in the case of William Haybern, the writ prayed for cannot issue.

Edward Telfair[134] Govr &c.
      v̄s.   ⎱ In Equity.
Samuel Brailsford & a^{ls}

The Court order that an injunction do issue from this Court to stay such monies in hands to the Marshall for the Georgia district, as have been or may be levied and received by virtue of any execution issuing from the Circuit Court

133. Originally written as "decided." An "iv" is written over "ec."
134. A partially erased "for" appears after "Telfair."

of the said District, at the suit of Samuel Brailsford & a^ls v̄s. James Spalding[135] and to detain the same in his hands until further order of this Court.

The Court proceeded to hear the Attorney General as counsel for William Hayburn on a motion for a mandamus directed to the circuit Court for the Pennsylvania district, to command the said Court to proceed on the petition of the said William Hayburn.
The Court informed the Attorney General that they will hold his motion under consideration, until the next term.

All business now undetermined is continued over to the next term.[136] and the Court is adjourned by Proclamation to the time and place by Law appointed.

At a Supreme Court of the United States held at Philadelphia (being the Seat of the National Government) on the first Monday in February and the fourth day of the said Month 1793.

Present

The Honorable John Jay Esquire Chief Justice

The Hon̄ble { William Cushing
James Wilson
John Blair &
James Iredell Esq^rs[137] }   Associate Justices

Proclamation is made and the Court opened.

Alexander Chisholm
Citizen of the State of South-
Carolina and Executor of
Robert Farquhar of the   In Case
same State deceased
    v^s
The State of Georgia

The Court agree to hear the Attorney General to morrow in support of his motion in this Cause made at the last term.

They assign Thursday next for hearing the Argument in the Cause of Ebenezer Kingsley and others v^s Thomas Jenkins removed into this Court by Writ of Error from the Circuit Court for Massachusetts district.

135. Originally "Shelding." The "h" has been altered to a "p" and an "a" is written over the "e."
136. Original entry ended here. Subsequently, Hand C added the remainder of the sentence.
137. Only five justices were present because only five held commissions at this time. Thomas Johnson, the sixth, had resigned on January 16, 1793.

Edward Telfair Esq.
Governor of the State
of Georgia in behalf of } Bill in Equity
said State
v.
Samuel Brailsford & ali.

On Affidavit filed stating the inability of James Spalding a person summoned to attend the Court as a witness in this Cause M.ʳ Dallas of Counsel for the State of Georgia moved the Court that a Commission be awarded to take the Deposition of said James Spalding to be read as evidence in this suit

The Court informed M.ʳ Dallas that they would hold his motion under advisement and acquaint him with their determination after hearing the Argument and when they should deliver their opinions on the demurrer filed in this cause. ___

A Return was this day made of the Commission awarded by this Court in the case of Jacob and Nicholas Van͜staphorst v.ˢ the State of Maryland with the depositions and other papers accompanying the same
Ordered,
That the said Commission be opened and together with the papers sent to this Court filed in the Clerks Office.

James Martin Esq.ʳ this day applied to the Court for permission to be sworn to the truth of a certain deposition accompanied by certain papers offered to the Court intended as he suggested as the foundation of a motion for a writ of error to be directed to the Supreme Judicial Court of the State of Massachusetts

The Court on perusal of the deposition with the papers annexed thereto refused the said application until certain expressions contained in the deposition offered imputing corrupt motives to the Judges of the said Supreme Court of Massachusetts be expunged.

The Court adjourned until to morrow at eleven 9Clock. ___ [138]

[———————————]

Tuesday, 5.ᵗʰ February 1793

Pursuant to Adjournment

The Honorable John Jay Esq.ʳ Chief Justice

The Honble {
William Cushing
James Wilson
John Blair
James Iredell Esq.ʳˢ
} Associate Justices

138. Reports were published about the Court's proceedings of February 4 in the *Gazette of the United States* (Philadelphia), February 6, 1793, and in the *New-York Journal* on February 9, 1793. A variant of this report appeared in the *Daily Advertiser* (New York) on February 7, 1793, and this was reprinted in the *Independent Chronicle* (Boston) on February 14, 1793.

Tuesday, 5th February 1793

Pursuant to Adjournment

The Honorable John Jay Esqr. Chief Justice

The Honble {
William Cushing
James Wilson
John Blair
James Iredell Esqr.
} Associate Justices

This day met at the City-Hall

Alexander Chisholm
Executor of Robert Farquhar decd
vs
The State of Georgia
} In Case

      The Court proceeded to hear the Attorney General in support of his motion in this cause but considering that no appearance had been entered on the part of the State of Georgia and regarding the question involved in the suit as highly important suggest to the Counsellors of the Court that if any are disposed to offer their sentiments on the subject now under Consideration the Court are willing to hear them.

      Proclamation being made the Court adjourned till tomorrow at eleven oClock.

Fine Minutes, February 5, 1793. (Cf. illustration of Original Minutes for February 5, 1793.) Courtesy National Archives.

This day met at the City-Hall

Alexander Chisholm
Executor of Robert Farquhar dec^d   }
    v^s   } In Case
The State of Georgia   }

The Court proceeded to hear the Attorney General in support of his motion in this cause but considering that no appearance had been entered on the part of the State of Georgia and regarding the question involved in the suit as highly important suggest to the Counsellors of the Court that if any are disposed to offer their sentiments on the subject now under Consideration the Court are willing to hear them.

Proclamation being made the Court adjourned till tomorrow at eleven °Clock.

[——————————]

Wednesday, 6th February 1793

Pursuant to adjournment the Court met this Morning at the City-hall

Present

The honorable John Jay Esqr Chief Justice

The Honble { William Cushing
             James Wilson   } Associate Justices
             John Blair &
             James Iredell Esq^rs }

Proclamation is made and the Court opened.

The Court proceeded to hear the Argument in the Cause of Edward Telfair &c^a in behalf of the State of Georgia v^s Samuel Brailsford & others and having heard Counsel postpone the further hearing of the same until to morrow.

The Court adjourn until tomorrow at eleven °Clock.

Thursday, 7th February 1793

Pursuant to Adjournment the Court met this morning at the City-Hall

Present

The honorable John Jay Esqr Chief Justice

The Honble { William Cushing
             James Wilson   } Associate Justices
             John Blair &
             James Iredell Esq^rs }

Edward Telfair Governor
of Georgia in behalf of said
State   } Bill in Equity
v.ˢ
Samuel Brailsford & al.ˢ

The Court proceeded to hear the further Argument of this Cause but the Counsel concerned not having finished the same it is adjourned until tomorrow at eleven ⁰Clock.

_____

Friday, 8ᵗʰ February 1793

Pursuant to Adjournment the Court this morning met at the City-Hall

Present

The Honorable John Jay Esq.ʳ Chief Justice

The hoñble { William Cushing
             James Wilson
             John Blair &
             James Iredell Esq.ʳˢ } Associate Justices

Edward Telfair Governor of Georgia
in behalf of said State
v.ˢ   } Bill in Equity
Samuel Brailsford & al.ˢ

The Court having heard the further Argument of this cause adjourn until tomorrow at eleven ⁰Clock. ‑
                        [——————————]

Saturday, 9ᵗʰ February 1793

Pursuant to Adjournment the Court met this Morning at the City=hall

Present

The Honorable John Jay Esq.ʳ Chief Justice

The Hoñble { William Cushing
             James Wilson
             John Blair &
             James Iredell Esq.ʳˢ } Associate Justices

On motion for the admission of James Martin Esq.ʳ the Attorney General of the United States laid before the Court certain printed Lists of Attornies in the Island of Jamaica (belonging to Great Britain) for several years with certain Certificates in proof of M.ʳ Martin's Citizenship in the State of New-York and of his admission to practice as a Counsellor in the Courts of Chancery and of the Supreme Court of the said State; also sundry letters in proof of the good moral and professional Character of M.ʳ Martin on which grounds the Attorney General moved for the admission of M.ʳ Martin to practice as a Counsellor of this Court— The Court informed the Attorney General that they would hold his motion under consideration.

Edward Telfair Governor of
Georgia &c.ᵃ
⎫
⎬ Bill in Equity
⎭
v̄.ˢ
Samuel Brailsford & Al.ˢ

The Argument of this cause was continued and this day was concluded.—

Ebenezer Kingsley & Al.ˢ
⎫
⎬ In Error from Massachusetts
⎭
v̄.ˢ
Thomas Jenkins

The Court proceeded to hear the argument of this Cause but the Counsel not having finished the same the Court adjourn until Monday next at eleven °Clock.

Monday, 11.ᵗʰ February 1793

Pursuant to adjournment the Court met this Morning at the City=hall

present

The Honorable John Jay Esq.ʳ Chief Justice

The hoñble ⎰ William Cushing
            ⎱ James Wilson
              John Blair &   ⎬ Associate Justices
              James Iredell Esq.ʳˢ

The Court proceeded to hear the further Argument of the Cause of Ebenezer Kingsley and others v̄.ˢ Thomas Jenkins but the same not being finished the further hearing of it is postponed until tomorrow at eleven °Clock to which time the Court adjourn.

Tuesday, 12.ᵗʰ February 1793

Pursuant to Adjournment the Court met this Morning at the City-hall

present

The hoñble ⎰ William Cushing
            ⎱ James Wilson
              John Blair &   ⎬ Associate Justices
              James Iredell Esq.ʳˢ

Proclamation is made and the Court opened.

The Chief Justice being prevented by indisposition[139] from attending Court this day the Justices present adjourn for the further hearing of the argument in the case of Ebenezer Kinglsey & al^i $\bar{v}^s$ Thomas Jenkins until tomorrow at eleven °Clock.

Wednesday, 13th February 1793

Pursuant to adjournment the Court met this morning at the City-hall

Present

The Honorable John Jay Esqr Chief Justice

The honble $\left\{ \begin{array}{l} \text{William Cushing} \\ \text{James Wilson} \\ \text{John Blair \&} \\ \text{James Iredell Esq}^{rs} \end{array} \right\}$ Associate Justices

The Counsel in the Case of Ebenezer Kingsley and others $\bar{v}^s$ Thomas Jenkins proceeded in their argument but not having closed the same The Court adjourn for the further hearing of the said argument until to-morrow at eleven °Clock.

Thursday, 14th February 1793

Pursuant to adjournment the Court met this morning at the City-hall

present

The Honorable John Jay Esqr Chief Justice

The honble $\left\{ \begin{array}{l} \text{William Cushing} \\ \text{James Wilson} \\ \text{John Blair \&} \\ \text{James Iredell Esq}^{rs} \end{array} \right\}$ Associate Justices

The Court this day informed Mr Martin (whose admission as Counsellor of this Court was moved for by the Attorney General on Saturday last) that as it appears that the Supreme Judicial Court of the State of Massachusetts have declined admitting him to practice as a Counsellor of that Court on the ground of his not appearing to that Court to be a Citizen of either of the United States and his having refused to be naturalized This Court will not thus incidentally determine so important a question as that involved in the motion of the Attorney General above referred to.

James Martin Esqr having expunged from the deposition offered to the

---

139. John Jay had been sick the month before. See "Commentaries," John Jay to William Cushing, January 27, 1793.

Court on Monday the 4th instant certain expressions reflecting on the Conduct of the Judges of the Supreme Court of the State of Massachusetts offers the same with the papers annexed and prays to be sworn to the truth of the said deposition as the ground of a Writ of Error to be directed to the aforesaid Judges to remove to this Court a certain proceeding on which an erroneous Judgment is stated to have been given by the Judges of the said Supreme Court to the prejudice of the rights of the said James Martin Esqr as a Citizen of the United States.

Ordered,

That the said James Martin Esqr be sworn to the truth of the said deposition and that it be filed with the papers annexed in the Clerks Office.

Ebenezer Kingsley & others)
v̄^{s} }
Thomas Jenkins   )

The Counsel concerned proceeded in the argument of this Cause but not having finished the same The Court adjourn for the further hearing of the said argument until tomorrow at eleven °Clock.

Friday, 15th February 1793

Pursuant to adjournment the Court met this morning at the City=hall

Present

The honorable John Jay Esqr Chief Justice

The honble { William Cushing
            James Wilson
            John Blair &
            James Iredell Esq^{rs} } Associate Justices

Ebenezer Kingsley and others)
v̄^{s} }
Thomas Jenkins   )

The Counsel concerned proceeded in the Argument of this Cause and finished the same on this day.

The Court announce that on Monday next they will determine the question agitated in the Case of Alexander Chisholm Executor of Robert Farquhar dec^d v̄^{s} The State of Georgia_ Whether either of the United States can be made a defendant in an Action at the suit of one or more individuals of another State?

The Court adjourned until tomorrow at eleven °Clock. _

Saturday, 16th February 1793

Pursuant to adjournment the Court met this morning at the City-Hall.

Present

The Honorable John Jay Esqr Chief Justice

The honble { William Cushing
James Wilson &
John Blair Esqrs[140] } Associate Justices

Thomas Pagan
v̄s
Stephen Hooper }

Mr Tilghman of Counsel for the Plaintiff moved for a second writ of Error in this Cause to remove the proceedings had in the same before the Supreme Judicial Court of the State of Massachusetts:

The Court having heard a Copy of the Record in this Case read and ^having considered the same are of opinion that the Writ applied for ought not to be granted.

The Court adjourn until Monday at eleven ọClock.

—————————

Monday, 18th February 1793

Pursuant to adjournment the Court met this morning at the City-Hall.

present

The honorable John Jay Esqr Chief Justice

The honble { William Cushing
James Wilson
John Blair &
James Iredell Esqrs } Associate Justices

Alexander Chisholm
Executor of Robert Farquhar
decd of South Carolina
v̄s
The State of Georgia } In case

The Court proceeded severally to give their opinions on the order moved for in this Cause on Saturday the 11th of August 1792 and argued by the

---

140. The reason for James Iredell's absence from this session of Court is unknown.

Attorney General on Tuesday the 5th instant.
On motion of the Attorney General
Ordered, that the consideration of the form of the order to be entered in this action be postponed until tomorrow.

Proclamation is made and the Court adjourned until tomorrow at eleven °Clock.

Tuesday, 19th February 1793

Pursuant to adjournment the Court met this morning at the City-Hall

Present

The Honorable John Jay Esqr Chief Justice

The honble { William Cushing / James Wilson / John Blair & / James Iredell Esqrs } Associate Justices

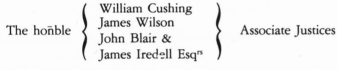

Ebenezer Kingsley & ali.
vs
Thomas Jenkins
} Error from the district of Massachusetts

The Court having heard and considered the arguments of Counsel in this Cause,
Order,
That the Judgment below of the Circuit Court for the District of Massachusetts in the said Cause be affirmed with costs — [141]

Alexander Chisholm Executor
of Robert Farquhar decd
vs
The State of Georgia
} In case

On Argument Ordered that the Plaintiff in this Cause do file his Declaration on or before the first day of March next.
Ordered, That certified Copies of the said declaration be served on the Governor and Attorney General of the State of Georgia on or before the first day of June next.
Ordered, That unless the said State shall either in due form appear or shew cause to the Contrary in this Court by the first day of the next term Judgment by default be entered against the said State.

---

141. Originally, the sentence ended with the word "affirmed." The phrase "with costs" appears to have been added subsequently, possibly by Samuel Bayard.

The Court adjourn until tomorrow at eleven ?Clock.

Wednesday, 20ᵗʰ February 1793

Pursuant to adjournment the Court met this morning at the City＝hall

Present

The Honorable John Jay Esqʳ Chief Justice

The Hoñble $\left\{\begin{array}{l} \text{William Cushing} \\ \text{James Wilson} \\ \text{John Blair \&} \\ \text{James Iredell Esqʳˢ} \end{array}\right\}$ Associate Justices

On motion of Mʳ Rawle for the admission of Samuel Roberts Esqʳ[142] Certificates of his having practised as a Counsellor of the Supreme Court of Pennsylvania and of having sustained a good professional and moral Character were
produced by Mʳ Rawle   The Court order that Mʳ Roberts be admitted as a
Counsellor of this Court and he is affirmed accordingly.

Edward Telfair Governor
of the State of Georgia &cᵃ $\left.\begin{array}{l} \\ \\ \end{array}\right\}$ Bill in Equity
$\bar{v}$ˢ
Samuel Brailsford & others

On Argument the Court are of opinion that if the State of Georgia has a
right to the bond in controversy her remedy is by action at Law   They direct
that the injunction continue until the next term and then be dissolved unless
the State shall sooner bring the said Action.

William Grayson & others $\left.\begin{array}{l} \\ \\ \end{array}\right\}$ Bill in Equity
$\bar{v}$ˢ
The State of Virginia

On motion by Mʳ Rawle to amend the bill filed in this suit
Leave is given by the Court to amend.
On motion, new process is awarded in this cause

Eleazer Oswald surviving
Administrator of John Holt decᵈ $\left.\begin{array}{l} \\ \\ \end{array}\right\}$ Summons in case
$\bar{v}$ˢ
The State of New York

---

142. Samuel Roberts (1763-1820), a Quaker by birth, was admitted to the Philadelphia bar in
1786 and to the Supreme Court of Pennsylvania bar in 1788. At the time of his admission to the
Supreme Court of the United States bar, Roberts lived in Philadelphia, but shortly thereafter he
moved to Lancaster. J. W. F. White, "The Judiciary of Allegheny County," *Pennsylvania Magazine
of History and Biography* 7 (1883): 158-59; Hinshaw, *American Quaker Genealogy*, 2:414; *MBBP*, p.
306; "Supreme Court List of Attorneys, 1742-1902," Records of the Eastern District, RG 33,
PHarH.

Proclamation having been previously made in the Words following "any person having authority to appear for the State of New-York in the above suit is required to appear accordingly" Thereupon it was moved by M.ʳ Cox of Counsel for the plaintiff and ordered by the Court that unless the said State appear by the first day of the next term to the above suit or shew cause to the contrary that Judgment be entered by default against the said State.

Proclamation having been made the Court is adjourned to the time and place by Law appointed.

At a Supreme Court of the United States held at Philadelphia (being the seat of the national Government) on the first Monday in August and the fifth day of the said month Anno Domini 1793: _

Present

The Honorable John Jay Esquire Chief Justice

The Hoñble { James Wilson · John Blair & · James Iredell[143] }   Esquires Associate Justices

Proclamation is made and the Court opened.

Letters Patent directed to the Honorable William Paterson Esquire bearing date the fourth day of March 1793 appointing him a Judge of the Supreme Court of the United States are now openly read and published in Court.[144]

Alexander Chisholm Executor of Robert Farquhar deceased v̄ˢ The State of Georgia   } In Case

By virtue of an Authority from the State of Georgia directed to Alexander J. Dallas and Jared Ingersoll Esquires the said Counsellors this day appeared to shew Cause why Judgment by Default should not be entered against the said State in the above suit

M.ʳ Dallas moved to postpone the argument of the Cause until the next term _

143. William Cushing missed both days of the August 1793 term. He had written to John Jay on July 22, 1793, and may have notified the chief justice of his intention not to attend (William Cushing to John Jay, July 22, 1793, not located but referred to in John Jay to William Cushing, August 6, 1793, Robert Treat Paine Collection, MHi). William Paterson, whose name is omitted here, is listed as present in the original minutes (see "Original Minutes," August 5, 1793). For an explanation of why some justices were listed as present before their letters patent were read and others were not listed until after the reading in Court, see the introduction to "Appointments to the Bench."

144. William Paterson replaced Thomas Johnson who had resigned on January 16, 1793.

The Court agreed to hold the motion under consideration.

The Court adjourned until to morrow at 11 °Clock. _

Tuesday 6ᵗʰ August 1793.

Pursuant to adjournment the Court met this morning at the City-Hall _

Present

The Honorable John Jay Esquire Chief Justice

The Honble ⎰ James Wilson ⎱
           ⎱ John Blair ⎰ Esquires Associate Justices
             James Iredell &
             William Paterson

James Martin Esqʳ laid before the Court a Writ of error issuing from the
office of the Clerk of this Court and directed to the Judges of the Supreme
Judicial Court of the State of Massachusetts which the Chief Justice refused to
allow but which Mʳ Martin contended ought to have been allowed by any
Judge of the Court to whom the Writ might have been presented and prayed
that it might now be allowed

The Court having heard Mʳ Martin in support of his motion were unanimously of opinion that circumstanced as this case is the Writ should not be
allowed.

Alexander Chisholm Executor ⎱
of Robert Farquhar decᵈ   ⎰
    v̄ˢ   ⎰ In Case
The State of Georgia   ⎰

By Consent of Parties expressed by their Counsel this Cause is continued to
the next term.

William Vassall complainant ⎱
    v̄ˢ   ⎰
The State of Massachusetts ⎰   On motion of the
                                  Plaintiff's Counsel these
                                  Causes are severally
Eleazer Oswald Administrator ⎱   continued to the next
of John Holt deceased   ⎰   term. _
    v̄ˢ   ⎰
The State of New-York   ⎰

On motion of the Attorney General for the admission of Ephraim Kirby,
Esquire,[145] of the State of Connecticut certificates are produced from Andrew

145. Ephraim Kirby (1757-1804), author of *Kirby's Reports* (Litchfield, Conn.: Collier & Adam,
1789), practiced law in Litchfield, Connecticut, from 1779 until 1803 except for a few months of
military service, 1782-1783. Alan V. Briceland, "Ephraim Kirby: Pioneer of American Law Reporting, 1789," *American Journal of Legal History* 16 (1972): 297-300, 318-19.

Adams Chief Justice and Roger Sherman and Eliphalet Dyer Associate Justices
of the Supreme Court of said State in proof of the good moral and professional
Character of said Ephraim Kirby and of the period of his admission to practice
as a Counsellor of said Court

Ordered,

That the said Ephraim Kirby, Esquire, be admitted to practise as a Counsellor of this Court   He is accordingly sworn and admitted.

Proclamation is made and the Court adjourned to the time and place by
Law appointed. _ [146]

At a Supreme Court of the United States holden at the City of Philadelphia,
the same being the present Seat of the National Government, on the first Monday in February and on the third day of said Month 1794. _

Present

The Honorable John Jay Esquire Chief Justice

The honble { William Cushing &
             James Wilson Esq^{rs}[147] } Associate Justices

A sufficient number of Justices to constitute a Quorum not being this day
convened, the Court is adjourned until tomorrow at 11 ºClock. _

Tuesday, 4th February 1794

Pursuant to adjournment the Court met this day at the City-hall

present

The Honorable John Jay Esquire Chief Justice

The Honble { William Cushing
            James Wilson &
            William Paterson Esq^{rs} } Associate Justices

Proclamation is made and the Court opened.

146. In a letter to Abigail Adams on August 10, 1793, her son Thomas mentioned that the
Court "having no business ready for trial sat but two days" (Adams Manuscript Trust, MHi). The
Court's term may have been shortened because of an outbreak of yellow fever in Philadelphia.
Alexander J. Dallas noted that "The Malignant Fever, which during this year, raged in the City
of Philadelphia, dispersed the great body of its inhabitants, and proved fatal to thousands,
interrupted, likewise, the business of the Courts; and I cannot trace, that any important cause was
agitated in the present Term." *Dallas*, 2:480.

147. William Paterson, John Blair, and James Iredell were absent for this court session. Paterson arrived on February 4, Blair on February 5, and Iredell missed the whole February term
because of illness. See "Commentaries," James Iredell to John Jay, January 21, 1794.

Letters patent bearing date the 28th day of January 1794 from the President of the United States constituting William Bradford of Pennsylvania Attorney General of the United States are now openly read and published in Court.

Letters patent bearing date the 28th day of January 1794 from the president of the United States appointing David Lenox[148] Marshall for the Pennsylvania District are now openly read and published in Court.

On motion of the Attorney General of the United ꞈStates
James Winchester[149] of the State of Maryland
Thomas. P. Carnes[150] of the State of Georgia and
William Edmund[151] of the State of Connecticut
are severally admitted to practice, as Counsellors of this Court and sworn to support the Constitution of the United States. ̲

The State of Georgia	} The Pleadings in this Suit are this day filed and issue joined between the parties to the same.
v[s]	
Samuel Brailsford	

On Motion of M[r] Tilghman of Counsel for the Defendant to amend, leave is given, with the Consent of the Counsel for the plaintiff, to insert the names of Robert William Powell and John Hopton as Co-defendants with Samuel Brailsford in the a̶r̶gre^ement[152] and pleadings filed as above mentioned and in the Venire issued in said suit.

---

148. David Lenox (1753-1828), a Revolutionary War veteran and aide-de-camp to Anthony Wayne, was a Philadelphia merchant. *The Society of the Cincinnati in the State of New Jersey* (Bethlehem: Times Publishing, 1960), p. 112; Biddle, *The Philadelphia Directory* (1791).

149. James Winchester (1772-1806), a Baltimore attorney, was admitted to the General Court of the Western Shore of Maryland in 1791. When admitted to the Supreme Court bar, Winchester represented Baltimore in the Maryland General Assembly. Judicial Conference, *Judges of the United States;* "Maryland Politics in 1796—McHenry Letters," *Publications of the Southern History Association* 9 (1905): 374; General Court of the Western Shore Docket and Minutes, October Term, 1791, p. 444, MdAA (information courtesy of Richard Richardson); *Votes and Proceedings of the House of Delegates of the State of Maryland, 1794* (Annapolis: Frederick Green, 1795), p. 1.

150. Thomas Petters Carnes (1762-1822), born in Maryland, had practiced law in Prince Georges County, Maryland, before he moved to Georgia in or about 1785. Carnes was admitted to the Georgia bar in February, 1786. When admitted to the Supreme Court bar, he was representing Georgia in the Third Congress, *BDAC;* Silas Emmett Lucas, Jr., *Some Georgia Company Records,* 3 vols. (Easley, South Carolina: Southern Historical Press, 1977), 1:21; Allan D. Candler, comp., *The Colonial Records of the State of Georgia,* 25 vols. in 28 parts (Atlanta: 1904-1916), vol. 19, part 2, *Statutes, Colonial and Revolutionary, 1774-1805* (Atlanta: Charles P. Byrd, 1911), 19:524.

151. William Edmund (1755-1838) established a law practice in Newtown, Connecticut, in 1782 and was still a resident of that town at the time of his admission to the Supreme Court bar. William Cothren, *History of Ancient Woodbury,* 3 vols. (1854-1879; reprint ed., Baltimore: Genealogical Publishing, 1977), 1:434-39.

152. Originally "argument." The "u" has been changed to an "re."

William Bradford, Jr. (1755-1795), second attorney general of the United States. By Charles Willson Peale (1741-1827). Oil on canvas, 1783. Courtesy Redwood Library and Athenaeum, Newport, Rhode Island.

The Jury impannelled and summoned in the above suit being called do now appear to wit

1 John Leamy	7 Owen Foulke junior
2 Joseph Anthony	8 Robert Smith
3 Samuel Hodgdon	9 Robert Ralston
4 Joseph Ball	10 Reynold Keen
5 Mathew M͓cConnell	11 Hugh Lenox
6 Thomas Ewing	12 John Stille

and are severally sworn or affirmed to try the issue joined between the said parties and a true Verdict to give according to evidence.

M͓r Dallas of Counsel for the plaintiff having opened the Cause, the Court adjourn for the further hearing of Counsel in the same until tomorrow at 11 ͦClock. ͟

Wednesday, 5͓th February 1794. ͟

Pursuant to Adjournment the Court this day met at the City-hall

present

The Honorable John Jay Esquire Chief Justice

The hoñble $\left\{ \begin{array}{l} \text{William Cushing} \\ \text{James Wilson} \\ \text{John Blair &} \\ \text{William Paterson Esq}^{rs} \end{array} \right\}$ Associate Justices

M͓r Edmund of Counsel for John Chandler a Citizen of the State of Connecticut this day moved for a Mandamus to the Secretary of War for the purpose of directing him to cause the said John Chandler to be put on the Pension List of the United States, as an invalid pensioner, conformably to the Order and Adjudication of the Honorable James Iredell and Richard Law Esquires Judges of the Circuit Court of the United States: ͟

The Court informed M͓r Edmund that when the trial of the Cause now before the Court should be finished they would hear him in support of his motion. ͟

The State of Georgia v̄s Samuel Brailsford & al͓s	The Court having heard M͓r Tilghman of Counsel for the Defendants adjourn for the further trial of the Cause until to morrow at 11 ͦClock. ͟

Thursday, 6th February 1794. _

Pursuant to adjournment the Court this day met at the City Hall

present

The Honorable John Jay Esquire Chief-Justice

The Honble { William Cushing
James Wilson
John Blair &
William Paterson Esq^{rs} } Associate Justices

On motion of Mr Tilghman _ John. C. Wells[153] is admitted to practice as an Attorney of this Court and is affirmed to support the Constitution of the United States.

| The State of Georgia
v̄^s
Samuel Brailsford & al^s | The Counsel proceeded in the trial of this Cause, but not having finished the same the Court adjourn until tomorrow at 11 °Clock. _ |

[————————]

Friday, 7th February 1794

Pursuant to adjournment the Court this day met at the City Hall

present

The Honorable John Jay Esquire Chief=Justice

The Honble { William Cushing
James Wilson
John Blair &
William Paterson Es^{rs} } Associate Justices

| The State of Georgia
v̄^s
Samuel Brailsford &al^s | The trial of the present Cause was this day concluded _ the Jury retired for a few minutes and on their return to the Bar by their Foreman Reynold Keen say they find a Verdict for the Defendants. _ |

The Court proceeded to hear Mr Edmund on the subject of his motion made on the 5th instant and agreed to hold the same under Advisement.

The Court adjourn until tomorrow at 11 °Clock. _

[————————]

153. John Craig Wells (d. before 1817), a Quaker by birth, was admitted to the Philadelphia bar in 1788 and to the Supreme Court of Pennsylvania bar in 1789. At the time of his admission to the Supreme Court of the United States bar, he resided in Philadelphia. *MBBP*, p. 322; Hinshaw, *American Quaker Genealogy*, 2:681; "Supreme Court List of Attorneys, 1742-1902," Records of the Eastern District, RG 33, PHarH; Hardie, *The Philadelphia Directory* (1794).

Saturday, 8th February 1794._

Pursuant to adjournment the Court this day met at the City Hall

Present

The Honorable John Jay Esquire Chief=Justice

The Honͦble ⎰ William Cushing ⎱
           ⎰ James Wilson   ⎱ Associate Justices
           ⎰ John Blair &   ⎱
           ⎰ William Paterson Esqʳˢ ⎱

Alexander. S. Glass & others Appelͭˢ
v̄ˢ
The Sloop Betsey[154] & Cargo &
Capͭ pierre Arcade Johannene

Appeal from[155] the Circuit Court for the District of Maryland

The Court, on motion of Mͬ Winchester, proceeded to hear the arguments of Counsel on the present appeal.

By an Agreement this Day filed the procters in behalf of the parties to the above suit consent that all exceptions to the manner of the appeal be waved and that the same shall be argued and decided on the Case as disclosed upon the face of the Record._

The Court adjourn until Monday at 11 ºClock

Monday, 10th February 1794._

Pursuant to adjournment the Court this day met at the City Hall

present

The Honorable John Jay Esquire Chief Justice

The Honͦble ⎰ William Cushing ⎱
           ⎰ James Wilson   ⎱ Associate Justices
           ⎰ John Blair and ⎱
           ⎰ William Paterson Esqʳˢ ⎱

Alexander. S. Glass & others
vˢ
The Sloop Betsey and Cargo &
Capͭ pierre Arcade Johannene

The Court this day heard Counsel on this appeal and for a further hearing of the said Appeal adjourn until to morrow at 11 ºClock._

154. The "t" is written over an "s."
155. The word "from" is written over "for."

Tuesday, 11ᵗʰ February 1794

Pursuant to adjournment the Court this day met at the City Hall

present

The Honorable John Jay Esquire Chief Justice

The Honble { William Cushing
James Wilson
John Blair &
William Paterson Esqʳˢ } Associate Justices

Alexander S Glass & others
v̄ˢ
The Sloop Betsey & Cargo &
Capᵗ pierre Arcade Johannene } The Court having heard Counsel in this appeal adjourn for the further hearing of the same until tomorrow at 11 ọClock.

[————————]

Wednesday, 12ᵗʰ February 1794

Pursuant to adjournment the Court this day met at the City Hall

present

The Honorable John Jay Esquire Chief Justice

The Honble { William Cushing
James Wilson
John Blair &
William Paterson Esqʳˢ } Associate Justices

Alexander S Glass & others
v̄ˢ
The Sloop Betsey & Cargo &
Capᵗ Pierre Arcade Johannene } The Court continued this day to hear Counsel in the present appeal, and adjourn until tomorrow at 11 ọClock. ‗

Thursday, 13ᵗʰ February 1794

Pursuant to adjournment the Court this day met at the City Hall

present

The Honorable John Jay Esquire Chief Justice

The Honble { William Cushing
James Wilson
John Blair &
William Paterson Esqʳˢ } Associate Justices

The Court proceeded to hear argument of Counsel on the motion of M.ʳ Edmund for a mandamus to the Secretary of War made on Wednesday the 5.ᵗʰ instant.

United States
v.ˢ
John Hopkins Esq.ʳ
} On motion of M.ʳ Tilghman the Court grant a rule to shew cause on friday next why a Mandamus should not issue directed to John Hopkins Esquire Commissioner of Loans for the District of Virginia requiring

him to admit Richard Smyth to subscribe to the Loan proposed by the United States in and by an act of the Congress of the United States entitled "An Act supplementary to the Act making provision for the debt of the United States" passed the 8.ᵗʰ day of May 1792 a certain certificate for the sum of 23,454 Dollars 76 Cents issued by the Commonwealth of Virginia bearing date prior to the 1.ˢᵗ day of January 1790 which Certificate after having been paid into the Treasury of the said Commonwealth was re=issued thereout in pursuance of an Act of the legislature of the said Commonwealth passed the 26.ᵗʰ day of December 1792._

Alexander Chisholm Ex̄or
of Robert Farquhar dec.ᵈ
v̄.ˢ
The State of Georgia
} The Attorney General moved the Court that Judgment be entered for the Plaintiff in this suit agreeably to the rule heretofore made in the same_.

The Court adjourn until tomorrow at 11 ºClock
[————————]
Friday, 14ᵗʰ February 1794

Pursuant to adjournment the Court this day met at the City Hall

present

The Honorable John Jay Esquire Chief=Justice

The Hon̄ble { William Cushing
James Wilson
John Blair &
William Paterson Esqʳˢ } Associate Justices

The Court having taken into consideration the motion of M.ʳ Edmund of the 5.ᵗʰ instant, and having considered the two Acts of Congress relating to the same, are of opinion that a Mandamus cannot issue to the secretary of War for the purposes expressed in the said motion._

Alexander Chisholm Ex̄or
of Robert Farquhar dec.ᵈ
v̄.ˢ
The State of Georgia
}

Alexander James Dallas & Jared Ingersoll Esquires having this day shewn cause why Judgment should not be entered against the state of Georgia in the above suit and the Court having duly considered the same are unanimously of opinion and accordingly direct that Judgment be entered in the said suit in favor of the plaintiff and on motion of the Attorney General do award a Writ of Enquiry to ascertain the Damages sustained by the said plaintiff by reason of the breach of promise and other defaults of the said Defendant.

The State of Georgia
v̄ˢ   } Bill in Equity
Samuel Brailsford & alˢ

On Motion of Mʳ Tilghman it is ordered by the Court that the bill filed in this suit be dismissed, and that the injunction issued in the same be dissolved with Costs. —

The State of Georgia
v̄ˢ   } Amic. Action in Case
Samuel Brailsford & alˢ

On Motion of Mʳ Tilghman, it is ordered by the Court that Judgment for the Defendants be entered in the above suit.

Ebenezer Kingsley & alˢ
v̄ˢ   } Error from the District
Thomas Jenkins   of Massachusetts.

On motion of Mʳ Lewis it is ordered by the Court that a special mandate do issue to the Circuit Court for the Massachusetts District in pursuance of the Act of Congress in such Case made and provided commanding the said Court fully to execute and carry into effect a Judgment heretofore obtained by the aforesaid Defendant against the said plaintiffs in Error in the Circuit Court aforesaid. —

United States
v̄ˢ   } The Attorney General proceeded to shew cause why a mandamus should not issue against the Defendant
John Hopkins Esqʳ   in the above suit.

The Court adjourn until tomorrow at 11 ºClock. —

Saturday, 15th February 1794. —

pursuant to adjournment the Court this day met at the City Hall

present

The Honorable John Jay Esquire Chief Justice

The Honble { William Cushing
              James Wilson
              John Blair &
              William Paterson Esqʳˢ } Associate Justices

On motion of Mr Lewis, the Honorable Samuel Dexter[156] of the State of Massachusetts is admitted to practice as a Counsellor of this Court & sworn to support the Constitution of the United States. _

United States	}	On motion by Mr Tilghman made on Thursday the
v̄^{s}		13 instant for a Mandamus to be directed to the De-
John Hopkins Esqr	)	fendant commanding him to do and execute the sev-

eral matters and things set forth in the rule aforesaid the Court after argument and full Consideration are of opinion that the right claimed by the petitioner in the present case does not appear sufficiently clear to authorise the Court to issue the Mandamus moved for.

The Court adjourn until Monday next at 11 ºClock. _

Monday, 17th February 1794. _

pursuant to adjournment the Court this day met at the City=Hall

present

The Honorable John Jay Esquire Chief=Justice

The hon̄ble { William Cushing
James Wilson
John Blair &
William Paterson Esq^{rs} } Associate Justices

United States	)	
v̄^{s}	}	Amicable Action on the Case
Yale Tod	)	

The Pleadings; and agreement of the Attorney General of the United States and the Attorney for the defendant being read and filed; and the Case argued

and the Court having ^also taken the same into Consideration are of opinion that Judgment be entered for the plaintiff in the above suit.

The Court adjourn until tomorrow at 11 ºClock. _

[————————]

156. Samuel Dexter (1761-1816) was admitted to the Worcester County, Massachusetts, bar in 1784 and the bar of the Massachusetts Supreme Judicial Court on circuit in Middlesex County, in May, 1787. When admitted to practice in the Supreme Court, he was a resident of Charlestown and a congressman from Massachusetts. *DAB;* Supreme Judicial Court [Record], 1787, p. 121v, MBSufC.

Tuesday, 18th February 1794

pursuant to adjournment the Court this day met at the City Hall

present

The Honorable John Jay Esq: Chief Justice

The hon̄ble ⎰ William Cushing ⎱
            ⎱ James Wilson   ⎰ Associate Justices
              John Blair &
              William Paterson Esqrs

Alexander. S. Glass & als   The Court this day published their final
    v̄s   decree in the present appeal which being
The Sloop Betsey & Cargo &   read & approved it is ordered that the
Capt pierre Arcade Johannene   same be registered: It is also further or-
                                 dered that an exemplification of the same
be transmitted to the Circuit Court for the District of Maryland.

Proclamation being made the Court adjourn to the time and place by Law appointed. —

Sam¹Bayard Clk

[————————]

At a Supreme Court of the United States holden at Philadelphia, the same being the present seat of the National Government, on the first Monday in August and on the fourth day of the said Month Anno Domini 1794. —

The Honorable James Wilson ⎱
            John Blair &   ⎰ Esquires[157]
            James Iredell

this day met at the City Hall, but a sufficient number of Justices to constitute a Quorum not appearing, the Court is adjourned until to-morrow at 11 ºClock. —

---

157. John Jay, William Cushing, and William Paterson missed the opening day of the August 1794 term. Paterson arrived the next day. Jay and Cushing did not attend the whole term. Jay was in England serving as envoy extraordinary to the Court of Great Britain. Cushing wrote to William Paterson of his intention to miss the August term, because of the extreme heat of a Philadelphia August. See "Commentaries," William Cushing to William Paterson, July 20, 1794; Frank Monaghan, *John Jay* (New York: Bobbs-Merrill, 1935), p. 372.

Tuesday, 5th August 1794.

Pursuant to adjournment the Court this morning met at the City-Hall

present

The Hon̄ble { James Wilson
John Blair
James Iredell &
William Paterson Esq^{rs} } Associate Justices

Proclamation being made the Court is opened.

Alexander Chisholm Exor
of Robert Farquhar dec^d
v^s
The State of Georgia

On motion of the Attorney General of Counsel for the Plaintiff the Court do award that the General Jury to be summoned at the next Court do enquire upon their Oaths and Affirmations what damages the plaintiff has sustained by reason of the premises, and the non-performance of the promises and assumptions in the declaration of the plaintiff contained, and that three months notice of the holding such enquiry be given to the Governor and Attorney General of the State of Georgia. _

On motion of the Attorney General,

Matthew McAllister, Esqr,[158] of the State of Georgia, was admitted to practice as a Counsellor of this Court, and sworn accordingly.

Joseph Thomas Esqr[159] of Pennsylvania, on motion of the Attorney General, was also admitted to practice as a Counsellor of this Court and affirmed accordingly. _

The General traverse Jury, summoned to attend the Court at the present term, being called, and no issues of fact appearing for trial, the Court dismiss them from any further attendance.

158. Matthew McAllister (1758-1823) was admitted to the Philadelphia bar in 1782 and his native York County bar in 1783. McAllister moved to Georgia about 1784 and was admitted to the Georgia bar in 1785. Soon thereafter he became the state's attorney general. He secured an appointment as attorney for the United States for the district of Georgia and was serving in that capacity when admitted to the Supreme Court bar. Harrison, *Princetonians*, 2:269-72; Carter and Glossbrenner, *History of York County*, p. 59; Robert and George Watkins, *A Digest of the Laws of the State of Georgia From Its First Establishment as a British Province Down to the Year 1798, Inclusive* (1800; reprint ed., Wilmington, Del.: Michael Glazier, 1981), p. 311.

159. Joseph Thomas (born 1765) was admitted to the Philadelphia bar in 1789 and to the Pennsylvania Supreme Court bar in 1791. Thomas, a Quaker by birth, lived in Philadelphia at the time of his admission to the Supreme Court bar. University of Pennsylvania, *Biographical Catalogue* (1894), p. 24; *MBBP*, p. 317; "Supreme Court List of Attorneys, 1742-1902," Records of the Eastern District, RG 33, PHarH; Hinshaw, *American Quaker Genealogy*, 2:666; Record Book, p. 637, Pine Street Meeting, Friends Monthly Meetings, Philadelphia, PHi; Hardie, *The Philadelphia Directory* (1794).

Proclamation being made the Court is adjourned to the time and place by Law appointed. ₋

[——————]

At a Supreme Court of the United States begun and held at Philadelphia in the State of Pennsylvania (being the seat of the National Government) on Monday the second day of February Anno Domini 1795. ₋

present

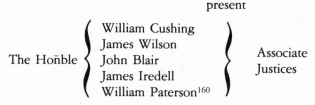

The Hoñble { William Cushing / James Wilson / John Blair / James Iredell / William Paterson[160] } Associate Justices

Proclamation is made and the Court opened.

The Marshall of the Pennsylvania District returns a Venire to him directed, which is read and filed. ₋

The Court excuse the absence of two of the petit Jurors, viz: Charles Evans and Robert Bethell.

On motion of the Attorney General J. Marshall[161] and Alexander Campbell,[162] Esquires, were admitted Counsellors of this Court, and they were immediately sworn as such.

The Jury were excused till Thursday next at ten ℃lock in the forenoon. ₋

Alexander Chisholm Ēxor of Robert Farquhar dec:d vs The State of Georgia } It is agreed by the Attorney General for the plaintiff that this Cause should continue open. ₋

160. John Jay, still in England as special envoy, missed the entire February 1795 term of Court. He did not return to the United States until May. Monaghan, *John Jay*, p. 405.

161. John Marshall (1755-1835), chief justice of the United States Supreme Court, 1801-1835, was admitted to the Fauquier County, Virginia, bar in 1780 and to the bar of the Virginia Court of Appeals in 1785. At the time of his admission to the Supreme Court bar, he practiced law in Richmond, Virginia. *DAB;* Virginia Court of Appeals Order Book, April 29, 1785, Vi; Leonard Baker, *John Marshall: A Life in Law* (New York: Macmillan, 1974), p. 160.

162. Alexander Campbell (d. 1796) began his law practice in the 1780s in northern Virginia, around Westmoreland and Essex Counties. In 1790 he moved his law practice to Richmond. When admitted to the Supreme Court bar, he was serving as United States attorney for the district of Virginia. Richmond *Virginia Gazette, and General Advertiser,* July 20, 1796; Alexander Campbell to Robert Carter, September 15, 1790, Carter Family Papers, ViHi (information courtesy of Lee Shepard); John P. Kennedy, *Memoirs of the Life of William Wirt,* 2 vols. (Philadelphia: Lea and Blanchard, 1850), 1:31-32; Francis T. Brooke, "A Narrative of My Life; For My Family," in Louise Pecquet duBellet, *Some Prominent Virginiania Families,* 4 vols. (1907; reprint ed., Baltimore: Genealogical Publishing, 1976), 2:358; Richmond *Virginia Gazette, and General Advertiser,* November 24, 1790; *SEJ,* 1:86, 88, 205.

Eleazer Oswald Administrator
of John Holt dec.ᵈ
v.ˢ
The State of New York
} Thursday next was
assigned for the trial
of this Cause. —

Ware
v.ˢ
Hylton
} On motion of Mʳ Tilghman this Cause
is continued. —

The Attorney General requests the opinion of the Court, whether it is necessary to procure the signature of an Attorney to an assignment of errors; of which the Court say they will consider.

The depositions of John Brown, John Lamb, Robert Bogardus, Robert Harper, and George Clinton, were opened in Court and ordered to be filed.[163]

The Court adjourned till 12 oClock tomorrow.
[————————]
Tuesday, 3ᵈ February, 1795. —

Pursuant to Adjournment, the Court met, this morning, at the City=Hall.

Present

The honͤble { James Wilson
John Blair
James Iredell
William Paterson[164]
} Esquires, Associate
Justices. —

Proclamation is made, and the Court opened.

The deposition of John M.ᶜKesson is opened, and ordered to be filed. —[165]

The Court is adjourned 'till ten ºClock tomorrow morning. —

Wednsday, 4ᵗʰ February 1795.

Pursuant to Adjournment, the Court met, this morning, at the City=Hall.

Present

The Honͤble { William Cushing
James Wilson
John Blair
James Iredell
William Paterson
} Esquires
Associate
Judges. —

163. These depositions were taken in the case of *Oswald v. New York.*

164. William Cushing missed parts of the February 1795 term because of illness. He was suffering from lip cancer. See "Commentaries," Jeremiah Smith to William Plumer, February 7, 1795; John Adams to Abigail Adams, February 9, 1795; and James Iredell to Hannah Iredell, March 6, 1795.

165. The deposition was taken in the case of *Oswald v. New York.*

Proclamation is made, and the Court opened.

The Court give notice to the Gentlemen of the Bar, that, hereafter, they will expect to be furnished with a statement, of the material points of the Case, from the Counsel on each side of a cause. —

Penhallow ⎱
    vᶢ   ⎰ this Cause is assigned for
Doane   ⎰ Friday next.

Mʳ Lewis read the Petition of John Corbley and others, confined, in the Goal of the City of Philadelphia, on Charges of High Treason, praying the Court to fix the time of their trial. — [166]

The Attorney General moves for the admission of Mʳ William Tilghman,[167] as a counsellor of this Court, and he is accordingly admitted and sworn. —

The Court is adjourned 'till ten ?Clock to morrow morning. —
[————————]
Thursday, 5ᵗʰ February, 1795.

Pursuant to adjournment, the Court met, this morning, at the City = Hall.

Present

The Hon̄ble ⎰ James Wilson
        ⎰ John Blair   ⎱ Associate
        ⎰ James Iredell   ⎰ Judges
        ⎰ William Paterson Esqʳˢ[168]

Proclamation is made, and the Court opened. —

The Jury are called.

William Moore Smith[169] was admitted, and sworn, a Counsellor of this Court. —

166. *Ex parte Corbley.*

167. William Tilghman (1756-1827) was admitted to the Maryland bar in 1783. At the time of his admission to the Supreme Court of the United States bar, he resided in Philadelphia. *DAB;* Hardie, *The Philadelphia Directory* (1794); Thomas Stephens, ed., *Stephens's Philadelphia Directory for 1796* (Philadelphia: W. Woodward, 1796).

168. See note 164 above.

169. William Moore Smith (1759-1821), admitted, in 1782, to the bars of Northampton County, Pennsylvania, and the Supreme Court of Pennsylvania, lived in Philadelphia at the time of his admission to the Supreme Court of the United States bar. *University of Pennsylvania Catalogue, 1749-1880,* p. 31; Chroust, *Rise of the Legal Profession,* 1:229; "Supreme Court List of Attorneys, 1742-1902," Records of the Eastern District, RG 33, PHarH; Stephens, *The Philadelphia Directory* (1796); Cornelius William Stafford, ed., *The Philadelphia Directory for 1797* (Philadelphia: W. Woodward, 1797).

Eleazer Oswald Administrator
of John Holt, deceased,   } This Cause
            v.ˢ   } Coming on
The State of New York

    1. John Barnes   6. John. G. Wachsmuth
    2. Wilson Hunt   7. Sallows Shewell
    3. Robert Gray   8. Samuel Clarkson
    4. Samuel Emory   9. John Melbeck
    5. James Barclay

  were sworn; and

    10. George Aston
    11. Adam Mendenhall
    12. Israel Pleasants were affirmed as Jurors.

John Dunlap and David Hall were sworn as Witnesses. —

    It is agreed by the Parties, that the Jury may give their Verdict tomorrow. —

Ware   } On motion of Mᵣ Campbell, for the defendant, to assign errors;
  v.ˢ   } Mᵣ Tilghman, for the plaintiff, declared, that the general Errors will
Hylton } be assigned. —

    The Court adjourned 'till eleven ºClock to morrow morning. —

Friday, 6ᵗʰ February, 1795.

Pursuant to adjournment, the Court met, this morning, at the City=hall.

Present

                { William Cushing
                { James Wilson
The honble { John Blair   } Associate
                { James Iredell   } Judges
                { William Paterson, Esqʳˢ

Proclamation is made, and the Court opened. —

Oswald
  v.ˢ   } The Jury find for the plaintiff five thousand three hundred
New=York } and fifteen dollars damages and six Cents Costs.

    The Petition of John Lockery, confined in the goal of this City on a Charge of High Treason, praying the Court to fix the time of his trial, was read by Mᵣ Moses Levy.[170]

    The Court proceeded to hear the argument on the petition of John Corbley & others.[171]

170. *Ex parte Lockery.*
171. *Ex parte Corbley.*

The Court proceeded to hear the Counsel in the case of Penhallow v̄ˢ Doane.

Adjourned till eleven ꝰClock tomorrow morning. _

Saturday, 7ᵗʰ February, 1795. _

Pursuant to adjournment, the Court met this morning, at the City=Hall.

Present

The Hoñble ⎨ William Cushing
James Wilson
John Blair
James Iredell
William Paterson, Esqʳˢ ⎬ Associate Justices

Proclamation is made, and the Court opened.

The Attorney General moved for a Rule to shew cause, why a mandamus to be directed to the Judge of the district of New=York to issue a warrant to apprehend Henry Barré, a deserter from the Perdrix, a corvette belonging to the Republic of France, should not issue. _ [172]

The Petitions of John Corbley and others,[173] and John Lockery,[174] being before the Court, and it being stated by the Attorney of the United States for the pennsylvania district, that the petitioners are charged with Treason, by them committed, against the United States, in the counties of Allegheny, Washington, Fayette, Bedford and Northumberland, within the district aforesaid; it is moved by Messʳˢ Levy and Lewis, of counsel with the petitioners, that special Circuit Courts, for the trial of criminal Causes, in Cases punishable with death, may be directed to be held at such convenient times and places, within the several Counties aforesaid, as the Court may deem most proper.

Adjourned 'till eleven ꝰClock on Monday Morning next.
[————————]
Monday, 9ᵗʰ February, 1795.

The Court met this morning at the City hall pursuant to adjournment.

present.

The Hoñble ⎨ William Cushing
James Wilson
John Blair
James Iredell
William Paterson, Esqʳˢ ⎬ Associate Justices

172. *United States v. Lawrence.*
173. *Ex parte Corbley.*
174. *Ex parte Lockery.*

Proclamation is made, and the Court opened.

The Court proceeded to hear the argument of Counsel in the case of Penhallow v̄s Doane's Adm̄ors.

Adjourned 'till eleven ºClock to morrow morning. —

Tuesday, 10ᵗʰ February, 1795.

Pursuant to adjournment, the Court met this morning at the City=Hall

present

The Hoñble ⎰ William Cushing ⎱ Associate
           ⎱ John Blair   ⎰ Justices
             James Iredell
             William Paterson Esqʳˢ175

Proclamation is made, and the Court opened.

The Court proceeded to hear Counsel in the case of Penhallow v̄ˢ Doane's Adm̄ors. —

Adjourned till ten ºClock tomorrow morning. —

Wednesday, 11ᵗʰ February 1795. —

Pursuant to adjournment, the Court met, this morning, at the City Hall.

present

The Hoñble ⎰ William Cushing ⎱ Esquires,
           ⎱ John Blair   ⎰ Associate
             James Iredell   Justices.
             William Paterson

Proclamation is made, and the Court opened.

The Court proceeded to hear the argument of Counsel in the case of Penhallow v̄s Done's Adm̄ors.

The Court adjourned 'till eleven ºClock to morrow morning. —

175. James Wilson was absent this day and all the subsequent days when *Penhallow v. Doane's Administrators* was being argued. Wilson had represented Doane when the case was being argued in the Court of Appeals in Cases of Capture under the Articles of Confederation in 1783. Henry J. Bourguignon, *The First Federal Court: The Federal Appellate Prize Court of the American Revolution, 1775-1787* (Philadelphia: American Philosophical Society, 1977), pp. 244-51.

Thursday, 12th February, 1795.

Pursuant to adjournment, the Court met this morning at the City Hall

present

The Honble { William Cushing } Esquires
            { John Blair   } Associate
            { James Iredell   } Justices
            { William Paterson }

Proclamation is made, and the Court opened.

The Court proceeded to hear the argument of Counsel in the Case of Penhallow v̄ˢ Doane's Adm̄ors. _

Adjourned 'till 11 ọClock tomorrow morning.

Friday, 13th February 1795. _

Pursuant to adjournment, the Court met this morning at the City Hall.

present

The honble { William Cushing } Esquires
           { John Blair   } Associate
           { James Iredell   } Justices. _
           { William Paterson }

Proclamation is made, and the Court opened.

The Court proceeded to hear the argument of Counsel in the case of Penhallow v̄ˢ Doane's Adm̄ors. _

The Court is adjourned till eleven ọClock tomorrow morning. _

Saturday, 14th February, 1795.

Pursuant to adjournment, the Court met this morning at the City Hall. _

present

The Honble { William Cushing } Esquires
           { John Blair   } Associate
           { James Iredell   } Justices
           { William Paterson }

Proclamation is made, and the court opened.

The Court proceeded to hear the argument of Counsel in the case of Penhallow vˢ Doane's Adm̄ors. _

On motion of M.ʳ Lewis, a habeas Corpus is ordered to issue to bring up John Hamilton and Thomas Sedgwick, both in the Custody of the Marshall of the Pennsylvania district, returnable on Monday Morning next at 12 ºClock. — [176]

The Court is adjourned till 11 ºClock on monday morning next.

Monday, 16ᵗʰ February 1795. —

Pursuant to adjournment, the Court met this morning at the City Hall

present

The honble	William Cushing John Blair James Iredell William Paterson	Esquires Associate Justices.

Proclamation is made, and the Court opened.

The Court proceeded to hear the argument of Counsel in the Case of Penhallow v̄.ˢ Doane's Adm̄ors.

By Consent of M.ʳ Lewis, on behalf of John Hamilton and Thomas Sedgwick, to bring up whom a habeas corpus issued on Saturday last, Ordered, that they be brought up tomorrow morning at eleven ºClock. — [177]

The Court is adjourned 'till eleven ºClock tomorrow morning. —

Tuesday, 17ᵗʰ February, 1795.

Pursuant to adjournment, the Court met, this morning, at the City=hall. —

present

The honble	James Wilson John Blair James Iredell William Paterson[178]	Esquires Associate Justices. —

Proclamation is made, and the Court opened.

---

176. *Ex parte Hamilton; Ex parte Sedgwick.*

177. Idem.

178. Because of illness, William Cushing missed Court sessions on February 17, 18, and 20. See note 164 above. He was specifically requested to attend the Court on February 21, however, to hear arguments in *Bingham v. Cabot.* A draft of an order or summons survives among the case papers although it was never formally read into the Court's record (*Bingham v. Cabot,* Appellate Jurisdiction Records, RG 267, DNA). Cushing attended all the rest of the sessions of the Court for its February term. This is the only instance of a justice being "summoned" to attend the Court during its first decade.

The Marshall for the pennsylvania district made return of a habeas corpus to bring up the bodies of John Hamilton and Thomas Sedgwick which was read and filed.[179]

The Court declared that all evidence on motions for a discharge upon bail must be by way of deposition, and not vivâ voce.

The Court is adjourned till eleven ºClock tomorrow morning. ___

[——————————]

Wednesday, 18th February 1795

Pursuant to adjournment, the Court met this morning at the City hall. ___

present

The honble { James Wilson
John Blair
James Iredell
William Paterson } Esquires
Associate
Justices

Proclamation is made, and the Court opened.

The Affidavits of Absalom Baird and Thomas Scott, on the habeas corpus brought for John Hamilton and Thomas Sedgwick, were taken in open Court and filed. ___ [180]

The Court proceeded to hear the argument of Counsel, on the motion for a mandamus to be directed to John Lawrence;[181] which being closed, they heard the Counsel on the habeas corpus to bring up John Hamilton and Thomas Sedgwick so far as it respects John Hamilton, at the termination of which Mr Lewis moved, on his behalf, that he might be discharged without bail.[182]

The Court was then adjourned until Friday morning next at eleven ºClock. ___

[——————————]

Friday, 20th February, 1795. ___

Pursuant to adjournment, the Court met this morning at the City Hall

present

The Honble { James Wilson
John Blair
James Iredell
William Paterson } Esquires
Associate
Justices.

Proclamation is made, and the Court opened.

179. *Ex parte Hamilton; Ex parte Sedgwick.*
180. Idem.
181. *United States v. Lawrence.*
182. *Ex parte Hamilton.*

The Court order John Hamilton to be discharged on bail, himself in four thousand dollars and two sureties in two thousand dollars each.

Mess.rs Presly Neville and Thomas Scott became the sureties, and, together with the said John Hamilton, enter into recognizance accordingly to appear at the next special or stated Circuit Court.[183]

Thomas Sedgwick was returned by consent.[184]

The Court is adjourned till eleven ⁰Clock tomorrow morning. —

[———————]

Saturday, 21.st February, 1795.

Pursuant to adjournment, the Court met this morning at the City hall.

present

The hoñble ⎰ William Cushing ⎱ Esquires
  James Wilson   Associate
  John Blair   Justices.
  James Iredell
  William Paterson

Proclamation is made, and the Court is opened.

The Court proceeded to hear the argument of Counsel in Bingham v.s Cabot

The Court adjourned till eleven ⁰Clock on Monday Morning next. —

Monday, 23.d February, 1795. —

Pursuant to adjournment, the Court met this morning at the City Hall

present

The hoñble ⎰ William Cushing ⎱ Esquires
  James Wilson   Associate
  John Blair   Justices.
  James Iredell
  William Paterson

Proclamation is made, and the Court is opened. —

The Court proceeded to hear the argument of Council in Bingham v.s Cabot.

The record, Writ, return, Citation and Assignment of Errors, in Olney Plaintiff in error v.s Dexter, and same Plaintiff v.s Arnold, were ordered to be filed. —

183. Idem.
184. *Ex parte Sedgwick*.

The Court give notice, that, tomorrow, they will give their opinions in Penhallow v̄ˢ Doane's Adm̄ors. —

Adjourned 'till one ọClock tomorrow afternoon. —

<hr>

Tuesday, 24ᵗʰ February 1795. —

Pursuant to adjournment, the Court met this afternoon at the City=Hall.

present

The hoñble ⎰ William Cushing ⎱ Esquires
⎱ John Blair ⎰ Associate
James Iredell Justices.
William Paterson[185]

Proclamation is made, and the Court is opened.

The Court proceeded to give their opinions in Penhallow v̄ˢ Doane's Adm̄ors when it was finally ordered That against all the plaintiffs in error, except George Wentworth, sixteen thousand three hundred and sixty Dollars and sixty eight Cents be recovered by the defendants in error, and the same sum against George Wentworth; and that against the plaintiffs in error the Costs of the Circuit Court be recovered, one half against George Wentworth, and the other half against the other plaintiffs in error; and that in this Court the parties pay their own Costs. —

The Court is adjourned till eleven ọClock tomorrow morning. —

<hr>

Wednesday, 25ᵗʰ February, 1795.

Pursuant to adjournment, the Court met this morning at the City Hall.

present

The hoñble ⎰ William Cushing ⎱ Esquires
⎱ James Wilson ⎰ Associate
James Iredell Justices. —
William Paterson[186]

Proclamation is made, and the Court is opened.

The Court proceeded to hear the argument of Council in Bingham v̄ˢ Cabot.

185. James Wilson was absent from this session, apparently because the Court planned only to give its opinions in *Penhallow v. Doane's Administrators*. See note 175 above.
186. The reason for John Blair's absence from this session of Court and from the remainder of the term is unknown.

M.ʳ Lewis moved for an habeas Corpus for Thomas Sedgwick and John Corbley, which was opposed by M.ʳ Rawle Attorney for the district of Pennsylvania.[187]

The Court adjourned till ten °Clock tomorrow morning. —

Thursday, 26.ᵗʰ February 1795

Pursuant to adjournment, the Court met this morning at the City Hall.

present

The Honble { William Cushing / James Wilson / James Iredell / William Paterson } Esquires Associate Justices.

Proclamation is made, and the Court is opened.

The Court proceeded to hear the argument of Counsel on the motion for an habeas corpus to bring up Thomas Sedgwick and John Corbley;[188] & Cur: Advis: vult. —

The Court then proceeded to hear the argument of Counsel in Bingham v̄.ˢ Cabot.

Adjourned till eleven °Clock tomorrow morning. —

Friday, 27.ᵗʰ February, 1795. —

Pursuant to adjournment, the Court met this morning at the City Hall.

present

The honble { William Cushing / James Wilson / James Iredell / William Paterson } Esquires Associate Justices.

Proclamation is made, and the Court is opened.

The Court declared, that, they being divided in opinion on the motion made by M.ʳ Lewis, on Wednesday last, for a habeas corpus to bring up Thomas Sedgwick and John Corbley, the motion could not be granted.[189]

The Court then proceeded to hear the argument of counsel in Bingham v̄.ˢ Cabot.

---

187. *Ex parte Sedgwick; Ex parte Corbley.*
188. Idem.
189. Idem.

The Court is adjourned till eleven °Clock tomorrow morning. ─
[───────────]
Saturday, 28ᵗʰ February 1795.

Pursuant to adjournment, the Court met this morning at the City Hall

present

The honble ⎨ William Cushing
James Wilson
James Iredell
William Paterson ⎬ Esquires
Associate
Justices. ─

Proclamation is made, and the Court is opened.

The Court proceeded to hear the argument of Counsel in Bingham v̄ˢ Cabot.

The Court is adjourned till Monday Morning next at 11 °Clock. ─

Monday, 2ᵈ March, 1795.

Pursuant to adjournment, the Court met this morning at the City Hall

present

The Honble ⎨ William Cushing
James Wilson
James Iredell
William Paterson ⎬ Esquires
Associate
Justices.

Proclamation is made, and the Court is opened.

The Court proceeded to hear the argument of Council in Bingham v̄ˢ Cabot, which being finished, they proceeded to give their opinions thereon, when it was finally ordered, that the judgment of the Circuit Court for the district of Massachusetts be reversed; and the Court being divided on the Question whether a venire facias de novo should issue, it is also ordered, that the writ do not issue. ─

Olney
v̄ˢ
Dexter

Same
v̄ˢ
Arnold ⎬ It is agreed to continue these causes. ─

Adjourned till eleven °Clock tomorrow morning. ─

Tuesday, 3ᵈ March, 1795.

Pursuant to adjournment the Court met this morning at the City hall

present

The Hoñble $\left\{\begin{array}{l} \text{William Cushing} \\ \text{James Wilson} \\ \text{James Iredell} \\ \text{William Paterson} \end{array}\right\}$ Esquires Associate Justices.

Proclamation is made, and the Court is opened.

The Mandamus to Judge Lawrence was refused after argument.[190]

Jansen &c. $\left.\begin{array}{l} \\ \bar{v}^\text{s} \\ \\ \end{array}\right\}$ Rule by consent, that &c (see Agreement) and inhibition
Talbot &c. awarded.

Penhallow
vs $\left\{\begin{array}{l} \end{array}\right.$ Special Mandate awarded, on motion of M.ͬ Tilghman, et exit.
Doane's Admͬors

Adjourned to the time and place by Law appointed. _

[——————]

At Philadelphia, in the State of Pennsylvania, being the present Seat of the national Government, on

Monday, 3.ͩ of August 1795. _

This being the day, by Law appointed, for holding a Supreme Court, and none of the Judges, but the honorable James Iredell, Esquire, appearing for that purpose, the Court is by him adjourned till one °Clock to morrow afternoon. _ [191]

Tuesday Afternoon
4.ᵗʰ of August 1795.

None of the Judges appearing to day agreeably to the adjournment, but the

190. *United States v. Lawrence.*

191. In a letter to John Jay dated "Wednesday Morning July 1795" (probably July 29), William Cushing wrote from New Jersey that he was rushing on to Philadelphia (John Jay Papers, NNC). Cushing did not attend the Court until August 5, however. James Wilson and William Paterson also did not appear in Court until August 5. John Blair missed the entire August term because of illness (see "Commentaries," John Blair to William Cushing, June 12, 1795). John Rutledge received official notice of his commission as chief justice too late to travel to Philadelphia in time for the opening of the August term. He did not arrive in Philadelphia until the evening of August 10 and then wrote to Iredell that he would not be in Court on August 11. See "Commentaries," *Argus* under date of July 27, 1795; *Philadelphia Gazette* under date of August 12, 1795, and John Rutledge to James Iredell, August 11, 1795.

honorable James Iredell, Esquire, the Court is by him adjourned 'till eleven °Clock tomorrow morning. —

Wednesday Morning
5th August 1795.

Pursuant to adjournment, the Court met this morning at the City Hall, to wit

The Honble { William Cushing
James Wilson
James Iredell
William Paterson } Esquires, Associate Judges. —

Proclamation is made and the Court is opened.

On motion of Edward Tilghman, Esquire, the Honorable Jacob Read, Esquire,[192] was admitted a Counsellor of this Court, and he was immediately sworn according to Law. —

On motion of Mr Duponceau, Joseph Clay, junr Esqr[193] was admitted a Counsellor of this Court, and he was immediately sworn according to Law. —

On motion of Mr Read, Henry De Saussure, Esqr[194] was admitted a Counsellor of this Court, and he was immediately sworn according to Law. —

The Marshall of the Pennsylvania District returns a venire facias which is filed. —

The depositions of Anthony McLeod, John Habersham and Gideon Davis Pendleton were opened in Court and filed. —[195]

Grayson et al ?
vs   } continued
The State of Virginia

Ware vs Hylton et al.? continued by Consent. —

Olney Pltff. in error vs Welcome Arnold continued by Consent. —

---

192. Jacob Read (1752-1816), born in South Carolina, was raised in Georgia, and was admitted to the South Carolina bar on March 23, 1773. Accepted at Gray's Inn later that year, he went to England for additional study of the law. Read returned to South Carolina in 1776 and was one of its senators at the time of his admission to the Supreme Court bar. *DAB;* N. Louise Bailey and Elizabeth Ivey Cooper, eds., *Biographical Directory of the South Carolina House of Representatives,* vol. 3 (Columbia: University of South Carolina Press, 1981), p. 597.

193. Joseph Clay, Jr. (1764-1811), born in Savannah, read law with George Wythe in Williamsburg. Admitted to the Georgia bar in February, 1786, he was practicing law in his native state when admitted to the Supreme Court bar. *DAB;* Candler, *Colonial Records of Georgia,* 19:524.

194. Henry William De Saussure (1763-1839), after admission to the Philadelphia bar in 1784, returned to his native South Carolina and was admitted to the bar at Charleston in 1785. At the time of his admission to the Supreme Court bar, De Saussure was director of the United States Mint, although he resigned almost at once. *DAB.*

195. In the case of *Hills v. Ross.*

Olney Pltff in error v̄s Edward Dexter continued by Consent. ＿

No issue of fact appearing for trial, the Jury are called and dismissed. ＿

Adjourned till 11 ºClock to morrow morning.

[————————]

Thursday Morning
6ᵗʰ of August 1795. ＿

Pursuant to adjournment, the Court met this morning at the City＝hall, viz͓ᵗ

The Hoñble ⎰ William Cushing ⎱ Esquires, Associate
⎱ James Wilson ⎰ Judges. ＿
⎰ James Iredell ⎱
⎱ William Paterson ⎰

Proclamation is made, and the Court is opened.

The Court proceeded to hear the argument of Counsel in the case of Talbot Pltff in error v̄s Joost Jansen. ＿

Adjourned 'till 11 ºClock tomorrow morning. ＿

——————————

Friday Morning
7ᵗʰ August 1795. ＿

Pursuant to adjournment, the Court met this morning at the City＝Hall, viz͓ᵗ

The hoñble ⎰ William Cushing ⎱ Esqͬˢ Associate Judges.
⎱ James Wilson ⎰
⎰ James Iredell ⎱
⎱ William Paterson ⎰

Proclamation is made, and the Court is opened.

The Court proceeded to hear the argument of Counsel in the case of Talbot Pltff in error v̄s Jansen.

Adjourned 'till eleven ºClock tomorrow morning. ＿

[————————]

Saturday Morning
8ᵗʰ August 1795. ＿

Pursuant to adjournment, the Court met this morning at the City＝Hall, viz͓ᵗ

The hoñble ⎰ William Cushing ⎱ Esqͬˢ Associate Judges. ＿
⎱ James Wilson ⎰
⎰ James Iredell ⎱
⎱ William Paterson ⎰

Proclamation is made, and the Court is opened.

The Court proceeded to hear the argument of Counsel in Talbot Pltff in error v̄s Jansen. _

Adjourned till 11 ºClock on Monday Morning next. _

[———————]
Monday Morning
10ᵗʰ August 1795. _

Pursuant to adjournment, the Court met this morning at the City-Hall, viz:

The Hoñble ⎨ William Cushing / James Wilson / James Iredell / William Paterson ⎬ Esqʳˢ Associate Judges.

Proclamation is made, and the Court is opened.

The Court proceeded to hear the argument of Counsel in the Case of Talbot Pltff in error v̄s Jansen. _

Adjourned 'till ten ºClock tomorrow morning. _

[———————]
Tuesday Morning
11ᵗʰ August 1795. _

Pursuant to adjournment, the Court met this morning at the City=Hall, viz:

The Hoñble ⎨ William Cushing / James Wilson / James Iredell / William Paterson ⎬ Esquires, Associate Judges.

Proclamation is made, and the Court is opened.

The Court proceeded to hear the argument of Counsel in Talbot, Pltff in error v̄s Jansen. _

Adjourned till 10 ºClock tomorrow morning. _

Wednesday Morning
12ᵗʰ August 1795. _

Pursuant to adjournment, the Court met this morning at the City=Hall, viz: _

The Hoñble ⎨ William Cushing / James Wilson / James Iredell / William Paterson ⎬ Esquires, Associate Judges. _

Proclamation is made and the Court is opened.

The Court proceeded to hear the argument of counsel in the case of Talbot Pltff in error v̄s Jansen.

Letters patent dated on the first of July last, appointing the honorable John Rutledge, Esquire, Chief Justice of the Supreme Court of the United States, during his good behaviour[196] and until the end of the next session of the Senate of the United States, were read and published in open Court; and thereupon he took the oath of office and the oath to support the Constitution of the United States; after which he took his seat on the bench. _ [197]

Adjourned till 10 ºClock tomorrow morning. _

———————————

Thursday Morning
13ᵗʰ August 1795. _

Pursuant to adjournment, the Court met this morning at the City Hall, viz!

The honorable John Rutledge Esq̄ʳ Chief Justice

The hoñble ⎧ William Cushing ⎫
            ⎨ James Wilson   ⎬ Esquires.
            ⎪ James Iredell   ⎪ Associate Judges.
            ⎩ William Paterson ⎭

Proclamation is made, and the Court is opened. _

The Court proceeded to hear the argument of Counsel in Talbot, Pltff in error v̄s Jansen. _

Adjourned till ten ºClock tomorrow morning. _

[———————————]
Friday Morning
14ᵗʰ August 1795. _

Pursuant to adjournment, the Court met this morning at the City=Hall, viz!_

The Honorable John Rutledge Esqʳ Chief Justice.

The hoñble ⎧ William Cushing ⎫
            ⎨ James Wilson   ⎬ Esquires
            ⎪ James Iredell   ⎪ Associate Judges. _
            ⎩ William Paterson ⎭

196. Although the commissions of all the justices included the phrase "during his good behaviour," this is the first time it is recorded in the fine minutes.

197. John Rutledge replaced John Jay who had resigned on June 29, 1795. See the introduction to "Appointments to the Bench" for a discussion of why John Rutledge was not listed as present on the day his commission was read.

Proclamation is made, and the Court is opened. _

The Court proceeded to hear the argument of Counsel in the Case of Talbot Pltff in error v̄s Jansen. _

Adjourned till ten °Clock tomorrow morning. _

Saturday Morning
15ᵗʰ August 1795. _

Pursuant to adjournment, the Court met this morning at the City Hall, viz͓ᵗ

The honorable John Rutledge Esqͬ Chief Justice

The honͭble ⎰ William Cushing ⎱
    ⎱ James Wilson ⎰ Esqͬˢ Associate Judges.
    ⎰ James Iredell ⎱
    ⎱ William Paterson ⎰

Proclamation is made and the Court is opened. _

Mͬ Lewis, one of the Counsel in the Case of Talbot Pltff in error v̄s Jansen, being indisposed, the Court is adjourned 'till ten °Clock on Monday Morning next.

Monday Morning
17ᵗʰ August 1795. _

Pursuant to adjournment, the Court met this morning at the City=hall, viz͓ᵗ

The honorable John Rutledge Esqͬ Chief Justice

The Honͭble ⎰ William Cushing ⎱
    ⎱ James Wilson ⎰ Esqͬˢ Associate Judges.
    ⎰ James Iredell ⎱
    ⎱ William Paterson ⎰

Proclamation is made and the Court is opened. _

Adjourned till tomorrow morning at 10 °Clock.

Tuesday Morning
18ᵗʰ August 1795. _

Pursuant to adjournment, the Court met this morning at the City=hall, viz͓ᵗ

The Honͭble John Rutledge Esqͬ Chief Justice

The honͭble ⎰ William Cushing ⎱
    ⎱ James Wilson ⎰ Esqͬˢ Associate Judges.
    ⎰ James Iredell ⎱
    ⎱ William Paterson ⎰

Proclamation is made and the Court is opened. —

The Court proceeded to hear the argument of Counsel in the Case of Talbot Pltff in error v̄s Jansen. —

Adjourned till 10 °Clock tomorrow morning. —

Wednesday Morning
19th August 1795

Pursuant to adjournment, the Court met this morning at the City Hall, viz.

The honble John Rutledge Esqr Chief Justice

The honble ⎰ William Cushing
⎱ James Wilson
  James Iredell
  William Paterson ⎰ Esquires Associate Judges. —

Proclamation is made and the Court is opened.

The Court proceeded to hear the argument of Counsel in the Case of Talbot Pltff in error v̄s Jansen. —

Adjourned till 10 °Clock tomorrow morning. —

Thursday Morning
20th August 1795. —

Pursuant to adjournment, the Court met this morning at the City hall, viz. —

The Honble John Rutledge Esqr Chief Justice

The honble ⎰ William Cushing
⎱ James Wilson
  James Iredell
  William Paterson ⎰ Esquires Associate Judges.

Proclamation is made and the Court is opened.

Cotton
v̄s
Wallace } On motion of Mr Read of Counsel for the defendant in error, Rule to return the record by the first day of January next. —

Hills et al
v̄s
Ross } On motion of Mr Read of Counsel for the defendant in error, Rule to return the record by the first day of January next. —

On motion of Mr Ingersoll, Jonathan Williams Condy, Esquire,[198] was ad-

---

198. Jonathan Williams Condy (1770-1828) was admitted to the Philadelphia bar in 1791 and to the Pennsylvania Supreme Court bar in 1792. Although not a Quaker by birth, he affirmed rather than swore when admitted to the Supreme Court bar. University of Pennsylvania, *Biograph-*

mitted a Counsellor of this Court, and he was immediately affirmed according to Law.﹘

Adjourned till tomorrow morning at ten ºClock.﹘

Friday Morning
21ˢᵗ August 1795.﹘

Pursuant to adjournment, the Court met this morning at the City hall, vizᵗ

The Hoñble John Rutledge, Esqʳ Chief Justice

The Hoñble $\left\{\begin{array}{l}\text{William Cushing}\\\text{James Wilson}\\\text{James Iredell}\\\text{William Paterson}\end{array}\right\}$ Esq̄ʳˢ Associate Judges.

Proclamation is made and the Court is opened.﹘

Mʳ Duponceau moved for a rule to shew cause why a prohibition should not go to Richard Peters Esqʳ Judge of the District Court of Pennsylvania to prohibit him from proceeding on a libel filed in the said Court by James Yard against Samuel. B. Davis and the Corvette or vessel of War called the Cassius.[199]

Adjourned till tomorrow morning at ten ºClock.﹘

Saturday Morning
22ⁿᵈ August 1795.﹘

Pursuant to adjournment, the Court met this morning at the City Hall vizᵗ

The Hoñble John Rutledge Esqʳ Chief Justice

The hoñble $\left\{\begin{array}{l}\text{William Cushing}\\\text{James Wilson}\\\text{James Iredell}\\\text{William Paterson}\end{array}\right\}$ Esqʳˢ Associate Judges.﹘

Proclamation is made and the Court is opened.

The Court proceeded to give their opinions in the Case of Talbot Pltff in error v̄s Jansen, when it was finally ordered, That the decree of the Circuit Court of South Carolina district pronounced on the fifth day of November in

ical Catalogue (1894), p. 26; *MBBP*, p. 258; "Supreme Court List of Attorneys, 1742-1902," Records of the Eastern District, RG 33, PHarH; *Record of Pennsylvania Marriages Prior to 1810*, 2 vols., reprint from *Pennsylvania Archives*, vols. 8 and 9 (1880; Baltimore: Genealogical Publishing, 1968), 1:53.
199. *United States v. Peters.*

the year of our Lord one thousand seven hundred and ninety four affirming the decree of the district Court of the same district pronounced on the sixth day of August in the year of our Lord one thousand seven hundred and ninety four be in all it's parts established and affirmed: — And it is further considered, ordered, adjudged and decreed, that the said William Talbot the plaintiff in error do pay to the said Joost Jansen the defendant in error, in addition to the sum of one thousand seven hundred and fifty five Dollars fifty three Cents for Demurrage and interest and eighty two dollars for Costs, in the decree of the said Circuit Court mentioned, Demurrage for the detention and delay of the said Brigantine De Vrouw Christina Magdalena at the rate of nine dollars and thirty three Cents lawful Money of the United States per diem to be accounted from the fifth day of November last past till the sixth day of June last, the day of the actual sale of the said Brigantine under the interlocutory order of this Court of the third day of March last past, to wit; for two hundred and thirteen days a Sum of nineteen hundred and eighty seven dollars and twenty nine Cents; and also interest at the rate of seven per centum per annum for two hundred and ninety days on the Sum of fifty one thousand eight hundred and forty five Dollars being the amount of the Sales of the Cargo of the said Brigantine heretofore sold by order and permission of the said district Court and making a Sum of two thousand eight hundred and eighty three dollars and forty two Cents and also a like sum of seven per Centum per annum on the amount sales of the said Brigantine De Vrouw Christina Magdalena under the order of this Court, that is to say interest for seventy seven days on the sum of eighteen hundred and twenty dollars from the said sixth day of June last making the sum of twenty six Dollars and eighty seven Cents the whole of which interest to be accounted to this day and making together the Sum of two thousand nine hundred and ten dollars twenty nine Cents lawful Money of the United States; And which said interest and demurrage makes together the Sum of four thousand eight hundred and ninety seven dollars fifty eight Cents in addition to and exclusive of the demurrage interest and Costs adjudged in the said Circuit Court of the United States for South Carolina district Also ninety one dollars and ninety three Cents for his Costs and Charges: And that the said Joost Jansen have execution of this judgment and decree by special mandate to the said Circuit Court and process agreeable to the Act of the Congress of the United States in that Case made and provided: And the said William Talbot in mercy and so forth. _

Wallace v̄s The Brig Cæsar et al!	On motion of M͟cClay for the defendant Rule to return the record by the first day of January next.

Adjourned till seven ⦵Clock this evening. _

Saturday Evening 22nd August 1795. ＿

Pursuant to adjournment the Court met at the City Hall viz!

The Hoñble John Rutledge Esquire Chief Justice

The hoñble $\left\{\begin{array}{l}\text{William Cushing}\\\text{James Wilson}\\\text{James Iredell}\\\text{William Paterson}\end{array}\right\}$ Esquires Associate Judges.

Proclamation is made and the Court is opened. ＿

The Court proceeded to hear the argument of Counsel on the motion for a prohibition to be directed to Richard Peters Esquire. ＿ [200]

Adjourned till Monday Morning next at nine ºClock. ＿

[――――――――]
Monday Morning
24th August 1795. ＿

Pursuant to adjournment, the Court met this morning at the City＝Hall, vizͭ

The Honorable John Rutledge Esqͬ Chief Justice

The hoñble $\left\{\begin{array}{l}\text{William Cushing}\\\text{James Wilson}\\\text{James Iredell}\\\text{William Paterson}\end{array}\right\}$ Esquires
Associate Judges.

Proclamation is made and the Court is opened.

Ordered,
That the Prohibition to be directed to Richard Peters, Esquire, Judge of the district Court of Pennsylvania, do issue. ＿ [201]

Adjourned to the time and place by Law appointed. ＿

[――――――――]

At Philadelphia, in the State of Pennsylvania, being the present seat of the national Government, on Monday the first day of February 1796. ＿

This being the day, by Law appointed, for holding a Supreme Court, and none of the Judges but the honorable James Wilson, Esquire, appearing for

200. Idem.
201. Idem.

Charles Lee, third attorney general of the United States, by Cephas Thompson (1755-1856). Oil on canvas, ca. 1810-1811. Courtesy National Portrait Gallery, Smithsonian Institution.

that purpose; the Court is by him adjourned 'till eleven ºClock tomorrow morning. __ [202]

Tuesday, February 2ⁿᵈ 1796.

None of the Judges but the Honorable James Wilson Esqʳ and the honorable William Paterson Esqʳ appearing pursuant to the adjournment of Yesterday, the Court is by them adjourned till tomorrow morning at 11 ºClock. __

Wednesday Morning, February 3ᵈ 1796. __

Pursuant to adjournment, the Court met this morning at the City Hall, to wit

The hon̄ble ⎰ William Cushing ⎱ Esquires
              ⎱ James Wilson   ⎰
              ⎰ James Iredell ⎱ Associate Judges
              ⎱ William Paterson ⎰

Proclamation is made and the Court is opened.

On motion of Edward Tilghman, Esqʳ the Attorney General of the United States, Charles Lee, Esquire, was qualified a Counsellor of this Court. __ [203]

On motion of Mʳ Lewis, Samuel Sitgreaves, Esquire,[204] of Pennsylvania, was admitted and sworn a Counsellor of this Court. __

---

202. Only four of the previous term's justices were still on the bench. James Wilson attended the opening session, William Paterson attended the next day, and William Cushing and James Iredell followed on the third. John Blair had resigned in October because of illness, and John Rutledge's appointment had been rejected by the Senate.

203. Charles Lee (1758-1815) was licensed to practice law in Virginia in 1781. At the time of his Supreme Court bar admission, Lee was attorney general of the United States. W. Hamilton Bryson, *The Virginia Law Reporters Before 1880* (Charlottesville: University Press of Virginia, 1977), pp. 85-86.

The first attorney general of the United States, Edmund Randolph, had his letters patent read into the record. William Bradford, who succeeded him, had been admitted previously as a counsellor of the Court. His letters patent were read in Court. Charles Lee, the newly appointed attorney general (Bradford died on August 23, 1795, and Lee was commissioned on December 10, 1795), was admitted to the bar of the Supreme Court, but the reading of his letters patent is not recorded in the minutes. Either Lee's letters patent were not read or the clerk just neglected to include the reading in the minutes.

204. Samuel Sitgreaves (1764-1827), admitted to the Philadelphia bar in 1783 and to the bar of the Supreme Court of Pennsylvania in 1785. A congressman from Pennsylvania, he lived in Easton, Pennsylvania, at the time of his admission to the bar of the Supreme Court of the United States. *University of Pennsylvania Catalogue, 1749-1880*, p. 31; *MBBP*, p. 311; "Supreme Court List of Attorneys, 1742-1902," Records of the Eastern District, RG 33, PHarH; Charles Lanham, *Biographical Annals of the Civil Government of the United States* (Washington, D.C.: James Anglim, 1876), p. 387.

The Attorney General of the United States proposed, for the consideration of the Court, that the Clerk of this Court should purchase for the use of this Court the Laws of the several States. _

Adjourned till eleven °Clock tomorrow morning. _

Thursday Morning
4ᵗʰ February 1796. _

Pursuant to adjournment, the Court met this morning at the City Hall, to wit,

The honble ⎰ William Cushing ⎱
           ⎰ James Wilson   ⎱ Esquires,
           ⎰ James Iredell   ⎱ Associate Judges. _
           ⎰ William Paterson ⎱

Proclamation is made, and the Court is opened.

Letters patent dated on the twenty seventh day of January one thousand seven hundred and ninety six appointing the honorable Samuel Chase, Esquire, of Maryland, one of the Associate Judges of this Court during his good behaviour, were read and published in open Court; and thereupon he took the oath of office, and the oath to support the constitution of the United States; after which he took his Seat on the Bench. _ [205]

On motion of Edward Tilghman, Esquire,
   Robert H. Dunkin,[206] of Pennsylvania, was admitted and sworn a Counsellor of this Court. _

The Court then proceeded to hear the argument of Counsel in the case of Thomas MacDonogh Pltff in error v̄s Citizen Dannery and the Ship Mary Ford.

Adjourned till 11 °Clock tomorrow morning. _

Friday Morning
5ᵗʰ February 1796. _

Pursuant to adjournment, the Court met this morning at the City Hall, to wit,

The honble ⎰ William Cushing ⎱
           ⎰ James Wilson   ⎱ Esquires
           ⎰ James Iredell   ⎱ Associate
           ⎰ William Paterson ⎱ Judges. _
           ⎰ Samuel Chase   ⎱

205. For a discussion of why Samuel Chase was not listed as present on the day his commission was read, see the introduction to "Appointments to the Bench."
206. Robert Henry Dunkin (1769-1808), admitted to practice before the Philadelphia bar in 1791, was a resident of Philadelphia and clerk of the corporation of the city at the time of his admission to the Supreme Court of the United States bar. Campbell, *History of the Friendly Sons of St. Patrick,* p. 401; *MBBP,* p. 265; Stephens, *The Philadelphia Directory* (1796); Stafford, *The Philadelphia Directory* (1797).

Proclamation is made, and the Court is opened. —

The Court proceeded to hear the argument of Counsel in the case of Thomas MacDonogh Pltff in error v̄s Citizen Dannery and the Ship Mary Ford.

The case of Benjamin Moodie Pltff in error v̄s the Mermaid et al. is assigned for argument for tomorrow.[207]

Adjourned till 11 ºClock tomorrow morning. —

[————————]
Saturday Morning
6ᵗʰ February 1796. —

Pursuant to adjournment, the Court met this morning at the City hall, to wit,

The hoñble	{ William Cushing James Wilson James Iredell William Paterson Samuel Chase }	Esquires Associate Judges. —

Proclamation is made, and the Court is opened. —

On motion of Mʳ Ingersoll,
   Robert Porter, Esquire,[208] was admitted a Counsellor of this Court, and he was accordingly sworn. —

The Court proceeded to hear the argument of Counsel in the Case of Ware Admor of Jones Pltff in error v̄s Hylton et al.

Adjourned till eleven ºClock on Monday morning next.

Monday Morning
8ᵗʰ February 1796. —

Pursuant to adjournment, the Court met this morning at the City Hall, to wit,

The Hoñble	{ William Cushing James Wilson James Iredell William Paterson Samuel Chase }	Esquires Associate Judges. —

207. The case was not argued until February 17, 1796.
   208. Robert Buell Porter (1768-1842) was admitted to practice at the Philadelphia bar in 1789 and to the Supreme Court of Pennsylvania bar in 1791. At the time of his admission to the bar of the Supreme Court of the United States, Porter lived in Philadelphia. *University of Pennsylvania Catalogue, 1749-1880*, p. 33; *MBBP*, p. 302; "Supreme Court List of Attorneys, 1742-1902," Records of the Eastern District, RG 33, PHarH; Stephens, *The Philadelphia Directory* (1796).

Proclamation is made, and the Court is opened. —

The Court proceeded to hear the argument of Counsel in the case of Ware Admor of Jones pltff in error v̄s Hylton et al. —

Adjourned till 11 ºClock tomorrow morning. —

Tuesday Morning
9ᵗʰ February 1796. —

Pursuant to adjournment, the Court met this morning at the City Hall, to wit,

The Hoñble ⟨ William Cushing / James Wilson / James Iredell / William Paterson / Samuel Chase ⟩ Esquires Associate Judges. —

Proclamation is made and the Court is opened. —

The Court proceeded to hear the argument of Counsel in the case of Ware Admor of Jones v̄s Hylton et al? —

Adjourned till eleven ºClock tomorrow Morning. —

[————————]
Wednesday Morning
10ᵗʰ February 1796. —

Pursuant to adjournment, the Court met this morning at the City Hall, to wit,

The Hoñble ⟨ William Cushing / James Wilson / James Iredell / William Paterson / Samuel Chase ⟩ Esquires Associate Judges. —

Proclamation is made and the Court is opened. —

The Court proceeded to hear the argument of Counsel in the Case of Ware Admor of Jones v̄s Hylton et al. —

Adjourned till eleven ºClock to morrow morning

Thursday Morning
11ᵗʰ February 1796. _

Pursuant to adjournment, the Court met this morning at the City Hall, to wit,

The Honble { William Cushing / James Wilson / James Iredell / William Paterson / Samuel Chase } Esquires Associate Judges. _

Proclamation is made and the Court is opened. _

The Court proceeded to hear the argument of Counsel in Ware Admor of Jones v̄s Hylton et al. _

Adjourned till 11 ºClock tomorrow morning. _

[————————————]

Friday Morning
12ᵗʰ February 1796. _

Pursuant to adjournment, the Court met this morning at the City Hall, to wit,

The honble { William Cushing / James Wilson / James Iredell / William Paterson / Samuel Chase } Esquires, Associate Judges.

Proclamation is made and the Court is opened. _

The Court proceeded to hear the argument of Counsel in the case of Ware Admor of Jones v̄s Hylton et al. _

Adjourned till 11 ºClock tomorrow morning.

Saturday Morning
13ᵗʰ February 1796. _

Pursuant to adjournment, the Court met this morning at the City Hall, to wit,

The Honble { James Wilson / James Iredell / William Paterson / Samuel Chase } Esquires Associate Judges. _

Proclamation is made and the Court is opened. _

On motion of Mr Read,

John Julius Pringle Esq[209] of South Carolina was admitted and sworn a Counsellor of this Court. _

On account of the illness of Judge Cushing the Court declined to hear any cause, and therefore adjourned till Monday Morning next at eleven °Clock. _

[———————]

Monday Morning
15th February 1796. _

Pursuant to adjournment, the Court met this morning at the City Hall, to wit,

The Honble ⎰ James Wilson / James Iredell / William Paterson / Samuel Chase ⎱ Esquires Associate Judges. _

Proclamation is made and the Court is opened. _

On account of the Continuation of Judge Cushing's illness and of the indisposition of Judge Paterson, the Court declined to hear any Cause, and therefore
Adjourned till tomorrow morning at 11 °Clock.

Tuesday Morning
16th February 1796. _

Pursuant to adjournment, the Court met this morning at the City Hall, to wit,

The honble ⎰ James Wilson / James Iredell / William Paterson / Samuel Chase ⎱ Esquires Associate Judges.

Proclamation is made, and the Court is opened.

On account of the continuation of the indisposition of Judge Cushing. and Judge Paterson, the Court declined the hearing of any Cause, and therefore Adjourned till eleven °Clock tomorrow Morning.

Wednesday Morning
17th February 1796. _

Pursuant to adjournment, the Court met this morning at the City Hall, viz!

209. John Julius Pringle (1753-1843) was admitted to the Charleston, South Carolina, bar in 1781. At the time of his admission to the Supreme Court bar, Pringle was attorney general of South Carolina and a resident of Charleston. *DAB.*

The hoñble { James Wilson / James Iredell / William Paterson / Samuel Chase } Esquires Associate Judges. _

Proclamation is made, and the Court is opened. _

Mʳ Read moved, that the Court would postpone the case of Benjamin Moodie, Pltff in error v̄s The Ship Mermaid et al. to be argued on Monday next. But his Motion was not granted, and the Court proceeded accordingly to the hearing of the argument thereof.

Ordered, unanimously by the Court, that the decree of the Circuit Court of the district of Massachusetts in the Case of Thomas McDonogh, Pltff in error, v̄s Citizen Dannery and the Ship Mary Ford be affirmed with Costs. _

Adjourned till tomorrow morning at 10 ºClock.

_____

Thursday Morning
18ᵗʰ February 1796. _

Pursuant to adjournment, the Court met this morning at the City Hall, viz!

The Hoñble { James Wilson / James Iredell / William Paterson / Samuel Chase } Esquires Associate Judges. _

Proclamation is made, and the Court is opened. _

The Court proceeded to hear the argument of Counsel in the Case of Benjamin Moodie Pltff in error v̄s The Ship Mermaid et al. _

On motion of Mʳ Ingersoll, a special mandate is awarded in the Case of Thomas MacDonogh Pltff in error v̄s Citizen Dannery and the Ship Mary Ford. _

Adjourned till tomorrow Morning at 10 ºClock.

_____

Friday Morning
19ᵗʰ February 1796. _

Pursuant to adjournment, the Court met this morning at the City Hall, Viz!

The Hoñble { James Wilson / James Iredell / William Paterson / Samuel Chase } Esquires Associate Judges. _

Proclamation is made and the Court is opened. _

The Court proceeded to hear the argument of Counsel in the Case of Benjamin Moodie Pltff in error v̄s The Ship Mermaid et al. ―

Adjourned till eleven ºClock tomorrow Morning. ―

[―――――――――]

Saturday Morning
20ᵗʰ February 1796. ―

Pursuant to adjournment, the Court met this morning at the City Hall, viz.ᵗ ―

The Hon̄ble { James Wilson
James Iredell
William Paterson
Samuel Chase } Esquires Associate Judges. ―

Proclamation is made, and the Court is opened. ―

The Court proceeded to hear the argument of Counsel in the case of Benjamin Moodie Pltff in error v̄s The Ship Mermaid et al.

The Case of Hills, May and Woodbridge v̄s Walter Ross is appointed for argument on Monday Morning next.

Adjourned till Monday Morning next at eleven ºClock. ―

Monday Morning
22ⁿᵈ February 1796. ―

Pursuant to adjournment, the Court met this morning at the City Hall, viz.ᵗ

{ James Wilson
James Iredell
William Paterson
Samuel Chase }

Proclamation is made, and the Court is opened.

On motion of the Attorney General of the United States, Alexander Hamilton Esqr.[210] of New York was admitted and sworn a Counsellor of this Court. ―

Adjourned till tomorrow morning at eleven ºClock. ―

[―――――――――]

210. Alexander Hamilton (1757-1804) was first called to the bar in July, 1782, as an attorney of the New York Supreme Court of Judicature. At the time he was admitted a counsellor of the Supreme Court, two days before his argument in *Hylton v. United States,* he was a resident of New York City. *DAB; PAH,* 3:122; 20:54.

Tuesday Morning
23ʳᵈ February 1796. —

Pursuant to adjournment, the Court met this morning at the City Hall, viz⁺ —

The Honble $\left\{\begin{array}{l}\text{James Wilson}\\\text{James Iredell}\\\text{William Paterson}\\\text{Samuel Chase}\end{array}\right\}$ Esquires Associate Judges. —

Proclamation is made, and the Court is opened. —

The Court proceeded to hear the argument of Counsel in the Case of Hylton, Pltff in error, v̄s The United States. —

Adjourned till tomorrow morning at eleven ⁰Clock. —

Wednesday Morning
24ᵗʰ February 1796. —

Pursuant to adjournment, the Court met this morning at the City Hall, viz⁺

The Honble $\left\{\begin{array}{l}\text{James Wilson}\\\text{James Iredell}\\\text{William Paterson}\\\text{Samuel Chase}\end{array}\right\}$ Esquires Associate Judges. —

Proclamation is made, and the Court is opened. —

The Court proceeded to hear the argument of Counsel in the Case of Hylton, Pltff in error, v̄s The United States. —

Adjourned till tomorrow morning at Eleven ⁰Clock. —

[———————]
Thursday Morning
25ᵗʰ February 1796. —

Pursuant to adjournment, the Court met this morning at the City Hall, viz⁺

The Honble $\left\{\begin{array}{l}\text{James Wilson}\\\text{James Iredell}\\\text{William Paterson}\\\text{Samuel Chase}\end{array}\right\}$ Esquires Associate Judges. —

Proclamation is made, and the Court is opened. —

The Court proceeded to hear the argument of Counsel in the Case of Hylton, Pltff in error, v̄s The United States. —

Adjourned till tomorrow morning at eleven °Clock. —

Friday Morning
26ᵗʰ February 1796. —

Pursuant to adjournment, the Court met this morning at the City Hall, viz⁺ —

The Honble { James Wilson / James Iredell / William Paterson / Samuel Chase } Esquires Associate Judges. —

Proclamation is made, and the Court is opened. —

The Court proceeded to hear the argument of Counsel in the case of Hills, May, and Woodbridge v̄s Walter Ross, and, after making some progress therein, they proceeded to hear the argument of Counsel in the case of John Wallace Pltff in error v̄s The Brig Cæsar and Cargoe and David Arnache. —

Adjourned till tomorrow morning at 11 °Clock. —

[———————————]
Saturday Morning
February 27ᵗʰ 1796. —

Pursuant to adjournment, the Court met this morning at the City Hall, viz⁺

The Honble { James Wilson / James Iredell / William Paterson / Samuel Chase } Esquires Associate Judges. —

Proclamation is made and the Court is opened.

The Court proceeded to hear the argument of Counsel in the Cases of John Wallace, plaintiff in error, v̄s The Brig Cæsar and Cargo and David Arnache — and Benjamin Moodie, Pltff in error, v̄s The Ship Favorite et al. which were agreed by Counsel to be argued together, as depending upon similar principles for their determination. —

Ordered, that the Clerk of this Court request the Secretary of State to grant for the Use of this Court a set of the Journals of the Congress of the United States up to the time of the commencement of the new Government; or, if that cannot be done, to permit them to be brought up to Court from time to time during the Session thereof, the Clerk returning them at the end of every session. —

Adjourned till Monday Morning next at Eleven °Clock. —

[———————————]

Monday Morning
29ᵗʰ February 1796. —

Pursuant to adjournment, the Court met this morning at the City Hall, to wit,

The Honble $\left\{ \begin{array}{l} \text{James Wilson} \\ \text{James Iredell} \\ \text{William Paterson} \\ \text{Samuel Chase} \end{array} \right\}$ Esquires Associate Judges.

Proclamation is made, and the Court is opened. —

Ordered, that the Judgment of the Circuit Court of South Carolina District, in the Case of Benjamin Moodie Esquire, Vice-Consul of his Brittanic Majesty, Pltff in error v̄s The Brig Favorite and her Cargo and Alexander Bolchos and others, be affirmed with Costs; and that the said defendants in error have execution thereof by special Mandate to be directed to the said Circuit Court. —

Ordered, That the Judgment of the Circuit Court of Georgia District, in the case of John Wallace Esqr Vice Consul of his Brittanic Majesty v̄s The Brig Cæsar and her Cargo and David Arnache and others, be affirmed with Costs; and that the said Defendants in error have special Mandate for execution thereof.

On motion of Mr Dallas, Rule on the Marshall of the District of South Carolina to make return of the process issued in the case of John Brown Cutting Administrator of Anne Paul Emanuel Sigismund de Montmorency Luxembourg v̄s The State of South Carolina within the first four days of the next ensuing term. —

The Court then proceeded to hear the argument of Counsel in the Case of Claude Delcol et al. Pltffs in error v̄s Jonathan Arnold. —

Adjourned till tomorrow morning at eleven ºClock. —

———————————

Tuesday Morning
March 1ˢᵗ 1796. —

Pursuant to adjournment, the Court met this morning at the City Hall, Vizt

The Honble $\left\{ \begin{array}{l} \text{James Wilson} \\ \text{James Iredell} \\ \text{William Paterson} \\ \text{Samuel Chase} \end{array} \right\}$ Esquires Associate Judges. —

Proclamation is made and the Court is opened.

The Court proceeded to give their opinions in the Case of Benjamin

Moodie, Pltff in error v̄s The Ship Mermaid et al. when it was finally
Ordered,

That the decree of the Circuit Court of South Carolina District in this Cause
be affirmed with Costs; and that the defendants in error have for Execution
thereof a special Mandate. _

The Court proceeded to hear the argument of Counsel in the case of Claude
Delcol et al. Plaintiffs in error v̄s Jonathan Arnold. _

Adjourned till tomorrow morning at eleven °Clock. _
[————————————]
Wednesday Morning
2ᵈ March 1796. _

Pursuant to adjournment, the Court met this morning at the City Hall, to
wit,

The hon̄ble ⎨ William Cushing / James Wilson / James Iredell / William Paterson²¹¹ ⎬ Esquires Associate Judges. _

Proclamation is made, and the Court is opened.

By consent of parties,
Ordered,

That the Judgment of the Circuit Court for the district of Georgia, in the
case of the Brig Everton and Cargo and John. B. Cotton, Pltffs in error, against
John Wallace, Esquire, Vice Consul of his Britannic Majesty, be affirmed with
Costs; and that the Question_ whether any and what Damages shall be recovered? do lie over for determination until the next Term of this Court.

The Court proceeded to hear the argument of Counsel in the case of Jeremiah Olney, Pltff in error v̄s Welcome Arnold. _

The Court appointed the Case of Geyer, Pltff in error v̄s John Michel and
the Ship Den Onzekeren and Cargo for argument for tomorrow, if the case
of Delcol et al. pltffs in error, v̄s Arnold cannot come on, on account of Judge
Chase continuing to be ill. _

Adjourned till tomorrow morning at eleven °Clock. _
[————————————]

211. According to a letter from James Iredell to Hannah Iredell on March 3, 1796 (see "Commentaries"), Samuel Chase was suffering from gout at this time and did not attend court again
until March 7.

Thursday Morning
3ᵈ March 1796. __

Pursuant to adjournment, the Court met this Morning at the City Hall, to wit,

The Hoñble { William Cushing } Esquires
            { James Wilson   } Associate
            { James Iredell   } Judges. __
            { William Paterson }

Proclamation is made, and the Court is opened.

The Court proceeded to hear the argument of Counsel in the cases of Geyer, Pltff in error v̄s John Michel and the Ship Den Onzekeren; and Benjamin Moodie Pltff in error v̄s The Ship Betty Cathcart and her Cargo and Jean Vidal et al. which were agreed by Counsel to be argued together, as depending upon similar principles for their determination.

Adjourned till tomorrow morning at 11 ºClock.

Friday Morning
4ᵗʰ March 1796. __

Pursuant to adjournment, the Court met this morning at the City Hall, to wit,

The Hoñble { William Cushing } Esquires
            { James Wilson   } Associate
            { James Iredell   } Judges. __
            { William Paterson }

Proclamation is made, and the Court is opened.

The Court proceeded to hear the argument of Counsel in the cases of Geyer, Pltff in error v̄s John Michel and the Ship Den Onzekeren; and Benjamin Moodie, Pltff in error v̄s The Ship Betty Cathcart and her Cargo and Jean Vidal et al. __

Adjourned till tomorrow morning at 11 ºClock. __

Saturday Morning
March 5ᵗʰ 1796. __

Pursuant to adjournment, the Court met this morning at the City hall, viz.ᵗ

The Hoñble { William Cushing } Esquires
            { James Wilson   } Associate
            { James Iredell   } Judges. __
            { William Paterson }

Proclamation is made and the Court is opened. —

The Court proceeded to hear the argument of Counsel in the Cases of Geyer, Pltff in error v̄s John Michel and the Ship Den Onzekeren; and Benjamin Moodie Pltff in error v̄s The Ship Betty Cathcart and her Cargo and Jean Vidal et al. —

Adjourned till Monday Morning next at eleven ꝑClock. —

Monday Morning
7ᵗʰ March 1796. —

Pursuant to adjournment, the Court met this morning at the City Hall, to wit,

The hoñble ⎰ William Cushing ⎱
⎱ James Wilson ⎰ Esquires
⎰ James Iredell ⎱ Associate
⎱ William Paterson ⎰ Judges. —
⎰ Samuel Chase ⎱

Proclamation is made and the Court is opened. —

The Court proceeded to give their Opinions solemnly in the Case of John Tyndale Ware, Adm̄or of William Jones the surviving partner of Farrel and Jones, Subjects of the King of Great Britain, against Daniel Lawrence Hylton and Company and Francis Eppes, Citizens of the State of Virginia, when it was finally ordered that Judgment be therein entered in the words following: —

Whereupon all and singular the premises being seen by the Court here and fully understood, and mature deliberation had thereon, because it appears to the Court now here, that in the record and process aforesaid and also in the rendition of the Judgment aforesaid upon the demurrer to the rejoinder of the defendants in error to the replication to the second plea, it is manifestly erred; it is considered that the said Judgment, for those errors and others in the record and process aforesaid, be revoked annulled and altogether held for nought And it is further considered by the Court here, that the plaintiff in error recover against the defendants two thousand nine hundred and seventy six pounds eleven shillings and six pence good British Money commonly called Sterling Money his debt aforesaid and his Costs by him about his Suit in this behalf expended and the said defendants in mercy &cᵃ But this Judgment is to be discharged by the payment of the Sum of five hundred and ninety six dollars and interest thereon to be computed after the rate of five per cent per Annum from the seventh day of July one thousand seven hundred and eighty two till payment besides the Costs and by the payment of such damages as shall be awarded to the plaintiff in error on a writ of Enquiry to be issued by the Circuit Court of Virginia to ascertain the sum really due to the plaintiff exclusively of the said Sum of five hundred and ninety six Dollars which was found to be due to the plaintiff in error upon the Trial in the said Circuit Court of the issue joined upon the defendant's plea of payment at a time when the Judgment of the said Circuit Court on the said demurrer was unreversed and in full force and vigor; and for the execution of this Judgment of the Court the cause aforesaid is remanded to the said Circuit Court of Virginia. ___

Mr Ingersoll moved for a prohibition on the libel and suit instituted by Thomas Smith in the district Court of the District of Virginia against Alexander Macauley and the Ship Charles Carter upon a Mortgage of the said Ship.[212]

Adjourned till tomorrow morning at 11 ºClock. ___

Tuesday Morning
8th March 1796. ___

Pursuant to adjournment, the Court met this morning at the City Hall, to wit,

The Hoñble {
William Cushing
James Wilson
James Iredell
William Paterson
Samuel Chase
} Esquires
Associate
Judges. ___

Proclamation is made, and the Court is opened.

Letters patent, dated on the fourth day of March in the Year of our Lord One thousand seven hundred and ninety six and of the Independence of the United States the twentieth, appointing the honorable Oliver Ellsworth, Esquire, of Connecticut, Chief Justice of this Court, during his good Behaviour, were read and published in open Court; and thereupon he took the oath of office and the oath to support the Constitution of the United States: after which he took his Seat upon the bench. ___ [213]

The Court then proceeded to give their opinions in the case of D. L. Hylton, Pltff in error v̄s The United States, when it was ordered, that the Judgment of the Circuit Court of Virginia district in the said Cause should be affirmed. ___

The Court then proceeded to hear the argument of Counsel in the case of Claude Delcol et al. Pltffs in error v̄s Jonathan Arnold. ___

Adjourned till tomorrow morning at 10 ºClock. ___
[—————————]

-----

212. *United States v. Judge of the District Court of the United States for the district of Virginia.*

213. Oliver Ellsworth replaced John Rutledge. See note 202 above. For a discussion of why Ellsworth was not listed as present on the day his commission was read, see the introduction to "Appointments to the Bench."

Wednesday Morning
9th March 1796. —

Pursuant to adjournment, the Court met this morning at the City Hall, to wit,

The Hoñble $\left\{\begin{array}{l} \text{James Wilson} \\ \text{James Iredell} \\ \text{William Paterson} \\ \text{Samuel Chase}[214] \end{array}\right\}$ Esquires Associate Judges. —

Proclamation is made, and the Court is opened.

The Court proceeded to hear the argument of Counsel in the case of Claude Delcol et al. Pltffs in error v̄s Jonathan Arnold.

Adjourned till tomorrow morning at eleven °Clock. —

Thursday Morning
10th March 1796. —

Pursuant to adjournment, the Court met this morning at the City Hall, to wit,

The hoñble $\left\{\begin{array}{l} \text{William Cushing} \\ \text{James Wilson} \\ \text{James Iredell} \\ \text{William Paterson}[215] \end{array}\right\}$ Esquires Associate Judges.

Proclamation is made, and the Court is opened.

Ordered, that the Case of Claude Delcol et al. Pltffs in error v̄s Jonathan Arnold lie over till the next term for argument upon the Question — How far are the owners responsible in damages? —

The Court proceeded to hear the argument of Counsel in the Cases of Geyer, Pltff in error v̄s John Michel and the Ship Den Onzekeren; and Ben-

---

214. Oliver Ellsworth was present for his oath of office and for the last day of the term to adjourn the Court, but he did not attend the Court on the intervening days as argument on some of the cases before the Court had preceded his appointment. We do not know why William Cushing missed this meeting of the Court. William Garrott Brown, *The Life of Oliver Ellsworth* (New York: Macmillan, 1905), p. 248.

215. Samuel Chase had been ill between March 2 and 7. See note 211 above. During that time the Court had heard *Geyer v. Michel* and *Moodie v. Ship Betty Cathcart*. When Chase returned to the bench, the Court heard *Delcol v. Arnold*. On March 10, the Court announced that *Delcol v. Arnold* was being held over to the next term. Chase may have been too ill to continue, or else he realized that *Delcol v. Arnold* was being held over and the Court would resume hearing the cases he had missed previously in which he could not participate, so he did not attend the rest of the term.

jamin Moodie, pltff in error, v̄s The Ship Betty Cathcart and her Cargo and Jean Vidal et al. _

Adjourned till tomorrow morning at ten ºClock. _

Friday Morning
11ᵗʰ March 1796. _

Pursuant to adjournment, the Court met this morning at the City Hall, to wit,

The Honble $\left\{\begin{array}{l}\text{William Cushing}\\\text{James Wilson}\\\text{James Iredell}\\\text{William Paterson}\end{array}\right\}$ $\begin{array}{l}\text{Esquires}\\\text{Associate}\\\text{Judges. \_}\end{array}$

Proclamation is made, and the Court is opened.

The Court proceeded to hear the argument of Counsel in the cases of Geyer, pltff in error, v̄s John Michel and the Ship Den Onzekeren; and Benjamin Moodie, pltff in error, v̄s The Ship Betty Cathcart and Cargo and Jean Vidal et al. _

Adjourned till tomorrow morning at ten ºClock. _

[————————]
Saturday Morning
12ᵗʰ March 1796. _

Pursuant to adjournment, the Court met this morning at the City Hall, to wit,

The Honble $\left\{\begin{array}{l}\text{William Cushing}\\\text{James Wilson}\\\text{James Iredell}\\\text{William Paterson}\end{array}\right\}$ $\begin{array}{l}\text{Esquires}\\\text{Associate}\\\text{Judges. \_}\end{array}$

Proclamation is made, and the Court is opened.

The Court proceeded to hear the argument of counsel in the Cases of Geyer, pltff in error, v̄s John Michel and the Ship Den Onzekeren; and Benjamin Moodie, pltff in error v̄s The Ship Betty Cathcart and Cargo and Jean Vidal et al. _

The Court proceeded to hear the argument of Counsel, on the motion of Mʳ Ingersoll for a prohibition on the libel and suit instituted by Thomas Smith in the District Court of the district of Virginia against Alexander Macauley and the Ship Charles Carter upon a Mortgage of the said Ship. _ [216]

---

216. *United States v. Judge of the District Court of the United States for the district of Virginia.*

Adjourned till Monday Morning next at ten ⁰Clock. _

[——————————]

Monday Morning
14ᵗʰ March 1796. _

Pursuant to adjournment, the Court met this morning in the Common Council Room of the Corporation of Philadelphia,[217] to wit,

The honble Oliver Ellsworth, Esqʳ Chief Justice

The honble $\left\{ \begin{array}{l} \text{William Cushing} \\ \text{James Wilson} \\ \text{James Iredell} \\ \text{William Paterson} \end{array} \right\}$ $\left. \begin{array}{l} \text{Esquires} \\ \text{Associate} \\ \text{Judges.} \_ \end{array} \right.$

Proclamation is made, and the Court is opened.

Ordered, that the decree of the Circuit Court of South Carolina district in the case of John Geyer pltff in error v̄s John Michel and the Ship Den Onzekeren and Cargo be affirmed with costs, but without damages. _

Ordered, that the decree of the Circuit Court of South Carolina District in the case of Benjamin Moodie, pltff in error, v̄s The Ship Betty Cathcart and Cargo and Laurent Vidal et al. be affirmed with Costs but without damages. _

Ordered, that the decree of the Circuit Court of South Carolina District in the case of Benjamin Moodie, Esqʳ pltff in error v̄s The Ship Phyn and Cargo and John Gaillard et al. be affirmed with Costs and that the defendants in error have a special mandate for execution. _

The Court then proceeded to hear the argument of Counsel on the motion of Mʳ Ingersoll for a prohibition on the libel and suit instituted by Thomas Smith in the district Court of Virginia District against Alexander Macaulay and the Ship Charles Carter upon a Mortgage of the said Ship; when it was
Ordered,
That the prohibition issue. _ [218]

Ordered,
That the motion of Mʳ Lewis, for a distringas to compel the appearance of the State of Virginia to the bill filed by William Grayson and others, lie over till the next Term. _ [219]

---

217. The February 1796 term of the Court had been the longest to date, lasting until March 14, 1796, the day of the opening of the Mayor's Court in Philadelphia. Since the Supreme Court ordinarily met in the Mayor's Courtroom in Philadelphia's City Hall, it had to move to a different location for March 14, which it did by meeting in the Common Council Room on the second floor of City Hall. Reeder, "First Homes of the Supreme Court," p. 585.
218. *United States v. Judge of the District Court of the United States for the district of Virginia.*
219. *Hollingsworth v. Virginia.*

Ordered,

That the cases of Jeremiah Olney Pltff in error v̄s Welcome Arnold, and Jeremiah Olney Pltff in error v̄s Edward Dexter lie[220] over till the next term. _

Ordered, on motion of Mʳ Pringle and by consent of parties that the writ of Error in the Case of Don Diego Morphy, Consul of his Catholic Majesty against the Ship Sacra Familia and Cargo and John Gaillard et al. be discontinued, and that no other Writ of Error be ever taken out therein. _

Ordered, that all the unfinished business of this Court be continued until the next term. _

Adjourned till the time and to the place by Law appointed. _

At the City hall in the City of Philadelphia (being the present seat of the National Government of the United States) on Monday the First day of August in the Year of our Lord one thousand seven hundred and ninety six, and of the Independence of the United States, the twenty first, The Court met.

present

The Honorable Oliver Ellsworth Esquire Chief Justice

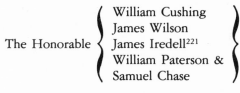

The Honorable { William Cushing / James Wilson / James Iredell[221] / William Paterson & / Samuel Chase } Esquires Associate Justices

Proclamation is made and the Court is opened.

The Marshall of Pennsylvania District makes return of a Venire for a special Jury, which is filed; and the Jurors being called, John Dunlap, Francis West, Richard Rundle, George Harrison, Curtis Clay[,] Philip Nicklin, William Crammond, Thomas W. Francis, John Simpson[,] John Hall, John Field, Joseph P Norris, George Bickham, Samuel Breck Junior, Israel Pleasants, John Kaighn, Emanuel Walker, Thomas Mackie, John Oldden, John Thompson, James Coxe, Isaac Penington, Joseph Sims, Peter Blight, Peter Kuhn, Joshua B. Bond, Thomas Hockley, William Montgomery, George Willing, Samuel Clarkson, Wilson Hunt, James Miller, Robert Wescott, Edward Shoemaker George Thompson, Samuel Meeker, Jonathan Jones, John Vaughan, William West, Norton Pryor Junʳ[,] George Lauman, Samuel Fisher, Jonathan Harvey, Patrick Moore[,] Benjamin W. Morris, John Duffield and David H Conyngham made default, and James Vanuxem was excused from further attendance on account of the ill state of his health.

220. The word "lie" is written over a period and a dash.
221. The "d" is written over an "l."

On motion of M.ʳ Ingersoll, John Y Noel Esquire²²² was admitted and sworn a Counsellor of this Court.

The List of Causes was called and several of them set down for argument.

The Jury are excused from further attendance till Saturday morning next at 9 o'Clock

Adjourned till to morrow morning at nine o'Clock.

[———————]

Tuesday Morning—
2.ⁿᵈ August 1796.

Pursuant to adjournment the Court met this morning at the City Hall, to wit,

The Honorable Oliver Ellsworth Esquire, Chief Justice

The Honorable { William Cushing / James Wilson / James Iredell / William Paterson / Samuel Chase } Esquires Associate Justices.

Proclamation is made and the Court is opened.

The Court proceeded to hear the argument of Counsel in the Case of John B Cotton vs John Wallace, and having made some progress therein they proceeded to hear the argument of Counsel in the case of Hills, May and Woodbridge and the Ship Elizabeth against Walter Ross.

Adjourned till to morrow morning at nine o'Clock.

[———————]

Wednesday Morning
3.ʳᵈ August 1796.

Pursuant to adjournment the Court met this Morning at the City Hall, to wit,

The Honorable Oliver Ellsworth Esquire, Chief Justice

The Honorable { William Cushing / James Wilson / James Iredell / William Paterson and / Samuel Chase. } Esquires associate Justices

222. John Young Noel (1762-1817) received his attorney's license in New Jersey in 1783 and practiced law in that state until he moved to Georgia, where he was admitted to the bar in 1788 (information courtesy of G-Ar). Noel, who served as solicitor general of Georgia until 1795 (information courtesy of G-Ar), was practicing law in Savannah when admitted to the Supreme Court bar. Harrison, *Princetonians,* 2:196-98.

Proclamation is made and the Court is opened.

The Court proceeded to hear the argument of Counsel in the Case of the Ship Elizabeth and Cargo and Hills, May and Woodbridge vs Walter Ross

Adjourned till to Morrow morning at nine o'Clock.

Thursday Morning
4ᵗʰ August 1796.

Pursuant to adjournment the Court met this morning at the City Hall, to wit

The Honorable Oliver Ellsworth Esquire, Chief Justice

The Honble. { William Cushing
James Wilson
James Iredell
William Paterson &
Samuel Chase } Esquires Associate Justices

Proclamation is made and the Court is opened

On motion of Edward Tilghman Esquire, Richard Stockton[223] and Andrew Kirkpatrick[224] Esquires, both of the State of New Jersey were admitted and sworn Counsellors of this Court

The Court proceeded to hear the argument of Counsel in the Case of the Ship Elizabeth and Cargo and Hills, Mary and Woodbridge against Walter Ross.

Adjourned till to morrow morning at nine o'Clock.

Friday Morning
5ᵗʰ August 1796.

Pursuant to adjournment the Court met this Morning at the State House,[225] to wit.

223. Richard Stockton (1764-1828) gained admission to the New Jersey bar in 1784. When admitted to the Supreme Court bar, Stockton had a thriving practice in that state. *DAB.*

224. Andrew Kirkpatrick (1756-1831) was admitted to the New Jersey bar in 1785. At the time of his admission to the Supreme Court bar, he lived in New Brunswick. *DAB.*

225. The Court usually met at the City Hall; why it met at the State House this day is not known. Possibly it changed quarters to allow alterations to the City Hall. Philadelphia had amended its government and elected a bicameral legislature in 1796. Alterations were being made in the meeting rooms of City Hall to accommodate two chambers rather than one. The Court returned to City Hall the next day. Reeder, "First Homes of the Supreme Court," p. 592; U.S. Department of Interior, National Park Service, "Historic Structures Report on Old City Hall, Independence National Historic Park, 1961," part 2, Architectural Data Section prepared by Lee Nelson, p. 10, typescript in Historian's Office, PPIn.

The Honorable Oliver Ellsworth Esquire, Chief Justice

The Honble. {
  William Cushing
  James Wilson
  James Iredell
  William Paterson &
  Samuel Chase
} Esquires Associate Justices

Proclamation is made and the Court is opened.

The Court proceeded to hear the argument of Counsel in the Case of Claude Delcol et al against Jonathan Arnold.

Adjourned till to morrow morning at nine o'Clock.

[————————]

Saturday Morning
6th August 1796.

Pursuant to adjournment the Court met this morning at the City Hall, to wit,

The Honorable Oliver Ellsworth, Esquire, Chief Justice

The Honble[226] {
  William Cushing
  James Wilson
  James Iredell
  William Paterson and
  Samuel Chase.
} Esquires Associate Justices

Proclamation is made and the Court is opened.

The Jury, who were required to meet on this day, are now dismissed.

The Petition of David Hunter praying the Court to continue the case of Hunter against Fairfax's lee. was read and the prayer of the Petition granted.

On motion of M.r Dallas for the Plaintiff a rule is granted on the Marshal of South Carolina District to return the Writ of Summons in the Case of Cutting against the State of South Carolina—

The Court proceeded to hear the argument of Counsel in the Case of Olney vs Arnold, and after making some progress therein, they proceeded to hear the argument of Counsel in the Case of Benjamin Moodie against the Ship Phœbe Ann and Cargo and Jean Bouteille et al.

Adjourned till Monday morning next at nine o'Clock.

[————————]

226. "The Honble" seems to be in Jacob Wagner's hand.

Monday Morning
8ᵗʰ August 1796.

Pursuant to adjournment the Court met this morning at the City Hall, to wit,

The Honorable Oliver Ellsworth Esquire, Chief Justice

The Honble. {
William Cushing
James Wilson
James Iredell
William Paterson &
Samuel Chase
} Esquires Associate Justices

Proclamation is made and the Court is opened.

The Court proceeded to hear the argument of Counsel in the Case of Benjamin Moodie against the Ship Phœbe Ann and Cargo and Jean Bouteille et al which being terminated they proceeded to hear the argument of Counsel in the Case of Benjamin Moodie vs the Ship Alfred and Cargo and Abraham Sasportas et. al. which being terminated they proceeded to hear the argument of Counsel in the Case of Benjamin Moodie vs the Ship Britannia and Cargo and Jean B Carvine et al.

Adjourned till to morrow morning at nine oClock.

[————————]

Tuesday Morning
9ᵗʰ August 1796.

Pursuant to adjournment the Court met this morning at the City Hall, to wit,

The Honorable Oliver Ellsworth Esquire, Chief Justice

The Honble. {
William Cushing
James Wilson
James Iredell
William Paterson &
Samuel Chase.
} Esquires Associate Justices

Proclamation is made and the Court is opened.

Ordered
That the Decree of the Circuit Court for South Carolina District in the Case of Benjamin Moodie against the Ship Phœbe Ann and Cargo and Jean Bouteille and others be affirmed with Costs: and a special Mandate is awarded.

Ordered
That the Decree of the Circuit Court for South Carolina District in the Case of Benjamin Moodie against the Ship Alfred and Cargo and John Antoine

Garriscan and others be affirmed with costs: and a special mandate is awarded —

Ordered

That the Judgment of the Circuit Court for South Carolina District in the Case of Benjamin Moodie against the Ship Britannia and Cargo and Jean B Carvine and others be affirmed with Costs: and a special mandate is awarded.

Ordered.

That the Judgment of the Circuit Court for South Carolina District in the Case of Benjamin Moodie against the Brig Eliza and Cargo and John Gaillard and others be affirmed with Costs: and a special mandate is awarded.

Ordered

That the Judgment of the Circuit Court for South Carolina District in the Case of Benjamin Moodie against the Brig Tivoly and Cargo and Abraham Sasportas and others be affirmed with Costs: and a special mandate is awarded.

Ordered

That the Judgment of the Circuit Court for South Carolina District in the Case of Benjamin Moodie against the Brig Eliza and Cargo and Paul Beltrimeux and others be affirmed with Costs: and a special mandate is awarded.

Ordered

That the Judgment of the Circuit Court for South Carolina District in the Case of Benjamin Moodie against the Snow Potowmack and Cargo and Jean B. Carvine and others be affirmed with Costs: and a special Mandate is awarded.

Mʳ Lewis renewed his motion for a Distringas to compel the State of Virginia to appear and answer William Grayson and others.[227]

The Court having heard the argument of Counsel in the case of John B Cotton Plaintiff in Error, against John Wallace, defendant in error, on the question, whether any and what damages shall be recovered? which question was referred to this term for determination — it is now finally ordered that the said defendant in Error recover as damages against the said Plaintiff in error the Sum of Two thousand seven hundred and eighty seven Dollars and thirty two cents being the Interest of thirty four thousand eight hundred and forty one Dollars[228] and fifty five Cents, the amount Sales of the Brig Everton and her Cargo from the fifth day of May one thousand seven hundred and ninety five, the day of the decree of the Circuit Court in the said cause being one year until the fifth day of May one thousand seven hundred and ninety six being one year[229] at the rate of eight per

227. *Hollingsworth v. Virginia.*

228. The "D" is written over an "S."

229. The interlineation, in a hand different from that of the text, seems to be in Jacob Wagner's handwriting.

Centum per annum; and also that the said Plaintiff in error do pay the costs accrued in this Cause since the last term: and a special mandate is awarded to carry this order into execution.

The Court proceeded to hear the argument of Counsel in the Case of Don Diego Pintado against the Ship San Joseph alias la Princesa de las Asturias and Jean Antoine Berard.

Adjourned till to morrow morning at nine o'Clock

Wednesday Morning
10th August 1796.

Pursuant to adjournment the Court met this morning at the City Hall. to wit,

The Honorable Oliver Ellsworth Esquire Chief Justice

The Honble. { William Cushing / James Wilson / James Iredell / William Paterson & / Samuel Chase } Esquire Associate Justices

Proclamation is made and the Court is opened.

Thomas Fennimore
vs
The United States[230]   } Error from the Circuit Court of New Jersey.

The Writ of error is returned and filed. The Attorney General on behalf of the United States agrees to acknowledge the service of a Citation, Mr E Tilghman for the Plaintiff assigns the Common Errors and the attorney General Joins in Error.

on motion of Edward Tilghman Esquire Richard Lake Esquire[231] of Pennsylvania was admitted and sworn a Counsellor of this Court

---

230. "States," which appears to have been written by someone other than the person who recorded the rest of the text, seems to be in Jacob Wagner's hand.

231. Richard Lake (1753-1798), son of an Edinburgh merchant, studied law in Scotland, where he was admitted to the Society of Writers to His Majesty's Signet in 1780. He moved to Pennsylvania in 1785 and was admitted to the bar of the Philadelphia Court of Common Pleas in 1793. At the time of his admission to the Supreme Court bar, he practiced law in Philadelphia. Shortly thereafter he moved to Kentucky. *The Society of Writers to His Majesty's Signet with a List of the Members* (Edinburgh: T. and A. Constable, 1936), p. 217; Thompson Westcott, *Names of Persons Who Took the Oath of Allegiance to the State of Pennsylvania* (Philadelphia: John Campbell, 1865), p. 105; *MBBP*, p. 285; Hardie, *The Philadelphia Directory* (1794); Stafford, *The Philadelphia Directory* (1797); obituary in Lexington *Kentucky Gazette,* December 26, 1798.

Ordered

That the decree[232] of the Circuit Court for the District of New York in the Case of Don Diego Pintado against the Ship San Joseph, alias la Princesa de la Asturias and Jean Antoine Berard be affirmed with Costs: and a special Mandate is awarded.

The Court proceeded to hear the argument of Counsel in the Case of Wisecart vs. Dauchy; and having made some progress therein they proceeded to hear the argument of Counsel in the Case of the United States against the Schooner La Vengeance and Jean Antoine Bernard de Rozier.

Adjourned till to morrow morning at nine o'Clock.

Thursday Morning
11th August 1796.

Pursuant to adjournment the Court met this Morning at the City Hall, to wit,

The Honorable Oliver Ellsworth Esquire Chief Justice.

The Honͦble. { William Cushing
James Wilson
James Iredell
William Paterson &
Samuel Chase } Esqrs Associate Justices

Proclamation is made and the Court is opened

Ordered

That the Judgment of the Superior[233] Court of Judicature, Court of Assize and Jail delivery for the County of Providence in the State of Rode Island in the Case of Jeremiah Olney Plaintiff in error, against Welcome Arnold be reversed with Costs.

Ordered

That the Judgment of the Superior Court of Judicature Court of Assize and Jail Delivery for the County of Providence in the State of Rhode[234] Island in the Case of Jeremiah Olney Plaintiff in error against Edward Dexter be reversed with Costs.

Ordered

That the Decree of the Circuit Court for the District of New York in the Case of the United States against the Schooner La Vengeance and Jean Antoine Bernard de Rozier be affirmed: and a special mandate is awarded.

232. The "r" is written over an "e."
233. The letters "erior" are written over a partially erased "reme." This change seems to be in the hand of Jacob Wagner.
234. The "h" is written over a partially erased "o."

John Brown Cutting adm̅. of
Ann Paul Emanuel Sigismund
de Montmorency Luxembourgh ⎱ In Case
    against
The State of South Carolina

Ordered

That the Plaintiff in this Cause do file his declaration on or before the tenth day of September next

Ordered

That certified copies of the said declaration be served on the Governor and Attorney General of the State of South Carolina on or before the first Day of November next

Ordered

That unless the said State shall either in due form appear or shew Cause to the contrary in this Court by the first day of the next term Judgment by default be entered against the said State.

Ordered

That the decree of the Circuit Court for South Carolina District in the Case of Claude Delcol and others Plaintiffs in error against Jonathan Arnold be affirmed with Costs: and a special mandate is awarded.

Ordered

That the Case of Samuel Emory[235] against David S Grenough be continued until the next term.

Ordered

That the Case of Thomas Fennimore against the United States be continued.

Adjourned till to morrow morning at nine o'Clock

Friday Morning
12th August 1796.

Pursuant to adjournment the Court met this Morning at the City Hall, to wit,

The Honorable Oliver Ellsworth, Esquire, Chief Justice[236]

The Hon̅ble. ⎰ William Cushing ⎱ Esqrs Associate Justices
    ⎰ James Wilson ⎱
    ⎰ James Iredell & ⎱
    ⎰ William Paterson[237] ⎱

235. The "o" is written over an "e."
236. The word "Justice" appears to have been written with a final "s" which has been altered to a flourish.
237. We do not know why Samuel Chase missed this session of Court.

Proclamation is made and the Court is opened.

Ordered

That the Decree of the Circuit Court for Georgia District in the Case of the Ship Elizabeth and Cargo and Hills, May,[238] and Woodbridge Plaintiffs in error against Walter Ross, defendant in error, pronounced on the fifth day of May one thousand seven hundred and ninety five be reversed[239] so far as the same respects the said Hills, May[240] and Woodbridge; and it is further ordered, that the said Hills May[241] and Woodbridge pay to the said Walter Ross thirty two thousand and ninety Dollars and fifty eight Cents the nett amount of the Sales of the Cargo of the said Ship and Five thousand six hundred and five Dollars and twelve Cents Interest thereon from the sixth Day of June in the Year one thousand seven hundred and ninety four to the twelfth day of August one thousand seven hundred and ninety six, making together the Sum of Thirty seven thousand six hundred and ninety five Dollars and seventy Cents: and that the said Hills May and Woodbridge do pay the Costs of Suit: and a Special mandate is awarded for execution.

Ordered

That when process at common Law or in equity shall issue against a State, the same shall be served on the Governor or Chief Executive Magistrate and Attorney General of such State.[242]

Ordered

That process of subpœna issuing out of this Court in any suit in equity shall be served on the defendant, sixty days before the return day of the said[243] process: and further, that if the defendant on such service of the Subpœna shall not appear at the Return day contained therein, the complainant shall be at Liberty to proceed ex parte.[244]

Ordered.

That the Decree of the Circuit Court of the United States in and for the Virginia District in the Case of Wisecart against Dauchy be affirmed with Costs: and a special Mandate is awarded.

M[r] Lewis withdrew[245] his motion for a Distringas to compel the State of

238. The "y" is written over a partially erased "ry." This change may have been made by Jacob Wagner.
239. Originally "reserved." The "v" is written over an "s," and the "s" is written over a "v." This change may have been made by Jacob Wagner.
240. See note 238.
241. Idem.
242. It is likely that this order was issued in response to the difficulty in serving a subpoena issued on March 14, 1796, in the case of *Moultrie v. Georgia.* See "Formulary," Subpoena in Equity, *Snipes et al. vs State of Georgia et al.*
243. Originally "suit." The "a" is written over a "u," and the "d" is written over a "t."
244. See note 242.
245. Originally "withdraw." The "e" is written over a partially erased "a." This change may have been made by Jacob Wagner.

Virginia to appear and answer the Bill fil'd on the Equity side of this Court by William Grayson and others. He then moved that an alias Subpœna might issue; which was granted.[246]

The Court proceeded to hear the argument of Counsel in the Cases of Louis Arcambal against Joseph Wiseman and Joseph Wiseman against Louis Arcambal; whereupon it was ordered that the decree of the Circuit Court of the United States in and for the Rhode Island District in the said two Causes be affirmed with Costs; and a special mandate is awarded.

Adjourned to the time and place by Law appointed.

[————————]

At the City hall in the City of Philadelphia (being the present seat of the National Government of the United States) on Monday the sixth day of February one thousand seven hundred and ninety seven and in the twenty first Year of the Independence of the United States the Court met.

Present

The Hnble.[247] { William Cushing
James Wilson
James Iredell
William Paterson &
Samuel Chase[248] }
Esquires
Associate Justices.[249]

Proclamation is made and the Court is opened.

The Jury returned by the Marshall for the District of Pennsylvania in Virtue
directed,
of a Venire facias to him for that purpose ^ being called,[250] Isaac Duncan[,] John Cooke, Adam Zantzinger, John Reily, John Massey, Francis West, Jacob Sperry, James Campbell, Joseph Sommerl, Abraham Kintzing, Charles Ross, John Miller Junior, John Paul, John Davis, Jacob Park[,] Godfrey Twells, Thomas Ryerson Henry Rice, Charles Gilchrist, James Bringhurst, Israel Cope, William Miller, Abijah Dawes,[251] Thomas Archer, Thomas Attmore[,] John R Baker, Paul Beck Junior, David Callighan[,] Samuel Clarkson, George R.

246. *Hollingsworth v. Virginia.*
247. "The Hnble" seems to be in Jacob Wagner's hand.
248. Oliver Ellsworth was absent during the February term because of illness. See "Commentaries," James Iredell to Hannah Iredell, February 9, 1797, and Jeremiah Smith to William Plumer, February 13, 1797.
249. "Esquires Associate Justices," written in a hand different from that of the rest of the text, seems to be in Jacob Wagner's handwriting.
250. The interlineation seems to be in Jacob Wagner's hand.
251. Originally "Daws." The "e" is written over an "s."

Chapman and Joseph Claiborn severally made default and James Cresson was excused from attendance.

The Case of

$$\left.\begin{array}{l} \text{Lessee of} \\ \text{Gist} \\ \quad \text{vs} \\ \text{Robinett} \end{array}\right\}$$

is continued to the next Term.

On motion of James Gibson[252] and Asher Robbins[253] were omitted[254] and sworn Counsellors of this Court.

Adjourned till to morrow morning at ten o'Clock.

Tuesday[255] Morning
February 7ᵗʰ 1797.

Pursuant to adjournment the Court met this morning at the City Hall, to wit

$$\text{The Honorable} \left\{\begin{array}{l} \text{William Cushing} \\ \text{James Wilson} \\ \text{James Iredell \&} \\ \text{Samuel}^{256} \text{ Chase}^{257} \end{array}\right\} \begin{array}{l} \text{Esquires, Associate} \\ \text{Justices} \end{array}$$

Proclamation is made and the Court is opened

The Court proceeded to hear the Argument of Counsel in the Case of Fennimore vs. the United States

---

252. James Gibson (1769-1856), a resident of Philadelphia at the time of his admission to the bar of the Supreme Court of the United States, had been a member of the Philadelphia bar since 1791. In 1793 he was admitted to the Supreme Court of Pennsylvania bar. Charles R. Hildeburn, ed., *Inscriptions in St. Peter's Church Yard, Philadelphia* (Camden, New Jersey: Chew, 1879), p. 34; Stafford, *The Philadelphia Directory* (1799); *MBBP*, p. 271; "Supreme Court List of Attorneys, 1742-1902," Records of the Eastern District, RG 33, PHarH.

253. Asher Robbins was born in 1761 in Wethersfield, Connecticut. He studied law in Rhode Island and was admitted to the bar there in 1792. That same year, he opened a law office in Providence; in 1795 he moved to Newport, where he remained until his death in 1845. Henry Reed Stiles, *History of Ancient Wethersfield*, 2 vols. (1904; reprint ed., Somersworth: New Hampshire Publishing, 1975), 2:574-75; *BDAC*.

254. In the original minutes, "admitted."

255. The clerk began to write "Thursday." The "ue" is written over a partially visible "hu."

256. "Samuel" is written over what might have been "James."

257. William Paterson may have decided not to attend on February 7, because the Court planned to hear argument in *Fennimore v. United States*, a case in which Paterson had ruled on circuit. 3 *Dallas* 364 (1797).

Chauncy Goodrich,[258] Pierpoint Edwards,[259] and Henry Wikoff[260] were admitted and sworn, as Counsellors of this court

On motion of Mr Goodrich the Cause of Calder against Bull is continued till the next term

Adjourned till to morrow morning at ten o'Clock.

[————————]

Wednesday Morning
8th February 1797.

Pursuant to adjournment the Court met this morning at the City Hall, to wit

The Hnble. { William Cushing / James Wilson / James Iredell / William Patterson & / Samuel Chase } Esquires associate Justices

Proclamation is made and the Court is opened.

John Brown Cutting Admor of the Prince of Luxembourg vs The State of South Carolina } Case

On Motion of Mr Ingersoll for the Plaintiff ordered,[261]
That Judgment by default be entered against the defendant.

Hunter vs Fairfax } The Attorney General joins in error.

258. Chauncey Goodrich (1759-1815), admitted to the bar in Connecticut in 1781, was a resident of Hartford and a member of Congress at the time he was called to the bar of the Supreme Court. *BDAC.*

259. Pierpont Edwards (1750-1826) began to practice law in New Haven in 1771. Edwards was living in New Haven and serving as attorney for the United States for the district of Connecticut when admitted to the Supreme Court bar. *DAB; SEJ,* 1:29-30; James McLachlan, *Princetonians: A Biographical Dictionary,* vol. 1, *1748-1768* (Princeton: Princeton University Press, 1976), p. 641.

260. Henry Wikoff (1770-1826) resided in Philadelphia at the time of his admission to practice before the Supreme Court of the United States. He had been admitted to the Philadelphia bar in 1791 and to the Supreme Court of Pennsylvania bar in 1793. *University of Pennsylvania Catalogue, 1749-1880,* p. 33; Stephens, *The Philadelphia Directory* (1796); Cornelius William Stafford, *The Philadelphia Directory for 1801* (Philadelphia: William W. Woodward, 1801); *MBBP,* p. 323; "Supreme Court List of Attorneys, 1742-1902," Records of the Eastern District, RG 33, PHarH.

261. The words "of Mr Ingersoll for the Plaintiff" fell within the braces as originally drawn. "On Motion" and "ordered" were added later.

Brown   ⎫
   vs   ⎬   Mʳ Barnes joins in error.
Van Braam ⎭

Wilson ⎫   Mʳ Tilghman moved to quash the Writ of error in this Cause on
  vs   ⎬   account of the Subject of dispute not being of such an amount as
Daniel ⎭   to give jurisdiction to this Court, _ Motion dismissed _

Adjourned till to morrow morning at ten o'Clock.

Thursday Morning
9ᵗʰ February 1797.

Pursuant to adjournment the Court met, this Morning at the City Hall, to
wit,

The Honble. ⎰ James Wilson   ⎱   Esquires associate
         ⎨ James Iredell   ⎬   Justices
         ⎩ William Paterson & ⎭
            Samuel Chase[262]

Proclamation is made and the Court is opened.

The Court proceeded to hear the argument of Counsel in the Case of Brown
vs Van Braam.

David Howell[263] was admitted and sworn a Counsellor of this Court.

The Jury were dismissed for the remainder of the Session.

Adjourned till to morrow morning at 10, o'Clock.
[———————]
Friday Morning
10ᵗʰ February 1797.

Pursuant to adjournment the Court met this morning at the City Hall, to
wit,

The Hnble. ⎰ James Wilson   ⎱   Esquires associate
         ⎨ James Iredell   ⎬   Justices
         ⎩ William Paterson & ⎭
            Samuel Chase

262. William Cushing may have absented himself because the Court was hearing *Brown v. Van Braam Houckgueest,* a case he had decided at the Rhode Island Circuit Court in Providence, in November, 1796 (Final Record, November 1796 term, CCD Rhode Island, RG 21, MWalFAR).
    263. David Howell (1747-1824) was admitted to the bar and began to practice in Rhode Island in 1768. At the time of his admission to the Supreme Court bar, he lived in Providence. *BDAC*; Ronald Vern Jackson, ed., *Rhode Island 1800 Census* (Salt Lake City: Accelerated Indexing Systems, 1972).

Proclamation is made and the Court is opened.

The Court proceeded to hear the Argument of Counsel in the Case of Brown vs Van Braam.

Cutting
vs }
The State of South Carolina

On motion of Mr Dallas of Counsel with the Plaintiff a[264] Writ of enquiry — of damages is awarded to enquire at the bar of this Court what[265] damages the Plaintiff has sustained by reason &c^a and that three months notice be given to the Governor and Attorney General of South Carolina of the holding of said enquiry.

Huger et al.
vs } Rule for a commission to be directed to John
The State of Georgia et. al. Julius Pringle, Henry William Dessaussure[,] Timothy Ford and Thomas Parker or any three or two of them, to examine Witnesses in the State of South Carolina. —

Rule for a Commission to be directed to Joseph Clay Junior, John Y. Noel, George Woodruff and   Stevens or any three or two of them to examine witnesses in the State of Georgia.

Rule for a Commission to be directed to Joseph Read, John Hallowell, John D. Coxe and Michael Keppele or any three or two of them to examine Witnesses in the State of Pennsylvania.

The Court proceeded to hear the argument of Counsel in the Case of Jennings et. al. vs the Brig Preseverence et al.

Adjourned till to morrow morning at 10 o'Clock

Saturday Morning
11th February 1797.

Pursuant to adjournment the Court met this morning to wit,

The Hñble. {
William Cushing
James Wilson
James Iredell
William Paterson &
Samuel Chase
} Esquires associate Justices

Proclamation is made and the Court is opened

---

264. Originally "at." The "t" is partially erased.
265. The "h" is written over an "a."

Hunter ⎫
vs ⎬ On motion of Mr Lee for the Defendant, Rule to argue the Cause
Fairfax ⎭ on[266] the 13th instant, or writ of Error to be nonpross'd

Ordered

That the Judgment of the High Court of Appeals for the State of Maryland in the Case of James Clerke Administrator of James Russell against Richard Harwood Junior be reversed, and that the judgment of the general Court of Maryland in the same cause be in all Things affirmed, and that the said James Clerke recover against the said Richard Harwood his Costs about the same suit expended in the general Court and Court of Appeals of Maryland and in this Court: and a Special mandate to General Court.

Adjourned till Monday Morning next at ten o'Clock.

Monday Morning
13th February 1797.

Pursuant to adjournment the Court met this morning, to wit,

The H̄nble. ⎰ William Cushing
⎱ James Wilson
⎰ James Iredell   ⎱ Esquires associate
⎱ William Paterson &   ⎰ Justices
⎰ Samuel Chase

Proclamation is made and the Court is opened.

Vassall ⎫
vs. ⎬
The State of Massachusetts ⎭

Ordered that this Cause be dismissed with Costs.

Hunter ⎫
vs ⎬
Fairfax ⎭

On motion of M[r] Lee for the Defendant
Ordered, That this cause be non pross'd with Costs; under the rule of Saturday the eleventh instant.

Brown ⎫
vs ⎬
Van Braam ⎭

Ordered that the Judgment of the Circuit Court for the District of Rhode

---

266. Originally "of." The "f" has been erased.

Island be affirmed with costs, and interest at the rate of six per cent per annum from the day of rendering the said judgment until this day, by way of damages.

Fennimore
vs
The United States

Rule for certiorari on a suggestion of diminution —

Grayson
Virginia[267]

On motion of M.[r] Lewis for the Complainant —

Rule for a commission to be directed to Charles Smith, John Hubley and William Montgomery Esquires, or any two of them to examine Witnesses in the borough of Lancaster in the State of Pennsylvania —

Rule for a commission to be directed to David Watts, William Alexander and John Lyon Esquires, or any two of them to examine Witnesses in the borough of Carlisle in the State of Pennsylvania —

Rule for a commission to be directed to John Woods, John Wilkins and George Wallace Esquires or any two of them, to examine Witnesses in the town of Pittsburg in the State of Pennsylvania

Rule for a commission to be directed to Daniel Delany, James Gibson and William Smith Esquires or any two of them to examine Witnesses in the City of Philadelphia.

Rule for a commission to be directed to the Honorable Samuel J. Cabal and Wilson Cary Nicholas Esquire[268] to examine Witnesses in the State of Virginia —

Rule for a commission to be directed to William Morton, William Murray and Andrew Holmes Esquires or any two of them to examine Witnesses in the State of Kentucky —

Wilson
vs
Daniel

M.[r] Tilghman appears as Counsel for the Defendant, waves all exception to the Writ of error and citation and alleges diminution of the record; and

Rule by consent that a certiorari be issued to either party as he shall elect; but it is understood that the Defendant be at liberty to withdraw his allegation of diminution and proceed to argument on the record as it now stands.

Jennings et al.
vs
The Brig Perseverance[269] et al.

267. *Hollingsworth v. Virginia.* In 1793 the original bill in equity was amended, and new process was awarded in the name of Levi Hollingsworth.

268. An "s" has been partially erased at the end of the word.

269. The "P" is written over a "T."

Ordered

That the decree[270] of the Circuit Court for the District of Rhode Island be affirmed with costs, and damages at the rate of six per cent per annum on the proceeds arising from the Sales of the said Brigantine and her Cargo after deducting the duties paid in the Custom House on the said Cargo and the Commission on the Sales, such interest to be calculated from the day of rendering the said decree until this day

On motion, Robert G. Harper[271] was admitted and sworn a Counsellor of this Court.

It is ordered by the Court, that the Clerk of the Court, to which any writ of error shall be directed, may make return of the same by transmitting a true Copy of the record[272] and of all proceedings in the cause under his hand and the Seal of the Court[273]

All the unfinished business is continued to the next term.

Adjourned to the time and place by Law appointed.

At the City hall in the City of Philadelphia on Monday the Seventh day of August one thousand seven hundred and ninety seven and in the Twenty second Year of the Independence of the United States, the Court met:

Present

The Honorable Oliver Ellsworth Esquire Chief Justice

The Honble. { William Cushing / James Iredell / William Patterson & / Samuel Chase[274] }   Esquires[275] / Associate Justices

---

270. Originally "degree." The "c" is written over a partially erased "g."

271. Robert Goodloe Harper (1765-1825) was admitted to the Charleston, South Carolina, bar in 1786. Harper was a congressman from South Carolina when admitted to the Supreme Court bar. Charles William Sommerville, *Robert Goodloe Harper* (Washington, D.C.: Neale, 1899), pp. 5, 7, 10.

272. Originally "records." The "s" is partially erased.

273. The *Philadelphia Gazette* on February 15, 1797, printed this order of the Court under the heading "For the information of Gentlemen of the bar in the United States" and over the name of "JACOB WAGNER, Clk. Sup. Ct. U. S." Also printed in the *Diary* (New York) on February 17, 1797. Wagner seems to have notified the clerks of the lower federal courts. See "Commentaries," Cephus Smith, Jr., to Jacob Wagner, July 15, 1797.

274. James Wilson did not attend the Court because he was fleeing his creditors. See "Commentaries," James Iredell to Hannah Iredell, August 11, 1797.

275. This word, in handwriting different from that of the rest of the text, seems to be written in the hand of Jacob Wagner.

Proclamation is made and the Court is opened,

The Marshall for the Pennsylvania District makes return of a Venire facias to him directed for summoning a Petit Jury, which was filed, and the Jury being called Alexander Cochrane, Derick[276] Peterson, Jesse Sharpless, Benjamin Scull, William Gibbs, Charles Massey, Francis West, Robert Westcott, William Colloday[,] Patrick Moore, Richard Mather, Pearson Hunt, John Whitehead, John Graham, Joseph Spencer, Raper Hoskins, Samuel Shaw Junior, Joshua B. Bond, John Aitkin, Jacob Knorr, Philip Hagner, Joseph Davidson[,] George Davis, Gavin Hamilton, John Taggert, Charles French, Nathan Field, George Lauman, Joseph Harbeson, Samuel Fulton, Samuel Shoemaker, George David Seckle, James Bacon, William Wood, Edward Smith[,] David Knox, James Simpson, Joseph Hertzog, John Morrell and Henry Muhlenberg severally made default.

It is ordered by the Court, that no record of the Court be suffered by the Clerk to be taken out of his Office but by the consent of the Court; otherwise to be responsible for it _

Hollingsworth et al.
vs   } is continued to the next term _
The State of Virginia

Lee. of Gist
vs   }
Robinett

On motion of M[r] Ingersoll, Rule upon the Clerk of the District Court of Kentucky District to shew cause, why the record is not returned _

Calder
vs   } continued by consent.
Bull

The Court proceeded to hear the argument of Counsel in the Case of Fennimore vs The United States, which being concluded, it was ordered by the Court, that the Judgment of the Circuit Court be affirmed with costs _

Adjourned to ten o'Clock to morrow Morning _ [277]

Tuesday Morning
8th August 1797.

Pursuant to adjournment the Court met this morning at the City Hall, vizt

---

276. The "i" is written over an "r."

277. The *Daily Advertiser* (Philadelphia) on August 8, 1797, noted the opening of the Court the day before.

The Honorable Oliver Ellsworth, Esquire, Chief Justice —

The Hoñble. $\begin{cases} \text{William Cushing} \\ \text{James Iredell} \\ \text{William Paterson \&} \\ \text{Samuel Chase} \end{cases}$ Esquires, associate Justices

Proclamation is made and the Court is opened

The Court ordered the enquiry of damages in the Case of Cutting vs The State of South Carolina to be now executed at the bar of the Court, and the Jury being called, come to wit, William Kinley, James Cruckshank, Robert Westcott, William Harlan, William Brown, Joseph Spencer, George Heberton, Samuel Richards, Gavin Hamilton, Job Butcher, Thomas Rogers and William Wood, who being impannelled, sworn and affirmed respectively, well and truly to enquire what damages the said Plaintiff hath sustained by reason of the Nonperformance of certain promises set forth in his declaration against the said State of South Carolina, Defendant, and to give a true verdict according to evidence, upon their oaths and affirmations respectively do say, that they find for the Plaintiff Fifty five thousand and two Dollars and eighty four Cents Damages by reason of &c — [278]

The Court proceeded to hear the argument of Counsel in the Case of Brown vs Barry.

Adjourned till to morrow morning at Ten o'Clock —

[————————]
Wednesday Morning
9th August 1797.

Pursuant to adjournment the Court met this Morning at the City Hall, viz.:

The Honorable Oliver Ellsworth Esqr Chief Justice

The Hoñble. $\begin{cases} \text{William Cushing} \\ \text{James Iredell} \\ \text{William Paterson} \\ \text{Samuel Chase} \end{cases}$ Esquires associate Justices.

Proclamation is made and the Court is opened.

The Court proceeded to hear the argument of Counsel in the Case of Brown vs. Barry.

Adjourned till to morrow morning at 10. o'Clock

---

278. The "&c —" is written over a partially erased ", and so forth."

Thursday Morning
10th August 1797.

Pursuant to adjournment the Court met this Morning at the City Hall in the City of Philadelphia viz!

The Honorable Oliver Ellsworth[279] Esq! Chief Justice

The Honble. { William Cushing
James Iredell
William Paterson &
Samuel Chase } Esquires associate Justices

Proclamation is made and the Court is opened

Franklin et. al.
vs
Rotch et al } is continued by consent.

The Court proceeded to hear the argument of Counsel in the case of Emory vs Greenough.

Hamilton et al.
vs
Moore }

On motion of M! E Tilghman Rule to shew cause why the Writ of error should not be amended; and on motion of M! Dallas rule to shew Cause, why the Writ of error should not be quashed

Adjourned till to morrow morning at 10. o'Clock.

Friday Morning
11th August 1797.

Pursuant to adjournment the Court met this morning at the City Hall, viz!

The Honorable Oliver Ellsworth[280] Esq! Chief Justice

The Honble. { William Cushing
James Iredell
William Paterson &
Samuel Chase } Esquires Associate Justices

Proclamation is made and the Court is opened

The Court proceeded to hear the argument of Counsel in the Case of Emory vs Greenough.

279. Originally "Ellswood." The letters "rth" are written over an erased "od." The correction seems to be in the hand of Jacob Wagner.
280. Idem.

On motion of M͏ͬ Ingersoll rule for final Judgment in the Case of Cutting vs The State of South Carolina

On motion of M͏ͬ Ingersoll rule for publication of the Commission returned from South Carolina in the Case of Moultrie et[281] al vs The State of Georgia, et al. _

Adjourned till to morrow morning at ten o'Clock.

[————————]

Saturday morning
12th August 1797.

Pursuant to · adjournment the Court met this Morning at the City Hall, viz͏ͭ

The Honorable Oliver Ellsworth Esq͏ͬ Chief Justice

The Hoñble.
{
William Cushing
James Iredell
William Paterson &
Samuel Chase
}
Esquires associate Justices

Proclamation is made and the Court is opened

The Court proceeded to hear the argument of Counsel in the Case of Emory vs Greenough.

Adjourned till to morrow morning at 10. o'Clock.

Monday Morning
14th August 1797.

Pursuant to adjournment the Court met this Morning at the City Hall, to wit;

The Honorable Oliver Ellsworth Esq͏ͬ Chief Justice

The Hoñble.
{
William Cushing
James Iredell
William Paterson &
Samuel Chase
}
Esquires Associate Justices

Proclamation is made and the Court is opened.

The Court proceeded to hear the Argument of Counsel in the Case of Emory vs Greenough.

Adjourned till Morrow Morning at 10. o'Clock

[————————]

281. The "et" has been written over a "v."

Tuesday Morning
15ᵗʰ August 1797.

Pursuant to adjournment the Court met this morning at the City Hall, to wit:

The Honorable Oliver Ellsworth Esqʳ Chief Justice

The Honͦble. {
William Cushing
James Iredell
William Paterson &
Samuel Chase
} Esquires Associate Justices

Proclamation is made and the Court is opened

The State of South Carolina
vs
The French Republic and
John Brown Cutting Admͬr.
of the Prince of Luxembourg
} Bill in equity.

It is ordered by the Court, that injunction be awarded to stay all further proceedings on a Judgment rendered at this present term in an action upon the case of John B. Cutting as Administrator of the Prince of Luxembourg[282] against the State of South Carolina, until the first day of January next; and it is further ordered by the Court, that injunction also be awarded to stay all further proceedings on said Judgment until the further order of this Court upon this condition, that the said State of South Carolina shall on or before the said first day of January next, bring into this Court the sum of Ten thousand eight hundred and fifty five Pounds eight shillings and five pence sterling money of the State equal of South Carolina, equal to   dollars,[283] together with the interest on the same at the rate of seven perCent per annum from the thirteenth day of March one thousand seven hundred and eighty nine to the time of payment into Court excepting and deducting from the amount of Interest one thousand Pounds of like money already paid to the said John Brown Cutting (which the said State by her Bill exhibited in this Court has acknowledged to be due and owing from her to the legal representative of the said Prince of Luxembourg or to the French Republic and has offered to deposit the same in this Court) and shall deposit the same in this Court subject to its further order and such decree as it may make respecting the same, and shall at the same time pay into this Court the Costs in the above Action.

Brown
vs
Barry
} Ordered that the Judgment of the Circuit Court be affirmed with Costs.

282. An "h" originally was written after the "g" and then erased.
283. The word "dollars," in handwriting different from that of the rest of the text, seems to be written in the hand of Jacob Wagner.

same
vs   } Same Order
same

same
vs   } Same Order
same

same
vs   } same Order
same

same
vs   } Same Order
same

Same
vs   } Same Order
same

Moultrie et. al.
vs   } On motion of William Tilghman Esquire, it is ordered, that the papers annexed to the commission issued to Joseph Clay Junior and others of the State of Georgia for the ex-
The State of Georgia et al

amination of Witnesses in this Ca˄se in the said State be detached from the said commission and annexed to the commission issued to John D Coxe and others of Pennsylvania to take the examination of Witnesses in the said cause in the City of Philadelphia.

Emory
vs   } continued by consent.
Greenough

Dorrance
vs   } continued
Van Horne's Lee

Wilson
vs   } continued
Daniel

Moultrie et al.
vs   } continued; and on motion of William Tilghman Esquire.
The State of Georgia et al.

Rule for Publication of the commission directed to Michael Keppele and others to examine Witnesses in the City of Philadelphia, as soon as it is returned.

Court et. al.
vs
Van Bibber

Ordered that the Judgment of the High Court of Appeals of the State of Maryland be reversed and that the Judgment of the general Court of Maryland in the same Cause be in all things affir[m]ed, and that the said Christopher Court and Company recover against the said Isaac Van Bibber as terre tenant of Mark Alexander his costs about the same suit expended in the General Court and Court[284] of Appeals of Maryland and in this Court and a special Mandate is awarded to the General Court.

Court et al.
vs
Wells

Ordered, that the Judgment of the High Court of Appeals of the State of Maryland be reversed and that the Judgment of the General Court of Maryland in the same Cause be in all things affirmed and that the said Christopher Court and Company recover against the said Cyprian Wells as terretenant of Mark Alexander their costs about the same suit expended in the General Court and Courts of Appeals of Maryland and in this Court, and a special mandate is awarded to the General Court,.

Court et. al.
vs
Robinson et. al.

Ordered, That the Judgment of the High Court of appeals of the State of Maryland be reversed and that the Judgment of the General Court of Maryland in the same cause be in all things affirmed and that the said Christopher Court and Company recover against the said Andrew Robinson and Alexander Robinson, terretenants of Mark Alexander, their costs about the same suit expended in the General Court and Court of Appeals of Maryland and in this Court and a special Mandate is awarded to the General Court.

Pepoon et al.,
vs
Jenkins

Edward Tilghman Esquire appears for the Defendant in error, and the cause is continued by consent.

Clerke et al.[285]
vs
Russell

M.r Ingersoll assigns the general errors and the cause is continued.

Hamilton et al.
vs
Moore

Ordered that the writ of error be non-pros'd.

All the unfinished ̶ business[286] is continued to the next term.

Adjourned to the time and place by law appointed.

[————————]

284. A partially erased "s" appears at the end of the word.
285. "Pepoon et al" was written first and then erased.
286. The letters "bus" are partially erased, and a dash and a small "bu" are written in and attached to the "siness." This change seems to have been made by Jacob Wagner.

At the City hall in the City of Philadelphia On Monday the fifth Day of February in the Year of our Lord one Thousand seven hundred and ninety eight and in the twenty second Year of the Independence of the United States the Supreme Court of the United States met agreably to Law[287]

Present

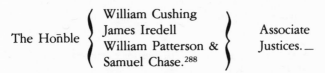

The Honble
{
William Cushing
James Iredell
William Patterson &
Samuel Chase.[288]
}
Associate
Justices. _

Proclamation is made and the Court is opened. _

The Marshal for the Pennsylvania District makes Return of a Venire Facias to him directed for summoning a Petit Jury which is filed and the Jury being called the following Persons only appear to wit_

Robert Ralston_ George Fox, Joseph Crukshank, William Ward Burrows, John Fries, Zaccheus Collins, Robert Smith, John Craig, James Barrand, Pattison Hartshorne_

And the said Petit=Jury is discharged until Saturday next. _

On Motion of Charles Lee Esquire The honble Uriah Tracy Esquire[289] of Connecticut is admitted and Sworn as a Counsellor of this Court_

John Coffin Jones
$\bar{v}^s$
Citizen Joseph Philippe
Letombe, Consul General
of the French Republic
}
In Case

The Marshal for the Pennsylvania District returns the Writ of Capias ad respondendum in this Cause issued and returnable here this Day as follows

287. A fine copy of the minutes for February, 1798, exists in the handwriting of David Caldwell, who had taken the rough notes at that term of Court. It is not known whether Samuel Bayard copied the fine minutes from Caldwell's version or whether Caldwell copied Bayard's version. The first four pages of Caldwell's version of the fine minutes are in Curator's Office, DUSC. The remaining nine pages are interleaved in the bound volume of original minutes (General Records, RG 267, DNA). We have noted differences between the Caldwell fine minutes and the fine minutes published here.

288. Oliver Ellsworth was ill at this time (see "Commentaries," Oliver Ellsworth to William Cushing, February 4, 1798; William Paterson to Euphemia Paterson, February 5, 1798; James Iredell to Hannah Iredell, February 5 and 8, 1798, and Abigail Adams to Hannah Cushing, March 9, 1798). James Wilson, in the middle of a personal financial crisis, was reported to be ill in North Carolina. See "Commentaries," William Paterson to Euphemia Paterson, February 5, 1798; and John Rutledge, Jr., to Edward Rutledge, February 25, 1798.

289. Uriah Tracy (1755-1807) was admitted to the bar in 1781 and began practice in Litchfield, Connecticut. He represented Litchfield in Congress, and was serving as senator from Connecticut when admitted to the Supreme Court bar. DAB.

"C. C. B. B. _ [290] so answers
"William Nichols
"Marshal _ "
On Motion of Mʳ Dallas _
Rule that the Plaintiff shew Cause why the Defendant should not be discharged upon common Bail _ and Friday next is appointed for the Argument of the Rule _

Wilson
vs
Daniel

Writ of Certiorari to the Circuit Court of Virginia returned _

Pepoon et al.
vˢ
Jenkins

Mʳ E. Tilghman joins in Error _

Bingham
vs
Cabot

Mʳ E. Tilghman appears as Counsel for the Defendant in Error and joins in Error _

The Court adjourns until Tomorrow Morning at ten of the Clock _

Tuesday Morning 6[291] February[292] 1798

Pursuant to Adjournment the Court met this Morning. to wit _

The honble {
William Cushing
James Iredell
William Patterson[293] &
Samuel Chase
} Associate Justices

Proclamation is made and the Court is opened _

On Motion of the honorable Uriah Tracy _ the honorable Peleg Sprague[294]

290. "C. C. B. B.": I have taken his body; bail bond entered.
291. A "1" was written just before the "6" but has been erased. In David Caldwell's version of the fine minutes, he wrote "6th."
292. In David Caldwell's version of the fine minutes, he abbreviated February as "Feb:"; February is abbreviated in this manner throughout his draft of the minutes of this term.
293. David Caldwell, in his version of the fine minutes, spelled Paterson with one "t" and spelled it that way throughout his draft of the minutes of this term.
294. Peleg Sprague (1756-1800) began practicing law in Worcester County, Massachusetts, in 1785. He was a resident of Keene, New Hampshire, and a member of Congress at the time of his Supreme Court bar admission. *BDAC.*

of the State of New-Hampshire is admitted and sworn as a Counsellor of this Court.

Franklin et al
v̄s
Rotch et al
} Sur Writ of Error. to Circuit Court of New-York[295]

It is agreed by Writing this Day filed_ that the Writ of Error be withdrawn and the Action closed upon Condition_ that William T. Robinson[296] give Bond for the Payment of three thousand two hundred Dollars payable the 5th. of 3rd. Month next (5th of March) in New=York or in Failure hereof that Samuel Franklin &Co. pay the Judgment of the Circuit Court at New York in this Case_ the Defendants to be exempt from all Costs_

Clarke et al.
v̄s
Russel
} Sur Writ of Error. to the Circuit Court of Rhode Island._[297]

The Court proceeds to hear the Arguments of Mr Edwards of Counsel for the Plaintiffs & of Mr Dexter of Counsel for the Defendant_

The Court adjourns until Tomorrow Morning at ten of the Clock._

Wednesday Morning
7th February. 1798._

Pursuant to Adjournment the Court met this Morning_ to wit

The Hon̄ble { William Cushing
James Iredell
William Patterson &
Samuel Chase } Associate Justices

Clarke et al
v̄s
Russel
}

The Court proceeds to hear the Arguments of Counsel in this Cause_ to wit_ of Mr E. Tilghman for the Defendant[298] and of Mr Ingersoll for the Plaintiffs_

295. In David Caldwell's version of the fine minutes, he wrote this phrase "Circt Ct New-York."

296. The first "n" is written over an "s."

297. In David Caldwell's version of the fine minutes, he wrote this phrase "Circt Ct of Rhode-Island_."

298. In David Caldwell's version of the fine minutes, he wrote "Deft."

Wilson
vs
Daniel

Certiorari to the Circuit Court of the Virginia District returned and filed __

Brailsford
vs
Georgia

Declaration filed ⅌ Morgan Atty __

The Court adjourns until Tomorrow Morning at ten of the Clock. __

Thursday Morning
8th. February. 1798. __

Pursuant to Adjournment the Court met this Morning __ to wit

The honble ⟨ William Cushing / James Iredell / William Patterson & / Samuel Chase ⟩ Associate Justices

Clarke et al
vs
Russel

The Court proceeds to hear the further Arguments of Counsel in this Cause to wit of Mr Ingersoll for the Plaintiffs __

Ordered that the Judgment of the Circuit Court of the United States in and for the Rhode Island District of the Eastern Circuit be reversed __ and __

A Venire facias de novo is awarded __

The Death of Joseph Nightingale is suggested __

On Motion of Jared Ingersoll Esquire the honorable William Gordon[299] of the State of New=Hampshire is admitted and sworn as a Counsellor of this Court

Calder
vs
Bull

The Death of Caleb Bull is suggested

The Court proceeds to hear the Arguments of Counsel in this Cause __ to wit __ of Mr Edwards for[300] for the Pltff.[301]

299. William Gordon (1763-1802), admitted to the bar in New Hampshire in 1787, opened a law practice in Amherst that same year. He was a member of Congress and a resident of Amherst at the time of his admission to the bar of the Supreme Court. *BDAC*.

300. David Caldwell's version of the fine minutes contains no crossed-out word.

301. In David Caldwell's version of the fine minutes, he abbreviated plaintiff as "Plff."

Jones
 v̄s
Letombe }

The Deposition of the Plaintiff taken before the Judge of the Massachusetts District is opened by the Court and filed —

The Court adjourns until Tomorrow Morning at ten of the Clock. —

***

Friday Morning
9th. February. 1798. —

Pursuant to Adjournment the Court met this Morning to wit

The hon̄ble { William Cushing
James Iredell
William Patterson &
Samuel Chase } Associate
Justices

Jones
 v̄s
Letombe }

Ordered that the Rule to shew Cause entered in this Cause on the first Day of the Session be corrected as follows —
On Motion of Mr Dallas —
Rule to shew Cause why the Defendant should not be discharged upon entering a common Appearance. —
And the Court proceeds to hear the Arguments of Counsel thereupon — to wit — of Mr Ingersoll for the Plaintiff —
Ordered that the Defendant be discharged upon entering a common Appearance —
By Direction of Mr Duponceau — the Appearance of Edward Livingston, Esquire, is entered for the Defendant —

Pepoon et al
 v̄s
Jenkins }

The Court proceeds to hear the Arguments of Counsel in this Cause. to wit — of Mr Dexter for the Plaintiffs —

The Court adjourns until toworrow[302] at ten of the Clock. —

***

302. In David Caldwell's version of the fine minutes, the word "Morning" appears after "tomorrow."

Saturday Morning
10th. February 1798.

Pursuant to Adjournment the Court met this Morning — to wit —

The Honble { William Cushing / James Iredell / William Patterson & / Samuel Chase. } Associate Justices

The Petit-Jury discharged to this Day being called the following Persons only appear — to wit —

George Fox — Josiah. H. Anthony — John Miller Jun! and James Ban —
The Petit Jury is discharged for the Remainder of the Session —

Pepoon et al
vs
Jenkins

The Court proceeds to hear the further Arguments of Counsel in this Cause to wit of M!. E. Tilghman for the Defendant —

The Court proceeds to hear the Arguments of Counsel in Support of the Jurisdiction of the Court in Suits against States — to wit — of M! W. Tilghman and M! Rawle — and of the Attorney General (M! Lee) against the Jurisdiction. — [303]

The Court adjourns until Monday Morning at ten of the Clock —

Monday Morning
12th. February 1798 —

Pursuant to Adjournment the Court met this Morning — to wit —

The Honble { William Cushing / James Iredell / William Patterson & / Samuel Chase } Associate Justices

Proclamation being made the Court is opened —

The Court adjourns without proceeding to Business until Tomorrow Morning at ten o'Clock.

---

303. This paragraph does not appear in David Caldwell's rough notes for this term; it does, however, appear in Caldwell's version of the fine minutes. The arguments heard by the Court involved the effect of the ratification of the Eleventh Amendment on cases already before the Court. These cases were *Hollingsworth v. Virginia, Moultrie v. Georgia,* and *Brailsford v. Georgia.*

Tuesday Morning
13th. February 1798. _

Pursuant to adjourment the Court met this Morning to wit. _

The Honͦble. { William Cushing / James Iredell / William Patterson & / Samuel Chase } Associate Justices

Proclamation being made the Court is opened

Calder
v̄s
Bull

The Court proceeds to hear the further Arguments of Counsel in this Cause_ to wit_ of Mͬ Nathaniel Smith[304] and Mͬ Tracy for the Defendant.

Wilson
v̄s
Daniel

The Court proceeds to hear the arguments of Counsel in this Cause[305] upon the Allegation of the diminution of the Record_ to wit of Mͬ E. Tilghman in support of it, and of Mͬ Lee (the Attorney General) and Mͬ Ingersoll against it. _

Bingham
v̄s
Cabot

The Court proceeds to hear the arguments of Counsel in this Cause, to wit, of the Attorney General[306] Mͬ Lee for the plaintiff and of Mͬ Dexter for the Defendant. _ [307]

The Court adjourns until tomorrow morning at ten of the Clock.

Wednesday Morning
14ͭͪ February 1798

Pursuant to adjournment the Court met this morning_ to wit,

The honͦble { William Cushing / James Iredell / William Paterson & / Samuel Chase } Associate Justices

Proclamation being made the Court is opened.

---

304. Nathaniel Smith (1762-1822) was admitted to the Litchfield County, Connecticut, bar in 1787. He was a member of Congress representing his home district of Woodbury, Connecticut, when he argued *Calder v. Bull* before the Supreme Court. There is no record of his admission to the Supreme Court bar. Dwight C. Kilbourn, *The Bench and Bar of Litchfield County, Connecticut, 1709-1909* (Litchfield, Conn., 1909), pp. 291-92; *BDAC*.

305. David Caldwell's version of the fine minutes includes a crossed-out "to wit."
306. In David Caldwell's version of the fine minutes, he wrote "Genͥ."
307. In David Caldwell's version of the fine minutes, he wrote "Defendt."

Hollingsworth
  v̄s
Virginia

The Court is of opinion, that, on consideration of the Amendment of the Constitution respecting Suits against States, it has no Jurisdiction of this Cause: _ [308]

It is therefore considered by the Court that the Bill be dismissed. _

Moultrie et al.
  v̄s
Georgia et al.

The Court is of opinion that on Consideration of the Amendment of the Constitution respecting Suits against States it has no Jurisdiction of this Cause:

It is therefore considered by the Court that the Bill be dismissed so far as respects the State of Georgia.

Brailsford
  v̄s
Georgia

The Court is of opinion that on Consideration of the Amendment of the Constitution respecting Suits against States it has no Jurisdiction of this Cause;

It is therefore considered by the Court that this Suit be discontinued. _

State of South Carolina
  v̄s
Cutting

Continued by Consent. _

Pepoon et al.
  v̄s
Jenkins

Ordered that the decree of the Circuit Court of the United States in and for the Massachusetts district of the Eastern[309] Circuit be affirmed. _

Bingham
  v̄s
Cabot

Ordered that the Judgment of the Circuit Court of the United States in and for the Massachusetts district of the Eastern Circuit be reversed. _

Wilson
  v̄s
Daniel

Continued. _

308. The Eleventh Amendment was ratified on January 8, 1798.

309. In David Caldwell's version of the fine minutes, the word "District" appears after "Eastern" and is crossed out.

Calder ⎱
  v̄s   ⎰ continued.
Bull ⎱

Gist ⎱
  v̄s   ⎰ continued.
Robinett ⎰

Dorance ⎱
  v̄s   ⎰ continued.
Van Horne ⎰

Gist ⎱
  v̄s   ⎰
Robinett ⎰

On motion of M.ʳ Ingersoll

Rule upon the Clerk of the District Court of the United States in and for the Kentucky district to shew Cause why the Record is not returned. ‗

Clerke &[310] al. ⎱
  v̄s   ⎰
Russell[311] ⎰

Ordered that the[312] Judgment of the Circuit Court of the United States in and for the Rhode Island district of the Eastern Circuit be reversed. ‗[313]

Moultrie &[314] al. ⎱
  v̄s   ⎰
Georgia &[315] al. ⎰

On motion of M.ʳ W. Tilghman for the Plaintiffs,

Ordered that the Bill filed in this Cause be dismissed without prejudice. ‗

Emory ⎱
  v̄s   ⎰
Greenough ⎰

Ordered that the Judgment of the Circuit Court of the United States in and for the Massachusetts district of the Eastern Circuit be reversed.

All the unfinished business is continued to the next Session. ‗

Adjourned to the time and place by Law appointed. ‗[316]

[―――――――――]

310. In David Caldwell's version of the fine minutes, he wrote "et" rather than an "&."
311. In David Caldwell's version of the fine minutes, he wrote "Russel."
312. In David Caldwell's version of the fine Minutes, the letters "Cler" appear after "the" and are crossed out.
313. In David Caldwell's version of the fine minutes, he wrote "with Costs."
314. In David Caldwell's version of the fine minutes, he wrote "et" instead of an "&."
315. Idem.
316. David Caldwell's version of the fine minutes ends here.

At the City hall in the City of Philadelphia (being the present Seat of the National Government of the United States) on Monday the Sixth Day of August in the Year of Our LORD One Thousand Seven Hundred and Ninety Eight and in the Twenty Third Year of the Independence of the United States, the Supreme Court of the United States met agreeably to Law

Present

The Honourable Oliver Ellsworth, Esquire, Chief Justice

The Honourable { William Cushing / James Iredell / William Paterson & / Samuel Chase[317] } Esquires, Associate Justices

Proclamation is made and the Court is opened

Wilson } The Court proceeded to hear the Attorney General of the United
v.ˢ   } States (Mʳ Lee) and Mʳ Ingersoll on the part of the Plaintiffs and
Daniel } Mʳ E. Tilghman on the part of the Defendant in Error.

The Court Adjourns untill Twelve o'Clock to Morrow.

Tuesday 7ᵗʰ August 1798.—

Pursuant to Adjournment the Court met at the City Hall, Vizᵗ—

Present

The Honourable Oliver Ellsworth, Esquire, Chief Justice

The Honourable { William Cushing / James Iredell / William Paterson & / Samuel Chase } Esquires, Associate Justices

Proclamation being made the Court is opened.—

Wilson } The Court having heard the Arguments of Counsel in this Case
v.ˢ   } Ordered That the Sentence of the Circuit Court for the Virginia
Daniel } District in said Case be reversed.—

Jones   }
v.ˢ   } Discontinued by directions of Plaintiff's Counsel (Mʳ Tilghman).
Letombe }

317. A very ill James Wilson, still trying to extricate himself from a continuing financial crisis, remained in North Carolina and did not appear for the August term. See "Commentaries," Samuel Johnston to James Iredell, July 28, 1798, and James Iredell to Hannah Iredell, August 6 and 9, 1798.

Gist
  v⁵   } Continued
Robinett

Dorance
  v⁵   } Continued
Van Horne

Irwin
  v⁵   } Continued by Consent
Lee of Sims

The Court Adjourns untill 11._ °'Clock to Morrow.

Wednesday 8ᵗʰ August 1798._

Pursuant to Adjournment the Court met at the City Hall, Vizᵗ_

Present.

The Honourable Oliver Ellsworth Esquire, Chief Justice

The Honourable { William Cushing
                  James Iredell
                  William Paterson &   } Esquires, Associate Justices
                  Samuel Chase

Proclamation being made the Court is opened

Clark
  v⁵   } Continued by Consent of Parties
Russell

Samuel Fowler &   On Motion of Mʳ Lewis
Joseph Lyman   Ordered That the Plaintiffs in the above Suit shew
  v⁵   cause by the First Day of next Term why a Venire
Abraham Miller Esqʳ   should not be awarded to summon a Jury from some
                         District of the United States other than the Districts
of Connecticut or of New York

Samuel Fowler &
Joseph Lyman   On Motion of Mʳ Lewis
  v⁵   Ordered That the Plaintiffs in the above Suit shew
Mary Lindsley   Cause by the First Day of next Term why a Venire
Samuel Lindsley   should not be awarded to summon a Jury from some
Ebenezer Lindsley   District of the United States other than the Districts of
Moses Mulford &   Connecticut or of New York.
John Seely

Calder vs Bull	The Court proceeded to give their Opinions in this Case seriatim Ordered That the Decree of the Supreme Court of the State of Connecticut be affirmed with Costs. __

United States v. Benjamin F. Bache	Mr Levy of Counsel for the Defendant files a sug- gestion in this Cause and thereupon moves for a pro- hibition to the Circuit Court for the Pennsylvania District to stay proceedings in said Case and that this

Motion be continued over to the next Term:
  Order'd by the Court

The Court having finished the business before it Adjourned to the Time
and place by Law appointed. __

At a Supreme Court of the United States held at Philadelphia (the same
being the present Seat of the National Government) on Monday the fourth
day of February in the Year of our Lord one Thousand Seven hundred and
Ninety Nine 1799

                          Present

The Honourable Oliver Ellsworth, Esquire Chief Justice

William Cushing
James Iredell   Esquires,
William Patterson &   Associate Justices
Bushrod Washington[318]

Proclamation being made the Court is Opened

Letters Patent from the President of the United States dated the 20th Day
of December 1798 constituting Bushrod Washington of Virginia an Associate
Justice of the Supreme Court of the United States are now openly read and
published __ [319]

Gist vs Robinett	On Motion of Mr Ingersoll this Cause Ordered to be continued under the Rule last made in the same __

Dorance vs. Vanhorne's Lee	On Motion of Mr Ingersoll ordered to stand over for the present

318. Samuel Chase had been ill since the start of 1799. See "Commentaries," Samuel Chase
to James Iredell, March 17, 1799.
319. Bushrod Washington replaced James Wilson who had died on August 21, 1798.

Irwine   ⎞ The Court directed the Record in this Case to be read, which
   vs.   ⎬ was done accordingly by M͛ Dallas Counsel on the[320] Part of the
Sims's Lee   ⎠ Plaintiff _

Fowler & Lyman ⎞
   vs.   ⎬ Rule made in this Cause this Day
Miller   ⎠ returned with Proof of Service _

Fowler & Lyman ⎞
   vs   ⎬ Rule
Lindeley et al͛ ⎠

The Court adjourns to 10 O Clock to Morrow.[321]

Tuesday 5ᵗʰ February 1799 _

Pursuant to Adjournment the Court met this Morning at the City Hall

Present

The Honourable Oliver Ellsworth Esquire Chief Justice

⎧ William Cushing   ⎞
⎨ James Iredell   ⎬ Esquires, Associate
⎪ William Patterson &   ⎨ Justices _
⎩ Bushrod Washington   ⎠

On Motion of M͛ Lewis the Court Ordered that the Name of John Hallowell should be erased from the List of Attornies and placed on that of Counsellors _ Agreeably to which Order M͛ Hallowell was affirmed and qualified
to act as a Counsellor of this Court

Irwine   ⎞ The Court proceeded to hear Argument in
   vs.   ⎬ this Case _
Sims's Lee   ⎠ Having heard M͛ Dallas on the part of the Plaintiff and M͛ Lee
              (Attorney General) on the part of the Defendant the Court ad-
journ the further hearing this Cause untill to Morrow at Ten O Clock

320. The words "on the" are written over "for."
321. Notice of the opening of the Supreme Court appeared in the *Aurora* (Philadelphia) on
February 5, 1799, in the *Commercial Advertiser* (New York) on February 6, and in the *Newport
Mercury* (Newport, Rhode Island), February 19, 1799.

Wednesday 6ᵗʰ February 1799

Pursuant to Adjournment the Court met this Morning at the City Hall.

Present

The Honourable Oliver Ellsworth Esquire Chief Justice —

$$\left.\begin{array}{l} \text{William Cushing} \\ \text{James Iredell} \\ \text{William Patterson \&.} \\ \text{Bushrod Washington} \end{array}\right\} \begin{array}{l} \text{Esquires, Associate} \\ \text{Justices} \_ \end{array}$$

On Motion of Mʳ E. Tilghman Mʳ William H. Todd[322] is admitted a Counsellor of this Court and qualified accordingly —

On Motion of Mʳ Lewis Josiah Ogden Hoffman Esquire[323] Attorney General of the State of New York is admitted a Counsellor of this Court and qualified accordingly

$$\left.\begin{array}{l} \text{Irwine} \\ \text{vs} \\ \text{Sims's Lee} \end{array}\right\} \begin{array}{l} \text{Mʳ Lee proceeded as Counsel for the Defendant in his Argument and having closed the same Mʳ Rawle proceeded to argue the Cause on the same Side} \end{array}$$

The Court adjourn untill Ten O Clock to Morrow

Thursday 7ᵗʰ February 1799

Pursuant to Adjournment the Court met this Morning at the City Hall

Present

The Honorable Oliver Ellsworth Esqʳ Chief Justice

$$\left.\begin{array}{l} \text{William Cushing,} \\ \text{James Iredell,} \\ \text{William Patterson \&} \\ \text{Bushrod Washington} \end{array}\right\} \begin{array}{l} \text{Esquires,} \\ \text{Associate Justices} \end{array}$$

322. William H. Todd (1771-1833) was admitted to the Philadelphia bar in 1793 and to the Supreme Court of Pennsylvania bar in 1795. Todd was a Philadelphia resident and clerk of its Select Council at the time of his admission to the Supreme Court of the United States bar. Edward L. Clark, comp., *A Record of the Inscriptions on the Tablets and Gravestones in the Burial Grounds of Christ Church, Philadelphia* (Philadelphia: Collins, 1864), p. 596; *MBBP,* p. 318; "Supreme Court List of Attorneys, 1742-1902," Records of the Eastern District, RG 33, PHarH; Stafford, *The Philadelphia Directory* (1799).

323. Josiah Ogden Hoffman (1766-1837) was admitted to the bar of the New York Supreme Court of Judicature in April, 1787. At the time of his Supreme Court admission, he was attorney general for the state of New York and lived in Albany. *DAB;* Hodge, Allen, and Campbell, *The New-York Directory* (1789); Ronald Vern Jackson and Gary Ronald Teeples, eds., *New York 1800 Census Index* (1974; reprint ed., Bountiful, Utah: Accelerated Indexing Systems, 1977).

Irwine ⎱   M[r] Rawle having continued his Argument in this Cause and
  vs. ⎰   finished the same M[r] Ingersoll on the same Side was directed to
Sim's's Lee ⎰ proceed

The Court adjourned untill to Morrow at Ten O Clock —

Friday 8th February 1799 —

Pursuant to Adjournment the Court met this Morning at the City Hall —

Present —

The Honorable Oliver Ellsworth Esquire Chief Justice

⎧ William Cushing   ⎫
⎨ James Iredell,   ⎬ Esquires, Associate
⎪ William Patterson &   ⎬ Justices —
⎩ Bushrod Washington   ⎭

Irwin ⎱   M[r] Ingersoll having closed his Argument this Morning M[r] E.
  vs. ⎰   Tilghman on the Part of the Plaintiff proceeded to argue the
Sims's Lee ⎰ Case, but not having finished the Court adjourn for the further
             hearing of the Cause untill to Morrow at Ten O'Clock

Saturday 9th February 1799 —

Pursuant to Adjournment the Court met this Morning at the City Hall

Present.

The Honorable Oliver Ellsworth Esquire Chief Justice

William Cushing
James Iredell
William Patterson &
Bushrod Washington

Irwin ⎱   M[r] Tilghman continued his Argument
  vs. ⎰   in this Case —
Sims's Lee ⎰

The Court adjourned untill Monday[324] next at Ten O'Clock

Monday 11th February 1799

The Court met this Morning pursuant to Adjournment at the City Hall —

---

324. Preceded by the word "to" which is erased.

Present

The Honorable Oliver Ellsworth Esquire Chief Justice

William Cushing
James Iredell,
William Patterson &
Bushrod Washington

Mossman & Mein
  v̄s. } Error from Georgia
Higginson sur͟g Ex͟r of } Record returned and filed
Greenwood & Higginson

Clarke } Error from Rhode Island
vs. } M͟r Howell on the Part of the Plaintiff proceeded to open the Case
Russell } but not having finished his Argument the Court adjourn untill to
Morrow at Ten O Clock

Tuesday 12ᵗʰ February 1799

Pursuant to Adjournment the Court met this Morning at the City Hall

Present.

The Honorable Oliver Ellsworth Esquire Chief Justice

{ William Cushing
  James Iredell,
  William Patterson &
  Bushrod Washington }

Clarke } M͟r Howell proceeded in his Argument and having concluded the
vs } same M͟r Robbins and M͟r Dexter were heard on the part of the
Russell } Defendant

The Court adjourn untill to Morrow Morning at Ten O Clock

Wednesday 13ᵗʰ February 1799 —

Pursuant to Adjournment the Court met this Morning at the City Hall

Present

The Honorable Oliver Ellsworth Esquire Chief Justice

{ William Cushing
  James Iredell, } Esquires
  William Patterson & } Associate Justices
  Bushrod Washington }

On Motion of M.ʳ Ingersoll Walter Franklin[325] was admitted as a Counsellor of this Court and was affirmed accordingly —

Clark
vs.
Russell } M.ʳ Tilghman was heard this Morning on the Part of the Defendant and M.ʳ Ingersoll on that of the Plaintiff

The Court adjourn untill to Morrow at 10 O Clock

Thursday Morning 14th February 1799 —

Pursuant to Adjournment the Court met this Morning at the City Hall

Present.

The Honorable Oliver Ellsworth Esquire Chief Justice

{ William Cushing
James Iredell,
William Patterson &
Bushrod Washington } Esquires, Associate Justices

Dorrance
vs
Vanhorne's Lee } On Motion of M.ʳ Ingersoll the Court order the Plaintiff in this Cause to assign Errors within two Days or that the Writ of Error be non pros'd.

Irwin
vs
Sims's Lee } M.ʳ Lewis on the Part of the Plaintiff having commenced his Argument in this Cause but from Indisposition not being able to finish the same the Court adjourn untill to Morrow at 10 O'Clock

Friday 15th February 1799

The Court pursuant to Adjournment met this Morning at the City Hall

Present

The Honorable Oliver Ellsworth Esquire Chief Justice

{ William Cushing
James Iredell
William Patterson &
Bushrod Washington } Esquires Associate Justices —

---

325. Walter Franklin (1773-1838), a New York-born Quaker, was admitted to the Philadelphia bar in 1793 and lived in Philadelphia at the time of his admission to the bar of the Supreme Court of the United States. Alexander Harris, *A Biographical History of Lancaster County* (1872; reprint ed., Baltimore: Genealogical Publishing, 1974), pp. 214-15; George R. Prowell, *History of York County Pennsylvania*, 2 vols. (Chicago: J. H. Beers, 1907), 1:487; Hinshaw, *American Quaker Genealogy*, 2:527; *MBBP*, p. 269; Stafford, *The Philadelphia Directory* (1799).

Irwine ⎫
vs. ⎬ M[r] Lewis pursued and closed his Argument
Sims's Lee ⎭ in this Cause

The Court adjourns untill to Morrow at 10 O Clock

Saturday 16th February 1799

Pursuant to Adjournment the Court met this Morning at the City Hall—

Present

The Honorable Oliver Ellsworth Esq[r] Chief Justice

William Cushing ⎫
James Iredell ⎬ Esquires
William Patterson & ⎬ Associate Justices
Bushrod Washington ⎭

On Motion of the Attorney General of the United States M[r] Hillhouse[326] of Connecticut was admitted as a Counsellor of this Court and sworn accordingly—

Fowler & Lyman ⎫ M[r] Lewis and M[r] J. O. Hoffman (atty Gen[l] of the State
vs. ⎬ of New York) appeared on the part of the Defendants
Miller ⎭ in said Causes in Support of the Rule made in the same
at the last Term.—

Same ⎫
vs. ⎬ M[r] Hillhouse shews Cause against granting the Rule,
Lindsley et al[s] ⎭ moved to be made absolute in said Causes—

The Court adjourn untill Monday Morning at Ten O Clock

Monday 18th February 1799

Pursuant to Adjournment the Court met this Morning at the City Hall.

Present

The Honorable Oliver Ellsworth Esquire Chief Justice

⎧ William Cushing ⎫
⎨ James Iredell ⎬ Esquires Associate
⎨ William Patterson & ⎬ Justices
⎩ Bushrod Washington ⎭

326. James Hillhouse (1754-1832), of New Haven, Connecticut, was serving in the Senate at the time of his admission to the Supreme Court bar. He was first admitted to the bar and commenced practice in New Haven in 1775. *DAB*.

Lyman & Fowler ⎫   The Court hearing the Arguments of Counsel on the
   vs.   ⎬   part as well of the Plaintiffs & the Defendants and duly
Miller   ⎭   considered the same —

Dorrance   ⎫
   vs   ⎬   Rule of the 14ᵗʰ Insᵗ made absolute
Vanhorne's Lee ⎭

Court adjourn to 11 O Clock to Morrow

Tuesday 19ᵗʰ February 1799

Pursuant to Adjournment the Court met this Morning at the City Hall

Present.

The Honorable Oliver Ellsworth Esquire Chief Justice

⎧ William Cushing   ⎫
⎨ William Patterson &   ⎬ Esquires, Associate
⎩ Bushrod Washington[327] ⎭ Justices —

Clark   ⎫   Ordered by the Court on Solemn Argument that the Circuit
  vs.   ⎬   Court for the Rhode Island District in this cause be reversed and
Russell ⎭   that a Venire de Nova be awarded

Irwin   ⎫   Ordered by the Court on solemn Argument that the Judge-
  vs.   ⎬   ment of the Circuit Court for the Pennsylvania District in this
Sims's Lee ⎭   Cause be affirmed and a Special Mandate awarded

Fowler & Lyman ⎫   Ordered by the Court that the Rule obtained and en-
   vs.   ⎬   tered in this Cause at the last Term be discharged —
Miller   ⎭

Fowler & Lyman   ⎫   Ordered by the Court that the Rule obtained and en-
   vs   ⎬   tered in this Cause at the last Term be discharg'd
Lindsley et alˢ ⎭

Mossman & Mein ⎫
   vs.   ⎬   Continued.
Higginson   ⎭

The Court adjourn to the Time and Place by Law appointed —

---

327. According to Alexander J. Dallas, James Iredell was absent "on account of indisposition."
Dallas, 3:412.

At the City Hall in the City of Philadelphia (being the present Seat of the National Government of the United States) on Monday the fifth day of August in the Year of our Lord one thousand Seven hundred and Ninety Nine, and in the Twenty ~~fou rth~~ third Year of the Independence of the United States the Supreme Court of the United States met agreeably to Law

The Honourable   William Patterson & ⎫
                   Samuel Chase[328]   ⎬ Esquires
                                        ⎭

met this Morning at the City Hall, but a Sufficient Number of Judges not appearing to constitute a Court; The Justices present adjourn untill to Morrow at Ten O Clock.

Tuesday 6th August 1799.

Pursuant to Adjournment the Court met this Morning at the City Hall

Present.

The Honourable Oliver Ellsworth Esquire Chief Justice

            William Patterson ⎫
            Samuel Chase &   ⎬ Esquires, Justices
            Bushrod Washington ⎭

Proclamation being made the Court was opened

State of New York   ⎫ M.r Hoffman Attorney General of the
     vs.   ⎬ State of New York appears on Behalf of
State of Connecticut & others ⎭ said State and having filed a Bill in Eq-
                              uity; thereupon moved that an Injunction might issue from this Court directed to Joseph Lyman and Samuel Fowler and their Agents Counsellors and Attornies enjoining the said Parties Defendants to stay all further proceedings commenced and prosecuted in the said Circuit Court by the said Lyman, Fowler &c untill further orders from the Supreme Court of the United States

Turner   ⎫ Ordered for Argument to
    vs   ⎬ Morrow —
Bank of North America ⎭

Mossman & Mein ⎫ On Motion of M.r Ingersoll — Ordered that the De-
     vs.   ⎬ fendant appear and join in Error by thursday Morning
Higginson   ⎭ next — 8th Continued

---

328. Oliver Ellsworth and Bushrod Washington, who were absent for the opening day of the term, arrived the next day. William Cushing and James Iredell missed the whole term because of illness. See "Commentaries," Samuel Johnston to Hannah Iredell, July 27, 1799; the *Philadelphia Gazette*, under date of August 5, 1799; Bushrod Washington to James Iredell, August 20, 1799; and James Iredell to [Sarah (Dolbeare)?] Gray, September 6, 1799.

Pierce and Harris ⎱ Ordered that the plaintiff appear and prosecute their
vs. ⎰ Writ of Error within the Term or suffer a non pros—
Ship Alligator and ⎰ Aug: 9th Non pros: ordered
B. Lincolm Esq:

Hazlehurst ⎱ Rule— On Motion of the Attorney General that the plain-
vs. ⎰ tiff appear and prosecute his Writ of Error within the Term
United States ⎰ or suffer a Non pros:

Coffin ⎱ Rule— On Motion of the Attorney General that the plaintiff appear
vs ⎰ and prosecute his Writ of Error within the Term or suffer a Non pros:
Same ⎰

Coffin ⎱ Rule— On Motion of the Attorney General that the Plaintiff ap-
vs. ⎰ pear and prosecute his Writ of Error within the Term or suffer a
Same ⎰ Non pros:

Geyer ⎱ Rule— On Motion of the Attorney General that the Plain-
vs. ⎰ tiff appear & prosecute his Writ of Error within the Term
United States ⎰ or suffer a Non pros:

Tunno ⎱ Rule— On Motion of the Attorney General that the Plaintiff ap-
vs. ⎰ pear and prosecute his Writ of Error within the Term or suffer a
Same ⎰ Non pros:

Miller ⎱ Rule— On Motion of the Attorney General that the Plaintiff ap-
vs. ⎰ pear and prosecute his Writ of Error within the Term or suffer a
Same ⎰ Non pros:

State of New York ⎱
vs. ⎰ M: Ingersoll appears for Defendants
State of Connecticut & ⎰
Lyman and Others ⎰

The Court adjourned untill to Morrow at Ten O Clock

Wednesday 7th August 1799

Pursuant to Adjournment the Court met this Morning at the City Hall

Present

The Honorable Oliver Ellsworth Esquire Chief Justice

William Patterson, ⎱
Samuel Chase and ⎰ Esquires, Associate Justices
Bushrod Washington ⎰

Turner ⎱ The Court proceeded to hear M: Ingersoll in be-
vs. ⎰ half of the Plaintiff in this Cause and M: Rawle on
Bank of North America ⎰ the part of the Defendant

| Turner vs. Dᵉ Caso Eurille | The Court directed Counsel to proceed in the Argument of this Case |

The Court adjourn untill to Morrow at Ten O Clock

Thursday 8ᵗʰ August 1799 —

Pursuant to Adjournment the Court met this Morning at the City Hall

Present

The Honorable Oliver Ellsworth Esquire Chief Justice

William Patterson
Samuel Chase &
Bushrod Washington } Esquires, Associate Justices

| Mossman & Mein vs. Higginson | Continued |

| Hazlehurst vs United States &c | Ordered for Argument to Morrow Morning or Non pros: |

9ᵗʰ Ordered by the Court that a Non pros: be entered in this Cause

| Coffin vs. Same | Ordered for Argument to Morrow Morning or Non pros: |

9ᵗʰ Ordered by the Court that a Non pros be entered in this Cause

| Coffin vs. Same | Ordered for Argument to Morrow Morning or Non pros: |

9ᵗʰ Ordered by the Court that a Non pros: be entered in this Cause —

| Geyer vs United States | Ordered for Argument to Morrow Morning or Non pros: |

9ᵗʰ Ordered by the Court that a Non pros: be entered in this Cause

| Tunno vs. Same | Ordered for Argument to Morrow Morning or Non pros: |

9ᵗʰ Ordered by the Court that a Non pros: be entered in this Cause

Miller }
vs.   } Ordered for Argument to Morrow
Same } Morning

9th Ordered by the Court that a Non pros be entered in this Cause —

State of New York }
vs.   } Court proceeded to hear Counsel on the Motion
State of Connecticut } for an Injunction made in this Cause —

Court adjourned untill to Morrow at Ten O Clock

Friday 9th August 1799 —

Pursuant to Adjournment the Court met at the City Hall

Present

The Honorable Oliver Ellsworth Esquire Chief Justice

William Patterson   }
Samuel Chase and   } Justices &c.[329]
Bushrod Washington   }

Turner   } On Argument the Court order and decree that the
vs.   } Judgement of the Circuit Court for the District of
Bank of North America } North Carolina in said Cause be reversed with
                         Costs —

Turner   } On Argument — The Court Order and decree
vs   } that the Judgement of the Circuit Court for the
Marquis De Casa Eurilla } District of North Carolina in said Cause be Re-
                           versed with Costs —

State of New York   } The Court having heard Counsel in Behalf
vs.   } of the parties complainant and Defendants in
State of Connecticut and } this Suit refuse the Injunction prayed for in
J. Lyman and Others   } this Cause —
                          Ordered that the Defendants Joseph Lyman
& Samuel Fowler plead, answer or demur to the bill filed in this Cause within
Sixty days —

The Court adjourns to the Time and place by Law appointed

[————————]

---

329. "&c." is written in a hand different from that of the rest of the text.

At a Supreme Court of the United to be holden agreeably to Law at Philadelphia (the same being the Seat of the National Government) on the first Monday being the third day of February in the Year of our Lord One Thousand eight hundred

Present

The Honorable   William Cushing & $\Big\}$ Esquires
                  William Patterson[330]

A Sufficient Number of Justices not being convened to constitute a Quorum. the Court is adjourned untill to Morrow at Eleven O Clock

Tuesday February 4th 1800

present

The Honorable   William Cushing & $\Big\}$ Esquires
                  William Patterson

A Sufficient Number[331] of Justices not being convened to form a Quorum the Court is adjourned untill to Morrow at Eleven O Clock

Wednesday February 5th 1800

present

The Honorable   William Cushing & $\Big\}$ Esquires
                  William Patterson

A Sufficient Number of Justices not being convened to form a Quorum the Court is adjourned untill to Morrow at Eleven O Clock

---

330. Only four of the previous term's justices attended the February 1800 term. James Iredell had died on October 20, 1799, and his replacement, Alfred Moore, did not intend to come to Philadelphia for this term. Bushrod Washington and Samuel Chase were en route to Philadelphia to join William Paterson and William Cushing. (See "Commentaries," William Paterson to Euphemia Paterson, February 2, 1800.) Chase was delayed by an accident (see "Commentaries," the *Philadelphia Gazette,* under date of February 3, 1800, and Samuel Chase to Hannah Chase, February 4, 1800). Oliver Ellsworth was in France serving as a special envoy of President Adams and missed the entire term. Michael Kraus, "Oliver Ellsworth," in *The Justices of the United States Supreme Court 1789-1969: Their Lives and Major Opinions,* ed. Leon Friedman and Fred L. Israel, 4 vols. (New York: R. R. Bowker, 1969), 1:233-34.

331. The clerk had begun to write this sentence on the line above, on a parallel with William Paterson's name, so the words "A Sufficient Number" are partially erased on that line.

Thursday February 6th 1800

pursuant to Adjournment the Court met this Morning

Present

The Honorable   William Cushing   ⎫
                     William Patterson,   ⎬ Esquires
                     Samuel Chase &   ⎭
                     Bushrod Washington

Proclamation is made and the Court is opened

Rutherford & al^s ⎫ Record returned and filed
vs   ⎬   On Motion of Mr Stockton of Counsel for the de-
Samuel R, Fisher   ⎨ fendants in Error —
& Miers Fisher   ⎭ Ordered — That the Writ of Error issued in this Case
                                be quashed with Costs —

The Court adjourned untill to Morrow at Ten O Clock[332]

Friday February 7th 1800

Pursuant to Adjournment the Court met this Morning

Present

The Honorable   William Cushing   ⎫
                     William Patterson   ⎬ Esquires
                     Samuel Chase &   ⎭
                     Bushrod Washington

Mossman & Mein   ⎫ On Motion of Mr Dallas of Counsel for the plaintiffs in
vs   ⎬ Error —
Higginson   ⎭   Ordered that the plaintiffs have Leave to amend their
                    Writ of Error by inserting the Return Day to which said
Writ was returnable —

Cooper   ⎫ plea filed and Issue
v̄s   ⎬   The Court proceed to hear the
Telfaire   ⎭ Argument in this Case

United States ⎫ Agreement of Counsel filed —
vs   ⎬ Writ of Error issued this day by Consent returnable as of
Topham   ⎭ this Term — Assignment of Errors and Joinder filed —

The Court adjourn untill to Morrow at Ten O Clock

---

332. The *Philadelphia Gazette* on February 6, 1800, noted that the Court had convened on that same day.

<u>Saturday February 8th 1800</u>

Pursuant to Adjournment the Court met this Morning

Present

The Honorable   William Cushing
                     William Patterson   } Esquires
                     Samuel Chase &
                     Bushrod Washington

Mossman & Mein
        v   } Continued by Order of the Court
Higginson

Cooper
   v̄s   } The Court proceeded to hear the Argument
Telfaire   of this Cause

Course
   v̄s   } Record returned and filed —
The Ex̄ors of Stead   Rule that the Defendants in Error do rejoin

Blane   Appeal from Virginia
   vs   }   Ordered that the Appeal from the Circuit Court for
Ship Charles Carter   the District of Virginia in this Case be dismissed —

The Court adjourn untill Monday at Ten O Clock

<u>Monday February 10th 1800</u>

Pursuant to Adjournment the Court met this Morning at the City Hall

Present

The Honorable   William Cushing
                     William Patterson   } Esquires
                     Samuel Chase &
                     Bushrod Washington

James Greenleaf   Error from Virginia
      vs   } Record returned and filed
Henry Banks   Agreement of Counsel   Assignment of Errors
                  and Joinder filed —

Paine & Bridgman
       vs   } Error from South Carolina
The United States   Record returned and filed —

United States
     vs.   } The Court proceeded to hear Counsel in this
Topham   cause —

The Court adjourn untill to Morrow at Ten O Clock

Tuesday February 11ᵗʰ 1800

The Court met this day at the City Hall pursuant to Adjournment

Present

The Honorable   William Cushing
William Patterson
Samuel Chase &   } Esquires
Bushrod Washington

United States ⎫
vs.   ⎬   The Court heard the further Arguments of
Topham   ⎭   Counsel in this Case —

The Court adjourn untill to Morrow at Ten O Clock

Wednesday February 12ᵗʰ 1800

Pursuant to Adjournment the Court met this Morning at the City Hall

Present

The Honorable   William Cushing
William Patterson
Samuel Chase &   } Esquires
Bushrod Washington

United States ⎫   The Court having heard the Parties in this Cause by their
vs.   ⎬   respective Counsel— Order and decree that the Sentence
Topham   ⎭   of the Circuit Court for the District of New York in said
Case be affirmed

Greenleaf ⎫
vs   ⎬   Continued
Banks ⎭

Paine & Bridgman ⎫   On Argument— Ordered that the Writ of Error is-
v̄s   ⎬   sued in this Case be quashed with Costs—
The United States ⎭

The Court adjourn untill to Morrow at Ten O Clock

<u>Thursday February 13th 1800.</u>

Pursuant to Adjournment the Court met this Morning at the City Hall

Present

The Honorable   William Cushing
                William Patterson   Esquires
                Samuel Chase &
                Bushrod Washington

Cooper   The Court having heard the parties in this Case by their respective
v̄s   Counsel; Order and decree that the Judgment of the Circuit Court
Telfaire   for the District of Georgia be affirmed with Costs.

Williamson   On Motion of Mr Ingersoll of Counsel for the plaintiff in Er-
vs.   ror _ Ordered that this Cause be continued till the next
Kincaid   Term _ the Writ of Error not to be a Supersedeas to the de-
                 cission of the Circuit Court _ The plaintiff in Error to be at
Liberty to shew to the Satisfaction of this Court that the Matter in dispute
exceeds the Sum or Value of two thousand Dollars exclusive of Costs[_] this
to be made to appear by Affidavits on ten days Notice to the Opposite party
or his Counsel in Georgia _ Rule as to Affidavits to be mutual _

State of New York
    v̄s
                     Continued _
State of Connecticut
Lyman & Others

The Court adjourn to the Time and place by Law appointed _

At a Supreme Court of the United States to be holden agreeably to Law at Philadelphia (the same being the Seat of the National Government) on the first Monday being the third day³³³ ^{4th} of August in the Year of our Lord One thousand eight hundred

Present

The Honorable   William Patterson &   Esquires
                Bushrod Washington³³⁴

A sufficient Number of Justices not being convened to constitute a Quorum the Court is adjourned by the Justices present till to Morrow Morning at ten O Clock

---

333. "4th" is written in pencil and may not be contemporary.
334. Oliver Ellsworth missed the entire term, because he was in France as envoy extraordinary. William Cushing was ill and therefore absent for the whole term (see "Commentaries," *Aurora*

Tuesday 5ᵗʰ August 1800

present

The Honorable   William Patterson &   ⎫
                  Bushrod Washington   ⎬   Esquires
                                        ⎭

A sufficient Number of Justices not being convened to constitute a Quorum the Court is adjourned till Morrow Morning at Ten O Clock

Wednesday 6ᵗʰ August 1800

Pursuant to Adjournment the Court met this Morning at the Court House[335]

Present

The Honorable   William Paterson   ⎫
                  Bushrod Washington &   ⎬ Esquires
                  Alfred Moore   ⎭

A sufficient Number of Justices not being convened to constitute a Quorum the Court is adjourned till to Morrow Morning at Ten O Clock

Thursday 7ᵗʰ August 1800

Pursuant to Adjournment the Court met this Morning at the Court House

Present

The Honorable   William Paterson   ⎫
                  Bushrod Washington &   ⎬ Esquires
                  Alfred Moore   ⎭

A sufficient Number of Justices not being convened to constitute a Quorum the Court is adjourned untill to Morrow Morning at Ten O Clock＿

---

under date of August 9, 1800, and Thomas B. Adams to William Cranch, August 15, 1800). Samuel Chase arrived in Philadelphia in time to attend Court on August 9. The *Aurora,* possibly for political reasons to discredit Chase, reported on August 8 and 9 that Chase's absence was caused by his delivering election speeches in Maryland (q.v. in "Commentaries"). The *Philadelphia Gazette* on August 12 noted that Chase's absence was due to illness (q.v. in "Commentaries"). William Paterson confirmed this report in a letter to Cushing on August 19, in which he mentioned that illness was the cause of Chase's delayed arrival in Philadelphia (q.v. in "Commentaries").

335. The County Court House completed in 1789 was the home of Congress when it met in Philadelphia. When Congress moved to Washington, D.C., in 1800, the Supreme Court of the United States, as well as the federal district and circuit courts for Pennsylvania, moved to the Court House, to the chamber vacated by the Senate. U.S. Department of Interior, National Park Service, "Historic Structures Report on Old City Hall, Independence National Historic Park, 1961," part 2, Historical Data Section prepared by David Kimball, p. 2, typescript in Historian's Office, PPIn.

Friday 8th August 1800

Pursuant to Adjournment the Court met this Morning at the Court House

Present

The Honorable   William Patterson
                 Bushrod Washington & } Esquires
                 Alfred Moore

A sufficient Number of Justices not being convened to constitute a Quorum the Court is adjourned untill to Morrow Morning at Ten O Clock

Saturday 9th August 1800

Pursuant to Adjournment the Court met this Morning at the Court House

Present

The Honorable   William Paterson
                 Bushrod Washington
                 Alfred Moore &   } Esquires
                 Samuel Chase[336]

A Commission[337] from the President, of the United States to Alfred Moore Esquire of North Carolina bearing date the tenth Day of December in the Year of our Lord one thousand Seven hundred and ninety nine & constituting the said Alfred Moore one of the Justices of the Supreme Court of the United States is now read in open Court[338]

Jones & others plffs' in Error ⎫   On hearing Counsel in this Case _ Or-
        vs   ⎬   dered that the Decree of the Circuit Court
Pearce Deft in Error   ⎭   in said Case be reversed

The Court adjourn untill Monday. Morning at ten O Clock

336. According to the order of seniority maintained in the list of justices present throughout the minutes of the first decade, Samuel Chase's name belongs before that of Bushrod Washington. The clerk continued to do this for the whole term, an error never made before by Samuel Bayard. This may indicate that Bayard did not take the original minutes from which the fine minutes were transcribed.

337. This is the first time a clerk has used the word "Commission." Previously, the clerks had noted that letters patent were read and published.

338. Alfred Moore replaced James Iredell who had died on October 20, 1799.

Monday 11th August 1800

Pursuant to Adjournment the Court met this Morning at the Court House

Present

The Honorable   William Paterson ⎫
                 Bushrod Washington ⎬ Esquires
                 Alfred Moore & ⎭
                 Samuel Chase

On Motion of Mr Rawle William Sergeant Esquire[339] is admitted a Counsellor of this Court

Mossman & Mein ⎫ The Court having heard the Parties in said Cause by
     vs.   ⎬ their respective Counsel Order the Decree of the Circuit
Higginson   ⎭ Court for the District of Georgia in said Case to be reversed it not appearing to the Supreme Court of the United States from the Record that the Circuit Court for the District of Georgia had Jurisdiction in said Case—

The Court adjourn untill to Morrow Morning at Ten O Clock

Tuesday 12th August 1800

Pursuant to Adjournment the Court met this Morning at the Court House

Present

The Honorable   William Paterson ⎫
                 Bushrod Washington ⎬ Esquires
                 Alfred Moore & ⎭
                 Samuel Chase

Mr Dallas laid before the Court a certified Copy of Proceedings had in the District Court held for the New York District in the Cases of M V Francis Fitzbonne & Peter Allard claiming to be admitted as Citizens of the United States and thereupon moved for a Rule to shew Cause why a Mandamus should not issue to the Judge of the District Court for the New York District commanding the said Judge to proceed to give Judgment in the said Cases— The Court having taken the said Motion into Consideration grant the Rule mov'd for—

339. William Sergeant (1776-1807), son of Jonathan Dickinson Sergeant, was admitted to the Philadelphia bar in 1795 and to the Supreme Court of Pennsylvania bar in 1796. He resided in Philadelphia at the time of his admission to the bar of the Supreme Court of the United States. Jordan, *Colonial and Revolutionary Families of Pennsylvania*, 2:658; note 63 above; University of Pennsylvania, *Biographical Catalogue* (1894), p. 34; *MBBP*, p. 310; "Supreme Court List of Attorneys, 1742-1902," Records of the Eastern District, RG 33, PHarH; Cornelius William Stafford, *The Philadelphia Directory for 1800* (Philadelphia: William W. Woodward, 1800).

Talbot
vs. } The Court proceeded to hear the Arguments of Counsel in this Case
Seaman

The Court adjourn untill to Morrow Morning at Ten O Clock

Wednesday 13th August 1800

Pursuant to Adjournment the Court met this Morning at the Court House

Present

The Honorable   William Paterson
Bushrod Washington
Alfred Moore &
Samuel Chase } Esquires

Talbot
vs } The Court heard Counsel in this Case
Seaman

Priestman
vs } The Court heard Counsel in this Case
United States

The Court adjourn untill to Morrow Morning at Ten O Clock—

Thursday 14th August 1800

Pursuant to Adjournment the Court met this Morning at the Court house

Present

The Honorable   William Paterson
Bushrod Washington
Alfred Moore &
Samuel Chase } Esquires

Baas
vs } The Court proceeded to hear the Argument of this Cause
Tingey

Olmstead & als
vs } Error from Pennsylvania
Clarkson   By an Instrument in Writing this day filed by Mr Lewis of Counsel for the plaintiffs in Error & Mr Ingersoll for the Defendant. it is agreed that a Writ of Error issue returnable to the first day of the present Session—

Blane
vs } Ordered that the Writ of Error issued in this Case be quash'd
Donald & Burton
and Others

Lambert ⎱
vs   ⎰ Ordered that the Writ of Error issued
Payne   in this Case be quash'd

Ross ⎱
vs. ⎰ Ordered that the Writ of Error issued
Maul   in this Case be quash'd

The Court adjourn untill to Morrow Morning at Ten O Clock

Friday 15ᵗʰ August 1800

Pursuant to Adjournment the Court met this Morning at the Court House

Present

The Honorable   William Paterson ⎫
                  Bushrod Washington ⎪
                  Alfred Moore &   ⎬ Esquires
                  Samuel Chase   ⎭

Course ⎫
vs   ⎬ On Motion of Mʳ Dallas Ordered that the Plaintiff have
Stead's Exors ⎭ Leave to amend her Writ of Error by inserting the true Teste
Day and the Record by stating the Court to which said Writ
was directed

Ordered That this Cause be continued to the next Term
the Writ of Error not to be a Supersedeas to the decision of the Circuit
Court_ The plaintiff in Error to be at Liberty to shew to the Satisfaction of
this Court that the Matter in Dispute exceeds the Sum[340] or Value of two
thousand Dollars exclusive of Costs this to be made to appear by Affidavit
on   days Notice to the opposite Party or their Counsel in Georgia_ Rule
as to Affidavits to be mutual_

Telfaire ⎫
vs   ⎬ Continued on Motion of Mʳ Dallas
Stead's Exors ⎭

Priestman ⎫
vs   ⎬ Ordered that the Decree of the Circuit Court for the Dis-
United States ⎭ trict of Pennsylvania in said Case be affirmed_

Talbot ⎫ Continued
vs   ⎬ On Motion of Mʳ Dallas Attorney for defendant in Error_
Seaman ⎭ Ordered that the Writ of Error issued in this Case shall not be
a Supersedeas to the payment of one Moiety of the Sales of the
Vessell and Cargo in Question after deduction of duties, Costs & Charges of
the said Vessell and her Cargo agreeably to the Order of the District Court
of New York and the Affirmance thereof by the Circuit Court_

340. The word "of" was written after "Sum" and then partially erased.

Baas ⎫ The Court having heard Counsel in this Case Order that the Decree
vs ⎬ of the Circuit for the Pennsylvania District in said Case be af-
Tingey ⎭ firmed —

Samuel Bayard Esquire having resigned the Office of Clerk of this Court —
It is Ordered that Elias B Caldwell[341] be appointed to the said Place and that
he give Bond for the faithful Performance of the Duties of the said Office

M[r] Caldwell appeared and took the Oath by Law prescribed and having
offered as Securities Elias Boudinot[342] and Joseph Reed[343] Esquires they are
approved and accepted by the Court

Ordered that M[r] Caldwell's Bond be deposited with the Register of the
Treasury of the United States and that he produce the Register's Receipt for
the same to this Court at their next Session — [344]

The Court having finished the Business depending before them adjourn to
the time and Place by Law appointed —

Sam[l] Bayard Clerk

---

341. See the introduction to "The Clerks and Their Record" for identification of Elias Boudinot Caldwell.

342. Elias Boudinot had been the guardian and mentor of Elias Boudinot Caldwell. For more
on their relationship, see the introduction to "The Clerks and Their Record."

343. Son of Pennsylvania's president and Revolutionary War leader of the same name, Joseph
Reed (1772-1846) was orphaned in 1785 and raised in the home of Jared Ingersoll. Reed studied
law, following his father's and guardian's footsteps, and was admitted to the Philadelphia bar in
1792. He served for many years as Philadelphia's recorder. William B. Reed, ed., *Life and Correspondence of Joseph Reed*, 2 vols. (Philadelphia: Lindsay and Blakiston, 1847), 2:416; John F.
Roche, *Joseph Reed: A Moderate in the American Revolution* (New York: Columbia University Press,
1957), p. 269n; *MBBP*, p. 305.

344. This receipt was listed as still in existence in a bound inventory entitled "Index of Records
& Papers in Supreme Court U. S. 20th Jan'y 1827" (General Records, RG 267, DNA). The
receipt has not been found.

Original Minutes

The original minutes are bound in a volume entitled

"Supreme Court of the United States
Original Minute Books
1790 to 1799
1805-'6-'7-'8-'10-'12-'13."

Included in this bound volume are the original minutes published here extending from February term, 1790, through August term, 1799. The original minutes for 1800 are missing and were listed as "Lost" in an inventory of the official record done in 1827.[1] As the title on the binding suggests, the volume of "Original Minute Books" is a gathering of disparate texts that eventually were transcribed into the fine minutes published in the preceding section. The "Original Minute Books" include John Tucker's original fine minutes, Samuel Bayard's original fine minutes for two terms, rough minutes of various clerks, and intermediate expansions of rough minutes; these are discussed in greater detail below. In a separate section following these original minutes, we publish numerous drafts of orders and motions, the wording of which parallels the original minutes but which are not bound with them.

The following table presents the sections into which we have divided the original minutes for publication and notes the creators of each. When handwriting appears in any of these sections that is different from that of the identified writer, we indicate the new hand at that point.

I.   Original Fine Minutes of John Tucker
     February 1790 term-February 1791 term

II. Original Fine Minutes of Samuel Bayard
     August 1791 term-February 1792 term

III. Samuel Bayard's Notes for Fine Minutes
     February 1792 term-August 1794 term

IV. Jacob Wagner's Notes for Fine Minutes
     February 1795 term-August 1797 term

V.   David Caldwell's Rough Notes for Fine Minutes
     February 1798 term
     Samuel Bayard's Expanded Notes for Fine Minutes
     February 1798 term

VI. Samuel Bayard's Rough Notes for Fine Minutes
     August 1798 term

Samuel Bayard's Expanded Notes for Fine Minutes
August 1798 term

VII.   Samuel Bayard's Notes for Fine Minutes
February 1799 term-August 1799 term

The original minutes in Sections I and II were written by John Tucker and Samuel Bayard on bound folio pages and represent the first attempt at a fine minute book. Bayard abandoned this first version of the fine minutes between February term, 1792, and August term, 1792, and oversaw its transcription into the fine minutes which are published in the preceding section of this volume. Sections III-VII present the notes which preceded transcription into finer form from February term, 1792, through August term, 1799. All of these notes were written on bound quarto pages except for the rough notes of Caldwell and Bayard in 1798, which were written on loose folio sheets. The first quarto signature, formed by folding a larger folio sheet, was titled by Bayard "Rough Minutes_ of the Proceedings of the Supreme Court of the United States_."

By publishing these original minutes, we are presenting their transformation through different stages before the clerk finally transcribed them into the fine minutes. Thus, for February term, 1792, we have Bayard's notes in Section III, the first fine version in Section II, and the final version transcribed into the fine minutes which are published in the preceding section of the present volume. For February and August terms, 1798, we have rough notes in Sections V and VI, expanded versions of those notes in the same sections, and the fine minutes which are published in the preceding section of this volume. Because no rough minutes survive for the period from February 1790 term through August 1791 term, the reader should refer to "Commentaries," *Pennsylvania Packet* under date of February 6, 1790. This newspaper report of the Court's meeting through February 5, 1790, is in a particularly detailed and unusually official form, which suggests that it might be a copy of the original, no longer extant, rough minutes.

We have had to adopt some special editorial procedures to prepare the original minutes for publication. First, the notes published in Sections III-VII generally were hastily written. It is, therefore, difficult to define a left margin for the text, and this, in turn, complicates our efforts to decide whether text has been indented, centered, or flushed left. For this reason, we standardize the placement of certain text. Case names are placed flush left; all datelines, the chief justices' names, and the word "present" preceding all lists of justices' names are centered. A second editorial complication is that some text cannot be transcribed with certainty either because of damage to pages or because of a tight binding that obscures words. Finally, we must point out that we do not repeat substantive notes for individuals or topics that have been annotated previously in the fine minutes.

D (DNA, RG 267, General Records). Transcribed from the original document, rather than a photocopy.

1. An 1827 inventory of "Minutes   Rough" lists as "Lost" the original minutes for 1800 through 1804 (General Records, RG 267, DNA); but the files of the curator of the Supreme Court include several folios of minutes in Elias B. Caldwell's hand spanning February 2, 1801, through February 10, 1801.

Original Fine Minutes of John Tucker
February 1790 Term
to February 1791 Term

At the Supreme Judicial Court of the United States, begun and held at New York, (being the Seat of the national Government) on the first Monday of February, and on the first day of said month Anno Domini 1790 —

Present.

The Honb^le John Jay Esqr Chief Justice —
The Honb^le William Cushing, and
The Honb^le James Willson, Esq^rs Associate Justices —

This being the day assigned by Law, for commencing the first Sessions of the Supreme Court of the United States, and a sufficient Number of the Justices not being convened, the Court is adjourned, by the Justices now present, untill to Morrow, at one of the Clock in the afternoon — [1]

Tuesday, Feby 2^d 1790 —

Present

The Honb^le John Jay Esqr Chief Justice

The Honb^le ⎨ William Cushing
James Willson, and
John Blair, Esq^rs Associate Justices

Proclamation is made and the Court is opened —

Letters patent to the Honorable John Jay Esqr bearing date the 26th day of Septr 1789. appointing him Chief Justice, of the Supreme Court of the United States, are openly read, and published in Court —

Letters patent to the Honb^le William Cushing Esq^[r] bearing date the 27th day of Septr 1789. appointing him associate Justice of the Sup. Court of the United States are openly read and published in Court

Letters patent to the Honb^le James Willson Esqr bearing date the 29th day of Septr 1789. appointing him Associate Justice of the Sup. Court of the United States, are openly read and published in Court

1. For what may be a printed version of the original rough minutes, see "Commentaries," *Pennsylvania Packet* under date of February 6, 1790.

Original Minutes, February 1, 1790, in the hand of John Tucker. Courtesy National Archives.

Letters patent to the Honb^{le} John Blair Esqr bearing Date the 30th day of Septr 1789. appointing him Associate Justice of the Sup. Court of the United States, are openly read and published in Court

Letters patent to Edmund Randolph of Virginia Esqr bearing date the 26th day of Septr 1789. appointing him Attorney General for the United States are openly read and published in Court __

Ordered, that Richard Wenman, be, and he is appointed Cryer of this Court.

Adjourned untill to morrow at one of the Clock in the Afternoon __ ²

[1790]
Wednesday Feby 3^d 1790 __ ³

Present

The Honb^{le} John Jay, Esqr Chief Justice __

The Honb^{le} { William Cushing
James Willson, and
John Blair, Esq^{rs} Associate Justices

Proclamation is made and the Court is opened

Ordered, that John Tucker Esqr of Boston, be the clerk of this court, __ That he reside, and keep his Office at the Seat of the national Government, and that he do not practise either as an att^y or a Counsellor in this Court while he shall continue to be Clerk of the same

The said John Tucker in open Court, takes the Oath of Office by Law prescribed to be taken by the Clerk of this Court, and an Oath to support the Constitution of the United States; and also gives Bond (approved of by the Court) to the United States, for the faithful discharge of his Duty as Clerk aforesaid, as by Law required

Ordered that the Seal of this Court shall be the Arms of the United States engraved on a circular piece of Steel of the Size of a Dollar, with these words in the margin __ "The Seal of the Supreme Court of the United States" __ And that the Seals of the Circuit Courts, shall be the Arms of the United States engraven on circular pieces of Silver of the Size of half a Dollar, with these words in the Margin Viz^t In the upper part "the Seal of the circuit Court, in the lower part the name of the district for which it is intended
Ordered, that the Clerk of this Court cause the before mentioned Seals to be made accordingly, and when done that he convey those for the circuit Courts to the District Clerks respectively __

2. Idem.
3. The number "90" is written over "89" in pencil; and the bracketed "1790" has been interlined in pencil. It is not known when these penciled alterations were made.

Adjourned to Friday the fifth day of Feb.y 1790 _ [4]

Friday Feb.y 5.th 1790 _

Present _

The Honb.le John Jay Esq.r Chief Justice

The Hoñble $\left\{\begin{array}{l} \text{William Cushing} \\ \text{James Willson, and} \\ \text{John Blair, Esq}^{rs} \text{ Associate Justices.} \end{array}\right.$

Proclamation is made, and the Court is opened

Elias Boudinot of New Jersey, Esq.r
Tho.s Hartley of Pensylvania and
Richard Harrison of New York Esq.rs $\Big\}$

are severally sworn as by Law required, and are admitted Counsellors of this Court.

Ordered, that (untill further Orders) if it shall be requisite to the admission of Attornies or Counsellors to practice in this Court; that they shall have been such for three years past in the Supreme Courts of the State to which they respectively belong, and that their private and professional Character shall appear to be fair

Ordered, that Counsellors, shall not practice as Attornies; nor Attornies as Counsellors in this Court.

Ordered, that they respectively take the following Oath, Viz.t I   do solemnly swear that I will demean myself (as an Atty. or Counsellor) of the Court uprightly, and according to Law; and that I will support the Constitution of the United States _

Ordered, that (unless and untill it shall be otherwise provided by Law) all Process of this Court shall be in the Name of "The President of the United States _

Adjourned untill monday the 8.th day of Feb.y 1790 _ [5]

4. See note 1 above.
5. Idem.

Monday Feby 8th 1790 —

Present

The Honb^{le} John Jay, Esqr Chief Justice —

The Honb^{le} { Willm Cushing
                     { James Willson, and
                     { John Blair Esq^{rs} Associate Justices

  Proclamation is made and the Court is opened —

Egbert Benson — John Lawrence — Theodore Sedgwick — William Smith — Morgan Lewis — James Jackson — Fisher Ames — George Thacher[—] Richard Varrick — and Robt Morris Esq^{rs} are severally sworn according to Law, and admitted <u>Counsellors</u> of this Court —

William Houston Esqr is also sworn as the Law directs, and is admitted an <u>Attorney</u> of this Court —

Adjourned to Tuesday the 9th day of Feby 1790 —

Tuesday Feby 9th 1790 — Present —

The Honb^{le} John Jay, Esqr Chief Justice —

The Honb^{le} { William Cushing
                     { James Willson and
                     { John Blair, Esq^{rs} Associate Justices.

Proclamation is made and the Court is opened.

Saml Jones — Abraham Ogden — Elisha Boudinot — Wm Paterson — Ezekiel Gilbert — and Cornelius [J]. Bogert Esq^{rs}[6] are severally sworn as the Law directs, and are admitted as <u>Counsellors</u> of this Court

Edward Livingston, and Jacob Morton Esq^{rs} — are severally sworn according to Law, and admitted <u>Attornies</u> of this Court —

Adjourned to Feby 10th 1790 —

6. The letters "Es" are written over an "ar."

Wednesday Feb.ʸ 10.ᵗʰ 1790—

Present.

The Honb.ˡᵉ John Jay Esq.ʳ Chief Justice

The Honb.ˡᵉ { William Cushing
              James Willson, and
              John Blair Esq.ʳˢ Associate Justices—

Proclamation is made and the Court is opened

Bartholom.ʷ De Haert— John Keep— Peter Masterton, and W.ᵐ Willcocks Esq.ʳˢ are now severally sworn as the Law directs, and are admitted <u>Attornies</u> of this Court—

New York Feb.ʸ 10.ᵗʰ 1790— Previous Proclamation being made, this Court is adjourned to the time and place appointed by Law

Jn Tucker Cler

At the Supreme Judicial Court of the United States, begun and held at New York (being the Seat of the national Government) on the first Monday of August, and on the second day of said Month Anno Domini 1790—

Present.

The Honb.ˡᵉ John Jay, Esq.ʳ Chief Justice—

The Honb.ˡᵉ { William Cushing
              James Willson
              John Blair, and
              James Iredell, Esq.ʳˢ Associate Justices

Proclamation is made and the Court is opened—

Letters patent to the Honb.ˡᵉ James Iredell Esq.ʳ bearing date the 10.ᵗʰ day of February 1790— appointing him one of the associate Justices of this Court are openly read and published in Court—

Ordered, that the Clerk of this Court procure a Seal for the Circuit Court of the State of Rhode Island and Providence Plantations, similar[7] to the circuit Seals ordered the last Term, and when done that he cause the same to be conveyed to the Clerk of the District of said State &c

Richard Bassett, and John Vining Esq.ʳˢ are severally sworn as the Law directs, and are admitted Counsellors of this Court

Adjourned to Tuesday the 3.ᵈ day of Aug.ᵗ 1790—

7. The "m" is written over an "l."

Tuesday Augt 3.^d 1790 —

Present.

The Honb.^{le} John Jay Esqr Chief Justice —

The Honble. { William Cushing
James Willson
John Blair, and
James Iredell, Esq.^{rs} Associate Justices

Proclamation is made and the Court is opened.

Barnabas Bidwell Esqr is sworn as the Law directs and is admitted a Counsellor of this Court.

New York Augt 3.^d 1790. Previous proclamation being made this Court is adjourned, next to meet at the time and place prescribed by Law

Jn Tucker Cler

At the Supreme Court of the United States begun and held at Philadelphia (being the Seat of the national Government) on the first Monday of February and on the Seventh day of said month Anno Dom. 1791 —

Present

The Honb.^{le} John Jay Esqr Chief-Justice —

William Cushing
James Willson, and   }   Associate Justices
James Iredell, Esq.^{rs}

Proclamation is made and the Court is opened —

Ordered, that the Counsellors and Attornies admitted to practice in this Court shall take either an Oath, or in proper Cases, an Affirmation of the Tenor prescribed by the Rule of this Court on that Subject made in Feby Term 1790 viz I   do solemnly swear or affirm (as the Case may be) that I will demean myself as an Attorney or Counsellor of this Court uprightly and according to Law; and that I will support the Constitution of the United States —

William Lewis Esqr is affirmed according to the Order of Court, and is admitted to practice as a Counsellor of said Court —

William Bradford Jr. and Alex.^r Wilcocks Esq.^{rs} having been proposed by the Attorney Genl of the United States for admission as Counsellors of this Court, they are sworn agreably to the Order thereof, and are admitted to practice accordingly

Miers Fisher Esqr having been proposed by the said Att.^y Genl for Admission as a Counsellor of this Court he is affirmed agreable to the Order therof and is admitted to practice accordingly.

Jonᵃ Dickenson Sergeant, Jared Ingersoll, Edwᵈ Tilghman, and James Munroe Esqʳˢ having been proposed by the Attʸ Genˡ of the United States for admission as Counsellors of this Court they are sworn agreable to the Order thereof and are admitted to practice accordingly

Adjourned to Tuesday the eighth day of Febʸ 1791.

Tuesday Febʸ yᵉ 8ᵗʰ 1791 —

Present

The Honbˡᵉ John Jay, Esqʳ Chief Justice —

William Cushing
James Willson, and   } Associate Justices
James Iredell, Esqʳˢ

Proclamation is made and the Court is opened.

The Chief Justice laid before the Court a Letter he had received from the Judge of the District Court of New=York, which was read and is in the words following viz. District of New York, Janʸ 20ᵗʰ 1791 — Sir, On complaint of the Collector, and proof on Oath, I committed Josiah Goreham Master of the Sloop Hiram to the Goal of this City on the 12ᵗʰ of November last for a Breach of the Revenue Laws aggravated by Perjury — Charles Seely his Mate had, a few days before been committed for landing and storing a Quantity of Coffee before Report or Entry, and in the Night time; and both have ever since remained in Confinement for want of Sureties for their appearance. An under Officer of the Customs was, about the time of the removal of Congress, suspended by the Secretary of the Treasury for malconduct in permitting Goods to be landed after Sunset — As there are circumstances which, in the opinion of the principal Officers, rendered any criminal Intention questionable; it was determined that a Judicial Enquiry should precede his Removal or Restoration. In the mean time, deprived of the means of Subsistence, he is importunate for a Tryal — Each of these Cases, and in general every Offence made subject to fine or corporal Punishment, one only excepted, are excluded from the Authority of the District Court by the Extent of the Punishment; and it's criminal Cognizance thus circumscribed, is a Burthen to the Community without any public Advantage — I think it therefore my Duty to make this Representation, that if the Supreme Court should conceive it proper, a special Circuit Court may be appointed for this district, and the Prisoners as the suspended Officer, be punished or relieved as Justice shall require I have the honor to be, with great Respect, sir, your most obedient humble Servant

James Duane

Honorable
The Chief Justice of the United States —

Thereupon Ordered, that a special Sessions of the Circuit Court be held at the City of New York, in and for the District of New York on the twenty first day of Feb.ʸ instant next; and that authenticated Copies of this Order be transmitted by the Clerk of this Court to the Judge to the Judge and the Clerk of the said District Court and to the Attorney of the United States for the said District

It appearing from the Information of the Att.ʸ Gen.ˡ that divers persons charged with Offences against the Laws of the United States are now confined in the Goal of the City of Philadelphia, and that as well for the Relief of the said Persons as of certain Seafaring Men who are detained as Witnesses, it would be expedient that a special Sessions of the Circuit Court should be speedily held, Ordered that a special Sessions of the said Court for the trial of criminal Causes be held at the City of Philadelphia in and for the District of Pensylvania on the Twenty first day of Feb.ʸ instant, next and that authenticated Copies of this Order be transmitted by the Clerk of this Court to the Judge, and the Clerk of the said district Court, and to the Attorney of the United States for the said District

Edward Burd — Luther Martin — William Barton — Moses Levy — John F. Mifflin — and Charles Heatly Esq.ʳˢ having been proposed by the Att.ʸ Gen.ˡ of the United States, for admission as Counsellors of this Court, they are sworn agreably to the Order thereof and are admitted to practice accordingly

William Rawle Esq.ʳ having been proposed by the said Att.ʸ Gen.ˡ for admission as a Counsellor of thi[s] Court, he is affirmed agreably to the Order thereof, and is admitted to practice accordingly —

Jasper Moylan — Alex.ʳ J. Dallas — Thomas Leaming J.ʳ — Peter S. Du Ponceau — Esq.ʳˢ having been proposed by the said Att.ʸ Gen.ˡ for Admission as Counsellors of this Court, they are sworn agreably to the Order thereof and are admitted to practice accordingly

John Todd J.ʳ Esq.ʳ having been proposed as aforesaid for admission as a Counsellor of this Court, he is affirmed according to their Order and is admitted to practice accordingly

Joseph Anderson, Joseph B. M.ᶜKean, and Benjamin Chew J.ʳ Esq.ʳˢ having been proposed by the Att.ʸ Gen.ˡ aforesaid for admission as Counsellors of this Court they are sworn agreable to the Order of Court and admitted to practice accordingly

John Caldwell, and Benjᵃ R. Morgan Esqʳˢ having been proposed by the said Attʸ Genˡ. for admission as Attornies of this Court[,] the said John is sworn, and the said Benjᵃ is affirmed according to the Order of Court and are admitted to practice accordingly

Nicholas and Jacob Vanstaphorst v. State of Maryland

The Marshall of the District of Maryland returns on the Summons in this Cause, that he has in Obedience to the Writ caused to be summoned the State of Maryland by serving a copy of the said Process on the Governor and Executive Council and Attorney Genˡ of the said State in presence of Joshua Barney and Robᵗ Dorsey

Luther Martin Esqʳ Attʸ Genˡ of the State of Maryland, having in Court directed John Caldwell Esqʳ to enter an appearance for the said State of Maryland; on motion of Edmund Randolph Esqʳ Attʸ Genˡ for the United States, of Council for the pltˢ Ordered that the said appearance be entered, and on like motion it was Ordered by the Court, that the said State plead in two months from the second day of this term or Judgment

Philadelphia Febʸ 8ᵗʰ 1791. This Court is adjourned, next to meet at the time and place appointed by Law

                                                              Jn Tucker Cler

Original Fine Minutes of Samuel Bayard
August 1791 Term
to February 1792 Term

At the Supreme Court of the United States, begun and held at Philadelphia (being the Seat of the National Government) on the first Monday in August and on the first day of the said Month, Anno Domini 1791.

Present—

The Honorable John Jay Esqre Chief Justice

The Honorable
{
William Cushing
James Wilson
John Blair and
James Iredell Esq^{rs}
}
Associate Justices—

Proclamation is made and the Court is opened—

Ordered— That Samuel Bayard be the Clerk of this Court in the place of John Tucker Esquire of Boston resigned; he is accordingly directed to give bond as by law directed, and is sworn to the faithful discharge of all the duties of his Office and to support the Constitution of the United States—

On motion of the Attorney General John D. Coxe Esquire is admitted to practice as a Counsellor of this Court and is sworn according to Law, and Order—

Nicholas & Jacob Vanstaphorst Pltffs
v̄s
The State of Maryland Def[d]^t
}
In Case

The Attorney General being of Counsel for the Plaintiffs moved the Court for a Commission to take the Depositions of certain Witnesses residing in Holland, with the consent of the Attorney and Counsel on the part of the Defendant States—

The Court refused the Commission until the Commissioners should be named—

The Court adjourned till to morrow at ten ?Clock.

Tuesday August 2ⁿᵈ 1791 _

Present

The Honorable John Jay Esquire Chief Justice _

The Honorable $\left\{\begin{array}{l}\text{William Cushing} \\ \text{James Willson} \\ \text{John Blair and} \\ \text{James Iredell}\end{array}\right\}$ Associate Justices

Proclamation is made and the Court is opened

On Petition David Leonard Barns Esquire of Taunton in the State of Massachusetts is admitted to practice as a Counsellor of this Court and is sworn accordingly _

On motion of William Bradford Junior Esqʳ Attorney General of Pennsylvania. Thomas Smith Esquire ~~Esquire~~ of Carlisle in Pennsylvania is sworn and Jacob R Howell is solemnly affirmed and are admitted to practice as counsellors in this Court, agreeably to Order.

William West Pltff in Error $\left.\begin{array}{l} \\ \\ \end{array}\right\}$
vs
David L. Barnes & others Defᵈᵗˢ

Mʳ Bradford offered to the Court a Writ, purporting to be a Writ of Error, Issued out of the Office of the Clerk of the Circuit Court for Rhode-Island District directed to that Court and commanding the return of the Judgment and proceedings rendered by them in this Cause to this Court with such return &c _

On motion of Mʳ Bradford of Counsel for William West the said Writ and papers annexed to it were read _

Mʳ Bradford moved for a rule that the Defendant rejoin to the errors assigned in this Cause _

David L. Barnes one of the Defendants and a Counsellor of this Court objected to the validity of the Writ in question and on that principle, to the rule moved for _ The arguments on both sides being heard, the Court informed the parties that they would consider the question.

The Court adjourned till ten ℃lock to morrow _

Wednesday August 3. 1791.

Present.

The Honorable John Jay Esquire Chief Justice

The Honorable { William Cushing
James Wilson
John Blair and
James Iredell Esqrˢ } Associate Justices

On motion of the Attorney General Charles Swift Esq[r] of the City of Philadelphia is admitted to practice as a counsellor of this Court, and is sworn agreeably to their Order.

And now bond is given with two sureties approved by the Court (viz Charles Pettit and John Nicholson Esquires) by Samuel Bayard their Clerk, for the faithful performance of the duties of his said Office &c. as by law directed _ Ordered that this Bond be delivered by Mr Bayard to the Treasurer of the United States, and that his receipt for the same be filed in the Clerks Office of this Court _

It appearing from the information of the Attorney General, that a certain Eleanor McDonald is confined in the Gaol of this City of Philadelphia charged with an Offence against the Laws of the United States, and that for the relief as well of the said Eleanor, as of such other Persons as may be charged with offences against the Laws of the United States it would be would be expedient that a special sessions of a circuit Court in and for the district of Pennsylvania should be speedily held.

Ordered _ that a special sessions of a circuit Court for the trial of criminal causes be held at the City of Philadelphia in and for the district of Pennsylvania on the fifteenth day of August instant; and that authenticated copies of this Order be transmitted by the Clerk of this Court to the Judge and to the Clerk of the said district and to the Attorney of the United States for said district _

William West Pltff
v̄s
David L. Barnes & others } In error _

The Court refused to grant the rule moved for, in this Cause yesterday, being unanimously of opinion, that writs of error to remove Causes to this Court from inferior ones, can regularly issue only from the Clerks Office of this Court _

Supreme Court of the United States _

Jacob Van Staphorst &
Nicholas Van Staphorst
v̄s
The State of Maryland } Rule _

It being suggested to the Court that several persons who are material Witnesses to both Parties in the above Cause reside in Amsterdam in Holland— It is therefore ordered on motion of M.ʳ Randolph of counsel for the Plaintiffs and with the consent of M.ʳ Ingersol of counsel for the Defendants, that a Commission do issue to Rutger [J]an Schimmelpenninck, Pieter Stadnitski and Hendrick Vollenhoven as Commissioners on the part of the Plaintiffs and to
                       Christian Van Eeghen
Nicolaas Bonds ᵔ P. C. Nahuys and Wilhem Willink as Commissioners on the part of the Defendants, for the purpose of taking the depositions of such Witnesses as shall be brought before them, so that one of the said Commissioners named on the part of the Plaintiffs and one of the said Commissioners named on the part of the Defendant do attend at the execution there of, and that the depositions so taken and certified under the hands and Seals of the Commissioners so taking the same shall be read and received as evidence on the trial of the above Cause—

                                                                    Sam¹Bayard Clk

At a Supreme Court of the United States begun and held at Philadelphia being the seat of the National Government on the first monday of February and on the Sixth day of said Month— Anno Domini 1792—

Present

The Honorable ⎰ James Wilson ⎱
               ⎱ John Blair and ⎰ Associate Justices
               ⎰ James Iredell Esqʳˢ ⎱

This being the day assigned for holding a Session of the Supreme Court of the United States, and a sufficient number of the Justices not being convened the Court is adjourned by the Justices now present until to morrow at twelve oClock—

Tuesday February 7.ᵗʰ 1792—

Pursuant to adjournment

The Honorable ⎰ James Welson and ⎱ Associate Justices
               ⎱ James Iredell Esqʳᵉ ⎰

This day met but a sufficient number of Justices not being convened to constitute a Court, the Justices now present adjourn until to morrow at twelve oClock—

Wednesday February 8th 1792

Pursuant to adjournment—

The Honorable { James Wilson and   } Associate Justices
             { James Iredell Esqres }

Met this day at the City Hall, but there not being a sufficient number of Justices convened the Court is adjourned by the Justices now present until to morrow at twelve oClock

Thursday February 9th 1792—

Pursuant to adjournment

The Honorable { James Wilson and   } Associate Justices
             { James Iredell Esqres }

This day met at the City Hall, but their not being a sufficient number of Justices convened; the Court is adjourned by the Justices now present until to morrow at twelve oClock—

Friday February 10th 1792—

Pursuant to adjournment—

The Honorable { William Cushing   }
             { James Wilson   } Associate Justices
             { John Blair and   }
             { James Iredell Esqres   }

This day met at the City Hall, and there now appearing a sufficient number of Justices convened to constitute a quorum, proclamation is made— and the Court opened—

No business being before the Court, it is adjourned until to morrow at eleven oClock—

Saturday February 11th 1792—

Pursuant to adjournment

The Honorable { William Cushing   }
             { James Wilson   } Associate Justices
             { John Blair and   }
             { James Iredell Esqrs }

Met this day at the City Hall—

Proclamation is made and the Court opened

Eleazor Oswald who survived ⎞
Elizabeth Holt Administrators ⎟
of John Holt deceased   ⎬ Summons in Case
  v̄s   ⎟
The State of New York   ⎠

And now the Return of the Marshall of the State of New York in this case is read in open Court by M.ͬ Sergeant of counsel for the Plaintiff— and a motion grounded thereon for a distringas to compell the appearance of said State—

The Court informed M̄.ͬ Sergeant, that they would consider his motion—

On motion of the Honorable Thomas Hartl[ey] Esquire, The Honorable William Few and Abraham Baldwin Esquires are admitted as Counsellers of this Court, and are Sworn accordingly—

On motion of the Attorney General The Honorable John W Kittera is admitted a counsellor of this Court and is Sworn accordingly—

By consent of Parties the Suit of
Jacob and Nicholas Vanstaphorst Plaintiffs ⎞
  v̄s   ⎬
The State of Maryland   ⎠

is continued over to the next term—

                                        for this day,
The business before the Court ⌃ being finished it is adjourned by proclamation until Monday at twelve O Clock—

                    Monday February 13. 1792—

                      Pursuant to adjournment

                          ⎛ William Cushing   ⎞
                          ⎟ James Wilson   ⎟
The Honorable   ⎨ John Blair and ⎬ Associate Justices
                          ⎝ James Iredell Esq.ͬˢ ⎠

    This day met at the City Hall—

Proclamation is made and the Court opened—

    On motion of M.ͬ Sergeant. H. H. Brackenridge Esquire is admitted a counsellor of this Court and is Sworn accordingly—

    The Court is adjourned by Proclamation until to morrow at one oClock—

Tuesday February 14_ 1792_

Pursuant to adjournment_

The Honorable { William Cushing
James Wilson
John Blair and
James Iredell Esq^{rs} } Associate Justices

This day met at the City Hall_

Proclamation is made and the Court opened_

The Clerk in obedience to an Order of the Court last term having produced a receipt from the Treasurer of the United States of his bond which he has given for the faithful performance of the duties of his said Office: and it being represented to the Court that agreeably to the practice of the Treasury, the said Bond ought to be lodged with the Register of the Treasury; the Court therefore direct that the said Bond be delivered to the said Register—

Eleazer Oswald who survived
Elizabeth Holt Administrators[8]
of John Holt deceased
  v̄s
The State of New York }

On motion of the Counsel for the Plaintiff lea[ve] is now given to withdraw the motion for a distringas v̄s the defendant State and for a discontinuance of the Suit to be enter'd therein

On motion of the Attorney General of the United States, George Read Esquire Attorney for the United States in the district of Delaware is admitted a counsellor of this Court is Sworn accordingly—

Proclamation being previously made the Court is adjourned to the time and place appointed by Law—

Sam^{l}Bayard

---

8. The letters "ors" are written over the letters "rix."

Samuel Bayard's Notes for Fine Minutes
February 1792 Term
to August 1794 Term

a Supreme Court of the United States begun & held at

At _^ Philadelphia, being the seat of the national government— on the first monday of February in & on the Sixth day of said Month— Anno Domini 1792.

Present.

The Hon^{bl} $\left\{ \begin{array}{l} \text{James Wilson}^9 \\ \text{John}^{10} \text{ Blair \&.} \\ \text{James Iredell} \end{array} \right\}$ Associate Justices

This being the day assigned for holding a sessions of the Supreme Court of the United States, & a sufficient number of the Justices not being convened, the Court is adjourned by the Justices now present until to morrow at twelve oclock—

Tuesday 7.th February 1792.

Pursuant[11] to adjournment

The Honble $\left\{ \begin{array}{l} \text{James Wilson \&} \\ \text{James Iredell Esq}^{rs} \end{array} \right\}$ Associate Justices

but
this day met _^ A sufficient number of Justices not being convened to constitute a Court; the Justices now present adjourn until to morrow at 12 oclock—

Wednesday 8 February 1792

Pursuant to adjournment—

The Honb^{le} $\left\{ \begin{array}{l} \text{James Wilson \&} \\ \text{James Iredell Esq}^{rs} \end{array} \right\}$ Associate Justices

this day
Met _^ at the City Hall, but there not being a sufficient number of Justices convened the court is adjourned, by the Justices now present until to morrow at 12 o'clock

9. An "ls" appears beneath the "so."
10. A "Wi" appears beneath the "Jo."
11. "Pursuant" is written over the word "Present."

Thursday 9ᵗʰ February 1792

Pursuant to adjournment—

The Honble { James Wilson & } Associate Justicess
              { James Iredell Esqʳˢ }

This day met at the City Hall but there not being a sufficient number of Justices convened—; the Court is ~~now~~ adjourned by the Justices now present until to morrow at 12 o'clock—

Friday 10ᵗʰ of February 1792—

Pursuant to adjournment.

The Honb^{le}. { William Cushing }
               { James Wilson   } Associate Justices
               { John Blair &   }
               { James Iredell Esqʳˢ }

This day met, at the city Hall, & there[12] now appearing a sufficient number of Justices convened to constitute a quorum; proclamation is made— & the Court opened—

No business being before the Court, it is adjourned until to morrow at 11. oclock

Saturday 11. February 1792.

Pursuant to adjournment.

The Honble { Wᵐ Cushing   }
              { James Wilson } Associate Justices
              { John Blair & }
              { James Iredell Esqʳˢ }

met this day at the City Hall—

Proclamation is made & the Court opened—[13]

Eleazor Oswald who[14]
survived— Elizᵗʰ Holt—
Admnrs. vs of John Holt decᵈ } Summons in Case
    v̄ˢ
The State of New York

---

12. The word "there" is written over "their."
13. The clerk wrote "11. Febʸ 1792." in the upper right corner of the next page in the original text.
14. An ampersand appears beneath the "w."

And now. the return of the Marshall of the State of New York in this case is read in open court by Mʳ Sergeant of counsel for the Pltffs— & a motion grounded thereon for a distringas to compel[15] the appearance of said State—

The Court informed Mʳ Sergeant, that they would consider his motion—

On motion of the Honᵇˡᵉ Thomas Hartley Esqʳ— The Honᵇˡᵉ William Few. & Abraham[16] Baldwin Esqʳˢ are admitted as Counsellors of this Court. & are sworn accordingly—

On motion of the Attorney General The Honᵇˡᵉ John W Kittera is admitted a counsellor of this Court & is sworn accordingly—

By consent of parties the Suit of

Jacob & Nicholas Vanstaphorst Pltff[s] ⎞
v̄s   ⎬
The State of Maryland   ⎠

is continued over to the next term—

The business before the Court. being finished it is adjourned, by proclamation until to morrow at 12 o'clock—

Monday 13. February 1792.

Pursuant to adjournment.

The Honᵇˡᵉ ⎧ WᵐCushing,
            ⎨ James Wilson   ⎬ Associate Justices
            ⎪ John Blair &
            ⎩ James Iredell Esqʳˢ ⎭

this day met. at the city Hall—

Proclamation is made & the Court opened—

On motion of Mʳ Sergeant. H. H. Brackenridge Esqʳ is admitted a counsellor of this Court. & is sworn accordingly—

The Court is adjourned by Proclamation until[17] to morrow at one oclock—

Tuesday 14 Febʸ 1792—

Pursuant to adjournment.

⎧ Wᵐ Cushing.
⎨ James Wilson   ⎬ Associate Justices
⎪ John Blair &
⎩ James Iredell Esqʳˢ ⎭

15. An "l" appears beneath the "e."
16. The "A" is written over an "a."
17. The word "to" was written first and then altered to read "until."

This day met at the city Hall _

Proclamation is made & the court opened _

⊗ ~~The Clerk having been ordered to receive from the Treasurer of the United States the bond given by said Clerk, jointly with his sureties Charles Pettit & John Nicholson Esqʳˢ, & left with the said Treasurer, & to having been order'd further, to deposit the same bond with the Register of the Treasury _ the said order is performed~~

₱ Judge Iredell[18]

⊗ The Clerk in obedience to an order of the Court last term, having produced a receipt from the Treasurer of the United States, of his bond which he has given for the faithful performance of the duties of his ~~said~~ office; & it being represented to the Court that agreeably to the practice of the Treasury the said bond ought to be lodged with the Register of the Treasury; the Court therefore direct that the said Bond be delivered to the said Register _

               who

Eleazer Oswald survived[19] Elizᵗʰ Holt

v̄ˢ

Administrator _ of John Holt. decᵈ.

v̄

State of New York[20]

⊗ ~~The court in this case informed the Attorney for the Plaintiff that~~
being returnable to August term last _
~~as the writ was not return'd until after the adjourment of the Court, at~~ last
said
~~the Term of August last _ they are of opinion that the cause is not before them &. that no rule can be grounded on the said writ _ ₱ Curiam _ but~~ Mʳ

On motion of the Counsel for the Plaintiff leave is now given to withdraw the motion for a distringas. v̄s the defendant State. & for a dis-
         of the suit
⊗ continuance ^ to enter'd therein
⊗ on motion of the Attʸ Genˡ of the United States. George Read Esqʳ Attʸ for the United States
the   for the   district.
in ^ ~~district of~~ Delaware ^ is admitted a counsellor of this Court & is sworn according[ly]

Proclamation being previously made the Court is adjourned to the time & place appointed by law _

---

18. James Iredell probably suggested the wording of the following paragraph, which corrects and clarifies the phrasing of the crossed-out version.

19. The letters "ved" have been substituted for a "ᵍ," which originally had followed the "i."

20. A brace originally was drawn to the right of the following:

"Eleazer Oswald surviᵍ

v̄ˢ

Administrator _ of John Holt.

v̄

State of New York."

A second brace, reproduced here, was drawn after interlining the word "who," altering "surviᵍ" to read "survived," and adding "Elizᵗʰ Holt _" and "decᵈ."

Monday August 6. 1792.

At a Supreme Court of the United States begun & held at Philad.ᵃ being
present
the ˄ seat of the National government on the first monday of August & on
the sixth day of the said month Anno Domini 1792.

Present

John Jay Esq.ʳ Chief Justice ̲

The Hon.ᵇˡᵉ ⎰ Wᵐ Cushing ⎱
          ⎱ James Wilson ⎰
          ⎰ John Blair ⎱ Esq.ʳˢ Associate Justices
          ⎱ James Iredell & ⎰
          ⎰ Thomas Johnson ⎱

Proclamation is made & the Court opened

Letters patent bearing date the seventh day of Nov.ʳ Anno domini 1791.
directed to the Hon.ᵇˡ Thomas Johnson of Maryland, constituting him an Associate Justice of the Supreme Court of the United States, are now openly read
& published in Court ̲

                                                                    is
On motion of the Att.ʸ Gen.ˡ of the US. John Hallawell Esq.ʳ as̶ ad-
to practice
mitted ˄ as an Attorney of this Court, & is solemnly affirm'd accordingly ̲

Jacob & Nicholas Vanstaphorst ⎰
          v̄   ⎰ In Case ̲
The State of Maryland   ⎰
                              the Att.ʸ General
Order'd on Motion of M̶r̶ R̶a̶n̶d̶o̶l̶p̶h̶ of counsel for the Plaintiffs, with con-
                                                            action
sent of Mʳ Ingersol of counsel for the defendant, that this c̶a̶u̶s̶e̶ be discontinued ̲ each party having agreed to pay their own costs ̲

Eleazer Oswald surviv.ᵍ ⎰
Adm̄nor of John Holt dec.ᵈ ⎰
          v̄   ⎰ In case ̲
State of New York.   ⎰

O̶n̶ ̶m̶o̶t̶i̶o̶n̶ ̶o̶f̶ Mʳ Ingersol of counsel for the Plaintiff Moves in this cause
for "a rule on the Marshall of the State of New York to return the writ issued
against the said State ̲ " The Court inform'd Mʳ Ingersol that they²¹ would
consider his motion ̲

_____

21. The word "we" appears beneath "they."

The Attorney General of the United States ~~gives~~ informs the Court ~~to be informed~~
that on Wednesday next to intends moving for a ma~~n~~damus ~~to be~~ directed[22] to
the circuit Court[23] for districts of Pennsylvania & N. York. commanding the said
~~proceed in the petition of William Hayburn, an invalid, applying to be put on~~
Courts _ to⊗ ~~give effect & operation to act of Congress passed at their last~~
~~the pension list~~ of the U. S.
~~session entitled "an act to provide & passed the 23. of Ma[rch] 1792 _~~

⊗ proceed in a certain petition of Wm Hayburn, applying ~~fo~~ to be put on the pension list of the
United States _ as in invalid Pensioner _

Proclamation is made & the Court adjourn'd until to morrow at ten
o'clock _

Tuesday 7. August 1792.

Pursuant to adjoinment

The Honble John Jay Esqr Ch. Justice

The Honble
{ W^mCushing
James Wilson
John Blair
James Iredell.
Thos Johnson }
Esq^rs Ass^t Justices

this day met at the City Hall.

Proclamation is made & the Court is open'd

Ebenezer Kingsley & a^ls
v̄
Thomas Jenkins
} Error from Masschustts

By consent of parties agreed that this cause be continued to the next term

~~Proclamation is made & the Court adjour'd until to morrow at 10 clock _~~

~~The Att^y Genl prays to be informed by the court of the~~ place ~~in~~ wh rules &
orders ~~of this court shall be obtain'd whether in the[24] court in Term time or~~
~~at the Clerks office _~~

The Attorney Genl moves the Court to be informed of the sytem of practice, by which the attornies

---

22. The letters "di" are written over "To."
23. "Court" is followed by a crossed-out comma.
24. The word "this" appears beneath "the."

in
& counsellors of this court shall regulate themselv[es] & of the place in which rules &ecauses here
depending shall be obtained—

The Court inform'd the Att.ʸ Gen.ˡ & they ~~request that if any of the~~ Gent.ⁿ
that if they
of the bar ^ have any remarks to offer on the subject of the mode of practice
here
to be adopted ~~by~~ this Court, ~~the~~ are willing to hear them—

Eleazer Oswald.⎫   On motion of M.ʳ Ingersol of counsel for the
surv.ᵍ Admnor of [J.] Holt ⎬   Plaintiff. order'd that the Marshall of the New
v̄s   ⎪   York district return the writ to him directed in
The State of New York ⎭   this cause before the adjournment of this Court,
                            if a copy of this ~~Court~~ rule shall seasonably be
                                                the
serv'd upon him or his deputy— or otherwise on the first day of ^ next term—
And that in case of default he do shew cause therefor, by affidavit taken before
one of the judges of the Judges of the united States—

Adjourned until tomorrow at 10 o'clock.

Wednesday 8. August 1792.

Pursuant to adjournment—

The Hon.ᵇˡᵉ John Jay Esq.ʳ Ch. Justice—

                    ⎧ W.ᵐCushing ⎫
                    ⎪ James Wilson ⎪
The Hon.ᵇˡᵉ   ⎨ John Blair   ⎬   Associate Justices
                    ⎪ James Iredell & ⎪
                    ⎩ Th.ˢ Johnson Esq.ʳˢ ⎭

met at the City Hall—

Proclamation is made & the Court opened—

                                                    of the Att.ʸ Gen.ˡ
The Chief Justice ~~informs the attorney Gen.ˡ~~ in answer to the motion ^ ~~of~~
made   informs him
^ yesterday, ^ & ^ the Bar that this Court ~~will~~ consider the practice of the
Courts of Kings Bench & of Chancery in England as ~~the~~ affording outlines
for
~~for~~ the practice of this Court & that they will from time to time make such
alterations therein as circumstances may render necessary—
                                                        ⊗
Edw.ᵈ Telfair for the ⎫   bill in Equity fil'd & motion ^
State of Georgia   ⎬ ⊗ by M.ʳ Dallas of counsel for the Gov.ʳ & State of Georgia—
v̄ˢ   ⎪   for an injunction to the Circuit Court ~~of~~ for the
Sam.ˡ Brailsford & al.ˢ ⎭   District: Georgia. to stay proceed.ᵍˢ in a certain
                                        has
                        cause ~~there~~ in w.ᵗ execution ^ issu'd—

the argument _{on} ~~of~~ this motion is postponed until to morrow —

Agreeably to his motion of monday last the Att.ʸ Gen.ˡ proceeded to shew cause why a mandamus should ^not^ issue to the circuit Courts of ~~New York &~~ Pennsyl.ᵃ districts for the purpose expressed in the said motion — The Court doubted of the power of the Att.ʸ Gen.ˡ to make this motion ex officio — The argument on this point is adjourned ~~until to morrow~~ —

Proclamation is made & the Court adjourned until to morrow at 10 o'clock

Thursday. August 9. —

Pursuant to adjourment —

The Hon.ᵇˡᵉ John Jay Esq.ʳ Ch. Justice

The Hon.ᵇˡᵉ
{
W.ᵐCushing
James Wilson
John Blair
James Iredell &
Thomas Johnson Esq.ʳˢ
}
Ass.ᵗ Justices

This morning met at the city Hall —

Proclamation is made & the Court opened —

Edw.ᵈ Telfair in behalf of the State of Geogia
v̄
Sam.ˡ Brailsfor'd & others.
}
Bill in Equity —
The Court proceeded to hear the argument on ~~of~~ the ^motion^ ~~motion~~ in this cause — & ~~haing~~ ^having^ heard Counsel ^on the same,^ ~~they~~ ~~postpone deciding on it until tomorrow~~ a future day.

adjourned until to morrow at 10 c'lock —

~~Procl~~

Friday 10ᵗʰ August —

Pursuant to adjournment —

The Honᵇˡᵉ John Jay Esq.ʳ Ch. Justice

The Hon.ᵇˡᵉ
{
W.ᵐ Cushing
James Wilson
John Blair
James Iredell &
Thomas Johnson Esq.ʳˢ
}
Assoc.ᵗ Justices.

This day met at the city Hall —

Proclamation is made &. the Court opened —

The Court proceeded to hear the Att.ʸ Gen.ⁱ in relation to ˄ the powers & extent of his office —

The Court adjourn until to morrow 10 c'lock

Saturday. August 11. 1792.

Pursuant to adjournment.

The Hon.ᵇˡᵉ John Jay Esq.ʳ Ch. Justice

The Hon.ᵇˡᵉ { W.ᵐCushing.
              James Wilson
              John Blair.
              James Iredell
              Thomas Johnson Esq.ʳˢ } Associate Justices

This day met at the city Hall —

Proclamation is made & the Court open'd —

Alex.ʳ Chisholm. Exor.
of Rob.ᵗ Farquhar. dec.ᵈ
v̄   } In case —
The State of Georgia

    Proclamation being previously made in the words following —
"Any person having authority to appear for the State of Georgia in the suit brought in this court²⁵ by Alex.ʳ Chisholm citizen of S. Carolina & Executor of Rob.ᵗ Farquhar ˄ of the same State deceas'd against the said State of Georgia — is required to come forth & appear accordingly — it was thereupon, moved by the Plaintiff by. Edm.ᵈ Randolph Esq.ʳ his counsel that unless the said state of Georgia shall after reasonable previous notice of this motion cause an appearance to be enter'd in behalf of the said State, on the fourth day of next term, or shall then shew cause to the contrary, judgment shall be enter'd against the said State & a writ of enquiry of damages shall be awarded —

    Order'd with consent of the Pltffs counsel, that the consideration of this motion be postponed until the first monday in Feb.ʸ next —

    The Court being divided in their opinions on the subject of the Att.ʸ Gen.ⁱ's authority ex officio to move the Court for a mandamus to the Circuit Court for the Pennsyl.ᵃ district, to correct the error complain'd of in the case of W.ᵐHayburn the writ ~~moved for is not granted~~ prayed cannot issue —

---

25. The words "the cause" appear beneath "this court."

Edwd Telfair Govr &c. ⎫

v̄   . ⎬ In Equity—

Sam.^lBrailsford & al.^s ⎭

                       from this Court.   such

The Court order that an injunction do issue ^ to stay ~~the~~[26] monies, in his[27]

                                          2.

       to   Geogia   € as have been or may be levied & receiv'd

hands ~~of~~ the Marshall for the ~~S.Carolina~~   district; ~~taken~~ ^ by virtue of any

                   1

        issuing from

execution ^ ~~from~~ the circuit Court for[28] the s.^d ~~at~~ District— at the suit of

                                  ames

Sam.^lBrailsford & al.^s v̄. ~~James~~[29] Spalding & to detain the same in his hands until further order of this ~~Court~~

The Court proceeded to hear the Att.^y Genl as counsel for. Wm Hayburn on a

                                   for the Pennsyl.^a district,

motion for a mandamus directed to the circuit Court ^ to command the s.^d Court to ~~do~~ proceed on the petition of the s.^d W.^mHayburn—

. The Court inform the Att.^y Genl that they ~~Court~~ will ~~consider~~, hold his motion under consideration, until the next Term—

All business now undetermind is continued over to the next term

Proclamation being previously made the Court is adjounn'd to the time & place by law appointed—

At a Supreme Court of the United States held at Philadelphia. (being the

                                the first

seat of the National Government) on ^ monday ~~the fourth d~~ in February & the fourth day of the said Month— 1793.—

                     Present.—

         The Honb.^{le} John Jay Esqr Ch. Justice—

              ⎧ W.^mCushing   ⎫

              ⎪ James Wilson.   ⎪   cociate

The Honble   ⎨ John Blair &   ⎬ Ass.^t Justices

              ⎩ James Iredell Esqr ⎭

Proclamation is made & the Court opened—

    26. The numeral "2" beneath this underlined phrase may have been placed there to remind the clerk to transpose this phrase with the following one under which "1" appears. He did not transpose them when he transcribed them into the fine minutes. For an instance of the clerk's reversing passages in which two phrases had been underlined and numbered, compare February 4, 1793, in the original and fine minutes.

    27. The word "the" appears beneath the letter "h."

    28. Beneath "for" appears "of t."

    29. The crossed-out "James" is written over what may have been "John."

Gen! to morrow,

Alex.ʳ Chisholm &c ⎫   The Court agree to hear the Att.ᵞ ^ on[30] support of his
    v̄.   ⎬   in this cause
The State of Georgia ⎭   motion made ^ at the last term ~~in this cause~~ — ~~to morrow~~ —

      hear
to ~~The~~ Cause of Jenkins v̄.ˢ Kinsley they assign to Thursday next — [31]
       2   2.   1.   1
                                                      als

⊗ They assign thursday next for ~~the~~ hearing ~~of~~ the argument in[32] the cause of Kingsley & v̄s. Jenkins
                                  into this Court,
~~from the~~ removed ^ by writ of error from the Circuit Court for Masschetts district —

E. Telfair Esq.ʳ Gov.ʳ of Georgia &c ⎫   On affidavit fild stating the inabil-
    v̄s.   ⎬   ity of James Spalding a person sum-
S. Brailsford & al.ˢ   ⎭   as a witness
                            mon'd to attend the Court ^ in this
                            cause — M.ʳ Dallas of counsel for the
State of Georgia — moved the Court — that a commission be awarded to take
      deposition   to be
the ~~testimony~~ of said James Spalding & ^ read as evidence in this suit —
    The Court informed M.ʳ Dallas that they would hold his motion under ad-
                       determination   & when they sh.ᵈ deliver
visement & acquaint him with their ~~opinion~~ after hearing the argument ^ on
their opinions ~~on the~~
the demurrer, ~~& when~~ [word inked out] ~~deliver'd~~ fild in this cause ~~& when they should deliver their opinion upon it~~ —

         was
    A return ~~is~~ this day made of the Commission ~~with the~~ awarded by this
Court, in the case of Jacob & Nicholas Vanstaphorst v̄s the State of Maryland —
with the depositions & other papers accompanying the same —
                              &   together with
    Order'd, that the said Commission be open'd ~~& fil'd~~ ^ & the papers sent to
this Court — fil'd in the Clk's office ~~of this Court~~ —

          this day
James Martin Esq.ʳ ^ applied to the Court ~~applies~~ for permission to be sworn
                    accompanied by certain papers ~~now~~
to the truth of a certain deposition ^ offer'd to the court, intended as he sug-
                                        to be
gested as the foundation of a motion for a writ of error ^ directed to the Supreme judicial Court of the State of Massachusetts —
         on perusal of the depostion with the papers annexd thereto,
    The court ^ rejected[33] the application until certain expressions containd in
         same
the ~~deposition offerd~~, imputing corrupt motives to the judges of the said Sup.
Cur of Massetts be expungd —

30. An "i" appears beneath the "o."
31. For the possible meaning of the numbers under this passage, see note 26 above.
32. The word "of" appears beneath "in."
33. A "c" appears beneath the "j."

Tuesday 5 February 1793

Pursuant to adjournment

of the Honble John Jay, Esqr Ch. Justice

[bracket] Wm Cushing
James Wilson
John Blair &
James Iredell Esq^rs [bracket] Ass^t Justices

The Honble

[The Court] met at the City Hall —

Alex^r Chisholm Ex^or.
of Robt Farquhar dec^d [bracket] In Case — The Court

The State of Georgia

... in support of his motion ...
the Att^y Genl ... for the ... considering

that no appearance had been enter'd on the
part of the State of Georgia regarding the question involved
in the suit, as highly important suggest to
the counsellors of the Court that if any are disposed
to offer their sentiments on the subject now under consideration
The Court are willing to hear them —
Proclamation being made the Court adjourns to morrow
at 11 oclock.

Original Minutes, February 5, 1793, in the hand of Samuel Bayard. (Cf. illustration of
Fine Minutes for February 5, 1793.) Courtesy National Archives.

The Court adjourn until to morrow at eleven o'clock＿

Tuesday 5 February 1793

Pursuant to adjournment＿

The Honble John Jay, Esqr Ch. Justice

The Honble $\left\{ \begin{array}{l} W^m \text{ Cushing} \\ \text{James Wilson} \\ \text{John}^{34} \text{ Blair \&} \\ \text{James Iredell Esq}^r\text{s.} \end{array} \right\}$ Ass^t Justices

This day met at the City Hall＿

Alex^r Chisholm Ex̄or.
of Robt Farquhar dec^d
v̄^s
The State of Georgia

In
Case＿
The Court direct＿ The argument of this cause
to be brought on＿ & is orderd＿ the Court having in this cause, in support of his motion, in

proceeded to hear

cause heard   in the same as

the same the Att^y Genl of counsel for the

but   the

Plaintiff, considerg that no appearance had been enter'd on the part of the
of Georgia   suit＿
state ＿ & regarding the question involv'd in the cause, as highly important
suggest to the Counsellors of the Court that if any are dispos'd to offer their
subject now under consideration＿
sentiments on the point now agitated The Court are willing to hear them＿.

Proclamation being made the Court adjourn till to morrow at 11 oclock.

Wednesday. 6. February 1793＿

Pursuant to adjournment＿ the Court met this morning at the City Hall＿

Present＿

The Honble. John Jay Esqr Ch: Justice

The Honble $\left\{ \begin{array}{l} W^m \text{ Cushing} \\ \text{James Wilson} \\ \text{John Blair \&} \\ \text{James Iredell Esqs} \end{array} \right\}$ Ass^t Justices

Proclamation is made & the Court open'd＿

Esq^t
The Court proceeded to hear the argument of the cause of Edwd Telfair &c.

---

34. "John" is written over "James."

in behalf of the State of Geogia v̄s Sam'Brailsford &alˢ _ & having heard Counsel ~~on~~ postpone the further hearing of the same until to morrow _

The Court adjourn until to morrow at 11. oclock

Thursday 7. Feby 1793

Pursuant to adjournment the Court met this morning at the city Hall _

Present _

The Honble John Jay Esqr Ch. Justice

The Honble ⎰ W^mCushing ⎱
⎱ James Wilson ⎰ Ass^te Justices _
⎰ John Blair & ⎱
⎱ James Iredell Esq^rs ⎰

Edwd Telfair Govr of Georgia ⎱
in & behalf of said State ⎰
v̄ ⎰ Bill in Equity
Sam'Brailsford & alˢ ⎱

the Counsel concern'd
The Court proceeded to hear the further argument of this Cause _ but ^
having finish'd
not ~~having~~ ^ the same, it is adjourned until to morrow _ at 11 o'clock _

Friday 8 Feby 1793.

Pursuant to adjournment the Court this morning met at the City Hall _

Present _

The Honble John Jay Esqr Ch. Justice

The Honble ⎰ W^mCushing ⎱
⎱ James Wilson ⎰ Ass^te Justices _
⎰ John Blair ⎱
⎱ James Iredell Esq^rs ⎰

Edwd Telfair Govr of Georgia &c ⎱
v̄ ⎰ Bill in Equity &c
Sam' Brailsford &a^ls ⎱

The Court having heard the further argument of this cause adjourn until to morrow at 11. oclocke _

Saturday 9th February 1793

Pursuant to adjournment the Court met this morning at the City Hall _

Present—

The Honble John Jay Esqr Chief Justice

The Honble { William Cushing / James Wilson / John Blair[35] / James Iredell Esq^rs }   Ass^te Justices

⊗   On motion for the admission of James Martin Esqr the Att^y Gen! laid before
                                          attornies—
the Court sundry certain printed lists of counsellors in the Island of Jamaica
(G. B). for several years previously to the year 1782 , certain certificates
         citizenship in State of
              N. York & of his   as   counsellor   the
in proof of M^r M's ˄ admission ˄ into the Courts of Chanc^y & Sup. Cur of
      said   also
the State of N Y. ˄ & sundry letters in proof of the good professional & moral
                   on these grounds
charater of Mr Martin & ˄ mov'd for his admission as a counsell[e]r of this
court— the Court inform'd[36] the Att^y Gen! that they w^d hold his motion under
consideration
On motion for the admission of James Martin Esqr — the Attorney General of the United States
laid before the Court certain printed lists of Attornies in the Island of Jamaica, (belonging to
                                                                          in proof
Great Britain), for several years, with certain certificates ˄ of M^rMartins citizenship in the State of
                                       as a counsellor
New York, & of his admission to practice ˄ in the Courts of Chancery, & of the Supreme Cour[t]
of the said State; also sundry letters in proof of the good moral & professional character of M^[r]
Martin— on which grounds, the Attorney[37] Genl mov'd for the Admission of Mr Martin to practice
as a counsellor of this Court— The Court inform'd the Att^y Gen! that they would hold his motion
under consideration—

Edwd Telfair Govr[38] of Georgia &c. }   The arg^t of this
            v̄   }   cause was continud
Sam^lBrailsford & al^s[39]   }   & closed this day—

Ebenenezer[40] Kingsley & Al^s }   In Error from Massachusettes—
            v̄   }   hear
Thomas Jenkins   }   The Court proceeded to ˄ the argument of
                                    this cause but not[41] having the counsel not
                                    having finishd the same— the Court adjourn
                                    until monday next— at 11. o'clock—

35. The letter "r" is written over an "l."
36. A "d" appears beneath the "m."
37. A "y" appears beneath the "o."
38. An "or" appears beneath the "r."
39. A smaller bracket encloses this line on the right side.
40. The letters "er" appear after the "b" and above the "e."
41. An "ha" appears beneath the "n."

<u>Monday 11. Feb.ʸ 1793.</u>

Pursuant to adjournment the Court met this morning at the City Hall—

Present

The Honble John Jay Esqr Ch. Justice—

The Honble ⎰ W^mCushing ⎱
⎰ James Wilson ⎱ Asst^e Justices—
⎰ John Blair ⎱
⎱ James Iredell Esqr ⎰

The Court proceed to hear the further argument. of the Cause— of Eben^r Kingsley & a^{ls} v̄ Thos Jenkins but, the same not[42] being finish'd, the further
                    postponed
hearing of it is ~~continued~~ until to morrow at 11 oclock.

<u>Tuesday 12. Feby 1793.</u>

~~Cour~~ Pursuant to adjournment the Court met this morning at the City Hall—

Present.

The Honble ⎰ W^mCushing ⎱
⎰ James Wilson ⎱ Asst^e Justices
⎰ John Blair & ⎱
⎱ James Iredell Esq^{rs} ⎰

Proclamation is made & the Court opened

~~The Court are informed that, th[ro'] indisposition, the attendance of the Chi~~
The Chief Justice ~~not~~ being prevented by indisposition from attending Court, this day. The Justices present adjorn ~~until~~ for the further hearing the argument of Eben^r Kingsley &a^{ls} v̄. Thos Jenkins, until to morrow at 11. oclock—

<u>Wednesday 13. Feb.ʸ 1793.</u>

Pursuant to adjournment the Court this morning met at the City Hall—

Present—

The Honble John Jay Esqr Ch. Justice

The Honble ⎰ W^mCushing ⎱
⎰ James Wilson ⎱ Asst^e Justices
⎰ John Blair ⎱
⎱ James Iredell Esq^{rs} ⎰

The Counsel in the case of Eben^r Kingsley &c. v̄s Thos Jenkins— proceeded in their argument. but not[43] having closed the same, The Cout adjourn for the

42. An "h" appears beneath the "n."
43. An "h" appears beneath the "n."

further hearing of the cause until to morrow at 11. o'clock ___

Thursday 14. February 1793 ___

Pursuant to adjournment the Court met this morning at the City Hall ___

Present ___

The Honble John Jay Esqr Cheif-Justice

The Honble ⎰ W.^mCushing
⎱ James Wilson
⎰ John Blair
⎱ James Iredell Esq.^{rs} ⎱ Ass.^{te} Justices ___

⊗

⊗

14. Feb.^y

this day   as a counsellor of this Court

~~It appearing to~~ The[44] Court informd M.^r Ma[r]tin (whose admission ‸ was movd for by the Att.^y Genl on Saturday last. ~~9th inst,~~) that as it appear[s] ~~to them,~~ that the Supreme Judicial Court.

the State of
~~Court~~ of ‸ Massachusetts have declined admitting him to[45] practice as a counsellor of that Court ___ on the ground of his not being a citizen of the United States, this Court will not thus incidentally

the
~~in regard to claim to~~
determine so important a question as that ~~of citizenship or not~~ ___ involv'd in the motion of the Att.^y Genl ~~for the~~ above referr'd to ___

James Martin Esqr ~~again offers to the Court. the papers~~ having expung'd from the deposition offer'd to this Court on Monday the 4th inst ___ certain expressions reflecting on the Conduct of the Judges of the Sup. Cur. of the State of Massc^{ts} offers the same with the papers annex'd and prays to be sworn to the
depositiⁿ   to be
truth of the said[46] ‸ as the ground of a writ of ‸ error ‸ directed to the afs^d Judges, to remove to this court a certain proceeding ~~on which an erroneous Jud~~ on which an erroneous Judg.^t is stated to have been given by the ~~said~~
said   reme Court.
Judges of. the ‸ Sup. ~~Cur. of the State of Massachusetts~~, to the prejudice of.
rights of the
the ‸ said James Martin Esqr as a citizen of the United States ___

truth of the
Order'd that the said James Martin Esqr be sworn to the ‸ said deposi-
& that it be fil'd.
tion ‸ ~~which is fil'd~~ with the papers annex'd in the Clerks office ___ [are] fil'd
in
~~with the Clerk's office~~ ___

---

44. The uppercase "T" originally had been lowercase.
45. The word "as" appears beneath "to."
46. The word "same" appears beneath "said."

Ebenezer Kingsley[47] & al[s]
v̄
Thomas Jenkins
} The counsel concernd ~~in this Cause~~ proceeded in the ~~further~~ agr[t][48] of this ~~same,~~ cause, but not not having finish'd the same, the Court adjourn for the further hearing of the ~~same~~ arg[t] until to morrow[49] at 11. oclock _

Friday 15. Feb[y] 1793 _

Pursuant to adjournment the court met this morning at the City Hall _

Present _

The Hon[ble] John Jay Esq[r] Ch. Justice

The Hon[ble] {
W[m]Cushing
James Wilson
John Blair
James Iredell Esq[rs]
} Asst[s] Justices

Kingsley
Ebenezer[50] ~~Jenkins~~ & al[s]
v̄
Thomas Jenkins
} The Counsel[51] concern'd proceeded in the argument of this cause, & finishd the same

The Court ~~inform~~ announce that on monday next they will determine the question agitated in the case of Alex[r] Chisholm v The State of Georgia _ Whether a state can be made a defendant in an action at the suit of one or more individuals of another State _

Adjourn'd until to morrow at 11. oclock,

Saturday. 16. Feb[y] 1793 _

Pursuant to adjournment the Court met this morning at the City Hall _

Present ~~the~~

The Hon[ble] John Jay Esq[r] Cheif Justice

W[m][52] Cushing
James Wilson &
John Blair Esq[rs]
} Asst[s] Justices _

47. An "l" appears beneath the "s."
48. In this case, an abbreviation for "argument."
49. A "to" appears beneath the "m."
50. A "T" appears beneath the first "E."
51. Originally written "Counsell."
52. "Jam" appears beneath the "W[m]."

Thomas Pagan ⎫   Mʳ Tilghman of counsel for the Plaintiff moved for a
   v̄ v̄   ⎬   2ⁿᵈ writ of error in this cause — to remove the proceed-
Stephen Hooper ⎭   ings had in the same before the Sup. Jud! Cour[t] of
the State of
   ˆMassachusetts —
         a copy of the   & considerd the same
   The Court having heard ~~the~~ ˆ record in this case read ˆ are of opinion that
writ applied for
they ~~cannot grant it~~ ought not to be granted.

~~Having finish'd the buseness laid before them~~
The Court adjourn until monday at 11: oclock

Monday 18 Febʸ 1793.

Pursuant to adjournn[~~men~~]t the Court met this morning at the City Hall —

Present.

The Honble. John Jay Esqʳ Ch. Justice

WᵐCushing ⎫
James Wilson ⎬   Assᵗᵉ Justices —
John Blair & ⎥
James Iredell Esqʳˢ ⎭

Alexː Chisholm Exͬor ⎫
of Robᵗ Farquhar decᵈ   ⎬   The Court proceeded to give their opinions sev-
of S. Carolina   ⎥   erally on the order moved for in this cause. on
   v̄ˢ   ⎥   saturday the 11. of August 1792. & argu'd by the
The State of Georgia ⎭   Attʸ Gen! on Tuesday the 5 inst.

On motion ~~order'd~~ of the Attʸ Gen! order'd that the consideration of the form
           to be enter'd —   action
of the order ~~mov'd for~~ in this ~~cause at⁵³ the last term~~ be postponed until to
morrow — to which time at 11. oclock

   the
~~The~~ Court adjourn —

Tuesday 19. Febʸ 1793.

Pursuant to adjournment the Court met this morning at the City Hall —

Present

The Honble. John Jay Esqʳ Ch. Justice

          ⎧ WᵐCushing   ⎫
The Honᵇˡᵉ ⎨ James Wilson   ⎬   Assᵗᵉ Justices
          ⎩ John Blair &   ⎥
            James Iredell Esqʳˢ ⎭

53. An "l" appears beneath the "a."

Ebenezer Kingsley & al^s ⎫ Error from ye dist of Massch^{tts}

v̄   ⎬ The Court having heard & consider'd the ar-

Thomas Jenkins   ⎭ guments of counsel in this cause

~~in this cause action~~

Order'd that the Judgment below, ˄ of the
Circuit[54] Court for the district of Massachusetts, be affirmed—

Alex.^r Chisholm E͞xor. ⎫ In case.— On argument.

of Robt Farquhar dec^d ⎬ Ordere'd that the Pltff in this cause do file his

v̄   ⎬ declaration on or before the first day of March

The State of Georgia ⎭ next—

Ordered that certified copies of the said decla-
ration be served on the Governor & Attorney General of the State of Georgia
on or before the first day of June next—

Ordered. that unless the said State, shall either in due form appear or shew

                                                    the
cause to the Contrary in this Court by the first day of ˄ next term Judgment
by default ~~ag~~ be enterd against the said State—

The Court adjourn until to morrow at 11. oclock

Wednesday 20. Feby 1793—

Pursuant to adjournment the Court met this morning at the City Hall—

Present.

The Honble John Jay Esqr Ch. Justice

The Honble ⎧ W^mCushing ⎫

          ⎨ James Wilson ⎬ Ass^{te} Justices—

          ⎨ John Blair ⎬

          ⎩ James Iredell Esq^{rs} ⎭

On motion of Mr Rawle for the admission of Sam.^lRoberts, Esqr certificates of
his having practis'd as a counsellor of the Sup. Cur. of Pennsylvania, & of

                                                    were producd by M.^rRawle—
having sustaind a good professional & moral charactor[55] ˄ — The Court[56] or-

   M.^rRoberts
der that ~~he~~ be admitted as a cou# sellor of this Court,[57] & he is affirm'd accordingly—

Edwd[58] Telfair Esqr Govr ⎫ Bill in Equity—

of the State of Georgia &c ⎬ On argument—[59]

v̄   ⎬ The Court are of opinion ~~that they cannot~~

Sam.^lBrailsford & al^s ⎭ ~~consider the merits of this controversy under~~

~~the present bill— they order that the injunction~~

54. The second "c" is written over a "t."
55. A "t" appears beneath the "o."
56. A "t" appears beneath the "r."
57. A "t" appears beneath the "r."
58. A "b" appears beneath the first "d."
59. The "n" is written over a "t."

~~issued do continue until~~ _ that if the State of Georgia has a right to the bond

they direct

in <u>controversy</u> her remedy is ~~at~~ by action at Law _ ˄ that the injunction con-

then be dissolved

tinue until the next term & ~~that~~ ˄ unless the State _ shall sooner bring the said

action ~~it shall be dissolved~~ _

W^mGrayson & al^s ⎱   Bill in Equity _
   v̄ the State of ⎰   on
Virginia.   Motion by M^rRawle to amend

suit _

            the bill _ fil'd in this ~~case~~ _

Leave is given by the Court to amend. _

On motion _ a new subpœna is awarded in this cause.

E. Oswald. surviving adm̄nor. ⎱   Summons in Case _
of J. Holt _ deceas'd   ⎰   Proclamation having been previously
   v̄^s   made in the words following "any person
The State of New York   having authority to appear for the state of

now

                   New York in the above suit _ is ˄ re-

quired to appear accordingly" _ thereupon it was mov'd by Mr Cox of counsel

& order'd by the Court   said

for the Plaintiff, ˄ that unless ~~an ap~~ the ˄ state appear by^60 the first day of next

to the above suit ˄

term ˄ or shew cause to the contrary ~~that~~ Judg^t be enter'd by default. against

the s^d State

Proclamation having been made the Court is adjourned to the time & place
by law appointed _

At a Supreme Court of the United States held at Philadelphia (being the seat
of the national Government) on the first monday of August & on the fifth day
of the said month. Anno: Domini. 1793 _

Present

The Honb^l John Jay Esqr Ch. Justice

The Hon^bles ⎰   James Wilson   ⎱
         ⎱   John Blair   ⎰   Ass^te Justices
         ⎰   James Iredell. &   ⎱
         ⎱   William Paterson Esq^rs ⎰

~~Alexander Chisholm &c~~ ⎱
   v̄s   ⎰   ~~In Case~~ _
~~The State of Georgia~~ ⎰

---

60. The word "on" appears beneath "by."

Letters patent directed to the Hon^bl W^mPaterson Esqr ~~appointing an ass~~ bearing date the fourth day of March 1793 _ constituting him a judge of the Sup. Cur of ye US. _ are now openly read & publish'd in Court _

Alexander Chisholm Exor &c
v̄s   } In Case
The State of Georgia

By virtue of an authority from the State of Georgia directed to Alex^r J. Dallas & Jared Ingersol[61] Esq^rs _ the said Counsellors this day appeared, to shew cause why Judgment by default should not be entered against the said State _ in[62] the above suit _

Mr Dallas moved to postpone the argumen of the cause until the next term _

The Court ~~took~~ held his motion under consideration _

Tuesday 6. August 1793.

Pursuant to adjournment

The Court met this morning at the City Hall _

Present.

The Honble John Jay. Esqr Ch. Justice.

James Wilson
John Blair
James Iredell &   } Associate Justices
W^mPaterson Esq^rs

James Martin Esqr laid before the Court ~~the~~ a writ of error issuing from this Court & directed to the Judges of the Sup. Jud. Court of the State of Massach^tts ~~to~~ which the Ch. Justice had refused to allow _ but which ~~allowance he app~~ re ded to be ~~incumbent on~~ M^rMartin contended ought to have been allowed by. any Judge of the Sup. Cur. of the US. to whom it might be presented _ The Court ~~are~~ were unanimously of opinion that ~~under~~ circumstanc'd as this case is the writ should not be allowed _

Alex^r Chisholm, Exor.
of Robert Farquhar dec^d   } This cause is continu'd
v̄^s   by consent of parties _
The State of Georgia   to ye next term _

61. The "I" is written over a "J."
62. The word "in" is written partly over the dash.

W^{m}Vassall comp^{lt} }   Proclamation is made
                                              to the next term
v   }   & the cause cont^d ˄ by consent

The State of Mass^{tts})   of the Counsel for ye Pltff —

E. Oswald. Admnor &c   }   cont^d
                                              ~~Agreed~~ by consent of
v̄^{s} }   Pltffs att^y ~~to continue~~

The State of New. York   /   ~~this cause~~ to ye next term —

                                        for the admission of Ephraim Kirby Esq of Connec^t
On Motion of Ed^d Randolph, ˄ certificates are producd from And^w Adams
                                                  Judges of the Sup. Cur. of the State of Connec^t —
~~Es~~Eliphalet[63] Dyer & Roger Sherma[n] Esq^{rs} ˄ in proof of the good pro-
                                                                                                       his
fessial & moral character of the said Eph^m Kirby — & of the time of ~~the~~ ad-
             practise in   s^d
mission to ˄ the ˄ Sup. Court ~~of Con[n]^t~~ —

     Order'd that E. Kirby Esqr be admitted to practise as a Counsellor of this
Court — &[64] he is ~~adm~~ sworn accordingly —

     At a Supreme Court of the United States held at the City of Philad^a (the
same being the present seat of the National government —) on the first monday of February & on the 3rd day of said Month —

                              Present.

               The Hon^{bl} John Jay Esqr Ch. Justice

Honb^{le} { William Cushing & }   Associate Justice
                   { James Wilson Esq^{rs} }

~~This day met at the but~~ a sufficient number of Justices not being
this day to constitute a quorum
                              Court is —
convened ˄ — they adjourned until to morrow at eleven o'clock —

                         Tuesday 4 Feb^y

                         Present —
                   John Jay. Ch. Justice

               W^{m}Cushing.   )
               James Wilson &   }   Ass^t Justices —
               W^{m}Paterson   )

     63. Originally "Esqr" was written after "Adams." The clerk crossed out the "Esqr" and wrote
the first letter of "Eliphalet" over the "q^r."
     64. The "&" is written over the dash.

The Commission of W Bradford read. dated 28 Jan.ʸ 1794.
That of David Lenox read― dated 28. Jan.ʸ 1794.

On motion of the Att.ʸ Gen.ˡ of y.ᵉ US.―
James Winchester of Maryland―
                        Georgia
Thos: P. Carnes. of ~~Delaware~~― &
W.ᵐ Edmund. of Connecticut admitted Counsellors of this Court―

State of Georgia ⎫   ~~In Case~~― In Assumpsit―
        v̄   ⎬   Issue join'd― non ass.ᵗ―
Sam.ˡBrailsford ⎭

~~The special Jury summon'd are~~

~~On~~ Motion of M.ʳ Tilghman to amend the a[g]reet. & pleading in this
cause― Leave is given by the Court to amend― ~~so as to~~ conformable to fact
& the venire issued in this case― Jury Sunm.ⁿᵈ & sworn &c. are
    John Leamy. Jos. Anthony, Sam.ˡHodgdon― ~~Christ.ʳ Marshall~~ Jos. Bale,
Math.ʷ M.ᶜConnell, Tho.ˢ Ewing, Owen Faulke Jun.ʳ, Rob.ᵗ Smith [Merc.ᵗ?][65] Robt.
Ralston., Reynold Keen., Hugh Lenox & Jn.º Stilley―
The Court having heard Counsel in[66] this cause but the same not being closed,
the Court adjourn until to morrow at 11. oclock

~~Tuesda~~ Wednesday. 5. Feb.ʸ[67]

Present

John Jay. Chief Justice

W.ᵐCushing.   ⎫
James Wilson ⎬ Ass.ᵗ Justices―
John Blair & ⎪
W.ᵐPaterson   ⎭

                                        be directed to
M.ʳ Edmund moves for a mandamus to ^ the Secretary of War in behalf of John
Chandler a citizen of the State of Connecticut to cause the said John Chandler
to be put on the pension list of the US. as an invalid pensioner. conformably
to the directions of James Iredell. & Rich'd Law. Judges of the Circuit Court
of the US. ~~for the~~
                                    when
                                    the
    The Court informed M.ʳ Edmund, that ~~af a~~ ^ cause ~~is~~ finish'd, they will hear
him in support of his motion―

65. This may be an abbreviation for merchant.
66. The word "on" appears beneath "in."
67. The clerk wrote the following list of justices present on a facing page with no reference
mark. We have moved the list to where it belongs.

State of Georgia. ⎫
   v̄s   ⎬ Arg^t continued —
Brailsford & al^s ⎭

Court adjourned until 11. o'clock

Thursday 6. Feby 1794.

Present as before

On motion of Mr Tilghman — John C. Wells is admitted to practise as an
attorney of this Court —

State of Georgia ⎫
   v̄   ⎬ Trial of ye cause continued —
Brailsford & al^s ⎭

The Court adjourn until 11. oclock

Friday.
~~Thursday~~ 7. Feby 1794.

Present as before —

State of Georgia ⎫
   v̄   ⎪ The trial of this cause cont^d
          ⎬ & finish'd — The Jury on their
S. Brailsford &al^s ⎪   to ye Bar. find —
Robt Wm Powel & ⎪ return ^ a verdict for the Defendants —
John Hopton ⎭

The Court proceeded to hear Mr Edmund on the subject of his motion made
                 postpone   further
on the 5. inst. &^{68} ~~adjourn~~ the ^ consideration of the same ~~fo until[l] to m~~ for
the present —

The Court adjourn until to morrow at. 11.

Saturday 8 Feby 1794.

Present as before —

Alex^r S Glass &al^s ⎫
   v^s ⎬ The^{69} Hearing of this cause
Sloop Betsy. ⎭   commenc'd —

      an agreement
By ~~article~~ this day filed — ~~it is agreed^{70} by~~ the proctors, in behalf of

---

68. The "&" is written over the word "but."
69. "The" is written over an "&."
70. A "g" appears beneath the "r."

to the above suit,   "consent
the parties ˰ aforesaid ˰ that ‗ all exceptions to the manner of the appeal, be
waved, ‗ and that the same shall be argued & decided on the case as disclosed
upon the face of the record" ‗

The Court having proceeded in this cause having but the[71] hearing of it
being unfinish'd adjourn for the further hearing of the same until monday at
11. ōclock ‗ [72]

Monday 10. Feb.ʸ 1794 ‗ [73]

Present ‗ as before

Alex.ʳ S. Glass. & al.ˢ v̄ˢ Sloop Betsy & cargo. & Capt.ⁿ Johannen	The argument of this appeal continued ‗

The Court adjourn until[74] to morrow at 11. oclock

Tuesday[75] 11. February 1794.

Present. as before

Glass & others v̄s Sloop Betsy &c P. A. Johannen. M.ʳ[76]	The hearing of this cause cont.ᵈ

The Court for the further hearing of yᵉ same adjourn until to morrow at
11. o'clock

Wednesday 12. February 1794.

Present as before

Glass & others v̄s The Sloop Betsy & Capt.ⁿ Johannen	The hearing of this appeal i[s] finish'd this day closed ‗

The Court adjourn until to morrow ‗ 11. oclock

71. The word "not" appears beneath "the."
72. The letters "oc" are written over a dash.
73. The "4" is written over a "3."
74. An "l" appears beneath the "i."
75. An "M" appears beneath the "T."
76. Abbreviation for "master" of a ship.

Thursday. 13. February 1794.

Edmund.

The Court to proceeded to hear Counsel on the motion of Mr ^ for a mandamus to the Sec^y of War of Mr Edmund, made on Wednesday ye 5 inst_

of Mr Tilghman is granted by the Court grant a rule

On.[77] Motion for a rule, on the Commiss^r of Loans for the Viginia Dist^r to shew cause why a mandamus should not issue to the John Hopkins Esqr &c[78]

for the

effect certain purposes stated in said rule_

Chisholm v. Geogia_ mot^n for Judg^t ℔ Mr Bradford_

The Court adjourn until 11. oclock to morrow

Friday. 14. Feby 1794.

Present. as before

The Court_ having taking into consideration the motion of Mr Edmund, of the 5 [int.] & having consider'd the 2 acts of Congress, relating to the same_ are of opinion that a writ of Mandamus cannot issue agai to the Sec^y of War for the purposes assign'd in sd motion_

Mrs Dallas & Ingersoll_ appear this day shew cause why a judgment should

the

not be enterd ag^t said State of Georgia at the suit of Geo Alex^r Chisholm Ex^r of Farquhar of[79] S. Carolina conformably[80] to ye rule enter'd in this case in[81] February Term last_

Alex^r Chisholm. &c   ⎫
              v̄   ⎬ Judgment,_ & writ of enquiry
The State of Georgia   ⎭ of damages awarded.[82]

Motion of Mr Tilghman_[83] for Judg^t of in Georgia vs Brailsford_ for the

dismission of the Bill

Defd^ts_ also for the ^ dissolution of the injunction in the cause, on[84] the Equity side of the Court &. with costs_   Order'd_

---

77. "O" is written over a lowercase "o."
78. The word "to" appears beneath "&c."
79. The "of" is written over a dash.
80. The letters "co" are written over a dash.
81. The "in" is written over a dash.
82. A dash appears beneath "aw."
83. "In" appears beneath the "Ti."
84. The word "of" appears beneath "on."

Kingley v[85] Jenkins._ in[86] Error from Mass[ts],

on											ordered that									do issue

Motion of M[r] Lewis_ ~~for~~ a special mandate ∧ to the Circ[t] C[t] ~~to proceed to execution_~~

~~Order'd_~~

⊗ for the Dist. of M. in pursuance of the act of Cong[r] in such case made & provd[d] command[g] y[e] s[d] C[t] fully to execute and carry into effect a ~~certain~~ Judg[t] heretofore obtain'd by the s[d] Def[t] v̄s the Pltffs in error afs[d] in the Circ[t] C[t] afs'd_

J. H.

M[r] Bradford_ proceeded on the part of ~~the U. S.~~ to shew cause why a mandamus sh[d] not issue in the Case[87] of the US. v̄s. J. Hopkins Esq[r]_

Having[88] heard counsel_ they adjourn until to morrow at 11. o'clock_

Saturday 15 February 1794_[89]

Present as before_

⊗ ~~On~~ arg[t] the Court are of opinion that the ~~mandamus~~ moved for on ~~thursday~~ ~~be directed to~~		~~&.~~ last, to ~~John Hopkins~~ for the ~~purposes ment[nd] in said motion cannot issue~~ as_ The right of ~~the person~~ apply[g] for ~~the Mand[s] writ.~~ is not ~~sufficently clear~~

in ~~authorize the Court~~ ∧ ~~granting the same~~ to ~~justify its issuing_~~

~~The Court cannot therefore grant the motion_~~

⊗ United States ⎫				On motion made by M[r] Tilghman on thurday the 13th day of Feb[y]
v ⎬				instant. for a mandamus to be directed to the Defd[t] commanding to
John Hopkins Esq[r] ⎭				do & execute the matters & things set forth in the rule afs[d] the Court
									after arg[t] & full consideration are of opinion that the right claimed by

the Petitioner in the present case does not appear sufficiently clear to authorize the Court to issue the Mandamus moved for_

Alex[r] S. Glass &c ⎫			~~Cur advisare vult of[90]~~ opinion
v̄s. ⎬			1. that the ~~Dist[t]~~ C[t] ~~has~~ is a ~~prize~~ Court. final ~~deter-~~
Sloop ~~Betsy~~ & cargo. ⎬			mination ~~postponed to~~ y[e] next session_
& Capt[n] ~~Johannen~~ ⎭			2. no ~~foreign~~ Court can ~~have any jurisd[n] in the US.~~
									~~wh[1]~~ except, by convention ~~of~~ y[e] ~~parties_~~

On Motion of M[r] Lewis_

Honb[le] S. Dexter. admitted as a counsellor of this Court.

The Court_ on motion of M[r] Hillhouse adjourn until monday next at 11. to

85. An "&" appears beneath the "v."
86. The word "on" appears beneath "in."
87. An "s" appears beneath the "C."
88. A "T" appears beneath the "H."
89. A "3" appears beneath the "4."
90. A dash appears beneath the word "of."

into further
take ~~under~~ consideration the case of the invalid pensioners of the Dist^r of
Connec^t_^{91}

Monday 17. February. 1794.

Present as before

United States. ⎫
  v̄s   ⎬   Amicable act^n on the Case instituted_
Yale Tod.d ⎭   On argument_ Judgment ℔ Quer[entes]^{92}

~~Glass & others~~ ⎫
  v̄   ⎬   The decision of the Court below revers'd_ & the record
~~Sloop Betsy &c~~ ⎭   remanded to the Dist^t Court of Maryland

Tuesday   ~~Order'd. ℔ Cu~~Judgment^{23} ~~for the Plaintiff~~
18_   ~~& That an exemplification of the^{94} decree of this Court in this cause~~
          ~~be transmitted to the Circuit Court for Maryland Dist.~~

Tuesday 18^{95} Feb^y

Present as before_

Alex^r S. Glass & others ⎫
  v̄s   ⎬   final decree in this case
The Sloop Betsy &c ⎭   this day read & approvd

Order'd that an exemplification of the same be transmitted to the circuit Court
                      the
for ˄ Maryland Dist^r_

                                        (the same being the
    At a Supreme Court of the United States holden at Philad^a ˄ on ~~mond~~
present seat of the Nat^l Gov^t)
the first monday in August & on the fourth day of said month_ Anno Do-
mini_ 1794.

~~Present.~~_

                James Wilson ⎫
The Hon^{bls} John Blair ⎬ Associate Justices_
                James Iredell. ⎭

91. *United States v. Todd.*
92. For the plaintiffs.
93. An "r" appears beneath the "J."
94. The letters "is" appear beneath the "e."
95. A "6" appears beneath the "8."

This day met at the City Hall but[96] a sufficient number of Justices to constitute a quorum, _{not appearing} the Court is adjourned until to morrow at 11. oclock.

Tuesday. 5. August. 1794.

~~The~~ Pursuant to adjournment.

The Court this morning met at the City Hall—

Present.

The Hon^{bl} { James Wilson
John Blair
James Iredell &
W^mPaterson Esq^{rs} } Associate Justices

Proclamation being made the Court is open'd.

Alex^r Chisholm &c
vs.
The State of Georgia

On Motion of the Att^y G[en].

~~Order'd~~ that— "a "2nd writ of ~~enqu~~[iry] do issue ~~in this~~
~~case to ascertain~~ the damages. ~~sustaind by the Pltff~~
~~by reason of the breach of~~ promise &c on ~~the part of~~
~~the Defd^t & that 3 months notice~~ of the time & ~~place of executing the same~~
~~be given,~~ to the same persons ~~on whom process was originally serv'd~~—
On[97] motion of the Att^y Gen! of counsel for the Pltff.
The Court do award that the Gen! jury to be summon'd at the next Court, do enquire upon their oath & affirmations what damages the Plaintiff has sustaind by reason of the premises & the non performance of the promises & assumption in the declaration of the plaintiff contain'd & that 3 months notice of the holding such enquiry be given to the Govr & Att^y Gen! of the State of Georgia.

Math^w McAllister of Georgia— swon as and.[98] Jos. Thomas of Pennsylvani affirm'd as Counsellors of this Court—

The Gen! traverse jury summon'd to attend this Court being call'd— & no
issues of fact appearing for trial, the Court dispense with ~~their~~ further Attendance _{of the jury.} during the present term—

---

96. An "f" appears beneath the "b."
97. A lowercase "o" appears beneath the uppercase "O."
98. The clerk originally had written "a C" but changed it to "and."

Jacob Wagner's Notes for Fine Minutes
February 1795 Term to
August 1797 Term

begun and
At a Supreme Court of the United States ᶺ held at Philadelphia in the State of Pennsylvania (being the seat of the National Government) on Monday the second day of February A. D. 1795.

Present

The Hoñble {
William Cushing
James Wilson
John Blair
James Iredell
William Patterson
} Associate Justices

Proclamation is made and the court opened

The Marshall of the Pennsylvania District returns a veniri to him directed, which is read and filed.

The Court excuse the absence of two of the Petit Jurors viz. Charles Evans and Robert Bethel.

Proclam ᶺtion is made and the court opened

The Marshall returns a veniri which is read & the Jury called.

The court excuse the absence of two of the Pettit Jurors viz.ᵗ Charles Evans and Robert Bethel.

On Motion of the Attʸ Genˡ Messʳˢ Marshall & ᶺAlexander Campbell are admitted Counsellors of this court & they are immediately sworn.

The Jury is excused till Thursday next at ten O Clock

Chisholm
vs
State of Georgia
} by Attʸ Genˡ for the Plᵗⁱᶠᶠ it is agreed ᶺ that ᶺthis cause it should continue open

Oswald
v
New York
} Thursday next ᶺwas assigned for [it?] the trial of this cause

Ware ⎞
v ⎟   On Motion of M.ʳ Tilghman
Hylton ⎠   this cause is continued.

Att.ʸ Gen.ˡ begs the opinion of the court whether it is necessary to procure the signature of an Attorney to an assignment of Errors; of which they said they would consider

Adjourn'd till twelve to morrow

                                                                dus
The depositions of John Brown, John Lamb, Robert Bogar ˄[letters inked out], Robert Harpur, and George Clinton were opened in court and ordered to be filed.

On motion of the Attorney General Mess J. Marshall and Alexander Campbell Esquires were admitted counsellors of this court; & they were immediately sworn, as such.

The Jury were excused till thursday next at ten OClock in the forenoon.

Chisholm ⎞
vs. ⎟   It is agreed by the Attorney General for the Pltff.
The State of Georgia ⎠   that this cause should continue open.

Oswald ⎞
vs ⎟   Thursday next was
The State of New York ⎠   assigned for the trial
                          of this cause.

Ware v ⎞
vs ⎟   On motion of M.ʳ Tilghman this
Hylton ⎠   cause is continued.

The Attorney General requests the opinion of the court, whether it is necessary to procure the signature of an Attorney to an assignment of errors; of which the court say they will consider.

The depositions of John Brown, John Lamb, Robert Bogardus, Robert Harpur, and George Clinton, were opened in court and ordered to be read. filed.

The Court adjourned till 12 OClock to morrow

Tuesday 3.ʳᵈ Feb.ʸ 1795

Pursuant to adjournment the Court Met this Morning at the city-hall

Present

The hnble ⎧ James Wilson ⎫
         ⎨ John Blair   ⎬ Esq.ʳˢ Asso-
         ⎪ James Iredell ⎪ ciate Justices
         ⎩ William Patterson ⎭

Proclamation is made and the court opened

The deposition of _∧ is[99] opened & _∧ filed
        John McKesson   ordered to be

The court is adjourned till ——————— ten OClock to morrow morning

Wednesday 4th Feby 1795.

Pursuant to adjournment the court met this morning at the City Hall

Present

The hnble $\left\{\begin{array}{l}\text{William Cushing}\\\text{James Wilson}\\\text{John Blair}\\\text{James Iredell}\\\text{William Patterson}\end{array}\right\}$ $\begin{array}{l}\text{Esquires}\\\text{Associate}\\\text{Judges}\end{array}$

Proclamation is made and the court opened.

The court give notice to the gentlemen of the Bar, that hereafter they will expect _∧ a statement of the material points of t̶h̶e̶ _∧ case from the counsel on each side of a cause.
to be furnished with ... the

Penhallow
vs
Doane
$\left.\begin{array}{l}\\\\\\\end{array}\right\}$ this cause is assigned for Friday next

Mr Lewis read the petition of John Corbley and others confined in the goal of the city of Philadelphia on charges f̶o̶r̶ of High Treason, praying[100] the court to fix the time of their trial

The Att^y Gen! moves for the admission of Mr William Tilghman as a counsellor of this court, and he[101] is i̶m̶m̶e̶d̶ accordingly admitted and sworn.

The court is adjourned till ten OClock to morrow morning.

Thursday 5 Feby 1795.

T̶h̶e̶ ̶C̶o̶u̶r̶t̶ ̶m̶e̶t̶ Pursuant[102] to adjournment _∧ this morning at the city Hall
the Court met

---

99. The "i" is written over an "&."
100. A crossed-out comma appears after "praying."
101. The "e" is written over the letters "is."
102. A lowercase "p" appears beneath the uppercase "P."

Present

	⎧ William Cushing ⎫	
	James Wilson	Esquires
The hnble ⟨	John Blair	Associate
	James Iredell	Judges
	⎩ William Patterson ⎭	

Proclamation is made and the court opened

The jury are called ~~and~~

~~in default~~

William Moore Smith was admitted and sworn a counsellor of this court

Oswald ⎫
  vs ⟩
New York ⎭

this cause coming on

John Barnes
Wilson Hunt
Robert Gray
~~George Aston~~
Samuel Emory
James Barclay
John G. Wachsmuth
Sallows Shewell
Samuel Clarkson
John Melbeck
     were sworn; and
George Aston
Adam Mendenhall
Israel Pleasants
     were affirmed as jurors

                 & David Hall were
John Dunlap ˄ sworn as a witnesses
~~David Hall sworn as a witness~~

It is[103] agreed by the parties that the jury may give their verdict to mrorrow

                                 for def
Ware ⎫ On motion of Mʳ Campbell ˄ to assign errors, Mʳ Tilghman for the
  vs ⟩ Pltff declared that the general errors will be assigned
Hylton ⎭

Adjourned till eleven OClock to morrow morning.

103. A smudged "Its" precedes "It is."

Friday Feby 6th

Pursuant to Adjournment the court met this morning at the city hall

---

The hnble ⎰ William Cushing ⎱ Present
         ⎱ James Wilson ⎰
         ⎰ John Blair   ⎱ Esquires
         ⎱ James Iredell ⎰
           William Patterson

Proclamation is made and the court opened —

Oswald ⎱
vs   ⎰ the jury find for the Plaintiff 5315 £ ~~cents~~ and 6/100 Doll.
New York ⎰ costs.
                                              Dollars Damages

                    confined in the goal of this city on a charge of High Trea[son]
The Petition of John Lockery ^ ~~and ot[h?] was read by Mr Levy~~ praying the
court to fix the time of his trial, was read by Mr M. Levy.

                    the argument on
The court proceeded to hear ^ the petition of John Corbley & others

The court proceeded to hear the counsel in the case of Penhallow v. Doane

Adjourned till eleven OClock tomorrow morning.

Saturday 7th Feby 1795.

Pursuant to adjournment the court met this morning
                              Present

The hble ⎰ William Cushing ⎱ Esq^rs
         ⎱ James Wilson ⎰
         ⎰ John Blair   ⎱ Associate
         ⎱ James Iredell ⎰ Justices
           William Patterson

Proclamation is made and the court opened —

                    a rule to shew cause why
The Att^y Genl moved for ^ a mandamus to be directed to the Judge of the
                    issue a warrant to
District of New York (to ^ apprehend Henry Barré[104] a deserter from the
Perdrix, a corvette belonging to the Republic of France) should not issue.

~~The Court proceeded to hear Messrs Lewis & Levy on behalf of John Corbley & others and Mr Rawle Att^y for the Pennsylvania District on behalf of the United States on the subject of the petition of said Corbley & others & on a motion made by their council~~

Adjourned till eleven OClock on Monday morning

104. A "y" appears beneath the "e."

Original Minutes, February 7, 1795, in the hand of Jacob Wagner. Courtesy National Archives.

& John Lockery

The petitions of John Corbley and others ˄ being before the court, and it being stated by the Attorney of the United States for the Pennsylvania District, that the petitioners are charged with treason by them committed against the United States[105] in the counties of Alleghany, Washington, Fayette, Bedford, and Northumberland, within the district aforesaid; it is moved by Messrs Levy and Lewis of counsel with the ~~prisoners~~ petitioners that special circuit courts for the trial of criminal causes in cases punishable with death may be directed to be held at such convenient times and places within the several counties afsd as the court may deem most proper

adjourned till 11 OClock on Monday Morning next.

Feby 9th 1795

The court met this morning at the City Hall pursuant to adjournment

Present

		William Cushing		
		James Wilson		Esquires
The Hnble	{	John Blair	}	associate
		James Iredell		justices
		William Patterson		

Proclamation is made and the court is opened—

the case of

The court proceeded to hear the argument of counsel in ˄ Penhallow vs Doane's Admors.

Adjourned till eleven OClock to morrow morning.

Feby 10th 1795.

Pursuan[t][106] to Adjournment the court met this morning at the city Hall

Present

		William Cushing		
		John Blair		Esqrs
The Hnble	{	James Iredell	}	Associate
		William Patterson		Justices

Proclamation is made and the court openened

The court proceeded to hear counsel in the case of Penhallow v. Doane's Admors.

105. An "s" appears beneath the "e."
106. The "t" is partially obliterated by an ink blot.

Adjourned till 10[107] OClock tomorrow morning

Wednesday 11th Feby 1795.

Pursuant to adjournment the court met this morning at the city hall

Present

The Hnble $\left\{\begin{array}{l}\text{William Cushing} \\ \text{John Blair} \\ \text{James Iredell} \\ \text{William Patterson}\end{array}\right\}$ $\begin{array}{l}\text{Esquires} \\ \text{Associate} \\ \text{Justices}\end{array}$

Proclamation is made & the court opened.

The Court proceeded to hear the argument of Counsel in the case of Penhallow v. Doane's Admors.

The court adjourned till 11 OClock to morrow morning.

Thursday 12th Feby 1795

Pursuant to adjourment the court met this morning at the city hall

Present

The Hnble $\left\{\begin{array}{l}\text{William Cushing} \\ \text{John Blair} \\ \text{James Iredell} \\ \text{William Patterson}\end{array}\right\}$ $\begin{array}{l}\text{Esquires} \\ \text{Associate} \\ \text{Justices}\end{array}$

Proclamation is made and the court opened _

The court proceeded to hear the argument of counsel in the case of Penhallow v. Doane.

adjourned till 11 OClock to morrow morning

Friday 13th February 1795

Pursuant to adjournment the court met this morning at the City Hall

Present

The hnble $\left\{\begin{array}{l}\text{William Cushing} \\ \text{John Blair} \\ \text{James Iredell} \\ \text{William Patterson}\end{array}\right\}$ $\begin{array}{l}\text{Esquires} \\ \text{Associate} \\ \text{Justices}\end{array}$

Proclamation is made and court is opened

107. A "2" appears beneath the "0."

The court proceeded to hear the argument of Counsel in the case of Pen-hallow vs. Doane's Admors.

The Court is adjourned till 11 OClock to morrow morning.

Saturday 14th Feby 1795.

Pursuant to adjournment the court met this morning at the City Hall

Present

The Hnble $\left\{\begin{array}{l}\text{William Cushing}\\ \text{John Blair}\\ \text{James Iredell}\\ \text{William Patterson}\end{array}\right\}$ Esquires Associate Justices

~~Mr Lewis mov~~

Proclamation is made and the court is opened

The Court proceeded to hear the argument of Counsel in the case of
Pe_nhallow v. Doane's Admors

On motion of Mr Lewis a habeas corpus is[108] ordered to issue to bring
up _____ John Hamilton & Thomas Sedgwick ^ rectble ^ Monday
both in the custody of the Marshall of the Pennsylvania district   on
next
Morning at 12 OClock.

                                                    morning
The court is adjourned till 11 OClock on Monday ^ next.

Monday Feby 16th 1795

Pursuant to adjournment the court met this morning at the City Hall

Present

The hnble $\left\{\begin{array}{l}\text{William Cushing}\\ \text{John Blair}\\ \text{James Iredell}\\ \text{William Patterson}\end{array}\right\}$ Esquires Associate Justices

Proclamation is made and the court is opened.

The Court proceeded to hear the argument of counsel in the case of Pen-hallow vs. Doane's Admors:

By consent of Mr Lewis on behalf of John Hamilton and Thomas Sedgwick, to bring up whom a habeas corpus[109] issued on Saturday last, Ordered, that

108. An "o" appears beneath the "i."
109. A partially erased comma follows "corpus."

they be brought up to morrow morning at eleven OClock ~~to morrow morning~~

The Court w~~ ~~ ^is^ as adjourned till eleven OClock to morrow morning.

Tuesday Feby 17.th 1794.[110]

Pursuant to adjournment the court met this morning at the City Hall

Present[111]

The Honble {
James Wilson
Wm John Blair
James Iredell
William Paterson
} Esquires Associate Justices —

Proclamation is made & the Court is opened

The Marshall for the Pennsylvania District made Return of a Habeas Corpus to bring up the Bodies of John Hamilton & Thomas Sedgwick which was read and filed.

The Court declared that all evidence on[112] motions for a discharge upon bail must be by way of deposition; and not viva voce.

The court is adjourned till 11 OClock to morrow morning.

Wednesday Feby 18th 1795.

Pursuant to adjournment the court met this morning at the city Hall.

Present

The Hnble {
James Wilson
John Blair
James Iredell
William Paterson
} Esquires Associate Justices

Proclamation is made and the court is opened.

habeas corpus brought by
on the ~~motion to discharge~~ John Hamilton & Thom Sedgwick
The affidavits of Absolem ^Baird and Thomas Scott ^were taken in open court and [*word inked out*] filed.

The Court proceeded to hear the argument of Council on the Motion for a mandamus to be directed to John Lawrence ~~at the termination~~ which being closed they heard the council on the habeas corpus to bring up John Hamilton

---

110. Jacob Wagner should have written "1795."

111. Hand G begins to record the minutes here and continues to do so through the word "Sedgwick" seven lines below, after which Jacob Wagner resumes.

112. An "i" appears beneath the "o."

and Thomas Sedgwick ~~at the termination of which M[r] Lewis on behalf of the~~
so far as it respects John Hamilton at the termination of which M[r] Lewis moved
on his behalf, that he might be discharged without bail

The court was then adjourned until friday morning next at 11 OClock

<u>Friday Feb[y] 20th 1795</u>

Pursuant to adjournment the court met this morning at the city hall.

Present

The hnble $\left\{\begin{array}{l}\text{James Wilson}\\\text{John Blair}\\\text{James Iredell}\\\text{William Patterson}\end{array}\right\}$ Esquires Associate Justices

Proclamation is made and the court is opened —

The Court ~~discharge~~[113] ^{agree to order} John Hamilton _^ ^{to be discharged} ~~on bail~~ on bail; himself in 4.000 Dollars
and two sureties in 2.000 Dollars each.

Mess[rs] Presly Neville, & Thomas Scott ~~Scott~~ became the sureties & together
with ~~be~~ _{^the} said John Hamilton enter into recognizance accordingly to appear at
the next ~~cir.~~ special _{^or} stated circuit court.

†
† Thomas Sedgwick was returned by consent.

The Court is adjourned till 11 OClock to morrow morning.

<u>Saturday Feb[y] 21st 1795</u>

Pursuant to adjournment the court met this morning at the city hall

Present

The hnble $\left\{\begin{array}{l}\text{William Cushing}\\\text{James Wilson}\\\text{John Blair}\\\text{James Iredell}\\\text{William Patterson}\end{array}\right\}$ Esquires Associate Justices.

Proclamation is made and the court is opened.

The Court proceeded to hear the argument of Counsel in Bingham v. Cabot.

The court adjourned till 11 OClock ~~to morrow~~ on Monday morning next

113. A crossed-out caret appears before "discharge."

<u>Monday Feby 23rd 1795.</u>

Pursuant to adjournment the court met this morning at the city hall

Present

The hnble {
William Cushing
James Wilson
John Blair
James Iredell
William Patterson
} Esquires Associate Justices

Proclamation is made and the court is opened.

The court proceeded to hear the argument of Council in Bingham v_ Cabot.

The record, writ, return, citation, & assignment of errors in Olney Pltff. in error v. Dexter & same Plttff. v. Arnold were ordered to be filed.

The court give notice that tomorrow they will give their opinions in ~~Doane vs.~~ Penhallow v. Doane's Adm̄ors

Adjourned till 1 OClock tomorrow after noon.

<u>Tuesday Feby 24th 1795.</u>

Pursuant to adjournment the court met this afternoon at the City Hall

Present

The H̄nble {
William Cushing
John Blair
James Iredell
William Patterson
} Esquires Associate Justices

Proclamation is made and the court is opened.

The court proceeded to give their opinions in Penhallow vs. Doane's
except George Wentworth
Adm̄ors when it was finally ordered That against all the Pltfs in error ^
~~by def. in~~ by def. in error   George Wentworth
16360 68/Cts Doll. be recovered, ^ and the same sum against [~~Each?~~] ^
the
and that against ^ pltffs in error the costs ~~be~~ of the Circuit Court be recovered one half against ^George Wentworth and the other half against the other Pltffs in error; and that in this[114] ~~Supr~~ Court the parties pay their own costs. ~~and~~

The court is adjourned till eleven OClock to-morrow morning

114. The word "the" appears beneath "this."

<u>Wednesday Feby 25th 1795.</u>

Pursuant to adjournment the court met this morning at the city hall

Present

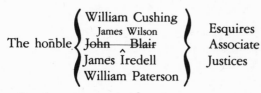

Proclamation is made and the court is opened,

The court proceeded to hear the argument of counsel in Bingham v. Cabot

Mr Lewis moved for an Habeas Corpus for Thomas Sedgwick and John Corbley which was opposed by Mr Rawle Att^y for the District of Pennsylvania

The court adjourned till ten OClock to morrow morning

<u>Thursday Feby 26th 1795.</u>

Pursuant to adjournment the court met this morning

Present

The hnble { William Cushing / James Wilson / James Iredell / William Paterson } Esquires Associate Justices

Proclamation is made and the court is opened. ~~the court~~

The court proceeded to hear the argument of Counsel on the motion for an habeas Corpus to bring up Thomas Sedgwick and John Corbley:
                                        & Cur— Advis. vult.

The court then proceeded to hear the argument of counsel in Bingham v Cabot ~~which being finished the court will consider~~

Adjourned till eleven OClock to morrow morning

<u>Friday Feby 27th 1795.</u>

Pursuant to adjournment the court this morning at the City Hall

Present

The hnble { William Cushing / James Wilson / James Iredell / William Paterson } Esquires Associate Justices

Proclamation is made and the court is opened.

The court declared, that, they being divided in opinion on the motion made by Mʳ Lewis on Wednesday last for a habeas Corpus to bring up Thomas Sedgwick and John Corbley, the motion could not be granted.

The court then proceeded to hear the argument of council in Bingham v. Cabot.

The Record in Joost Jansen v was this day filed

The Court is adjourned till 11 OClock to morrow morning.

Saturday Febʸ 28ᵗʰ 1795.

(23ʳᵈ) [115]

Pursuant to adjournment the court met this morning at the City Hall

Present

The hnble $\left\{ \begin{array}{l} \text{William Cushing} \\ \text{James Wilson} \\ \text{James Iredell} \\ \text{William Patterson} \end{array} \right\}$ $\left\{ \begin{array}{l} \text{Esquires} \\ \text{Associate} \\ \text{Justices} \end{array} \right.$

Proclamation is made and the court is opened

The Court proceeded to hear the argument of Counsel in Bingham vs Cabot.

at 11 OClock
The court is adjourned till Monday Morning next in ^

Monday March 2ⁿᵈ 1795

Pursuant to adjournment the court met this morning at the City Hall.
Proclamation is made and the court is opened

Present

The hnble $\left\{ \begin{array}{l} \text{William Cushing} \\ \text{James Wilson} \\ \text{James Iredell} \\ \text{William Patterson} \end{array} \right\}$ $\left\{ \begin{array}{l} \text{Esquires} \\ \text{Associate} \\ \text{Justices} \end{array} \right.$

Proclamation is made and the court is opened.

The Court proceeded to hear the argument of Council in Bingham v Cabot,
they
which being finished, the court proceeded to give their opinions thereon,
circuit
when it was finally ordered that the Judgment of the District Court [words
for the District of Massachusetts
inked out] ^ Massachusetts in this Court be reversed; and the Court being di-

115. The clerk may have written "(23ʳᵈ)" to indicate that February 28 was the twenty-third day of the term.

vided on the question whether a venire facias de novo should issue, it
is also
~~was~~ ˄ ordered that the writ do not issue.

Olney v Dexter. Same v. Arnold it is agreed to continue these causes.

Adjourned till eleven OClock to morrow morning.

Tuesday March 3ʳᵈ 1795

Pursuant to adjournment the court met this morning at the City Hall

Present

The ħnble $\left\{\begin{array}{l}\text{William Cushing} \\ \text{James Wilson} \\ \text{James Iredell} \\ \text{William Patterson}\end{array}\right\}$ $\begin{array}{l}\text{Esquires} \\ \text{Associate} \\ \text{Justices}\end{array}$

Proclamation is made and the court is opened.

was
The Mandamus to Judge Laurence ˄ refused after argument

~~Talbot~~ v. Jansen
                                    & inhibition awarded
    Rule by consent (see ~~agreement~~ ˄

Penhallow v. Doanes Admᵒʳˢ ~~Mandate~~ awarded on motion of Mʳ Tilghman

~~Adjourned to the time and place by law appointed~~

Jansen &ᶜ v. Talbot &ᶜ Rule by consent, that &ᶜ (See Agreement) & inhibition awarded.

Penhallow v Doane's Admᵒʳˢ: Special mandate awarded on motion of Mʳ
Tilghman — et exit.

Adjourned to the time and place by law appointed.

At Philadelphia, in the State of Pennsylvania being the present seat of the
national government on

Monday 3ʳᵈ of August 1795[116]

This being the day by law appointed for holding a Supreme Court, and none

---

116. Jacob Wagner introduces this section of the original minutes with a title which reads,
"Rough Minutes of the proceedings of the Supreme Court of the U. States Commencing at August
Term 1795."

Tuesday March 3.d 1795

Pursuant to adjournment the court met this morning at the City Hall

Present { William Cushing } Esquires
The Honble { James Wilson . } Associate
{ James Iredell } Justices
{ William Patterson }

Proclamation is made and the court is opened.

The Mandamus to Ludg Lawrence was refused after argument

~~Talbot v. Jansen~~
~~Rule by consent (see Agreement~~
~~Penhallow v. Doanes ~~ ~~Special Mandate awarded on~~
~~motion of Mr. Tilghman~~
~~Adjourned to the time and place~~
~~by law appointed~~

Jansen &c. v. Talbot &c. Rule by consent, that &c. (See Agreement) & inhibition awarded.

Penhallow v. Doanes Admors: Special mandate awarded on motion of Mr. Tilghman.
et exit. Adjourned to the time and place by Law
appointed.

Original Minutes, March 3, 1795, in the hand of Jacob Wagner. Courtesy National Archives.

of the Judges, but the honorable James Iredell Esq.ʳ appearing for that purpose;
by him
the court is ˄ adjourned till one OClock to morrow afternoon —

~~Tuesday Afternoon 4 Sept.ʳ 1795~~
~~Pursuant to~~

Tuesday Afternoon[117]
4 August 1795

None of the Judges appearing to day agreeably to the adjournment; but the
by him
honorable James Iredell Esq.ʳ The court is ˄ adjourned till eleven OClock to
morrow morning ~~at eleven OClock~~.

Wednesday Morn.ᵍ
5 August 1795

Pursuant to adjournment the Court met this morning at the city Hall, to
wit:

The hnble. { William Cushing / James Wilson / James Iredell / William Paterson } Esq.ʳˢ Associate Judges

Proclamation is made and the Court is opened.

Edw.ᵈ   Esq.ʳ
On motion of M.ʳ ~~Re ad~~ Tilghman, ˄ The hnble Jacob Read Esq.ʳ was admitted a counsellor of this court and he was immediately sworn according[118]
to law.

a counsellor of this Court & he was
On motion of M.ʳ Duponceau, Joseph Clay jun.ʳ Esq.ʳ was admitted & ˄ immediately sworn according[119] to law

Esq.ʳ a counsellor of this court
On motion of M.ʳ Read, Henry W.ᵐ DeSaussure ˄ was admitted ˄ and he
was immediately sworn according[120] to law.

The Marshal[121] of the Pennsylvania District returns a venire facias which
is
~~was~~ ˄ filed.

---

117. "Morn" appears beneath "After."
118. The "a" was written over a period.
119. Idem.
120. Idem.
121. A second "l" is partially erased at the end of the word "Marshal."

The depositions of Anthony McLeod, John Habersham and Gideon Davis Pendelton were opened in court & filed.

Grayson et al^s
    vs   } continued
The State of Virginia

Ware vs. Hylton et al. continued by consent.

Olney Pltff in error vs. Welcome Arnold continued by consent

Olney Pltff in error vs. Edward Dexter continued by consent

(insert the following)
    No issue of fact appearing for trial the jury are called & dismissed.

Adjourned till 11 OClock tomorrow morning

Thursday Morn^g
6 August 1795

Pursuant to adjournment the Court met this morning at the city hall, vizt

The hnble {
William Cushing
James Wilson
James Iredell
William Paterson
} Esq^{rs} Associate Judges.

Proclamation is made and the court is opened.

The court proceeded to hear the argument of counsel[122] in the case of Talbot Pltff in error vs. Joost Jansen.

               morrow
Adjourned till eleven OClock to ^ morning

Friday Morn^g
7 Augt 1795

Pursuant to adjournment the court met this morning at the city hall, viz.

The hnble {
William Cushing
James Wilson
James Iredell
William Paterson
} Esq^{rs} Associate Judges.

Proclamation is made and the court is opened.

The court proceeded to hear the argument of counsel in the case of Talbot,

122. The letters "cil" appear beneath "sel."

Pltff. in error vs. Jansen.

Adjourned till eleven OClock tomorrow morning.

Saturday Morn⁸
8ᵗʰ Aug.ᵗ 1795

Pursuant to adjournment the court met this morning at the City Hall, viz.

The hᵗnble { William Cushing / James Wilson / James Iredell / William Paterson } Esquires Associate Judges

Proclamation is made and the court is opened.

The court proceeded to hear the argument of counsel in Talbot, Pltff in error vs. Jansen.

Adjourned till 11 OClock on Monday morning next.

Monday, Morn⁸
10 Aug.ᵗ 1795

Pursuant to adjournment the court met this morning at the city hall, viz.

The hᵗnble { William Cushing / James ~~Iredell~~ Wilson / James Iredell / William Paterson } Esqʳˢ Associate ~~Justices~~ Judges

Proclamation is made and the court is opened.

The Court proceeded to hear the argument of counsel[123] in the case of Talbot, Pltff. in error vs Jansen.

Adjourned till ten OClock to morrow morning.

Tuesday Morn⁸
11 Aug.ᵗ 1795

Pursuant to adjournment the Court met this morning at the City Hall, viz.

The hᵗnble { William Cushing / James Wilson / James Iredell / William Paterson } Esqʳˢ Associate Justices

Proclamation is made and the court is opened

123. Idem.

The Court proceeded to[124] hear the argument of counsel[125] in Talbot, Pltff. in error vs. Jansen.

Adjourned till 10 OClock tomorrow morning.

<u>Wednesday Morn^g</u>
<u>12 August 1795</u>

Pursuant to adjournment the Court met this morning at the City Hall, viz.

The ħnble ⎧ William Cushing ⎫ Esquires
⎨ James Wilson ⎬ Associate
⎪ James Iredell ⎪ Judges
⎩ William Paterson ⎭ ~~Justices~~

Proclamation is made and the Court is opened.

The Court proceeded to hear the argument of counsel in the case of Talbot, Pltff. in error vs. Jansen.

Letters patent dated on the first of July last, ~~directed to the honorable John~~
                                the honorable John Rutledge Esqr
~~Rutledge Esqr,~~ [*word inked out*] appointing ⁁ ~~him~~ Chief Justice of the Supreme
                                        his
Court of the United States during ⁁ good behaviour, and until the end of the
next Session of ~~Congress~~ the Senate of the United States, were read and pub-
        thereupon   he
lished in open court; and ~~he~~ ⁁ ~~came at the same time a~~ ⁁ took the oath of office
and the oath to support the constitution of the United States; after which he
took his seat on the bench.

Adjourned till 10 OClock to morrow morning.

<u>Thursday Morn^g</u>
<u>13th Augt 1795.</u>

Pursuant to adjournment the court met this morning at the City Hall, viz

The Honorable John Rutledge Esqr Chief Justice

The ħnble ⎧ William Cushing ⎫ Esquires
⎨ James Wilson ⎬ Associate
⎪ James Iredell ⎪ Judges
⎩ William Paterson ⎭ ~~Justices~~.

Proclamation is made and the court is opened.

124. An uppercase "C" appears beneath the "t."
125. The letters "sel" are written over "cil."

The Court proceeded to hear the argument of counsel[126] in Talbot, Pltff, in error vs Jansen.

Adjourned till 10 — OClock to morrow morning.

Friday Morning
14th Aug: 1795

Pursuant to adjournment the court met this morning at the City Hall, viz.

The honorable John Rutledge Esq: Chief Justice

The hnble $\left\{\begin{array}{l}\text{William Cushing}\\\text{James Wilson}\\\text{James Iredell}\\\text{William Paterson}\end{array}\right\}$ Esquires Associate Judges

Proclamation is made and the court is opened.

The Court proceeded to hear the argument of Counsel in The case of Talbot, Pltff. in error vs. Jansen.

Adjourned till 10 OClock to morrow morning.

Saturday Morning
15th Aug: 1795

Pursuant to adjournment the court met this morning at the City Hall, viz

The hnble John Rutledge Esq: Chief Justice

The hnble $\left\{\begin{array}{l}\text{William Cushing}\\\text{James Wilson}\\\text{James Iredell}\\\text{William Paterson}\end{array}\right\}$ Esquires Associate Judges

Proclamation is made and the court is opened

M: Lewis, one of the counsel[127] in the case of Talbot, Pltff. in error vs. Jansen, being indisposed, the court is adjourned till 10 OClock on Monday morning next.

Monday Morning
17th August 1795

Pursuant to adjournment the court met this morning at the City Hall viz:

126. Idem.
127. Idem.

The ħnble John Rutledge Esqʳ Chief Justice

The ħnble ⎰ William Cushing ⎱ Esquires
          ⎱ James Wilson   ⎰ Associate
          ⎰ James Iredell   ⎱ Judges
          ⎱ William Paterson ⎰

Proclamation is made and the court is opened.

Adjourned till to morrow morning at ten OClock.

Tuesday Mornᵍ
18ᵗʰ Augᵗ 1795

Pursuant to adjournment the court met this morning at the City Hall, viz.

The ħnble John Rutledge Esqʳ Chief Justice

The ħnble ⎰ William Cushing ⎱ Esquires
          ⎱ James Wilson   ⎰ Associate
          ⎰ James Iredell   ⎱ Judges
          ⎱ William Paterson ⎰

Proclamation is made and the court is opened.

The court proceeded to hear the argument of counsel in The case of Talbot, Pltff. in error vs. Jansen

Adjourned till 10 OClock to morrow morning.

Wednesday Morning
19ᵗʰ August 1795

Pursuant to adjournment the court met this morning at the City Hall, viz.

The ħnble John Rutledge Esqʳ Chief Justice

The ħnble ⎰ William Cushing ⎱ Esquires
          ⎱ James Wilson   ⎰ Associate
          ⎰ James Iredell   ⎱ Judges
          ⎱ William Paterson ⎰

Proclamation[128] is made and the court is opened.

The court proceeded to hear the argument of counsel in the case of Talbot, Pltff. in error vs. Jansen.

Adjourned till 10 OClock tomorrow morning

---

128. An uppercase "T" appears beneath the "P."

Thursday Morning
20ᵗʰ August 1795

Pursuant to adjournment the Court met this morning at the City Hall, viz.

The hnble John Rutledge Esqʳ Chief Justice

The hnble {	William Cushing }	Esquires
	James Wilson {	~~Chi~~
	James Iredell {	Associate
	William Paterson }	Judges

Proclamation is made and the court is opened.

Cotton } On motion of Mʳ Read ^of counsel^ for def. in error
v
Wallace } Rule to return ^the^ record by the first day of ^January^ next.

Hills et al. ~~Woodbridge~~ } On motion of Mʳ Read of counsel for [*words inked out*] ^the defendent in^ error,
vs.
Ross } rule to ~~shew cause~~ ^return^ record by the 1ˢᵗ day of January next.

On motion of Mʳ Ingersoll, Jonathan William Condy ^Esqʳ^ was admitted a counsellor of this court and he was immediately ~~sworn~~ affirmed according[129] to law.

adjourned till tomorrow morning at ten OClock

Friday Morning
21ˢᵗ August 1795

Pursuant to adjournment the court met this morning at the City Hall, viz.

The hnble John Rutledge, Esqʳ Chief Justice

The hnble {	William Cushing }	Esquires
	James Wilson {	Associate
	James Iredell {	Judges
	William Paterson }	

Proclamation is made and the court is opened.

Mʳ Duponceau moved for a rule to shew cause why a prohibition should not go to Richard Peters Esqʳ Judge of the district Court of Pennsylvania to

---

129. A period appears beneath the "a."

by James Yard
prohi him from proceeding on[130] a libel filed in the said court ˄ against Samuel
B. Davis and the corvette or vessel of war called the Cassius ˄

adjourned till to morrow morning at ten OClock.

Saturday Morning
22 August 1795

Pursuant to adjournment the court met this morning at the city hall, viz.

The hnble John Rutledge Esqr Chief Justice

The hnble { William Cushing } Esquires
          { James Wilson   } Associate
          { James Iredell   } Judges
          { William Paterson }

Proclamation is made and the court is opened.

The court proceeded to ~~hear the argument of counsel~~ give their opinions
in the case of Talbot, Pltff. in error vs. Jansen, when it was finally ordered
that ~~the decree of the circuit court of South Carolina be affirmed~~ (see record)

Wallace   ) On motion Mr Clay for the def. _
    vs.   {   ˄ Rule to return the record by the 1st day of
The Brig Cæsar et al.) Jany next.

Adjourned till 7 OClock this evening

~~vs~~   )
~~Brig Cæsar & cargo~~ {
~~& al.~~   )

~~adjourned till 7 OClock this evening~~[131]

Saturday Evening
22nd August 1795

Pursuant to adjournment the court met at the City Hall, viz.

The hnble John Rutledge Esqr Chief Justice

The hnble { William Cushing } Esquires
          { James Wilson   } Associate
          { James Iredell   } Judges
          { William Paterson }

---

130. The word "on" is written over "in."

131. This crossed-out passage appears on the verso of the page with entries for Saturday morning, August 22, 1795.

Proclamation is made and the court is opened

The court proceeded to hear the argument of counsel on the motion for a prohibition to be directed to Richard Peters Esq‍ʳ

Adjourned till Monday Morning next at nine OClock

Monday Morning
24ᵗʰ August 1795

Pursuant to adjournment the court met this morning at the City Hall, viz.

The ĥnble John Rutledge Esqʳ Chief Justice

The ĥnble $\left\{\begin{array}{l}\text{William Cushing}\\ \text{James Wilson}\\ \text{James Iredell}\\ \text{William Paterson}\end{array}\right\}$ Esquires Associate Judges

Proclamation is made and the court is opened

Ordered that the Prohibition to be directed to J̶u̶d̶ ̶g̶e̲ ^Richard Peters Esqʳ Judge of the District ^Court of Pennsylvania, do issue.

Adjourned to the time and place by law appointed.

At Philadelphia, in the State of Pennsylvania, being the present seat of the National Government, on Monday the first day of February 1796.

This being the day by law appointed for holding a Supreme ^Court and none of the Judges but the honorable James Wilson Esqʳ appearing for that purpose; the Court is by him adjourned till eleven OClock tomorrow morning.

Tuesday February 2ⁿᵈ 1796

A̶g̶r̶e̶e̶a̶b̶l̶y̶ ̶t̶o̶ ̶t̶h̶e̶ ̶a̶d̶j̶o̶u̶r̶n̶m̶e̶n̶t̶ None of the Judges but the Honorable James Wilson Esqʳ and ^the Honorable William Paterson ^Esqʳ appearing pursuant to the adjournment of yesterday; the court is o̶p̶e̶n̶e̶d̶ by them a̶n̶d̶ ̶t̶h̶e̶n̶ ̶i̶m̶m̶e̶d̶i̶a̶t̶e̶l̶y̶ adjourned till tomorrow morning at 11 OClock.

Wednesday Morning
Feb.ʸ 3ʳᵈ 1796

Pursuant to adjournment the Court met this Morning at the City Hall to wit:

The honble ⎰ William Cushing ⎱ Esq.ʳ Chief Justice [132]

The hnble ⎰ James Wilson / James Iredell / William Paterson ⎱ Esquires / Associate Judges

Proclamation is made and the court is opened.

On motion of M.ʳ Edward Tilghman Esquire, the Attorney General of the United States, Charles Lee Esquire, was qualified a Counsellor of this Court.

On motion of M.ʳ Lewis, Samuel Sitgreaves, Esq.ʳ of Pennsylvania was admitted and sworn [as?] a counsellor of this court.

The Attorney General of the United States proposed for the consideration of the court, that the Clerk of this court should purchase for the use of this court the laws of the several states.

Adjourned till eleven OClock to morrow morning.

Thursday Morning
4 February 1796.

Pursuant to adjournment the court met this morning at the City Hall, to wit,

The hnble ⎰ William Cushing ⎱ Esq.ʳ [133]

⎰ James Wilson / James Iredell / William Paterson ⎱ Esquires / Associate Judges

Proclamation is made and the court is opened.

Letters Patent dated on the twenty seventh day of February January one thousand seven hundred and ninety six appointing the Honorable Samuel Chase Esq.ʳ of Maryland, one of the Associate Judges of this court during his good behaviour were read and published in open court; and thereupon he

132. Originally the braces were drawn around the names of Wilson, Iredell, and Paterson. Cushing, who had been commissioned chief justice on January 27, 1796, declined the appointment on February 2, 1796. When the clerk realized that Cushing was not chief justice, the braces were extended to enclose Cushing's name.

133. Braces drawn around the names of Wilson, Iredell, and Paterson were extended to enclose Cushing's name. The words "Chief Justice," originally written after "Esq.ʳ," have been erased. See note 132 above.

took the oath of office and the oath to support the constitution of the United States; after which he took his seat upon the bench

On motion of Edw.ᵈ Tilghman Esquire Robert H. Dunkin of Pennsylvania was admitted and sworn a counsellor of this court

The court then proceeded to hear the argument of counsel in the case of Thomas MacDonogh, Pltff. in error vs. Citizen Dannery and the Ship Mary Ford.

adjourned till 11 OClock to morrow morning.

Friday Morning
5ᵗʰ February 1796

Pursuant to adjournment the court met this morning at the City Hall, to wit

The hnble {
William Cushing
James Wilson   Esquires
James Iredell   Associate
William Paterson   Judges
Samuel Chase
}

Proclamation is made and the court is opened —

The court proceeded to hear the argument of counsel in the case of Thomas MacDonogh Pltff. in error vs. Citizen Dannery and the Ship Mary Ford.

The case of Benjamin Moodie, Pltff in error vs. the Mermaid et al. is assigned for argument for to morrow

Adjourned till 11 OClock to morrow morning

Saturday Morning
6 Febʸ 1796.

Pursuant to adjournment the court met this morning at the City Hall, to wit

The hnble {
William Cushing
James Wilson   Esquires
James Iredell   Associate
William Paterson   Judges
Samuel Chase
}

Proclamation is made and the court is opened

On motion of Mr Ingersoll Robert Porter Esqr was admitted a Counsellor of this court and he was accordingly sworn

The Court proceeded to hear the argument of Counsel in the case of
Ware, admᵒʳ of Jones
Jon̲es, Pltff. in error vs. Hylton et al.

Adjourned till eleven OClock on Monday morning next.

Monday Morning
8 Feb.ʸ 1796.

Pursuant to adjournment the court met this morning at the City Hall, to wit

The hnble $\left\{\begin{array}{l} \text{William Cushing} \\ \text{James Wilson} \\ \text{James Iredell} \\ \text{William Paterson} \\ \text{Samuel Chase} \end{array}\right\}$ Esquires Associate Judges

Proclamation is made and the court is opened

The court proceeded to hear the argument of Counsel in the case of
Ware, adm̄or of Jones
~~Ware~~
Jon̄﹏es, Pltff. in error vs. Hylton et al.

Adjourned till eleven OClock tomorrow morning.

Tuesday Morning
February 9 Feb.ʸ 1796

Pursuant to adjournment the court met this morning at the city Hall, to wit.

The ħnble $\left\{\begin{array}{l} \text{William Cushing} \\ \text{James Wilson} \\ \text{James Iredell} \\ \text{William Paterson} \\ \text{Samuel Chase} \end{array}\right\}$ Esquires Associate Judges

Proclamation is made and the court is opened.

The court proceeded to hear the argument of Counsel in Ware Adm̄or of Jones vs. Hylton et al.

Adjourned till eleven OClock tomorrow morning.

Wednesday Morning
10 February 1796.

Pursuant to adjournment the court met this morning at the City Hall, to wit;

The ħnble $\left\{\begin{array}{l} \text{William Cushing} \\ \text{James Wilson} \\ \text{James Iredell} \\ \text{William Paterson} \\ \text{Samuel Chase} \end{array}\right\}$ Esquires Associate

~~Pursuant to adjournment the court met this morning~~

Proclamation is made and the court is opened

The court proceeded to hear the argument of counsel ~~in the case of counsel~~ in the case of Ware admor of Jones vs. Hylton et al.

Adjourned till eleven OClock to morrow morning

Thursday Morning
11 Feb? 1796

Pursuant to adjournment the court met this morning at the City Hall, to wit,

The h͠nble.[134] { William Cushing
James Iredell
James Wilson[135]
William Paterson
Samuel Chase } Esquires Associate ~~Justices~~ Judges

Proclamation is made and the court is opened.

The court proceeded to hear the argument of Counsel in Ware, admor of Jones vs. Hylton et al.

Adjourned till 11 OClock tomorrow morning

Friday Morning
12th February 1796

Pursuant to adjournment the court met this morning at the City Hall, to wit,

The h͠nble { William Cushing
James Wilson
James Iredell
William Paterson
Samuel Chase } Esquires Associate Judges

Proclamation is made and the court is opened.

The court proceeded to hear the argument of Counsel in the case of Ware, Admor of Jones vs. Hylton et al.

Adjourned till 11 OClock tomorrow morning.

---

134. The contraction bar is drawn below the baseline.

135. In order of seniority, James Wilson belongs before James Iredell in the list of justices. This clerical error was corrected in the fine minutes.

Saturday Morning
13th February 1796

Pursuant to adjournment the court met this morning at the City Hall, to wit,

The hnble ⎰ William C ⎱ Associate
⎱ James Wilson ⎰ Judges
⎰ James Iredell ⎱
⎱ William Paterson ⎰
⎰ Samuel Chase ⎱

Proclamation is made and the court is opened.

On motion of Mr Read, John Julius Pringle Esqr ~~Attorney General~~ of South Carolina, was admitted and sworn a Counsellor of this Court.

On account of the illness of Judge Cushing the Court declined to hear any cause and therefore ~~adjourned to th~~
Adjourned till Monday Morning next at eleven OClock.

~~15 Feby 1796 Mr Read took away the record in the Den Onzekeren~~.

Monday Morning
15 February 1796

Pursuant to adjournment the court met this morning at the City Hall, to wit,

The hnble ⎰ James Wilson ⎱ Esquires
⎱ James Iredell ⎰ Associate
⎰ William Paterson and ⎱ Judges.
⎱ Samuel Chase ⎰

Proclamation is made and the court is opened

On account of the continuation of Judge Cushing's illness and of the indisposition of Judge Paterson, the court declined to hear any cause and therefore Adjourned till tomorrow morning at 11 OClock.

Tuesday Morning
16 February, 1796

Pursuant to adjournment the Court met this morning at the City Hall, to wit,

The hnble ⎰ James Wilson ⎱ Esquires
⎱ James Iredell ⎰ Associate Judges.
⎰ William Paterson ⎱
⎱ Samuel Chase ⎰

Proclamation is made and the court is opened.

On account of the continuation of the indisposition of Judge Cushing and Judge Paterson the court declined the hearing of any cause and therefore Adjourned till eleven OClock to morrow morning.

Wednesday Morning
17 Feb.ʸ 1796

Pursuant to adjournment the court met this morning at the City Hall, viz.

The hnble ⎰ James Wilson ⎱ Esquires
         ⎨ James Iredell ⎬ Associate
         ⎱ William Paterson ⎰ Judges
           Samuel Chase

Proclamation is made and the court is opened.

M.ʳ Read moved that the Court would Postpone the case of Benj— Moodie, Pltff. in error vs. the Ship Mermaid et al to be argued on Monday next.
But his motion was not granted and the court accordingly proceeded to
    hearing of the
the ^ argument thereof.

               unanimously by the court
Ordered ^ that the decree of the circuit Court of the District of Massachusetts in the case of Thomas M.ᶜDonogh, Pltff. in error vs. Citizen Dannery and the Ship Mary Ford be affirmed with costs.

Adjourned till to morrow morning at 10 OClock.

Thursday Morning
18 February 1796

Pursuant to adjournment the Court met this morning at the City Hall, viz.

The hnble ⎰ James Wilson ⎱ Esquires
          ⎨ James Iredell ⎬ Associate
          ⎱ William Paterson ⎰ Judges
            Samuel Chase

Proclamation is made and the court is opened.

The court proceeded to hear the argument of Counsel in the case of Benj— Moodie, Pltff. in error vs. The Ship Mermaid et al.

On motion of M.ʳ Ingersoll a special Mandate is awarded in the case of Thomas MacDonogh, Pltff. in error vs Citizen Dannery & the Mary Ford.

Adjourned till to morrow morning at 10 OClock.

<u>Friday Morning</u>
<u>19 Feb.ʸ 1796</u>

Pursuant to adjournment the Court met this morning at the City Hall, viz_

The hnble ⎰ James Wilson ⎱ Esquires
⎱ James Iredell ⎰ Associate
⎰ William Paterson ⎱ Judges
⎱ Samuel Chase ⎰

Proclamation is made and the court is opened.

The court proceeded to hear the argument of Counsel in the case of Benj_ Moodie, Pltff. in error vs. The Ship Mermaid et al.

Adjourned till eleven OClock tomorrow morning.

~~Judge Chase has the record of the British Debt Cause 20 Feb.ʸ 1796~~

<u>Saturday Morning</u>
<u>20 Feb.ʸ 1796</u>

Pursuant to adjournment the Court met this morning at the City Hall, viz.

⎰ James Wilson ⎱ Esquires
⎱ James Iredell ⎰ Associate
⎰ William Paterson ⎱ Judges
⎱ Samuel Chase ⎰

Proclamation is made and the court is opened

The Court proceeded to hear the argument of Counsel in the case of Benj. Moodie Pltff. in error vs. The Ship Mermaid et al.

The case of ~~the Elizabeth~~ Hills, May and Woodbridge vs Walter Ross. is appointed for argument on Monday morning next.

Adjourned till Monday Morning next at eleven OClock

<u>Monday Morning</u>
<u>22[136] Feb.ʸ 1796</u>

Pursuant to adjournment the Court met this morning at The City Hall, viz.

The hnble ⎰ James Wilson ⎱ Esquires
⎱ James Iredell ⎰ Associate
⎰ William Paterson ⎱ Judges
⎱ Samuel Chase ⎰

Proclamation is made and the court is opened.

136. A zero appears beneath the second "2."

On motion of the Attorney General of the United States Alexander Hamilton Esq.ʳ of New York was admitted and sworn a counsellor of this court.

Adjourned till tomorrow morning at 11 OClock.

Tuesday Morning
23 Feb.ʸ 1796

Pursuant to adjournment the Court met this morning at the City Hall, viz—

The hnble { James Wilson
James Iredell
William Paterson
Samuel Chase } Esquires Associate Judges

Proclamation is made and the court is opened.

The Court proceeded to hear the argument of Counsel in the case of Hylton, Pltff. in error vs. The United States

Adjourned till to morrow morning at eleven OClock

Wednesday Morning
24 Feb.ʸ 1796

Pursuant to adjournment the Court met this morning at the City Hall, viz—

The hnble { James Wilson
James Iredell
William Paterson
Samuel Chase } Esquires Associate Judges

Proclamation is made and the Court is opened.

The Court proceeded to hear the argument of Counsel in the case of Hylton, Pltff— in error vs. The United States.

Adjourned till tomorrow morning at 11 10 OClock.

Thursday[137] Morning Feb.ʸ 25ᵗʰ 1796

Pursuant to Adjournment the Court met this Morning at the City Hall viz

The Hon.ᵇˡᵉ { James Wilson
James Iredell
W.ᵐ Paterson
Samuel Chase } Esq.ʳˢ Associate Judges—.

Proclamation is made & the Court opened

---

137. Hand G begins to record the minutes here.

The Court proceeded to hear the Argument of Counsel in the Case of Hylton Plff— in Error v̄s The United States.

Adjourned till to Morrow Morning at 11 oClock.

Friday Morning
Feb.ʸ 26ᵗʰ 1796—

Pursuant to Adjournment the Court met ~~pursuant~~ this Morning at the City Hall viz.

The
Honᵇˡᵉ
{ James Wilson
James Iredell
William Paterson
Samuel Chase }
Esquires, Associate
Judges

Proclamation is made & the Court opened. — [138]

The court proceeded to hear the argument of Counsel in the case of Hills, May, and Woodbridge vs. Walter Ross and after making some progress therein they proceeded to hear the argument of Counsel in the case of ~~Hills, May and~~
John Wallace, Pltff. in error vs.
The Brig Cæsar and cargo and David Arnache.
~~Woodbridge vs. Walter Ross.~~

Adjourned till tomorrow morning at 11 OClock.

Saturday Morning
Feb.ʸ 27ᵗʰ 1796

Pursuant to adjournment the Court met this morning at the City Hall, to wit,

The hnble
{ James Wilson
James Iredell
William Paterson
Samuel Chase }
Esquires
Associate
Judges

Proclamation is made and the Court is opened

The court proceeded to hear the argument of Counsel in the cases of John Wallace, Pltff. in error, vs. The Brig Cæsar and Cargo and David Arnache and Benjamin Moodie, Pltff. in error vs. The Ship Favorite et al— which were agreed by Counsel to be argued together, as depending upon similar principles for their determination.

Ordered, that the Clerk of this court request the Secretary of State to grant for the use of this court a set of the Journels of the ~~Journe~~ Congress of the United States up to the time of the commencement of the New Government;

138. On the next line, Wagner again begins to take the minutes.

or, if that cannot be done, to permit them to be brought up to court ^ during
the session thereof, & to be re turned at the end of every Session.
from time to time
the Clerk returning them

Adjourned till tomorrow mornin monday morning next at eleven OClock.

Monday Morning
29th Feby 1796

Pursuant to adjournment the court met this morning at the City Hall, to wit,

The hnble ⎨ James Wilson   ⎬ Esquires
           James Iredell   Associ[-]
           William Iredell Patterson   ate
           Samuel Chase   Judges

Proclamation is made and the court is opened.

Ordered, that the de cree *judgment* of the Circuit Court of South Carolina District in the case of Benjamin Moodie Esquire, Vice Consul of his Britannic Majesty, Plaintiff in error vs. The Brig Favorite and her cargo and Alexander Bolchos and others, be affirmed with costs and that the said Benjamin Moodie *defendants in error* have execution thereof by special Mandate, to be directed to the said Circuit Court.

Ordered, that the de cree *judgment* of the Circuit Court of Georgia District in the case of John Wallace Esquire, Vice Consul of his Britannic Majesty vs. The Brig Cæsar and her cargo and David Arnache and others, be affirmed with costs and that the said John Wallace ^ have a execution thereof by special Mandate, to be directed to the next Circuit Court of Georgia District. *defendants in error* *for execution thereof*

On motion of Mr Dallas, Rule on the Marshall of the District of South Carolina to make return of the process issued in the case of John Brown Cutting, Administrator of Anne Paul Emanuel Sigismund de Montmorency Luxembourg vs. the State of South Carolina, within the first four days of the next ensuing term.

The Court then proceeded to hear the argument of Counsel in the case of Claude Delcol et al. Pltff. in error vs. Jonathan Arnold.

Adjourned till tomorrow morning at eleven OClock_

Tuesday Morning[139]
March 1ˢᵗ 1796 _

Pursuant to Adjournment the Court met this Morning at the City Hall viz

The Honᵇˡᵉ { James Wilson
James Iredell
Willᵐ Paterson
Samuel Chase } Esqʳˢ Associ[-] ate Judges _

Proclamation is made & the Court opened. _ [140]

The court proceeded to give their opinions in the case of Benjamin Moodie, Pltff. in error against The Ship Mermaid et al. when it was finally ordered,

of S. C. District
That the decree of the Circuit Court ᐱ in this cause be affirmed with costs

for   thereof a
and that the defendants in error have ᐱ execution ~~of this order by~~ special mandate.

The court proceeded to hear the argument of Counsel in the case of Claude Delcol et al. Plaintiffs in error against Jonathan Arnold

Adjourned till to morrow morning at eleven OClock.

Wednesday Morning
2 March 1796

Pursuant to adjournment the court met this morning at the City Hall, to wit,

The ħnble { William Cushing
James Wilson
James Iredell
William Paterson } Esquires
Associate
Judges

Proclamation is made and the court is opened.

By Consent of parties,
Ordered,
That the Judgment of the Circuit Court for the District of Georgia, in the case of the Brig Everton and Cargo and John B. Cotton, Pltff.s in error, against John Wallace, Esquire, Vice Consul of His Britannic Majesty, be affirmed with costs, and that the question whether any and what damages shall be recovered, do lie over for determination until the next Term of this court.

The Court proceeded to hear the argument of Counsel in the case of Jeremiah Olney, Pltff. in error against Welcome Arnold.

139. The beginning of this entry is written by Hand G.
140. Wagner resumes taking the minutes on the next line.

The court appointed the case of Geyer, Pltff. in error vs. John Michel and the Ship Den Onzekeren and cargo for argument for to morrow, if the case of Delcol et al. Pltffs in error vs Arnold cannot come on, on account of Judge Chase continuing to be ill.

Adjourned till to morrow morning at eleven OClock.

Thursday Morning
3 March 1796

Pursuant to adjournment the court met this morning at the City Hall, to wit,

The hnble $\left\{\begin{array}{l} \text{William Cushing} \\ \text{James Wilson} \\ \text{James Iredell} \\ \text{William Paterson} \end{array}\right\}$ Esquires Associate Judges

Proclamation is made and the court is opened

The court proceeded to hear the argument of Counsel in the cases of Geyer, Pltff. in error vs. John Michel and the Ship Den Onzekeren; and Benjamin ~~Grayson et al.~~ Moodie, Pltff. in error, vs. The Ship Betty Cath_ ~~vs.~~cart and her cargo and ~~& The State of Virginia~~ Jean Vidal, et al, which were agreed by Counsel to be argued together, as depending upon similar principles for their determination.

Adjourned till tomorrow morning at eleven OClock.

Friday Morning
4 March 1796

Pursuant to adjournment the Court met this morning at the City Hall, to wit,

The hnble $\left\{\begin{array}{l} \text{William Cushing} \\ \text{James Wilson}^{141} \\ \text{James Iredell} \\ \text{William Paterson} \end{array}\right\}$ Esquires Associate Judges

Proclamation is made and the court is opened

The Court proceeded to hear the argument of Counsel in the cases of Geyer, Pltff. in error vs. John Michel and the Ship Den Onzekeren; and Benjamin Moodie, Pltff. in error vs. The Ship Betty Cathcart and her cargo and Jean Vidal et al.

Adjourned till tomorrow morning at 11 OClock.

141. An "Ir" appears beneath the "W."

Saturday Morning[142]
March 5th 1796

Pursuant to Adjournment, the Court met this Morning at the City Hall, viz[143]

The hnble { William Cushing
James Wilson
James Iredell
William Paterson } Esquires Associate Judges.

Proclamation is made and the court is opened.

The court proceeded to hear the argument of Counsel in the cases of Geyer Pltff. in error vs. John Michel and the Ship Den Onzekeren; and Benjamin Moodie Pltff. in error vs. The Ship Betty Cathcart and her cargo and Jean Vidal et al.

Adjourned till Monday Morning next at eleven OClock.

Monday Morning
7th March 1796

Pursuant to adjournment the court met this morning at the City Hall, to wit

The hnble { William Cushing
James Wilson
James Iredell
William Paterson
Samuel Chase } Esquires Associate Judges

Proclamation is made and the court is opened.

The court proceeded to give their opinions solemnly in the case of ^(British debt)

(see memor.)

John Tyndale Ware, Admor of William Jones the surviving partner of Farrel and Jones, subjects of the King of Great Britain, against Daniel Lawrence Hylton and company and Francis Eppes, citizens of the State of Virginia, when it was finally ordered that judgment be therein entered in the words following.

Whereupon all and singular the premises being seen and by the court here and fully understood and mature deliberation had thereon, because it appears to the court now here, that in the record and process aforesaid and also in the rendition of the Judgment aforesaid upon the demurrer to the rejoinder of the defendants in error to the Replication to the second plea it is manifestly erred; it is considered that the said Judgment for those errors and others in the record and process aforesaid be revoked annulled and altogether held for nought and it is further considered by the court here, that the Plaintiff in error recover against the defendants two thousand nine hundred

---

142. The beginning of this entry is written by Hand G.
143. Wagner resumes taking the minutes on the next line.

and seventy six pounds, eleven shillings and six pence good British money commonly called sterling money, his debt aforesaid and his costs by him about his suit in this behalf expended and the said defendants in mercy &c But this Judgment is to be discharged by the payment of the sum of 596 dollars and interest thereon to be computed after the rate of 5 per cent. per annum from the 7th day of July 1782[144] till payment besides the costs and by the payment of such damages as shall be awarded by ˄ to the Plaintiffs in error on a writ of enquiry to be issued by the Circuit Court of Virginia to ascertain the sum really due to the Plaintiff, exclusively of the said sum of five hundred and ninety six dollars, which was found to be due to the Plaintiff in error upon the trial in the said Circuit Court of the issue joined upon the defendants plea of payment at a time when the Judgment of the said Circuit Court on the said demurrer was unreversed and in full force and vigor; and for the execution of this judgment of the court the cause aforesaid is remanded to the said Circuit Court of Virginia.[145]

On motion

Mr Ingersoll moved for a prohibition on the libel and suit instituted by Thomas Smith in the District Court of the District of Virginia against Alexander Macaulay and the Ship Charles Carter upon a mortgage of the said Ship.

Adjourned till to morrow morning at eleven OClock.

Tuesday Morning[146]
8 March 1796

Pursuant to adjournment the Court met this morning at the City Hall, to wit,

The hnble { William Cushing
              James Wilson   } Esquires
              James Iredell   } Associate
              William Paterson   } Judges.
              Samuel Chase   }

Pursuat Proclamation is made and the court is opened.

(here insert what is in the opposite page, m[ark]ed *)

* Letters patent, dated on the fourth day of March in the year of our Lord one thousand seven hundred and ninety six and of the Independence of the United States the twentieth, appointing the honorable Oliver Ellsworth, Esquire, of Connecticut, Chief Justice of this Court, during his good behaviour,[147] were read and published in open court; and thereupon he took the oath of office and the oath to support the constitution of the United States: after which he took his seat upon the bench.

144. The "8" is written over a "9."
145. This decree was written on a larger piece of paper which was affixed with sealing wax to the verso of the preceding page.
146. The clerk seems to have entered the proceedings of this sitting of the Court on the next page in the book and then removed it leaving only a thin margin of paper with a few word fragments legible. He then tipped in a new page with the proceedings of Tuesday written on it. Because this tipped-in page stuck out further on the right margin, it is frayed and the ends of some words are lost.
147. The "u" is written over an "r."

The court then proceeded to give their opini[ons] in the case of D. L. Hylton, Pltff. in error vs. The Uni[ted] States, when it was ordered, that the Judgme[nt] of the Circuit Court of Virginia District in the said cause should be affirmed.

The court then proceeded to hear the argume[nt] of Counsel in the case of Claude Delcol et al Pltff.'s in error vs. Jonathan Arnold

Adjourned[148] till to morrow morning at 10 OClo[ck]

Wednesday Morning
9th March 1796

Pursuant to adjournment the court met this morning at the City Hall, to wit,

The hnble $\left\{\begin{array}{l}\text{James Wilson}\\\text{James Iredell}\\\text{William Paterson}\\\text{Samuel Chase}\end{array}\right\}$ Esquires Associate Judges.

Proclamation is made and the Court is opened.

The court proceeded to hear the argument of Counsel in the case of Claude Delcol et al. Pltff. in error vs. Jonathan Arnold.

Adjourned till to morrow morning at 11 OClock.

Thursday Morning
10 March 1796

Pursuant to adjournment the court met this morning at the City Hall, to wit,

The hnble $\left\{\begin{array}{l}\text{William Cushing}\\\text{James Wilson}\\\text{James Iredell}\\\text{William Paterson}\end{array}\right\}$ Esquires Associate Judges

Proclamation is made and the court is opened.

Ordered that the case of Claude Delcol et al. Pltff. in error v⁵ Jonathan Arnold, lie over till the next term for argument, upon the question, how far are as to the damages to be the owners responsible in damages? allowed.

The court proceeded to hear the argument of Counsel in the cases of Geyer, Pltff. in error vs John Michel and the Ship Den Onzekeren; and Benjamin

148. An "r" appears beneath the "n."

Moodie, Pltff. in error v.⁵ The Ship Betty Cathcart and her cargo and Jean Vidal et al.

Adjourned till to morrow morning at ten OClock.

Friday Morning
11 March 1796

Pursuant to adjournment the court met this morning at the City Hall, to wit,

The hnble { William Cushing / James Wilson / James Iredell / William Paterson } Esquires Associate Judges

Proclamation is made and the court is opened.

The court proceeded to hear the argument of Counsel in the cases of Geyer, Pltff. in error v.⁵ John Michel and the Ship Den Onzekeren; and Benjamin Moodie, Pltff— in error v.⁵ The Ship Betty Cathcart and cargo and Jean Vidal et al.

Adjourned till to morrow morning at ten OClock—

Saturday Morning
12 March 1796

Pursuant to adjournment the court met this morning at the City Hall, to wit,

The hnble { William Cushing / James Wilson / James Iredell / William Paterson } Esquires Associate Judges.

Proclamation is made and the court is opened.

The court proceeded to hear the argument of Counsel in the cases of Geyer, Pltff. in error vs. John Michel and the Ship Den Onzekeren; and Benjamin Moodie, Pltff— in error vs. The Ship Betty Cathcart and cargo and Jean Vidal et al.

The court proceeded to hear the argument of Counsel on the motion of M.ʳ Ingersoll for a prohibition on the ~~suit~~ libel and suit instituted by Thomas Smith in the District Court of the District of Virginia against Alexander Macaulay and the Ship Charles Carter upon a Mortgage of the said Ship.

                     Monday   next
Adjourned till ~~tomo_rrow~~ morning ^ at 10 OClock.

Monday Morning
14[149] March 1796

Pursuant to adjournment the court met this morning in the Common Council Room of the Corporation of Philadelphia, to wit,

The hnble Oliver Ellsworth, Esq.ʳ Chief Justice

The hnble. { William Cushing / James Wilson / James Iredell / William Paterson } Esquires Associate Judges —

Proclamation is made and the court is opened.

⊗ ~~Ordered that the decrees of the Circuit Court in the cases of Geyer, Pltff. in error vs. John Michel and the Ship Den Onzekeren, and Benjamin Moodie, Pltff. in error vs. The Ship Betty Cathcart and cargo and Jean Vidal et al. with cost but w[i]t be affirmed with costs but without any damages. (in copying this make them seperate)~~

⊗ ordered, that the decree of the Circuit Court of South Carolina District in the case of John Geyer, Pltff. in error vs. John Michel and the ship Den Onzekeren and cargo be affirmed with costs, but without damages.

Ordered, that the decree of the Circuit Court of South Carolina District in the case of Benjamin Moodie, Pltff. in error vs. The Ship Betty Cathcart and cargo and Laurent Vidal et al. be affirmed with costs, but without damages.

Ordered, that the ~~Judgmen~~ decree of the Circuit Court of S_ C_ District in the case of Benjamin Moodie, Esq.ʳ Pltff. in error, vs the Ship Phyn and cargo and John Gaillard et al. be affirmed with costs and that the defend. in error have a special mandate for execution.

The Court then proceeded to hear the argument of Counsel ~~in the case of~~ on the motion of M.ʳ Ingersoll for a prohibition on the libel and suit instituted by Thomas Smith in the District Court of Virginia District against Alexander Macaulay and the Ship Charles Carter upon a mortgage of the said Ship, when it was
Ordered
That the Prohibition issue.

Ordered,
That the motion of M.ʳ Lewis, for a distringas to compel the appearance of the State of Virginia ~~be in the~~ to on the Bill filed by William Grayson and others, lie over till the next term.

149. The "4" is written over a "3."

ordered, that the decree of the Circuit Court of South Carolina District in the case of John Geyer, Pltff. in error vs. John Michel and the ship Den Onzekeren and cargo be affirmed with costs, but without damages.

Ordered, that the decree of the Circuit Court of South Carolina District in the case of Benjamin Moodie, Pltff. in error vs. The Ship Betty Cathcart and cargo and Laurent Vidal et al. be affirmed with costs, but without damages.

Monday Morning
14 March 1796

Pursuant to adjournment the court met this morning in the Common Council Room of the Corporation of Philadelphia, to wit,

The hnble Oliver Ellsworth, Esq.r Chief Justice

The hnble. {
William Cushing
James Wilson
James Iredell
William Paterson
} Esquires
Associate
Judges

Proclamation is made and the court is opened.

Ordered that the ~~judgments~~ decrees of the Circuit Court in the cases of ~~Geyer~~ John Geyer, Pltff. in error vs. John Michel and the Ship Den Onzekeren and cargo; and Benjamin Moodie, Pltff. in error vs. The Ship Betsy Cathcart and cargo and Laurent Vidal et al. ~~with costs but without~~ be affirmed with costs but without ~~any~~ damages.
(in copying this make them separate)

Ordered that the ~~judgment~~ decree of the Circuit Court in the case of Benjamin Moodie, Esq.r Pltff. in error, vs the Ship Phyn and cargo and

Original Minutes, March 14, 1796, in the hand of Jacob Wagner. Courtesy National Archives.

Ordered,

That the cases of Jeremiah Olney, Pltff___ in error vs. Welcome Arnold and Jeremiah Olney Pltff. in error vs Edward Dexter lie over till the next term.

and by consent of ˏparties[150]   writ of error in
Ordered on motion of M.ʳ Pringle ˆO̶r̶d̶e, that ˏ the case of Don Deigo[151]
Consul of His Catholic Majesty
Morphy ˏ against the Ship Sacra Familia and cargo and John Gaillard et al. be discontinued, and that no other writ of error be ever taken out therein.

Ordered, that all the unfinished business of this Court be continued until the next term.

Adjourned till the time and to the place by law appointed.

United States[152] ⎫
    vs.   ⎬ Prohib. issued 24[153] Aug.ᵗ 1795
Rich.ᵈ Peters ⎭

Talbot Pltff. in error ⎫
    vs   ⎬ Spl. Mand. issued 22[154] Aug.ᵗ 1795
Jansen ⎭

Hills et al. ⎫ ⎫
   v.ˢ   ⎬ ⎬ serv.ᵈ copies of rule to return
Walter Ross ⎭ ⎮ record on M.ʳ Duponceau on the
Cotton ⎫ ⎮ 26
   vs   ⎬ ⎭
Wallace ⎭

At the City Hall in the City of Philadelphia (being the present seat of the National Government of the United States) on Monday the first day of August in the year of our Lord one thousand seven hundred and ninety six and of
first
the Independence of:___ the United States the twentyt̶ ̶h,[155] the Court met.

Present

The Honorable Oliver Ellsworth Esq.ʳ Chief Justice

             ⎧ William Cushing   ⎫
             ⎪ James Wilson   ⎪ Esquires
The H̄nble ⎨ James Iredell   ⎬ Associate
             ⎪ William Paterson, and ⎪ Justices
             ⎩ Samuel Chase   ⎭

150. The caret positioned "parties" at the page's edge.
151. An "ie" appears beneath the "ei."
152. The clerk left a few pages blank and then wrote these notes on cases.
153. A "5" appears beneath the "4."
154. A "4" appears beneath the second "2."
155. Originally the clerk had written "twentieth" but the "ie" was changed into a "y."

Proclamation is made and the Court is opened.

The Marshal[156] of Pennsylvania District makes return of a venire for a special jury, which is filed; and the jurors being called, John Dunlap, Francis West, Richard Rundle, George Harrison, Curtis Clay, Philip Nicklin, William Grammond, Thomas W. Francis, John Simpson, John Hall, Samuel C[oates], John Field, Joseph P. Norris, George Bickham, Samuel Breck jun[r] Israel Pleasants, John Kaighn, Emanuel Walker, Thomas Mackie, John Oldden, John Thompson, James Coxe, Isaac Penington, Joseph Sims, Peter Blight, Peter Kuhn, Joshua B. Bond, Thomas Hockley, William Montgomery, George Willing, Samuel Clarkson, Wilson Hunt, James Miller, Robert Wescott, Edward Shoemaker, George Thompson, Samuel Meeker, Jonathan Jones, John Vaughan, William West, Norton Pryor jun[r][,] George Lauman, Samuel Fisher, Jonathan Harvey, Patrick Moore, Benjamin W. Morris, John Duffield and David H. Conyngham were made Default; and James Vanuxem was excused from further attendance on account of the ill state of his health.

On motion of M[r] Ingersoll, John Y. Noel Esquire was admitted and sworn a Counsellor of this Court.

The list of causes was called and several of them set down for argument.

The Jury are excused from further attendance till Saturday morning next at 9 OClock.

Adjourned till to morrow morning at nine OClock.

Tuesday Morning
2 August 1796

Pursuant to adjournment the Court met this morning at the City Hall, to wit,

The H̄nble Oliver Ellsworth Esquire Chief Justice

The H̄nble { William Cushing / James Wilson / James Iredell / William Paterson / Samuel Chase } { Esquires Associate Judges Justices. }

Proclamation is made and the court is opened.

The Court proceeded to hear the argument of Counsel in the case of John B. Cotton vs. John Wallace, and having made some progress therein they proceeded to hear the argument of Counsel in the case of Hills, May and Woodbridge and the Ship Elizabeth against Walter Ross.

156. A second "l" was erased.

Adjourned till tomorrow morning at nine OClock.

<u>Wednesday Morning</u>
<u>3 August 1796</u>

Pursuant to adjournment the Court met this morning at the City Hall, to wit,

The H̄nble Oliver Ellsworth Esq.ʳ Chief Justice

The H̄nble ⎰ William Cushing ⎱
⎱ James Wilson ⎰ Esquires
⎰ James Iredell ⎱ Associate
⎱ William Paterson, and ⎰ Justices
⎰ Samuel Chase ⎱

Proclamation is made and the court is opened.

The Court proceeded to hear the argument of Counsel in the case of the Ship Elizabeth and cargo and Hills, May and Woodbridge vs. Walter Ross.

Adjourned till to morrow morning at nine OClock.

<u>Thursday Morning</u>
<u>4 Aug.ᵗ 1796</u>

Pursuant to adjournment the Court met this morning at the City Hall, to wit,

The H̄nble Oliver Ellsworth Esq.ʳ Chief Justice

The H̄nble ⎰ William Cushing ⎱
⎱ James Wilson ⎰ Esquires
⎰ James Iredell ⎱ Associate
⎱ William Paterson ⎰ Justices
⎰ Samuel Chase ⎱

Proclamation is made and the court is opened.

On motion of Edward Tilghman Esq.ʳ— Richard Stockton and Andrew Kirkpatrick, Esquires, both of the State of New Jersey, were admitted and sworn Counsellors of this Court.

The court proceeded to hear the argument of Counsel in the case of The Ship Elizabeth and cargo and Hills, May and Woodbridge against Walter Ross.

Adjourned till to morrow morning at nine OClock.

Friday Morning
5 Aug! 1796

Pursuant to adjournment the court met this morning at the State House, to wit,

The Hnble Oliver Ellsworth Esq! Chief Justice

The Hnble {
William Cushing
James Wilson
James Iredell
William Paterson, and
Samuel Chase
} Esquires Associate Justices

Proclamation is made and the court is opened.

The court proceeded to hear the argument of Counsel in the case of Claude Delcol et al. against Jonathan Arnold.

Adjourned till to morrow morning at nine OClock.

Saturday Morning
6 Aug! 1796

Pursuant to adjournment the court met this morning at the City Hall, to wit,

The Hnble Oliver Ellsworth Esquire Chief Justice

The Hnble {
William Cushing
James Wilson
James Iredell
William Paterson
Samuel Chase
} Esquires Associate Judges

Proclamation is made and the Court is opened.

The jury, who were required to meet on this day, are now dismissed.

The Petition of David Hunter praying the Court to continue the case of Hunter against Fairfax's lee, which was granted and the prayer of the petition granted.

On motion of M! Dallas for the Plaintiff a rule is granted on the Marshal of South Carolina District to return the writ of Summons in the case of Cutting against the State of South Carolina.

The Court proceeded to hear the argument of Counsel in the case of Olney vs. Arnold, and after making some progress therein, they proceeded to hear the argument of Counsel in the case of Benjamin Moodie against the Ship Phœbe Ann and cargo and Jean Bouteille et al.

Adjourned till Monday Morning next at nine OClock.

<u>Monday Morning</u>
<u>8 Aug.ᵗ 1796</u>

Pursuant to adjournment the court met this morning at the City Hall, to wit,

The Hnble Oliver Ellsworth Esq.ʳ Chief, Justice

The Hnble ⎰ William Cushing ⎱ Esquires
⎰ James Wilson ⎱ Associate
⎰ James Iredell ⎱ ~~Judges~~
⎰ William Paterson ⎱ Justices
⎰ Samuel Chase ⎱

Proclamation is made and the court is opened.

The court proceeded to hear the argument of Counsel in the case of Benjamin Moodie vs. The Ship Phœbe Ann and cargo and Jean Bouteille et al. which being terminated they proceeded to hear the argument of Counsel in the case of Benjamin Moodie vs. The Ship Alfred and cargo and Abraham Sasportas et al. which being terminated they proceeded to hear the argument of Counsel in the case of Benjamin Moodie ~~Plain~~ vs. The Ship Britannia and cargo and Jean B. Carvine et al.

Adjourned till to morrow morning at nine OClock.

<u>Tuesday Morning</u>
<u>9 Aug.ᵗ 1796</u>

Pursuant to adjournment the court met this morning at the City Hall, to wit,

The hnble Oliver Ellsworth Esquire, Chief Justice

The hnble ⎰ William Cushing ⎱ Esquires
⎰ James Wilson ⎱ Associate
⎰ James Iredell ⎱ Justices
⎰ William Paterson ⎱
⎰ Samuel Chase ⎱

Proclamation is made and the court is opened

Ordered
         Decree   for
That the ~~Judgment~~ of the Circuit Court ~~of~~ South Carolina District in the case of Benjamin Moodie against the Ship Phœbe Ann and cargo and Jean Bouteille and others be affirmed with costs: and a special mandate is awarded.

Ordered

Decree   for
That the J̶u̶d̶g̶m̶e̶n̶t̶ of the Circuit Court o̶f̶ South Carolina District in the
                                                                                              Antoine
case of Benjamin Moodie against the ship Alfred and cargo and John ˄ Gar-
riscan and others be affirmed with costs: and a special mandate is awarded.

Ordered

                                            for
That the Judgment of the Circuit Court o̶f̶ ˄ South Carolina District in the
case of Benjamin Moodie against the Ship Britannia and cargo and Jean B.
Carvine and others be affirmed with costs: and a special mandate is awarded.

Ordered

                                            for
That the Judgment of the Circuit Court o̶f̶ South Carolina District in the
case of Benjamin Moodie against the Brig Eliza and cargo and John Gaillard
and others be affirmed with costs: and a special mandate is awarded.

Ordered

                                            for
That the Judgment of the Circuit Court o̶f̶ ˄ South Carolina District in the
case of Benjamin Moodie against the Brig Tivoly and cargo and Abraham
Sasportas and others be affirmed with costs: and a special mandate is awarded.

Ordered

                                            for
That the Judgment of the Circuit Court o̶f̶ ˄ South Carolina District in the
case of Benjamin Moodie against the Brig Eliza and cargo and Paul Beltri-
meaux and others be affirmed with costs: and a special mandate is awarded.

Ordered

                                            for
That the Judgment of the Circuit Court ˄ o̶f̶ South Carolina District in the
case of Benjamin Moodie against the B̶r̶i̶g̶ ̶E̶l̶i̶z̶a̶ ̶a̶n̶d̶ Snow Potowmack and
cargo and Jean B. Carvine and others be affirmed with costs: and a special
mandate is awarded.

M.ʳ Lewis renewed his motion for a Distringas to compel the State of Vir-
ginia to appear t̶o̶ and answer William Grayson and others i̶n̶ ̶a̶ ̶s̶u̶i̶t̶ ̶i̶n̶ ̶e̶q̶u̶i̶t̶y̶.̶

The Court having heard the argument of Counsel in the case of John B.
Cotton, Plaintiff in error, against John Wallace, defendant in error, on the
question, whether any and what damages shall be recovered? which question
was referred to this term for determination,— it is now finally ordered, that
the said defendant in error recover as damages against the said Plaintiff in
                  t̶w̶o̶ ̶t̶h̶o̶u̶s̶a̶n̶d̶ ̶a̶n̶d̶ ̶n̶i̶n̶e̶t̶y̶ ̶d̶o̶l̶l̶a̶r̶s̶ ̶&̶ ̶f̶o̶r̶t̶y̶ ̶n̶i̶n̶e̶ ̶c̶e̶n̶t̶s̶ two thousand seven
error the sum of t̶h̶r̶e̶e̶ ̶t̶h̶o̶u̶s̶a̶n̶d̶ ̶f̶i̶v̶e̶ ̶h̶u̶n̶d̶r̶e̶d̶ ̶a̶n̶d̶ ̶f̶i̶f̶t̶e̶e̶n̶ ̶d̶o̶l̶l̶a̶r̶s̶ ̶a̶n̶d̶ ̶e̶l̶e̶v̶e̶n̶
hundred and eighty seven dollars and thirty two cents
c̶e̶n̶t̶s̶ being the interest on thirty four thousand eight hundred and forty one
dollars and e̶l̶e̶v̶e̶n̶ ̶c̶e̶n̶t̶s̶ fifty five cents, the amount sales of the Brig Everton
and her cargo from the fifth day of May one thousand seven hundred and

ninety five, the date of the decree of the Circuit Court in the said cause
<u>until the 5th day of May one thousand seven hundred & ninety six</u>
being one year, ~~three months and four days~~ at the rate of eight per centum
per annum; and also that the said Plaintiff in error do pay the costs accrued
in this cause since the last term: and a special mandate is awarded to carry this
order
de~cree into execution.

~~The court is adjourned till to morrow morning at nine OClock.~~

The court proceeded to hear the argument of counsel in the case of Don
Diego Pintado against The Ship San Joseph alias la Princesa de las Asturias
and Jean Antoine Berard.

Adjourned till to morrow morning at nine O Clock.

Wednesday Morning
10 Aug.ᵗ 1796

Pursuant to adjournment the court met this morning at the City Hall

The Hoñble Oliver Ellsworth Esquire Chief Justice

	William Cushing	
	James Wilson	Esquires
The Honble	James Iredell	Associate
	William Paterson	Judges
	Samuel Chase	

Proclamation is made and the court is opened.

Tho.ˢ Fennimore	
vs	Error from the Circuit
The United States	Court of New Jersey

/// The writ of error is returned and filed. The Attorney General on behalf of
the United States agrees to acknowledge the service of a citation. M.ʳ E. Tilghman for the plaintiff assigns the common errors and the Attorney General joins
in error.

On motion of Edward Tilghman Esq.ʳ, Richard Lake Esq.ʳ of Pennsylvania
was admitted and sworn a counsellor of this court.

Ordered

decree
/// That the ~~Decree Judg~~ment of the Circuit Court ~~of the U[n]~~ for the District of New York in the case of Don Diego Pintado against the ^Ship San
Joseph, alias la Princesa de las Asturias and Jean Antoine Berard be affirmed
with costs: and a special Mandate is awarded.

The court proceeded to hear the argument of Counsel in the case of Wisecart vs. Dauchy; and having made some progress therein they proceeded to

hear the argument of Counsel in the case of the United States against the Schooner La Vengeance and Jean Antoine Bernard de Rozier.

Adjourned till to morrow morning at nine OClock.

Thursday Morning
11 Augᵗ 1796

Pursuant to adjournment the court met this morning at the City Hall, to wit,

The Honble Oliver Ellsworth Esqᵣ Chief Justice

Cushing

The Hnble { William Paterson
James Wilson
James Iredell
William Paterson
Samuel Chase } Esquires Associate Justices

Proclamation is made and the court is opened.

Ordered
That the Judgment of the Superior Court of Judicature, Court of Assize and Jail delivery for the County of Providence in the State of Rhode Island in the
Plaintiff in error
case of Jeremiah Olney against Welcome Arnold be reversed with costs.

Ordered
That the Judgment of the Superior Court of Judicature, Court of Assize and
in the case of Jeremiah Olney Plaintiff in
Jail Delivery for the County of Providence in the State of Rhode Island be
error against Edward Dexter
reversed[157] with costs.

Ordered that the Decree of the Circuit Court for the District of New York in the case of the United States against the Schooner La Vengeance and Jean Antoine Bernard de Rozier be affirmed: and a special mandate is awarded.

John Brown Cutting, Admᵒr of
Ann Paul Emanuel Sigismund de
Montmorency Luxembourg } In case
    against
The State of South Carolina

Ordered
That the Plaintiff in this cause do file his declaration on or before the 10ᵗʰ day of September next.

157. The first ''r'' is written over an ''a.''

Ordered

/// That certified copies of the said declaration be served on the Governor and Attorney General ~~General~~ of the State of South Carolina on or before the 1ˢᵗ of November, next.

Ordered

That unless the said State shall either in due form appear or shew cause to the contrary in this court by the first day of the next term Judgment by default be entered against the said State.

Ordered

///   decree   for

That the ~~Ju_dgment~~ of the Circuit Court ~~of~~ ₍for₎ South Carolina District in the
                                      Plaintiffs in. error

case of Claude Delcol and others ₍against₎ against Jonathan Arnold be affirmed with costs: and a special mandate is awarded.

Ordered

///   Emory

That the case of Samuel ~~Er_ror~~ against David S. Grenough be continued until the next term.

Ordered

/// That the case of Thomas Fennimore against the United States be continued.

Adjourned till to morning at nine OClock.

Friday Morning
12 Augᵗ 1796

Pursuant to adjournment the Court met this morning at the City Hall, to wit,

The ħnble Oliver Ellsworth, Esquire, Chief Justice

The H̄nble { William Cushing / James Wilson / James Iredell and / William Paterson ~~and~~ / ~~Samuel Chase~~ } Esquires Associate Justices

Proclamation is made and the court is opened

Ordered

                                      Georgia

That the Decree of the Circuit Court ~~ofor~~ ~~South Ca_rolina~~ District in the case of The Ship Elizabeth and cargo and Hills, May, and Woodbridge Plain-
                                    on

tiffs in error against Walter Ross, ₍defendant₎[158] in error ₍be₎ rever sed;

158. An "e" appears beneath the "a."

as same respects the said Hills, May, and Woodbridge

and it is further ordered that the said Hills May and Woodbridge pay to the said Walter Ross ~~three~~ thirty two thousand and ninety dollars and fifty eight cents the nett amount of the sales of the cargo of the said Ship and five thousand six hundred and five dollars and twelve cents interest thereon from the sixth day of June in the year one thousand seven hundred and ninety ~~six~~ four to the twelfth day of August one thousand seven hundred and ninety six, making together the sum of thirty seven thousand six hundred and ninety five dollars and seventy cents ~~with costs of suit~~: and that the said Hills, May and Woodbridge do[159] pay the costs of suit: and a special mandate is awarded for execution.

Ordered,

That when process at common law or in equity shall issue against a State, the same shall be served ~~on~~ on the Governor or Chief Executive Magistrate and Attorney General of such State.

Ordered,

                   out

That process of subpœna issuing ^ of ~~a~~ this court in any suit in equity shall be served on the defendant, sixty days before the return day of the said process: and further, that if the defendant on such service of the Subpœna shall not appear at the return day contained therein; the complainant shall be at Liberty to proceed ex parte.

Ordered

That the Decree of the Circuit Court of the United States in ~~the~~ and for the Virginia District in the case of Wisecart against Dauchy be affirmed with costs: and a special Mandate is awarded.

M.ʳ Lewis withdrew his motion for a Distringas to compel the State of Virginia to appear and answer the bill filed on the Equity side of this Court by William Grayson and others. He then moved that an alias subpœna might issue; which was granted.

The Court proceeded to hear the argument of Counsel in the cases of Louis Arcambal against Joseph Wiseman, and Joseph Wiseman against Louis Arcambal; whereupon it was ordered, That the decree of the Circuit Court of the
            in and for the Rhode Island District
United States ^ in the said two Causes be affirmed with costs: and a special Mandate is awarded.

Adjourned to the time and place by law appointed.

---

159. The "d" is written over a "t."

At the City Hall, in the City of Philadelphia (being the present seat of the National Government of the United States) on Monday the sixth day of February one thousand seven hundred and ninety ~~six~~ seven and in the twenty first year of the Independence of the United States, the Court met:

Present

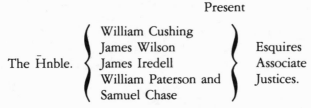

The Hnble. {
William Cushing
James Wilson
James Iredell
William Paterson and
Samuel Chase
} Esquires Associate Justices.

Proclamation is made and the court is opened.

The jury, returned by the Marshall for the District of Pennsylvania in virtue of a venire facias to him for that purpose, being called, Isaac Duncan, John Cooke, Adam Zantzinger, John Reily, John Massey, Francis West, Jacob Sperry, James Campbell, Joseph Sommerl, Abraham Kintzing, Charles Ross, John Miller jun.ʳ John Paul, John Davis, Jacob Park, Godfrey Twells, Thomas Ryerson, Henry Rice, Charles Gillchrist, James Bringhurst, Israel Cope, William Miller, Abijah Dawes, Thomas Archer, Thomas Attmore, John R. Baker, Paul Beck jun.ʳ David Callighan, Samuel Clarkson, George R. Chapman and Joseph Claiborn severally made default, and James Cresson was excused from attendance.

†
†   The case of Lee of Gist vs. Robinett is continued to the next term.

On motion, James Gibson and Asher Robbins were admitted and sworn Counsellors of this Court,

Adjourned till to morrow morning at ten OClock

Tuesday Morning
7 Feb.ʸ 1797.

Pursuant to adjournment the court met this morning at the City Hall, to wit,

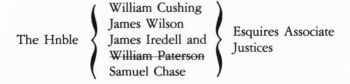

The Hnble {
William Cushing
James Wilson
James Iredell and
~~William Paterson~~
Samuel Chase
} Esquires Associate Justices

Proclamation is made and the Court is opened

The court proceeded to hear the argument of Counsel in the case of Fennimore vs. The United States

Chauncy Goodrich, Pierpoint Edwards, and Henry Wikoff were admitted and sworn, as Counsellors of this court.

On motion of M͏ͬ Goodrich, the cause of B Calder against Bull is continued till the next term —

Adjourned till tomorrow morning at ten OClock

Wednesday Morning
8͏ᵗʰ February 1797.

Pursuant to adjournment the court met this morning at the City Hall, to wit

The Hnble.
$\left\{\begin{array}{l} \text{William Cushing} \\ \text{James Wilson} \\ \text{James Iredell} \\ \text{William Paterson and} \\ \text{Samuel Chase} \end{array}\right\}$ Esquires Associate Justices.

Proclamation is made and the Court is opened.

John Brown Cutting Adm̄or of
the Prince of Luxembourg
vs.
The State of South Carolina
$\left.\phantom{\begin{array}{l}x\\x\\x\\x\end{array}}\right\}$ Case.

On motion ˄ Ordered
        of M͏ͬ Ingersoll for the Plaintiff
That Judgment by default be entered against the defendant.[160]

Hunter
vs
Fairfax
$\left.\phantom{\begin{array}{l}x\\x\\x\end{array}}\right\}$ the Attorney General joins in error.

Brown
vs
Van Braam
$\left.\phantom{\begin{array}{l}x\\x\\x\end{array}}\right\}$ M͏ͬ Barnes joins in error.

Wilson
vs.
Daniel
$\left.\phantom{\begin{array}{l}x\\x\\x\end{array}}\right\}$ M͏ͬ Tilghman moved to quash the writ of error in this cause, on account of the subject of dispute not being of such an amount as to give jurisdiction to this court. — Motion dismissed.

Adjourned till to morrow morning at ten OClock.

---

160. The "a" is written over an "e."

Thursday Morning
9 Feb.ʸ 1797.

Pursuant to adjournment the court met this morning at the City Hall, to wit,

The Hnble. { James Wilson
            James Iredell
            William Paterson and
            Samuel Chase } Esquires
                           Associate
                           Justices

Proclamation is made and the court is opened.

The Court proceeded to hear the argument of Counsel in the case of Brown vs. Van Braam.

David Howell was admitted and sworn a Counsellor of this court.

The jury were dismissed for the remainder of the session.

Adjourned till to morrow morning at 1OClock.[161]

~~Wedn~~
Friday Morning
10ᵗʰ Feb.ʸ 1797.

Pursuant to adjournment the court met this morning at the City Hall, to wit,

The Hnble. { James Wilson
            James Iredell
            William Paterson and
            Samuel Chase } Esquires Associate
                           Justices.

Proclamation is made and the court is opened.

The Court proceeded to hear the argument of Counsel in the case of Brown vs. Van Braam.

Cutting
    vs
The State of South Carolina[162]

On motion of Mʳ Dallas of Counsel for the with Plaintiff a writ of enquiry of damages is awarded to enquire at the bar of this court what damages the Plaintiff has sustained by reason &ᶜ and that three months notice be given to the Governor and Attorney General of South Carolina of the holding of said enquiry.

---

161. The clerk entered the time as it appears above but may have meant to write "10 OClock."
162. The words "Cutting vs The State of South Carolina" were squeezed into the left margin.

Huger et al.	Rule for a commission to be directed to John
vs.	Julius Pringle, Henry William Dessaussure;
The State of Georgia et al.	Timothy Ford, and Thomas Parker or any
	three or two of them, to examine witnesses

in the State of South Carolina.

Rule for a commission to be directed to Joseph Clay junior, John Y. Noel, George Woodruff and   Stevens, or any three or two of them, to examine witnesses in the State of Georgia.

Rule for a commission to be directed to Joseph Read, John Hallowell, John D. Coxe and Michael Keppele or any three or two of them, to examine witnesses in the State of Pennsylvania

The Court proceeded to hear the argument of Counsel in the case of Jennings et al. vs. The Brig Perseverence et al.

~~Ordered by consent, That the case of Dorrance vs. Van Horne's lee be continued~~.

Adjourned till to morning at 10 OClock.

Saturday Morning
11th Feby 1797 —

Pursuant to adjournment the Court met this morning, to wit,

The Hnble {
William Cushing
James Wilson
James Iredell
William Paterson and
Samuel Chase
} Esquires Associate Justices

Proclamation is made and the court is opened

Hunter	On motion of Mr Lee for the defendant rule to argue the cause on
vs	the 13th instant, or writ of error to be nonpross'd.
Fairfax	

Ordered,[163]

That the ~~Decree of~~ Judgment of the High Court of Appeals for the State of Maryland in the case of James Clerke, Adm^{or} of James Russell, against Richard Harwood Junr be reversed, and that the judgment of the General Court of Maryland in the same cause be in all things affirmed, and that the said James Clerke recover against the said Richard Harwood his costs about

---

163. A penciled rule is placed between "nonpross'd" and "Ordered."

the same suit expended, in the General Court _& Court of Appeals of Maryland
and ~~of~~ _{in} this Court: and a sp.ᴸ. Mand. to Genˡ Cᵗ

Adjourned till Monday Morning next at ten OClock.

Monday Morning
13ᵗʰ Febʸ 1797.

Pursuant to adjournment the Court met this morning, to wit,

The Hnble. { William Cushing
James Wilson
James Iredell
William Paterson and
Samuel Chase } Esquires Associate Justices

Proclamation is made and the Court is opened.

Vassall
vs.
The State of Massachusetts }

Ordered That this cause be dismissed with costs.

Hunter
vs
Fairfax }

On motion of Mᵣ Lee for the defendant Ordered, That this cause be non
pross'd _{with costs} under the rule of Saturday the 11ᵗʰ instant —

Brown
vs
Van Braam }

Ordered That the Judgment of the Circuit Court for the District of Rhode
Island be affirmed with costs, and interest at the rate of six per cent per annum
from the day of rendering the said judgment until this day, by way of damages.

Fennimore
vs.
The United States } ~~Rule for certiorari on a~~
~~suggestion of diminution =~~

~~Edward Tilghman Esqᵣ appears as Coun~~

Rule for certiorari on a suggestion of diminution.

Grayson) On motion of M͏ͬ Lewis for the Complainant, Rule for a commission
   vs.   } to be directed to Charles Smith, John Hubley and William Mont-
Virginia) gomery, Esquires, or any two of them, to examine witnesses in the
            borough of Lancaster in the State of Pennsylvania

Rule for a commission to be directed to David Watts, William Alexander and John Lyon Esquires or any two of them, to examine witnesses in the borough of Carlisle in the State of Pennsylvania

Rule for a commission to be directed to John Woods, John Wilkins and George Wallace Esquires or any two of them, to examine witnesses in the town of Pittsburg in the State of Pennsylvania.

Rule for a commission to be directed to Daniel Delany, James Gibson, and William Smith, Esquires, or any two of them to examine witnesses in the City of Philadelphia.

Rule for a commission to be directed to the Honorable Samuel J. Cabal and Wilson Cary Nicholas Esquire, to examine witnesses in the State of Virginia

Rule for a commission to be directed to William Morton, William Murray and Andrew Holmes Esquires, or any two of them to examine witnesses in the State of Kentucky.

Wilson) M͏ͬ Tilghman appears as Counsel for the defendant, waves all ex-
  vs.   }   and
Daniel) ception to the writ of error and citation ˄ alleges diminution of the
         record; and

            Rule ~~rule~~ by consent that a certiorari be issued to either party as he shall elect; but it is understood that the defendant be at liberty to withdraw his allegation of diminution and proceed to argument on the record as it now stands.

Jennings et al.
   vs.   }
The Brig Perseverance et al)

    Ordered
          Decree
That the ~~Judgment~~ of the Circuit Court for the District of Rhode Island be affirmed with costs, and damages at the rate of six per cent. per annum on the proceeds arising from the sales of the said Brigantine and her cargo, after deducting the duties paid in the custom house on the said cargo and the com-
                      such
mission on the sales, ~~t~~he interest to be calculated from the day of rendering the said decree until this day.

On motion, Robert G. Harper was admitted and sworn a Counsellor of this Court.

It is ordered by the Court, That the Clerk of the Court, to which any writ of error shall be directed, may make return of the same by transmitting a true copy of the record and of all proceedings in the cause under his hand and the seal of the Court.

All the unfinished business is continued to the next term.

Adjourned to the time and place by law appointed.

At the City Hall in the City of Philadelphia on Monday the 7ᵗʰ day of August 1797 and in the twenty second day of year of the independence of the United States, the court met:

Present

The hnble Oliver Ellsworth Esqʳ Chief Justice

The hnble ⎰ William Cushing ⎱
           ⎱ James Iredell ⎰ Associate Justices
             William Paterson and
             Samuel Chase

Proclamation is made and the Court is opened

The Marshall for the Pennsylvania District makes return of a venire facias j[uratores?] to him directed for summoning a petit jury, which was filed; and the jury being called Alexander Cockrane, Derrick Peterson, Jesse Sharpless, Benjamin Scull, William Gibbs, Charles Massey, Francis West, Robert Westcott, William Colloday, Patrick Moore, Richard Mather[,] Pearson Hunt, John Whitehead, John Graham, Joseph Spencer, Raper Hoskins, Samuel Shaw junʳ Joshua B. Bond, John Aitkin, Jacob Knorr, John Henderson Philip Hagner, Joseph Davidson, George Davis, Gavin Hamilton, John Taggert, Charles French, Nathan Field, George Lauman, Joseph Harbeson, Samuel Fulton, Samuel Shoemaker[,] George David Seckel, James Bacon, William Wood, Edward Smith, David Knox, James Simpson, Joseph Hertzog, John Morrell and Henry Muhlenberg severally made default.

It is ordered by the Court, That no record of the Court be suffered by the Clerk to be taken out of his office but by the consent of the Court; otherwise to be responsible for it.

Hollingsworth et al. vs
       vs.   ⎬ is continued to the next term
The State of Virginia

Lee of Gist ⎰ On motion of Mʳ Ingersoll, Rule upon the Clerk of the District
     vs.   ⎬ Court of Kentucky District to shew cause, why the record is not
Robinett   ⎱ returned.

Calder ⎫
  vs. ⎬ continued by consent.
Bull ⎭

The Court proceeded to hear the argument of Counsel in the case of Fennimore vs. The United States, which being concluded it was ordered by the Court,[164] that the Judgment of the Circuit Court be affirmed with costs.

Adjourned to ten OClock tomorrow morning.

Tuesday Morning 8 Augᵗ 1797.

Pursuant to adjournment the Court met this morning at the City Hall, viz.

The Hnble ̲ Oliver Ellsworth Esqʳ Chief Justice

The Hnble. ⎧ William Cushing ⎫ Esquires
⎨ James Iredell ⎬ Associate
⎩ William Paterson ⎭ Justices
    Samuel Chase

Proclamation is made and the Court is opened

The Court ordered the enquiry of damages in the case of Cutting vs. The State of South Carolina to be now executed at the bar of the Court; and the jury being called come, to wit; William Kinley, James Cruckshank, Robert Westcott, William Harlan, William Brown, Joseph Spencer, ~~John~~ George Heberton, Samuel Richards, Gavin Hamilton, Job Butcher, Thomas Rogers &[165]
impannelled
William Wood; who being ~~ele̲cted tried and~~ sworn and affirmed respectively, [~~upon~~] [*letters inked out*] well and truly to enquire what damages the said Pltff ̲ hath sustained by reason of the non performance of certain promises set forth in his declaration against the said State of South Carolina, defendant, and to give a true verdict according to evidence, upon their oaths and affirmations
        find for the Plaintiff   & 84 Cts
respectively do say that they ̲ 55002. Doll. ̲ damages and ~~eight damages and 8 Cts cost~~[s]. by reason of &ᶜ ~~and judgment~~ [is].

The Court proceeded to hear the argument of counsel in the case of Brown vs. Barry.

Adjourned till to morrow morning at 10 OClock

---

164. The letters "Fe" appear beneath "Cou."
165. The "&" is written over a comma.

Wednesday Morning 9 Aug.ᵗ 1797.

Pursuant to adjournment the Court met this morning at the City Hall, viz.

The Hnble Oliver Ellsworth Esquire Chief Justice

The Hnble ⎰ William Cushing ⎱ Esquires Associate
          ⎰ James Iredell   ⎱ Justices.
          ⎰ William Paterson ⎱
          ⎱ Samuel Chase   ⎰

Proclamation is made and the Court is opened.

The Court proceeded to hear the argument of Counsel in the case of Brown vs_ Barry.

Adjourned till to morrow morning at 10 OClock.

Thursday Morning 10 Aug.ᵗ 1797.

Pursuant to adjournment the Court met this morning at the City Hall in the City of Philadelphia, viz.

The Honble_ Oliver Ellsworth Esq.ʳ Chief Justice

The Honble. ⎰ William Cushing   ⎱ Esquires
            ⎰ James Iredell   ⎱ Associate
            ⎰ William Paterson and ⎱ Justices
            ⎱ Samuel Chase   ⎰

~~Pur~~ Proclamation is made and the Court is opened.

Franklin et al. ⎫
     vs.   ⎬ is continued by consent.
Rotch et al.   ⎭

The Court proceeded to hear the argument of Counsel in the case of Emory vs. Greenough.

Hamilton et al ⎫ On motion of M.ʳ E. Tilghman rule to shew cause why the
     vs.   ⎬ writ of error should not be amended; and on motion of
Moore   ⎭ M.ʳ Dallas rule to shew cause why the writ of error should
                 not be quashed.

Adjourned till to morrow morning at 10[166] OClock.

166. A "9" appears beneath the "1."

Friday Morning 11 Aug.ᵗ 1797 _

Pursuant to adjournment the Court met this morning at the City Hall, viz.

The Hoñble. Oliver Ellsworth Esq.ʳ Chief Justice

The Hoñble
{
William Cushing
James Iredell
William Paterson and
Samuel Chase
}
Esquires
Associate
Justices

Proclamation[167] is made and the Court is opened.

The Court proceeded to hear the argument of Counsel in the case of Emory vs. Greenough.

On motion of M.ʳ Ingersoll rule for final judgment in the case of Cutting vs. The State of South Carolina.

On motion of M.ʳ Ingersoll rule for publication of the commission returned from South Carolina in the case of Moultrie et al. vs. The State of Georgia et al.

Adjourned till to morrow morning at 10 OClock.

Saturday Morning
12ᵗʰ Aug.ᵗ 1797.

Pursuant to adjournment the Court met this morning at the City Hall, viz.

The Hoñble. Oliver Ellsworth Esq.ʳ Chief Justice

The Hoñble
{
William Cushing
James Iredell
William Paterson and
Samuel Chase
}
Esquires
Associate
Justices

Proclamation is made and the Court is opened.

The Court proceeded to hear the argument of Counsel in the case of Emory vs. Greenough.

Adjourned till to morrow morning at 10 OClock _

167. The letters "lc" appear beneath "cl."

Monday Morning 14 Augt 1797.

Pursuant to adjournment the Court met this morning at the City Hall, to wit:

The Hoñble Oliver Ellsworth Esqr Chief Justice

The Honble. { William Cushing / James Iredell / William Paterson and / Samuel Chase } Esquires Associate Justices.

Proclamation is made and the Court is opened:

The Court proceeded to hear the argument of Counsel in the case of Emory vs. Greenough.

Adjourned till to morrow morning at 10 OClock —

Tuesday Morning 15 Augt 1797.

Pursuant to adjournment the Court met this morning at the City Hall, to wit:

The Hnble Oliver Ellsworth Esqr Chief Justice

The Hoñble { William Cushing / James Iredell / William Paterson and / Samuel Chase } Esquires, Associate Justices.

Proclamation is made and the Court is opened.

The State of South Carolina
   vs.
The French Republic and John } Bill in equity
Brown Cutting, Adm̃or of of the
Prince of Luxembourg

It is ordered by the Court, that injunction be awarded to stay all further proceedings on t̲he judgment rendered at this present term, in an action upon the case of John B. Cutting as Administrator of the Prince of Luxembourg against the State of South Carolina, until the first day of January next; and it is further ordered by the Court, that injunction also be awarded to stay all further proceedings on said judgment until the further order of this court upon this condition, that the said State of South Carolina shall, on or before the said first day of January next; bring into this court the sum of ten thousand eight hundred and fifty five pounds eight shillings and five pence sterling money of

equal to[168]
the State of South Carolina ^ together with the interest on the same at the rate of seven per cent per annum from the thirteenth day of March one thousand seven hundred and eighty nine to the time of payment into court excepting and deducting from the amount of interest one thousand pounds of like money already paid to the said John Brown Cutting (which the said state by her bill exhibited in this court has acknowledged to be due and owing from her to the legal representative of the said Prince of Luxembourg or to the French Republic and has offered to deposit the same in this court) and shall deposit the same in this court subject to its further order and such decree as it may make respecting the same; and shall at the same time pay into this court the costs in the above action.

Brown
vs   Ordered that the judgment of the Circuit Court
Barry   be affirmed with costs.

Same
vs   same order.
same

same
vs   same order.
same

same
vs —   Ordered, that the judgment of the Circuit Court
same   be affirmed with costs

same
vs.   same order.
same

same
vs.   same order.
same

Moultrie et al.
vs.   On motion of William Tilghman Esq[r] it is or-
The State of Georgia et al.   dered, that the papers annexed to the com-
                              mission issued to Joseph Clay junior and oth-
                              ers of the State of Georgia for the
examination of witnesses in this cause in the said State be detached from the said commission and annexed to the commission issued to John D. Coxe and others of Pennsylvania to take the examination of witnesses in the said cause in the city of Philadelphia —

168. Wagner left a blank for the equivalent amount in dollars.

Emory
vs.   } continued by consent.
Greenough

Dorrance
vs.   } continued.
Van Horne's lee,

Wilson
vs.   } continued
Daniel

Moultrie et al.
vs.   } continued; and on motion of William Tilgh-
The State of Georgia et al.   man Esq[r] rule for publication of the commis-
sion directed to Michael Keppele and others
to examine witnesses in the City of Philadel-
phia, as soon as it is returned.

Court et al.
vs.   } Ordered that the judgment of the High Court of Appeals of
Van Bibber   the State of Maryland be reversed and that the judgment of
the General Court of Maryland in the same cause be in all
things affirmed, and that the said Christopher Court and Com-
pany recover against the said Isaac Van Bibber as terretenant of Mark Alex-
ander his costs about the same suit expended in the General Court and Court
of Appeals of Maryland and in this Court and a special Mandate is awarded
to the General Court.

Court et al.
vs.   } Ordered, That the judgment of the High Court of appeals
Wells   of the State of Maryland be reversed and that the judgment
of the General Court of Maryland in the same cause be in all
things affirmed and that the said Christopher Court and com-
pany recover against the said Cyprian Wells as terretenant of Mark Alexander
their[169] costs about the same suit expended in the General Court and Court of
appeals of Maryland and in this court; and a special mandate is awarded to the
General Court.

Court et al.
vs.   } Ordered, That the judgment of the High Court of appeals
Robinson et al _   of the State of Maryland be reversed and that the judgment
of the General Court of Maryland in the same cause be in
all things affirmed and that the said Christopher Court and
company recover against the said C̶y̶ Andrew Robinson and Alexander Robin-
son, terretenants of Mark Alexander, their costs about the same suit expended
in the General Court and Court of Appeals of Maryland and in this Court;
and a special Mandate is awarded to the General Court.

169. The letters "is" appear beneath "ei."

Pepoon et al. vs. Jenkins.	M̶r̶ ̶T̶il̶ Edward Tilghman Esqr appears for the defendant in error, and the cause is continued by consent.
Clerke et al. vs. Russell	Mr Ingersoll assigns the general errors and the cause is continued.
Hamilton et al. vs. Moore	Ordered, That the writ of error be non-pros'd.

All the unfinished business is continued to the next term.

Adjourned to the time and place by law appointed.

David Caldwell's Rough Notes and
Samuel Bayard's Expanded Notes for
Fine Minutes
February 1798 Term

David Caldwell's Rough Notes for Fine Minutes —————
February 1798 Term

6. Feb: 1798.

Court opened &c.

Present as Yesterday —

On Motion of the honorable Uriah Tracy— the honble Peleg Sprague of the
State of New-Hampshire is admitted as an ~~Attorney of~~ Counsellor of this Court
and takes the Oath in that Case prescribed to[170] be taken

Nathaniel Russell $\Big\}$ Sur App. f^rm Circ^t C^t
vs   Rhode Island D^t
Clarke & Nightingale

The Court proceed to hear the Argument of Counsel in this Cause—
Mr Edwards for Plffs. Mr Dexter Dft.

adj^d to ten tomorrow

7th Feb: 1798.

Court opened &c—

Present The Honble. William Cushing $\Big\}$
            James Iredell   Associate
            William Paterson &   Justices—
            Samuel Chase

Russel $\Big\}$
vs
Clarke & Nightingale

---

170. The word "by" was written first and then altered to read "to."

The Court proceeds to hear the Argument of Counsel in this Cause_ to wit_ M͞ ̶D̶e̶x̶t̶e̶r̶ Edward Tilghman for Dfts. and M͞ Ingersoll for Plff_

adj^d to 10. Tomorrow_

8^th171 Feb: 1798.

Court is opened &c. Present as Yesterday

Russel
vs
Clarke & Nightingale }

Ordered that the Judgment of the Circuit Court of the United States in and for the Rhode-Island District be reversed_ and a Venire facias de novo is awarded_

̶I̶t̶ ̶i̶s̶ ̶s̶u̶g̶g̶e̶s̶t̶e̶d̶ ̶t̶h̶a̶t̶ The Death of Joseph Nightingale is suggested_

Jared Ingersoll
On Motion of ̶E̶d̶w̶a̶r̶d̶ ̶T̶i̶l̶g̶h̶ ̶m̶a̶n̶ Esquire. the honble William Gordon Esquire of New-Hampshire is admitted as a Counsellor of this Court.

Calder
vs
Bull }

The^172 Death of Caleb Bull one of the Defendants is suggested by M͞ Edwards

and the Court proceed to hear the Arguments of Counsel in this
M͞ Edwards
Cause_ to wit ^ _ for Plff

John Coffin Jones.
vs
P. Letombe Consul &c. }

Deposition of Plff. filed_

9. Feb: 1798.

Court open[s] &c.

Present as Yesterday

Jones
vs
LeTombe }

---

171. The "8" is written over a "7."
172. "The" is written over "It is."

Ordered that the Rule to shew Cause entered in this Cause on the first Day of the Session be corrected as follows —

On Motion of M.ʳ Dallas —

Rule to shew Cause why the Dft. should not be discharged upon entering a Common Appearance —

And the Court proceed to hear the Argument of Counsel thereupon to wit — of M.ʳ Ingersoll — for Plff.

Ordered that the Def.ᵗ be discharged upon entering a Common Appearance —

M.ʳ Edward Livingston appears for the Deft: by Direction of M.ʳ Duponceau —

Pepoon et al)
   vs   }
Jenkins   )

The Court proceeds to hear the Argument of Counsel in this Cause — to wit. of M.ʳ Dexter for the Plaintiff —

10. Feb: 1798.

Court opened &c. present as Yesterday —

Proclamation being made the Persons summoned and returned to serve as Petit-Jurors are respectively called — and the following Persons appear to wit — and the Petit-Jury is thereupon discharged for the Remainder of the Session —

Pepoon et al)
   vs   }
Jenkins   )

The Court proceed to hear the further Arg.ᵗˢ of Counsel in the Cause to wit of M.ʳ E. Tilghman for Dft.

13. Feb: 1798 —

Court opened &c — Present as Yesterday —

Calder)
  vs   }
Bull   )

The Court proceeds to hear the Arguments of Counsel in this Cause to wit — of M.ʳ Nathaniel Smith for and th[e] Def.ᵗ M.ʳ Tracey — for Dft.

Wilson)
  vs   }
Daniel)

The Court proceed to hear the Arguments of Counsel in this C[au]se _ to wit M.r E. Tilghman _ for Plff. & the Atty Gen! M.r Lee for the Def.t

Bingham
  vs
Cabot

The Court proceed to hear the Arguments of Counsel in this Cause. to wit the Atty Gen! M.r Lee for Plff _ And of M.r Dexter for Dft.

14. Feb: 1798.

Court opened &c. Present as Yesterday _

~~In all Cases of Equity~~ _ Hollingsworth vs Virg.a

The Court is of opinion _ that on Consideration of the Amendment of the Constitution respecting Suits against States _ it has no Jurisdiction of this Cause _ It is therefore considered by the Court that the Bill be dismissed _

Moultrie et al.
  vs
Georgia. et al.

Same Entry with the Addition of. "so far as respects the State of Georgia _ "

Brailsford
  vs
Georgia

The Court is of Opinion _ that on Consideration of the Amendm.t of the Constitution respecting Suits against States it has no Jurisdiction of this Cause _ It is therefore considered by the Court that this Suit be discontinued _

S.o Carolina
  vs
Cutting

continued by Consent _

Pepoon
  vs
Jenkins

Ordered that the Decree ^of_____ be affirmed _

Bingham
  vs
Cabot

of _____
Ordered that the Judgment ˄ be reversed —

Wilson ⎫
vs   ⎬
Daniel ⎭

continued

Calder ⎫
vs   ⎬
Bull   ⎭

Continued

Emory   ⎫
vs   ⎬   continued
Greenough ⎭

Gist   ⎫
vs   ⎬   continued
Robinett ⎭

Dorance   ⎫
vs   ⎬   Continued
Van Horne ⎭

Gist   ⎫
vs   ⎬
Robinett ⎭

On Motion of Mʳ Ingersoll — Rule upon the Clerk of the District Court of Kentucky District to shew Cause why the Record is not returned —

Clarke et al. ⎫
vs   ⎬
Russel   ⎭

Ordered that the Judgment of _____ be reversed with Costs —

Moutrie et al ⎫
vs   ⎬   continued
             ⎭

On Motion of Mʳ W. Tilghman for Plff. Leave to amend —

Moultrie[173] ⎫
vs   ⎬
_____   ⎭

173. From this point, Caldwell wrote the entries for February 14 on a separate slip of paper headed "Wēnsday 14 Feb: 1798."

W. Tilghman

M: ~~Dexte_r~~ for

~~Mr Moul~~

On Motion ~~of M: M~~ the Plff ordered that the Bill filed in this Cause
filed be dismissed
~~be filed~~ without Prejudice ___

Emory

vs

Greenough

Ordered that the Judgment of _____ be reversed ___

All unfinished Business con:

adj° to Time & Place by Law appointed.

Samuel Bayard's Expanded Notes for Fine Minutes ———
February 1798 Term

At the City Hall in the city of Philadᵃ on monday the 5.ᵗʰ day of Febʸ in
the year of our Lord one thousand seven hundred & ninety eight ___ & in the
twenty second year of the independence of the U. S. the Sup. Court of the
U S. met agreeably to Law ___

Present. ___

The Honbˡˢ

W. Cushing.
James Iredell
W. Paterson ___ &
SamˡChase

Esqʳˢ Associate[174] Justᵉˢ

Proclamation is made & the Court is open'd

The Marshall for the Pensylvania Dis: makes return of a venire facias to him
directed for summoning a petit Jury, which is fil'd & the jury being called the
following persons only appear ___ Viz: Rob: Ralston. Geo. Fox[,] Jos. Crukshank, William. Ward. Burrows ___ John Fries ___ Zaccheus Collins Rob: Smith[,]
John Craig. James Barrand, [Pa]ttison Hartshorne And the said pettit jury is
discharg'd until Saturday next ___

On motion of Charles Lee Esq: the Honᵇˡ Uriah Tracy is admitted & sworn
as a counsellor of this Court ___

---

174. A "t" appears beneath the second "a."

John Coffin Jones.   } In Case
    vs   The Marshall for the Pennsylvania District returns
Citizen Jos. Philippe   the writ of capias ad respondendum in this cause
Letombe — Consul Gen!   issued &ret^{ble} here this day as follows —
of the French Republic   C. C.   B. B. so answers —
                        William Nicholls. Marshall,

On Motion of Mr Dallas — Rule that the Pltff shew cause why the defendant should not be discharg'd on Common bail & friday next is appointed for the arg^t of the Rule.

Wilson.   }
   vs   }   Writ of Certiorari to the Circuit
Daniel   }   Court of Virginia returne'd —

Pepoon & als. }
    v^s   }   Mr Tilghman joins in Error —
Jenkins   }

Bingham. }   Mr E. Tilghman appears as Counsel
   vs.   }   for the defendant in Error & joins
Cabot   }   in Error —

The Court adjourns until to morrow morn^g at 10 oclock —

Tuesday Morn^g 6. Feby 1798.

Pursuant to adjourn^t the Court met this morn^g — viz. —

               W. Cushing Esqr }
The Hon^{bls} —   J. Iredell   }
              W. Patterson   }   Esq^{rs} Associate Justices
              S. Chase   }

Proclamation is made & the Court is open'd —

On motion of the Hon^{bl} Uriah Tracy Esq. the Honb^{le} Peleg Sprague of the State of New-Hampshire is admitted & sworn as a Counsellor of this Court —

Franklin & al^s }
    vs   }   Sur. writ of error to the Circ^t
Rotch et als. }   Court of New York —

It is agreed by writing this day filed that the writ of error be withdrawn & the action closed upon condition, that Wm T. Robinson, give bond for the pay^t of three thousand two hundred dollars — payable the 5th of 3rd month next (5 March) in New York or in. failure hereof that Sam^lFranklin &C^o pay the Judg^t of the Circuit Court at New York in this case — the Defendan^{ts} to be exempt from all costs —

Clarke ⎫
  vs ⎬ Sur writ of error ~~from~~ ^to^ the ~~Cl~~
Russell ⎭ Circuit Court of Rhode Island

The Court proceeds to hear the arguments of Mr Edwards of Counsel for the Plaintiffs & of Mr Dexter of Counsel for the defend.^t^

The Court adjourns until to morrow Morn.^g^ at 10 o'clock —

Wednesday. Morn.^g^ 7. Feby 1798.

Pursuant to adjourn.^t^ — the Court met this morn.^g^ to wit —

The Honb.^les^ ⎰ W. Cushing ⎱ Esq.^rs^ Associate Justices —
           ⎱ J. Iredell ⎰
             W. Paterson &
             S. Chase

Clarke ⎫ The Court proceeds to hear the Arguments of Counsel in this cause
 vs. ⎬ to wit of Mr E. Tilghman for the defendant — & of Mr Ingersoll
Russell ⎭ for the Plaintiffs —

Wilson ⎫ Certiorari to the Circ.^t^ Court of the
  vs ⎬ Virginia district — return'd & filed —
Daniel ⎭

Brailsford ⎫
   vs   ⎬ Declaration filed ㄆ Morgan Att.^y^
Georgia ⎭

The Court adjourns until to morrow morn.^g^ at 10 o'clock —

Thursday 8. Feby 1798.

Pursuant to adjourn.^t^ the Court met this morn.^g^ to wit —

The Honble ⎰ W. Cushing. ⎱ Esq.^rs^ associate Justices —
             James Iredell
             W. Paterson. &
             S. Chase

Clarke & al. ⎫ The Court proceeds to hear the further arguments of Coun-
   vs   ⎬ sel in this cause to wit of Mr Ingersoll for the Pltfs.
Russell ⎭

Order'd — that the Judgment of the Circuit Court of the U. S. in & for Rhode Island Dist. of the Eastern Circuit be <u>reversed</u> — & — a venire facias de Novo is awarded —

the death of Joseph Nightingale is suggested —

On motion of Jared Ingersoll Esq.ʳ the Hon.ᵇˡ W. Gordon of the State of New Hampshire is admitted & sworn as a counsellor this Court —

Calder
 v̄s   } The death of Caleb Bull is suggested —
Bull

The Court proceeds to hear the arguments of Counsel in this cause — to wit of M.ʳ ~~Ingersoll~~ Edwards for the Pltff —

Jones.
 v̄s   } The deposition of the Plaintiff taken before the Judge of the Massachusetts Dist.ʳ is opened by the Court & filed —
Letombe

The Court adjourns until to morrow at 10. o'clock —

[———————————]

Friday. 9. Feb.ʸ 1798.

Pursuant to adjourn.ᵗ —[175] the Court met this morn.ᵍ — to wit — as before —

Jones.
 v̄s.   } Order'd that the rule to shew cause entered in this cause on the first day of this session be corrected as follows —
Letombe

On Motion of M.ʳ Dallas —

Rule to shew cause why the defendant should not be discharged upon entering a common appearance — And the Court proceeds to hear the arguments of Counsel thereupon to wit of M.ʳ Ingersoll for the Plaintiff —

Order'd that the Defd.ᵗ be dischar[ged?] upon entering a common appearance — By direction of M.ʳ Duponceau the appear[ance?] of Edward Livingston Esq.ʳ is entere'd for the Defd.ᵗ —

Pepoon & al.
 v̄s   } The Court proceeds to hear the arguments counsel in this cause to wit — of M.ʳ Dexter for the Plaintiffs —
Jenkins

The Court adjourns until to morrow. at 10 o'clock —

Saturday 10. Feb.ʸ 1798.

Pursuant to adjourn.ᵗ the Court met this morn.ᵍ — Present as before —

The pettit Jury discharg'd to this day being called the following persons only appear to wit Geo. Fox, Josiah. H. Anthony, John Miller Jun.ʳ & James Barr. —

The Pettit Jury is discharg'd for the remainder of the session —

Pepoon & al.
 v̄s   } The Court proceeds to hear the further arg.ᵗˢ of Counsel in this cause viz. of M.ʳ Tilghman for the defd.ᵗˢ —
Jenkins

---

175. An "s" appears below the superscripted "t."

The Court proceeds to hear the arguments of Counsel in support of the Jurisdiction of the Court in suits against States to wit of M.ʳ Tilghman &M.ʳ Rawle — & of the Att.ʸ Gen.ˡ (M.ʳLee) against the Jurisdiction.

The Court adjourns until Monday Morn.ᵍ at 10 o'clock —

Monday Morn.ᵍ 12. Feb.ʸ 1798.

Pursuant to adjourn.ᵗ the Court met this morn.ᵍ —

Present as before

Proclamation is made & the Court open'd

The Court adjourns without proceeding to business until to morrow morn.ᵍ at 10. —

Tuesday. 13. Feb.ʸ 1798.

Pursuant to adjourn.ᵗ the Court met this morn.ᵍ — Present as before —

Proclamation is made & the Court opened —

Calder
v̄ˢ
Bull
} The Court proceeds to hear the arg.ᵗˢ of counsel in this cause — to wit of M.ʳ Nathaniel Smith & M.ʳ Tracy for the Defd.ᵗ —

Wilson
v̄ˢ
Daniel
} The Court proceeds to hear the arguments of Counsel in this Cause upon[176] the allegation of the diminution of the Record — viz. of M.ʳ Tilghman in support of it — & of M.ʳ Lee — (the Attorny Gen.ˡ) &M.ʳ Ingersoll against it —

Bingham
v̄ˢ
Cabot
} The Court proceeds to hear the arguments of Counsel in this cause viz — of the Att.ʸ Gen.ˡ M.ʳ Lee — for the Pltff — & of M.ʳ Dexter for the Defd.ᵗˢ —

The Court adjouns until to morrow morn.ᵍ at 10 o'clock —

Wednesday. Morn.ᵍ — 14. Feb.ʸ 1798.

Pursuant to adjourn.ᵗ the Court met this Morn.ᵍ to wit — Present as before —

Proclamation being made the Court is open'd,

Hollingsworth
v̄s
Virginia
} The Court is opinion that on consideration of the amend.ᵗ of the Constitution respecting suits against States it has no jurisdiction of this cause —

It is therefore consider'd by the Court that this bill be dismissed —

---

176. The letters "up" are written over the letters "int."

Moultrie & al.⎞   The Court is[177] of opinion that on Consideration of the
$\bar{v}^s$ ⎬   amendment of the Constitution respecting suits agai[s]
Georgia &al.   ⎠   States, it has no jurisdiction of this cause

by
It is therefore considered ~~that~~ the Court that this bill be dismissed so far as respects the State of Geogia _

Brailsford ⎞   The Court is of opinion that on consideration of the amend-
$\bar{v}s$ ⎬   ment of the Constitution respecting ~~States~~ suits against States _
Georgia   ⎠   it has no jurisdiction of this cause. _

It is therefore considered by the Court that this ~~Cause~~ suit be discontinu'd _

State of S. Carolina ⎞
$\bar{v}s$ ⎬   Cont^d by consent _
Cutting   ⎠

Pepoon et al. ⎞   Order'd that the decree of the Circuit Court of the
$\bar{v}$ ⎬   U. S. in & for the Massachusetts district, of the Eastern
Jenkins.   ⎠   Circ^t _ be affirm'd _

Bingham ⎞   Order'd that the judg^t of the Circ^t Court of the U S. in & for
v^s ⎬   the Massachusetts district, of the Eastern Circ^t _ be <u>revers'd</u> _
Cabot.   ⎠

Wilson ⎞
v   ⎬   Cont^d _
Daniel ⎠

Calder. ⎞
$\bar{v}$ ⎬   cont^d _
Bull   ⎠

Gist _ $\bar{v}$s. ⎞   Cont^d _
Robinett   ⎠

Dorance   ⎞
$\bar{v}^s$ ⎬   Cont^d _
Vanhorne's Lee ⎠

Gist.   ⎞   on motion ofM^r Ingersoll _
$\bar{v}^s$ ⎬   Rule upon Clerk of the District Court of the U. S. in & for the
Robinett   ⎠   Kentucky Dist. to shew cause why the Record is not return'd

177. The word "of" appears beneath "is."

Clarke et[178] al. }   Order'd that the Judg[t] of the circ[t] Court of the U. S. in
$\bar{v}^s$ & for the Rhode Island district of the Eastern Circuit—
Russell   be reversed—

Moultrie et al. }   On motion of M[r] W. Tilghman
$\bar{v}^s$ for the Plaintiffs—
Georgia et al[s]

Order'd that the Bill filed in this cause be dismiss'd without prejudice—

Emory }   Order'd that the judg[t] of the Circuit Court of the U. S. in &
$\bar{v}s$ for the Massachusetts distr. of the Eastern Circuit— be re-
Grenough   versed—

All the unfinish'd business is continued to the next session—

Adjourn'd to the time & place by laws appointed—

(Minutes of this[179] session made by M[r] David Caldwell— Clerk of Circ[t] Court of Pennsyl[a]).[180]

---

178. The "e" is written over an "a."

179. Originally the clerk wrote "the."

180. David Caldwell did not receive a formal appointment as clerk of the federal district and circuit courts for Pennsylvania until after his father's death on November 26, 1798. David Caldwell did act as clerk, however, during the period when his father's health was declining. (See introduction to, and note 29 for, "The Clerks and Their Record.") It is not known whether Bayard wrote this passage before or after Caldwell's formal appointment.

Samuel Bayard's Rough Notes and Expanded Notes for Fine Minutes August 1798 Term

Samuel Bayard's Rough Notes for Fine Minutes ——————————
August 1798 Term

<u>Minutes of the Sup. Cur. U. S.</u>—

<u>Monday. 6. Aug. 1798.</u>

Present. The Hon^{les}

The Ch. Just. of the U. S. |

W. Cushing.
J. Iredell.
W. Paterson. & } Esq^{rs}—
S. Chase.

Wilson)
v^s   } The Court proceeded to hear M̶r̶ ̶T̶i̶l̶g̶h̶m̶a̶n̶ ̶o̶f̶ ̶c̶o̶u̶n̶s̶e̶l̶ ̶f̶o̶r̶ ̶t̶h̶e̶ &
Daniel) M^rLee the Att^y Genl of the U S & M^rIngersoll on the part of the Plt^{ff} & Mr Tilghman for ye Defe^{ts} in error—

The Court adjournd until to morrow at ten O'clock—

<u>Tuesday. 7. Aug. 1798.</u>

The Court met pursuant to adjo[urnm]t[^{ts}] & proceeded to hear the Counsel in the case of

Wilson.)
v̄s   } Orderd that
Daniel) The sentence of the ^circut Court ^ b̶e̶l̶o̶w̶ ̶b̶e̶ ̶r̶e̶v̶e̶r̶s̶e̶d̶— for the Virginia Dist in said case be reversed—

Jones)
vs   } the cause discontinued by consent
Letombe) of the Plff's Att^y—

f̶o̶r̶ ̶a̶ rule to shew cause. w̶h̶y̶.
^should not issue
M^rLevy. moves f̶o̶r̶ ̶a̶ ̶p̶r̶o̶h̶i̶b̶i̶t̶i̶o̶n̶ ^ to the Circ^t Court— t̶o̶ ̶s̶t̶a̶y̶ ̶p̶r̶o̶c̶e̶e̶d̶i̶n̶g̶s̶ in the case of t̶h̶e̶ U. S. v̄s. B. F. B̶a̶c̶h̶e̶— depend^g in the said C̶o̶u̶r̶t̶—

T̶h̶e̶ ̶C̶o̶u̶r̶t̶ ̶a̶d̶j̶o̶u̶r̶n̶'̶d̶ ̶u̶n̶t̶i̶l̶ ̶t̶o̶ ̶m̶o̶r̶r̶o̶w̶ ̶a̶t̶ ̶1̶0̶ ̶o̶'̶c̶l̶o̶c̶k̶.

Wednesday. 8 Aug. 98

The Court met pursuant to adjournm.ᵗ

Present as before__

Clarke vˢ Russell__ cont.ᵈ by consent.

__Motion ⅌ MʳLewis for a certiorari. to the Judges of the   Court__
of   in the cases of__

Calder ⎱   the Court proceeded to give their opinions seriatim
v̄   ⎰   Ordered__
Bull   the Judgᵗ of th[e] Sup. Cur. of Connecᵗ the U [letter inked out] that
                              the State of
                the decree of the Sup. Cur of ∧ Connecᵗ be affirmed with costs. __

U. S. vs. B. F. Bache
                  moves
M̶r̶L̶e̶v̶y̶.̶ p̶r̶a̶y̶s̶ that the motion made yesterday in the case of the U S. vs. Bache
may be continued until next term__

    Order'd by the Court

U. States ⎱   files a suggestion in this case & thereupon
v̄   ⎰ MʳLevy of Counsel for the Defdᵗˢ ∧ moves for a prohibition to
B. F. Bache ⎰ the Circᵗ for the Pennsylᵃ Distᵗ to stay proceedings in said case__
                              motion
            & that the said ∧ be contᵈ until next term__
    Order'd by the Court__

s[ee?]. Motion of Mʳ Lewis on file__

Samuel Bayard's Expanded Notes for Fine Minutes ———
August 1798 Term

At a Supreme Court of the United States holden at Philadᵃ (the same being
the present seat of[181] the National Governᵗ) on monday the 6. day of August
in the year of our Lord 1798. __ [182]

                              Present. __

            The Honᵇˡᵉ. Oliver Elsworth Esqᵗ Ch. Justice

        William Cushing   ⎫
        James Iredell   ⎬ Esqʳˢ associate Justiᶦˢ⁾
        William Paterson & ⎭
        Samˡ Chase

The C̶ Proclamation being made the Court is opened __ [183]

181. A ")" was written first, then an "o" was superimposed on it.
182. The letters "an" appear beneath the numbers "179."
183. The letters "n'd" appear beneath the "d__."

Wilson ⎫
v̄s. ⎬   The Court proceeded to hear Counsel on this case — viz. M.ʳ
Daniel ⎭   Lee — (Att.ʸ Gen.ˡ of[184] the U — S.) &M.ʳ Ingersoll on the part of
    the Pltff — & M.ʳ Tilghman on that of the defd.ᵗ

The Court adjourn'd until 12 o'clock to morrow —

[————————]

Tuesday 7. August 1798

The Court met pursuant to adjourn.ᵗ —

Present as yesterday —

Wilson ⎫
v̄ˢ ⎬   The Court having heard the
Daniel ⎭   arguments of Counsel in this case

                                         for
Order'ᵈ that the sentence of the Circuit Court of the Virginia District in said
case be revers'd —

Jones ⎫
v̄ˢ ⎬   Discontinu'd by direction's of the
Letombe ⎭   Plaintiffs Counsel — (M.ʳ E. Tilghman)

The Court adjourn'd until to morrow at 11. oclock —

————————

Wednesday. 8 August. 1798.

The Court met pursuant to adjourn.ᵗ

Present as on yesterday —

Clark ⎫
v̄s. ⎬   Continued by consent of[185] parties —
Russell ⎭

Sam.ˡFowler & ⎫
Joseph Lyman
v̄s
Abraham Miller ⎬ ⎫ On motion of M.ʳLewis
                            Order'd. that the Plaintiffs in each of the above suits
Same.
v̄s   shew cause by the first day of next term why venire's
                      should not be awarded to summon juries from some
Mary Lindsley ⎬ ⎭   of
Sam.ˡLindsley.   District of the U.States other than[186] the Dist.ʳ of Con-
Eben.ʳ Lindsley   necticut or of N. York.
Moses. Mulford &
John Seely.

184. The letter "o" is written over " —)."
185. The word "of" is written over a dash.
186. A "t" appears beneath the "n."

Calder ⎫   The Court proceeded to give
  v̄ ⎬   their opinions in this case seriatim
Bull ⎭

Order'd — That the decree of the Supreme Court of the State of Connecticut be affirmd with costs —

Irwin ⎫
  v̄ ⎬   Cont^d by consent.
Lee of Sims ⎭

United States. ⎫   McLevy of counsel for the defendant files a suggestion
  v̄ ⎬   in this cause & thereupon moves for a prohibition to the[187]
B. F. Bache ⎭   Circuit Court of the U. S.tates for the Pennsyl^a District to
stay proceedings in said case — & that this motion be continued over to the next ~~Court~~ Term. Order'd by the Court —

All unfinish'd business is continu'd over to the next term —

Proclamation being made the Court is adjourn'd to the time & place by Law appointed —

Sam^lBayard

---

187. The "t" is written over an uppercase "C."

Samuel Bayard's Notes for Fine Minutes
February 1799 Term to
August 1799 Term

At a Supreme Court of the United States held at Philedelphia (the same being the present seat of the National Gov.[t]) on Monday the fourth day of February in the year of our Lord One thousand seven hundred & ninety nine —

Present. — [188]

The Hon.[ble] Oliver Elsworth[189] Esq.[r] Ch — Justice

$$\left\{ \begin{array}{l} \text{W.[m]Cushing} \\ \text{James Iredell} \\ \text{W.[m]Paterson \&} \\ \text{Bushrod Washington} \end{array} \right\} \text{Esq.[rs] Ass.[t] Justices}$$

Procelamation being made the Court is open'd —

Letters patent from the President of the United States, dated the 20th day of of Dec.[r] 1798. constituting Bushrod Washington of Virginia an associate Justice of the Supreme Court of the United States, are now openly read & publish'd —

Gist
v̄s
Robinett } On motion of M.[r] Ingersoll this cause order'd to be continud under the rule[190] last made in the same —

Dorance.
v̄s
Vanhorne's L̄ee } On motion of M.[r] Ingersoll order'd to be continued stand ov over[191] for the present —

Irwin's
v̄s
Sims's L̄ee } The Court directed the Record in this case to be read, which was done accordingly by M.[r] Dallas ^Counsel on the part of the Pltff —

---

188. A "t" appears beneath the second "e."
189. The "l" is written over an "s."
190. An "f" appears beneath the "r."
191. The "o" is written over a dash.

Fowler & Lyman ⎫ Rules made in these causes,[193] this
    v̄ˢ   ⎬ day returnd with proofs of
Miller   ⎭ service ~~on the~~

Same Pltffs[192] ⎫
    vˢ   ⎬   ~~Same~~
Lindsley & alˢ ⎭

The Court adjourns to 10 _ o'clock tomorrow

[—————————]

Tuesday. 5. Febʸ 1799.

Pursuant to adjournᵗ the Court met this mornᵍ at the City Hall _

Present as on yesterday _

On motion of Mʳ Lewis the Court order'd that the name of John Hallowell should be erased from the list of attornies & placed on that of Counsellors _ Agreeably to which order, Mʳ Hallowell was affirm'd & qualify'd to act as a Counsellor of this Court _

Irwins   ⎫ The Court proceeded to hear
   v̄ˢ   ⎬ Argument in this case _
Sims's Lee ⎭

Having heard MʳDallas on the part of the Pltff. &Mʳ Lee (Attʸ Genˡ) on the part of the Defdᵗ _ the Court adjourn the further hearing of this cause until to morrow at 10. o'clock _ [194]

[—————————]

Wednesday. 6 Febʸ 1799.

Pursuant to adjournᵗ the Court met this mornᵍ at the city Hall _

Present as before _

On motion of Mʳ E. Tilghman. Mʳ William H. Tod. is admitted a counsellor of this Court. & qualify'd accordingly _

On motion of Mʳ Lewis _ Josiah. Ogden Hoffman Esqʳ, Attorney Genˡ of the State of New York, is admitted a counsellor of this Court & qualify'd accordingly _ [195] ᛫

Irwins   ⎫ Mʳ Lee proceeded as counsel for the Defdᵗ, in his argument
   v̄ˢ   ⎬ & havng the closed the same _ Mʳ Rawle proceeded to argue
Sims's L̄ee ⎭   on
               the cause ~~of~~ the same side _

The Court adjourn until 10 'oclock to morrow _

[—————————]

192. The "P" is written over a dash.
193. The clerk originally placed these cases in separate braces, but then drew one large brace to enclose both. As a result, he made the words in this clause plural.
194. The letters "don" are written in the lower right-hand corner of the page.
195. The letter "a" is written over "to."

Thursday. 7. Feby 1799

Pursuant to adjourn^t[196] the Court met this morn^g at the City Hall_

Present as before_

Irwin   }   Mr Rawle having continued his argument[197] in this cause, &
vs   }   finish'd the[198] same Mr Ingersoll on the same side was directed
Sims's Lee   }   to proceed_

The Court adjourn'd until to morrow at 10. o'clock

Friday. 8. Feby 1799.

Pursuant to adjourn^t the Court met this morn^g at the City Hall_

Present as before

Irwin   }   Mr Ingersoll on the having closed his argument this morn^g
vs   }   Mr E. Tilghman on the part of the Pltff_ proceeded to argue
Sims's Lee   }   the case, but not having finish'd the Court adjourn for the fur-
               }   ther hearing of the cause until to morrow at 10 o'clock

---

Saturday. 9. Feby 1799.

Pursuant to adjourn^t the Court met this morn^g at the City Hall_

Present as on yesterday_

Irwin   }
vs   }   Mr Tilghman continu'd his arg^t
Sims's Lee   }   in this case.

                                    next
The Court adjourn'd until to monday[199] ^ at 10 o'clock_

Monday. 11. Feby 1799.

The Court met this morn^g[200] at 10 oclock pursuant to adjourn^t, at the city Hall_

Present as before_

Mossman & Mein   }
v̄^s   }
                   }   Error from Georgia
Higginson surv^g   }   Record return'd & fil'd_
Ex̄or of Greenwood & }
Higginson   }

196. A "^t" also appears above the "o."
197. A "g" appears beneath the "r."
198. The "e" is written over "is."
199. The word "morrow" appears beneath "monday."
200. A baseline "g" appears beneath the "g."

| Clark | Error from R. Island—
| v̄ˢ | MᶜHowell on the part of the Pltff proceeded to open this case—
| Russell | but not having finish'd his argument, the Court adjourn until to morrow at 10 o'clock—

Tuesday 12. Febᵞ 1799.

Pursuant to adjournᵗ the Court met this mornᵍ at the City Hall—

Present as before—

| Clark | MᶜHowell proceeded in his argrument²⁰¹ & having concluded the
| v̄s | same, Mᵣ Robbins &MᶜDexter were heard on the part of the
| Russell | Defdᵗ—

The Court adjourn until to morrow mornᵍ at 10 o'clock—

Wednesday 13. Febᵞ 1799.

Pursuant to adjournᵗ the Court met this mornᵍ at the City Hall—

Present as before

On motion of Mᵣ Ingersoll, ~~the~~ Walter Franklin was admitted as a Counsellor of this Court & was affirm'd accordingly—

| Clark | Mᵣ Tilghman was heard this mornᵍ— on the part of the Defdᵗ &
| v̄ˢ | Mᵣ Ingersoll on that of the Pltff—
| Russell |

The Court adjourn until to morrow at 10 oclock—

Thursday Mornᵍ 14. Febᵞ 1799.

Pursuant to adjournᵗ the Court met this mornᵍ at the City Hall—

Present as before—

| Dorance | On motion of Mᵣ Ingersoll. the Court order the
| v̄s | Pltff— in this cause to assign errors within 2 days— or
| Vanhorne's L̄ee | that the writ of error be non. pros.'d—

| Irwin | rule
| v̄ˢ | Mᵣ Lewis on the part of the Pltff having ~~fro~~ commenc'd his
| Sims's L̄ee | argument in this cause, but from indisposition not being able to finish the same the Court adjour[n] until to morrow at 10. o'clock—

---

201. The clerk originally wrote "argᵗ" but then crossed out the "ᵗ" and added the letters "ru-nent."

Friday 15. Feb.ʸ 1799.

The Court pursuant to adjourn.ᵗ met this morn.ᵍ at the City Hall —

Present as before

Irwin
v̄ˢ } Mʳ Lewis pursu'd & closed his
Sims's Lee } argument in this cause —

The Court adjourn until to morrow. at 10. o'cloc[k]

Saturday — 16. Feb.ʸ 1799.

Pursuant to adjourn.ᵗ the Court met this morn.ᵍ at the City Hall —

Present as before

On motion of the Att.ʸ Gen.ᶦ of the U. S. Mʳ Hillhouse, of Connec.ᵗ was admitted as a counsellor of this Court & sworn accordingly.

Fowler & Lyman)
v } Mʳ Lewis, &Mʳ J. O. Hoffman (Att.ʸ Gen.ᶦ of the State
Miller } } the part
Same } } of N. Y.). appear'd on[202] ~~behalf~~ of the Defd.ᵗˢ ~~to~~ said
v } } causes in support of the rule made in the same at the
Lindsley & als.) last term —

Mʳ Hillhouse, & shew'd cause against granting the rule mov'd to be made absolute in said causes —

The Court adjourn until Monday Morn.ᵍ at — 10. o'clock —

Monday. 18. Feb.ʸ 1799.

Pursuant to adjourn.ᵗ the Court met this morn.ᵍ at the City Hall —

Present as before

Lyman. & Fowler.[203]
v̄ˢ
Miller } The Court having the arguments of Counsel on the
part — as well of the Pltffs — & the Defd.ᵗˢ — & duly con-
Same } sider'd the same —
v
Lindsley & als

                                                        made absolute
Dorance. v̄ˢ. Vanhone's Lee. — Rule of the 14. Ins.ᵗ ~~non. pro~~

---

202. The "o" is written over an "i."
203. The "w" is written over an "l."

Court adjourn to 11 _ oclock _ to morrow _

Tuesday. 19. Feb.ʸ 1799.

Pursuant to adjourn.ᵗ the Court met this morn.ᵍ _ at the city Hall _

Present <s>as before</s> _

O. Elsworth. Esq.ʳ Ch. Just.

W. Cushing
W. Paterson _   }   Esq.ʳˢ associate Justices _
B. Washington

Clark.
  v.ˢ   }   Order'd by the Court _ on solemn argumnt that the Judg.ᵗ of the
Russell   Circ.ᵗ Court for the Rhode Island. District in this cause be revers'd
   & that a venire de novo be awarded _

Irwin
  v.ˢ   }   Order'd by the Court on solemn arg.ᵗ that the Judg.ᵗ of the
Sims Lee   Circuit Court for the Pennsylvania Dist. in this cause be Affirm'd _ & a special mandate awarded _

Fowler & Lyman
  v.ˢ   }   Order'd by the Court that the rule obtain'd & enter'd
Miller   in this cause at the last term be discharg'd _

Same
  v   }   Same entry _
Lindsley & als.

Mossman & Mein
  v̄.ˢ   }   Continu'd _
Higginson

Peirce & Harris v̄.ˢ _ Ship Alligator. & B. Lincoln. _ Cont.ᵈ _

The Court adjourn to the Time & place by Law appointed _

[————————]

At a Supreme Court of the U _ States _ held at Philadelphia (the same being the present seat of the National Govern.ᵗ) on Monday the 5.ᵗʰ day of August. in the year of our Lord one thousand seven hundred. & ninety nine _

Present _

The Hon.ᵇˡᵉ _   W. Patterson & }   Esq.ʳˢ
   Sam.ˡChase

There Met this morn.ᵍ at the City Hall but a sufficient number of Judges not appearing to constitute a Court the Justices present adjourn until to morrow at 10 o'clock _

Tuesday. 6. August 1799.

Pursuant to adjourn! the Court met this morn⁸ at the City. Hall._ Present_

Oliver. Elsworth Esqʳ Ch. Just.

Wm Patterson.
Sam¹Chase &   } Esqʳ
Bushrod Washington

Proclamation being made the Court was opene'd_ State of N. Y. vs. State

of Connec! ^& others M! Hoffman Att! Gen! of the State of N. Y. appears on behalf
of said & ^having filed a bill, in Equity; thereupon mov'd_ (see motion on file).

Turner
vs   } order'd for argument to morrow
Bank of N. A.

Mossman & Mein) On motion of M! Ingersoll
vs   }   join in error
Higginson   ) Order'd that the defd! appear & ~~plead~~ by thursday morn⁸
                  next_ 8ᵗʰ_ continued_

Peirce & Harris   ) Order'd that the Pltff appear & prosecute their writ of
vˢ   } error within the term or suffer a non. pros._
Ship Alligatior & } Aug. 9.ᵗʰ_ non. pros. order'd_
B. Lincoln²⁰⁴ Esqʳ.

Hazlehurst) Rule_ on motion of the Att! Gen! that the plaintiff appear &
vs.   }   within the Term
U. States.) prosecute his writ of error ^or_ suffer a non. pros._

Coffin)
vs   } Same entry_
Same   )

Coffin)
vs   } 2ⁿᵈ²⁰⁵ actⁿ Same entry_
Same   )

Geyer)
vs   } Same entry_
Same)

204. An "m" appears beneath the "n."
205. An "S" appears beneath the "2."

Tunno
vs } Same entry—
Same

Miller
vs } Same entry—
Same

Lyman & others
State of. N. Y. v̄ˢ State of Connecticut &[206] Mʳ Ingersoll appears for defendants—

The Court adjourn'd until to morrow at 10— o'clock—

Wednesday. 7. August. 1799.

Pursuant to adjournᵗ the Court met this mornᵍ at the City Hall—

Present—

Oliver Elsworth Esqʳ

WᵐPatterson
SamˡChase. & } Assᵗ Justices
B. Washington Esqʳˢ

Turner
v̄ˢ } The Court proceeded to hear Mʳ Ingersoll in behalf of the Pltff in this cause & Mʳ Rawle on the part of
Bank of N. America. } the Defdᵗ—

Turner
v̄ˢ } The Court directed Counsel to proceed in the argᵗ[207] of this case
Dᵉ Caso Enrille

The Court adjourn until to morrow at 10 oclock—

Thursday. 8. August. 1799.

Pursuant to adjournᵗ the Court met this mornᵍ— at the City Hall—

Present—

Oliver Elsworth Esqʳ Ch. Just.

WᵐPatterson
SamˡChase } Assᵗ Justices
B. Washington Esqʳˢ

206. A dash is drawn beneath the "&"
207. A "g" appears beneath the "a."

Mossman & Mein ⎫
  $\bar{v}^s$ ⎬   ~~Cont~~ Continued _
Higginson   ⎭

Hazlehurst. ⎫ Order'd for arg.ᵗ to morrow
  $\bar{v}s$ ⎬ morning. or Non. pros. _
U. States _ & ⎭

9ᵗʰ Order'd by the Court that a Non: pros: be enter'd in this cause _

Same in the 5 other cases _ same entry _

State of N. York ⎫
        v   ⎬   Court proceeded to hear Counsel on the motion
State of Connecticut ⎭   for an injunction made in this cause _

Court adjourn'd until to morrow at 10 o'clock

Friday. 9 Aug. 1799

Pursuant to adjd.ᵗ the court met at the City Hall _ Present as before

Turner ⎫ On argument the Court order. & decree that the
  $\bar{v}s$ ⎬ Judg.ᵗ of the Circuit C.ᵗ for the Dist of N. C. _ in said
Bank of N. America ⎭ Cause be <u>revers'd</u>. with costs _

Turner ⎫
  $\bar{v}^s$ ⎬   Same entry _
Marquis De Casa Enrille ⎭

State of New York ⎫   Court having
        $\bar{v}$ ⎬ The ~~proceeded to~~ heard[208] Counsel in behalf. of
State of Connecticut & ⎨ the parties complainant[209] & defend.ᵗ in[210] this
J. Lyman & others ⎭ suit _ refuse the ~~motion for~~ injunction pray'd for
                                    in this cause _

                                                    plead ~~answ~~
  ~~Rule~~ Order'd _ that the defendants. _ J. Lyman & S. Fowler ^ answer
or demur
^ to the bill filed in this cause within 6.0 days. _

Court adjourns to the time & place by law. appointed _

---

208. Originally the word "hear" had been written. The "d" was added to it.
209. A "t" appears beneath the second "n."
210. A dash appears beneath the "i."

Drafts Relating to
Court Proceedings

The drafts of orders, motions, proclamations, and judgments printed in this section exist as separate sheets of paper scattered throughout the official record; they have been given titles and dates that reflect their eventual incorporation in the minutes of the Court. Thus, the first document in the section is a draft of the rules of admission to the bar and of issuance of process. These rules have been dated February 5, 1790, the date that they were recorded in the fine minutes. The source note for each document, in addition to the usual information as to its location and condition, provides the identity of the person who drafted it. The individuals who have been identified as contributing to the composition of these documents include not only the clerks—Samuel Bayard and Jacob Wagner—but also Chief Justices John Jay and Oliver Ellsworth, and Attorney General Edmund Randolph. As with the original minutes, the hastily scrawled character of these manuscripts results in the absence of an identifiable left margin; we therefore standardize indentations assuming a regularity of margin.

Rules for Admission and Issuance of Process ——————————
February 5, 1790

ordered that (untill further order) it shall be requisite to the admission of attornies or counsellors to practice in this court, that they shall have been such for 3 Years past in the Sup. Courts of the States to which they respectively belong_ and that their private & professional Characters shall appear to be fair _

ordered that counsellors shall not practices as attornies, nor Attornies as Counsellors in this Court. ⊗

⊗That they respectively ~~be sworn to demean themselves faithfully~~ take the following oath viz! I. a. b. do solemnly swear that I will demean myself as an Attorney (or Counsellor[)] of this court uprightly and according to Law_ and that I will support the Constitution of the U. S._

                             should   be
ordered that (unless, and untill, it ~~be~~ otherwise ^ provided by Law) all Process shall be in the name of "The President of the United States" _

Df (DNA, RG 267, Records of the Office of the Clerk). In John Jay's hand. Damage to the document is the cause for supplying a conjectural reading.

Request and Order for a Special Circuit Court ─────────
February 8, 1791

The Ch. Justice [*letters inked out*] laid before the Court a Letter he had rec^d from the Judge of the District ~~of~~ Court of new York, which Was read and is in the words following vizt (here insert it verbatim)

District of New York
Jany 20th 1791:

Sir

On complaint of the Collector and proof on oath, I committed Josiah Goreham master of the sloop Hiram to the goal of this City on the 12th of November last for a breach of the revenue laws aggravated by perjury. Charles Seely his mate had, a few days before, been committed for landing and storing a quantity of Coffee before report or entry, and in the night time, and both have ever since remaind in confinement for want of Sureties for their appearance.

An under oficer of the customs was, about the time of the removal of Congress, suspended by the secretary of the treasury for malconduct in permitting goods to be landed after sunset. As there are circumstances which, in the opinion of the principal officers, rendered any criminal intention questionable; it was determined that a Judicial enquiry should precede his removal or restoration. In the mean time, deprived of the means of subsistence, he is importunate for a trial.

Each of these cases, and in general every ofence made subject to fine or corporal punishment, one only excepted, are excluded from the authority of the district court by The extent of the punishment; and it's criminal cognizance, thus circumscribed, is a burthen to the community without any public advantage.   I think it therefore my duty to make this representation, that if the supreme Court should conceive it proper, a special circuit may be appointed for this district, and the Prisoners as well as the suspended oficer, be punished or relieved as Justice shall require.

I have the honor to be_ with great respect_   Sir   Your most obedient   humble Servant

Ja^t Duane

Honorable
    The Chief Justice of the United states_

Thereupon ordered that a special Session of the circuit Court be held at the city of new York in and for the District of new York on the twenty first Day of Feby Instant next; And that ₐ Copies of this order be transmitted by the Clerk of this Court to the Judge and the Clerk of the said District Court, and to the Attorney ~~General~~ of the U. S. for the said District_

authenticated

The order for the special session of the Circuit Court for the District of New York is in John Jay's hand: Df (DNA, RG 267, Records of the Office of the Clerk). Although the letter requesting the special session was found in a different box, it is reproduced here as an insert according to Jay's instructions: ARS (DNA, RG 267, Records of the Office of the Clerk).

Motion and Rule in *West v. Barnes* ————————————
August 2 and 3, 1791

Wm West v Dav^d L. Barnes & others

Mr Bradford offered to the Court a writ purporting to be a writ of Error issuing out of the office of the Clerk of the ~~District~~ circuit Court for Rhode Island District, directed to that Court & commanding the Return of the Judgment & Proceedings rendered by them in this Cause, to this Court,— together with such Return &c^a

on Motion ~~for~~ of [M]^r Bradford of Counsel for [W]^m [West] the said writ & Papers annexed ^to it^ were read—

~~on Motion of the same~~ Mr Bradford moved ~~that the~~ for a Rule that the Def^{ts} rejoin to the Errors assigned by the Pltff in this Cause—

David L. Barnes one of the Def^t & a Counsellor of this Court objected ~~that~~ to the Validity of the Writ in Question, and on that Principle to the Rule moved for— the arguments on both sides being heard the court informed the parties that they would [determing?] the Question— adjourned &c

Wm West v Dav^d L. Barnes &c

The Court refused to grant the Rule moved for yesterday in this Cause, being unanimously of opinion that writs of Error to [*letters inked out*] remove ^to this Court^ ~~ones.~~ Cause[s] ^from inferiour ~~Jurisdictions courts~~ can regularl[y] issue only from the Clerks office of this Court[1]

drawn by the Chief Justice— & approv'd by his associates—

Sam^lBayard Clk— of the
Supreme Court of the United States:

Df (DNA, RG 267, Appellate Jurisdiction Records, Papers in Undocketed Appellate Cases: *West v. Barnes*). Endorsed as "Originals of Orders of the Sup. Cur." In John Jay's hand except where noted. Damage to this document affects legibility.

1. The lines following this are in the hand of Samuel Bayard.

Order on a Motion in *Oswald v. New York* ————————————
August 7, 1792

on mo. of Mr I. ordered that the Marshall of   District return ye writ directed to him ~~issued~~ in this Cause before the adjournm^t of this Court, if a Copy of this Rule shall seasonably be serv^d upon him or his Depy— or otherwise on the first Day of the next Term— And that in Case of Default, he do shew on the s^d first Day of next Term

Cause therefor ^ by Aff^t taken before one of the [*word inked out*] Judges of the United States

Df (DNA, RG 267, Original Jurisdiction Records: *Oswald v. New York*). In John Jay's hand. The date is written in pencil on the verso of the document.

Rules of Practice ———————————————————————————
August 8, 1792

informs

The Chief-Justice announces to the Attorney Genera[l] in answer to his motion of yesterday, & to the Bar, that this Court rule consider the practice of the Courts of Kings Bench, & of Chancery in England as affording the outlines
for   and that they will from Time to Time
of the Practice of this Court, reserving to themselves the power of makeng[1]
                            therein
such alterations ^ as the precedents of circumstances in this Country may render necessary —

August. 8. 1792

Df (DNA, RG 267, Records of the Office of the Clerk). Samuel Bayard wrote this document, including the interlined "therein;" the rest of the interlineations may have been written by John Jay. Damage to the document is the cause for supplying the conjectural reading.
   1. The "e" is written over an "i."

Proclamation in *Chisholm v. Georgia* ———————————————
August 11, 1792

Any person having Authority to appea[r for?] the State of Georgia in The Suit broug[ht in this?] Court by   against the said [state is?] required to come forth and appear according[ly].

oyer. &c—

Any person having authority to appear [for the?] State of Georgia in the suit brought in [this court?] by Alexander Chistolm citizen of Sout[h Carolina?] &
                                   same   said
Executor of Robert Farquhar of the said [state?] deceased against the ^ State of Georgia [is required?] to come forth & appear according[ly.]

Df (DNA, RG 267, Original Jurisdiction Records: *Chisholm v. Georgia*). In Samuel Bayard's hand. Damage to the document is the sole cause for supplying conjectural readings.

Orders in *Chisholm v. Georgia*
August 11, 1792

1.[1]

Chisholm exr &c
vs   } In case
The State of Georgia

This day came the plaintiff by E R. [his counsel?] and thereupon his excellency E. T. esqr governor &c. of the [state?] of Georgia, and attorney general thereof, on whom the [marshall?] of the District of Georgia has returned service of the or[iginal summons?] in this cause, were solemnly called but came not.

Proclamation being made &c[2]

                thereupo[n]   E. R.

Whereupon it was ^ moved by [the plain?]tiff by ^ his counsel aforesaid, that unless the said state of Geor[gia shall?] after reasonable previous notice

    motion

of this order being served on the [governor?] attorney or solicitor general of the said state for the time being, cau[se an appea?]rance to be entered in behalf of the said state on the fourth da[y of next?] term, or shall then shew cause to the contrary, judgment shall [be entered?] against the said state, and a writ of inquiry of damage[s shall be?] awarded.

    with the consent of the pltfs counsel

Ordered, that the consideration of [this motion?] be postponed, until the first monday in february [next.?]

2.[3]

Chisholm exr &c
vs   } In case.
The State of Georgia

This day came the plaintiff by [E. R. his?] counsel; and it appearing from the return of the marshal [for the?] district of Georgia, that the original summons in this cause [having been?] served on his excellency E. T. esqr governor &c of the said [state?] or   esqr attorney general of the said state, [and no appea?]rance being now entered in behalf of the said state.

It was moved by the plai[ntiff by?] his counsel aforesaid, that &c as before.

Df (DNA, RG 267, Original Jurisdiction Records: *Chisholm v. Georgia*). In Edmund Randolph's hand. Damage to the document is the sole cause for supplying conjectural readings.

    1. This number, "1," which appears at the top of the first page of a folio, may have been a page number or an indication that what followed was the first of two alternate wordings for an entry in *Chisholm v. Georgia*. The second page of the folio begins with a "2," which may indicate a page number or the second of two alternate wordings.

    2. See preceding "Proclamation in *Chisholm v. Georgia* August 11, 1792."

    3. See note 1 above.

Order in *Glass v. Sloop Betsey* ————————————————
February 18, 1794

1. ordered that this ~~Proceedings~~ cause be and it is hereby remanded to the District Court for Maryland District
ordered that an Exemplification of the Decree of this Court in this Cause be transmitted to the circuit Court for Maryland District—

Df (DNA, RG 267, Appellate Jurisdiction Records: *Glass v. Sloop Betsey*). In John Jay's hand.

Order on a Motion in *Chisholm v. Georgia* ————————
August 5, 1794

And now on motion
of
On motion of the Att[y] Genl, ^ counsel for the plntf, the [C]ourt do award
Gen[era]l
that the ^ Jury to be summoned at the next [Court?] do enquire upon their oaths & affirmations. [what d?]amages the plntf has sustain'd. by reason [of the premises and the?] nonperformance of the promises & assumptions [in?] the declaration of the Plntf contained, & that 3 M^os notice of the ~~executi~~ holding such Enquiry be given to the Govr & Attorney General of the state of Georgia.

Df (DNA, RG 267, Original Jurisdiction Records: *Chisholm v. Georgia*). In Samuel Bayard's hand. This document is damaged which affects legibility.

Judgment in *Ware v. Hylton* ————————————————————
March 7, 1796

Whereupon all and singular the Premises being seen by the Court here and fully understood and mature deliberation had thereon because it appears to the Court now here that in the Record and Process aforesaid and also in the Rend[i]tion of the Judgment afs^d upon the Demurrer to the Rejoinder of the Defendants in Error to the Replication to the second Plea it is manifestly erred it is considered that the said Judgm^t for those Errors and others in the Record and Process aforesaid be revoked annulled and alltogether held for nought and it is further considered by the Court here that the Pltff in Error recover against the Defts Two thousand nine Hundred and Seventy Six Pounds Eleven Shillings and Six Pence good Brittish money commonly called Sterling Money his debt afs^d and his Costs by him about his Suit in this behalf expended and the said Defendants in Mercy &c But this Judgment is to be discharged by the Payment of the ~~damages~~ Sum of 596 dollars and Interest thereon to be computed after the rate of 5 pr Cent pr Ann from the 7th day of July 1782 till

by th[e]
Payment besides the Costs and ~~on~~ Payment of such Damages as shall be awarded to the Pltff in Error on a Writ of Inquiry to be issued by the Circuit Court of Virginia to ascertain the Sum really[1] due to the Plaintiff ˄ ~~in Error in Consequence of the Reversal of the said Judgm^t on the Demurrer aforesaid~~⊗

⊗ (exclusively of the said Sum of 596 dollars w^h was found to be due to the Pltff in Error upon the Trial in the ~~Cir~~ said Circuit Court of the Issue joined upon the Defendants Plea of Payment at a time when the Judgment of the said Circuit Court on the said Demurrer was unreversed and in full Force and Vigor), and for the execution &c (as above)_ [2]

and for the Execution of the Judgment of the Court the Cause aforesaid is remanded to the said Circuit Court of Virginia_

Costs allowed.[3]

Df (DNA, RG 267, Appellate Jurisdiction Records: *Ware v. Hylton*). Written in an unknown hand. Damage to the document is the cause for supplying the conjectural reading.
    1. A crossed-out caret appears before the word "really."
    2. From the crossed-out closing parenthesis to the dash is in a different, unknown hand.
    3. "Costs allowed" in Jacob Wagner's hand.

Order in *Cutting v. South Carolina* ——————————————
August 15, 1797

The State of South Carolina	
v^s	In Chancery
John B. Cutting Adm^{rs} of the	Augt Term 1797.
Prince of Luxembourgh	

    It is ordered by the Supreme Court of the United States, this 15th day of Augt in the year 1797, that Injunction be awarded to stay all further proceedings on a judgment rendered at this present ~~Aug~~ Augt Term, in an Action upon the Case of John B. Cutting as administrator of the Prince of Luxembourgh against the State of South Carolina, until the first day of January [next?]; And it is further ordered by the said Court that Injunction[1] also be awarded to stay all further proceedings [o?]n said judgement until the further order of this Court upon this condition, that the said State of South Carolina shall on or before the said first day of January next bring into this Court the sum of £8381,,13. Sterling money of South Carolina with the interest thereof from the 7th day of Septr 1785_ at the rate of 5 p[^{r}?] Cent^m per Ann_ from the 7[th?] day of Septr 1785 till the 13 Day of March 1789 of £10855, 8. 5_
the s^d State
Sterling money of ˄ South Carolina together with the interest on [the?] same at the rate of 7 p^r C^t per ann[um?] from the 13 day of March 1789 to t[ime?]

of payment into Court excepting & deduct[ing] from the Amount of interest
One thous[and] pounds of like money already paid to the [said?] John B. Cutting, (which _{the}said State by her bill exhibited in this Court has acknowledged
to be due & owing from h[er?] to the legal representative of the said Prin[ce]
of Luxembourgh or to the French Repu[blic] ~~who makes claim to the same,~~
and h[as?] offered to deposit the same in this cour[t] and _{shall deposit} the same in this
Court subject to [its?] further order & such decree as it [may make?] respecting
the same; and shall at the sa[me?] time pay into this Court the costs in th[e]
above action.

Df (DNA, RG 267, Original Jurisdiction Records: *Cutting v. South Carolina*). In Oliver Ellsworth's
hand. This document is damaged which affects legibility.
    1. The "I" is written over an "i."

Judgment in *Hollingsworth v. Virginia, Moultrie v. Georgia*, and *Brailsford v. Georgia*
February 14, 1798

The court is[1] _{on consideration of} of opinion that ~~since~~ the amendment of the Constitution
respecting _{Suits ~~of private persons~~ against} ~~ye Suability of~~ States, it has ~~not~~ no Jurisdiction of this cause _{it is} [*letters inked out*] therefore Considered by the Court that the bill be dismissed

Df (DNA, RG 267, Original Jurisdiction Records: *Hollingsworth v. Virginia*). In an unknown hand.
    1. The word "is" is written over "are."

Order Appointing Elias B. Caldwell Clerk of the Supreme Court
August 15, 1800

Samuel Bayard, Esquire, having resigned the Office of the Clerk of this
Court_ It is ordered that Elias B. Caldwell be appointed to the said place,
and that he give bond for the faithful performance of the duties of the said
Office_
    Mr Caldwell appeared and took the Oath by law prescribed and having of-
fered as securities Elias Boudinot and Joseph Reed Esquires, they are approved
and accepted by the Court.
    Ordered that Mr Caldwell's bond be deposited with the Register of the
Treasury of the United States, and that he produce the Registers receipt for
the same to this Court at their next Session_

15th August 1800._

Df (DNA, RG 267, Records of the Office of the Clerk). In an unknown hand.

Docket

The first volume of the engrossed docket of the Supreme Court presents a history of litigation between February term, 1791, and February term, 1808. The docket is organized by term. Each case was recorded under the term when it was first docketed and then a record was maintained of subsequent actions in that case until final disposition. In publishing the docket book, we exclude all cases docketed after August term, 1800, and all entries dated after 1800 in cases initiated previously.

The engrossed docket was begun after Samuel Bayard became clerk of the Court. If there was an earlier version of the docket during the clerkship of John Tucker, it has not survived.[1] Below is a table tracing changes in handwriting through the engrossed docket. Some of the hands which appear in the fine minutes also appear here, and they have been identified by the use of the same letter designation. Hands have been associated with entries for particular terms; this means, for example, that all actions dated in August term, 1795, were entered by Hand C, irrespective of the term when the case had been docketed originally. As with the fine minutes and original minutes, we annotate individually in the text those instances where another hand is identifiable that does not fit this table.

Hand C	Case titles and entries for February 1791 term-February 1796 term
Hand C	Titles for cases first docketed August 1796 term ending with case title for *United States v. La Vengeance*
Jacob Wagner	Titles for cases first docketed August 1796 term beginning with case title for *Fennimore v. United States*
Jacob Wagner	Entries for August 1796 term
Jacob Wagner	Case titles and entries for February 1797 term-August 1797 term
Jacob Wagner	Titles for cases first docketed February 1798 term
Samuel Bayard	Entries for February and August 1798 terms beginning with *Hollingsworth v. Virginia* (first docketed in February term, 1793) and ending with *Wilson v. Daniel* (first docketed in August term, 1796)
Hand F	Entries for February and August 1798 terms beginning with *Moultrie v. Georgia* (first docketed in February term, 1797) and ending with *Pierce v. Ship Alligator* (first docketed in August term, 1798)
Hand F	Titles for cases first docketed August 1798 term

Hand F   Case titles and entries for February 1799 term-August 1800
                                         term

Samuel Bayard   All notations of costs paid in conjunction with litigation

This table reveals that the official clerk of the Court, Samuel Bayard, was directly involved
in the production of only a small part of the engrossed docket. In the annotations which point
out deviations from the above table, however, the reader will see that Samuel Bayard and
(during Bayard's absence in England) acting clerk Jacob Wagner made additions and corrections to the work of other scribes. As was the case with the fine minutes, this indicates an
active clerical superintendence. The reader also may notice for February and August 1800
terms the number of entries probably made after Bayard left as clerk, indicating that he may
have let his clerical duties in Philadelphia slip as he established himself in Westchester County,
New York.

Originally, the docket book was paginated and the term of the Court was used as a running
head. We do not reproduce the page numbers or running heads, but instead indicate the
beginning of each new term of the Court. Therefore, when cases are cross-referenced by page
in the original, we report the fact in annotations. We also eliminate the number beside each
case that was assigned for filing purposes in the nineteenth century. We reproduce vertical
and horizontal rules as closely as possible to the way that they appear on the page. When the
original text crosses over a vertical line, we adopt a rule that dictates placement in the block
where most of it lies. We also retain the diagonal, three-line marks (///) next to case names,
which seem to indicate the conclusion of action in those cases.

D (DNA, RG 267, General Records). Transcribed from the original document, rather than a photocopy.

1. An 1827 inventory of "Rough   Dockets" lists as "Lost" the original dockets for the entire first decade of the
Court's existence (General Records, RG 267, DNA), but we have located rough dockets for 1798. These are published
in "Notes for Docket Entries."

February Term 1791

Morton, Att?   Nicholas Vanstaphorst & ⎫
                                Jacob Vanstaphorst   ⎬   Summons in Case.
                                      v̄ˢ   ⎪
Caldwell. Attʸ   The State of Maryland   ⎭

                                Writ returned
                                Narr. filed
                                Plea . . . d̄o
                                Replⁿ . . . d̄o
            ///   Ordered, by consent of parties, that a Commission
                                do issue to Rutger Jan Schimmelpennenck, Peter
                                Stadnitski, Hendrick Vollenhoven, Commissioners on
                                the part of the Plaintiffs— and to Christian Van
                                Eighen, Nicholas Bonds, P. C. Nahuys[1] and Willem

1. The letters "yh" appear beneath the "hu."

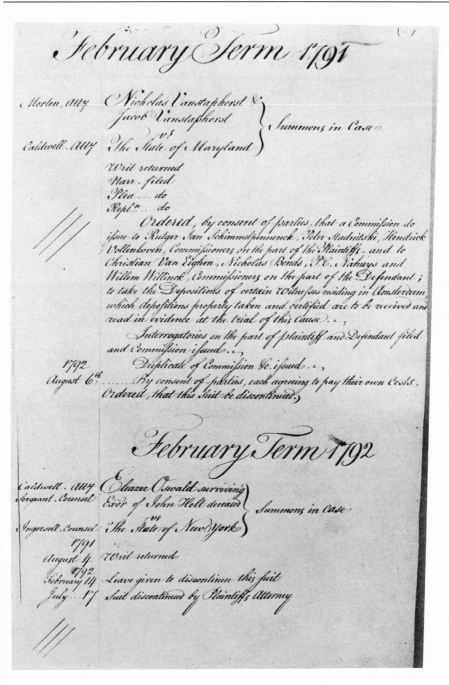

Docket Book, February term, 1791. Courtesy National Archives.

Willinck, Commissioners on the part of the Defendant; to take the Depositions of certain Witnesses residing in Amsterdam, which depositions properly taken and certified are to be received and read in evidence at the trial of this cause. _

Interrogatories on the part of plaintiff and Defendant filed and Commission issued. _

Duplicate of Commission &c. issued. _

1792
August 6th.

By consent of parties, each agreeing to pay their own Costs, Ordered, that this Suit be discontinued.

February Term 1792

Caldwell. Att^y
Sergeant. Counsel

Ingersoll. Counsel

Eleazer Oswald surviving
Ex̄or of John Holt deceased
vs
The State of New York
} Summons in Case

1791
August 4 | Writ returned

1792
February 14 | Leave given to discontinue this suit

/// July 17 | Suit discontinued by Plaintiffs Attorney

August Term 1792

In Equity

Randolph. Counsel

John Collet
v̄s
James Collet
} In Error, from the Circuit Court for the Pennsylvania District

/// 1792
June 30 | Writ returned with the record
Discontinued by order of Mr Randolph Counsel for the plaintiff.

Edward Telfair
Governor of the
State of Georgia in
behalf of said State   Bill in Equity filed praying an
    v̄ˢ   injunction to stay Monies in
Samuel Brailsford   the hands of the Marshall for
& others   the District of Georgia

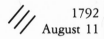

1792
August 11 | An injunction ordered, as prayed in the Complainant's bill, to stay the monies in Controversy in the hands of the Marshall for the Georgia district until the further order of this Court.

1793
February 4 | Demurrer to the Bill filed — 6ᵗʰ February ordered for Argument.

   "   20 | The Court order that the injunction continue until the next term and then be dissolved unless the State of Georgia shall sooner bring her Action for the Bond in Controversy

1794
February 14 | Plaintiffs Bill dismissed and the Injunction dissolved with Costs

Randolph,
Ingersoll. Counsel   Ebenezer Kingsley,   Error from the
Hallowell. Attʸ   Silas Pepoun   Circuit Court
                            and Anna Bingham.   for the District
Lewis.Tilghman. Counsel   v̄s   of Massachusetts
                            Thomas Jenkins

/// | On solemn argument,
    Judgment of the Court below affirmed with Costs.

Hallowell. Attʸ   Alexander Chisholm
Randolph. Counsel   Ex̄or of Robert Farquhar decᵈ   Summons
                                vˢ   in Case
                            The State of Georgia

1792	
August 11	On motion of Plaintiffs Counsel ordered that the rule now moved for to compel the appearance of the State of Georgia be postponed for Consideration until the next term.
1793	
February 5	The Court heard the Attorney General in support of his Motion in this Cause
19	Ordered on argument that Judgment by default be entered against the State of Georgia in this suit unless she appear or shew cause to the Contrary by the first day of next term.
August 6	Continued by consent of plaintiffs Counsel.
1794 February 13	On motion of the Attorney General of the United States the Court direct that Judgment be entered for the Plaintiff and award a Writ of Enquiry of damages.
1794 August 5	On motion of the Attorney General of Counsel for the plaintiff the Court do award that the General Jury to be summoned at the next Court do enquire upon their Oaths & Affirmations what damages the plaintiff has sustained by reason of the promises and the Non-performance of the promises and assumptions in the declaration of the Plaintiff contained and that three months notice of the holding such Enquiry be given to the Governor and Attorney General of the State of Georgia. _
1795 February 2	Continued.
" August	Continued Costs paid
1796 March 14	Continued
Aug.ᵗ	continued
1797 Feb.ʸ	cont.ᵈ
1797 Aug.ᵗ	cont.ᵈ

February Term 1793

Morgan

Hollingsworth[2]
[Wil̂liam Grayson] & others ⎞
$\overline{v}^s$ ⎬ Bill in Equity
The State of Virginia   ⎠

/// 1792
December 4 | Bill of the Complainants＿ and the Return of the Marshall for the Virginia District filed.＿

1793
February 20 | On motion of M᷊ Rawle, Leave is given to amend the Bill and new process awarded.

July 3 | Process issued in the name of Levi Hollingsworth and others against the Commonwealth of Virginia.＿

1794 February 18 | Continued

" August 5 | Continued

1795 February | Continued

August 5 | Continued

1793. July 16. | The date of the return of subpœna on the amended bill; the time of the filing of which is supposed to be the 5ᵗʰ of August 1793.[3]

1796 March 12 | M᷊ Lewis moves for a distringas to compel the appearance of the State.

Aug᷊ 12. | M᷊ Lewis withdraws his motion for a distringas, and in lieu thereof moves for an alias subpœna, which is granted, et exit.

1797 February 13. | On motion of M᷊ Lewis for the complainant, rule for a commission to be directed to Charles Smith, John Hubly and William Montgomery, Esquires, or any two of them to examine witnesses in the borough of Lancaster in the State of Pennsylvania; for a commission to be directed to David Watts, William Alexander and John Lyon, Esquires or any two of them, to examine witnesses in the borough of Carlisle in the

---

2. Interlineation and brackets in hand of Jacob Wagner.
3. This entry in the hand of Jacob Wagner.

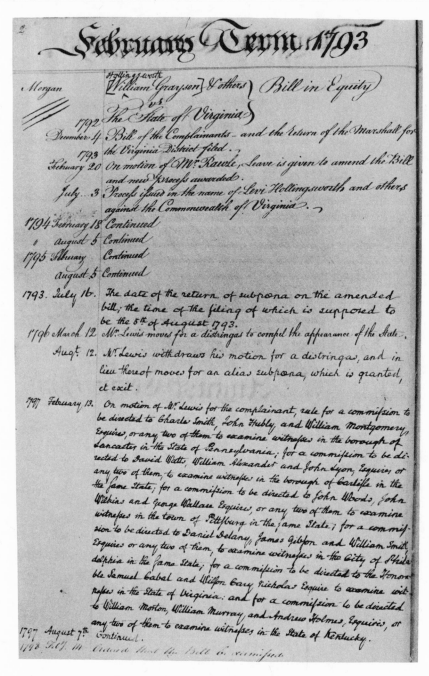

Docket Book, February term, 1793. Courtesy National Archives.

the same State; for a commission to be directed to John Woods, John Wilkins and George Wallace Esquires, or any two of them to examine witnesses in the town of Pittsburg in the same State; for a commission to be directed to Daniel Delany, James Gibson and William Smith, Esquires or any two of them, to examine witnesses in the City of Philadelphia in the same State; for a commission to be directed to the Honorable Samuel Cabal and Wilson Cary Nicholas Esquire to examine witnesses in the State of Virginia: and for a commission to be directed to William Morton, William Murray and Andrew Holmes, Esquires, or any two of them to examine witnesses in the State of Kentucky.

1797 August 7th	Continued.
1798. Feby 14.	Ordered. that the Bill be dismissed.

Caldwell

///

Morgan

	Eleazer Oswald (who survived Elizabeth Holt, Administrators &c. of John Holt deceased) Citizen and Inhabitant of the State of Pennsylvania $\bar{v}^s$ The State of New-York	} In case

1793 February 4	The Marshall for the New-York District returns his service of the process issued in the above suit.
" 20	On motion of Mr Cox, Ordered that unless the State of New York appear by the first day of next term to the said action or shew Cause to the contrary Judgment by default be entered against the said State.
August 6	The Cause continued by consent of the Attorney for the Plaintiff.
1794 February 18	Continued
" August	Continued
1795 February 5	Non Assumpsit & payment by Leave and Issue And now to wit, on the same day, a Jury being called

come, to wit, John Barnes, Wilson Hunt, Robert Gray, Samuel Emory, James Barclay, John. G. Wachsmuth, Sallows Shewell, Samuel Clarkson, John Melbeck, George Aston, Adam Mendenhall, and Israel Pleasants, who being impannelled, tried, sworn and affirmed to speak the truth of and Concerning the premises, upon their Oaths and Affirmations do say, that they find for the Plaintiff 5315 dollars damages and 6 cents costs.

" Eodem die. Judgment nisi.

August Term 1793

Hallowell.	William Vassall, subject of the King of Great Britain $\bar{v}^s$ The State of Massachusetts } Bill in Equity

1793 June 4	Subpœna issued.
August 5	Writ returned by the Marshall for the Massachusetts district
1794 February 18	Continued
" August	Continued
1795 February	Continued
" August	continued
1796 February	continued
Aug[t]	Continued
1797 13 Feb[y]	Suit dismissed with costs.

Morgan. Hallowell.	The State of Georgia $\bar{v}^s$ Samuel Brailsford[4] } In case

1793 June 3	Agreement filed
August 6	Continued by order of Court with the Consent of Parties.

---

4. A partially erased "& others" appears after "Brailsford."

1794 February 4	Narr. Plea and Replication filed and Issue

On motion of M[r] Tilghman of Counsel for the Plaintiff, the Counsel for the Defendant consenting, Leave is given by the Court to insert the Names of Robert William Powell and John Hopton as defendants with Samuel Brailsford

" 8

And now to wit of the Term of February in the Year of our Lord 1794 comes David Lenox Marshal for the Pennsylvania District and returns here in Court a certain Jury of the District who being elected and sworn or affirmed Viz[t] John Leamy Joseph Anthony Samuel Hodgdon Joseph Ball Matthew M[c]Connell Thomas Ewing Robert Smith Robert Ralston Reynold Keen Hugh Lenox and John Stille on their Oaths and Owen Foulke junior on his solemn Affirmation do by their Foreman Reynold Keen respectively _ say that they find a Verdict for the Defendants.

14

On Motion of M[r] Tilghman the Court order that Judgment be entered for the Defendants[5]

February Term 1794

Alexander. S. Glass & others v̄[s] The Sloop Betsey and Cargo and Captain Pierre Arcade Johannen	}	Appeal from the Circuit Court for the Maryland District.

1794 January 24	Appeal filed
February 5	Appellants file their Petition of Appeal
8	.Appellee files his Petition to dismiss the Appeal
"	Agreement of Proctors filed
18	Final Decree of the Court read and filed
	Def[ts] costs p[d] 20 Doll[s]

5. The clerk partially erased an entry which appears in the left-hand column and looks like "1798 Feb[y] 7 [*words illegible*]."

Hallowell. Att^y

John Tyndale Ware
Adm̄nor of William Jones
the surviving partner of
Farrel and Jones — subjects
of the King of Great Britain
v̄^{s}
Daniel Lawrence Hylton &
company & Francis Eppes
Citizens of the State of Virginia

Error from the
Circuit Court for
the Middle Cir-
cuit and District
of Virginia

1794 February 18	Continued
August	Continued
1795 February	Continued
August 5	Continued by consent
1796 March 7	Judgment reversed and Cause remanded. See the Minutes of that day.
Costs p^d	

Bradford Att^y General

United States:
v^s
John Hopkins Esqr

Motion for
a Mandamus to
the Defendant

1794 February 13	Motion made and Rule obtained to shew Cause why the Writ should not issue.
14	Cause shewn, and the Case argued.
15	The Court of Opinion that the Writ ought not to issue.

Morgan. Att^y

Hallowell. Att^y

United States
v̄^{s}
Yale Tod

Amicable Action for
Money had and
received to the plaintiff's Use

1794 February 17

Case and Pleadings drawn and filed
    The Court having heard the Case argued by Coun-
sel and duly considered the same are of Opinion and
accordingly direct that Judgment be entered for the
plaintiff

February Term, 1795.

William Bingham, Plaintiff in error,
$\bar{v}^s$
John Cabot, Andrew Cabot,
Joseph Lee, George Cabot,
Moses Browne,
israel Thorndike,
Francis Cabot, Samuel Cabot,
Jonathan Jackson, Joshua Ward
and Stephen Cleveland,
defendants in error,

} Error from the Circuit Court of Massachu- setts

///

1795 March 2

Ordered, that the Judgment of the Circuit Court for the district of Massachusetts be reversed; and Venire facias de novo refused.

Wt of Error	3.60
Recog:	60[6]
drawing C[i]t:	80
p[d].	5.0

///

John Penhallow, Joshua Wentworth
Ammi Ruhamah Cutter, Nathaniel
Fulsom, Samuel Sherburne, senior,
Thomas Martin, Moses Woodward,
Neal M[c]Intire, George Turner,
Richard Champney, Robert Furness,
and George Wentworth, Plaintiffs
in error,
$\bar{v}^s$
David Stoddard Grenough, and
Anna his wife, and Isaiah Doane,
Adm[n]ors of Elisha Doane,
deceased, defendants in error,

} Error from the Circuit Court of the District of New = Hampshire

1795 February 24

Ordered, that against all the plaintiffs in Error, except George Wentworth, sixteen thousand three hundred and sixty dollars and sixty eight Cents be recovered

6. The "6" is written over a "5."

by the defendants in error, and the same Sum against
George Wentworth; and that against the plaintiffs in
error the Costs of the Circuit Court be recovered,
one half against George Wentworth and the other
half against the other plaintiffs in error; and that in
this Court the parties pay their own Costs. ⎯

1795 March 3ᵈ | Special Mandate awarded, and exit.

Costs pᵈ

| United States ⎯v̄ˢ⎯ John Lawrence, Judge of the district of New=york | Motion for a Rule to show Cause, why a mandamus should not issue. |

1795 March 3ᵈ | Rule refused.

| United States ⎯v̄ˢ⎯ John Hamilton and Thomas Sedgwick | Habeas Corpus. |

1795 February 20 | John Hamilton discharged on bail; and Thomas Sedg-
wick returned by Consent.

| United States ⎯v̄ˢ⎯ Thomas Sedgwick and John Corbley | Motion for a habeas Corpus. |

1795 February 27 | Motion refused.

| Jeremiah Olney, Plaintiff in error, ⎯v̄ˢ⎯ Welcome Arnold, defendant in error, | Error from the Superior Court of Judicature, Court of Assize and Jail delivery for the County of Providence in the State of Rhode Island. |

1795 March 2 | Continued.

August 5 | Continued by Consent.

1796 March 14	Continued
August 11.	Judgment affirmed with costs: and spl. mand. et exit
Costs p^d	

Jeremiah Olney, Plaintiff in error, $\bar{v}^s$ Edward Dexter, defendant in error	Error from the Superior Court of Judicature, Court of Assize and Jail delivery for the County of Providence in the State of Rhode Island.

1795 March 2	Continued.
August 5	Continued by consent.
1796 March 14	Continued
August 11.	Judgment affirmed with costs: and spl. mand. et exit.
Costs p^d.	

William Talbot, Plaintiff in error, $\bar{v}^s$ Joost Jansen, defendant in error	Error from the Circuit Court of South Carolina District.

1795 March 3^d ///	Rule by Consent, that the Magdalena shall be sold, without prejudice to either party, by the Marshall, and the proceeds lodged in the Bank of Carolina, subject to the definitive Sentence of this Court: and that the Court below be inhibited from proceeding, except so far as respects such Sale.—
August 22	Ordered, that the decree of the Circuit Court of South Carolina district, pronounced on the fifth day of November in the Year of our Lord One thousand seven hundred and ninety four, affirming the decree of the district Court of the same district pronounced on the sixth day of august in the Year of our Lord one thousand seven hundred and ninety four, be in all it's parts established and affirmed: And it is further

Considered, ordered, adjudged and decreed, that the said William Talbot, the plaintiff in error do pay to the said Joost Jansen the defendant in error, in addition to the Sum of one thousand seven hundred and fifty five dollars fifty three Cents for demurrage and interest and Eighty two Dollars for Costs, in the decree of the said Circuit Court mentioned, demurrage for the detention and delay of the said Brigantine De Vrouw Christina Magdalena at the rate of nine dollars and thirty three Cents, lawful Money of the United States per diem, to be accounted from the fifth day of November last past till the sixth day of June last, the day of the actual Sale of the said Brigantine under the interlocutory order of this Court of the third day of march last past, to wit, for two hundred and thirteen days, a Sum of Nineteen hundred and eighty seven dollars and twenty nine Cents; and also interest at the rate of seven per Centum per annum for two hundred and ninety days on the Sum of fifty one thousand eight hundred and forty five dollars, being the amount of the Sales of the Cargo of the said Brigantine heretofore sold by order and permission of the said district Court, and making a Sum of two thousand eight hundred and eighty three dollars and forty two Cents and also a like Sum of seven per Centum per annum on the amount Sales of the said Brigantine De Vrouw Christina Magdalena under the Order of this Court, that is to say, interest for seventy seven days on the Sum of Eighteen hundred and twenty dollars from the said sixth day of June last making the Sum of twenty six dollars and eighty seven Cents the whole of which interest to be accounted to this day and making together the Sum of two thousand nine hundred and ten dollars twenty nine Cents lawful money of the United States; And which said interest and demurrage makes together the Sum of four thousand eight hundred and ninety seven Dollars fifty eight Cents in addition to and exclusive of the demurrage interest and Costs adjudged in the said Circuit Court of the United States for South Carolina district, also ninety one Dollars and ninety three Cents for his Costs and

Charges: And that the said Joost Jansen have execution of this Judgment and decree by special Mandate
to the said Circuit Court and process agreeable to the
Act of the Congress of the United States in that Case
made and provided: And the said William Talbot in
mercy and so forth:＿ and spl. mand. et exit.[7]

Costs p.^{d}

August Term. 1795.

///

| John. B. Cotton, Plaintiff in error, v̄.^{s} John Wallace, defendant in error | Error from the Circuit Court of Georgia District |

1795 August 20 | On motion of Mr Read for Defendant Rule to return Record by the first day of January next.

1796 January 7 | Return of Record filed.

" March 2 | Judgment affirmed with Costs and the Question＿ Whether any and what damages shall be recovered? to lie over until the next Term.

August 9. | Ordered, That the said defendant in error recover as damages against the said Plaintiff in error the sum of two thousand seven hundred and eighty seven dollars and thirty two cents, being the interest on thirty four thousand eight hundred and forty one dollars and fifty five cents, the amount sales of the Brig Everton and her cargo from the fifth day of May one thousand seven hundred and ninety five, the date of the decree of the Circuit Court in the said cause until the fifth day of May one thousand seven hundred and ninety six, being one one year, at the rate of eight per centum per annum; and also, that the said Plaintiff in error do pay the costs accrued in this cause since the last term: and a special mandate is awarded to carry this order into execution: et exit.

7. Jacob Wagner added "and spl. mand. et exit."

///

	John Wallace, plaintiff in error, vs Brig Cæsar and Cargo and David Arnache	Error from the Circuit Court of Georgia District.—

1795 August 22	On motion of M[r] Clay for the defendants Rule to return Record by the first day of January next.—
1796 January 28	return of record filed.
February 29	Judgment affirmed with Costs: and spl. mand. et exit.[8]
	Costs p[d]

///

	The United States vs Richard Peters, Esquire, Judge of the District Court in and for the Pennsylvania District.—	Motion for a Prohibition

1795 August 24th	Rule for a prohibition granted et exit.[9]
	Costs p[d]

///

	Ship Elizabeth and Cargo and Hills, May, and Woodbridge, Plaintiffs in error vs Walter Ross	Error from the Circuit Court of Georgia District

1795 August 20	On motion of M[r] Read for the defendant, Rule to return Record by the first day of January next.
1796 January 7	Return of Record filed.
" March 3	Rule by consent, that depositions be taken before any Justice, or Judge of any of the Courts of the United States, or before any Chancellor, Justice, or Judge of

8. Jacob Wagner changed a period to a colon and added "and spl. mand. et exit."
9. The phrase "et exit" was added, probably by Jacob Wagner.

a Supreme or Superior Court, Mayor or Chief Magistrate of a City, or Judge of a County Court or Court of Common pleas of any of the United States, on twenty days notice, if the Notice is given in one State of a Witness or Witnesses to be examined in another, otherwise ten days notice, to either party or to the Agent, proctor or Counsel of either party at or nearest to the place where such deposition shall be taken and be used in the argument of the above Cause; and that if the defendant in error, using due diligence, shall not be able to obtain the deposition of Gideon Davis Pendleton late of Savannah, Attorney at Law and Notary public, his the said Gideon Davis Pendleton's deposition taken on the twenty third day of June 1795 before Nathaniel Pendleton, Esquire, District Judge of Georgia, and now remaining with the Clerk of the Supreme Court of the United States, marked on the back "Walter Ross v̄s Ship Elizabeth filed 5 Augͭ 1795 Z," a Copy of which signed as a Copy by Edward Tilghman is in the possession of the plaintiffs in error, shall be given in evidence if otherwise competent and subject to all legal exceptions, except as to the mode of taking the same: Notice to the British Consul at Charleston to be good for Witnesses examined on the part of the plaintiffs in error at the latter place.

August 12.

Ordered, That the Decree of the Circuit Court for Georgia District, pronounced on the 5ᵗʰ May 1795, be reversed, so far as the same respects the said Hills, May and Woodbridge; and it is further Ordered, That the said Hills, May and Woodbridge pay to the said Walter Ross thirty two thousand and ninety dollars and fifty eight cents, the nett amount of the sales of the cargo of the said ship, and five thousand six hundred and five dollars and twelve cents, interest thereon from the 6ᵗʰ day of June 1794 to the 12ᵗʰ day of August 1796, making together the sum of thirty seven thousand six hundred and ninety five dollars and seventy cents, and that the said Hills, May and Woodbridge do pay the costs of suit: and a special mandate &ᶜ et exit.

Daniel L. Hylton ⎫ Error from the
vs   ⎬ Circuit Court of
The United States ⎭ Virginia District.

1796 March 8 | Judgment affirmed: _ [10]

/// | Argued Feb 23ᵈ _ 24ᵗʰ & 25ᵗʰ 1796 _ [11]

February Term 1796

John Brown Cutting Admͬor
of Ann Paul Emanuel Sigismund
de Montmorency Luxembourg ⎫ Summons
vs   ⎬ Case
The State of South Carolina ⎭

///

1796. | Alias summons issued[12]

August 11. | Rule to file declaration on or before 10ᵗʰ Septͬ next.

same day, | Rule, That certified copies of the declaration be served on the Governor and Attorney General of South Carolina on or before the 1ˢᵗ Novͬ next.

same day. | Rule, That unless the said state shall either in due form appear or shew cause to the contrary in this court by the first day of next term, Judgment by default be entered against the said State.

1797 Febͽ 8. | Rule, That judgment by default be entered against the defendant.

Febͽ 10. | Rule, That a writ of enquiry of damages be awarded to enquire at bar what damages the Pltff. has sustained by reason &ͨ and that three months notice be given to the Governor and Attorney General of South Carolina of the holding of said enquiry.

Augͭ 8ᵗʰ | Verdict for 55002 Dollars and 84 Cents.

11ᵗʰ | Rule for final judgment.

Costs pᵈ |

10. This phrase originally was followed by a colon and a dash and then by a short phrase, now erased, of which only the ending, "et exit," is still legible.
11. This phrase was written in pencil and may not be contemporary.
12. This phrase was written by Jacob Wagner.

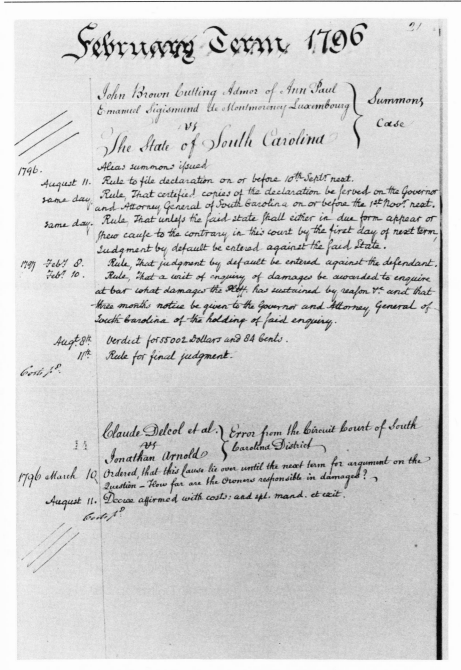

February Term 1796

21

John Brown Cutling Admor of Ann Paul
Emanuel Sigismund de Montmorency Luxembourg } Summons
Case

vs

The State of South Carolina

1796.   Alias summons issued
August 11.   Rule to file declaration on or before 10th Septr. next.
same day   Rule, That certified copies of the declaration be served on the Governor
              and Attorney General of South Carolina on or before the 1st Novr. next.
same day.   Rule, That unless the said state shall either in due form appear or
              shew cause to the contrary, in this court by the first day of next term,
              Judgment by default be entered against the said State.
1797 Feby. 8. Rule, That judgment by default be entered against the defendant.
     Feby. 10. Rule, That a writ of enquiry of damages be awarded to enquire
              at bar what damages the Plff. has sustained by reason &c. and that
              three months notice be given to the Governor and Attorney General of
              South Carolina of the holding of said enquiry.
August 8th   Verdict for 55002 Dollars and 84 Cents.
       11th   Rule for final judgment.
Costs 1s.

Claude Delcol et al. } Error from the Circuit Court of South
                       Carolina District
vs
Jonathan Arnold
1796 March 10 Ordered, that this cause lie over until the next term for argument on the
              Question – How far are the Owners responsible in damages?
August 11.   Decree affirmed, with costs: and spl. mand. et exit.
Costs 1s.

Docket Book, February term, 1796. Courtesy National Archives.

Claude Delcol et al. ⎞
vs   ⎬ Error from the
Jonathan Arnold   ⎠ Circuit Court
                        of South Carolina
                        District

1796 March 10 | Ordered, that this Cause lie over until the next term for argument on the Question— How far are the Owners responsible in damages?—

/// August 11. | Decree affirmed with costs: and spl. mand. et exit.

Costs p^d.

///

John Geyer   ⎞
vs   ⎬ Error from the
John Michel and the ⎮ Circuit Court of
Ship Den Onzekeren ⎮ South Carolina
and Cargo et al.   ⎠ District.

1796 March 14 | Judgment affirmed with Costs but without Damages: and spl. mand. et exit[13]

Costs p^d.

///

Benjamin Moodie   ⎞
vs   ⎬ Error from the
The Ship Betty Cathcart and ⎮ Circuit Court of
Cargo and John Vidal et al. ⎠ South Carolina
                            District.

1796 March 14 | Judgment affirmed with Costs but without Damages: and spl. mand. et exit.[14]

Costs p^d.

////

Benjamin Moodie   ⎞
vs   ⎬ Error from the
The Ship Mermaid   ⎮ Circuit Court of
and Cargo and   ⎮ South Carolina
John Gaillard et al. ⎠ District

1796 March 1 | Judgment affirmed with Costs: and spl. mand. exit.[15]

---

13. Jacob Wagner changed a period to a colon and added "and spl. mand. et exit."
14. Idem.
15. Jacob Wagner changed a period to a colon and added "and spl. mand. exit."

///

Benjamin Moodie
v̄s
The Brig Eliza
and Cargo and
John Gaillard et al.

Error from the
Circuit Court of
South Carolina
District. __

1[16]

1796 March 14 | Continued

August 9. | Decree affirmed with costs: and spl. mand. et exit

///

Benjamin Moodie
v̄s
The Ship Phyn and Cargo
and John Gaillard et al.

Error from the
Circuit Court of
South Carolina
District.

1796 March 14 | Judgment affirmed with Costs: and spl. mand. et exit[17]

///

Benjamin Moodie
v̄s
The Brig Tivoly
and Cargo and
Abraham Sasportas et al.

Error from the
Circuit Court of
South Carolina
District.

2[18]

1796 March 14 | Continued

August 9. | Decree affirmed with costs: and spl. mand. et exit.

///

Benjamin Moodie
v̄s
The Ship Alfred and Cargo
and John Garriscan et al.

Error from the
Circuit Court of
South Carolina
district. __

3[19]

1796 March 14 | Continued

August 9. | Decree affirmed with costs: and spl. mand. et exit.

16. This number is in pencil. A penciled number appears next to all the cases decided on August 9, 1796, in which Benjamin Moodie was a party.

17. Jacob Wagner changed a period to a colon and added "and spl. mand. et exit."

18. See note 16 above.

19. Idem.

///	Benjamin Moodie v̄s The Brig Favorite and Cargo and Alexander B[o]lchos and others	} Error from the Circuit Court of South Carolina District. _
1796 February 29	Judgment affirmed with costs: and spl. mand. et exit.[20]	
Costs p^d		

///	Benjamin Moodie v̄s The Ship Britannia and Cargo and Jean B. Carvine et al.	} Error from the Circuit Court of South Carolina District.
4[21]	1796 March 14	Continued
	August 9.	Decree affirmed with costs: and spl. mand. et exit.

///	Benjamin Moodie v̄s The Snow Potowmack and Cargo and Jean B. Carvine et al.	} Error from the Circuit Court of South Carolina District.
5[22]	1796 March 14	Continued
	August 9.	Decree affirmed with costs: and spl. mand. et exit.

///	Benjamin Moodie v̄s The Brig Eliza and Cargo and Paul Beltrimeaux et al.	} Error from the Circuit Court of South Carolina District
6[23]	1796 March 14	Continued
	Augt 9.	Decree affirmed with costs: and spl. mand. et exit.

20. Jacob Wagner changed a period to a colon and added "and spl. mand. et exit."
21. See note 16 above.
22. Idem.
23. Idem.

7[24]

///	Benjamin Moodie v̄s The Ship Phœbe Ann and Cargo and Jean Bouteille et al.	Error from the Circuit Court of South Carolina District
1796 March 14	Continued	
Aug.ᵗ 9.	Decree affirmed with costs: and spl. mand. et exit.	

///	Don Diego Morphy v̄s The Ship Sacra Familia and Cargo and John Gaillard et al	Error from the Circuit Court of South Carolina District.
1796 March 14	On motion of M.ʳ Pringle, Rule by consent that this Cause be discontinued, and that no other Writ of Error be ever taken out therein. —	

///	Thomas Mac Donogh v̄s Citizen Dannery and the Ship Mary Ford et al.	Error from the Circuit Court of Massachusetts District
1796 February 17	Judgment affirmed with Costs: and spl. Mand. et exit.[25]	
Costs p.ᵈ		

///	David Hunter v̄s George Goodtitle, Lessee of Denny Fairfax	Error from the Circuit Court of Virginia District.
1796 March 14	Continued	
Aug.ᵗ	Continued	
1797 Feb.ʸ 8.	M.ʳ Lee on behalf of the defendant joins in error.	
Feb.ʸ 11.	Rule obtained by the defendant for argument on the 13ᵗʰ instant or writ of error to be non-pros'd.	
Feb.ʸ 13.	Rule for a non-pros. with costs.	

24. Idem.
25. Jacob Wagner changed a period to a colon and added "and spl. Mand. et exit."

///

The United States
v̄s
The Judge of the
District Court
of the United States
for the district
of Virginia.

} Motion for
a prohibition. —

1796 March 14 | Prohibition granted, et exit.[26]

Costs p^d

August Term 1796. —

John Doe, Lessee of
Nathaniel Gist
v̄s
Joseph Robinett

} Error from the
district Court of
Kentucky District. —

1796 Aug^t | Continued.

1797 Feby 6. | Continued.

Augt 7. | On motion of Mr Ingersoll, Rule upon the Clerk of the District Court of Kentucky District to shew cause, why the record is not returned.

1798. Feby 14 | On Motion of Mr Ingersoll Rule upon the Clerk of the District Court of Kentucky District to shew cause why the record is not returned.

Augt 7. | Continued

1799 Feby 4 | On Motion of Mr Ingersoll continued under the Rule last made

///

John Dorrance
v̄s
Cornelius Vanhorne's
Lessee

} Error from the
Circuit Court of
Pennsylvania District.

1796 Aug^t | Continued.

1797 Feb^y | cont^d

Augt 15.[27] | cont^d

26. The phrase "et exit" may have been added by Jacob Wagner.
27. The clerk partially erased a ditto mark to the left of "Aug^t."

1798.[28] Feb.ʸ 14.	Cont.ᵈ
" Aug. 7.	Cont.ᵈ—
1799 Feb.ʸ 14	Rule to assign Errors within two Days or that the Writ of Error be non pros.ᵈ
18th	Ordered by the Court that the aforesaid rule be made absolute

///
Don Diego Pintado
v̄s
The Ship San Joseph, alias
La Princesa de Asturias and
Jean Antoine Berard
} Error from the Circuit Court of New York District

1796 August 10. — Decree affirmed with costs: and spl. Mand. et exit.

Costs p.ᵈ

///
Adrian Wiscart,
Augustin Deneufville, &
Peter Robert Deneufville
v̄s.
Alexis Francis and
Joseph Dauchy[29]
} Error from the Circuit Court of Virginia District.

1796 Augᵗ 1ˢ — Record filed—

Augᵗ 12th — Decree affirmed with Costs: and spl. Mand: et exit

///
The United States
v̄s
The Schooner La Vengeance
and Jean Antoine Berⁿard
de Rozier.[30]
} Error from the Circuit Court of New York District._

1796 August 11. — Decree affirmed: and spl. Mand. et exit.

Costs p.ᵈ

///
Thomas Fennimore
vs.
The United States.
} Error from the Circuit Court of New Jersey District.

28. The clerk partially erased the letters "Feb" which appear beneath "1798."
29. This case name and entry were written by Hand F.
30. The interlined "n" and "de Rozier" are probably in the hand of Jacob Wagner.

1796 August 11.	Continued.
1797 Feb.ʸ 13	Rule for a certiorari on a suggestion of diminution.
1797 July 19ᵗʰ	Certiorari exit.
Aug.ᵗ 7ᵗʰ	Judgment affirmed with costs.
Sept.ʳ 21ˢᵗ	Special Mandate exit.
///	Samuel Emory vs. David S. Grenough } Error from the Circuit Court of Massachusetts District.
1796 Aug.ᵗ 11.	Continued.
1797 Feb.ʸ	Cont.ᵈ
Aug.ᵗ 15.	Cont.ᵈ by consent.
1798 Feb.ʸ 14.	Ordered that the Judgment of the Circuit Court for the Massachusetts District be reversed.
///	Joseph Wiseman vs. The Ship Nuestra Señora del Carmen and cargo and John Jutan, agent of Jean Antoine Garriscan, and Louis Arcambal. } Error from the Circuit Court of Rhode Island District.
1796 Aug.ᵗ 12ᵗʰ	Decree affirmed with costs: and spl. mand. et exit.
Costs p.ᵈ	
///	The Ship Nuestra Señora del Carmen and cargo and John Jutan, agent of John Antoine Garriscan, and Louis Arcambal vs. Joseph Wiseman. } Error from the Circuit Court of Rhode Island District.
1796 Aug.ᵗ 12ᵗʰ	Decree affirmed with costs: and spl. Mand. et exit.
///	William Wilson vs. Thomas Daniel } Error from the Circuit Court of Virginia District.
1796 Aug.ᵗ	Continued.

1797 _ 13. Feb.ʸ	Mʳ Tilghman appears as counsel for the defendant, waves all exception to the writ of error and citation and alleges diminution of the record; and Rule by consent, that a certiorari be issued to either party as he shall elect; but it is understood, that the defendant be at liberty to withdraw his allegation of diminution and proceed to argument on the record as it now stands.
Augᵗ 3ʳᵈ	Certiorari issued on the part of defendant.
Augᵗ 15.ᵗʰ	Continued.
1798 Feb.ʸ 7.	Certiorari returned & filed
Feb.ʸ 14.	Continued
Augᵗ 7.	Ordered that the Sentence of the Circuit Court for the Virginia District be reversed.

February Term 1797.

///	Alexander Moultrie, Isaac Huger and William Clay Snipes, vs. The Governor, Attorney General and Treasurer of the State of Georgia on behalf of the said State, and Nicholas Long, Thomas Glasscock, Ambrose Gordon, Thomas Cummings, James Gunn, David Murray Washington, Matthew McAllister and George Walker.	Bill in Equity.

10 Feb.ʸ 1797.	Rule for a commission to be directed to John Julius Pringle, Henry William DeSaussure, Timothy Ford and Thomas Parker or any three or two of them, to examine witnesses in the State of South Carolina.
eod. die.	Rule for a commission to be directed to Joseph Clay junʳ[,] John Y. Noel, George Woodruff and Stevens, or any three or two of them, to examine witnesses in the State of Georgia.
eod. die.	Rule for a commission to be directed to Joseph Read, John Hallowell, John D. Coxe and Michael Keppele or any three or two of them, to examine witnesses in the State of Pennsylvania.

1797 Aug? 11th	Rule for publication of the Commission returned from South Carolina.
15th	Ordered, That the papers annexed to the commission issued to Joseph Clay junior and others of the State of Georgia, for the examination of witnesses in this cause, in the said State, be detached from the said commission and annexed to the commission issued to John D. Coxe and others of Pennsylvania to take the examination of witnesses in the said cause in the City of Philadelphia.[31]
eod. die	Ordered, that this cause be continued and that publication be made of the execution of the commission directed to Michael Keppele and others to examine witnesses in the City[32] of Philadelphia, as soon as it is returned.
1798 Aug? 14th	The Court is of Opinion that on Consideration of the*[33] Amendment of the Constitution respecting Suits against States that it has no Jurisdiction of this Cause
	It is therefore considered by the Court that the Bill be dismissed so far as respects the State of Georgia _

///

James Clerke, Admor of James Russel: vs. Richard Harwood jun?	Error to the High Court of Appeals of Maryland.

| 1797 11th Feb? | Ordered, That the Judgment of the High Court of Appeals of the State of Maryland be reversed and that the judgment of the General Court of Maryland in the same cause be in all things affirmed, and that the said James Cerke recover against the said Richard Harwood his costs about the same suit expended in the General Court and Court of Appeals of Maryland and in this Court: and a special mandate is awarded to the General Court, et exit. |
| Costs p? | |

31. A partially erased phrase, "State of Pennsylvania," appears beneath "City of Philadelphia."

32. A partially erased word, "State," appears beneath "City."

33. The material that follows was continued on the lower part of the facing page, which the clerk indicated by writing "* cont^d on ye other Side."

///

John Brown
vs.
Andreal E. Van Braam
Houckgueest.
} Error to the
Circuit Court of
Rhode Island District

1797 Feb.ʸ 7.

Feb.ʸ 13.   M.ʳ Barnes for the defendant joins in error.

Ordered, That the judgment of the Circuit Court for the District of Rhode Island be affirmed with costs, and interest at the rate of six per cent. per annum from the day of rendering the said judgment until this day by way of damages: and spl. Mand. et exit.

Costs p.ᵈ

///

Thomas Jennings and John
L. Venner:
vs.
Louis Arcambal and the Brig
Perseverence and cargo.
} Error to the
Circuit Court of
Rhode Island
District.

1797 13 Feb.ʸ

Ordered, That the decree of the Circuit Court be affirmed with costs and damages at the rate of six per cent. per annum on the proceeds arising from the sales of the said Brigantine and her cargo after deducting the duties paid into the custom-house on the said cargo and the commission on the sales, such interest to be calculated from the day of rendering the said decree until this day: and spl. mand. et exit.

Costs p.ᵈ

///

Christopher Court and Company
vs.
Isaac Van Bibber, terre-tenant of
Mark Alexander
} Error to the
High Court
of Appeals
of Maryland

1797 Aug.ᵗ 15ᵗʰ

Ordered, That ˄the judgment of the High Court of Appeals of the State of Maryland be reversed, and that the judgment of the General Court of Maryland in the same cause be in all things affirmed, and that the said Christopher Court and company recover against the said Isaac Van Bibber as terretenant of Mark Alexander his costs about the same suit expended in the General Court and Court of Appeals of Maryland and in this court: and a special mandate is awarded to the General Court, et exit.

Christopher Court and Company	Error to the
vs.	High Court
Cyprian Wells, terre-tenant of	of Appeals
Mark Alexander.	of Maryland

1797 Aug.[t] 15th

Ordered, that the judgment of the High Court of
be reversed, and that the judgment of the
Appeals of the State of Maryland ^ in the same
General Court of Maryland
cause be in all things affirmed, and that the said Christopher Court and company recover against the said Cyprian Wells as terretenant of Mark Alexander their costs about the same suit expended in the General Court and Court of Appeals of Maryland and in
to the General Court,
this court: and a special mandate is awarded ^ et exit.

Christopher Court and Company	Error to the
vs.	High Court
Andrew Robinson and Alexander	of Appeals
Robinson, terretenants of Mark	of Maryland.
Alexander.	

1797 Aug.[t] 15th

Ordered, That the judgment of the High Court of
and that the judgment of the General
Appeals of the State of Maryland be reversed ^ and
Court of Maryland in the same cause be in all things affirmed
that the said Christopher Court and company recover against the said Andrew Robinson and Alexander Robinson, terretenants of Mark Alexander, their costs about the same suit expended in the General Court and Court of Appeals of Maryland and in this Court; and a special mandate is awarded to the General Court, et exit.

John Calder and	Error to the
Jannet Calder	Supreme Court of
vs.	errors of
Caleb Bull	Connecticut.
and Abigail Bull	

1797 _ 7th Aug.[t]   Cont.[d] by consent.

1798 Feb.[y] 9th.   The Death of Caleb Bull suggested

14   Continued

| | Aug.ᵗ 8ᵗʰ | Ordered that the Decree of the Supreme Court of the State of Connecticut be affirmed with costs |

Cotsp.ᵈ

August Term 1797.

	No. 1.	James Brown ⎱ Error to the Circuit Court
		vs ⎰ of Virginia District.
Mʳ Morgan		James Barry
	1797 Aug.ᵗ 8ᵗʰ	Mʳ Morgan joins in error.
	15.ᵗʰ	Judgment affirmed with costs.

Costs p.ᵈ

	No. 2.	James Brown ⎱ Error to the Circuit Court
		vs. ⎰ of Virginia District.
Mʳ Morgan		James Barry
	1797 Aug.ᵗ 8ᵗʰ	Mʳ Morgan joins in error.
	15ᵗʰ	Judgment affirmed with costs.

Costs p.ᵈ

	No. 3	James Brown ⎱ Error to the Circuit Court
		vs. ⎰ of Virginia District.
Mʳ Morgan		James Barry
	1797 Aug.ᵗ 8ᵗʰ	Mʳ Morgan joins in error
	15.	Judgment affirmed with costs.

Costs p.ᵈ

	No. 4.	James Brown ⎱ Error to the Circuit Court
		vs. ⎰ of Virginia District.
Mʳ Morgan		James Barry
	1797 Aug.ᵗ 8ᵗʰ	Mʳ Morgan joins in error
	15ᵗʰ	Judgment affirmed with costs.

Costs p.ᵈ

	No. 5	James Brown ⎱ Error to the Circuit Court
		vs. ⎰ of Virginia District.
Mʳ Morgan		James Barry

1797 Aug.ᵗ 8ᵗʰ | M.ʳ Morgan joins in error.

15ᵗʰ | Judgment affirmed with costs.

Costs p.ᵈ

///

Silas Pepoon and Anna Bingham vs. Thomas Jenkins. } Error to the Circuit Court of Massachusetts District.

1797 Aug.ᵗ 15ᵗʰ | Edward Tilghman Esq.ʳ appears for the defendant in error and the cause is continued by consent.

1798 Feb.ʸ 14ᵗʰ | Ordered that the Decree of the Circuit Court of the United States in and for the Massachusetts District of the Eastern Circuit be affirmed

/// N.º 6.

M.ʳ Morgan

James Brown vs. James Barry } Error to the Circuit Court of Virginia District.

1797 Aug.ᵗ 8ᵗʰ | M.ʳ Morgan joins in error.

15ᵗʰ | Judgment affirmed with costs.

Costs p.ᵈ

///

M.ʳ Morgan.

Samuel Franklin, William T. Robinson, John Taylor, Simon Metcalfe, Christopher Miller and John Blagge vs. William Rotch, Samuel Rodman, William Rotch junior and Benjamin Hussey } Error to the Judges of the Circuit Court of New York District.

1797 _ 10ᵗʰ Aug.ᵗ | continued by consent.
The[34] Plaintiff assigns the General Errors
The Def.ᵗˢ plead in Nullo est erratum and issue is joined thereon.

1798. 6ᵗʰ Feb.ʸ | Agreed between the parties that the Writ of Error be
and the action closed
withdrawn ˄ on the following conditions, That William T. Robinson give Bond for the payment of 3200 dollars payable the 5ᵗʰ of 3.ᵈ Mo: next in New York

34. From this point Samuel Bayard seems to have written the entries through the end of the February 6, 1798, entry.

with condition of failure that Samuel Franklin and Comp.ᵞ pay the Judgment of the Circuit Court at New York upon this case The Defendants to be exempt from all legal Costs. (vide agreement filed).

The State of South Carolina
vs.
The French Republic and } Bill in equity.
John Brown Cutting, Adm̄or
of the Prince of Luxembourg

1797 Aug.ᵗ 15.ᵗʰ   It is ordered, that injunction be awarded to stay all further proceedings on a judgment rendered at this present term, in an action upon the case of John B. Cutting as Adm̄or of the Prince of Luxembourg against the State of South Carolina, until the first day of January next; and it is further ordered by the Court, that injunction also be awarded to stay all further proceedings on said judgment until the further order of this court, upon this condition, that the said State of South Carolina shall, on or before the said first day of January next, bring into this Court the sum of ten thousand, eight hundred and fifty five pounds, eight shillings and five pence sterling money of the State of South Carolina, equal to forty six thousand, five hundred & twenty three dollars & twenty five cents. ~~dollars~~,[35] together with the interest on the same at the rate of seven per cent per annum from the thirteenth day of March one thousand seven hundred and eighty nine to the time of payment into Court, excepting and deducting from the amount of interest one thousand pounds of like money, already paid to the said John B. Cutting (which the said State by her bill exhibited in this Court has acknowledged to be due and owing from her to the legal representative of the said Prince of Luxembourg or to the French Republic, and has offered to deposit the same in this court) and shall deposit the same in this court, subject to its further order and such decree as it may make respecting the same; and shall at the same time pay into this Court the costs in the above action.

35. The phrase, "forty six thousand, five hundred & twenty three dollars & twenty five cents," was added after the initial entry on this day and the word "dollars" was crossed out. The clerk apparently had left a blank space before the word "dollars" so that he could insert the specific amount later.

///   John Innis Clarke and Joseph ⎫   Error to the
        Nightingale   ⎬   Circuit Court
            vs.   ⎭   of Rhode Island.
        Nathaniel Russell

1797 August 15.ᵗʰ   Mʳ Ingersoll assigns the general errors and the cause
                     is continued[36]

1798 Augᵗ 15   continued.[37]

1799. Febʸ 19.[38]   Ordered that the Judgement of the Circuit Court
                     of the United States in and for the Rhode Island Dis-
                     trict of the Eastern Circuit be reversed and a Venire
                     Facias de Novo is awarded

                     Costs pᵈ

///   Archibald Hamilton and ⎫   Error to the Circuit
        John Hamilton   ⎬   Court of Georgia.
            vs.   ⎭
        William Moore

1797 Augᵗ 10ᵗʰ   On motion of Edward Tilghman Esqʳ rule to shew
                     cause why the writ of error should not be amended;
                     and on motion of Mʳ Dallas rule to shew cause why
                     the writ of error should not be quashed.

15ᵗʰ   Ordered, that the writ of error be non-pros'd.

                     February Term 1798.

Mʳ Caldwell   ///   John Coffin Jones   ⎫
                         vs.   ⎬
Livingston   Citizen Joseph   ⎬   Capias Case
                     Philippe Letombe   ⎬   Bail
                     Consul General of the   ⎬   90,000 dollars.
                     French Republic   ⎭

1798 Febʸ 8ᵗʰ   Plaintiff's Deposition filed   C C & B B so
                     Answers[39]   William Nichols Marshall

36. The clerk partially erased an entry which appears in the left-hand column and looks like "[1798?]
Febʸ 8ᵗʰ."
37. This word seems to have been written by Samuel Bayard.
38. This date seems to be in the hand of Samuel Bayard.
39. Hand F wrote from this point to the June 20, 1798 entry.
"C C & B B so Answers": I have taken his body; bail bond entered. It is a response to the *capias*
issued.

Feb.y 9th | On Motion of M.r Dallas Rule to shew Cause why the Defendant should not be discharged upon entering a Common Appearance —

Ordered that the defendant be discharged on entering a Common Appearance.

By direction of M.r Duponceau the Appearance of Edward Livingston is entered for the Defendant —

1798
June 20th.40 | Discontinued by Edward Tighman and Jared Ingersoll Esquires in writing filed

/// | William Bingham
Pltff. in error
vs.
John Cabot, surviving partner of Andrew Cabot, Moses Brown, Israel Thorndike, Joseph Lee, Jonathan Jackson, Samuel Cabot, George Cabot, Joshua Ward and Stephen Cleveland } Error to the Circuit Court of Massachusetts.

1798. Feb.y 14.41 | Ordered that the Judgement of the Circuit Court of the United States in and for the Massachusetts District of the Eastern Circuit be reversed —

/// | Samuel Brailsford, Indorsee of James Spalding
vs.
The State of Georgia. } Summons in case. served42

Narr filed43

1798. Feb.y 14.44 | The Court is45 of Opinion that on Consideration of the Amendment of the Constitution respecting Suits against States it has no Jurisdiction of this Cause

It is therefore Ordered by the Court that this Suit be discontinued.

40. This date and the entry for it seem to have been written by Samuel Bayard.
41. This date seems to be in the hand of Samuel Bayard.
42. This word seems to have been written by Hand F.
43. This phrase was written by Hand F.
44. This date seems to be in the hand of Samuel Bayard.
45. The word "are" appears beneath "is."

August Term 1798.

Morgan

Ingersoll

///

William Irwine
plaintiff in Error
    vs.
John Fenn Lessee
of Charles Sims
Defendant in Error

} Error from the
Circuit Court of the
United States for the
Pennsylvania District

1798 Augt 4th | Record returned
The Plaintiff by Benjamin R. Morgan his Attorney assigns the General Errors _ Defendant joins in Error

8th | Continued by Consent

1799 Feby 19 | On solemn Argument it is ordered, adjudged and decreed by the Court that the Judgement of the Circuit Court of the United States for the Pennsylvania District be affirmed and Special Mandate awarded

Costs p^d
by Plf^t in error _

Howell

Robbins
Dexter
Tilghman

///

John Innis Clarke surviving
Partner of Clarke & Nightingale
    vs.
Nathaniel Russell

} Error from the
Circuit Court of
the Rhode Island
District

1798 Augt 6th | Record returned and filed _
Bill of Exceptions filed to be annexed to the Record
Defendant by Edward Tilghman his Attorney pleads in Nullo est Erratum.

8th | Continued by Consent of Parties

1799 Feby 19th | On solemn Argument ordered by the Court, that the Judgement of the Circuit Court for the Rhode Island District be reversed and that a Venire Facias de Novo be awarded

Gibbs & Channing
of Newport _ R. I.
will pay costs _

S. B^46 rec^d Costs.

46. Samuel Bayard.

Hillhouse		Samuel Fowler & Joseph Lyman
	///	vs.
Hoffman Lewis		Abraham Miller

1798 Aug.[t] 8th

On Motion of M.[r] Lewis

Ordered that the Plaintiff's shew cause by the first day of the next Term why a Venire should not be awarded to summon a Jury from some District of the United States other than the District of Connecticut and New York

1799 Feb.[y] 4th Rule returned with proof of Service

Feb.[y] 19 Ordered by the Court on Argument that the above Rule be discharged

S. B[47] rec.[d] Costs.

Hillhouse		Samuel Fowler and Joseph Lyman
		vs.
Hoffman Lewis		Mary Lindslay, Samuel Lindslay, Ebenezer Lindslay, Moses Milford, John Seely
	///	

1798 Aug.[t] 8th

On Motion of M.[r] Lewis

Ordered that the Plaintiff shew Cause by the first day of the next Term why a Venire should not be awarded to summon a Jury from some District of the United States other than the Districts of Connecticut and New York

1799 Feb.[y] 4th Rule returned with Proof of Service

Feb.[y] 19th Ordered by the Court on Argument that the above Rule be discharged —

S. B[48] rec.[d] Costs.

///

Levy.	United States	Suggestion for a Pro-
	vs.	hibition to the Circuit
	Benjamin Franklin Bache	Court of the United States for the Pennsylvania District.

47. Idem.   48. Idem.

1798 Aug.ᵗ 8ᵗʰ	Continued

| 1799[49] | Abated by Death of the defendant _ |

| /// | Edward John Pierce and Abel Harris Appellants vs. Ship Alligator and Benjamin Lincoln Esq.ʳ } Error to the circuit Court of the United States for the Massachusetts District |

| 1798 Aug.ᵗ 18ᵗʰ | Record returned
Assignment of Errors by Edward S.ᵗ Loe Livermore Attorney for Appellants[50] filed with the Record. |

| 1799 Feb.ʸ[51] | Continued. _ |

| 1799 Aug.ᵗ | Rule to prosecute within the Term or Non Pros: |

| Aug.ᵗ 9ᵗʰ. | Ordered that a Non Pros: be entered _ |

February Term 1799.

| /// | Richard Downing Jennings vs. James Read surv.ᵍ Ex̄or of Joseph Carson dec.ᵈ } Error from the Circuit Court of the United States for the Pennsylvania District _ |

| 1799 Feb.ʸ 4ᵗʰ. | Record returned & filed
    Ordered and decreed by the Court by Consent of Counsel that the several Decrees of the Circuit Court and of the District Court, so far as the same Decree that the said District Court had not Jurisdiction to carry into Effect the Decree of the Court of Appeals shall be reversed, annulled and made void and that the cause be remanded to the District Court that such proceedings may ^be therein had in all other Respects as to Law and Right shall appertain
    The Defendant in Error being at Liberty to contend before the District Court of Pennsylvania as |

49. This date and entry may have been written by Samuel Bayard.

50. Edward St. Loe Livermore (1762-1832) opened a law office in Concord, New Hampshire, in 1783. He was living in Portsmouth, New Hampshire, when he submitted this assignment of errors for filing with the record of *Pierce v. Ship Alligator*. There is no record of his admission to the Supreme Court bar. *BDAC*.

51. This date and the entry for it were written by Samuel Bayard.

Matter of Defence on the Merits or to the Form of Proceedings that the Libel should first have been filed in the District Court of New Jersey, but not to make the Decision of the Judge on that point a Ground of excepting to the Jurisdiction of the said District Court of Pennsylvania

Costs to await the Event of the Cause—

Morgan.[52]

///

James Mossman (surv^g Ex̄or of James Houston) & William Mein vs. William Higginson surv^g Partner of Greenwood Higginson	}	Error from the Circuit Court of the United States for the District of Georgia—

1799 Feby 11th	Record returned & filed
18th	Continued.
" Aug^t	Rule on the Defendant to appear and plead by the 8th Instant
Augt 8th	Continued—
1800— Feby 7.[53]	Order'd that the Plaintiffs have leave to amend their writ of error by inserting the return day to which said writ was returnable—
" 8.	Continued by order of Court.—
" August. 11.	Judgment of the Circuit Court revers'd—

August Term 1799—

State of New York vs. State of Connecticut and Andrew Ward, Jeremiah Halsey, Samuel Fowler, Joseph Lyman & Others[54]	}	Bill in Equity

52. This word is in the hand of Samuel Bayard.
53. This date and the following entries for this case are in the hand of Samuel Bayard.
54. The entries for this case in August 1799 term were cross-referenced by page number to entries for the same case in February 1800 term and August 1800 term. Hand H, who wrote the numbers, also appears in the docket after 1800, and it is not known whether the cross-referencing occurred before or after that date.

1799 June 22ᵈ	Bill filed —
1799 Augᵗ	The Court refuse⁵⁵ the Injunction prayed for in this Cause. Ordered that the Defendants J. Lyman and S. Fowler &c &c⁵⁶ plead, answer or demur to the Bill filed in this Cause within Sixty days —
1800. Febry 13 — ⁵⁷	Contᵈ

Thomas Turner survᵍ Partner
of John Wright Stanly and
Wright Stanly
    vs.
President & Directors of the
Bank of North America
} Error from North Carolina

1799 Augᵗ 2ᵈ	Record filed —
1799 Augᵗ	Ordered and decreed by the Court that the Judgement of the Circuit Court for the District of North Carolina in this [suit?] Cause be Reversed with Costs.

///

Thomas Turner Admor of
Wright Stanley decᵈ
    vs
Marquis De Caro Eurilla
} Error from North Carolina

Morgan.⁵⁸

1799 Augᵗ 5ᵗʰ	Record filed —
Augᵗ	Ordered and Decreed by the Court that the Judgement of the Circuit Court for the District of North Carolina be Reversed with Costs —

///

Robert Hazlehurst
    vs.
United States
} Error from South Carolina

1799 July 27ᵗʰ	Record filed
Augᵗ 9	Non pros: Special Mandate issued

55. A partially erased "d" is visible at the end of the word.
56. This "&c" may be in Samuel Bayard's hand.
57. This date and the entry for it were written by Hand I. This hand also appears in the docket after 1800, and it is not known whether this entry was added before or after that date.
58. This word is in Samuel Bayard's hand.

///	John Geyer vs United States }	Error from South Carolina.
1799 July 27th	Record filed	
Augt 9th	Non Pros: Special mandate issued	
///	Ebenezer Coffin vs. United States }	Error from the Circuit Court of the United States for the District of South Carolina
1799 July 27th59	Record filed	
Augt 9th	Non pros: Special Mandate issued	
///	Ebenezer Coffin vs United States }	Error from the Circuit Court of the United States for the District of South Carolina
1799 July 27th	Record filed	
Augt 9	Non pros: Special Mandate issued	
///	Thomas Tunno vs. United States }	Error from the Circuit Court of the United States for the District of South Carolina
1799 July 27th	Record filed	
Augt 9th	Non Pros: Special Mandate issued	
///	James Miller vs United States }	Error from the Circuit Court of the United States for the District of South Carolina
1799 July 27th	Record filed	
Augt 9th	Non pros: Special Mandate issued	

59. A partially erased "3rd" appears beneath "7th."

February Term 1800

Mossman & Mein ⎱
    vs   ⎰ Error from Georgia
Higginson

1800[60] Feby 8th | Continued —

1800 Augt 11.[61] | The Court having heard the parties in said cause by their respective Counsel, Order the Decree of the Circuit Court for the District of Georgia in said cause to be reversed, it not appearing to the supreme Court of the United states from the Record that the Circuit Court for the District of Georgia had jurisdiction in said cause —

State of New York ⎱
    vs   ⎰ Bill in Equity
State of Connecticut[62]

Continued

Basil Cooper ⎱
    vs   ⎰ Error from Georgia
Edward Telfaire

7th Febr^y | plea filed & Issue

13th Feb^y | Ordered and decreed by the Court that the Judgment of the Circuit Court for the district of Georgia be affirmed with Costs

John G Williamson ⎱
    vs   ⎰ Error from Georgia
Maria Kincaid[63]

13th Feb^y | On Motion of Mr Ingersoll of Counsel for the plaintiff in Error. — Ordered that the Cause be con-

---

60. "1800" was written by Hand I. This hand also appears in the docket after 1800, and it is not known whether this was added after that date.

61. This date and the entry for it were written by Hand I. This hand also appears in the docket after 1800, and it is not known whether this entry was added before or after that date.

62. The entries for this case in February 1800 term were cross-referenced by page number to entries for the same case in August 1799 term and August 1800 term. Hand H, who wrote the page numbers, also appears in the docket after 1800, and it is not known whether the cross-referencing occurred before or after that date.

63. The entries for this case in February 1800 term were cross-referenced by page number to an entry for the same case in August 1800 term. Hand H, who wrote the numbers, also appears in the docket after 1800, and it is not known whether the cross-referencing occurred before or after that date.

tinued till the next Term — the Writ of Error not to be a Supersedeas to the decision of the Circuit Court — The plaintiff in Error to be at Liberty to shew to the Satisfaction of this Court that the Matter in dispute exceeds the Sum or[64] Value of two Thousand dollars exclusive of Costs — This is to be made to appear by Affidavit on ten days Notice to the opposite Party or her Counsel in Georgia — Rule as to Affidavits to be mutual

August 15.th[65]   Continued by consent.

Elizabeth Course
vs   } Error from
The Exors of Benjamin Stead) Georgia

Record returned & filed

12th Feby   Ordered that the Writ of Error in this Case be quash'd with Costs —

The United States)
vs   } Appeal from New York
George Topham   )

7th Feby   Agreement of Counsel filed — Errors assigned and Joinder in Error
Writ of Error issued by Consent retble as of this Term
    Judgment of the Circuit Court for the district of New York affirmed

Costs pd

Thomas Blane   )
vs   } Error from Virginia[66]
Ship Charles Carter)

8th Feby   Ordered by the Court that the Appeal from the Circuit Court for the Virginia District be dismissed —

64. A partially erased "f" appears beneath the "r."
65. This date and the entry that follows were written by Hand J. This hand also appears in the docket after 1800, and it is not known whether this was added after that date.
66. The word "Virginia" was written by Hand K. This hand also appears in the docket after 1800, and it is not known whether this was added after that date.

///

| | Walter Rutherford & Others vs Samuel R. Fisher & Myers Fisher | Error from the Circuit Court of New Jersey |

Feby 6th | Ordered that the Writ of Error issued in this Case be quashed with Costs

Costs p^d.

| James Greenleaf vs Henry Banks | Error from Virginia |

Feby 10th | Record returned & filed — Agreement of Counsel with Assignment of Errors and Joinder filed

12th | Continued

August 9th,67 | Continued —

///

| Paine & Bridgman vs The United States | Error from South Carolina |

Feby 10th | Record returned & filed — plea filed & Joinder in Error

12th | Ordered that the Writ of Error in this Case be quashed

August Term 1800 —

| The State of New York vs The State of Connecticut^68 |

1800 August 14th | Continued by Consent

15 | Demurrer filed

---

67. This date and the entry for it were written by Hand J. This hand also appears in the docket after 1800, and it is not known whether this was added after that date.

68. The entries for this case in August 1800 term were cross-referenced by page number to entries for the same case in August 1799 term and February 1800 term. Hand H, who wrote the numbers, also appears in the docket after 1800, and it is not known whether the cross-referencing occurred before or after that date.

	~~John G Williamson~~ vs ~~Maria Kincaid~~[69]
~~1800 August 15th~~	Continued by Consent
	~~James Greenleaf~~ vs ~~Henry Banks~~[70]
1800 Augt 9th	Continued
	Thomas Blane vs Donald & Burton & T. Burton
1800 Augt 2d	Record returned and filed
14	Writ of Error quashed _
	Doe Lee of Lambert vs Reuben Payne Error from Virginia[71]
1800 Augt 2d	Record returned & filed
14	Writ of Error quashed
	David Ross vs Thomas Maul
1800 Augt 2d	Record returned & filed
14th	Writ of Error Quash'd
	Whitehead Jones & Others Plff vs Henry Ward Pearce
1800 Augt 9th	Decree below reversed

69. The entry for this case in August 1800 term was cross-referenced by page number to entries for the same case in February 1800 term. Hand L, who wrote the numbers, also appears in the docket after 1800, and it is not known whether the cross-referencing occurred before or after that date.

70. Idem.

71. The phrase "Error from Virginia" was written by Hand K. This hand also appears in the docket after 1800, and it is not known whether this was added after that date.

Elizabeth Course
vs
The Ex̄ors of Benjⁿ Stead

On Motion of Mʳ Dallas— Ordered that the Plaintiff have Leave to amend her Writ of Error by inserting the true Teste Day— and the Record by stating the Court to which said Writ was directed—

Ordered— That this Cause be continued to the
next Term the Writ of Error not to be a Supersedeas
to the decision of the Circuit Court— The Plaintiff
in Error to be at Liberty to shew to the Satisfaction
of this Court that the Matter in dispute exceeds the
Sum or value of Two Thousand Dollars exclusive of
Costs— this to be made to appear by Affidavit on
 days Notice to the opposite party or their Counsel
in Georgia—

Rule as to affidavits to be mutual—

Edward Telfaire
vs
The Ex̄cors of Benjamin Stead

1800 Augᵗ 15ᵗʰ On Motion of Mʳ Dallas this Cause is continued—

William Priestman
vs
The United States

1800 Augᵗ 15ᵗʰ Decree below affirmed with Costs

John Baas
vs
Thomas Tingey

1800 Augᵗ 15ᵗʰ Decree below affirmed with Costs

Gideon Olmstead & others
vs
Matthew Clarkson

1800 Augᵗ 14ᵗʰ   Writ of Error issued by Consent of Counsel on
Agreement[72] in Writing filed

15 Continued

72. A partially erased "in Writing" appears beneath "on Agreement."

Ingersoll[73]

Dallas.[74]

Silas Talbot Commander of the United Ship Constitution vs Hans F Seaman Claim[r] of The Amelia	Error from New York

1800 Aug[t] 14th

Continued by Order of Court —

On Motion of M[r] Dallas Attorney for defendant in Error — Ordered that the Writ of Error issued in this Case shall not be a Supersedeas to the Payment of one Moiety of the Sales of the Vessell and Cargo in Question after deduction of duties, Costs and Charges of the said Vessell & her Cargo agreeably to the Order of the District Court of New York and the Affirmance thereof by the Circuit Court

---

73. This word seems to be in the hand of Samuel Bayard.
74. Idem.

Notes for Docket Entries

The only notes for docket entries that survive are those published below for February and August terms, 1798.[1] The notes for February are on a single folio sheet in the hand of David Caldwell, who also kept the rough minutes for that term. Caldwell's list includes all cases mentioned in the minutes during that term. The cases, however, are not given in the order of their appearance in the minutes; rather, they are listed in chronological order according to their date of first docketing. This organization would have facilitated the transfer to the docket of minute entries for the term. Samuel Bayard and Hand F used Caldwell's notes as a guide to record the appropriate entry under each case in the engrossed docket.[2] The two diagonal lines to the left of each case name may have been used to indicate that entry into the docket was finished.

Bayard's docket notes for August term, 1798, are on a folded, full-sized folio sheet. As with Caldwell's list, Bayard's presents the cases heard in August in the order in which they appear in the engrossed docket. Bayard mistakenly included *Emory v. Greenough* and *Franklin v. Rotch* both of which had been concluded in February term, 1798. The diagonal, three-line marks (///) to the left of some case names indicate the conclusion of a case in August term, 1798. The purpose of the check marks next to some case names is not known.

1. An 1827 inventory of "Rough   Dockets" lists as "Lost" the original dockets for the entire first decade of the Court's existence (General Records, RG 267, DNA).

2. See table of handwriting in headnote to "Docket."

David Caldwell's Docket Entry Notes ————————————
February 1798 Term

List of Causes — Sup: C. Feb: 1798.

// Hollingsworth et al vs State of Virginia (Sat:
// Lessee of Gist vs Robinett
// Dorance vs Van Horne's Lee
// Emory vs Greenough
// Wilson vs Daniel
// Moultrie et al vs State of Georgia
// Calder vs Bull —
// Pepoon et al vs Jenkins

// Franklin et al vs Rotch et al. Settled
// Cutting vs State of S.º Carolina _
// Russel vs Cl[e]rke et al.
// Jones vs Letombe
// Bingham vs Cabot
// Brailsford vs State of Georgia _

D (DNA, RG 267, General Records).

Samuel Bayard's Docket Entry Notes ————————
August 1798 Term

Causes depending in the Sup. Cur of y.ᵉ U. S.

Aug. Term. 1796.

Gist.
   v̄.ˢ   }   Cont.ᵈ _ 7 Aug. 98:
Robinete.

Dorance
   v̄s.   }   Cont.ᵈ 7 Aug. _ 98.
Vanhorne's Lee.

/// Emory.
   v̄s.   }   Settled _
   Grenough.

/// Wilson
√   vs   }   Sentence below revers'd _
   Daniel

7 Aug. 98.

Feb.ʸ Term 1797.

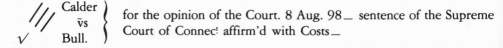

/// Calder
√   v̄s   }   for the opinion of the Court. 8 Aug. 98 _ sentence of the Supreme
   Bull.   Court of Connec.ᵗ affirm'd with Costs _

Aug. Term. 1797.

Franklin. & al[s]
   v̄s.   Vide. an agree[t] to withdraw this action _ on certain con-
Rotch & als.   dition _ q[ly] if conditions comply[d] with _

Feb[y] Term. 1798.

Jones
  v̄s   discontinue'd.
Letombe.

August Term: 1798.

Irwin
  vs   Cont[d] _ by consent _
Lee of Sims.

7 Aug. 98.

Clark v
  v̄s   Cont[d] by consent
Russell.

8. Aug. 98.

U. States
  v[s]
B. F. Bache.

Fowler &
Lyman
  v̄s.
Miller.

Same
  v̄[s]
Lindsley & al[s].

D (DNA, RG 267, General Records).

Admission to the Bar

After the letters patent of the justices and attorney general had been read, a crier and clerk appointed, and seals ordered, the Court in February, 1790, next turned its attention to the organization of the Court's bar. On February 5 it established rules regarding criteria for admission, a distinction between attorneys and counsellors, and an appropriate oath. On February 7 of the following year, the justices made provision for an affirmation (in lieu of an oath) for admission to the bar.

The attorneys and counsellors admitted during the Court's first term came from as far south as Georgia and as far north as the District of Maine. More than one-half came from New York, and close to one-third came from New Jersey and Massachusetts. There is some question as to how they established their qualifications for the bar.[1] It is unlikely that they would have brought with them written evidence meeting the Court's requirements, which were not stated until February 5, five days before the term's end. The certificates[2] and character references that survive for three applicants in February, 1790, were prepared during that short interval. How did the rest of the applicants verify their credentials? It is possible that either a justice or some credible witness provided evidence of their qualifications. The minutes of the Court do not record who moved the admission of attorneys and counsellors either in February term or August term, 1790. In the latter term, all applicants for the bar brought to the Court either certificates or character references or both.

The admission procedure changed markedly when the Court moved to Philadelphia in February, 1791. On the first day of the term, a large number of lawyers appeared for admission to the bar but lacked the appropriate paperwork. Edward Burd, prothonotary of the Supreme Court of Pennsylvania and one of the group applying for admission, immediately supplied the requisite certificate for twenty-two applicants. But they still had to present evidence of good character. Six of the twenty-two individuals were admitted that first day: four on the basis of offices that they held or had held involving legal expertise; one after being vouched for by Associate Justice James Wilson, who had not wanted to vouch for anyone; and one, Jared Ingersoll, on the basis of his recognized eminence as a lawyer. This episode was particularly important because, during the discussion of who would be admitted, Chief Justice Jay explained that the Court would not allow members of the Supreme Court bar to vouch for other lawyers.[3] As a result, after the admission of William Lewis, the first counsellor admitted on February 7, 1791, counsellors and attorneys were almost always admitted on motion of the attorney general of the United States. This latter practice was followed fairly consistently during the period when Jay was chief justice; it changed, however, after his resignation. From August, 1795, through August, 1800, the members of the Court's bar, with very few exceptions, moved the admission of applicants.

The most comprehensive source for ascertaining membership in the Supreme Court bar is the minutes, which include most of the attorneys and counsellors admitted. Some counsellors, however, do not appear in the minutes: for example, Arthur Lee, Alexander White, and Samuel Johnston are listed only on the parchment counsellor roll.[4] Conversely, the three rolls with signatures of lawyers admitted to the Supreme Court bar are incomplete. The parchment counsellor roll, begun by clerk John Tucker, was abandoned after February term, 1792, and the next signature was not added until 1801. The parchment attorney roll which Tucker began is complete through February 8, 1791. After that date, Samuel Bayard began to have attorneys sign their names in a bound attorney roll. John Caldwell and Benjamin R. Morgan, two of the attorneys who had already signed the parchment attorney roll, also signed the bound attorney roll.[5]

The parchment counsellor and attorney rolls are each composed of a long sheet of heavy parchment, with slight discoloration at the edges. The signatures and dates on the counsellor roll are quite faded and difficult to read, while those on the attorney roll are more legible despite some fading. At the top of these parchment rolls, John Tucker recorded the oaths of, respectively, a counsellor and an attorney; Samuel Bayard made minor revisions in each reflecting the Court's rule allowing affirmations in February, 1791. The bound attorney roll consists of a long, narrow bound volume with the oath or affirmation of an attorney at the top of the first page in the hand of Samuel Bayard.

The clerks of the Supreme Court also maintained files of certificates and character references. The former usually certified prior admission to a state's highest court. By perusing this section, a reader can see that the files of certificates and character references are incomplete. An endorsement page is all that survives of a certificate for John W. Kittera (admitted as a counsellor on February 11, 1792). Endorsements on some manuscripts indicate that originally more documents belonged in the file and are now missing. Finally, it should be noted that documentation is published here for two individuals—Sampson Levy and Anthony Morris—never admitted to the bar of the Supreme Court, but whose certificates and character reference were found in the papers of that Court's clerk.

1. For a detailed discussion of some of the issues raised here, see James R. Perry and James M. Buchanan, "Admission to the Supreme Court Bar, 1790-1800: A Case Study of Institutional Change," *Supreme Court Historical Society Yearbook* (1983), pp. 10-16.

2. As used in the present volume, "certificates" refers to documents filed by applicants that vouched for their having practiced in the highest courts of their states.

3. See "Commentaries," Edward Burd to Jasper Yeates, February 8, 1791; see also "Certificates and Character References," Certificate of Twenty-Two Individuals, Admitted as Attorneys and Counsellors, February 7 and 8, 1791, and Certificate of Sixteen Individuals, Admitted as Attorneys and Counsellors, February 8, 1791.

4. See the parchment counsellor roll published in this section.

5. When Elias B. Caldwell became clerk, he instituted some changes in the use of these three rolls. First Caldwell, possibly confused by the existence of a parchment as well as a bound attorney roll, had newly admitted members of the bar sign both through the end of 1801. It should be noted that the Court passed an order on August 12, 1801, allowing counsellors to be admitted as attorneys ("Minutes of the Supreme Court of the United States, 1790-1805," in General Records, RG 267, DNA); thereafter, most lawyers were admitted as both. Until the end of 1801, counsellor/attorneys signed the parchment counsellor and attorney rolls as well as the bound attorney roll. After 1801, Caldwell abandoned the bound attorney roll entirely and had counsellor/attorneys sign only the parchment rolls through February 11, 1805. After that date, the parchment attorney roll was never used again. Beginning that same term, Caldwell began to have newly admitted counsellors sign either the parchment counsellor roll or what had formerly been the bound attorney roll. It may have been at this time that both were relabeled. The interlined phrase "& Counsellor" was added to the oath/affirmation preceding the signatures in the former bound attorney roll; "and Attorney" was interlined in the oath/affirmation preceding the signatures in the parchment counsellor roll. After February 20, 1807, the parchment counsellor roll was never used again; the newly designated bound attorney/counsellor roll was continued. This first volume was used until 1852 when the need for more space led to the use of a new one.

Signatures of Counsellors and Attorneys Admitted

Parchment Counsellor Roll ——————————————————

A Roll of Counsellors sworn in the Supreme
Court of the united States.

(or affirm as the Case may be)[1]

I ...... do solemnly swear that I will demean myself as a <u>Counsellor</u> ^ of this
Court uprightly and according to Law; and that I will support the Constitution
of the united States.

1. Elias Boudinot   5th Feby 1790
2. Thos. Hartley   5th Feby 1790
3. Rich: Harison,   5 Feby 1790
4. Egbt Benson_   Feby 8th 1790.
5. John Laurance   Feby 8th 1790
6. Theodore Sedgwick   Feby 8th 1790
7. William Smith_   Feby 8th 1790
8. MornLewis_.   Feby 8th 1790
9. Jas Jackson   Feby 8th 179[0].
10 Fisher Ames   Feby 8. 1790
11. George Thatcher   Feby 8th 1790
12. Richd Varick   Feby. 8. 1790
13. Robt Morris   Feby 8th 1790.
14. Samuel Jones   9th February 1790
15 Abm Ogden   9th Febry 1790.
16 Elisha Boudinot   9 feb. 1790_
17. Wm Paterson   9th Feby 1790.
18. Ezekiel Gilbert   9th Feby 1790
19. Corns [J] Bogert   9 Feby 1790
20. Arthur Lee[2]   Feby 1790[3]
21. Richd Bassett   Augt 2d 1790
22. John Vining   August 2d 1790
23 Barnabas Bidwell   Aug. 3rd 1790[4]
24. WmLewis_   Feb: 7th 1791.

25. WmBradford Jun.   Feb[y 7.] _
   1791.
26. Alexr Wilcocks   7th feb[y?] 1791
27. Miers Fisher   7 Feb 1791
28. JonaDSergeant
29. Jared Ingersoll.   7th Feby 1791
30. Edwd Tilghman   Feby 7. 1791
31. Jas Monroe   7. Feby. 1791.
32. EdwBurd   feb 8:[5] 1791
33. Luther Martin   Feb 8th 1791
34. W.Barton.   Feby 8th 1791
35. Moses Levy.   8. Feby 1791
36. John F. Mifflin   Feby 8. 179[1]
37. Chas Heatly   Feby 8th 1791_
38. W.Rawle.   Feby 8th 1791.
39. Jasper Moylan   8th feby 179[1]
40. A. J. Dallas.   8 Feb. 1791
41. Thos Leaming Junr   8 Feby
   [17]91_
42. Peter S. Du Ponceau.
43. John Todd Junr   8th Feby.
   1791.
44. Jos. B. McKean_   Febr 8:
   1791.
45 Jos:Anderson   8th Feby 179[1]

46 Benjamin Chew j[r?] 8ᵗʰ Febʸ 1791
47. AlexʳWhite⁶ 8ᵗʰ Febʸ 1791
48. SamˡJohnston⁷ 8. Febʸ 1791.⁸
49. John D.Coxe 1. Augᵗ 1791 _⁹
50 David L. Barnes_ Aug[s?]ᵗ 2ᵈ 1791
51. Thomas Smith 2ᵈ Augᵗ 1791.
52 Jacob R Howell 2 Aug 1791 _

53. Charles Swift 3ᵈ Augˢᵗ 1791
54. W Few Fe[b] 11ᵗʰ 1792
55. Jᵒ W: Kittera Febʸ 11ᵗʰ 1792.
56. AbrBaldwin Febʸ 11ᵗʰ 1792
57. [HH] Bracken[ri]dge Febʸ 13ᵗʰ 1792 _
58. Geo. Re[a]d Junʳ Febʳʸ 1[5]. 1792.

D (DNA, RG 267, Records of the Office of the Clerk). Transcribed from the original document, rather than a photocopy.

1. Interlined passage added by Samuel Bayard some time after February 7, 1791, when the Court established a rule allowing attorneys and counsellors to take either an oath or an affirmation.

2. Born in Westmoreland County, Virginia, Arthur Lee (1740-1792) studied law at Lincoln's Inn and the Middle Temple and in 1775 was admitted to the bars of the Court of King's Bench and of the Circuit. Lee lived at Lansdown, his Virginia estate, at the time of his Supreme Court bar admission. *DAB;* Edward Alfred Jones, *American Members of the Inns of Court* (London: Saint Catherine Press, 1924), p. 123; Edmund Jennings Lee, *Lee of Virginia, 1642-1892* (1895; reprint ed., Baltimore: Genealogical Publishing, 1974), pp. 254-55; *Tyler's Quarterly Historical and Genealogical Magazine* 14 (1932-1933): 69.

3. After the February term ended in 1790, several newspapers published the names of counsellors and attorneys admitted to the Court. One group of newspapers published the names in the chronological order of their admission. Interestingly, all of them omitted the name of Richard Harison, and they varied in the spelling of the name of Balthazar DeHaert. The latter appeared as "Bath. de Haert" in the *New-York Journal* of February 11, 1790; as "Balthazar De Hart" in the *Pennsylvania Mercury* (Philadelphia) of February 16, 1790; as "Barth. de Haert" in the *Gazette of the United States* (New York) of March 6, 1790; and as "Balthazar De Hart" in the *Georgia Gazette* (Savannah) of March 18, 1790. The *Daily Advertiser* (New York) published a chronological list of lawyers admitted on February 10 and 11, 1790.

Another group of newspapers printed the names by state of residence. All of them omitted the name of Morgan Lewis. See "Commentaries," *Federal Gazette* under date of February 11, 1790.

4. For newspaper reports of the admission of counsellors at the August 1790 term of the Court, see "Commentaries," *Gazette of the United States* under date of August 4, 1790, and the citations given there.

5. The "8" is written over a "7."

6. Alexander White (ca. 1738-1804) was born in Frederick County, Virginia. He studied law in England, being admitted to the Inner Temple in 1762 and Gray's Inn in 1763. White returned to Virginia in 1765 and established a practice in his native Frederick and surrounding counties. By 1772, he had been appointed deputy king's attorney for the neighboring Berkeley County. At the time of his admission to the Supreme Court bar, White was a congressman from Virginia. *DAB;* Jones, *American Members of the Inns of Court,* p. 216; Willis F. Evans, *History of Berkeley County, West Virginia* (n.p., 1928), p. 224.

7. Samuel Johnston (1733-1816) was born in Dundee, Scotland, and emigrated with his family to North Carolina in 1735. He read law with Thomas Barker at Edenton in 1754 and soon after began his own career there. Johnston was a senator from North Carolina when admitted to the Supreme Court bar. *DAB;* R[obert] D. W. Connor, *Samuel Johnston, Governor of North Carolina, 1787-1789* (Raleigh: Edwards & Broughton, 1912), p. 6.

8. After the February 1791 term, several newspapers printed the names of counsellors and attorneys admitted to the Court. They arranged them by state of residence. See "Commentaries," *Gazette of the United States* under date of February 23, 1791.

9. The admission of John D. Coxe as a counsellor was reported as part of the proceedings of the Court on August 1, 1791. The admission of David Leonard Barnes as a counsellor was reported as part of the proceedings of August 2. See notes under those days in the "Fine Minutes" for newspaper citations. On August 5, 1791, the *General Advertiser* (Philadelphia), after reporting on the proceedings of August 2 and 3 (Tuesday and Wednesday), noted the admission of counsellors on those two days. Reprinted in the *United States Chronicle* (Providence), August 18, 1791. When reprinting this information in their paper of August 6, 1791, the editors of the *Pennsylvania Mercury* (Philadelphia) mistakenly assumed that, because the admissions had been listed in the *General Advertiser* after the proceedings of Wednesday, the admissions had all occurred on that day.

Parchment Attorney Roll

A Roll of Attornies sworn in the Supreme Court of the united States

or affirm (as the Case may be)[1]

I ...... do solemnly swear ^ that I will demean myself as an <u>attorney</u> of this Court uprightly, and according to Law; and that I will support the Constitution of the united States.

> W^mHoustoun   8th Feby 1790 _
> Edward Livingston   9th Feby 1790
> Jacob Morton   9th Feby 1790. _
> Balth^r De Haert   10th February 1790
> J W Keese _   10th February 1790
> Peter Masterton   10 Febru^y 1790.
> Wm Willcocks.   10th February _ 1790.[2]
> John Caldwell   8th February 1791 _
> Benjamin R Morgan   8th February 1791[3]

D (DNA, RG 267, Records of the Office of the Clerk). Transcribed from the original document, rather than a photocopy.

1. Interlined passage added by Samuel Bayard some time after February 7, 1791, when the Court established a rule allowing attorneys and counsellors to take either an oath or an affirmation.
2. See note 3 to the counsellor roll.
3. See note 8 to the counsellor roll.

Bound Attorney Roll ─────────────────────────────────

Month	day	year.	
			I ...... do solemnly swear (or affirm as the case may be) that I will demean myself as an Attorney of this Court, uprightly, and according to law, and that I will support the Constitution of the United States ─
February N. York	8th	1790.	
" "	9th	"	
" "	"	"	
" "	10th	"	
" "	"	"	
" "	"	"	
" "	"	"	
Philadª Febʸ:	8th	1791.	John Caldwell
"	"	"	Benjamin R Morgan
August.	6.	1792.	⊗John[1] Hallowell
			⊗Tranferr'd by order of Court to the list of Consellors ─ Feb 5, 1799[2]
Febʸ	6	1794	Jnº C. Wells

D (DNA, RG 267, Records of the Office of the Clerk).

1. Samuel Bayard began to cross out the first name of John Hallowell, who on February 5, 1799, was admitted by the Court as a counsellor; instead, Bayard appended a note to that effect.

2. The note of John Hallowell's transferal to the counsellor roll is in Samuel Bayard's hand; the date is in pencil and could have been written by Bayard.

Certificates and Character References

Certificate of William Smith ──────────────
Admitted as a Counsellor February 8, 1790

I certify that William Smith /of South Carolina/ has practised in the Supreme Court of the State of South Carolina as Counsellor & attorney during the space of three years & upwards.
New York. Feb.ʸ 8. 1790.

Aedanus Burke[1] ⎞
one of the Judges of the ⎰
Supreme Court of the State[2] ⎰
of South Carolina ⎠

RS (DNA, RG 267, Records of the Office of the Clerk).
   1. Aedanus Burke was in New York on this date as a congressman from South Carolina.
   2. A partially erased "Certi" appears to the left of this line.

Certificate and Character Reference of Elisha Boudinot ─────
Admitted as a Counsellor February 9, 1790

Application having been made unto me John Chetwood Esq.ʳ one of the Justices of the Supreme Court of Judicature in and for the State of New-Jersey by Elisha Boudinot Esq.ʳ Attorney and Counsellor at Law in the said State to give him a Certificate of his having practised in those Characters in the said Court for upwards of three years last past ⎯ I do hereby certify that the said Elisha Boudinot Esq.ʳ has for upwards of that term practised as an Attorney and Counsellor at Law with reputation in the said Supreme Court ⎯ and that he hath always sustained a fair moral Character ⎯ Witness my hand this 8ᵗʰ day of February ⎯ 1790 ⎯

John Chetwood

The Honorable ⎯
The Justices of the Supreme Court ⎱
of the United States

ARS (DNA, RG 267, Records of the Office of the Clerk).

Certificate and Character Reference of Cornelius [J]. Bogert — Admitted as a Counsellor February 9, 1790

I hereby certify that Cornelius [J] Bogart has practised as Counsellor at Law in the Supreme Court of the State of New York upwards of three years, and that he sustains a fair moral and professional character —
Feby 9th — 1790

Rob: Troup[1]

Troup
City of New York ss: The above named Robert ^ being duly sworn deposeth and saith that the contents of the aforegoing certificate are true

Rob: Troup.

Sworn this 9th ~~1790~~
of Feby 1790
  Before me

  Samuel Jones Recorder
  of the City of New York

ARS (DNA, RG 267, Records of the Office of the Clerk). Entirely in the hand of Robert Troup except for the signature and title of Samuel Jones.
  1. Robert Troup is not known to have held any official post that would have authorized him to sign Cornelius Bogert's certificate.
  Robert Troup (1757-1832) was an attorney in New York City in 1790. Admitted to the bar in 1782, he had studied law with John Jay. Both Troup and Bogert had graduated from King's College (later Columbia), Bogert in 1773 and Troup in 1774. *DAB;* [Robert] Hodge, [Thomas] Allen, and [Samuel] Campbell, eds., *The New-York Directory and Register for the Year 1789* (New York: 1789); Paul M. Hamlin, *Legal Education in Colonial New York* (New York: New York University, Law Quarterly Review, 1939), p. 134.

Certificate and Character Reference of Richard Bassett — Admitted as a Counsellor August 2, 1790

Delaware State ss.   To all to whom these ᵱsents[1] shall come
        I William Killen Chief Justice of the Supreme Court within the
        said State send Greeting. I do hereby certify; That the Honor-
SEAL   able Richard Bassett Esqr now a member of the Senate House
        of Congress of the united States, for the State of Delaware
        afores^d hath been, for upwards of twelve years last past, and yet
is, a practising Attorney of record in the said Court; and as such hath, during all that [*letters inked out*] time, demean'd himse[lf] with decency and becoming respect to the Court, and as far as it hath come to my knowledge; with fidelity to his Clients. Given under my hand and seal at Dover in Kent County in the

State afores[d] the Twenty Fifth Day of May in the year of our Lord One Thousand Seven Hundred and Ninety.

William Killen.

ARS (DNA, RG 267, Records of the Office of the Clerk).
  1. The word meant is "presents."

Certificate of John Vining ——————————————————
Admitted as a Counsellor August 2, 1790

This is to Certify That John Vining Esquire Member of the House of Representatives of the United States from the Delaware State in or about the Year 1783 was Admitted to practise as an Attorney and Counsel in the several Courts of that State and hath continued so to Act regularly until his Attendance in Congress given under our hands at New York this Second day of August. 1790—

Geo[:]Read[1]
Rich[d] Bassett[2]

ARS (DNA, RG 267, Records of the Office of the Clerk). This certificate seems to have been written in the hand of Richard Bassett and co-signed by George Read.
  1. George Read was in New York on August 2, 1790, as senator from Delaware.
  2. Richard Bassett, a senator from Delaware, had just been admitted to the Supreme Court bar.

Certificate and Character Reference of Barnabas Bidwell ————
Admitted as a Counsellor August 3, 1790

New Haven   July 30th— 1790

Sir,

The bearer hereof is Barnabas Bidwell Esq[r] of this town, a gentleman of the law, of a fair unblemished character, of excellent abilities & eminent acquirements in the law, and other branches of the arts and sciences— He is an attorney and counsellor at our superior Court, of more than three years standing, and hath been admitted a counsellor and attorney at the circuit Court of this District— It is his wish to be admitted a counsellor at the Supreme Court—.[1] His merit is such, that I am certain, his admission will be highly gratifying to all, who have the pleasure of an acquaintance with him—. I have the honor to be with very great respect.
    your most Obed[t] & v[e]ry H°Serv

Pierpont Edwards

Hon[ble] John Jay—

ARS (DNA, RG 267, Records of the Office of the Clerk).

1. Originally Pierpont Edwards wrote "Supreme Judicial Court" which he changed to the present reading by partially erasing the last two words and writing "Court" over them.

Certificate of Twenty-two Individuals ————————————
Admitted as Attorneys or Counsellors February 7 and 8, 1791

I certify that the Gentlemen hereafter mentioned have been severally admitted and practised in the Supreme Court of the Commonwealth of Pennsylvania as Attornies and Counsellors thereof above the term of three Years.

Witness my Hand the seventh day of february 1791.

EdwBurd ProtSupCur

Penns[a]

Alexander Wilcocks.	Peter Stephen Duponceau
William Bradford.	Benjamin Chew junior
Jonathan Dickinson Sergeant.	Thomas Leaming
Jared Ingersoll.	Joseph Anderson
Miers Fisher.	
Edward Tilghman —	
Moses Levy	
Jasper Moylan	
William Rawle	
Charles Heatley	
Alexander James Dallas	
John Caldwell Att[1]	
William Barton	
John Todd junior. Counsellor[1]	
John F Mifflin	
Joseph B M{c}Kean Counsellor[1]	
Benjamin R Morgan Att[1]	
Edward Burd Counsellor[1]	

ARS (DNA, RG 267, Records of the Office of the Clerk).

Alexander Wilcocks, William Bradford, Jonathan Dickinson Sergeant, Jared Ingersoll, Miers Fisher, and Edward Tilghman were admitted as counsellors on February 7, 1791. For Edward Burd's explanation of why these were the only six on his list admitted to the Supreme Court bar on February 7 while the rest were admitted on February 8, see "Commentaries," Edward Burd to Jasper Moylan, February 8, 1791.

Moses Levy, Jasper Moylan, William Rawle, Charles Heatly, Alexander James Dallas, William Barton, John Todd, John F. Mifflin, Joseph McKean, Edward Burd, Peter Du Ponceau, Benjamin Chew, Thomas Leaming, and Joseph Anderson were admitted as counsellors on February 8, 1791.

John Caldwell and Benjamin Morgan were admitted as attorneys on February 8, 1791.

1. "Att" to the right of the names of John Caldwell and Benjamin Morgan and "Counsellor" to the right of the names of John Todd, Joseph McKean, and Edward Burd may not be in Burd's writing.

Certificate of Sixteen Individuals ——————————————————
Admitted as Attorneys or Counsellors February 8, 1791

s[1]	Edward Burd c[2]	September Term 17.78
s	William Barton c	2[d] October 1779
s	Moses Levy c	10th April 1780
s	John F. Mifflin c	September Term 1781
s	Charles Heatly c	September Term 1783
af[d3]	William Rawle c	2[d] October 1784
s	Jasper Moylan c	April Term 1785
s	John Caldwell a[4]	11th July 1785
s	Alexander J. Dallas c	13th July 1785
s	Thomas Leaming c	September Term 1785
s	Peter Stephen Duponceau c	28th January 1786
af[d]	John Todd junior __ c	11[[h?]] January 1787
	Joseph B McKean c	[2][d] April 1787
s.	Joseph Anderson c	5th April 1787.
af	Benjamin Morgan J[r] a	5th July 1787
s	Benjamin Chew J[r] c	July Term 1787

I Edward Burd Esquire Prothonotary of the Supreme Court of the State of Pennsylvania Do Certify that the foregoing Gentlemen were severally admitted a[s] Attornies in the same Court agreeably [to?] the da[tes?] affixed to their several and respective names [an]d a[lso?] took the Oaths or Affirmations prescribed by Law

> In Witness whereof I have hereto set [my?] hand and affixed the
> SEAL   Seal of the same [S]upreme Court at Philadelphia this Eighth day
> of February in the year of our Lord MDCCXCI.

Edw:Burd ProtSupCur

ARS (DNA, RG 267, Records of the Office of the Clerk). We have bracketed words in the certification signed by Edward Burd because the seal covers part of the text.

John Caldwell and Benjamin Morgan were admitted as attorneys and the rest were admitted as counsellors. For further information pertaining to the admission of these individuals to the bar of the Supreme Court, see "Commentaries," Edward Burd to Jasper Yeates, February 8, 1791.

1. Sworn.
2. Counsellor.
3. Affirmed.
4. Attorney.

s Edward Burd   c   September Term 1778
s William Barton   c   2d October 1779
s Moses Levy   c   10th April 1780
s John F. Mifflin c   September Term 1781
s Charles Heatly   c   September Term 1783
af William Rawle   c   2d October 1784
s Jasper Moylan   c   April Term 1785
s John Caldwell   a   11th July 1785
s Alexander J. Dallas c   13th July 1785
s Thomas Leaming   c   September Term 1785
s Peter Stephen Duponceau 28th January 1786
af John Todd junior c   11th January 1786
s Joseph B. McKean c   28th April 1787
s Joseph Anderson   c   3d April 1787
af Benjamin Morgan Jr a   5th July 1787
s Benjamin Chew Jr c   July Term 1787

I Edward Burd Esquire Prothonotary
of the Supreme Court of the State of Pennsylvania
Do Certify that the foregoing Gentlemen were severally
admitted as Attorneys in the same Court agreeably
the d   affixed to their several and respective names
        took the Oaths or Affirmations prescribed by
In Witness whereof I have hereto set
        and affixed the Seal of the same
Supreme Court at Philadelphia this Eighth
day of February in the year of our Lord
MDCCXCI.   Edw Burd Prothy

Certificate of Sixteen Individuals signed by Edward Burd, February 8, 1791. Courtesy of National Archives.

Character References of Edward Burd ————————
Admitted as a Counsellor February 8, 1791

Philad.ᵃ Feb. 8. 1791

Gentlemen

From a very long and intimate Acquaintance with Edward Burd Esqᶠ. in private life and at the Bar I am able to recommend him as a Gentleman of unimpeachd Moral Character and competent Abilities as a Lawyer

I have the honour to be   Gentlemen   Your most obedᵗ servᵗ

James Biddle
Presidᵗ Com. Pleas of
Philadᵃ County —

From my knowledge of Mʳ Burds Moral & professional Character I readily join in recommending him to be admitted as a Counsellor in the Supreme Court of the United States —

Alexʳ Wilcocks
Recorder of the City of
Philadelphia —

Philadᵃ 8ʰ feb[r?] 1791

ARS (DNA, RG 267, Records of the Office of the Clerk).

Character References of John Todd, Jr. ————————
Admitted as a Counsellor February 8, 1791

John Todd junʳ Esqʳ having practised for some years as Attorney and Counsellor at Law in the Court of Common Pleas in which I have presided, I can safely recommend him as being qualified, both in point of Knowledge in his profession, and moral Character, to practise in the Supreme Court of the United States —

Edwᵈ Shippen

Philadelphia 8ᵗʰ Febry 1791 —

From my Knowledge of the Moral and Professional Character of Mʳ John Todd Junʳ I freely join in the above Recommendation —

Alexʳ Wilcocks

Philadᵃ 8ᵗʰ febʸ 1791 —

ARS (DNA, RG 267, Records of the Office of the Clerk).

Certificate and Character Reference of Joseph B. McKean ———
Admitted as a Counsellor February 8, 1791

I Edward Burd Esquire prothonotary of the Supreme Court of the Commonwealth of Pennsylvania Do Certify that at a Supreme Court held at Philadelphia for the said State the Second day of April in the year of our Lord One
thousand seven hundred and eighty seven On motion of Mʳ Bradford Joseph
B. MᶜKean Esquire was Admitted an Attorney of the same Court, and took
the Oath prescribed by Law

          In Witness whereof I have hereto set [m]y hand and affixed the
   SEAL   Seal [o]f the said. Supreme Court at Philadelphia the Seventh
          [day?] of February in the year of our Lord MDCCXCI.

                                 Edw:Burd protSupCur Pennsᵃ

Joseph B. MᶜKean Esqʳ is in my Opinion well worthy of being admitted to
practise as Counsel in the Supreme Court of the United States; both as to his
legal Abilities and moral Character —

                                   Edwᵈ Shippen

                                   7. Febry 1791.

ARS (DNA, RG 267, Records of the Office of the Clerk). We have bracketed readings in the
certification signed by Edward Burd because the seal covers part of the text.

Certificate and Character Reference of John D. Coxe ———
Admitted as a Counsellor August 1, 1791

We I̶ do certify that John D. Coxe. Esquire has been admitted & practised the
                                       Philadelphia
Law in the Court of Common Pleas for the County of ‸ & the Supreme Court
   Commonwealth
of this ‸ for many Years & that he has always supported a fair Character[1] as a
Practitioner & a man of Morality & Integrity —
   Philadᵃ Augᵗ 1 1791 —

                            James Biddle Preidᵗ[2]
                            Com Pleas Philadᵃ County

                            Alexʳ Wilcocks Recorder
                            of the City of Philadᵃ

ARS (DNA, RG 267, Records of the Office of the Clerk). Written by Alexander Wilcocks and
co-signed by James Biddle.
   1. The letter "r" is written over a "d."
   2. The word meant is "President."

Petition for Admission by David L. Barnes ————
Admitted as a Counsellor August 2, 1791

To the Honorable the Judges of the Supreme Court of the United States of America holden at Philadelphia on the first monday of August Anno Domini 1791 —
David Leonard Barnes —
  Humbly shews
That he has been a practising Attorney regularly sworn & admitted in the Supreme Judicial Court of the Commonwealth of Massachusetts for more than Three years last past — Wherefore he prays that he may be admitted a Counsellor of this Honorable Court — and as in duty bound will pray —

David L. Barnes

ARS (DNA, RG 267, Records of the Office of the Clerk).

Certificate and Character Reference of Jacob R. Howell ———
Admitted as a Counsellor August 2, 1791

The under-written, Chief Justice of the Supreme court of the Commonwealth of Pennsylvania, certifies, that Jacob R, Howell Esquire was admitted an Attorney & Counsellor at Law in the said court in the year 1787, and hath ever since practised therein with fidelity and reputation; that he is acquainted with the moral character of the said Jacob R, Howell, and knows it to be fair and good; and that his abilities in the Law and conduct in life — are very respectable. Signed at Philadelphia August 1st 1791. —

Thos M:Kean

ARS (DNA, RG 267, Records of the Office of the Clerk).

Certificate of Abraham Baldwin ————
Admitted as a Counsellor February 11, 1792

I do Certify that I have known the Honorable Abraham Baldwin esquire one of the Representatives for[1] the State of Georgia in the Congress of the United States as a practitioner of Law in the Superior Courts of the said State from the Year one thousand seven hundred and eighty four.

Jas Jackson
Counsellor at Law
Supreme Court United State[s]

Philadelphia }
11th Feby 1792 }

ARS (DNA, RG 267, Records of the Office of the Clerk).
  1. The word "for" is written over the word "of."

Document for Admission of John W. Kittera ──────────
Admitted as a Counsellor February 11, 1792

[*In the papers from the office of the clerk in Record Group 267 at the National Archives a page exists with the endorsement* "John W. Kittera_ Certificate of Edw ª Burd Esqʳ." *The document for which this is the endorsement is missing.*]

Certificates and Character Reference of John Hallowell ──────────
Admitted as an Attorney August 6, 1792

I Edward Burd Esquire Prothonotary of the Supreme Court of the State of Pennsylvania Do Certify that at a Supreme Court held at Philadelphia for the said State on the Second day of July in the year of our Lord One thousand Seven hundred and eighty nine On Motion of Mʳ Fisher_ John Hallowell Esquire was admitted an Attorney of the said Court, and took the Affirmation prescribed by Act of Assembly

> In Witness whereof I have hereto [s]et my hand and affixed the
> SEAL   Seal [of?] the same Supreme Court at Philadelphia the first day
> of August in the year of our Lord MDCCXCII.

Edw:Burd: ProtSupCurPennsª

Pennsylvania ss.

The under-written certifies, that John Hallowell Esquire has practised as an Attorney and Counsellor at Law in the Supreme court of Pennsylvania for three years last past with fidelity as well to the court as to the client, and with reputation to himself; and also that he sustains a good moral character. Philadelphia. August 2ª 1792.

ThoˢM:Kean

ARS (DNA, RG 267, Records of the Office of the Clerk). We have bracketed readings in the certification signed by Edward Burd because the seal covers part of the text.

Certificates and Character Reference of Samuel Roberts ──────────
Admitted as a Counsellor February 20, 1793

I certify that at a Supreme Court held at Philadelphia for the State of Pennsylvania on the twenty fourth day of September in the year of our Lord one thousand seven hundred and eighty eight on Motion of MʳLewis Samuel Roberts Esquire was admitted an Attorney of said Court and took the oath prescribed by Law.

SEAL

In witness whereof. I have hereto set my Hand and affixed the Seal of the said Supreme Court at Philadelphia the nineteenth day of february in the year of our Lord one thousand seven hundred and ninety three

Edw:Burd prot

The underwritten, Chief Justice of the Supreme court of the State — of Pennsylvania, certifies, that Samuel Roberts Esquire was admitted an Attorney & Counsellor at Law in the said Supreme court above four years past; that he has behaved during that period with fidelity to the Court and Client, and reputation to himself, and that his moral character is fair and unspotted. Given at Philadelphia the 20th day of February 1793. —

Thos M:Kean

ARS (DNA, RG 267, Records of the Office of the Clerk).

Certificate and Character Reference of Ephraim Kirby ————
Admitted as a Counsellor August 6, 1793

State of Connecticutt S: Litchfield 3d June. 1793

These certify that Ephm Kirbie Esqr of this Town has been regalarly admitted as a Councellor & Practitioner at Law agreably to ye Laws of this State, & has practiced as such before ye Supr Court with Reputation for more than twelve Years last past, is esteamed a well studied Lawyer. & Supports a fair & unblemished Charrecter

℣ Andw Adams cheif Justice of ye SuprCourt —

ARS (DNA, RG 267, Records of the Office of the Clerk).

The minutes of the Supreme Court indicate under the August 6, 1793, admission of Ephraim Kirby that certificates were also produced from Roger Sherman and Eliphalet Dyer, associate justices of the Superior Court of Connecticut. These have not been found.

Certificate of John C. Wells ————
Admitted as an Attorney February 6, 1794

I Edward Burd Esquire prothonotary of the Supreme Court of the State of Pennsylvania Do Certify that at a Supreme Court held at Philadelphia for the said State the Second day of October One thousand seven hundred and ninety Before the Honorable Thomas McKean Esquire Doctor of Laws Chief Justice and his Associates Justices of the same Court On Motion of Mr Rawle John

Craig Wells Esquire was admitted an Attorney of the said Court, and duly took the Affirmation prescribed by Law

SEAL

In Witness whereof I have hereto set my hand and affixed the Seal of [t]he said Supreme Court at Philadelphia the fifth day of August in the year of our Lord MDCCXCIII.

Edw:Burd Prot SupCur
Penn[a]

ARS (DNA, RG 267, Records of the Office of the Clerk). We have bracketed one reading because the seal obscures the text.

According to the endorsement on this certificate, a document from Thomas McKean supporting the admission of John C. Wells was originally included. We have not found it.

Certificate and Character Reference of William Tilghman ——— Admitted as a Counsellor February 4, 1795

I do certify That William Tilghman Esquire is a practising Attorney and Counsel in the Supreme Court of the State of Pennsylvania and is unquestionably of good moral and professional Character.

Edw[d] Shippen

Philadelphia 3[d] febry 1795 —

ARS (DNA, RG 267, Records of the Office of the Clerk). Endorsed as "filed 4th Feb[y] 1795."

Certificate and Character Reference of William M. Smith ——— Admitted as a Counsellor February 5, 1795

I Edward Burd Esquire Prothonotary of the Supreme Court of the Commonwealth of Pennsylvania Do Certify that at a Supreme Court held at Philadelphia for the said. State the Eighteenth day of April in the year of our Lord one thousand seven hundred and eighty two, before the Honorable Thomas McKean Esquire Chief Justice and his Associates Justices of the same Court On motion, William Moore Smith Esquire, was admitted an Attorney of the same Court, and took the Oath prescribed by Law.

SEAL

In Witness whereof I have hereunto set my hand and affixed the Seal of the same Supreme Court at Philadelphia the Sixth day of Feb[r]uary in the year of our Lord MDCCXCII.

EdwBurd prot

William Moore Smith Esquire is well known to me: he has behaved as an Attorney and Counsel in the Supreme Court of this State for some years past with Honor and Ability
6. Febry 1792.

Edw.d Shippen
Tho Mifflin
W.mBradford.

ARS (DNA, RG 267, Records of the Office of the Clerk). Endorsed as "filed 5th Feby 1795."

Certificate and Character Reference of Jonathan W. Condy ——
Admitted as a Counsellor August 20, 1795

I Edward Burd Esquire Prothonotary of the Supreme Court of the Commonwealth of Pennsylvania, hereby certify that at a Su-

SEAL preme Court held at Philadelphia for the said Commonwealth the second day of April in the Year of Our Lord one thousand seven Hundred and ninety two before the Honourable Thomas M.cKean Esquire Doctor of Laws, Chief Justice, and his Associates, Justices of the said Supreme Court Jonathan Williams Condy Esquire was on Motion of M.r Sergeant admitted an Attorney of the said Court, and took the affirmation prescribed by Law — In Witness whereof I have hereto set my Hand and affixed the Seal of the said Supreme Court at Philadelphia the eleventh day of April[1] A D — MDCCXCV —

EdwBurd prot

I do certify That Jonathan Williams Condy Esquire is of good moral and professional Character —

Edw.d Shippen

20th August 1795

ARS (DNA, RG 267, Records of the Office of the Clerk). Endorsed as "filed 20th Aug.t 1795."
   1. The word "April" is written over "Feb."

Certificate of Samuel Sitgreaves ——
Admitted as a Counsellor February 3, 1796

I certify that at a Supreme Court held at Philadelphia for the State of Pennsylvania the eleventh day of April in the year of our Lord one thousand seven hundred and Eighty five on Motion of M.r Ingersoll Samuel Sitgreaves Esquire was admitted an Attorney of the said Court and took the Oath prescribed by Act of Assembly

In witness whereof I have hereto set my hand and affixed the
SEAL   Seal of the said Supreme Court at Philadelphia the second day
of february in the Year of our Lord MDCCXCVI.

Edw:Burd ProtSupCur
Penns^a

Certificates and Character Reference of Robert H. Dunkin ——— Admitted as a Counsellor February 4, 1796

I Edward Burd Esquire prothonotary of the Supreme Court of the Commonwealth of Pennsylvania Hereby Certify that a Supreme Court held at Philadelphia for the said Commonwealth the third day of September in the Year
of our Lord One thousand seven hundred and Ninety two before the Honorable Thomas McKean Esquire Doctor of Laws Chief Justice and his Associates Justices of the said Supreme Court Robert Henry Dunkin Esquire was on
Motion of Mr Tilghman admitted an attorney of said Court and took the Oath
prescribed by Act of Assembly.

In Witness whereof I have hereto set my hand and affixed the
SEAL   Seal of the said Supreme Court at Philadelphia this Eleventh Day
of January in the Year of our Lord MDCCXCVI

Edw:Burd prot

The undersigned certifies, that Robert Henry Dunkin Esquire has been duly
admitted and sworn an Attorney at Law in the Supreme court of the Commonwealth of Pennsylvania for upwards of three years past, and hath practised
as such with fidelity & reputation, and justly sustains a fair and good moral
character. Given at Philadelphia the 22^d day of January 1796._

Tho^sM:Kean

Certificates and Character Reference of Robert Porter ——— Admitted as a Counsellor February 6, 1796

I Edward Burd Esquire Prothonotary of the Supreme Court of the State of
Pennsylvania Do Certify that at a Supreme Court held at Philadelphia for the
said State the Seventh day of April in the year of our Lord One thousand

Seven hundred and ninety one Before the Honorable Thomas McKean Esquire Doctor of Laws Chief Justice and his Associates Justices of the same Court On motion of Mr Sergeant Robert Porter Esquire was admitted an Attorney of the same Court and duly took the Oath prescribed by Law

SEAL In Witness whereof I have hereto set my hand and affixed the Seal of the same Supreme Court at Philadelphia the fourteenth day of April in the year of our Lord MDCCXIV.[1]

EdwBurd Prot SupCur
Penns^a

The under-written certifies, that Robert Porter Esquire has been admitted & duly sworn an Attorney at Law in the Supreme court of the Commonwealth of Pennsylvania for five years past, that he hath conducted himself in his practise as such with fidelity as well to the court as to the Client and reputation to himself, and sustains a fair & good moral character. Given at Philadelphia the 22^d day of January 1796._

Tho^sM:Kean

ARS (DNA, RG 267, Records of the Office of the Clerk). Endorsed as "filed 6 Feby 1796."
1. Edward Burd recorded the date in roman numerals incorrectly as 1714. He apparently meant to write "MDCCXCIV" or "MDCCXCV."

Certificate of Richard Lake
Admitted as a Counsellor August 10, 1796

I Certify that at a Supreme Court held at Philadelphia for the State of Pennsylvania the first day of April in the year of our Lord One thousand seven hundred and ninety three Before the Honorable Thomas McKean Esquire Doctor of Laws Chief Justice and his Associates Justices of the same Court On motion of Mr Todd Richard Lake Esquire was admitted an Attorney of the said Supreme Court and duly took the Oaths required by Law

SEAL In Witness whereof I have [here]to set my hand and affixed [t]he Seal of the same Supreme Court at Philadelphia the fifteenth day of April in the year of our Lord MDCCXCIII.

Edw:Burd ProtSupCur
Penns^a

ARS (DNA, RG 267, Records of the Office of the Clerk). We have bracketed readings because the seal obscures part of the text.

Certificate of James Gibson ————————————
Admitted as a Counsellor February 6, 1797

I Edward Burd Esquire prothonotary of th[e] Supreme Court of the Commonwealth of Pennsylvani[a] Hereby Certify that at a Supreme Court held at
Philadelphia for the said Commonwealth the Sec[ond] day of September in the
year of our Lord one thousand Seven hundred and ninety three Before the
Honorable Thomas McKean Esquire Doctor of Laws Chief Justice and his associates Justices of the said Supreme Court James Gibson Esquire was on motion of Mr Sergeant admitted an attorney of said Court and t[ook?] the Oath
to support the Constitution [of the State?] and the U[nited Sta]tes an[d] [*words
missing*]

> In Witness whereof I [have hereto?] [se]t my hand and affixed
> SEAL   the [Seal of?] [the] said supreme Court at philade[lphia] this first
> day of August in the Year of our Lord MDCCXCVI.

EdwBurd prot

ARS (DNA, RG 267, Records of the Office of the Clerk). Damage to the right edge of the page
is the major cause for supplying conjectural readings. In addition, the seal has partially obscured
some words.

Certificate of Henry Wikoff ————————————
Admitted as a Counsellor February 7, 1797

I certify that at a Supreme Court held at Philadelphia for the State of Pennsylvania the seventh day of January in the Year of our Lord one thousand
seven hundred and ninety three On Motion of Mr Ingersoll Henry Wikoff
Esquire was admitted an Attorney of said Court and took the Oath prescribed
by Law.

> In witness whereof I have hereto set my Hand and affixed the
> SEAL   Seal of the said Supreme Court of Philadelphia the thirtieth day
> of April in the year of our Lord MDCCXCV.

Edw:Burd ProtSupCur
Penns^a

ARS (DNA, RG 267, Records of the Office of the Clerk). Endorsement mentions "Certificates"
enclosed; we have discovered only this document.

Certificates and Character Reference of William H. Todd ————
Admitted as a Counsellor February 6, 1799

I Edward Burd Esquire prothonotary of the Supreme Court of the Commonwealth of Pennsylvania Hereby Certify that at a Supreme held at philadelphia for the said Commonwealth the fifth day of January in the Year of

our Lord one thousand Seven hundred and ninety five before the honorable Thomas McKean Esquire Doctor of Laws Chief Justice and his Associates Justices of the said Supreme Court William Tod Esquire was on Motion of Mr Coxe admitted an attorney of said Court and took the Oath prescribed by the act of assembly as an Attorney and also the Oath to support the Constitution of the united States [pres]cribed by Act of congress

> In Witness whereof I have hereto set my hand and affixed the
> SEAL   Seal of [the?] said Supreme Court at philadelphia [thi?]s fifteenth
> day of February in the Year of our Lord MDCCXCVI

Edw.Burd Prot

I do hereby certify, that William Todd Esquire has been admitted an Attorney and Counsellor at Law in the supreme court of Pennsylvania more than two years last past, that he has practised as such with reputation to himself, fidelity to the court and to the client, and that he sustains a good moral character. Given under my hand at Philadelphia the 5th day of February 1799:__

Tho^sM:Kean

ARS (DNA, RG 267, Records of the Office of the Clerk). We have bracketed readings because the seal covers part of the text.

Certificates and Character Reference of Walter Franklin ———
Admitted as a Counsellor February 13, 1799

I Edward Burd Esquire prothonotary of the Supreme Court of the Commonwealth of pennsylvania Hereby Certify that at a supreme Court held at Philadelphia for the said Commonwealth the first day of September in the Year of our Lord one thousand Seven hundred and ninety four Before the honorable Thomas McKean Esquire Doctor of Laws Chief Justice and his associates Justices of the said Supreme Court Walter Franklin Esquire was on Motion of Mr Chew admitted an Attorney of said Court and took the Solemn Affirmation prescribed by Law and also to Support the Constitution of the State and of the United States

> In Witness whereof I have hereto set my hand and affixed the
> SEAL   seal of the said Court at Philadelphia this Eleventh day of April
> in the Year of our Lord MDCCXCVIII

EdwBurd Prot

I do certify That Walter Franklin Esquire has been a practicing Attorney and Counsel in the Supreme Court of Pennsylvania for some time past; and is a Gentleman of sufficient professional Abilities, and good moral Character__

Edw^dShippen__

11th february 1799__

ARS (DNA, RG 267, Records of the Office of the Clerk).

Certificates and Character Reference of William Sergeant ——— Admitted as a Counsellor August 11, 1800

I Edward Burd Esquire Prothonotary of the Supreme Court of the Common-wealth of Pennsylvania hereby Certify that at a Supreme Court held at Phila-delphia for the said Commonwealth the fifth day of September anno Domini one thousand seven Hundred and ninety six Before the Honorable Thomas M[c]Kean Esquire Doctor of Laws, Chief Justice and his Associates Justices of the said Supreme Court William Sergeant Esquire was on Motion of M[r] In-gersoll admitted an Attorney of said Court and took the oath prescribed by Act of Assembly

> In Witness whereof I have hereto set my hand and affixed the
> SEAL   seal of said Supreme Court at Philadelphia this Eleventh day of
> February in the year of our Lord MDCCC—

EdwBurd Prot

The undersigned Certifies that William Sergeant has been a practicing At-torney in the Supreme Court of the State of Pennsylvania since September 1796 and has always sustained a good Moral Character.

Given under my Hand at Philadelphia this 11th Day of August 1800

Thomas Smith[1]

ARS (DNA, RG 267, Records of the Office of the Clerk).
1. Thomas Smith was admitted to the Supreme Court bar on August 2, 1791.

Certificate of Sampson Levy ——————————— No Record of Admission to Supreme Court Bar

I certify that at a Supreme Court held at Philadelphia for the State of Pennsylvania the second day of July one thousand seven hundred and
eighty ^eight Sampson Levy Esquire on the Motion of M[r] Ingersoll was admitted an Attorney of the said Court and took the oath prescribed by Law   Witness my Hand the eighteenth day of february in the year of our Lord MDCCXCI.

Edw:Burd ProtSupCur
Penns[a]

ARS (DNA, RG 267, Records of the Office of the Clerk).
   Sampson Levy, Jr. (1761-1831), born and raised in Philadelphia, read law with his brother Moses, who was admitted to the bar of the Supreme Court on February 8, 1791. Sampson Levy was admitted to the Philadelphia bar in 1787 and to the bar of the Supreme Court of Pennsylvania in 1788. His name does not appear on the counsellor roll, on either of the two attorney rolls, nor in the fine minutes. Henry Samuel Morais, *The Jews of Philadelphia* (Philadelphia: Levytype, 1894), pp. 39, 41; *MBBP*, p. 287; "Supreme Court List of Attorneys, 1742-1902," Records of the Eastern District, RG 33, PHarH.

Certificates and Character Reference of Anthony Morris ——— No Record of Admission to Supreme Court Bar

I Edward Burd Esquire prothonotary of the Supreme Court of the State of Pennsylvania Do Certify that at a Supreme Court held at Philadelphia for the said State the twenty fourth day of September in the year of our Lord One thousand seven hundred and eighty eight On Motion of M.ʳ Lewis — Anthony Morris Esquire was admitted an Attorney of the same Court and took the Affirmation prescribed by Act of Assembly.

In Witness whereof I have hereto set my hand and affixed th[e] Seal of the said Supreme Court [a]t Philadelphia the Ninth day of August in the year of our Lord MDCCXCII.

SEAL

Edw. Burd ProtSupCur

The under-signed certifies, that Anthony Morris, of the city of Philadelphia
                                    admitted
Esquire, has been ‸ and practised as an Attorney & Counsellor at Law in the Supreme court of the State of Pennsylvania for two years last past & upwards, that he has conducted himself with fidelity to the court and to the Client and reputation to himself, and deservedly sustains a good moral character. Given under my hand at Philadelphia the 8.ᵗʰ day of August 1792. —

ThoˢM:Kean

ARS (DNA, RG 267, Records of the Office of the Clerk). Endorsed as "filed 11. Augᵗ 92 — ." Conjectural readings have been supplied where the document is damaged and where the seal obscures part of the text.

Anthony Morris (1766-1860) was admitted to the Philadelphia bar in 1787 and to the Supreme Court of Pennsylvania bar in 1788. There is no record of Morris being admitted to the Supreme Court bar on the counsellor roll, on either of the two attorney rolls, or in the fine minutes, but this certificate and character reference on his behalf were filed in 1792. *DAB*; "Supreme Court List of Attorneys, 1742-1902," Records of the Eastern District, RG 33, PHarH.

Formulary

The bound formulary published here was begun by Samuel Bayard. It is not known whether he intended it to be a compilation for personal use or one meant to be an official part of the Supreme Court's record. Certainly, he did not include in it models of all forms used by the Court. During the time before Bayard's departure for England, forms were entered directly in the bound volume, generally by Bayard himself. Forms for the period when Bayard was in England and one from the period after his return were tipped into the volume. After 1800 Elias B. Caldwell began to enter forms. Annotations to the forms indicate who wrote them.

Three-quarters of the forms are either for actual Supreme Court cases or for process issuing from the Supreme Court. The rest are for process in the Supreme Court of Pennsylvania or the Circuit Court for the district of Pennsylvania; these were probably meant to be used as models for Supreme Court forms. Where a form has been entered without an actual Supreme Court case name, we have attempted to identify a case for which the form might have been created. We proceeded on the assumption that the forms were entered chronologically (with the noted exception of the form for *Pierce v. Ship Alligator*). We then looked for Supreme Court cases that would have required forms in the chronology of the formulary. Finally, we searched through the extant record to compare the formulary "model" with actual documents in the suspected cases. We record our conclusions in the notes to forms. The role played by these forms in the development of Supreme Court process will be discussed more extensively in the case volumes to be published later in this series.

The cover of the formulary includes a haphazard collection of titles and names, as if used as a practice sheet. The various entries, many of them rubbed or crossed out, appear in this order:

Supreme Court of
Precedents _
Precedents
Precedents,
Precedents
Supreme Court of the[1]
United States[2]
Formulary
Clerk's office
E. B. Caldwell
1801.

The different styles of handwriting on the cover are difficult to distinguish. All of the lines from "Supreme Court of" through "Clerk's office" appear to have been written by Samuel Bayard; Elias B. Caldwell added his signature and "1801." Inside the front cover, Samuel Bayard wrote "Sam¹Bayard's: formulary＿."

As with the original minutes, this formulary presents special editorial problems. Extensive damage and hasty execution have necessitated conjecture in transcription; this is annotated where it occurs. Because we are printing seriatim forms that were originally written on separate pages of a bound volume, we supply lines to separate them visually.

D (DUSC, Office of the Curator). Transcription was from the original document, rather than a photocopy.
  1. Partly covers another repetition of "Precedents."
  2. Partly covers "Prece[dents]."

Commission to take ⎰
depositions &c.[1]   ⎱

United States of America ⎰
in the Supreme Court.   ⎱   The Presd.t of the United States for[2]

To A. B. C D. &c. Esquires＿ greeting
Know ye that in confidence of your fidelity & prudence, We have[3] appointed you, & by these presents do give you, any three or two of you, full power & authority, diligently to examine, A B. C D &c = or [all witnesses whatsoever].[4] upon certain interrogatories to be exhibited to you＿ as well on the part of John Thomson complainant as on the part of Gelbert Venables defendant,[5] or either of them＿ And therefore we command you any three or two of you that at certain days & places to be appointed by you for that purpose, you do cause the said witnesses to come before you, & then & there examine each of them apart. upon the said interrogatories upon their respective
                      or solemn affirmations
corporal oaths ^ first taken before you or[6] any two of you, & to take such their examinations & reduce them to writing, & when you shall so have taken them you are to send the same to the Judges of the Supreme Court of the United States, ~~held~~ at Philadelphia, (being the seat of the National government) closed up & under your seals, or the seals of any three or two of you distinctly & plainly set, together with the said Interrogatories & this writ.
And you, & every of you, are required, before you act in, or be present at the swearing or examining of any witness or witnesses, severally to take the oath (or solemn affirmation as the case may be) first speciefied in the schedule hereunto annexed,

  1. This form written and signed by Samuel Bayard.
  2. The "for" is written over the word "to."
  3. The words "We have" are written over "The S."
  4. Brackets are in the original.
  5. The Supreme Court did not hear a case by this name. This form and the commissioner's and clerk's oaths which follow were probably used as models for the commission issued in *Vanstaphorst v. Maryland.* See "Fine Minutes," August 3, 1791; and "Docket," February term, 1791.
  6. A dash appears beneath the "o."

And full power & authority is hereby given to ~~any~~ you or any three, two, or one of you, jointly & severally to administer such oath to the rest, any two or three of you upon the holy evangelists— And it is furthe[r][7] required that all & every the Clerk or Clerks, employed in taking writing, transcribing, or engrossing the deposition, or depositions, of the witnesses to be examined by virtue of these presents, shall before he or they be permitted to act as Clerks as aforesaid, or be present at such examination, severally take the oath last specefied in the said schedule annex'd—

And full power & authority is also given unto you or any of you, jointly or severally to administer such oath, (or affirmation) to such Clerk or Clerks— on the holy Evangelists—

Given under the seal of the said Supreme Court of the United States— Witness the Hon[ble] John Jay Esq[r] Chief-Justice of said Court. at.[8] Philad[a]. this _____ day of _____ in the year of our Lord _____ & of the Independence ~~of the Independence~~ & sovereignty of the United States the _____

Sam[l]Bayard Clk

A. B.— Compl[ts] Att[y]—

Commissioners oath[9]

You shall ~~truly~~, according to the best of your knowlege, truly, faithfully, & without partiality to any or either of the parties in this cause, take the Examinations & depositions of all & every witness & witnesses produced & examined by virtue of these Commission hereunto annexed, upon the interrogatories now produc'd & left with you,/ ~~& you shall not publish, disclose or make known, to any person, or persons whatsoever, except the Clerk or Clerks by you employed & sworn to secrecy in the execution of this Commission, the Contents of all or any of the depositions of the witnesses or any of them to be taken by you & the other Commissioners named, or any of them by virtue of this Commission until publication shall pass by rule or order of the Supreme Court of the United States/~~— so help you God.

Clerks oath[10]

You shall truly, faithfully, & without partiality to any or either of the parties in this cause, take & write down, transcribe & engross, the depositions of all

---

7. Because the document is damaged, a conjectural reading is supplied.
8. The "at" is written over the word "in."
9. Written by Samuel Bayard.
10. Idem.

& every witness, & witnesses, produced before, & examined by the Commissioners or any of them named in the Commission hereunto annexed, as far forth as you are directed & employed, by the said Commissioners, or any of them, to take & write down, transcribe & engross, the said depositions or any of them, & you shall not publish, disclose, or make known to any person or persons whatsoever, the contents of all or any of the depositions of the witnesses or any of them, to be taken, written down transcribed & engrossed, by you, or whereunto you shall have recourse or be any ways privy until publication shall pass by Rule or order of the Sup. Cur. of the United States so help you God.

<u>Writ of _ Error.</u>[11] }

United States ss.

The President of the United States To the Judges of the Circuit Court ~~Greeting~~ of the United States for the[12] district of New Hamshire Greeting _ Because that in the record & proceedings & also in the rendering of the Judgment of a plea which is in the said Circuit Court before you or some of you between Elizabeth Wallend[ee?]d plaintiff & S. S. defendant[13] in a plea of debt a manifest error hath happened to the great damage of the said S. S and others as by their complaint appears. We being willing that Error if any hath been, should be duly corrected and full & speedy justice done to the parties aforesaid in this behalf _ do command you if Judgment be therein given that then under your seal distinctly & openly you send the record & proceedings, with all things concerning the same to the Supreme Court of the United States together with this writ, so that you have the same at the seat of government of the United States on the first Monday of February next in our s^d Supreme Court to be then & there held for the s^d United States that the record & proceedings afore^sd being inspected the said Supreme Court may cause further to be done therein to correct that error what of right & according to the laws & customs of the said United States should be done   Witness the Hon^bl John Jay Esquire chief Justice of the Supreme Court this 5th day of August in the year of our Lord &c & the 16 of our Independance

S B.[14] Clk

---

11. Idem.

12. The words "for the" are written over the word "greeting."

13. This form for a writ of error seems to have been the model for the one issued on February 10, 1792, in *Kingsley v. Jenkins* (Appellate Jurisdiction Records, RG 267, DNA). It may also have been the model for a writ of error in the case *Elizabeth Wallingford v. Samuel Sherburne,* decided in May 1791 term by the United States Circuit Court for the district of New Hampshire, although there is no record of such a writ having been requested (Law Case Files, and Final Record, CCD New Hampshire, RG 21, MWalFAR).

14. Samuel Bayard.

Summons }

United States ss.

The President of the United States to the Marshall of the District of _____ Greeting —

You are hereby commanded to summon A.B. _____ of the State of _____ so that the said _____ appear before the Chief Justice, & the Associate Justices of the Supreme Court of the United States, at Philadelphia, (being the seat of the National government) on _____ on the _____ day of _____ next _____ at a Supreme Court to be then & there holden for the United States, to answer _____ A.B _____ of a plea of _____ & have you then & there this writ —

Given under the seal of the said Supreme Court of the United States, as witness the Honorable John Jay Esqr. Doctr. of Laws Ch. Justice of the said Supreme Court, at Philada. aforesaid this _____ day of (the last day of the preceeding term) Anno Domini one thousand seven hundred, ninety _____ & of the Independence of the United States the _____

J.B. Clk

Formulary, "Summons." Courtesy Office of the Curator, Supreme Court of the United States.

Summons[15] }

United States ss.

The President of the United States to the Marshall of the District of _____
Greeting _

You are hereby commanded to summon. AB. _____ or the State of ___

so that the said _____ appear before the ˄Chief Justice, & the Associate Justices
of the Supreme Court of the United States, at Philadelphia, (being the seat of

the National government) on _____ on the first[16] ˄mon day of _____
next _

i̶n̶ ̶t̶h̶e̶ ̶y̶e̶a̶r̶ ̶&̶c̶ _ at a Supreme Court o̶f̶ ̶t̶h̶e̶ to be then & there holden for
the United States, to answer _____ AB _____ of a plea of _____ &
have you then, & there this writ _

Given under the seal of the said Supreme Court of the United States, as

witness the Honorable John Jay Esq[r] Doct[r] of Laws Ch. Justice of o̶u̶r̶ [ye] said
Supreme Court, at Philad[a] aforesaid. this _____ day of (the last day of the
preceding term) Anno Domini one thousand seven hundred, & ninety two &
of the independence of the United States the sixteenth _

                                                                    S. B.[17] Clk

_____

Mandamus[18] { to W. A. &. E. S. Justices of the peace to
             { proceed, on the complaint of J. F. & give judg'[:]

Pennsylvania ss. _

George the II. &c to William Atwood and Edward Shippen Esq[rs] & to each
of them _ Greeting

Whereas J. Foulke, Collector of the excise for the City and County of
Philad[a] in due & legal manner constituted & appointed lately to wit the eighteen day of May in the year of our Lord one thousand seven hundred &

forget seven obtained a certain summons under y̶o̶u̶r̶ [the] hand & seal of you or one
of you against Peter Berry of the City of Philad[a] Cordwainer for the offence
of retailing, less than one quart of rum delivered at one time & to one person,
committed ag[t] an act of Gen[l]Assembly of the afs[d] Province, entitled an act for

_____

15. Written by Samuel Bayard, this form for a summons appears to be a model for the one
issued on February 8, 1792, in *Chisholm v. Georgia* (Original Jurisdiction Records, RG 267, DNA).

16. The word "first" is written over a line which originally had indicated a blank space to be
filled in subsequently.

17. Samuel Bayard.

18. This mandamus appears to be a copy of one issued in 1747 by the Supreme Court of the
province of Pennsylvania. It and the one that follows were probably copied by Samuel Bayard in
anticipation of Supreme Court action in *Ex parte Hayburn*. See "Fine Minutes," August 6 and 9,
1792.

laying an excise on Wine Rum Brandy and other spirits. And Whereas W^mTroller one of the Constables of the city afs^d aftwd^s to wit on the 19. Day of of the month afs^d, did appear before you the said W. A. & E. S. aldermen of the city afsd, & to you did return that he had duly summond the afs^d P. B. to appear before you & answer the complaint afs^d ag^t the s^d P. B.— Nevertheless, you the said aldermen of the city afs'd not being ignorant of the premises, but your duty[19] in this behalf, little regarding, the hearing & determining the complaint afs^d have altogether refused & still do. refuse in contempt of us, & to the great damage of the said J. F. as from his complaint we have received— We therefore willing that due & speedy justice in this behalf be done as is Just, do command you & firmly enjoin you, that immediately after the receipt of this writ, you proceed to hear & determine the complaint afs^d & full & speedy justice in that behalf you administer to the said J. Foulke. or shew cause to the contrary thereof, lest for your default complaint to us may again be made—

And how you shall execute this writ our command, you make known to the Justices of our Suprume Court of our Proveince of Pennsyl^a at our Supreme[20] Court, to be held at Philad^a for the said Province the 24. day of Septr next, & that you have then & there this writ—

Witness the Honb^le J. Kinsey[21] Esqr. Chief Justice of our S^d Sup. Court— &c &c

J. Read Prot.^y

Allow^d ℔ J. Kinsey.
5 M^o 2 day. 1747.

Madamus to restore
a Clergyman to his Pastorship.[22] }

Pennsylvania ss. —
The Commonwealth of Pennsyl^a to. A. B.   CD. &.c. Greeting—
Whereas the Rev'd. W. Marsha[ll][23] hath been duly elected & appointed

19. The words "you did" had been written initially in the place where "your duty" appears.
20. The letters "em" are written over the letters "un."
21. "K" is written over an "R."
22. This mandamus appears to be a copy of one which may have been used in the Supreme Court of Pennsylvania. In July, 1790, the Supreme Court of Pennsylvania heard a case involving a Reverend William Marshall, who in 1786 had been barred by some of the elders from preaching at Scots' Presbyterian Church. Samuel Bayard appears to have copied this mandamus in anticipation of Supreme Court action in Ex parte Hayburn. J. Thomas Scharf and Thompson Westcott, History of Philadelphia, 1609-1884, vol. 2 (Philadelphia: L. H. Everts, 1884), pp. 1274-76; "Fine Minutes," August 6 and 9, 1792.
23. A conjectural reading is supplied because the clerk wrote the name "Marshall" to the very edge of the page and the last two letters are missing.

Minister pastor & preacher by the religious Society or members of the Scotts Presbyterian church or associate congregation inhabiting in the said city or places thereunto adjacent, to perform divine service for the said religious society in a certain church or meeting house situate in Spruce street in the said City of Philad.ª in the County of Philad.ª appropriated for the religious worship of the said Society—

Nevertheless— you the said AB. CD &c have refused to admit the said W. M. to the use of the pulpit. in the said church or meeting house, for the purpose of performing divine service therein for the said religious society as by their complaint, we have understood. We therefore willing that due & speedy justice should be done in this behalf as is reasonable, do command you that you restore the said W. M. to the use of the pulpit in the said church or meeting house as Pastor Preacher or minister in order to perform divine service therein for the said religious society, or signify to us cause to the contrary thereof lest in default of complaint should come to us repeated— And how you shall execute this our command certify to us at a Sup. Court to be held at Philad.ª for the State of P. the 2nd day of Ap.ł next— returning to us this our writ— Witness &c

---

Venire for a special Jury/[24]

United States ss:

The President of the United States to the Marshall for the Pennsylvania District Greeting— You are hereby commanded that you cause to come before the Justices of the Supreme Court of the United States at the said Supreme Court to be held at Philad.ª for the said United States the _____ day of __ next, twenty four honest & lawful men of your district named in the panel to this writ annexed to wit— AB. CD. E F. &c— by whom the truth of the matter may be better known— to make a certain jury of the country between _____ L M. _____ & R. S. _____ because as well the said L. M. as the said _____ R S. between whom the contention is have put themselves on upon the said Jury.— And have you then & there the names of that jury & this writ—

Witness the Honᵇˡᵉ John Jay Esqʳ Ch. Justice of the said Supreme[25] Court at Philad.ª the _____ day of _____ in the year of our Lord— 179__ & of the independence of the US. the _____

S. B.[26] Clk.

---

24. Written by Samuel Bayard, this form for a venire to call a special jury appears to have been the model for the one issued in *Georgia v. Brailsford.* Although the actual venire has not been found, the above case was the only one in the Supreme Court during this period which was decided by a special jury. 3 *Dallas,* 1 (1794); "Fine Minutes," February 4, 5, and 6, 1794.

25. The letters "em" are written over "un."

26. Samuel Bayard.

Venire for a grand & ⎱
common jury—[27]   ⎰

United States ss.—

(LS)[28]   The President of the United States to the Marshall of the Pennsylvania
          District Greeting—

We command you that you cause to come before the Judges of our Circuit
Court of the United States in & for the Pennsylvania District of the middle
Circuit at a session of our same Court to be held at Philadelphia in the district
aforesaid on the eleventh day of April next at ten of the Clock in the forenoon
of the same day twenty four honest & Lawfull men of your said district by
whom the Truth of the several Matters & things then & there to be given
them in charge may be better known & enquired of to serve as Grand Jurors
& also a number of honest & lawfull men not less than forty eight & not
exceeding sixty to serve as petit Jurors & to do, execute & perform all &
singular those things which on behalf of the United States shall be then &
there enjoy ^n ed them— And have you then there the Names of those whom
you shall so cause to come & be you then there together with your Ministers
& bring with you this Precept

Witness the Honorable John Jay Esquire Chief Justice of our Supreme Court
this twelfth day October in the seventeenth year of the Independance of the
United States.—

Form of a special mandate to carry into effect the Judg[t] of a C[ir?]t. Court—
on an affirmance of s[d] Judg[t] in the Sup Cur. US.

United States ss—   (drawn[29] by M[r] Lewis[30])

The President of the US. to the Judges of the Cir[ci?][31] C[t] for the Eastern

27. The portion of this form for a venire to call a common jury appears to have been the
model for the venire facias issued August 5, 1794, in *Oswald v. New York* (Original Jurisdiction
Records, RG 267, DNA). On the same date, a "General traverse jury" summoned to attend the
Supreme Court was dismissed for lack of any case to be tried. This jury, which may have been
called in anticipation of a trial in the above case, would probably have been summoned by a
venire issued at the February term, 1794. Although no record of the issuance of such a venire
exists, it was most likely at this time that the above form was entered in the formulary. (See "Fine
Minutes," August 5, 1794.)

28. Before this point, Samuel Bayard wrote; this seal and the rest of the form probably were
written by Hand B, although it is possible that they were written by Hand A.

29. Above "drawn" appears a partially erased "(draun."

30. William Lewis, member of the Supreme Court bar (see "Fine Minutes," February 7, 1791).
On motion of Lewis, the Supreme Court ordered a special mandate issued to the United States
Circuit Court for the district of Massachusetts commanding it to execute judgment obtained in
that court by the defendant in *Kingsley v. Jenkins* (see "Fine Minutes," February 14, 1794). This
form for a special mandate appears to be a model for the one issued in the above case. Although
the original has not survived, it was received, and execution was issued by the United States Circuit
Court for the district of Massachusetts on June 13, 1794. Final Record, May 1792 term, CCD
Massachusetts, RG 21, MWalFAR.

The parenthetical phrase, "drawn by M[r] Lewis," is in the hand of Jacob Wagner. The rest of

Form of a special mandate to carry into effect the Judg. of a Circ.
Court — on an affirmance of d Judg. in the Sup. Cur. U.S.

United States ss—   (Drawn by Mr. Lewis)

The President of the U.S. to the Judges of the
Circ.t Ct. for the Eastern Ct. ~~between~~ & for the — Dist. Greeting

Whereas A.B. late of —— Deft. lately in the Circ.t
Ct. for the — ~~Dist.~~ ~~recovered~~ by Judg.t of said Court recovered
according to the form of the Act of Congress in such case made
and provided, recovered against C.D. of — Deft. the sum of ——
Doll.s & cents — lawful money of the U.S. for his damage — &
Doll.s for his costs by the s.d A.B. sustained in a certain suit
ag.t C.D. afs.d prosecuted — as by the inspection of the record &
proceedings thereof which were brought into the Sup. Cur. of s.d
U.S. by virtue of a writ of error issuing from said Ct. appears
on record — which s.d record judg.t after.d in the s.d Sup. Cur. at
Philad.a was in all things affirm.d — And thereupon the said
Sup. Cur. Considering that all things which in the said Circ.t Ct.
are lawfully transacted and adjudg.d sh.d be carried into due &
speedy execution — You therefore are hereby commanded that
such ~~proceedings~~ execution & proceedings be made ~~thereon~~ the
said judg.t in the s.d Circ.t Ct. before you, for the damages & costs
afs.d as according to the laws of the U. States ought to be made

Witness the hon.ble J. J. Esq. Chief Just.k of the s.d Sup.
Cur. at Ph. the — day of — in the year — & of the indep.t
of the U.S. the ———— ————   J. B. Clke

Formulary, "Form of a special mandate . . . ." Courtesy Office of the Curator, Supreme
Court of the United States.

C[t] & the in & for the _____ Dist. Greeting[32]

Whereas A. B. late of _____ Dist._ lately in the Circ[t] C[t] for the ___ Dist. recover'd by Judg[t] of said Court re[cover]ed according to the form of the Act of Congress in such case made and provided, recovered against_ CD. of _____ Dist. the sum of _____ Dll[s]_ & cents_ lawful money of the US. for his damages_ & _____ Dll[s] for his costs by the s[d] AB. sustaind in a certain suit ag[t] CD. afs[d] prosecuted_ as by the inspection of the record & proceedings thereof which were brought into the Sup. Cur of y[e] US. by virtue of a writ of error issung from said C[t] appears on record_ which s[d] record judg[t] aftw[ds] in the s[d] Sup. Cur. at Philad[a] was in all things affirm'd_ And thereupon the said Sup. Cur. considering that all things which in the said Circ[t] C[t] are lawfully transacted and adjudg'd sh[d] be carry'd into due & speedy exon._ You therefore are hereby commanded that such proceedings execution & proceedings be made thereon the said judg[t] in the s[d] Circ[t][33] C[t] before you, for the damages & costs afs[d] as according to the laws of[34] the UStates ought to be made

Witness the Hon[b][e] J. J. Esq[r] Ch Just. of the s[d] Sup Cur. at Ph. this _____ day of _____ in the year _____ & of the independ[ce?] of the US. the _____ _

                                                                S. B.[35] Clk

---

> Form of a special mandate to the circuit court to carry into effect the sentence of the district, circuit, & supreme courts in an admiralty case[36]
> Drawn by hnble J. Read Esq[r][37] of Charleston[38]

United States

The President of the United States [to?] the Judges of the Circuit Court for

the document appears to be in the handwriting of Samuel Bayard.

31. A "t" appears beneath the second "c."

32. A dash appears beneath "Greeting."

33. The letters "Cir" are written over "C[t]."

34. The word "of" is written over an ampersand.

35. Samuel Bayard.

36. The actual special mandate in *Talbot v. Jansen* apparently has not survived. It is not in the records of the Supreme Court of the United States, and the case papers of the United States Circuit Court for the district of South Carolina for this period were destroyed by fire.

This document has been tipped into the bound formulary. Because of damage or trimming or both, the outer edge of the first page of this form for a special mandate is missing text on some lines. The first two pages are damaged at the bottom because they extended outside the edge of the bound formulary. Damage to the document thus is the major cause for supplying conjectural readings.

37. Jacob Read, member of the Supreme Court bar. See "Fine Minutes," August 5, 1795.

38. From the beginning of the title through here is in the hand of Jacob Wagner. With three exceptions which have been noted, the rest of this form is in the handwriting of Jacob Read.

the Southern Circuit of the United States & for the District of South Car[o]lina
Greeting_ Whereas Joost Jansen a Citizen of the United Netherlands late
master of the Brigantine de Vrouw Christina Magdalen[a] of Amsterdam on
behalf of himself & of Messrs Westen [&?] Ehrmann of Amsterdam owners of
the said Briga[n]tine & also [in?] behalf of the owners of her Cargo being also
Citizens of the Unted Netherlands on or about the 20^t[^h]^]^39 of June 1794,
    Exhibit &   Special   of U. S for^40
did ^ file his libel in the [*word inked out*] ^ District Court ^ of South Carolina
Distri[ct] having & holding Exclusive original Cognizance of a[ll] Civil Causes
of Admiralty & Maritime Jurisdicti[on] against the said Brigantine & Cargo &
also ag^st Edw^[d] Ballard late Commander of the private Pilot Boat [or] schooner
of War Called L'ami de la Liberté & ag^st al[l] & every person or
                or pretending   Title
persons Whomsoever Claiming ^ any Right or ^ To the said Brigantine &
                                 having been
Cargo_ for Recovery of the same Brigantine & Cargo as ^ unlawfully &
        on the high seas
P[ir]atically taken ^ by the said Edwd Ballard as in an[d] by the said Libel more
fully & at large appears, And Whereas the Usual Process having Issued the
                                pretending & stiling hims[elf] a
said Edwd Ballard made default and When a   Certain William Talbot ^
Citizen of the French Republic
~~appeared & in or about the~~ & Captain & Commander of the private Vessel of
War Called the Lami de la point a Pitre & pretended to be duly Commissioned
Armed Equipped & Appointed under Authority of the French Republic for &
in behalf of himself & the owners officers & Mariners of the said private
   [who pre?]tended also to be Citizens of the s[ai]d Rep[ublic]
[vesse]ll of War a[r] ^ [appears] [*words missing*] June 1794 filed a Claim to the
                          protest &
said Brigantine & Cargo [a]s his Prize & also his ^ plea to the Jurisdictin of
    District^41   Protest &
the said ^ Court_ And Whereas the Party Libellant by his Procter filed his
Replication to the said Claim & Plea & it was in [*letters missing*]ch [s]ort Pro-
                   of witnesses [hav &?]
             Examinations ^ taken
ceeded that after all [acts?] Propounded ^ & Publication passed & the term
                        fully & argued &
[probatory?] Closed the said ~~libel Claim & Plea~~ Cause was ^ heard before the
    District^42
said ^ Court And the said District Court on or about the [6]^th day of August
1794._^43 did adjudge order & Decree "that the Claim of the said William
Talbot Exhibitted & filed in this Cause with his protest to the Jurisdiction of

39. The number "20" was written over what appears to be the number "17."
40. Caret and interlineation in hand of Jacob Wagner.
41. Idem.
42. Idem.
43. The "4" is written over a "5."

should
the Court ∧ be dismissed with Costs the said Claim not being supported. by
the Evidence produced & being Irrelevant to the points in Issue" And further
did Decree and order "that the said Brigantine de Vrouw Christin[a] Mag-
delena with her Tackle Furniture & Apparel & the Cargo on board her at the
time of her seizure & detention be delivered over to the [acter] in the Cause
in behalf of the original owners of the same" — And Wheras the said William
Talbot not satisfied with the said Decree [an]d in or about the _____ 11ᵗʰ
                1794—
day of August agreeable to the Act of the ~~Congress of the~~ Unted States in
                                                    [i]n the said District Court
Congrress assembled did lodge & file: his Writ   of Error ∧ Whereby the
          Proceedings
said ∧ final sentence & Judgment— were Removed into the Circuit Court for
South Carolina District And did assign Error. in the said Circuit Court & pray
~~for~~ a Reversal of the said Sentence & Decree of the said District Court and
the said Joost Jansen having joined in Error the same Cause came to be heard
                which was begun to be holden
before that Circuit Court ∧ ~~held~~ for South [Carolina?] [*words missing*] 25ᵗʰ d[ay]
                              fully Argument & fully
of October 179[4—] And after ∧ hearing the said Cause "The Court being of
opinion that there was⁴⁴ no Error either in Law or in Fact in the final Judgment
& Decree pronounced by the Judge of the District Court in the said Cause on
the 6ᵗʰ day of August 1794, the same was by Decree of the said Circuit
          pronounced in the 5ᵗʰ day of November 1794
Court ∧ Established & affirmed in all its parts & to stand in its full force
strength & Effect the said Cause for Error assigned. notwithstanding— And
by the said Circuit Court
          Considered
it was ∧ further ∧ ordered adjudged & Decreed ~~by the said Circuit Court~~ That
the said William Talbot shoud pay to the said Joost Jansen the sum of Two
Guineas pr diem to be accounted from the 6ᵗʰ day of August to the sᵈ 5ᵗʰ day
          in the Year aforesaid
of November ~~1794~~— as damage & demurrage of the said Vessel & also seven
per Centum Interest in the proceeds of the Cargo of the said Brigantine to be
accounted. from the said sixth day of August to the said 5ᵗʰ day of Novʳ to
wit for 9[6] 91 days demurrage of the said Brigantine at Two Guineas per
Diem the sum of Eight hundred & forty Eight Dollars 25 Cents & for Interest
for Three Months Vizᵗ from the 6ᵗʰ of⁴⁵ August to the 5ᵗʰ of Novem[ʳ] on
12097.3.3
~~£1297.3.3~~ lawful money of Sᵒ·Carolina equal to the Sum of 51.845 Dollars of
                                                                    Dollars
the United States being the proceeds of the said Cargo the Sum of 907. ∧ 28
                                    Dollars
Cents & making in the Whole the Sum of 1755. ∧ 53 Cents and also the Sum
of Eighty Two Dollars for the Costs & Charges which the said Joost Jansen

44. The word "was" is written over "is."
45. The "o" is written over an "A."

had Sustained by Reason of the said Writ of Error & appeal_ And Whereas the said William Talbot not Satisfied with the said Decree of the said Circuit Court in or about the s^d fifth day of November 1794_ agreeably to the Act of the United States in Congress assembled did lodge & file his writ of Error
in the said Circuit Court Whereby the said ^Proceedings final sentence Judgment & Decree were Removed into the Supreme Court of the United States ~~held at Philadelphia the same being the present seat of the National Gouvernment~~ and. did assign Error in the said Supreme Court & pray ~~for~~ a Reversal of the said sentences Judgments & Decrees ~~might be Reversed~~ of the said Circuit Court And the said Joost Jansen having Joined in Error, The Same Cause came on to be
heard ~~in~~ ^Before the Honourable the Supreme Court of the United States in this present Term ~~And~~ Whereupon ~~as with~~ ^after full argument of the said Cause ^duly the premises being Considered For that it appear[e]d to the said Supreme Court ~~of the U S~~, that there is no Error ~~either in Law or in fact~~ in the said Final Judgment & Decree of the s^d Circuit Court It was ordered adJudged[46] & Decreed, (Here follows Decree Verbatim) as by ^the Inspection of the Record & proceedings which were brought into the Sup Court of the U S, by Virtue of the said Writ of Error issuing from the said Court & the Final Judgment & Decree of the said Supreme Court fully appears,_ of Record And thereupon the said Supreme Court Considering_
That all things which in the said Circuit Court of South Carolina ^District & District are lawfully transacted & adjudged as well as those things which are lawfully traansacted & adjudged in the said Supreme Court shoud be carried into Speedy Execution   You ~~are~~ therefore are hereby Commanded That such execution & proceedings be made in the said Judgments & Decrees in the said Circuit Court before you for the delivery of the said Vessell & Cargo (if the Same or any part thereof yet Remain to be   delivered) ^or of the proceeds and am^t sales thereof & for the pa^y[t] of the said Several Sums of_ Demurrage Interest Damages & Costs aforesaid as. ^to Right & Justice appertain and to according ~~to~~ to the Laws of the United States ought to be made the s^d Writ of Error Notwithstanding.

Witness the Honourable John Rutlege Esqr Chief Justice of the said Supreme Court at Philadelphia this twenty Second day of August in the Year of our Lord One Thousand Seven hundred & Ninety Five & of the Independency of the U; S; the ~~20th~~_ Twentieth

J Wagner[47] D^y Clk Sup Cur
U S,

---

46. The "ad" was added to the word "Judged."
47. Jacob Wagner.

Snipes et al.
vs   } Subp. in Equity
State of Georgia et al[48]

The President of the United States to the Governor of the State of Georgia.
on behalf of the said State
and the Attorney General and Treasurer of the said State ^ and to David
Murray Washington, also to James Gun, Matthew McAllister and George
Walker, also to Nicholas Long, Thomas Glasscock and Ambrose Gordon,
Greeting: For certain causes offered before the honorable the Supreme Court
of the United States holding Jurisdiction in equity, you are hereby commanded
and strictly enjoined, that laying all other matters aside and notwithstanding
any excuse, you personally be and appear before the said Supreme Court hold-
ing jurisdiction in equity on the first Monday in August next at Philadelphia
being the present seat of the national government of the United States, to
answer concerning those things, which shall be then and there objected to you,
and to do further and receive what the said Supreme Court holding jurisdiction
in equity shall have considered in this behalf and this you may in no wise omit
under the penalty of five hundred dollars: Witness the Honorable Oliver Ells-
worth Esquire, Chief Justice of the said Supreme Court at Philadelphia the
fourteenth day of March in the year of our Lord one &c[49]

Smith
vs   } Prohib.[50]
Macaulay

The President of the United States to the Judge of the District Court of the
United States in and for the District of Virginia Greeting: You are hereby
prohibited, that you hold not plea in the said District Court, proceeding as a
Court of Admiralty and maritime jurisdiction, of a certain libel and suit com-
menced and prosecuted by Thomas Smith of the District aforesaid against the
of the same district
Ship, called the Charles Carter, and against Alexander Macaulay ^ as the owner
to the Supreme Court of the United States
of the same district
of the same Ship, whereof the said Alexander Macaulay[51] complains ^ that

48. As this case proceeded, the litigants' names were used interchangeably by the clerk of the Supreme Court. Historically, the case is known as *Moultrie v. Georgia*.

This subpoena was written by Jacob Wagner. The sheet of paper on which it was written has been pasted onto a page of the formulary volume.

49. The Court issued the subpoena on March 14, 1796. This is the only March that Ellsworth was chief justice before the Court took further action in this case. See *Huger et al. vs The State of Georgia et. al.*, "Fine Minutes," February 10, 1797.

50. On March 14, 1796, the Supreme Court ordered a prohibition to issue in the case of *Smith v. Ship Charles Carter*. The sheet of paper on which this prohibition was written by Jacob Wagner has been pasted onto a page of the formulary volume.

51. A caret, which has been crossed out, appears after "Macaulay."

in the said District Court

the said Thomas Smith draws him into plea before you, proceeding as a court of Admiralty and maritime jurisdiction: Witness. &c

———————

United States ss.

The President of the United States To the Judges of the Circuit Court for the Circuit of the United States in and for the District of Massachusetts[52]

Greeting,

Whereas Benjamin Lincol[n] Collector of the District of Boston and Charleston within the District of Massachusetts in the Name and Behalf of the United States of America did exhibit and file his Libel in the District Court of the

in &

United States ^ for the Massachusetts District ~~having and holding exclusive original Cognizance of all civil Causes of Admiralty and Maritime Jurisdiction;~~ against the Ship Alligator, her Tackle, Apparel and Furniture & against Edward John Pierce & Abel Harris for the following Causes Viz That sundry Good[s] Wares & Merchandizes of foreign Growth and Manufacture of the Value of four hundred Dollars were unladen & delivered from the said Ship Alligator in the Night Time & not in open Day & without a Permit from the Collector

being

aforesaid for that Purpose, the said Goods ^ ~~being of Foreign Growth and Manufacture and~~ subject to the Payment of ^ duties to the United States and that the said Goods, Wares and Merchandizes were brought into the Port of Boston in said Ship Alligator and that the Duties to which said Goods were subject were not paid or secured to be paid to the said United States as by the said Libel more fully and at large appears, And whereas the usual Process having issued the said Edward John Pierce & Abel Harris appeared & filed their Claims to said Ship, her Tackle, Apparel & Furniture, and it was in such Case proceeded upon, that after all Acts propounded &c &c the said District Court did order, adjudge and Decree that the said Ship Alligator, her Tackle Apparel & Furniture be and remain forfeited & be distributed as the Law directs — And whereas the said Edward John Pierce & Abel Harris not satisfied with the said Decree ~~did lodge & file his Writ of Error in the said District Court whereby the said Proceedings & final Sentence & Judgement were removed into the Circuit Court for Massachusetts District;~~ claimed an Appeal to the Circuit Court of the United States for the District aforesaid, which was granted by the said District Court & the said Cause came on to be heard before

———————

52. The large sheet containing this form was originally folded in half lengthwise and affixed to the inside of the front cover of the formulary. The right edge of the sheet protruded beyond the edge of the bound volume and was damaged. Sometime after 1800, this sheet was removed from the inside of the front cover, refolded so that the damaged edge was protected, and tipped into the back of the bound formulary. When this was done, part of the document with text written on it stuck to the sealing wax that had been used to affix it to the front cover and the page was torn. Damage to the document is the sole cause for supplying conjectural readings.

Samuel Bayard signed this form, which was written by Hand F. Bayard is probably responsible for crossing out passages and interlining revised wording.

the ᴬ^{said} Circuit Court for the District aforesaid & after fully hearing the said Cause & the Evidence produced _ It was considered by the said Circuit Court that the Decree of the said District Court be affirmed & that the said Ship be and remain forfeited & be distributed as the Law directs, all which Proceedings by the Inspection of the Record & Proceedings thereof which were brought into the [Sup]reme Court of the United States by virtue of a Writ of Error issuing from the said Supreme Court appears of Record _ And whereas a Day was given to the said Parties b[y] the Judges of the said Supreme Court untill Friday the Ninth day of August in the year of our Lord one Thousand seven hundred & Ninety nine to wit to the said Edwa[rd] John Pierce & Abel Harris to prosecute the said Writ of Error against the said Benjamin Lincoln _ At which day before the Judges of the said Supreme Court the said Benjamin Lincoln came by Charles Lee his Attorney and the said Edward John Pierce & Abel Harris altho' solemnly called came not but made default, nor have th[ey] further prosecuted yᵉ said Writ of Error against the said Benjamin Lincoln And therefore It is considered by the said Supreme Court that the said Benjamin Lincoln go the[re]upon without day &cᵃ And that the Judgement of the Circuit Court aforesaid should in all Things be affirmed and remain in full Force & Effect the said Caus[es] & Matters for Error alledged in said proceedings in any Wise Notwithstanding And further by the said Supreme Court it was considered that the sai[d] Ship Alligator and her Tackle, Apparel and Furniture should be and remain forfeited and be distributed as the Law directs and t[hat] the said Benjamin Lincoln should recover against the said Edward John Pierce & Abel Harris the Sum of   Dollars &   Cen[ts] for the⁵³ Costs and Charges which the said Benjamin Li[ncoln] [ha?]s sustained by Reason of the delay of the Execution of the Judgement aforesaid on pretence of the Prosecutio[n] [*words missing*] [of] Error & that yᵉ said Benjamin Lincoln may have Execution thereof as by yᵉ Record more fully appear[s] [*words missing*] so that all things in yᵉ said Circuit Court lawfully transacted & adjudged should be carried into due & [*words missing*] therefore Command you that such Execution & proceedings thereon may be had as according to yᵉ Laws & Constituti[on] [*words missing*] & yᵉ State of Massachusetts ought to issue & be had yᵉ Writt of Error aforesaid notwithstanding Witness The honorable Oliver Ellsworth Esqʳ Chi[ef Justice of the] Supreme Court at Philadelphia the ninth day of August Anno Domini one thousand seven hundred & Ninety nine _ ⁵⁴

SamˡBayard
Clk Sup. Cur. U. S

---

53. The letters "ir" have been partially erased following the word "the."
54. This form was set up so that the last few lines of text were indented on both sides to leave room for the seal on the left and Samuel Bayard's signature on the right.

Orders and Rules

Compiled by Samuel Bayard before he resigned the office of clerk, this list of orders and rules differs somewhat from the set of rules eventually published during the nineteenth century. The published rules were probably taken from a handwritten listing through 1838.[1] The latter manuscript includes as rules of the Court the following orders that Bayard left out of his listing:

1) February 3, 1790: the appointment of John Tucker as clerk and the requirement that he reside and maintain an office in the capital[2];
2) February 5, 1790: the oath for attorneys and counsellors;
3) February 5, 1790: the order that process run in the name of the president;
4) February 7, 1791: the allowance of affirmation;
5) August 15, 1800: the order in *Course v. Stead*.

Bayard's compilation appears to have been made sometime between his return from England in spring, 1798, and his resignation in August, 1800. It may have been a last-minute effort on his part to put the Court's record in order before leaving the office of clerk.

D (DNA, RG 267, Records of the Office of the Clerk). Written on a folded, full-size folio sheet.

1. In this handwritten listing (Office of the Curator, DUSC), a rule of August 8, 1792, is incorrectly dated as August 8, 1791. This mistake was repeated in the early published editions of Supreme Court rules. Samuel Bayard recorded the date correctly in his compilation.

2. Samuel Bayard may have viewed these orders as applying to Tucker only. If not, he certainly would not have wanted to call attention to the fact that his own absenteeism during much of his clerkship violated one of the Court's rules.

Orders and Rules relative to the practice of the Sup: Court of the U.States —

90
Feb.ᵧ 3ᵈ 1789. Ordered that the Clerk does not practice as an Attorney or
in this Court
Counsellor ∧ while in office —

Feb.ᵧ 5ᵗʰ 1790 — Ordered, that (untill further orders) it shall be requisite to the admission of Attornies or Counsellors to practice in this Court; that they shall have been such for three years past in the Supreme Courts of the State to which they respectively belong, and that their private and professional character shall appear to be fair —

Ordered, that Counsellors shall not practice as Attornies; nor Attornies as Counsellors in this Court.

August 8th 1792 _ The Chief Justice informs the Bar, that this Court Consider the practice of the Courts of Kings Bench and of Chancery in England as affording outlines for the practice of this Court _

Feby 4th 1795 _ The Court give notice to the Gentlemen of the Bar. that hereafter, they will expect to be furnished with a statement of the material points of the case, from the Counsel on[1] each side of a cause _

    17.th 1795 _ The Court declared that all evidence. on motions for a discharge upon bail must be by way of deposition, and not viva voce _

Augt 12th 1796 _ Ordered, that when Process at Common Law, or in Equity shall issue against a State, the same shall be served on the Governor or Chief Executive Magistrate and Attorny Genl of such State _

1796 _ Augt 12th Ordered, that Process of Subpena issuing out of this Court in any suit in Equity shall be se_^ved on the Defendant, sixty days before the return day of the said process; and further, that if the Defd.^t on such service of the Sup.^a shall not appear at the return day contained therein, the Compl.^t shall be at liberty to proceed ex parte _

[1]797 _ Feby 13th It is ordered by the Court, that the Clerk of the Court, to which any writ of Error shall be directed, may make return of the same by transmitting a true copy of the Record, and of all proceedings in the cause under his hand and the seal of the Court _

    Augt 7 _ It is ordered by the Court, that no Record of the Court be suffered by the Clerk to be taken out of his office but by the consent of the Court; otherwise to be responsible for it _

1. An "e" has been erased after the "n."

Inventory of Case Papers

Before Samuel Bayard resigned as clerk, an inventory of case papers was made, which appears to be in his handwriting. Written on a very long, folded folio sheet, the listing begins with cases docketed in February, 1791, continues with cases from February, 1796, through February, 1800, and then concludes with cases from February, 1792, through August, 1795. We do not know why Bayard arranged the terms of the Court in this order. Cases within each term are, for the most part, presented in the order in which they were docketed. Inasmuch as this inventory omits cases docketed in August term, 1800, it may have been compiled between February and August of that year. Like the list of orders and rules, this inventory may have been part of Bayard's effort to put the Court's record in order before turning it over to the new clerk. It may also have been meant as a checklist for what was to be taken in the move of the capital (and the Court) from Philadelphia to the District of Columbia.

The symbols in the left margin have been reproduced as they appear in the original inventory. Their function is unknown.

D (DNA, RG 267, Records of the Office of the Clerk). The words "Common Place" appear on the verso of this document; they are in an unknown handwriting and may not be contemporary.

List of papers belonging to the office of the Clerk of the Supreme Court of the United States.

Feb. 1791 —

Vanstraphorst's vs State of Maryland —
   The Record —

Feb. 1796 — Records — in the following Cases —

Benj. Moodie, (British Consul) vs Ship Betsy Cathcart &c —
Same Pltff — vs Ship Mermaid &c —
Same — vs Brig Eliza &c & John Guillard —
Same vs Ship Phyn &c —
Same vs Brig Tivoly &c —
Same vs Ship Alfred[1] &c
Same vs Brig Favorite &c —

   1. The "A" is written over an "E."

Same vs Ship Britannia
Same vs Snow Potowmack &c＿
Same vs Brig Eliza & cargo & Paul Beltrimeux & al.
Same vs Phœbe Ann &c＿
Don Di[ego] Morphy vs Ship Sacra Familia [&c]
Thoˢ M[c?]Donough vs Citizen Danery &c＿
Hunter vs Lessee of Denny Fairfax＿
Geyer vs John Michel & Ship Don Onzekeron.
John B. Cutting Admʳ of Ann Paul Emanuel Sigᵈ &c v
     State of South Carolina
∠ Claud Delcol et al. v Jon: Arnold＿

Augᵗ 1796.

Dauchy & Wiscart &c²
Don Diego Pintado v Ship San Joseph &c
Thoˢ Fennimore v UStates＿
Louis v Arcambal＿³
Arcambal [v?] Louis＿⁴
Dorance & Vanhorn⁵
X Gist v Robinett   Copy
X UStates v La Vengeance
X Emory v Grenough
⦋ Wilson v Daniel

Febʸ 1797＿

Moultrie v State of Georgia＿
X Clerke Admʳ of Russell v Harwood
Brown v Van Braam＿
Jennings [&?] Vennet Arcambal & Brig Per＿⁶
3 Records of the Tentˢ Court & Cº v the Ten[a]nts of Alexander
Calder v Bull

Augᵗ Term 1797＿

X Brown v Barry
X Pepoon et al: v Jenkins＿

2. The case referred to is *Wiscart v. Dauchy.*
3. The case referred to is *Wiseman v. Arcambal.* "Louis v Arcambal" does not appear anywhere in the record of the Supreme Court, so the clerk himself made the mistake.
4. The case referred to is *Arcambal v. Wiseman.* "Arcambal v Louis" does not appear anywhere in the record of the Supreme Court, so the clerk himself made the mistake.
5. This refers to an action filed in *Vanhorne's Lessee v. Dorrance.*
6. The case referred to is *Jennings v. Brig Perseverance.* "Thomas Jennings and John L. Venner: vs. Louis Arcambal and the Brig Perseverance and cargo" is the name that appears in the engrossed docket.

X Franklin &c v Rotch___
The State of South Carolina v John B. Cuttng
X Clarke & Nightingale vˢ Russell___
∠ Hamilton v Moore

Feb.ʸ Term 1798___

X J. C. Jones v Letombe
Bingham v Cabbot et al:
X Brailsford [Ind^(er)?] v State of Virginia.[7]

Aug.ᵗ Term 1798___

∠ Irwine v Sims___
Clarke &c v Russell
∠ Fowler & Lyman v Miller
∠ D.º Lindslay et[8] al[9]
∠ UStates v B F. Bache
X Pierce v Ship Alligator

Feb.ʸ 1799.

Jennings v Read Ex.ʳ &c
⊥ Mossman & Mein v Higginson &c

Aug.ᵗ 1799___

⊥ State of N York___ vˢ Connecticut &c
Turner v Bank of N. A.
D.º v Marquiss De Caso Enrilla___
Hazlehurst v UStates
Geyer v UStates___
Coffin v UStates 2___
Fenno v D.º[10]
Miller v D.º

---

7. The case referred to is *Brailsford v. Georgia*. We have discovered no document in the record of the Supreme Court labeled "Brailsford Ind^(er) v State of Virginia" so the clerk does not appear to have copied an incorrect name. There were, however, three cases involving states which came before the Court in February, 1798: *Hollingsworth v. Virginia, Moultrie v. Georgia,* and *Brailsford v. Georgia.* The clerk accidentally may have confused the names.

In the engrossed docket the case name appears as "Samuel Brailsford, Indorsee of James Spalding vs. The State of Georgia."

8. The "e" has been written over what appears to be an ampersand.

9. The case referred to is *Fowler v. Lindsley.*

10. The case referred to is *Tunno v. United States.*

Feb.ʸ 1800—

Cooper v Telfaire—
⤫ Williamson v Kincaid
⤫ Course v Ex.ʳˢ of Stead—
∠̸ UStates v Topham—
∠̸ Blane v Carter
Rutherford et al: v Fisher
∠ Greenleaf v Banks   Copy
∠̸ Paine & Bridgeman v UStates

Feb.ʸ 1792—

⤫ Oswald Ex. of Holt v NYork—

Aug.ᵗ 1792.

Collet v Collet—   Copy
Felfaire & Brailsford—¹¹
Kingsley et al: v Jenkins—
Chisholme v Georgia—

Feb⁽ʸ⁾ 1793

Grayson v Vi[r]ginia¹²
Oswald v NYork—

Aug.ᵗ 1793

∠ Vassall v Massachusetts

Feb.ʸ 1794

Glass et al: v Sloop Betsey & Cargo—
Ware Ex.ʳ &c v Hylton—
∠ UStates v Hopkins—
D.º¹³ v.ˢ Todd—

Feb.ʸ 1795

Bingham v Cabbot et al:
P[e]nhallow v Stoddart—¹⁴

11. The case referred to is *Georgia v. Brailsford.* "Edward Telfair Governor of the State of Georgia in behalf of said State v̄ˢ Samuel Brailsford & others" is the name of the case which appears in the engrossed docket.
12. The "r" has been written over a "g."
13. The "D" is written over a "U."
14. The case referred to is *Penhallow v. Doane's Administrators.* One of the administrators was David Stoddard Greenough. We have found no document in the record of the Supreme Court labeled "Penhallow v. Stoddart."

∠ [UStates] v Lawrence Judge &c
　D° v Hamilton & Sedgwick
　D° v Sedgwick & Cor[b]ley
　Olney v Arnold
　D°[15] v Dexter
　Talbot v Jansen

　Aug.t 1795 —

　J. B Cotton v Wallace
　Wallace v Brig Cesar & Cargo —
　UStates v Peters
　Hills &c v Ross
　Hylton v UStates —

15. The "D" is written over an "Ol."

Glossary of Legal Terms

The definitions appearing below have been drawn from three sources: Giles Jacob, *A New Law-Dictionary,* 10th ed. rev. and enl. by J. Morgan (London: W. Strahan and W. Woodfall, 1782); John Bouvier, *Bouvier's Law Dictionary,* rev. by Francis Rawle (Boston: Boston Book, 1897); and, Henry C. Black, *Black's Law Dictionary,* 4th ed. rev. (St. Paul, Minnesota: West Publishing, 1968). Context was the most important criterion in deciding which definitions to print. Only those meanings used in the text have been included. The contemporary eighteenth century definitions in Jacob have been preferred over those in Bouvier or Black, except where the latter contain clearer and more concise definitions with essentially the same meaning. In cases where a definition is carried forward from an earlier to a more recent dictionary, only the earlier source has been cited. Alternate spellings appearing in the text are in brackets after the preferred spelling.

Action on the case: A common law remedy generally to recover damages for an injury committed without force, or which results indirectly from the action of the defendant. Bouvier, s.v. "trespass on the case."

Administrator: A person appointed by the court to manage and distribute the estate of an intestate. Bouvier, Black.

Affidavit: A written statement sworn before a person having the authority to administer an oath. Jacob.

Affirm: 1) To confirm the judgment of a lower court; 2) to make a solemn religious declaration in the nature of an oath. Bouvier.

Alias subpoena: A second or further subpoena issued after the first has been sued out without effect. Jacob.

Alias summons: A second or further summons issued after the first has been sued out without effect. Jacob.

Amicable action: An action brought by the mutual consent of the parties. Black.

Answer: In equity, a written defense made by the defendant to the complainant's bill. Bouvier.

Appeal: The removal of a cause from a court of inferior to one of superior jurisdiction, for the purpose of review and retrial. Bouvier.

Appearance: The formal proceeding by which a defendant submits himself to the jurisdiction of the court. Bouvier.

Appellant: The party taking an appeal from one court to another. Black.

Assignment of errors: The written statement of the plaintiff-in-error alleging errors in the proceedings of the court below. Bouvier.

At bar: Before the court. Black.

Bill in equity: The initial pleading by the complainant in an equity suit, containing the names of the parties, a statement of facts, the allegations of wrongdoing, and a prayer for relief. Bouvier.

Capias or *capias ad respondendum:* That you take to answer (Lat.); a writ by which actions were frequently commenced and which commanded the sheriff to take the defendant, keep him safe, and produce his body in court on a certain day to answer the plaintiff. Black.

Case: See action on the case.

Certiorari: A writ issued by a superior to an inferior court, requiring the latter to send to the former some proceeding therein pending, or the record and proceedings in some case already terminated where the procedure is not according to the common law. Bouvier.

Chancery: A court of general equity jurisdiction. Bouvier.

Citation: A judicial writ commanding a person to appear on a certain day and do something therein specified, or show cause why he should not. Bouvier.

Commission: An instrument issued by a court or other competent tribunal to authorize a person to take depositions or perform any other action so specified within. Bouvier.

Common appearance: The filing of bail on the part of a defendant when served with an arrest warrant. Jacob, s.v. "appearance."

Common error: An error for which there are many precedents. Black, s.v. "error."

Complainant: A party asking for legal redress; a plaintiff in an equity suit. Bouvier, Black.

Complaint: In criminal law, the allegation made before a magistrate that a person has committed some specified offense. Bouvier.

Curia advisare vult: The court will advise (Lat.); an entry in the record indicating the continuance of a cause until a final judgment should be rendered. Bouvier, Black.

Declaration: A plaintiff's first pleading in an action at law, being a formal statement of the facts constituting the cause of action. Black.

Decree: The judicial decision of a case by a court of equity or admiralty. Bouvier.

Default: Nonperformance of a duty; nonappearance in court by a defendant or plaintiff on an assigned day; failure of any party to take a required step to advance his cause. Jacob, Bouvier, Black.

Defendant: The party sued in a personal action. Jacob.

Defendant-in-error: The party against whom a writ of error is sued out. Bouvier.

Demurrage: Payment for delay of a vessel beyond the time allowed for loading, unloading, or sailing. Bouvier.

Demurrer: In equity, an allegation by the defendant stating that even if the facts alleged in the pleading be true, they are insufficient for the complainant to proceed upon or to oblige the defendant to answer. Bouvier, Black.

Deposition: The written testimony of a witness, not in open court, in answer to interrogatories and intended to be used in a trial. Jacob, Bouvier.

Diminution (of the record): Incompleteness of the record of a case as sent from an inferior to a superior court. Bouvier.

Discharge (of a rule): To vacate. Bouvier.

Discontinuance: The interruption in proceedings occasioned by the plaintiff's failure to continue the suit from day to day until conclusion. Jacob. Bouvier.

Dismiss without prejudice: To dismiss, as of a bill of equity, without impairing the right of the complainant to sue again on the same cause of action. Black, s.v. "dismissal without prejudice."

Distringas: A writ commanding the sheriff to seize a defendant's goods and chattels, usually to compel an appearance in court. Bouvier, Black.

Enter: To formally place anything before the court, or upon the record, usually in writing. Black.

Equity: A branch of remedial justice by and through which relief is afforded suitors in the courts of equity. Originating in the Curia Regis, the great court in which the English king administered justice in person, equity overcame limitations in common law by permitting all persons having an interest in the case to be made parties, by framing pleadings so as to present the whole case, and by allowing a variety of remedies. Bouvier.

Eodem die: On that day (Lat.). Black.

Error: See writ of error.

Errors: See assignment of errors.

Ex officio: From office (Lat.); the power a person has, by virtue of the office, to do certain acts. Jacob, Black

Ex parte: Of the one part (Lat.); done by or for one party. Jacob, Black.

Exception: An objection made to a decision of the court in the course of a trial. In admiralty or equity, a formal written allegation that some pleading or proceeding in a cause is insufficient. In common law, a written statement of objections to the decision of the trial court upon a point of law is a bill of exceptions. Upon issuance of a writ of error, the bill of exceptions is filed with the appellate court and serves to place before the court information about the trial which could not be included in the record. Bouvier, Black.

Execution: A writ directing an officer to carry into effect the court's final judgment or decree. Bouvier.

Executor: A person appointed to carry into effect a last will and testament. Bouvier.

Exemplification: An official transcript of a document from public records, authenticated as a true copy. Black.

Exit or *et exit:* It goes forth (Lat.); a docket entry signifying the issue of process. Black.

Gaol, (goal): Jail; prison for temporary confinement. Black.

General jury, general traverse jury: See petit jury.

Habeas corpus: You have the body (Lat.); a writ directed to a person detaining another and commanding him to produce the body of the prisoner at a certain time and place. Bouvier.

In case: See action on the case.

In error: See writ of error.

In nullo est erratum: In nothing is there error (Lat.); a plea by which the defendant-in-error affirms there is no error in the record. Bouvier, Black.

Inhibition: A writ to forbid a judge from further proceeding in a cause depending before him. Jacob.

Injunction: A kind of prohibition generally issued by a court of equity to stay proceedings in courts at law. Jacob.

Interlocutory: Something intervening between the commencement and the end of a suit which decides some point or matter, but is not a final decision of the whole controversy. Black.

Interrogatories: A series of formal written questions used in the judicial examination of a party or a witness. Black.

Joinder or *joinder in error:* In proceedings on a writ of error, a denial of the errors alleged in the assignment of errors. Jacob.

Joinder in demurrer: The answer to a demurrer. Bouvier.

Judgment: The decision of the court on proceedings instituted therein. Bouvier.

Judgment nisi: A judgment which is to stand, unless the affected party appears and shows cause, or takes other appropriate measures to avoid it or cause its revocation. Black, s.v. "nisi.".

Lessee: A person who holds an estate by virtue of a lease. Bouvier, Black.

Letters patent: An instrument granted by the government to convey a right or authority to an individual. Bouvier.

Libel: In admiralty, the initial pleading on the part of the plaintiff, corresponding to the declaration, bill, or complaint. Bouvier, Black.

Mandamus: A high prerogative writ, usually issuing out of the highest court of general jurisdiction, directing any natural person, corporation, or inferior court to do a specific thing pertaining to their office or duty. Bouvier.

Moiety: The half of anything. Jacob.

Motion: An application to the court by a party, or his counsel, in order to obtain some rule or order of court. Jacob, Bouvier.

Narratio: A plaintiff's declaration, being a narrative of the facts relied upon. Bouvier, Black.

Non assumpsit: He did not undertake (Lat.); in personal actions, the defendant's plea that he did not promise that which is alleged. Jacob, Bouvier.

Non pros, non pros'd, or *non prosequitur:* He does not pursue (Lat.); the failure of the plaintiff to prosecute his action, or any part of it, within a certain time, and the judgment in such instance that the plaintiff pay costs. Bouvier, Black.

Order: A written direction of a court not included in a judgment. Bouvier.

Panel: The roll or piece of parchment, containing the names of jurors summoned to decide a case, which the sheriff must return to the court with the venire facias. Bouvier.

Per curiam: By the court (Lat.); a phrase often used to distinguish the opinion or decision of the court from that of a single judge. Bouvier.

Per querentes: For the plaintiffs (Lat.). Black, s.v. "querens."

Petit jury: A body of men sworn to declare the facts of a case as presented by the evidence. Bouvier, s.v. "jury."

Plaintiff: The party who brings a personal action. Black.

Plaintiff-in-error: The party who sues out a writ of error. Black.

Plea: That which either party alleges for himself in court. In common law, a pleading, especially the first pleading on the part of the defendant. In equity, a special answer arguing that the suit should be dismissed, delayed, or barred. Jacob, Bouvier, Black.

Pleadings: The formal allegations by the parties of their respective claims and defenses, for the judgment of the court. Black.

Precept: A writ directed to the sheriff commanding him to perform a specific act. Bouvier.

Process: A formal written command issued by authority of law; the means by which a defendant is compelled to appear in court. Bouvier, Black.

Proctor (procter): In admiralty, a person employed to manage a cause. Bouvier.

Prohibition: A writ issued to an inferior court commanding it to cease all proceedings in a cause, upon suggestion that jurisdiction is lacking. Bouvier.

Recognizance: An obligation of record, entered into before some court or authorized officer, with a condition to do some particular act. Bouvier.

Record: A written history of a suit from beginning to end, including the conclusion of law. Black.

Rejoin: To answer a plaintiff's replication. Black.

Rejoinder: The defendant's answer to the plaintiff's replication. Jacob.

Remand: To send a cause back to the same court from which it came for further action. Bouvier, s.v. "remanding a cause."

Replication: A reply made by the plaintiff to the defendant's plea, or in equity to the defendant's answer. Black.

Return: The act of a sheriff in delivering back to the court a writ, notice, or other paper which he was directed to serve or execute, with a brief account of his actions under the mandate; also, the indorsement made by the sheriff upon the writ or paper. Black.

Reverse: To vacate, set aside, or make void. Bouvier.

Rule: An order made by a court. Rules of court are either general or special: the former are the laws by which the practice of the court is governed; the latter are special orders made in particular cases. Bouvier, s.v. "rule of court."

Seriatim: In a series (Lat.). Bouvier.

Service: The execution of a writ or process. Bouvier.

Shew cause or *show cause:* To appear as directed, and present the court with reasons why something should not be done by the court. Black.

Special jury: A jury selected with the assistance of the parties, usually to try matters of great importance; consisting of forty-eight freeholders from which each side strikes twelve names, and from the remainder the jury is selected. Jacob, Bouvier, s.v. "jury."

Special mandate: An order issued by an appellate court, upon the decision of an appeal or a writ of error, directing the lower court to take action on or make disposition of a case. Black.

Stay: The act of arresting a judicial proceeding by the order of a court. Black.

Subpoena: Under penalty (Lat.); a writ issued to call a witness to appear and testify in court. In equity, a writ for calling a defendant to appear and answer the complainant's bill. Jacob, Bouvier.

Suggestion: A statement, formally entered on the record, of some fact or circumstance which will materially affect the further proceedings in the cause, or which is necessary to be brought to the knowledge of the court in order for the proper disposition of the cause, but which, for some reason cannot be pleaded. Black.

Summons: A writ commanding the sheriff to notify a party to appear in court on a specified day to answer a complaint. Bouvier.

Supersedeas: A writ to stay proceedings at law. Jacob.

Sur: On. Black.

Surety: A person who binds himself to pay money or perform any other act for another. Bouvier.

Terre tenant: A person who has the actual possession of the land. Jacob.

Teste: The concluding clause of a writ beginning with the word "Witness . . ." and including the date executed. Bouvier, s.v. "teste of a writ."

True verdict: The voluntary conclusion of the jury after deliberate consideration. Black.

Venire, venire facias, venire facias juratores: That you cause to come (Lat.); a judicial writ directed to the sheriff to cause a jury of the neighborhood to appear to try a suit at issue. Jacob, Black.

Venire de novo or *venire facias de novo:* A new writ of venire facias, awarded when the proper effect of the first has been frustrated, or the verdict has become void, or when a judgment is reversed. Bouvier.

Viva voce: With the living voice (Lat.); given orally in open court. Bouvier.

Warrant: A writ issued by an authorized officer, directing a sheriff, or other officer, to arrest a person therein named, charged with committing some offense, and to bring him before the proper judicial authorities. Bouvier.

Writ: A mandatory precept, issued by and in the name of the sovereign or state, commanding something to be done touching a suit or action. Jacob, Bouvier.

Writ of error: A writ issued out of a court of appellate jurisdiction, directed to the judges of a court of record in which final judgment has been given, commanding them to send the record to the appellate court in order that some alleged error in the proceedings may be corrected. Bouvier.

Writ of inquiry (enquiry) of damages: A writ issued to the sheriff upon a judgment by default commanding him to summon a jury to enquire what damages the plaintiff has sustained. Jacob.

Signs and Abbreviations

This list includes only those eighteenth-century signs and abbreviations that might not be recognized easily by the modern reader. The list begins with a presentation of signs and then continues with abbreviations. When an abbreviation appears in the text of this volume with the same letters but in different forms, we only record it once in this list; thus, the word "against" might be abbreviated as "agt" or "ag⁴," but in this list only "agt" would be given. In general, all superior letters have been dropped to the baseline with only one exception ("and" for "answered"). Plural forms of these abbreviations also have been eliminated; so too have variants due to different capitalization.

9	A sign used at the end of a word to replace the letters "us" or "os" or "ost."
℗	A sign used at the end of a word to replace "is" or "es" or, more generally, any word ending.
℔	per
℔	Per
⊗	A reference mark, called an obelisk.

& ali(s)	and others		*affe*	affectionate
& als	and others		*affece*	affectionate
&c	et cetera		*affect*	affectionate
&ca	et cetera		*affecte*	affectionate
acknowd	acknowledged		*affectte*	affectionate
actn	action		*afft*	affidavit
adjd	adjourned		*afsd*	aforesaid
adjdt	adjournment		*aftwds*	afterwards
adjo	adjourned		*agreet*	agreement
adm	administrator		*agst*	against
admnor	administrator		*agt*	against
admnr	administrator		*amic*	amicable
admor	administrator		*and*	answered
admr	administrator		*Annapl*	Annapolis
af	affirmed		*Annaps*	Annapolis

app	appeal	*et als*	and others
appelts	appellants	*evg*	evening
argt	argument	*ex*	executor
att	attorney	*excors*	executors
atty	attorney	*exec*	executor
AV	August	*exon*	execution
chancy	chancery	*exor*	executor
Chs Town	Charleston	*exr*	executor
Congr	Congress	*favd*	favored
cir	circuit	*favr*	favor
circt	circuit	*feds*	federalists
cirt	circuit	*frd*	friend
cit	citation	*frm*	from
claimt	claimant	*G*	God
cler	clerk	*G.B.*	Great Britain
clk	clerk	*h*	humble
commissr	commissioner	*hb*	humble
comn	commission	*hble*	humble
complt	complainant	*hl*	humble
compts	compliments	*hle*	humble
cont	continued	*hond*	honored
contd	continued	*IA*	January
ct	court,	*inst*	instant
	circuit	*int*	instant
cty	county	*IV*	June, July
cur	court	*jud*	judgment
currt	current	*lee*	lessee
D	Dear	*ler*	letter
decd	deceased	*M.*	Massachusetts
def	defendant	*mands*	mandamus
defdt	defendant	*memor*	memorial
defend	defendant	*mo*	most, month,
defendt	defendant		motion
defets	defendants	*N.A.*	North America
deft	defendant	*narr*	narratio
deld	delivered	*non asst*	non assumpsit
depy	deputy	*non pro*	non prosequitur
dft	defendant	*ob*	obedient
do	ditto	*obet*	obedient
dr	dear	*obt*	obedient
dt	district	*oppy*	opportunity
dy	deputy	*oth*	other
eno	enough	*p*	president
et ali(s)	and others	*P.*	Pennsylvania

pact	packet	*sert*	servant
plff	plaintiff	*spl mand*	special mandate
plft	plaintiff	*ss*	scilicet (Lat.):
plts	plaintiffs		to wit
prohi	prohibit	*st*	servant
prohib	prohibition	*sunmnd*	summoned
prot	prothonotary	*sup*	supreme
provdd	provided	*supa*	subpoena
PTK	Potomac	*surg*	surviving
Ptmk	Potomac	*svt*	servant
qy	query	*tents*	tenants
r	received	*vy*	very
rd	received	*wch*	which
recog	recognizance	*wd*	would
rectble	returnable	*wh*	which
regd	regard	*whh*	which
repln	replication	*wod*	would
retble	returnable	*wt*	writ
sernt	servant